COLT ARCHÆOLOGICAL INSTITUTE PUBLICATIONS

The Early Bronze Age Sanctuary at Ai (et-Tell)

No. 1

JOSEPH A. CALLAWAY

with the assistance of

WILLIAM W. ELLINGER, III

A Report of the
Joint Archæological Expedition to Ai (et-Tell)

BERNARD QUARITCH LTD
11 GRAFTON STREET, NEW BOND STREET, LONDON

MADE AND PRINTED IN GREAT BRITAIN BY
WILLIAM CLOWES & SONS, LIMITED, LONDON, BECCLES AND COLCHESTER

The Joint Archæological Expedition to Ai (et-Tell)
is sponsored by
The American Schools of Oriental Research, Cambridge, Massachusetts
and the following consortium:

Sponsoring Institutions

1964–1966–1968–1969–1970

The Southern Baptist Theological Seminary
Louisville, Kentucky

Perkins School of Theology
Dallas, Texas

Harvard Semitic Museum
Cambridge, Massachusetts

1964

Drew Theological Seminary
Madison, New Jersey

1966–1968

Asbury Theological Seminary
Wilmore, Kentucky

1968

Waterloo Lutheran University
Waterloo, Ontario, Canada

1968–1969

The Palestine Exploration Fund
London, England

1969–1970

Evangel College
Springfield, Missouri

Participating Institutions

Furman University
Greenville, South Carolina

Berkeley Divinity School
New Haven, Connecticut

The Lutheran Seminary
Gettysburg, Pennsylvania

Cumberland College
Williamsburg, Kentucky

Lawrence University
Appleton, Wisconsin

Samford University
Birmingham, Alabama

Golden Gate Baptist Theological Seminary
Mill Valley, California

Cincinnati Bible Seminary
Cincinnati, Ohio

St. Lawrence University
Canton, New York

Baldwin-Wallace College
Berea, Ohio

Middle East College
Beirut, Lebanon

The Nicol Museum of Biblical Archæology
Louisville, Kentucky

PERSONNEL OF THE EXPEDITION

The excavation was carried out by a supervisory staff drawn from supporting institutions; a few salaried employees who performed highly specialized tasks, such as surveying, drafting, and drawing pottery; hired technicians from the West Bank who had experience in the techniques of excavating; and hired laborers from the village of Deir Dibwan. A comparative listing of the personnel along with the supervisory staff follows.

DISTRIBUTION OF PERSONNEL

Year	Supervisory Staff	Technicians	Laborers
1964	12	12	70
1966	24	12	90
1968	29	10	125
1969	32	10	120
1970	11	2	20

SUPERVISORY STAFF, 1964–1970

Administration

Joseph A. Callaway	*Director, 1964–1970*
Kermit Schoonover	*Associate Director, 1964–1969*
Hassan A. Awad	*Assistant to the Director, 1968, 1969*
Bryan Dare	*Business Manager, 1968, 1969*

Field Excavations: et-Tell

Norman E. Wagner	*Supervisor of et-Tell Excavations, 1968*
James R. Kautz, III	*Supervisor of et-Tell Excavations, 1969*

SITE A

Joseph A. Callaway	*Site Supervisor, 1964*
Yusef Labadi	*Assistant Supervisor, 1964*
Kermit Schoonover	*Site Supervisor, 1968*
Derrek Hines	*Assistant Supervisor, 1968*

SITE B

Robert J. Bull	*Site Supervisor, 1964*
William J. A. Power	*Site Supervisor, 1964*
Dorothea Ward Harvey	*Site Supervisor, 1966*
James R. Kautz, III	*Site Supervisor, 1968; Assistant Supervisor, 1966*
David A. Smith	*Assistant Supervisor, 1966*
Carole Bohn	*Assistant Supervisor, 1968*
Michael Hagebusch	*Site Supervisor, 1969*

SITE C

Kermit Schoonover	*Site Supervisor, 1964, 1966*
George G. Ramey	*Assistant Supervisor, 1966*
Lloyd Neve	*Assistant Supervisor, 1966*
Fr. Thomas Duerr	*Assistant Supervisor, 1966*
R. Lansing Hicks	*Assistant Supervisor, 1966*

SITE D

Joseph A. Callaway	*Site Supervisor, 1964*
Kenneth L. Vine	*Site Supervisor, 1966*
James M. Ward	*Assistant Supervisor, 1966*

SITE G

G. Herbert Livingston	*Site Supervisor, 1966*
Subri Abadi	*Assistant Supervisor, 1966*
Loal Ames	*Assistant Supervisor, 1966*

SITE H

G. Herbert Livingston	*Site Supervisor, 1968*
David L. Newlands	*Assistant Supervisor, 1968*

SITE K

G. Herbert Livingston	*Site Supervisor, 1968*
George A. Turner	*Assistant Supervisor, 1968*
David L. Newlands	*Site Supervisor, 1969*
Charles Ferris	*Assistant Supervisor, 1969*

SITE J

Karen Randolph Joines	*Site Supervisor, 1968, 1969*
Sandra Brenner	*Assistant Supervisor, 1968*
Gilbert Romero	*Assistant Supervisor, 1969*
J. Maxwell Miller	*Assistant Supervisor, 1969*
Fred Downing	*Assistant Supervisor, 1969*

Field Excavations: Khirbet Haiyan, SITE E

Murray B. Nicol	*Supervisor, Site E Sounding, 1964*
Robert E. Cooley	*Site Supervisor, 1969*
Daniel William O'Connor	*Assistant Supervisor, 1969*
Peyton R. Helm	*Assistant Supervisor, 1969*

Field Excavations: Khirbet Khudriya, SITE F

Kyle M. Yates, Jr.	*Supervisor of Khudriya Excavations, 1966, 1968*
Billie Hanks, Sr.	*Assistant Supervisor, 1966 (Church), 1968 (Tombs)*
Amin Barhoom	*Assistant Supervisor, 1966 (Tombs)*

Robert W. Crapps   *Assistant Supervisor, 1966 (Tombs)*
G. Willard Reeves   *Assistant Supervisor, 1968 (Church)*
Glendon Grober   *Assistant Supervisor, 1968 (Tombs)*

Field Excavations: Khirbet Raddana, SITES R, S

Robert E. Cooley   *Site Supervisor, 1969*
D. Gwynn Davis, Jr.   *Assistant Supervisor, 1969*
David L. Newlands   *Site Supervisor, 1970*
Burton MacDonald   *Assistant Supervisor, 1970*

CAMP ADMINISTRATION

Mrs. Joseph A. Callaway   *Camp Director, 1964–1970*
Mrs. James R. Kautz   *Assistant Camp Director, 1966*
Mrs. Carl C. Hughes   *Dietitian, 1968*
Mrs. Robert E. Cooley   *Assistant Camp Director, 1969*
Edward Tango   *Assistant Camp Director, 1969*

TECHNICAL DEPARTMENT

William W. Ellinger, III   *Supervisor of Technical Department, 1969, 1970;
                                    Architect, 1966, 1969, 1970*
Terry Ball   *Architect, 1964*
T. Furman Hewitt   *Assistant Architect, 1964*
Carl C. Hughes   *Architect, 1968*
Lex Gropper   *Assistant Architect, 1968*
Ronald E. Hill   *Photographer, 1964; Recorder, 1964*
James M. Ward   *Photographer, 1966*
Tim Olive   *Photographer, 1968*
John C. Trever   *Photographer, 1969*
Ralph Doermann   *Assistant Photographer, 1969*
Howard Bream   *Recorder, 1966*
Mrs. George G. Ramey   *Assistant Recorder, 1966*
Willard W. Winter   *Recorder, 1968, 1969*
Mrs. Carol Hicks   *Assistant Recorder, 1968, 1969*
Mrs. James R. Kautz   *Assistant Recorder, 1969*
Mrs. Lotta Gaster   *Recorder, 1969, 1970*
Mrs. David L. Newlands   *Recorder, 1970*
Michelle Johnston   *Artist, 1964*
Fr. Albert Moore   *Artist, 1966*
Earl Stieler   *Artist, 1968, 1970*
Mrs. Marcia Ellinger   *Artist, 1969, 1970*
Fred A. Reddel   *Assistant Artist, 1969*
James McCain   *Draftsman, 1968, 1969*

Hassan Mamlouk   *Formatore,* 1968, 1969, 1970
C. Dwight Townes   *Research Assistant,* 1968, 1969
David L. Newlands   *Research Assistant,* 1970
George R. Glenn   *Field Geologist and Soils Engineer,* 1970
Bertrand Glenn   *Assistant Field Geologist,* 1970

PREFACE

The list of institutions supporting the Expedition to Ai and the list of persons participating in the excavations indicate the extensive investment of resources, time, and even life itself in a major excavation. An undertaking such as the Ai Expedition simply could not be brought to completion without the generous, and, in many cases, dedicated labor of many people. The listing of names and responsibilities is a small and inadequate way of recognizing individual contributions. However, it records the many-sided indebtedness of both the writer and those who make use of the present report to a select group of persons drawn from varied academic, national, and religious backgrounds and united in a common, scholarly endeavor.

The support and encouragement of G. Ernest Wright, President of the American Schools of Oriental Research, and Thomas D. Newman, Administrative Director, have contributed substantially to the publication of this report. Grants of Foreign Currency Funds were obtained through Smithsonian Institution, 1968–1970, with their assistance, and the excavation project has been one of their concerns from the time of its inception.

Indebtedness to Mr. Kennedy B. Schmertz, Director of the Foreign Currency Program of Smithsonian Institution and Mr. Kenneth D. Whitehead, Deputy Director, for the Smithsonian grants specified in the Introduction is gladly acknowledged. The scope of excavations at Ai would have been severely restricted without these grants, and the completion of this report would have been delayed considerably.

Specific research on the nature and extent of Egyptian involvement in the EB III sanctuary at Ai was made possible by a grant of $1,000 from the American Philosophical Society (Penrose Fund, No. 4701) in 1968. The results of that research are incorporated in Chapters VII–VIII.

Final preparation of the present report was supported in part by a grant of $5,000 from the Lucius N. Littauer Foundation, Harry Starr, President. This was a matching funds grant to the National Endowment for the Humanities, for which the writer is indeed grateful.

The Endowment is supporting the preparation of reports June 1, 1971–May 31, 1973 in Project No. H–4903 with a two-year budget of $14,700, which has expedited the appearance of this volume. The findings and conclusions, however, do not necessarily represent the views of the Endowment.

An important contribution to the comfort and well-being of the expedition staff was a first-aid station and household pharmacy stocked by Dr. James Childers, Louisville, Kentucky. As Medical Adviser to the expedition, he contributed appreciably to lowering the incidence of minor illnesses, and, consequently, to man-days lost in the field.

Many scholars interested in archaeology have visited the site at Ai, and contributed to an interpretation of the results of the excavations. The writer gladly acknowledges, however, special indebtedness to Ruth Amiran, whose interest in Ai dates back to 1934 when she joined the Marquet-Krause staff in her first excavation; to the late Père Roland de Vaux, whose interest in the site dates back to 1935 when he first arrived in Jerusalem; to G. Ernest Wright, who excavated with W. F. Albright at Bethel when Marquet-Krause conducted her second campaign at Ai in 1934; and to Kathleen M. Kenyon, whose discoveries at Jericho excited the interest of the writer in resuming work at Ai in 1961 during a seminar at the Institute of Archaeology in London.

Kermit Schoonover, Associate Director of the expedition, and Director of the American School of Oriental Research in Jerusalem, 1968–1969, has borne more than his share of the burdens of the project, and has worked constantly with the writer to clarify interpretations of field work and maintain a sense of balance in reconstructions included in this report. William W. Ellinger, III, the Architect and Supervisor of the Technical Department maintained an orderly arrangement of all materials for study, and assisted the writer in organizing and assembling the components of this report. All plans and sections were prepared by Mr. Ellinger, and Mrs. Marcia Ellinger prepared the final drawings of all pottery and objects.

All plans and drawings of the Marquet-Krause sites and pottery were taken from *Les Fouilles de 'Ay (et-Tell)*, published by Paul Geuthner, Paris, 1949. Acknowledgement of each item is included with its presentation in the report. Mrs. Lotta Gaster translated pottery descriptions from French originals in *Les fouilles de 'Ay (et-Tell)* for the pottery lists accompanying these drawings.

The pottery drawings in the text-figures were assembled in London by H. Dunscombe Colt, who gave generously of his time in arranging the format of the report. The writer is indebted to Mr. Colt for his contribution to the presentation of this volume, and for inclusion of it in the Colt Archaeological Institute series of publications.

Continuous local support of the Ai Expedition has come from the Nicol Museum of Biblical Archaeology, Louisville, Kentucky, and Mrs. Virginia Nicol of Atlanta, Georgia. President Duke K. McCall of The Southern Baptist Theological Seminary has constantly supported the expedition in every way possible, as have local friends, among whom Dr. C. Dwight Townes, Mr. and Mrs. Ralph V. Brown and Mr. and Mrs. Charles L. Westray must be mentioned. Mrs. Rogers Merhoff of Louisville has done the final typing of the manuscript. The contributions and encouragement of these friends are gratefully acknowledged.

JOSEPH A. CALLAWAY

Louisville, Kentucky

CONTENTS

LIST OF PLATES

LIST OF TEXT FIGURES

ABBREVIATIONS AND BIBLIOGRAPHY

Albright 1932   W. F. Albright, 'The Excavation of Tell Beit Mirsim. Part I, The Pottery of the First Three Campaigns,' *Annual of the American Schools of Oriental Research*, Vol. XII. New Haven: Yale University Press, 1932.

Albright 1935   W. F. Albright, 'Palestine in the Earliest Historical Period,' *Journal of the Palestine Oriental Society*, Vol. XV (1935).

Albright 1965   William F. Albright, 'Some Remarks on the Chronology of Palestine before about 1500 B.C.,' *Chronologies in Old World Archaeology*, Robert W. Ehrich, ed. Chicago: University of Chicago Press, 1965, pp. 47–60.

Amiran 1965   Ruth Amiran, 'Khirbet Kerak Ware at Ai,' *Israel Exploration Journal*, Vol. 17, No. 3 (1967), pp. 185–186.

Amiran 1968   Ruth Amiran, 'Two Canaanite Vessels Excavated in Egypt with Egyptian "Signatures",' *Israel Exploration Journal*, Vol. 18 (1968), pp. 241–243.

Amiran 1969   Ruth Amiran, *Ancient Pottery of the Holy Land*. Jerusalem: Massada Press, 1969.

Amiran 1970   Ruth Amiran, 'The Egyptian Alabaster Vessels from Ai,' *Israel Exploration Journal*, Vol. 20, Nos. 3–4 (1970), pp. 170–179.

Amiran Early Arad   Ruth Amiran and Others, *Early Arad, The Chalcolithic Settlement and the Early Bronze City*. Plates of report in the press at time of writing.

Callaway 1962   Joseph A. Callaway, 'The Gezer Crematorium Re-Examined,' *Palestine Exploration Quarterly* (July–Dec., 1962), pp. 104–117.

Callaway 1964   Joseph A. Callaway, *Pottery from the Tombs at Ai (et-Tell)*. London: Colt Archaeological Institute, Monograph No. 2, 1964.

Callaway 1965   Joseph A. Callaway, 'The 1964 Ai (et-Tell) Excavations,' *Bulletin of the American Schools of Oriental Research*, No. 178 (Apr., 1965), pp. 13–40.

Callaway and Nicol 1966   Joseph A. Callaway and Murray B. Nicol, 'A Sounding at Khirbet Haiyan,' *Bulletin of the American Schools of Oriental Research*, No. 183 (Oct., 1966), pp. 12–19.

Callaway 1969   Joseph A. Callaway, 'The 1966 Ai (et-Tell) Excavations,' *Bulletin of the American Schools of Oriental Research*, No. 196 (Dec., 1969), pp. 2–16.

Callaway 1970   Joseph A. Callaway, 'The 1968–1969 Ai (et-Tell) Excavations,' *Bulletin of the American Schools of Oriental Research*, No. 198 (Apr., 1970), pp. 7–31.

de Contenson 1956   H. de Contenson 'La céramique chalcolithique de Beersheba: étude typologique,' *Israel Exploration Journal*, Vol. 6 (1956), pp. 163–179, 226—238.

de Vaux 1947   R. P. de Vaux and R. P. Steve, 'La première campagne de fouilles à Tell el-Far'ah, près Naplouse,' *Revue Biblique*, Tome LIV, No. 4 (Oct., 1947), pp. 573–589.

de Vaux 1948   R. P. de Vaux and R. P. Steve, 'La seconde campagne de fouilles à Tell el-Far'ah, près Naplouse,' *Revue Biblique*, Tome LV (Oct., 1948), pp. 544–580.

de Vaux 1949   R. P. de Vaux and R. P. Steve, 'La seconde campagne de fouilles à Tell el-Far'ah, près Naplouse,' *Revue Biblique*, Tome LVI, No. 1 (Jan., 1949), pp. 102–138.

de Vaux 1951   R. P. de Vaux, 'La troisième campagne de fouilles à Tell el-Far'ah, près Naplouse,' *Revue Biblique*, Tome LVIII, No. 3 (July, 1951), pp. 393–430.

de Vaux 1952   R. P. de Vaux, 'La quatrième campagne de fouilles à Tell el-Far'ah, près Naplouse,' *Revue Biblique*, Tome LIX, No. 4 (Oct., 1952), pp. 551–583.

de Vaux 1955   R. P. de Vaux, 'La cinquième campagne de fouilles à Tell el-Far'ah, près Naplouse,' *Revue Biblique*, Tome LXII (Oct., 1955), pp. 541–589.

de Vaux 1961   R. P. de Vaux, 'Les fouilles de Tell el-Far'ah,' *Revue Biblique*, Tome LXVIII (Oct., 1961), pp. 557–592.

de Vaux 1966   R. P. de Vaux, 'Palestine in the Early Bronze Age,' *The Cambridge Ancient History*, Vol. I, Part 1, rev. ed. Cambridge: The University Press, 1966.

Dothan 1957   M. Dothan, 'Excavations at Meser 1956,' *Israel Exploration Journal*, Vol. 7 (1957), pp. 217–228.

Emery 1949   Walter B. Emery, *Great Tombs of the First Dynasty*, Vol. I. Cairo: Government Press, 1949.

Emery 1961   W. B. Emery, *Archaic Egypt*. Penguin Books, 1961.

Emery 1962   W. B. Emery, *A Funerary Report in an Egyptian Tomb of the Archaic Period*. Leiden: Nederlands Instituut voor het Nabije Oosten, 1962.

Engberg 1934   R. M. Engberg and G. M. Shipton, *Notes on the Chalcolithic and Early Bronze Age Pottery of Megiddo*. Chicago: The Oriental Institute of the University of Chicago, 1934.

Fitzgerald 1935   G. M. Fitzgerald, 'Beth-shan: Earliest Pottery,' *Museum Journal*, Vol. XXIV, No. 1 (1935), pp. 5–32.

Garstang 1928   John Garstang, 'El Tell: Ai.' Report on the 1928 soundings at Ai to the Department of Antiquities, Jerusalem, Sept. 21, 1928, 5 pages (unpublished).

Garstang 1932   John Garstang, 'Jericho: City and Necropolis,' *Annals of Archaeology and Anthropology*, Vol. XIX. Liverpool University, 1932.

Garstang 1936   John Garstang, 'Jericho, City and Necropolis,' *Annals of Archaeology and Anthropology*, Vol. XXIII. Liverpool University, 1936.

Grintz 1961   Jehoshua M. Grintz, ''Ai Which is Beside Beth-aven: A Re-examination of the Identity of 'Ai,' *Biblica*, Vol. 42 (1961), pp. 201–216.

Guy 1938   P. L. O. Guy, *Megiddo Tombs*. Chicago: The University of Chicago Press, 1938.

Hayes 1964   William C. Hayes, 'Chronology: Egypt—to End of Twentieth Dynasty,' *The Cambridge Ancient History*, rev. ed., Vols. I & II. Cambridge: The University Press, 1964.

Hennessy 1967   J. B. Hennessy, *The Foreign Relations of Palestine During the Early Bronze Age*. London: Colt Archaeological Institute, 1967.

Kantor 1956   Helene J. Kantor, 'Syro-Palestinian Ivories,' *Journal of Near Eastern Studies*, Vol. XV, No. 3 (July, 1956), pp. 153–174.

Kantor 1965   Helene J. Kantor, 'The Relative Chronology of Egypt and its Foreign Correlations before the Late Bronze Age,' *Chronologies in Old World Archaeology*, Robert W. Ehrich, ed. Chicago: University of Chicago Press, 1965.

Kelso 1968   James L. Kelso, 'The Excavation of Bethel (1934–1960),' *The Annual of the American Schools of Oriental Research*, Vol. XXXIX. Cambridge, Mass.: The American Schools of Oriental Research, 1968.

Kenyon 1952   Kathleen M. Kenyon, 'Excavations at Jericho,' *Palestine Exploration Quarterly* (Jan.–June, 1952), pp. 4–6, 62–82.

Kenyon 1960   Kathleen M. Kenyon, *Excavations at Jericho*, Vol. I. London: British School of Archaeology in Jerusalem, 1960.

Kenyon 1965   Kathleen M. Kenyon, *Excavations at Jericho*, Vol. II. London: British School of Archaeology in Jerusalem, 1965.

Koeppel 1940   R. Koeppel, *Teleilat Ghassul*, II. Rome: Pontifical Biblical Institute, 1940.

Lapp 1966   Paul W. Lapp, 'The Cemetery at Bab edh-Dhra', Jordan,' *Archaeology*, Vol. 19, No. 2 (Apr., 1966), pp. 104–111.

Lapp 1968   Paul W. Lapp, 'Bab edh-Dhra' Tomb A 76 and Early Bronze I in Palestine,' *Bulletin of the American Schools of Oriental Research*, No. 189 (Feb., 1968), pp. 12–41.

Lapp 1970   Paul W. Lapp, 'Palestine in the Early Bronze Age,' *Near Eastern Archaeology in the Twentieth Century*, edited by James A. Sanders. Garden City, N.Y.: Doubleday, 1970. pp. 101–131.

Loud 1948   Gordon Loud, *Megiddo II, Seasons of 1935–39*, Chicago: University of Chicago Press, 1948.

McCown 1947   C. C. McCown, *Tell en-Nasbeh I: Archaeological and Historical Results*. Berkeley and New Haven: The Palestine Institute of Pacific School of Religion and The American Schools of Oriental Research, 1947.

Macalister 1902   R. A. S. Macalister, 'Report on the Excavation of Gezer,' *Palestine Exploration Fund Quarterly Statement* (1902), pp. 317–364.

Macalister 1912   R. A. S. Macalister, *The Excavation of Gezer*, 3 vols. London: J. Murray, 1912.

Mallon, 1934   Alexis Mallon, *Teleilat Ghassul*, *I*, with Robert Koeppel, Rene Neuville, *et al.* Rome: Pontifical Biblical Institute, 1934.

Marquet-Krause 1933   J. Marquet-Krause, 'The Excavations at El-Tell.' Report of the 1933 Rothschild Expedition to the Department of Antiquities, Jerusalem, 1933, 3 pages (unpublished).

Marquet-Krause 1934   J. Marquet-Krause, 'Les fouilles du Baron Edmond de Rotschild à Et-Tell, Année 1934.' Report to the Department of Antiquities, Jerusalem, November, 11 1934, 5 pages (unpublished).

Marquet-Krause 1935   Judith Marquet-Krause, 'La deuxième campagne de foilles à 'Ay (1934). Rapport sommaire. *Syrie*, Tome 16 (1935), pp. 325–345.

Marquet-Krause 1949   Judith Marquet-Krause, *Les fouilles de 'Ay (et Tell) 1933–35*, 2 vols. Paris: P. Geuthner, 1949.

Ory 1935   J. Ory, 'Excavations at Ras el-'Ain,' *Quarterly of the Department of Antiquities of Palestine*, Vol. V (1935–1936).

Parr 1956   Peter J. Parr, 'A Cave at Arqub el-Dhahr,' *Annual of the Department of Antiquities of Jordan*, Vol. III (1956), pp. 61–73.

Perrot 1955   Jean Perrot, 'Excavations at Tell Abu Matar, near Beersheba,' *Israel Exploration Journal*, Vol. 5, Nos. 1–3 (1955), pp. 17–40, 73–84, 167–189.

Perrot 1961   Jean Perrot, 'Une tombe à Ossuaires à Azar,' *Atiqot*, Vol. III (1961), pp. 1–83.

Petrie 1901   W. M. Flinders Petrie, *The Royal Tombs of the Earliest Dynasties*, Part II. London: The Egypt Exploration Fund, 1901.

Petrie 1913   W. M. Flinders Petrie, *Tarkhan I and Memphis V*. London: Bernard Quaritch, 1913.

Petrie 1927   Flinders Petrie, *Objects of Daily Use*. London: British School of Archaeology in Egypt, 1927.

Petrie 1937   Flinders Petrie, *Stone and Metal Vases*. London: British School of Egyptian Archaeology, 1937.

Prausnitz 1955   M. W. Prausnitz, 'Ay and the Chronology of Troy,' *Annual Report*, Institute of Archaeology, University of London, 1955.

Pritchard 1962   James B. Pritchard, *Gibeon, Where the Sun Stood Still*. Princeton: Princeton University Press, 1962.

Quibell 1913   J. E. Quibell, *Excavations at Saqqara (1911–1912): The Tomb of Hesy*. Cairo: Institut Francais d'Archéologie Orientale, 1913.

Quibell 1923   J. E. Quibell, *Excavations at Saqqara (1912–1914): Archaic Mastabas*. Cairo: Institut Francais d'Archéologie Orientale, 1923.

Reisner 1931   G. A. Reisner, *Mycerinus: The Temple of the Third Pyramid at Giza*. Cambridge, Mass.: Harvard University Press, 1931.

Saller 1965   S. Saller, 'Bab edh-Dhra',' *Liber Annuus*, XV (1964–1965), pp. 137–219.

Shipton 1939   G. M. Shipton, *Notes on the Megiddo Pottery of Strata VI–XX*, Chicago: University of Chicago Press, 1939.

Vincent 1937   L. H. Vincent, 'Les fouilles d'et-Tell='Ai,' *Revue Biblique*, Tome XLVI (Apr., 1937), pp. 231–266.

Wampler 1947   J. C. Wampler, *Tell en-Nasbeh II: The Pottery*. Berkeley and New Haven: The Palestine Institute of Pacific School of Religion and the American Schools of Oriental Research, 1947.

Wheeler 1954   Sir Mortimer Wheeler, *Archaeology from the Earth*, London: Penguin Books, 1954.

Wright 1937   G. Ernest Wright, *The Pottery of Palestine from the Earliest Times to the End of the Early Bronze Age*, New Haven: American Schools of Oriental Research, 1937.

Wright 1958   G. Ernest Wright, 'The Problem of Transition Between the Chalcolithic and Bronze Ages,' *Eretz Israel*, Vol. V (1958), pp. 37–45.

Wright 1970   G. Ernest Wright, 'The Significance of Ai in the Third Millennium B.C.,' *Archaologie und Altes Testament* (Festachrift fur Kurt Galling), A. Kuschke und Ernst Kutach, eds. Tubingen: J. C. B. Mohr (Paul Siebeck), 1970, pp. 299–319.

Wright 1971   G. Ernest Wright, 'The Archaeology of Palestine from the Neolithic Through the Middle Bronze Age,' *Journal of the American Oriental Society*, Vol. 91, No. 2 (Apr.–June, 1971), pp. 276–293.

G. R. H. Wright 1966   G. R. H. Wright, 'A Method of Excavation Common in Palestine,' *Zeitschrift des Deutschen Palästina-Vereins*, Bd. 82 (1966), pp. 113–124.

Yeivin 1934   S. Yeivin, 'The Masonry of the Early Bronze People,' *Palestine Exploration Fund Quarterly Statement* (1934), 189–191.

INTRODUCTION

ORGANIZATION AND OBJECTIVES OF THE EXPEDITION

THE ORIGINS OF THE EXCAVATIONS AT AI

The Joint Archaeological Expedition to Ai (et-Tell) was organized in 1963 by Lawrence E. Toombs, Kermit Schoonover, and the writer. Toombs and the writer were members of the Shechem Expedition, directed by G. Ernest Wright. The final season of excavation at Shechem was scheduled to be the summer of 1964, so the new expedition to Ai was conceived as a redeployment of staff as well as a result of the training system incorporated in the objectives of the parent expedition. Schoonover entered into the planning of the new expedition as spokesman for the Perkins School of Theology, whose faculty members in the Department of Old Testament wished to become involved in an archaeological expedition. Wright encouraged the organization of the new expedition, and gave his support in obtaining endorsement by the American Schools of Oriental Research. The Semitic Museum at Harvard was brought into the organization as a sponsor under Wright's leadership.

Selection of the site of Ai may be traced to the influence of a seminar in which Toombs and the writer participated during the winter of 1961–1962. The seminar in archaeology was led by Kathleen M. Kenyon at the Institute of Archaeology of London University. The Early Bronze Age in Canaan had been an interest of the writer for some time, so a study of the site of Ai was undertaken as a seminar project. Of special interest was the pottery from the tombs, which was culturally related to contemporary tombs at Jericho. The study continued beyond the seminar, and resulted in a monograph, *Pottery from the Tombs at 'Ai (et-Tell)*, published in 1964. With three years of study invested, Ai was naturally the first candidate for selection as a site to be excavated.

The last excavation at Ai occurred from 1933 through 1935 with French support. The expedition terminated abruptly in the midst of plans to continue work in 1936 when the Director, Mme. Judith Marquet-Krause, died on July 1, 1936. Consequently, the French had rights to continue the excavation if they elected to do so, and there were reports that André Parrot might take the responsibility. World War II, followed by the Arab–Israeli war of 1948, delayed indefinitely any resumption of work, and Parrot continued his excavation at Mari.

James B. Pritchard, a member of the W. F. Albright Expedition to Bethel in 1934 when Marquet-Krause worked at the nearby site of Ai, became interested in resuming the Ai excavations in 1954. His plan was furthered when the French conceded their rights at Ai in the spring of 1955 (see Pritchard 1962, 4–5). With support for an excavation project at Ai by the University Museum of the University of Pennsylvania, he obtained from G. Lankester Harding, the Director of the Department of Antiquities in Jordan, a promise to issue a license to excavate the site. However, when Pritchard arrived in Jerusalem to secure the license, Harding suggested that he select a new site which had not been excavated. The advantages of the proposal appealed to Pritchard, and he decided in favor of el-Jib (Gibeon).

The writer's interest in Ai was made known to Père Roland de Vaux of École Biblique in Jerusalem in 1962, during the second season of excavations at Jerusalem. De Vaux graciously agreed to inquire again about French intentions with regard to the site of Ai. The response came in the fall of 1962, and again the French generously conceded their claims at Ai to the new expedition which was being formed. This formality lay behind the talks among Toombs, Schoonover, and the writer at the Society of Biblical Literature meeting in December, 1963, when a decision was reached to organize the expedition and begin excavations in 1964.

An application for a license to excavate at Ai was filed with Dr. Awni Dajani, Director of Antiquities of Jordan, on March 6, 1964. Mrs. Crystal Bennett, Acting Director of the British School in Jerusalem, assisted in filing the application, and in obtaining Dr. Dajani's approval.

The Department of Antiquities, upon receipt of a license fee of 300 Jordan Dinars ($840), approved the application and issued License No. 70 on April 1, 1964. A permit was issued to authorize excavations at et-Tell, where sites would be opened at the sanctuary, the palace, the lower city fortifications, and the Iron Age village in an effort to complete the work begun by Marquet-Krause. A second permit authorized excavation at Khirbet Haiyan, a site on the south edge of Deir Dibwan, mentioned in publications as a possible location of biblical Ai (see Grintz 1961, 216).

The initial expedition was scheduled from May 4 through June 24, 1964 in order to permit Toombs and the writer to assume supervisory responsibilities at Shechem on June 25th. However, one month prior to the departure for work at Ai, unforeseen circumstances forced Toombs to withdraw from participation in the expedition and the writer was obliged to assume full responsibility for direction of the excavation. Schoonover served as Associate Director with specific responsibilities of dealing with personnel and officials of the local government.

OBJECTIVES AND WORK ACCOMPLISHED

The objectives of the expedition set forth in the application for a license to excavate were as follows:

1. To obtain precise stratification and building plans of the Early Bronze Age sanctuary, acropolis, and the Iron Age I village, which were excavated by Marquet-Krause.
2. To discover the nature and sequence of the Early Bronze Age fortifications, as well as any Iron Age I fortifications which might have escaped identification in the previous excavations.
3. To explore the vicinity of et-Tell for unidentified sites, and to excavate significant sites in the region which have been proposed as candidates for biblical Ai.
4. To recover an archaeological profile of et-Tell into which the information from previous excavations could be organized, integrated, and published.

All excavations during the 1964 and 1966 seasons were located on the upper terraces of the *tell*, above contour line 835 in Fig. 3. Sites A, B, C, and D were opened either within or adjunct to significant areas excavated by Marquet-Krause, implementing Objectives No. 1 and 2 above. The overall purpose was to complete an archaeological study of the sanctuary, the acropolis, the lower city fortifications, and the Iron Age village before any new sites were opened.

Excavation of the sanctuary was completed in 1964, and the lower city and acropolis sites were completed in 1966 (see Callaway 1965, 16–21; 1969, 2–16). Site G, located in Fig. 3, was excavated in 1966 to ascertain the extent of the Iron Age village on the east slope of the *tell*. Also the Iron Age village site was enlarged to a total of twenty five-meter squares in 1966, which practically covered the unexcavated area between the Marquet-Krause site, indicated by parallel line shading in Fig. 3, and contour line 850. A trench was cut through a wide stone terrace bordering Site B on contour line 850 with the objective of obtaining a vertical profile showing the sequence of structures covered by the terrace.

The profile was obtained, and the terrace was found to be Byzantine in origin. In the process of making this discovery, an Iron Age I house with a hewn stone roof-support pillar was partially uncovered beneath the terrace. A decision was made to remove a large area of the terrace, which reached a width of fifteen meters in places, and to obtain a complete plan of the house. Therefore, excavation of the Iron Age village continued in 1968 and 1969.

Pursuit of Objective No. 2 required the opening of new sites along the lower east side of the *tell*. once the sites on the upper terraces were completed. The fortifications and related structures of the extreme lower city were unknown. Three sites, designated H, K, and J, were opened in 1968 along the city wall from the southeast corner, Site K, around to the lowest part of the city at Site J, overlooking the deep Wadi el-Jaya.* Site K was enlarged in 1969 on the inside of the city wall to obtain evidence of houses or other structures possibly built against the wall.

Site H yielded a stretch of EB III city wall eight meters wide and stood seven meters high from its base on bedrock (Callaway 1970, 25–26, Fig. 13). A sequence of EB I–III gates was found at Site J, along with two EB III towers guarding a cleverly designed 'zig-zag' entrance (*ibid.*, pp. 19–24). A second major gate used in EB I–II was discovered at Site K, at the southeast corner of the *tell*. Fortified by a circular tower dominating the corner, this gate apparently allowed a straight-forward entry into the city along the left side of the tower (*ibid.*, pp. 26–27). When the EB II city was destroyed, possibly by an earthquake, the gate at Site K was blocked in the EB III rebuilding of the city wall.

When Site K was enlarged in 1969, a large open reservoir dating to EB III was found in the bend of the city wall with its dam constructed against the east wall and the blockage of the Corner Gate. A one-meter wide layer of red clay, imported from the fields outside the city and cleared of large stones, was carefully built into the dam to seal in the impounded water. Large stones were set into the inner face of the dam, and a tightly fitted surface of flat stones, set also in red clay, completed the paving inside the reservoir (*ibid.*, pp. 28–31).

One additional gate dating to EB I was discovered in exploration of the city wall system in 1968 and 1970. A one-meter wide passage was found in Area VII at Site A, as shown in Fig. 84, in Wall C. The passage was straight through the wall, but the approach road outside the city led along the north side of Tower C of the Citadel to Wall C, turned sharply left for some ten meters to the gate, then turned right into the Citadel Gate. The gate was blocked in EB II when the city wall was widened on the outside and became our Wall B, shown in Fig. 85.

* The Wadi el-Jaya is also called the Wadi el-Asas (or Asis) two kilometers east of et-Tell, and has been designated 'Asas' in preliminary reports. However, the Survey of Palestine Sheet 17–14, 1:20,000, indicates that 'el-Jaya' is the preferred designation of the *wadi* north and immediately east of et-Tell.

Significant new information about the EB city fortifications has emerged from close study of the Citadel and Lower City Sites. There are four distinct EB city wall phases instead of three, as Marquet-Krause, and the writer, previously held. Wall C in Fig. 84 is the EB I fortification which continues to Site C. The EB II fortification is Wall B, shown in Fig. 85. At Site C, it is the 5.50 meter wide rebuild of Wall C noted in 1964 (Callaway 1965, 28–31). Further exploration of the structure at Site C in 1970 confirms that the original fortification was 5.00 meters wide, and that the rebuild was on the inside of the city, as opposed to the outside at Site A. These two phases are now Walls C and B, and the two outer walls at Site C, designated B and A (*ibid.*, 29, Fig. 10), are now A and A¹ dating to EB IIIB and IIIA respectively.

Objective No. 3 of the expedition was to examine sites primarily in the vicinity of et-Tell previously proposed at various times as possible sites of biblical Ai (see Grintz 1961, 201–203, for a review of proposed sites). The first place selected was Khirbet Haiyan, located as Site E at the south edge of Deir Dibwan in Fig. 2. A sounding was made at Haiyan in 1964, as indicated earlier, and occupation evidence from first century Roman through Omayyad was identified (see Callaway and Nicol 1966, 12–19). Because the sounding was quite limited in size, the site was enlarged in 1969 to obtain representative data. A total of twelve five-meter squares was excavated in front of the evergreen oak and *weli* of Sheikh Abu Rukba, where numerous sherds and tessera lay on the surface of the ground. The findings of 1964 were confirmed by the more extensive excavation, because the earliest dated object identified was a coin of Agrippa I. Fifth- and sixth-century Byzantine buildings were the earliest structures.

Khirbet Khudriya, another site proposed as biblical Ai, was selected for excavation in 1966. A stone baptismal font projecting from the earth in an olive orchard led to the location of fourteen five-meter squares during the first season. The site, designated F in Fig. 2, yielded a tightly knit church complex consisting of a nave, sacristy rooms, an apse, and possibly a living area around a paved court. Khudriya was possibly a monastery, dating to the fourth to sixth centuries by coin evidence.

Expansion of the site in 1968 to a lower terrace on the northwest, overlooking the Wadi el-Asas (the same as Wadi el-Jaya north of et-Tell) led to the discovery of an industrial area. Spread out along the terrace were an olive press, a wine press with a series of storage vats, three large cisterns, and a storage cave adapted from an earlier Roman tomb. In the north face of the Wadi el-Asas was discovered a total of twenty-three tombs ranging in date of usage from Late Hellenistic to Omayyad. One MB II tomb was brought to the attention of the Director by a local landowner, and subsequently excavated. This tomb, designated F8, was about one kilometer east of Khudriya.

Finally, a salvage excavation at Khirbet Raddana, in the north edge of Bireh in Fig. 1, was conducted in 1969 and 1970. Construction of a subdivision road at the site uncovered two hewn stone pillars, obviously part of a house, and containing pottery contemporary with the pillar building at Site B dating to early Iron Age I. Two large pillar buildings excavated as Sites R and S in 1969–1970 confirmed that the ruin was in fact an Iron Age I village. They rested on top of the spectacular hill location of the site, with agricultural terraces visible round the crest and on the slopes. Two springs at the foot of the slopes on the north and south apparently provided the water supply, in addition to cisterns associated with the houses.

Raddana was not one of the sites originally planned for excavation, but the discoveries made there may be quite significant in elucidating the cultural context of biblical Ai. Raddana may, in fact, be biblical Beeroth, one of the Hivite cities mentioned in Josh. 9:17.

Objective No. 4, the organization and integration of information from previous excavations in reports of the present expedition, will be accomplished in varying degrees in the process of publishing the reports.

FINANCING AND BUDGET

The initial plan of financing the excavations at Ai was by subscription on the part of sponsoring institutions, and by contributions toward the maintenance of staff members by participating institutions. Usually the participating institutions covered the expenses of members from their schools. The rationale of the plan was that sponsoring institutions would furnish leadership for the excavation, and that eventually they would share in the publication of the reports. This would give them a role commensurate with the outlay of more money than participating institutions contributed. During the first two expeditions, each sponsor was asked to subscribe $3,000 toward the budget, and other institutions were asked to contribute $500 toward the maintenance of each staff member they sent out. In addition to this, the Director solicited contributions from individuals, corporations, and foundations.

Five expeditions have now been fielded, and five budgets subscribed. The budgets tended to escalate each season, partly due to expanded operations and partly to inflation. The total budget for each expedition was as follows:

1964:	$15,000
1966:	$20,000
1968:	$39,000
1969:	$55,310
1970:	$13,350

The Six-Day-War, which occurred in 1967, altered both the budget and the plan of financing. The site of Ai was suddenly within the Israeli occupied territory, under military government. Inflation in both wages and maintenance costs added significantly to budget requirements. Also, the constant possibility of renewed hostilities threatened the project and made it expedient to complete the excavation with all haste. Financing the larger scale and more expensive operations was assisted substantially by grants of Foreign Currency Funds obtained through the Smithsonian Institution by the American Schools of Oriental Research. The grants amounted to $19,000 in 1968, $50,000 in 1969, and $8,000 in 1970.

All major excavations were completed in 1969, leaving the 1970 season for processing of finds, completion of data-gathering, site and general surveys, architectural drawings, and photographs. Included in the 1970 budget was compensation for an architect and artist to work full-time in the preparation of materials for final reports.

THE EXCAVATION REPORTS

A prospectus of the total publication project

This volume is the first of several required to set forth the results of the excavations at Ai (et-Tell) and other sites mentioned above. Et-Tell is a very shallow and sprawling site, making it convenient to divide into topical components instead of the more usual cross-section reports of phases. Where the Iron Age village is located, there are no meaningful remains of the Early Bronze Age city underneath; and where there is no succeeding settlement, the Early Bronze Age ruins lie in shallow deposits from surface to bedrock. The reports presently envisioned are, therefore, as follows:

1. *The Early Bronze Age Sanctuary at Ai (et-Tell)*, the present report on Site A.
2. *The Early Bronze Age Citadel and Lower City at Ai (et-Tell)*, a report on the citadel at Site A, the lower city fortifications at Site C, and the Postern Gate tower complex excavated by Marquet-Krause in 1935.
3. *The Early Bronze Age Acropolis at Ai (et-Tell)*, a report on Site D, called 'the palace' by Marquet-Krause.
4. *The Early Bronze Age Reservoir and East Gates at Ai (et-Tell)*, a report on the reservoir and Corner Gate at Site K, the east wall at Site H, and the Wadi Gate at Site J.
5. *The Early Bronze Age Pottery at Ai (et-Tell)*, an analytical and technical study of the pottery from all of the sites published in Vols. I–IV.
6. *The Iron Age I Village at Ai (et-Tell)*, a report on Site B.

Also the excavations of nearby sites conducted simultaneously with the work at et-Tell will require the following additional reports:

7. *Excavations at Khirbet Haiyan, near Ai (et-Tell)*, a report on Site E, a Byzantine village southeast of et-Tell, and at the south edge of modern Deir Dibwan.
8. *Excavations at Khirbet Khudriya, near Ai (et-Tell)*, a report on Site F, a Byzantine monastery and twenty-three related tombs from the Roman and Byzantine periods. Khudriya is located two and one-half kilometers east of et-Tell, on the south edge of the Wadi el-Asas opposite Rammun (Rimmon).
9. *Excavations at Raddana, in Bireh*, a report on the Iron Age I village in the north edge of modern Bireh, at Ramallah.

Also the excavations of nearby sites conducted simultaneously with the work at et-Tell will require the following additional reports:

Composition of Volume I

The present volume on the sanctuary is a report of the archaeological evidence as observed and recorded. An attempt is made to keep the writer's conclusions and reconstructions detached from the evidence on which they are based. The evidence itself is, of course, the result of observation, which is interpretation. Nevertheless, it is not interpretation to the degree that the evidence cannot be used by persons who may see reason to propose different reconstructions. The objective is to present the findings in a manner which will allow the writer's conclusions to be evaluated critically without destroying the validity of the evidence itself.

The report is organized and presented as follows:

1. Introduction to the excavation project.

2. A description of the site and the excavations conducted by Garstang, Marquet-Krause, and the present expedition, with an introduction to the excavation terminology and techniques employed.

3. An analysis of phases and stratification.

4. A presentation of the evidence of Phases I–II, and a discussion of the Pre-Urban stratum.

5. The evidence of Phase III, the Building C stratum.

6. Phase IV, the construction phase of the Building B stratum.

7. Phase V, the destruction phase of the Building B stratum.

8. Phase VI, the construction phase of the Building A stratum.

9. Phase VII, remodeled Building A, or the Sanctuary A stratum, and Phase VIII, the destruction layer of Sanctuary A, taken from Marquet-Krause 1949.

10. Summary tables of strata and layers.

The plates of photographs follow the summary tables.

Drawings of pottery, objects, building plans, and sections are incorporated in the chapters dealing with the major periods of the site, except for sketch plans, the Master Section, and plans of the major building phases located in the fold-out section at the end of the text. The former are placed in the text-sections of the report to make reference more convenient for the reader. Some degree of quality in the production of the drawings is sacrificed, but this seems warranted in view of the difficulty often encountered in making constant reference to drawings included in the plate section of reports.

Pottery drawings are presented at a scale of 1:4, unless otherwise indicated. The traditional method of showing a cross-section with interior features on half of the drawing and exterior profile and features on the other half is followed. The section appears regularly on the left side of the drawing except for plates of material from other sources. All artifacts are presented from the perspective of light sources emanating from the upper left side of the object. Shading of pottery and object drawings is to be understood in the light of this convention. All original drawings of pottery and objects were produced at a scale of 1:1, and reduction to the published scale was by photographic technique.

The fragmentary nature of the sanctuary remains required that all pottery with any characteristic feature at all be preserved. The scarcity of undisturbed deposits and their yield of artifacts made it imperative that almost every sherd be saved. Consequently, the only discards were weather-worn or otherwise undistinguished body sherds which could serve no useful purpose in either the report or research as now understood. There were very few discards, therefore, because many body sherds which could not be meaningfully presented in a drawing were saved. Most of these undrawn sherds are described in the pottery lists, where the descriptions add interesting variations to evidence presented in drawings.

Generally, the plates of photographs appear in the order of the chronological sequence of the site, i.e., from the Pre-Urban Stratum through the Sanctuary A Stratum. Some deviation resulted from arranging photographs of different sizes so as to take maximum advantage of the available space. Most photographs were taken with a Rolleiflex camera equipped with f2.8 Planar lens. Almost all field photographs were taken late in the afternoon, after the areas were free of bright sunlight. Details could be captured in photographs more clearly in twilight shadow than in bright sunlight where the contrast between light and shadow could not be effectively controlled. Photographs of entire sites were taken in sunlight. Objects were photographed outdoors in light shade, utilizing natural instead of artificial light.

Plans and sections will be explained in the next chapter. Field plans were produced at a scale of 1:50, and sections at a scale of 1:25, both drawn in the field on millimeter graph paper and later transferred to linen cloth.

I

THE SITE AND THE EXCAVATIONS

LOCATION

The site of Ai (et-Tell) is about two kilometers east of Beitin (Bethel), and about fifteen kilometers north-northeast of Jerusalem, as shown in Fig. 1. The only practical approach from Jerusalem is by way of the Nablus Road, passing through Bireh (Ramallah). About one and one-half kilometers north of Bireh a right turn is taken to the Taiyiba-Jericho road. Another right turn about one and one-half kilometers farther takes one through Beitin and to Deir Dibwan, where the improved road ends. A left turn at the monument, erected at the entrance of Deir Dibwan by the Ai Expedition, leads to the *tell*, about one-half kilometer up a long hill to the west. The site of Ai is located at the highest point of the ridge overlooking Deir Dibwan and the vast wasteland of dry hills and valleys stretching eastward to the Jordan Valley. From the summit of the *tell* there is a commanding view of the east and south. The green line of the Jordan River can be seen in the expanse of its valley, and the north end of the Dead Sea is visible on a clear day. Landmarks clearly discernible in the south are the Mount of Olives, Anata, Tell el-Ful, er-Ram, Jaba, and Nebi Samwil.

In ancient times, the site was approached from the east. An unimproved road leads east from Deir Dibwan, past Khirbet Khudriya, located in Fig. 2, to an intersection with the Roman road which connected Rammun (Rimmon) and Mukhmas (Michmash). This road probably preserves a pre-exilic route, reflected in Isa. 10:28f, which traced the advance of the Assyrian invaders past Rimmon, Ai, Michmash, Anathoth, and to a point before Jerusalem. Another unimproved route leads southeast from Deir Dibwan, past Khirbet Haiyan, toward Mukhmas, following sections of a Byzantine road connecting Mukhmas, Haiyan, Burj Beitin (located on a hill between Bethel and Ai) and Beitin. The two routes seem to preserve a tradition of access to Ai from the east and southeast. Four gates in the Early Bronze Age city wall at Sites J, K, A, and the Marquet-Krause Lower City reflect this orientation in EB I–III.

THE TELL

The *tell* is a polygon-shaped mound covering an area of 110,410 square meters (Marquet-Krause 1934) or 110.4 dunams (about 27.5 acres). It was formed by the original line of city walls built in EB I. The first wall was rebuilt and widened in EB II. EB IIIA and IIIB walls were built in succession against the outside of the original one, resulting in a final triple-wall construction. At the time the last wall was built a considerable depth of debris had accumulated over the inner area of the *tell*. The last wall effectively buttressed the accumulating mound on all sides, which gradually assumed its present shape by capturing wind-blown dust and decaying debris from the houses of its inhabitants. At Site H, the EB IIIB wall still stands seven meters high, approximately its original height. These walls shaped the original Early Bronze Age city, preserving its form to this day by

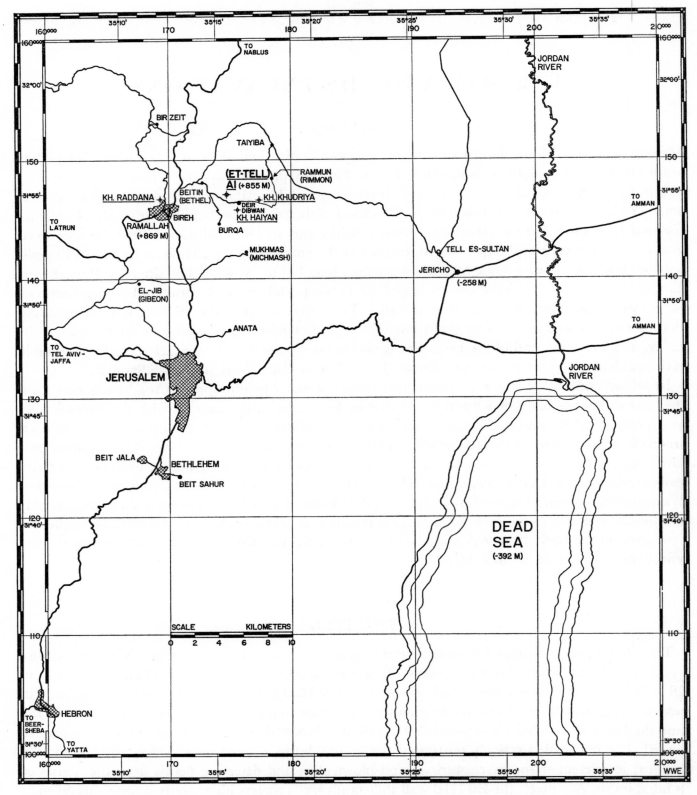

Fig. 1. The region of Ai (et-Tell). Sites excavated 1964–1970 are indicated by crossed circles.

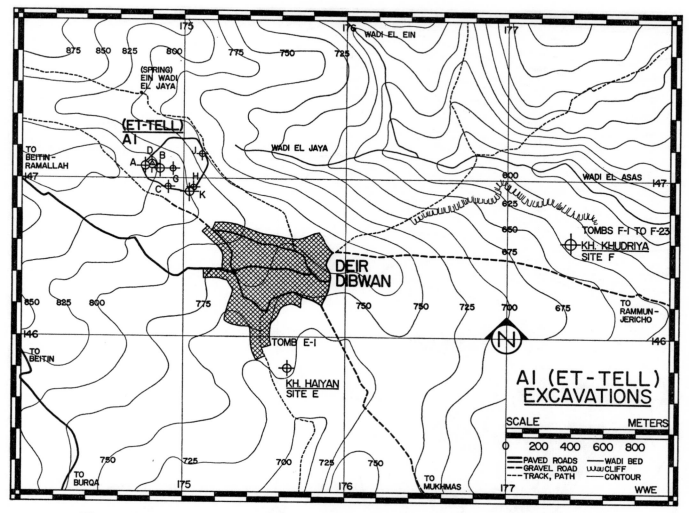

Fig. 2. The immediate region of Ai (et-Tell) with sites excavated 1964–1970.

their incredible durability. From the south, about one kilometer away, the ruins have the appearance of a giant grave, which in fact they are.

On the north and east sides, the deep Wadi el-Jaya drops precipitously as much as 100 meters from the acropolis elevation. The bottom of the *wadi* cannot be seen from the northeastern line of city walls due to the abrupt drop over step-like rock terraces. The *wadi* branches opposite the acropolis, with one branch leading toward Beitin, and the other encircling the *tell* and leading back toward Deir Dibwan. Thus the *tell* crowns the end of a long ridge rising from the east, and lies sprawled over its highest point, reaching a height of 850 meters above sea level at the acropolis. The fortifications follow the edge of the *wadi* on the north and west sides, taking advantage of the natural defenses afforded by the steep outside approaches. Fig. 3 shows that the city walls were built along defensible contours leading downhill from the acropolis and enclosing the wide lower terraces in a fan-shaped polygon. Outside the city, the terraces change abruptly to rough slopes of the ravines surrounding the site.

Thus the *tell* drops away toward the east in a succession of fairly regular terraces, down to Site J,

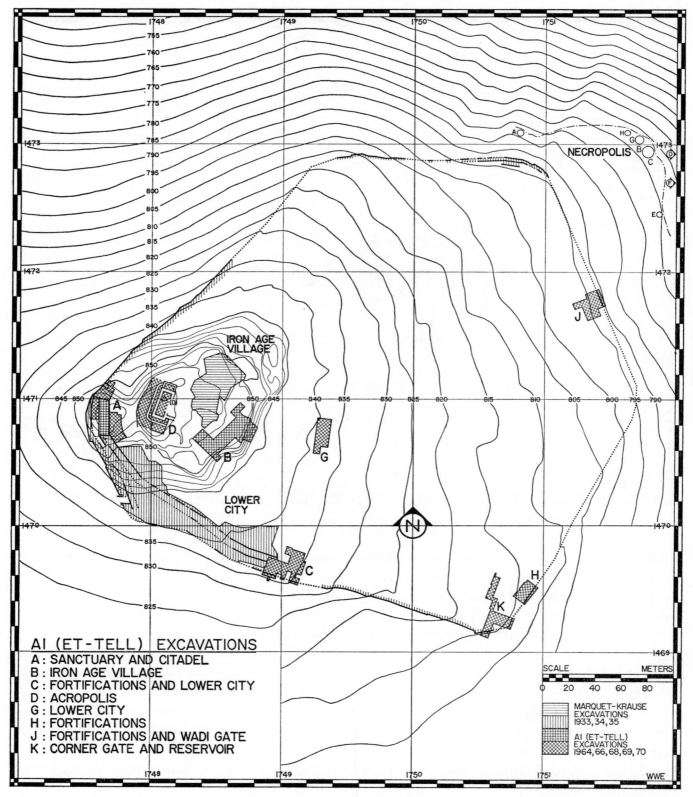

Fig. 3. Plan of et-Tell with sites excavated 1964–1970.

the lowest point overlooking the *wadi*. A change in elevation from 850 meters above sea level at Site D to 795 at Site J is noted, a difference of some 55 meters. In fact, one cannot see the acropolis area from Site J because of the bulging terraces which lie between them.

Roads within the city can be located in part by evidence at the four gates, and in part by the contours of the *tell*. A path now leads from a point between the Corner and Wadi Gates, on the lower east side, almost straight up the slope of the *tell* toward Site G. Terraces on the slopes of the city converge at the vertical line of the path, suggesting the preservation of a major route within the ancient city. Above contour line 835, the road probably 'zig-zagged' up the terraces on the steep approach to the acropolis. Also there is a wide, level terrace on the inner side of the north wall, stretching from the Citadel Gate down the edge of the *wadi* toward the northeast turn of the city wall just north of the Wadi Gate. This appears to be a natural road bounded on the outside by the city wall and on the inside by sheer bedrock rising abruptly to higher levels inside the city. Thus two probable major routes within the city brought the lower east side into communication with the upper levels, and lateral streets possibly branched off. Another road led along the inside of the lower city from the Citadel Gate to the Postern Gate. This road continued toward Site C via Ch. 239 of Marquet-Krause 1949, Pl. C, and probably east to the Corner Gate.

THE SITE A BUILDINGS

Nestled in the extreme western bend of the city wall system, the Site A buildings were set apart from the rest of the EB city. The acropolis buildings at Site D faced east with a panoramic view of the entire city spread out on the terraces below. However, Site A was located behind the Site D complex and hidden from the lower city. Situated on the west end of an hour-glass shaped contour the east end of which supported the Site D buildings at an elevation of 850 meters, Site A occupied a location inferior to that of Site D. From the perspective of status, however, the location was more desirable than that of the lower city, because it was adjacent to the Site D building complex, and was a component of the acropolis unit.

The Site A buildings were not an articulated unit with the acropolis, since the Site D complex was heavily fortified by its own enclosure walls. Instead, Site A was actually integral with the city wall system at a strategic point in the fortifications. Furthermore, each building phase, even that of Sanctuary A, used the wall of a related citadel phase for its western wall. Thus the Site A buildings were integral in structure with the citadel and city wall system, although they were adjacent to the acropolis complex. One might infer a special significance to these buildings from the fact that they were at the rear of the acropolis, yet their exclusion from the fortified enclosure at Site D implies that they were more expendable in any crisis situation than the central buildings at Site D. The destiny of the Site A buildings was inseparably linked with that of the citadel. The logical inference is that their functions were also related.

Four phases of fortification towers were associated with the Site A buildings. First, a semi-oval structure, Tower C, projected outward from Wall C, as indicated in Fig. 84, and guarded the east side of the approach road to the Citadel Gate. Building C was built along the inside of Wall C opposite Tower C, using the inner face of the city wall for its roof support on the west side. Second, Tower B, a rectangular projection outside Wall B in Fig. 85, blocked the approach road to the

Citadel Gate because the gate was eliminated in Wall B and presumably relocated elsewhere in this phase. Inside the city, Building B was constructed against the inner face of Wall B, reusing the unit of rooms of Building C located north of Wall B in Fig. 84. Building B was apparently a domestic house with a courtyard and outdoor fireplace unrelated to the citadel structures.

The third fortification was Tower A, associated with Building A as drawn in Fig. 86. This tower measured 8 × 30 meters, and was situated on the ruins of earlier Walls C and B. Wall A, the new city fortification associated with Tower A, was constructed west of the tower and around the projecting ruins of the earlier strong points. Tower A thus sat above and overlooking the city wall, guarding the approach to the city where broken terraces of bedrock stepped down to a broad shallow valley on the western side. Building A was constructed on a deep fill against the inner face of Tower A, and possibly was the residence of a priestly family associated with Temple A on the acropolis.

Tower A[1] was the fourth phase of fortifications, and it was associated with Sanctuary A. A new city wall was built outside Wall A, as shown in Fig. 87, and buttresses were added around the north end of Tower A, strengthening the fortification at a point where bedrock dropped away sharply toward the valley on the west. Sanctuary A probably served no functional role with the rebuilt tower. In fact, the evidence suggests that the sanctuary housed a syncretized Egyptian cult, and thus was probably a royal shrine of the ruler of Ai. The garrison posted at the citadel, therefore, insured the safety of the shrine and at the same time protected the vulnerable northwest bend in the city fortifications. Sanctuary A may have been a small city-state shrine, as Wright suggests on the analogy of the Nippur temples in the third milennium, B.C. (Wright 1970, 316). An alternative interpretation, however, is that Sanctuary A was a symbol of government imposed upon the people from the outside, and, therefore, would be something less than the religious center of a city-state league.

THE GARSTANG EXCAVATION AT THE SANCTUARY SITE, 1928

John Garstang excavated eight trenches at et-Tell in 1928, at least one of which was at the sanctuary site. The trenches are located in Fig. 4 which was traced from Garstang's field sketch plan submitted to the Department of Antiquities on September 21, 1928 (see Garstang 1928, Sketch Plan 'Et Tell, September 20, 1928').* Garstang's drawing of the *tell* included only the upper part, because the 'footpath' at 'Trench A bis' seems to be located at Site C in Fig. 3. His 'Trench A bis' apparently intersected the outer face of Wall A in area C IV (see Callaway 1965, 29, Fig. 10), near the eastern extremity of the Marquet-Krause excavations (see Marquet-Krause 1949, Pl. XCV, *coupe* A–B).

The two large circular contours in the upper part of the plan represent the acropolis, with the Site D complex on the right where the large circle encloses three small ones, and Site A on the left, represented by the spiral contour. Trench E apparently cut into the northern side of the heap of stones covering the sanctuary (see Marquet-Krause 1949, Pl. I:2). Trench D, against the EB wall outside the sanctuary, is the shallow depression in the side of the *tell* visible in Marquet-Krause 1949,

* The writer is indebted to Dr. Y. Rahmani of the Rockefeller Museum and Miss Hannah Katzenstein of the Israel Museum for providing access to the Garstang report.

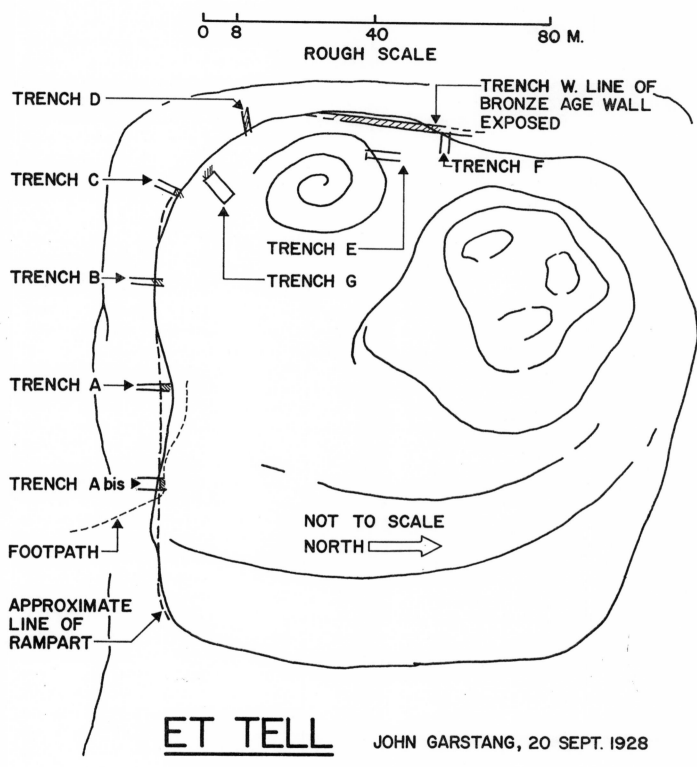

Fig. 4. Map of soundings made by John Garstang.

Pl. I:1, right at the beginning of the heap covering the sanctuary in the upper left. Thus Garstang's Trench E was the only sounding which penetrated the sanctuary area inside the city.

The only record concerning Trench E consists of a sentence in the report to the Department which is as follows: 'Interior Trench E was not instructive owing to interference with the site, it would appear, during the war of 1915–1917, when this spot was used as an artillery observation point' (Garstang 1928, 3). Probably told by local people that the site had been used as an artillery observation point during World War I, Garstang was asked to remove certain debris and restore the area to usable condition. Since he was a British citizen, and the disturbance of the area was attributed to British military occupation, he apparently was obliged to comply with the wishes of the owners.

Garstang reported that the site of et-Tell pertained 'entirely to the Bronze Age,' and as evidence he deposited the following in 'five labelled boxes':

1. 'A selection of pottery fragments marked as from their respective trenches'
2. 'several fossils'
3. 'part of a tile and a sample of mud and pottery agglomerate' (Garstang 1928, 3).

The writer has found one box of pottery fragments in the storeroom of the Rockefeller Museum. However, there was no key to the numbers written on the sherds distinguishing provenance among the eight trenches. The numbers run from 1.250 through 1.368, and are found on pottery, fossils, and one sample of soil. Some numbers are missing. There is a statement in Garstang 1931, 356, that 'a considerable proportion of L.B.A.i' wares were found, including 'a Cypriote wish-bone handle,' with a parenthetical note that they were left 'in the collection of the American School.'

Apparently, the exact provenance of each of the five boxes of artifacts was not recorded, because one would expect eight boxes from eight trenches. Also, it is likely that the collection left at the American School was selected from the five boxes without regard to provenance, since the excavator seems to have been interested only in finding what he claims to have left at the School. The undistinguished collection of Byzantine, Iron Age I, and Early Bronze sherds stored at the Rockefeller Museum would therefore be the discards from the 'five labelled boxes,' and would be relatively useless as evidence for evaluating Garstang's conclusions. A search of the American School attic has not turned up the crucial collection reportedly left there.

An observation can be made regarding the Rockefeller Museum collection, however. Garstang noted in his report to the Department of Antiquities that the site of et-Tell '. . . proves to pertain entirely to the Bronze Age,' but he did not specify which Bronze Age. It is too much to assume that he meant Early Bronze Age, because he noted in Garstang 1931, 356, that '. . . as usual, M.B.A. wares were most abundant.' Actually, there is not one Middle Bronze Age sherd in the collection. That he called Early Bronze Age pottery Middle Bronze in 1928 now seems probable. Even Marquet-Krause, who learned field methods with Garstang one season at Jericho before beginning at et-Tell, noted in her first report to the Department of Antiquities that the outer city wall 'seems to have been built about the XIXth century B.C.' (Marquet-Krause 1933, 1). She did note that 'the overwhelming majority of potsherds found in the burned layer of the acropolis building dated to the Bronze Age, although 'a small number of sherds could be attributed to the M.B.I. period' (p. 2). She seems to have attributed the outer city wall to 'the XIXth century B.C.' on the basis of Garstang's report, because she apparently cleared his Trench F there in 1933. Garstang, therefore, had

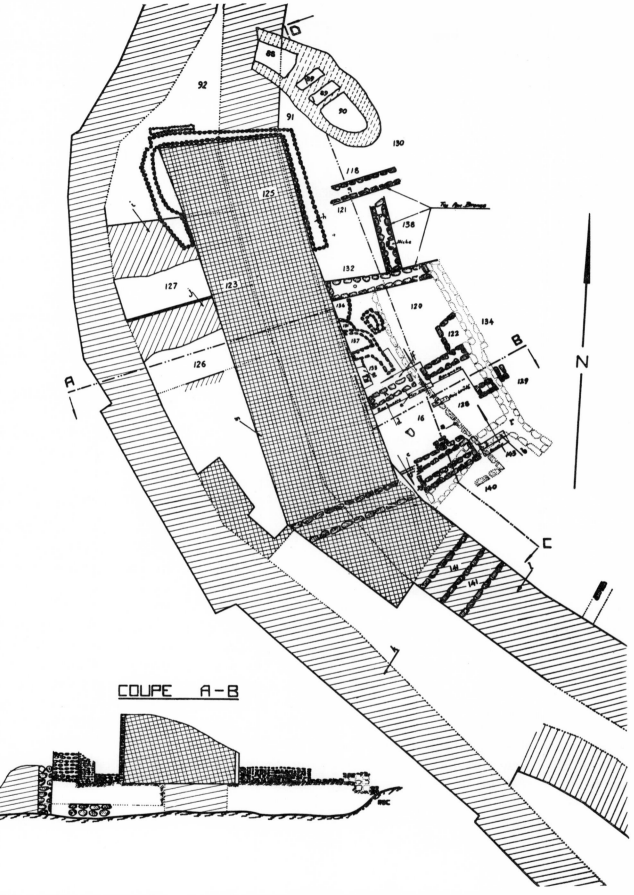

COUPE A-B

Fig. 5. A composite plan of the Site A buildings (after Marquet-Krause 1949, Pl. XCIII).

not clearly distinguished Early Bronze from Middle Bronze pottery in 1928. It is quite probable that what he called 'L.B.A.i' was Early Bronze also, although one can never know until the American School collection is found.

THE MARQUET-KRAUSE EXCAVATION OF THE SANCTUARY, 1933–1935

The first expedition

Three different areas at et-Tell were selected for exavation by the Rothschild Expedition in its first season, from September 11 to November 13, 1933. As outlined by Marquet-Krause, they were as follows:

1. 'near the northwest corner of the outer enclosure wall';
2. 'on the summit of the mound';
3. 'in the necropolis outside the city proper'; (Marquet-Krause 1933, 1).

A plan of the sites excavated in 1933 shows the acropolis building largely uncovered, and one field of the Iron Age village on the east side of the acropolis opened. There is no plan of the site mentioned in No. 1 above. The interim report submitted to the Department of Antiquities described the results of Objective No. 1 as follows:

'The outer city wall is built of large unhewn blocks of stone and is founded on bedrock. It seems to have been built about the XIXth century B.C.' (Marquet-Krause 1933, 1).

The sanctuary, apparently, was not excavated in 1933, because the field 'near the northwest corner of the outer enclosure wall' seems to have been a continuation, or merely clearance, of Garstang's Trench F.

The second expedition

A remarkable second campaign of six months, from the first of June to the first of December, resulted in the discovery of the sanctuary in 1934 (Marquet-Krause 1949, 13). The discovery of the sanctuary '. . . fut le résultat inespéré d'un travail long et difficile. Situé au Sud-Ouest du palais, sur un terrain moins élevé, l'emplacement disparaissait complètement sous un amas de pierres de 6 mètres de haut, couvrant une surface plus ou moins circulaire de 20 ares environ. Cet amas faisait penser à une tour (*midgal*) dominant la vue du Sud-Ouest . . .' (Marquet-Krause 1949, 16, Pl. I:2)

The heap of stones deterrent to excavation actually preserved the sanctuary in good condition, as the terrace of stones at Site B preserved the Iron Age I houses excavated in 1968–1969 (see Callaway 1970, 12–19). When the walls of the tower were seen under the stones at the sanctuary site, efforts were concentrated, and '. . . avec une moyenne de 80 à 100 hommes, durant un long mois, nous acharnâmes à transporter les pierres.' Attention was focused upon the tower first, because there is mention of the 'petite chambres' found in the tower structure which were difficult to define exactly, to the extent that they were not drawn on the tower plan (Marquet-Krause 1949, 17). Nevertheless, there seemed to be a casemate type infrastructure of the tower that claimed the interest of the excavator before the sanctuary itself was discovered.

A reconstruction of the elusive tower rooms was attempted by Vincent, apparently a frequent visitor at the site and the 'archaeologist on call' when problems arose. His sketch plan and section

(Vincent 1937, 247) show a casemate-type structure with walls '. . . de 2 mètres à 2 m. 50 d'épaisseur . . .' (Marquet-Krause 1949, 17) which was smoothly faced on the exterior, but had no finished inner face in the row of inner 'rooms.' Marquet-Krause speculated that the room-like structures were built to strengthen the tower structure and allow a height of up to 15 meters to be reached in the original building. The tower, therefore, was a part of the fortifications, and was not a functional part of the sanctuary, other than its west wall (see Marquet-Krause 1949, 17).

The most impressive discovery of 1934 was the sanctuary constructed against the tower. Apparently the south room was discovered first, because the preliminary report describes its censers, the charred timber thought by Vincent to be an *asherah*, and the masses of broken pottery before the contents of the north room are mentioned. Actually, the depth of debris above Room 116, the south room, was not great, as can be seen in Pl. X.1. A pyramid of stones was heaped over Room 120 and its altar, probably causing the workers to reach occupation levels there last.

Photographs of the rooms of the sanctuary with their bins and ledges indicate that the entire floor plan was uncovered before probes into the earlier layers were begun. Pl. XIV shows the series of rooms reconstructed in the isometric of Pl. XCIV. The basic integrity of stratification assigned to the terminal sanctuary phase is therefore affirmed, particularly in Rooms 116, 120, 122, 128, 133, and Bins 131, 136, and 137.

Very little is known, however, about the complex of walls and rooms north of the sanctuary. The excavator failed to see a blocked doorway in her Wall o, the north wall of the sanctuary, which communicated with Room 132 in an earlier phase of the building (see Callaway 1965, 23, Fig. 5). Consequently the tripartite plan suggested a second sanctuary, with a special niche in the east side of Wall p (Marquet-Krause 1949, Pl. XCIII). Marquet-Krause preferred the theory that priests of the deity housed in the sanctuary probably were quartered there (Marquet-Krause 1949, 19). Objects indicating the function of the rooms were almost completely lacking, leaving any reconstruction of the area mostly to conjecture.

Garstang's Trench E seems to have penetrated this part of the sanctuary site, which may account for the radical destruction found there in 1934. His report, furthermore, indicated that the area had been disturbed prior to his excavation by the installation of an artillery observation post during World War I. Thus the area comprised of Rooms 118, 121, 130, 132, and 138 seems to have been destroyed beyond any reconstruction before Marquet-Krause reached the site.

Two further observations about the 1934 excavations may be useful at this point. First, the description of fill layers underneath the sanctuary (designated Sanctuary A in 1935, Marquet-Krause 1949, 29), indicates that probes were sunk to bedrock in Rooms 116 and 120. The thickness of earth and debris under the sanctuary is reported to have varied from 2.30 meters in the south end of the site to 1.60 meters in the north, as represented in Pl. XCIII, *coupe* C–D. Thus the earlier systematic clearance of the articulated walls, rooms, and floors of the sanctuary was succeeded by less careful and unsystematic probing of the fill underneath. The major walls and the altar of the sanctuary were left standing on rough balks of earth extending into the rooms in irregular projections. Reconstructions of the earlier structures and their stratigraphy were based, therefore, upon disconnected evidence which would be less accurate than that of the first sanctuary.

Second, three levels of stratification were defined at the conclusion of the 1934 excavation (Marquet-Krause 1949, 20). The levels were numbered from bottom to top, thus Level I represented the earliest structures on the site; Level II designated the intermediate occupations and buildings; and Level III was the uppermost, or latest structure, i.e., the sanctuary. Levels II and III are marked on the photograph in Pl. XXII.2, which is a view of the north side of Wall o and the east side of the tower. The wall designated 'm' in the photograph extends below Level II, and therefore represents Level I. The difficulties with this stratification will be seen later. The definition of three levels rests partly upon the evidence north of Wall o, radically disturbed by Garstang's Trench E and the British artillery observation post. It seems that a sequence of walls was worked out in the area north of Wall o which was related to a succession of floor and fill layers in Room 120.

Only Level III was designated a sanctuary in 1934. There was no doubt in the excavator's mind that this level was a sanctuary, and that it dated to Early Bronze III. However, the Egyptian alabasters found in Level III were recognized in later study as parallel in form and materials with alabasters dating to the Egyptian IInd and IIIrd Dynasties, a period much earlier than the dates assigned to Level III. Marquet-Krause was then dating the termination of the sanctuary and acropolis to ca. 2000 B.C. Therefore she concluded that the alabasters of Level III must have been kept from an earlier sanctuary, '. . . contemporain de la première phase de notre Cité, à l'aurore de l'Ancien Bronze' (Marquet-Krause 1949, 20). This is noted because the disparity between the date of the alabasters and the context in which they were found seems to have influenced the identification of earlier phases as sanctuaries. At the time Levels I and II were excavated in 1934, however, the inclination was to identify only Level III as a sanctuary.

The third expedition

A relatively short third expedition was fielded from the end of August to November 15, 1935. More workers were employed, reaching a number of 160, over against the top number of 80 mentioned in the report of the second expedition.

Most of the 160 workers were employed at sites other than the sanctuary, principally at the Iron Age village and the lower city excavations.

Very little was reported about the excavation of the sanctuary, though it is evident that some work was continued there. Mention is made of finding three knife handles of carved bone and an alabaster cup in the removal of a collapsed wall. This was near the niche in the south wall of the sanctuary where a carved ivory handle of a knife, along with its sheath, were found in 1934. The bone handles and alabaster appeared to belong to an earlier level than that of the ivory handle, found in Level III.

The sanctuary, with its three levels identified in 1934, seems to have become the type site for stratifying EB remains over the entire *tell* by 1935. However, the 'Level' designations were not continued, and without explanation, new strata designations appear. Level III, the sanctuary discovered in 1934, became Sanctuary A; Level II was called Sanctuary B, and Level I, the earliest in point of time, was Sanctuary C (see Marquet-Krause 1949, 29).

Reconstruction of a typology of pottery forms associated with these three phases became a primary concern. This reflects, perhaps, the intense interest in Tell Beit Mirsim and Bethel (see Albright 1932 and Kelso 1968, 54–81). Jar rims and necks characteristic of the Sanctuary A period are illustrated on Pl. XXXI.1; Sanctuary B pottery is shown on Pl. XIX and a type-sequence of ledge-handle forms from Sanctuaries A, B, and C is displayed on Pl. XX.1. The phasing of the

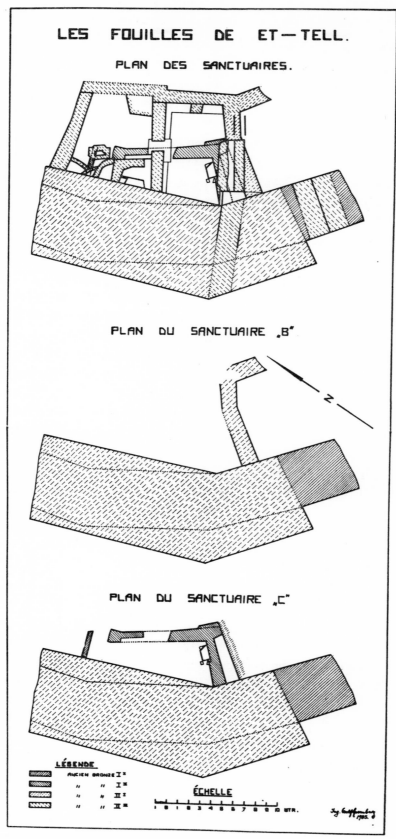

Fig. 6. The Marquet-Krause reconstruction of Sanctuaries A, B, and C (after Marquet-Krause 1949, Pl. XCVIII).

sanctuary site, and subsequent analysis of pottery forms associated with each phase, apparently became normative for the entire *tell*.

The floor of Sanctuary B, shown in Pl. XVIII.1, 2, was associated with Wall 'r', which served Sanctuaries A and B, as Pl. XCVIII indicates. Thus Sanctuary B was thought to cover an area in only one room equal to that of the three rooms of Sanctuary A (Marquet-Krause 1949, 29). Sanctuary B in Pl. XCVIII was not adequately understood, as evident from the incomplete plan. The basis for identification seems to have been the floor in Room 116, constructed of packed earth on a sequence of fill layers, rather than a discernible sequence of wall structures.

A third structure, designated Sanctuary C, was found under the floor of Sanctuary B. The walls are drawn in Pl. XCVIII, where only one room is outlined. The east wall, however, is parallel with an earlier, six-meter wide city wall, outlined under the tower structure on the west. Against the south wall was a rectangular stone-paved platform thought to be a place for offerings (Marquet-Krause 1949, 30, illustrated on Pl. XX. 2). The platform was constructed '. . . de deux briques et de pierres plates irrégulières, parmi lesquelles se trouvait une pierre noire d'espèce inconnue à Ay, donc importée' (Marquet-Krause 1949, 30). Pottery from the third sanctuary seemed more primitive than that of Sanctuaries A and B, and the forms were more limited.

Finally, upon reaching bedrock some four meters below the top of the ruins of Sanctuary A, sherds similar to those of Sanctuary C were found. Note was made that some could be traced to 'l'époque énéolithique,' however.

Mme. Marquet-Krause died on July 1, 1936, before the report of the third expedition was published. She was in the midst of making plans to return to et-Tell for a fourth season of work. Her objectives at et-Tell were not accomplished, although it seems that the sanctuary excavation was essentially completed. The last report concluded with a summary of phases and successive layers, indicating that firm conclusions had been reached (Marquet-Krause 1949, 31). There was, therefore, a complete excavation of the sanctuary, with the exception of the intended reconstruction of its history which apparently the excavator planned to do at the conclusion of the project.

THE JOINT ARCHAEOLOGICAL EXPEDITION TO AI, 1964–1970

The excavation of Site A

A careful salvage operation was conducted at Site A, located in Fig. 2, from May 4 until June 24, 1964. For some twenty-eight years, the site had remained open to the ravages of nature, man, and animals, exactly as it had been left in November, 1935. Marquet-Krause left the major walls of Sanctuary A standing upon their balks of earth, and the altar of the sanctuary was intact. However, the sides of the balks had eroded, primarily on the upper side, leaving the scant remains of Sanctuary A rather mutilated. More substantial remains of the lower phases were preserved, proving fortunate because most of the problems in the interpretation of the site involved Sanctuaries B and C.

Remains of the site were completely excavated in 1964, and the present volume is the result of that expedition. The fortification towers and associated city walls were explored in 1968, but no additional knowledge of the buildings was gained. The sequence of towers strengthened the EB city wall system at the sharp bend of the wall around the acropolis, a vulnerable spot in the defenses of the city because the terrain outside provided a rather easy approach to the city wall. The towers, therefore, were erected to dominate the area and secure the acropolis. A detailed report on them will appear in a subsequent volume devoted to the city fortifications and gates.

Since the general purpose of the present expedition was to carry forward the work terminated abruptly by the untimely death of Marquet-Krause, the first four sites, opened in 1964, were located at strategic places in the previous excavations. Site A, located in Fig. 3, is the sanctuary. The objective at Site A was to obtain a precise stratigraphy by careful excavations of the earth supporting the remaining walls of Sanctuary A. A secondary objective was to discover enough pottery and objects associated with the various layers and phases to determine the distinguishing characteristics of each phase. In the event that the phasing by Marquet-Krause was accurate, the current finds could simply be added to those already known from Sanctuaries A–C. If the phasing were modified, however, there remained the possibility of associating finds from the Marquet-Krause expedition with current discoveries by typology, making possible in any case a report which would include all the pottery and objects from the site in one convenient volume.

Layout and technique

Because of the piecemeal nature of remains to be removed, control over the excavation at all times was imperative. 'Control' means the systematic removal of layers identified and numbered prior to removal. This was attempted with the following layout and technique.

First, the site was divided into manageable areas. Usually, in undisturbed sites, the areas are arbitrary units of convenient and controllable size. Five-meter squares have become basic units in many excavations, because a supervisor can observe at all times the activity in a unit of that size. The principle of close supervision, not the size of the area, is primary. In the case of the sanctuary site, a grid of regular squares was not feasible, because each room of Sanctuary A had parts excavated to bedrock. The only places where balks could be maintained were underneath the main walls of Sanctuary A, which remained intact.

Consequently the major rooms of Sanctuary A became the basic areas of the site, and the balks on which the walls stood limited the areas. Four areas, assigned Nos. I–IV on the sketch plan in Fig. 81, were laid out accordingly. The space covered by an area throughout the excavation of all phases is indicated by diagonal-line shading between the major walls associated with the area number.

Area I was bordered on the north by Wall E, and by Wall C on the west. Its south side was indistinct, because everything had been removed to bedrock, except a small area alongside Wall C, located at the left end of the plan. A II (i.e., Site A, Area II) included all of the first room of Sanctuary A, enclosed by Wall E on the south, Wall C–Tower A on the west, Wall H on the north, and Wall P on the east. A III included the second room and the enclosure around the altar, the wall of which had been removed previously. The south enclosure was Wall H, reaching from the juncture with Wall P on the east to Tower A on the west; Tower A bordered the west side; Wall M was the north limit; and a ledge of bedrock, already exposed except for a thin layer of earth, limited the east side of the area. A IV reached from Wall M on the south, alongside Tower A on the west, to a ledge of bedrock skirting the north extremity of Wall O in a semi-circle to the east. Thus the north and east sides of A IV were indistinct.

Second, a master balk connecting all four areas was located along the east face of Tower A. This balk had continuous layers traceable along the length of the entire site. The section drawn from the balk became the Master Section, a kind of anchor section for all the lateral sections running east-west along the dividing balks between areas. Actually, the master balk along the east face of the tower was the only possible one for its purpose. Outcroppings of exposed bedrock surrounded the site from the north, across A IV from Tower Buttress A[1] (see Fig. 81), around the east side of A III, A II, and almost across A I to Wall C on the southwest. No north-south section was possible along the east side of the site. Also, large areas of A II and A III had been removed to bedrock along the north-south line of Wall F, located in the middle of the site, so no significant connected section could be drawn there.

Along Tower A, however, the end of the Wall M balk between Areas III and IV rested against the face of the tower and connected with layers under it. The Wall H balk, between Areas II and III, likewise abutted the tower and supported the left side of the Sanctuary A altar. Dramatically striated fill under the tower extended into the Wall H balk. At the south end of the site was the Wall E balk, between Areas I and II, connecting at the extreme south end of the master balk. The Wall F balk in Areas I and II lay parallel with the city wall, and was associated with the master balk at three points, i.e., the balks under Walls E, S, and H. A close correlation of layers in all of the balks with those in the master balk was possible, and control of the removal of layers was maintained through this correlation.

Because the identification of layers in the Master Section controlled the removal of layers in each area, a system of *layer* identification numbers was employed in labeling all artifacts. The section provided the vertical location of the layer, and, where there were installations or buildings, the horizontal plan located important features within the layer. Locus numbers were assigned to important objects to locate the place on the horizontal plan of the layer where they were found. Thus the primary designation of provenance was the layer number, which indicated the place in vertical sequence from which artifacts were taken; locus numbers were secondary designations, indicating horizontal location within the layer.

Technical terms and their meaning

A working definition of the term 'layer' may be helpful at this point, because it is preferred over the more usual term 'locus' as a primary designation of provenance. Normally, a layer is an observable entity of earth or other deposit which has a distinct homogeneity and occurs within a definable vertical sequence. A layer conforms to its natural 'bedlines' which controlled its formation in the first place (see Wheeler 1954, 54f.), and these bedlines, controlling excavation of the layer, are drawn to scale on a vertical profile.

The term 'locus' also indicates a definable natural unit, usually related to a structure such as a floor, a wall, or an installation of some kind. But, as G. R. H. Wright points out, in some instances it is 'not inevitably comprehended in a uniform deposit of debris' (G. R. H. Wright 1966, 120). Historically, finds designated by the term 'locus' have received their orientation from building plans instead of vertical sections of layer deposits. This seems to be the significance of published profiles of walls in older reports having no layer lines connecting the walls. In recent years, the term has come to be associated more closely with layers and sections which extend beyond the confines of houses, but it continues to reflect a past usage less compatible with section-controlled excavation than the term 'layer.'

Layers were identified in the sanctuary area by scraping and cleaning the edge of cuts made by Marquet-Krause. They were thus seen in vertical sequence and labelled before each successive layer was removed by working from the point of definition at the edge of the cut across the horizontal space of the respective areas. Numbers were assigned in the order of removal, i.e., from top to bottom, so that layer numbers occurred in the exact reverse of the sequence of original deposits. Layer numbers were therefore working designations later incorporated into the phasing of the site after bedrock was reached.

'Phase' is another term preferred in this report to the more usual 'stratum.' A phase is an observable combination of layers in the earth which seems to represent a definite historical entity beyond that indicated by a layer. There are, for instance, architectural phases where a building complex is constructed, used, modified, or destroyed. There are also phases of abandonment, prior to or between architectural phases. Essentially, phases are assigned on the basis of section analysis. In this report, the evidence of the Master Section, designated A–A in Fig. 83, is primary. 'Phase,' therefore, seems to be a compatible term to use with 'layer' in a section-controlled excavation technique.

The term 'stratum,' on the other hand, has not been related to observed sections primarily. Stratum usually indicates a particular historical period represented by artifacts found in a combination of loci. G. R. H. Wright notes that stratum does not always, in usage, identify a physical entity in the earth. He cites as evidence this statement in the Megiddo reports: 'Stratum X was strongly represented both stratigraphically and ceramically throughout the excavated areas' (G. R. H. Wright 1966, 122, from Shipton 1939, 17). The corollary of this, Wright observes, is that it would have been possible for Stratum X to exist throughout the excavated areas even had it not been represented stratigraphically.

His point and his corollary are somewhat misleading, because Shipton seems to be referring to architectural remains as 'stratigraphic' evidence. Obviously he regarded pottery as evidence of a stratum also, even in the absence of building remains, and that would be technically 'stratigraphic.' More precisely, the term indicates a physical entity in the earth, because some evidence of this entity gives rise to the identification. However, stratum may mean more than the physical entity demonstrates, because, as Wright perceptively notes, it is 'an hypostatizing of the actual.' A section may demonstrate evidence of a stratum, but in usage, the term has had enough of the character of an hypostasis to make it unsuitable as the equivalent of phase.

Admittedly, phasing entirely from the evidence of drawn sections has its limitations and liabilities. It demands carefully supervised excavation techniques which assure proper identification and separation of layers. Also, an experienced field archaeologist is required for the drawing of sections. This task is accomplished with the collaboration of the area and site supervisors as well as the architect, but the section must be done by one who has had enough experience to recognize the ordinary structures and installations of antiquity from various and sometimes odd perspectives. It is not enough to draw what is obvious, because what is obvious may not be coherent. The hidden part of structures, which may not be obvious to an inexperienced person, become apparent to one who has seen them before, so that a cut into the rubble core of a wall can be recognized even before the faces are revealed, or brick structures which have merged with the earth of their ruins become in-telligible.

To a certain extent the section which is properly drawn is an hypostasis, like the concept of stratum discussed above. A section drawn by a novice, or by a third party, such as an architect, whose training has not been in excavation techniques, can be quite as incoherent and meaningless as pottery analysis by an untrained staff member would be. The difference, therefore, between the concepts of stratum and phase is not that one is an hypostasis and the other is not, but that the latter, when equivalent to an observed physical entity in the earth seems to be more subject to inde-pendent critical judgment than the former. The former has often been clothed in so much inter-pretation that factual evidence and interpretation are inseparable in reports. In the last analysis, however, the reliability of either depends upon the person who produces them, as the writer was so aptly reminded by the late Père Roland de Vaux.

The concept of stratum as a designation for a historical period is not to be retired, however. Stratum continues to have relevance, because it incorporates meaning beyond that inherent in the term phase. In the understanding and usage of the term employed here, a stratum consists of a phase or combination of phases, as phases consist of combinations of layers. Layers, it should be noted further, consist of a combination of sub-layers, which are actually the raw data recorded in field sections and record books. A stratum, therefore, is erected upon the demonstrable evidence of a building-block sequence, beginning with sub-layers painstakingly excavated and recorded in the field, and moving through the combination of layers and phases. The primary evidence for a stratum is a homogeneous combination of phases or layers representing a period of history, and the secondary evidence is that of pottery and artifacts, elucidating the chronology and culture of the stratum. A stratum, in the present report, is related to an observed section, and is based upon a sequence of visual analyses which seem to the writer to contain more checks and balances than the system of erecting strata upon the evidence of loci alone.

II

AN ANALYSIS OF PHASES AND STRATIFICATION

SYMBOLS ON PLANS AND SECTIONS

Plans of building phases

The symbols and designations of features on building plans are illustrated largely on the sketch plan in Fig. 81. Areas within the site are indicated by site designations, i.e., 'A,' followed by the area number in Roman numerals. The area designations are underlined, as <u>A I</u>, <u>A II</u>, etc., and the space included in a particular area is shaded with diagonal lines in the same unit with the designation. Walls are indicated by an upper case letter inside an elongated diamond symbol oriented to align with the related wall. Different alphabetical designations are assigned for each radical change in wall direction, but the same letter with numerical superscript is used where a wall continues straight or in the same general direction, but with a change in construction or phase. Examples are Walls F, F^1, F^2, and F^3 in A II and A III.

A heavy, continuous line is used to indicate the face of a wall, and a dashed line traces an assumed projection or former continuation, or in some cases, the joining of wall fragments. Combination dashed and dotted lines are used to indicate portions of plans taken from the Marquet-Krause report. Walls and related installations, such as bins and enclosures, are assigned letter designations in the same alphabetic series. Special installations, however, have the letter designation enclosed in a circle instead of the diamond symbol used for walls. Special structures, such as Tower A, associated with Wall A, have letter designations enclosed in a square diamond symbol. The letter designations are generally assigned in the order in which the structures were encountered in the excavation and recorded in the field notebooks.

Elevations were taken at points marked with a cross ($+$), and the elevation is given in meters above sea level. Brief notes associated with elevations describe the places where the reading was taken, i.e., 'bedrock,' 'floor,' 'base' (of wall), etc. The datum point for all elevations is the north rectangular-top column base of the 'plan du palais,' Marquet-Krause Pl. XCII, elevation No. 5: 854.20 meters above sea level.

Sections of balks and walls

Sections are designated by upper case letters also, but the letters are in a separate series and are enclosed in squares. The area covered by a section is indicated by a broken line connecting two squares which contain the same letter, such as A–A, B–B, etc. Orientation of the section is indicated by arrows pointing from the squares in the direction toward which one views the balk drawn in the section. Section designations do not correspond to wall designations, because profiles may be drawn on two sides of the balk on which a wall is located such as C–C and E–E, located on either side of the Wall H balk. A balk, however, may be identified by the primary designation of the wall on top of it, e.g., Wall F, and not $F–F^1$.

Sections have their own category of letter designations because they make up a closely correlated body of data whose primary significance is in their inter-relatedness. The relation of sections to walls is secondary; walls located on top of balks at Site A just happened to be there. The presence of these walls caused the previous excavator to leave the balks in order to preserve the walls.

Symbols used to designate features in individual sections are evident in the Master Section, shown in Fig. 83. The wall symbols employed on plans also locate the same walls on the section. Only the top and bottom courses of Tower A are drawn near the Sanctuary A altar. The extent of the tower is indicated by a symbol with arrows pointing toward its top and bottom extremities. Wall M was removed in the course of excavation; the symbol with two arrows indicates its location and width. Section B–B at the Wall M balk, located horizontally in Fig. 81, is located vertically at the point where B–B joins the Master Section balk in Fig. 83.

Layers, or sub-phases, are numbered serially from top to bottom in the order of excavation, and are indicated by Arabic numerals enclosed in circles. Where there appears to be sufficient change in the material character of a layer to warrant localized distinction, lower case alphabetical postscripts are added to the numerical designation. Phases, unlike layers, are numbered in the order of their historical occurrence, i.e., from bottom to top, and are indicated by Roman numerals in hexagonal symbols. Phase separation lines in the section are heavy, while layer separation lines are drawn lightly, i.e., except those marking off phases. The sides of balks left unexcavated are indicated by vertical lines made of a series of slight curves with small 'v' shaped connections pointing towards excavated areas. The same indicates unexcavated balks on horizontal plans. Balks which were removed are located by broken lines associated with their respective wall symbols. Where certain installations or significant areas were not excavated, phase and sub-phase lines are connected across the unexcavated space by dashed lines to show assumed continuations.

A system of shading is devised to indicate the different character and appearance of layers. This is symbolic rather than pictorial, because the bedlines of layers are important in the presentation of evidence and are therefore sharply defined and emphasized. Actual bedlines were often less clearly differentiated. Generally, compact deposits are indicated by alternating horizontal and vertical triple lines. Small triangles interspersed in the shading indicates an incidence of stones or pebbles. Ashy earth is normally represented by diagonal lines, and layers with heavy deposits of ashes are shaded with dots in addition to the diagonal lines. This, in general, is the rationale behind the shading, which is purely symbolic. The shading can be associated with photographs, as Section A–A and Pl. II.1, for more realistic correlation of the symbolic with the actual.

A small sketch plan accompanies each section and locates its horizontal coverage with diagonal-line shading. The locations correspond to those indicated on the sketch plan in Fig. 81. More precise locations can be found by referring to plans of the various phases, or relevant photographs can be sought out among the plates where visual identification is possible. The section orientation is indicated by the arrow-shaped symbols containing the individual section letter designations on each small sketch plan.

THE MASTER SECTION OF THE SITE

Section A–A, shown in Fig. 83, connects with balks touching all areas of the site, and preserves a record of all phases of its history as noted. Areas I and II are connected via the lateral Section G–G, a profile of the north face of the Wall E balk. Area I, south of the Wall E balk, joins Section G–G via Section H–H, a profile of the west face of the Wall F balk running parallel with the master balk from Area I to Area III. The Wall S balk in Area II connects Section H–H with the master balk midway of the area, and relates the significant platform, called the 'altar' of Sanctuary C by Marquet-Krause, to the stratigraphy of the rest of the site. Section E–E, the south face of the Wall H balk in Area II, ties the north end of Section H–H to the master balk, and provides crucial evidence for distinguishing Phases III and IV. Across Area III, the south face of the Wall M balk, profiled in Section B–B, is the key to stratigraphy in Areas III and IV. This is supplemented by specialized Sections C–C and D–D between Wall F² and the east side of the Building A enclosure, and Section I–I of Area IV, between Tower A and Wall O on the north side of the Wall M balk.

The Master Section, therefore, is integrated with all of the sections of the site, and its stratigraphy is closely correlated with them. The twelve major layers, or sub-phases, of earth and occupation debris of this section cover all of the phases represented in various degrees on the area sections. They range from Layer 1, the scanty remains of Sanctuary A left from previous excavations, to Layer 12, a compact yellow-to-brownish clay found in broken places on bedrock. The twelve layers fall into seven distinct phases. An eighth phase is added from the Marquet-Krause report of the destruction evidence from Sanctuary A, completing the profile of five general historical periods, or strata. Using terminology introduced in part by Marquet-Krause, the strata with phase and layer equivalents are as follows:

Stratum	Phase	Significance	Layers	Period
Pre-Urban	I	First structure on site	12	EB IB (Wright; Proto-Urban B, Kenyon)
	II	Pre-city occupation	11–10	Same
Building C	III	First major building; new city fortifications, Wall C and Tower C	9b–8	EB IC (Wright; EB I, Kenyon)
Building B	IV	Remodeled and expanded building; widened fortifications, Wall B and Tower B	7a–7	EB IIA
	V	Destruction phase of Building B	6–5	EB IIB
Building A	VI	Second major building; new city fortifications, Wall A and Tower A	4–2	EB IIIA
Sanctuary A	VII	Remodeled building for sanctuary; strengthened Tower A¹; new fortification, Wall A¹	1	EB IIIB
	VIII	Destruction phase of Sanctuary A, termination of EB city	M-K report	EB IIIB

This summary of stratigraphy may be compared with that of Marquet-Krause, which was not meticulously defined from a system of sections, yet in general agrees with the results stated above. Where it does not agree, it is not opposed to the present analysis. Her summary gives the successive phases from upper to lower as follows (Marquet-Krause 1949, 31):

1. Une couche de cendres correspondant à la déstruction du sanctuaire A: 33 cm.
2. Sol du sanctuaire A: 15 cm.
3. Cendres et débris correspondant à la déstruction du sanctuaire B: 60 cm.

4. Sol de terre battue du sanctuaire B: 20 cm.
5. Cendres et débris correspondant à la déstruction du sanctuaire C: 55 cm.
6. Une couche de terre rouge (*Khamra*) mélangée à de toutes petites pierres, recouverte d'une mince couche de terre battue très rustique, et ayant servi de soubassement au sanctuaire C: 50 cm.
7. Une couche de terre mêlée de cendres formant remblai: 80 cm.
8. Enfin dans la partie nord, nous avons trouvé les vestiges d'un muret construit à même le roc.

Modifications of the Marquet-Krause stratigraphy are as follows:

1. Two structural phases of 'Sanctuary A' are now identified; the latter is designated Sanctuary A, while the former is simply Building A.
2. 'Sanctuary B' is now Building B, and is identified as a remodeled and expanded version of the earlier Building C.
3. 'Sanctuary C' is Building C, the first major urban structure.
4. 'Les vestiges d'un muret construit à même le roc' is identified as part of a house belonging to the pre-urban phase of occupation at the site.

At the time of excavation in 1964, it seemed better to assign Marquet-Krause's 'C' and 'B' to two phases of 'B' (Callaway 1965, 19), but thorough analysis of all sections now indicates two distinct building plans in A II–I, representing EB I and II respectively. Therefore, the designations 'C' and 'B' are retained, but as designations of buildings and not sanctuaries.

Three phases of Building A are identified on the evidence of the present section analysis and that of the Marquet-Krause report. Two structural phases are evident in the analysis of sections in Area III, although the artifacts recovered from the second phase are negligible. It seems desirable, however, to present the two phases separately, even though artifacts in the latter phase are few. The terminal, or third, phase is defined by artifacts recovered by Marquet-Krause from the floor, altar, and other installations in the debris of the final destruction of the site. All of this evidence is therefore taken from her report, because nothing of this phase remained to be excavated by the present expedition.

The phases, with the exception of Phase VIII noted above, are distinguished in the physical evidence represented by the sections, so that strata are erected upon observable evidence. Layers making up the phase entities are also observable, and provide sub-divisions within certain phases. The breakdown of individual phases into component layers enables the assignment of relative importance to specific layers. Distinctions within layers were made also in the course of excavation. Pottery, objects, and organic remains found on floor surfaces were not lumped in with everything which derived from the entire layers as they appear on sections, but were given sub-layer designations. These distinctions will be noted in the detailed presentation of the various layers and phases. The layer sub-divisions, however, are not drawn on the master or auxiliary sections because excessive sub-layer lines would complicate the presentation of overall stratigraphy.

Phases I–II, the Pre-Urban stratum

A compact yellow-to-brownish clay found in pockets and broken places in bedrock is designated Phase I. It is apparently all that remains of the original earth on the site. The particular break in which Layer 12 may be seen is located between Sections E and F in Fig. 83, on the left of the meter scale in Pl. IV.1. Another break is on the right of the scale in the same photograph. This is the shape of the original terrain of the site, before any building at all took place. Similar breaks in bedrock may be seen on the outside of the *tell* in Pl. I, where terrace-like projections step down to the valley on the northwest. The breaks at Site A tilt upward at the outer edge, where the terrain drops sharply toward the valley, and the clay of Layer 12 is the residue captured behind the inclined outer edge of the rock layer. The tilt of the rock preserved the layer from natural erosion keeping the site denuded of any other original deposits. The cultural artifacts in Layer 12 are few, therefore, because of the piecemeal nature of its remains. Theoretically, the artifacts could range in date of origin from prehistory down to the beginning of Phase II. Actually, they seem to derive from the building of the Phase II structure.

Phase II, on the other hand, is an occupation phase, the first on the site. The only structural evidence represented on the Master Section is Wall R in Area III. This may be seen more clearly in Pl. II.2, where it rests on bedrock in the center of the area, as Marquet-Krause noted (see Marquet-Krause 1949, 31).

The west end of the wall is built on top of Layer 12 where it enters the balk under Tower A. Stones can be seen in the layer in Fig. 83 on the right side of the wall, and apparently one flat stone was used as a base for construction of the wall. The stone does not align with the superstructure of the wall, indicating that the left side of the first building stone rested on the clay of Layer 12. The clay is visible in Pl. III.1, at the lower left side of Wall R.

Across the unexcavated area to the left of Wall R in Fig. 83, Layer 12 continues on bedrock as the only remaining deposit of original earth. This is covered by Layers 11 and 10, apparently contemporary with the use of Wall R because they abut the side of the wall. These layers level the area south of Wall R to a point in Area II visible in Fig. 83 where a downward slope toward the south begins. The downward slope begins at the same point for both layers, probably indicating that it is not due to erosion. Erosion would cut away the top of Layer 10, presumably, but not Layer 11, if the layers were deposited in a continuous period of occupation as the evidence indicates. The slope is probably due, therefore, to the increased decline in the surface of bedrock.

No evidence of a counterpart wall to Wall R was found in Areas II or III. The stones on the north side, illustrated in Pl. III.1, would make a rough functional surface for a small house, although it is probable that the occupants lived on that side, and that the other wall of the hut is to be found in Area IV. Wall R does, in fact, bend to the north as Wall Y, as though it encloses a room on the north. A few stones on bedrock in the middle of Area III may indicate a second room east of the bend in Wall R, on level ground. The small area in the northwest corner of Area III enclosed by Wall R is very rough and sloping toward the west, and would be more suitable as a court, or common area for adjacent rooms. A counterpart wall to Wall R is probably located in the unexcavated area shown in Fig. 83, therefore, and a second hut was possibly constructed east of the bend in Wall R, and utilized the same wall.

The grey ashy fill of Layers 11 and 10 was apparently deposited over a considerable period of time. A distinction was made in the layers on the basis of stone content and an identifiable bedline north of Section F–F in Area II. However, numerous thin layers with ashy bedlines were definable in places, indicating tip layers of debris thrown on the edge of the stony decline of bedrock by the occupants of the Wall R house. South of Section F–F in Area II, it was almost impossible to separate even two layers, as Pl. VIII.3 indicates. The thick grey layer behind the center section of the meter scale rests upon Layer 12 at the bottom, and is covered by the red stony fill of Layers 9a and 9. However, in Pl. VI.2, Layer 10, on which the meter scale is lying, is separated from Layer II by an ashy bedline characterized by a pebbly surface. The two layers are therefore the result of a continuous process of depositing ashy refuse probably covering a considerable period of time.

The slope of the surface of Layer 10 in Area II suggests the absence of a retainer wall, such as the city wall, at the south end of the site. This feature is not as clearly shown in the Master Section as in Section H–H, Fig. 8, where Layer 11 lenses out on bedrock under the later Wall E, and Layer 10 tips downward to a point farther down the slope. In any case, the filling of the south end of the site begins with Layer 9a, when a terrace was constructed to retain the depth of fill necessary to level the area with the surfaces in Area III. Phase II, on the other hand, represents a period when only Area III and the north half of Area II were used, and when there was no city wall on the west of the site. The paucity of building remains, when considered alongside the abundance of ashy debris in Layers 11 and 10, suggests that the inhabitants were practically campers on the site.

The stone semi-circle in Pl. VI.2, 3 was set in a trench cutting through layers 10 and 11, and is therefore later. This will be discussed in the analysis of Section F–F. Also, the evidence of Phase II presented here should not be confused with 'Sanctuary C' of Marquet-Krause (see Marquet-Krause 1949, 30, 31), located under 'Sanctuary B,' but associated with the stone platform 'offering table' (Marquet-Krause 1949, Pl. XX:2). This platform is the one above the semi-circle of stones in Pl. VI.2, 3, and is associated with Layers 8 and 9 in Section F–F. Phase II is associated with 'les vestiges d'un muret construit à même le roc' found 'dans la partie nord,' apparently Wall R in A III (Marquet-Krause 1949, 31).

Phase III, the Building C stratum: the first city and major structure

There is no compelling evidence of destruction on top of Layer 10, possibly due to the absence of anything to burn or destroy. No accumulation of artifacts was taken from the surface of the layer. The fill of Layer 9 covered Layer 10 completely, including Wall R, and there is a clean transition from one to the other. Fine grey dust in the bedline of Layer 9 suggests that plants were growing on the surface when the fill was dumped over it.

Layer 9 is a distinctive red stony fill apparently imported from the valley just south of the city wall. A deep accumulation of red earth which eroded over the millennia from the stony hills on either side is found in the valley. Its distinctive color is evident in Pl. III.2, a view of Area II, and a closer view in Pl. IV.1 shows the sharp differentiation from Layers 10 beneath and 7 above. Generally, the layer is uniformly deep red in color with a consistent content of small stones.

However, Layer 9a at the left end of Section A–A seems to be a rough fill of large stones mixed with the same red earth. The predominance of stones causes the earth to appear lighter in color, but it is the same earth as that in Layer 9. Apparently the large stones were brought in to fill the sloping area at the south end of the site and level it for the fill of Layer 9. The beginning of Layer 9a can be seen at the left end of the meter scale in Pl. VI.2.

When the south end of the site was leveled against Wall D², drawn in Section H–H, the red stony earth of Layer 9 was spread over the entire site as foundation for the Building C structure. This is Marquet-Krause's Sanctuary C. A split in the level of surfaces between Areas II and III was built at Wall Q, and can be followed on the Master Section. Area III was filled to cover Wall R, as Pl. II.2

illustrates, and a surface was prepared on the red fill leveled against Wall Q. The left, or south, side of Wall Q, however, was built about 25 centimeters lower than the north, or right, side in Section A–A. The wall is built on Layer 9 on both sides, as indicated in the section. Pl. V.1 illustrates the south face of the wall, with the stones of the wall on Layer 9 behind the later fill of Layer 7 visible on the upper left of the meter scale.

The confusing split in levels of the Layer 9 surface has occasioned difficulties in distinguishing Marquet-Krause's Sanctuaries B and C, because the Building C surface is on Layer 9 in Area II, while the Building B surface is on Layer 7. However, both B and C apparently use the same surface in Area III. Because the two phases utilize some of the same walls and floors, it seemed desirable to the writer in 1965 to propose two phases of the same stratum rather than to think in terms of two distinct building periods (see Callaway 1965, 16–21), which Marquet-Krause proposed. It is clear now that the two phases represent two distinct historical periods.

A distinctive feature of the Building C foundation is the employment of a special saucer-shaped fill underneath certain structures. One of these, designated Layer 8, is drawn on the right side of Section A–A, in Area III. The left edge of the saucer form is under Wall W, and Wall X is over the deepest part. There may have been at one time a third wall off the right side of the section at the north edge of the fill. The fill is very compact and ashy, approaching in compactness the Phase IV fill of Layer 7, but different because of its ashy content. Layer 8 is not to be confused with Layer 7, a buff compact clay devoid of ashy content. The former is always a mixture of clay and ashes, and always in a saucer shape under a special installation which it supports. Furthermore, the saucer form of the fill is always set in a depression in Layer 9 allowing the surface of 8 to remain level with 9 beyond the special filled area.

Wall C, the first city wall, seems to have been constructed after the termination of Phase II, but before the Building C phase structure was erected. A foundation trench is cut through Layers 11 and 10 as indicated in the Master Section, and is covered by Layer 9a. A more detailed analysis of the association of the first city wall with the Phase III structure will be given in connection with Section F–F, Fig. 9. The foundation trench was filled with grey, not red, earth, as Pl. VII.2 indicates, on the right side of the meter scale. The same grey earth has dried and fallen away from the trench in Pl. VIII.3, against Wall C on the left. The sequence seems to be as follows:

1. The Phase II Pre-Urban stratum was terminated with Layer 10.
2. Layers 10 and 11 were cut through to bedrock by the new occupants of the site who built Wall C, the first city wall. Construction of the city wall preceded construction of the first major building, and the foundation trench was filled with the grey earth excavated for construction of the wall.
3. Layers 9a and 9 were imported as fill to level the site for Building C after the city wall was built. This would be a continuation of the same general operation of city building, so that the wall construction belongs in Phase III, but the wall was built prior to construction of Building C.

Phase IV, the construction phase of the Building B stratum

Building C was remodeled, as we shall see in the analysis of Area II stratification, and Layer 7 of the Master Section was laid over the Phase III surface of Layer 9. The new fill is as distinctive as the red stony earth of the earlier layer. This is a very compact and gritty buff clay imported specially for the room in Area II. Pl. IV.1, 2 illustrates the layer above the meter scale in IV.1, and underneath the scale in IV.2. An ashy layer marks the surface of the Building B floor on top of Layer 7 in both photographs.

The floor on the right side of Wall Q in Fig. 83, constructed on top of Layers 8 and 9 and used in Phase III, seems to have been reused in Phase IV. This floor is covered by the same kind of radical destruction debris as that on the surface of Layer 7, and the ruins of Wall Q are found in its debris. The Phase III surface of Layer 9 in Area II was covered lightly with ashes, but there was nothing comparable to the depth of ashes and degree of burning found on the Phase IV surfaces.

Phase V, the destruction phase of the Building B stratum

Layer 6 across the entire master balk is characterized by evidence of ashes and debris from a holocaust which terminated Building B. Stones from Wall Q are broken down into calcined masses as illustrated in Pl. IX.2, behind the half-meter scale. On the floor at the base of the scale, a calcined lump was recovered in which a small jar was cemented to the side of a large store-jar fragment. This is shown in Pl. XV.1, and Pl. XV.2 indicates that the intense heat actually caused the trapped moisture to boil through the cement-like mass and create a lava-like deposit.

Ashes with bits of charred timbers are evident on the Phase V floor in Area II, on top of Layer 7 in Pl. IV.2. The wood of the timbers has been identified as *Quercus calliprinos*,* an evergreen oak which now has almost disappeared from the region. Only one tree of this kind still grows in the vicinity of the *tell*. The tree may be found beside the tomb of Sheikh Abu Rukba at Khirbet Haiyan. Timbers from this species of tree have been found at Sites C and D also, suggesting that it was quite plentiful during the periods of Buildings C and B.

Where the EB III Tower A is associated with Layer 6, it rests upon the destruction debris of Building B. Wall C, associated with the Building B floor, is covered by the tower at Section F in Fig. 83. The corner of the tower is shown above the balk of Section F in Pl. III.2, and Wall C disappears under the end of the tower. The black line of the Layer 6 floor can be seen under the tower toward Wall C. Wall Q is covered by the Sanctuary A altar in Pl. IX.1, and the floor on the right of the base of Wall Q extends under the meter scale and the tower. The two fragmentary brick walls on the right of the altar in Section A–A are crushed by the weight of the tower above them. Layer 6, therefore, is definitely associated with the inner face of Wall C, Wall Q, and brick Walls W and X, all of which are earlier than the tower and Building A. Wall C was rebuilt and widened on the outside in Phase IV, making the association of Layer 6 with Wall B, although the undisturbed inner face was reused in the Wall B phase.

Layer 5 is evident only in the Sanctuary A altar balk of Section A–A, although the layer is traced in lateral sections. It seems to belong with the destruction debris of whatever superstructure there was of Building B. Wall Q seems to have been constructed of bricks upon a wide stone base, as Section A–A indicates. The bricks turned reddish in the fire which destroyed the building, and Layer 5 contains the remains of their collapse along with ashes and other debris. Individual bricks are

---

* The writer is indebted to Miss Cecil Western, of the Ashmolean Museum, Oxford, for examining and identifying the charred wood remains taken from Layer 6 of the sanctuary.

shown *in situ* on Wall Q in Pl. V.2, and the spaces where small branches of evergreen oak bound the bricks together are discernible.

Phase V apparently separates from the first layer of Phase VI, as shown on Section A–A, along a line of loose small stones probably belonging with the leveling operation in preparation for erecting Building A. The balk is shown in Pl. IX.1, and the line of separation begins above the topmost stone of Wall Q on the right side. Below that line, as is evident in Pl. IX.2, the deposit is more firm and is interspersed with charred wood fragments which appear to lie in the natural position of repose from the collapse of the building. Layers 5 and 6 therefore are undisturbed destruction debris from the burning and collapse of Building B.

Phase VI, the first phase of the Building A stratum.

The only evidence of Sanctuary A on the Master Section is the altar in Area III, built against the side of Wall H. The entire unit is constructed above the ruins of Wall Q, used in Phase III–V. Layers 3 and 4 are redistributed debris from the destruction of Building B, used to level and fill the site for the construction of the Phase VI building. Both layers are ashy rubble whose tiplines can be seen in Pls. IX.1 and X.1. Layer 3 is important because it is the foundation layer for the construction of Wall H. Layer 2 lies under the *huwwar* surface illustrated in Pl. XVII, below and in front of the surface at the top of the altar. Layer 2 and its surface are associated with Wall H, but not necessarily with the three stones on the right side of the altar which are all that remain of Enclosure 133 around the altar.

The Layer 2 surface, if extended, is level with the threshold of the entrance in Wall H, and approximately level with the threshold of a passageway in Wall M shown in Pl. XVIII. 4. This seems to be a surface associated with the passageway in Wall M before it was blocked in Phase VII, and the entrance in Wall H. The raised altar of stones built upon Layer 1, therefore, is later, as well as the wall of Enclosure 133, shown in Fig. 5, around the altar. The altar and enclosure were not there in Phase VI. The only installation which could belong in Phase VI is a stone-bordered floor area under the enclosure wall in Pl. XX.2. Insufficient evidence of the stones visible in Pl. XX.2 remained from the Marquet-Krause excavation to draw the unit in a section, but this assignment of the floor unit to Phase VI seems plausible on the evidence of the photograph and the *huwwar* surface on top of Layer 2.

The implications of this interpretation are significant, because the Phase VI structure does not have the components of a sanctuary, such as the altar and enclosures of the Phase VII building. The stone-bordered platform, or floor area, in the southwest corner of Area III was possibly a special area of the room, but no evidence of a sanctuary function remains. The distinctive, raised altar of Phase VII is a new development without an antecedent structure in Phase VI, unless a Phase VI raised structure was removed for construction of the later one.

Phase VII, the remodeled building for Sanctuary A

The plaster surface on Layer 1 is laid against the wall stones on the right side of the altar, and the raised part of the altar against Tower A. These are obviously contemporary, and apparently new in Phase VII. If the entire enclosure wall is represented by the three stones which remain, then the altar and enclosure were built in Phase VII on the fill of Layer 1. We shall see in the analysis of

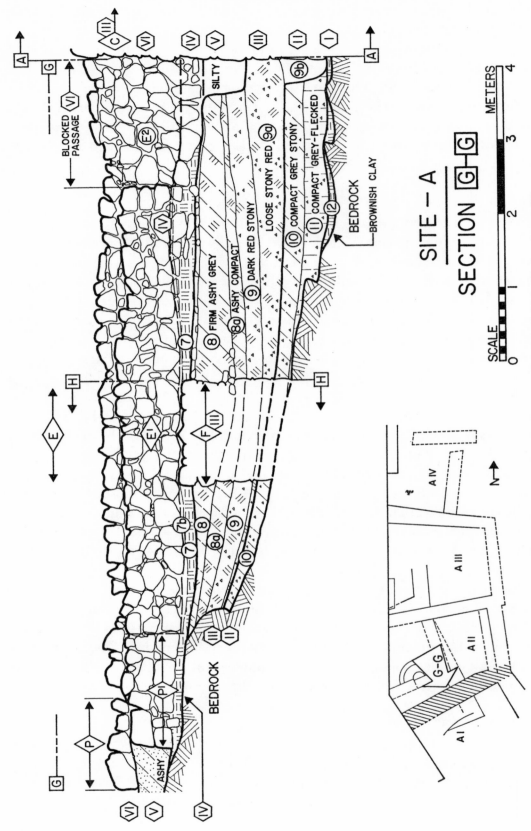

Fig. 7. Section G–G, the north face of the Wall E balk in Area II.

Section B–B that a passageway in Wall M was blocked in Phase VII, and that Marquet-Krause's Enclosure 136, showing in Fig. 5, was built across the corner of Area III, enclosing the corner formed by the blocked entrance. Consequently, Enclosure 136 is Phase VII, as well as the wall around the altar room, No. 133. Enclosures 131 and 137 are probably Phase VII structures also, and not Phase VI.

Phase VIII, the destruction phase of Sanctuary A

All artifacts assigned to this phase are those taken from the floors, enclosures, ledges, and altar of the Sanctuary A structure in what apparently was its final phase. Pl. XX.1, 2, a photograph of the Sanctuary A structure after it was cleared, suggests the basic integrity of the phase. Some earlier artifacts may be included, but they do not invalidate the significant collection from Phase VIII.

SECTION G–G IN AREA II

The stratigraphy of Areas I–II

The Wall E balk between Areas I and II preserves most clearly the distinctions among the earliest phases of the site, so the analysis of area sections begins with its profile, shown in Fig. 7. There is nothing different in Layers 12–10, i.e., Phases I–II, from that found in the Master Section. Layer 12 is in broken places in bedrock, retained by the upward tilt of the edges of rock layers stepping down the west side of the *tell*. Layers 11 and 10 reach a cumulative depth of 60 centimeters in the depression east of Wall C, because the decline in surface of bedrock from Area III caused the deposits to settle into the area.

A discussion of the association of Wall C with Layers 11 and 10 will be given in the analysis of Section F–F, Fig. 9, because it preserves the most demonstrable evidence. A foundation trench, designated Layer 9b, is found in Section G–G at the end where the Master Section is joined. The earth in Layer 9b is grey, not red, because the wall was built before the red fill of Layers 9a–9 was deposited. Layer 10, the latest in Phase II, is fairly level on the surface in Section G–G and without evidence of erosion, which indicates that the occupants of the site were probably replaced by the Phase III inhabitants without any appreciable period of abandonment. In fact, there may not have been even one season of winter rains in the transition period, because there is no evidence of even minor erosion of the surface of Layer 10. Some erosion would be expected if the continuous process of dumping from the huts in Area III had ceased for even one or two years before the city wall was constructed.

Phase III, the saucer-shaped fill phase

As was noted above, Wall C is first in the sequence of Phase III structures at the site. Layer 9b is the loose fill in the foundation trench of Wall C, excavated from Layers 10 and 11 for construction of the wall, then replaced. The fill layers supporting the Building C structure are on top of the foundation trench, and Layer 9a, a loose stony red fill described above, is immediately on top of Layer 10 and the foundation trench of the city wall. This was apparently imported to level the south end of the site for the better quality *khamra* fill of Layer 9, completing preparation for actual construction of the building. A feature pointed out in the Phase III fill in the Master Section is found at this point in the sequence of layers. There is a wide saucer-shaped fill of ashy grey earth, packed into a depression in the surface of Layer 9 reaching from Wall C on the right side of the section to the top of a ledge of bedrock on the left side. This is made up of two similar layers supporting Wall F and the *huwwar* surface associated with it.

Wall F is built upon Layer 8a, an ashy fill more compact than Layer 8. The layer ends in a feather edge against Wall C on the right, although the end of the layer is cut through by a deep washout which will be explained later. Layer 8a seems to be especially for the south end of Area II, and Area I across the balk from Section G–G, because this part of the site required the deepest fill and, consequently, the best foundation for structures erected upon it.

On either side of Wall F is the second fill designated Layer 8, although the two sides are not constructed of the same kind of earth. The fill on the left side of Wall F is a stony brown earth. Apparently outside the building enclosed by Wall F, this structure has an exposed outdoor surface. A thick dark line indicating the location of this surface can be seen in Pl. VI.1 underneath the *huwwar* surface in the left foreground. The stones covered by the *huwwar* and running at a right angle to the balk are those of Wall F.

Layer 8 on the right side of Wall F can be seen in Pl. VI.3, underneath the wall in the background of the photograph. In the balk this appears as a compact ashy grey layer like Layer 8 in Area III. On top of it is a thick *huwwar* surface imbedded with stones reaching from Wall F to Wall C on the right, across the washout. This surface is inside the building enclosed by Wall F on the left, or east, and Wall D¹ across the balk in Area I. This is the structure which Marquet-Krause called Sanctuary C.

Phase IV, the Wall E¹ phase

A radical remodeling took place in Areas II–I in Phase IV, the Building B phase, although the Phase III structures in Areas III–IV continued in use. Layer 7, of the same gritty buff clay of Layer 7 in the Master Section, covered the Phase III surfaces and leveled Area II for a *huwwar* surface over the stone base of Wall F. The surface is shown in Pl. VI.1 on top of Wall F, extending to Wall C in the background. The stones of Phase III Wall F can be seen in the left center of the photograph, where the fill and surface are cut away. The same wall and fill are shown in Pl. III.2, under the meter scale. Wall E¹, of course, has been removed in both photographs.

With the fill brought up over the base of Wall F and surfaced with *huwwar*, the room was extended on top of the ledge of bedrock shown on the left side of the section. Wall E¹, new in Phase IV, was constructed across the south end of Area II to a point on the ledge of bedrock where a second incline begins toward the left. The wall is substantially built of large field stones, laid with a rubble core. This wall is about 1.50 meters wide, slightly wider than Wall Q at the north side of Area II. An entrance on the right side against Wall C is built into the Phase IV wall. The entrance is actually 1.75 meters wide, suggesting that it was an open passageway without doors.

The shape of the Building B structure was therefore altered in Area II in Phase IV, because Wall E¹ cut off the south corner of the Phase III room between Walls G and D¹, and added the large area east of Wall F.

Phase V cannot be shown satisfactorily in Section G–G, because this phase is the destruction debris of Building B which accumulated on the floor against Wall E¹. Evidence of this phase was almost

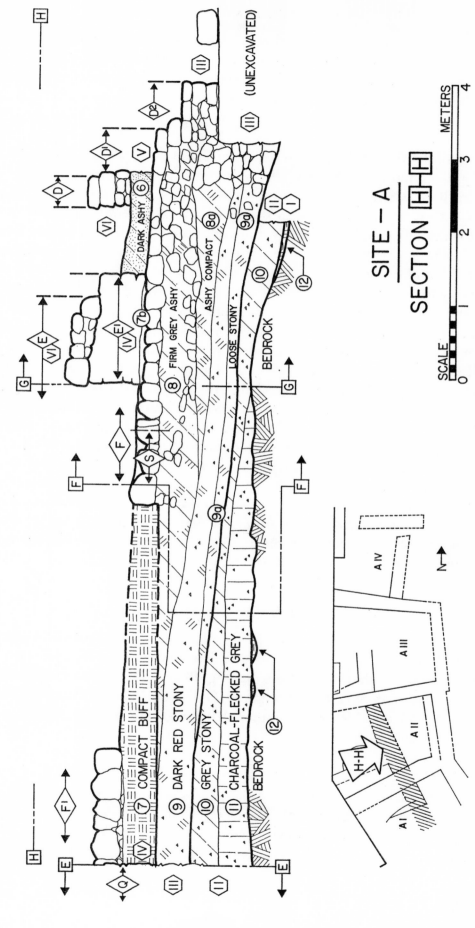

Fig. 8. Section H–H, the west face of the Wall F balk in Areas I–II.

SITE – A

SECTION H–H

SCALE

METERS

0 1 2 3 4

Key labels within figure:

(UNEXCAVATED)

DARK ASHY.

FIRM GREY ASHY.

ASHY COMPACT

LOOSE STONY

BEDROCK

COMPACT BUFF

DARK RED STONY

GREY STONY

CHARCOAL-FLECKED GREY

BEDROCK

⑦ ⑧ ⑨ ⑩ ⑪ ⑥ ⑦b ⑧a ⑨a

N→

A I A II A III A IV

H–H

completely missing because the previous expedition removed everything to bedrock right up to the side of Wall E¹ as is evident in Marquet-Krause 1949, Pl. XX:2, across the upper left of the photograph. There was enough fragmentary evidence to indicate that the destruction debris of Building B had been against the base of Wall E¹, and on the surface associated with the wall.

Phase VI

The foundation fills of the first phase of Building A lay against Wall E¹, as Marquet-Krause's Pl. XX:2 shows. The light-colored line against Wall C in the background is her Sanctuary A surface, and reaches across Wall E¹ where a change in the style of courses can be detected. This phase is represented in Section G–G by the blockage in the Phase IV passageway against Wall C, and a heightening of Wall E¹ as indicated by the heavy line under the top course of stones. This addition to Wall E¹, designated E, is narrower than the original wall, as Section H–H indicates, and not entirely on the original line of the wall.

Wall E¹ can be picked out in Marquet-Krause, Pl. XII:2, across the dark trench from the left end of a wooden plank in the foreground. The wall bends to the left underneath the double walls constructed on top, and abuts Wall C which is covered in the left background. Wall E is extended toward the east, the left in Section G–G, as indicated by the location of Wall P. Wall P¹, which shows in the plan of Phase VI as a ledge inside of Wall P, is the top of the Phase IV wall drawn in Section E–E. This wall was reused in Phase VI as a ledge along the base of the later wall.

On the right side of Section G–G, under the blockage of the Phase IV entrance, is the washout referred to earlier. This is a rather deeply eroded spot against Wall C and partly filled with silt. The erosion occurred before the passageway was blocked, and, of course, after Wall E¹ was constructed. The washout is therefore Phase IV or later, because the wall and entrance were constructed in Phase IV. Obviously the erosion occurred after the room ceased to be used, because its presence would have been an intolerable obstruction in the passageway. Therefore its *terminus a quo* is most likely the Phase V destruction of Building B, and *terminus ad quem* the construction of the first Building A phase. The washout suggests that a considerable interval of time could have elapsed between the Phase V destruction and reconstruction of the site in Phase VI.

SECTION H–H IN AREAS I–II

The only profile reaching into Area I is Section H–H in Fig. 8. This runs parallel with the Master Section through Areas II–I and connects by way of lateral Sections G–G, F–F, and E–E. The major significance of Section H–H is that distinctions among Phases III–V are clearly represented, supplementing the information derived from Section G–G discussed above. Phase II is represented only by fill in Layers 10 and 11 which slopes rather sharply toward bedrock from a point about 1.50 meters south of the Wall H balk.

Phase III, the Wall F phase

An interesting series of fill layers is found in Areas II–I underneath the Phase III structures. The surface of Layer 10 slopes toward the south, on the right side of Section H–H. The fill is placed on top of the sloping surface, and is retained by a terrace-like structure, Wall D², at the end of the site. The terrace appears to be on bedrock, and is strengthened on the inner side by a fill of loose stones which probably allowed seepage water to drain away.

Layer 9a, the fill of large stones in loose red earth, is laid over Layer 10 in a surprisingly thin deposit which tails off to a point about 1.50 meters from the Wall H balk. This is the place where the slope begins. Then Layer 9 is placed over 10 on the left side of the section and over 9a on the right side, raising the level of the entire area about 50 centimeters, but still requiring more fill at the south end against Wall D². The grey ashy compact fill of Layer 8a, a part of the first saucer-shaped fill in Section G–G, was placed on top of the south end of Layer 9, and thickened against Wall D² to bring the lower end of the site to a rough level for the construction of Wall F.

Wall F was founded on Layer 8a, the fill upon which a thick *huwwar* floor was constructed in Section G–G. The base stones of Wall F standing above the floor level extend to Wall D¹, which is above D², but angle toward the north for additional terrace support. The line of Wall F may be seen in Pl. III.2, on the right side of the meter scale, and Wall D¹ is the row of stones in the foreground which turns left at the lower end of Wall F. The angled stone in the balk across Area II is in line with Wall F, and on the same level, as seen in the photograph. The wall on top of the single stone, designated F¹, is a Phase IV structure associated with Layer 7 which appears in the Master Section, while the single stone is associated with Layer 9.

Phase IV, the Wall F¹ phase.

In the Master Section, Layer 7 is the foundation of the Phase IV structure whose floor abuts Wall Q. This is the same Layer 7 on the left side of Section H–H, under Wall F¹. However, the right side of Layer 7 is above 8, associated with Phase III. The buff compact fill of Layer 7 therefore covers the Phase III surface on Layers 9 and 8, in Sections A–A and G–G, and this also covers the base stones of Wall F as illustrated in Pl. VI.1, described in the analysis of Section G–G. The significant new development in Phase IV is that the base stones of Wall F are completely covered by Layer 7, and a surface for the new structure enclosed by Wall E¹ is extended eastward to the ledge of bedrock noted in Section G–G.

The profile through Wall E¹ in Section H–H indicates that it is constructed on the surface of Layer 7 on the same level as Wall F¹ on the left side of the section. A single tilted stone underneath Wall F¹, covered by Layer 7, was pointed out in Pl. III.2 as probably a fragment of the Phase III Wall F. The stone can be seen more clearly in Pl. IV.1, on the red layer under the middle of Wall F¹, on the right and above the meter scale.

There is no standing wall on the right side of Wall E¹ in Section H–H, but a wall stood there in Phase IV, This was probably Wall D¹, because the surface in Pl. VI.1 extends to D¹, and no terrace which would support a wall in Phase IV remained beyond Wall D¹.

Phase V is represented only by the deep ashy layer against Wall E¹ and under Wall D. This is the same evidence of destruction of Building B as Layer 6 in the Master Section. Unfortunately, most of Phase V was removed before the present expedition began work.

Phase VI is found in two places only as represented in the section. Wall E is constructed for the most part on top of Wall E¹ but more narrow than the Phase IV wall. Wall D is on the thick layer of ash remaining from Phase V. A few more courses of Wall D¹ probably supported this wall at the time of its construction. These walls are a part of the construction of the first phase of Building A.

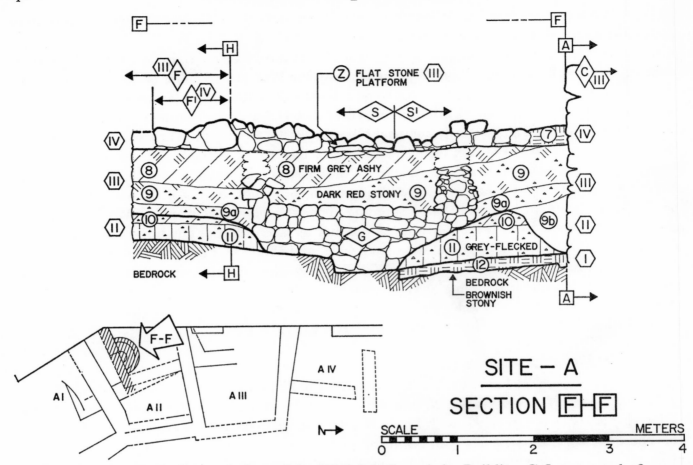

Fig. 9. Section F–F, the north face of the Wall S balk and the Building C flat stone platform in Area II.

SECTION F–F IN AREA II

Two important problems in the stratigraphy of the site are encountered in Section F–F, shown in Fig. 9. The first is the founding of Wall C, the first city wall; and the second is the problem of Marquet-Krause's Sanctuary C altar, identified with the platform of flat stones in Pl. VI.2,3. Phases II–III are involved in the first problem, and Phase III is involved in the second. Consequently, they are the major points of interest in the following discussion of the section.

Phase III, the first urban phase

Section F–F is the best profile at the site abutting directly against Wall C, the first city wall. Section G–G also joins Wall C, but the washout down to Layer 9a and previous excavations disrupt the section where it touches the wall.

The right side of the section, abutting Wall C, is illustrated in Pl. VII.2. On the left side of the meter scale are the stones of the semi-circular Wall G underlying the platform shown in Pl. VI.3, designated an altar by Marquet-Krause. The base of Wall C is on the right side of the scale, reaching almost to bedrock at the end of the Wall S¹ balk behind the scale. The balk under Tower A terminates against Wall C on the extreme right side of the photograph. The exact spot shown in detail in this photograph can be seen in relation to Walls C and Tower A in Pl. II.1, behind the semi-circle of stones on the left side of the photograph, and in the dark place above bedrock under the junction of Wall C in the left background and Tower A whose corner covers Wall C.

Four layers of earth against Wall C in Pl. VII.2 can be identified. The topmost layer, above the top section of the meter scale and sloping downward against the stones on the left, is No. 9a, a fill of red earth and stones described in the analysis of the Master Section. This can be traced against Wall C in the photograph, and into the balk on the right, under Tower A. Underneath it is the foundation trench of Wall C, cut through Layers 10 and 11, and the undisturbed section of those layers on the left side of the meter scale. The foundation trench, Layer 9b, is a fairly wide cut beginning just above and to the left of the upper white section of the scale in Pl. VII.2, and sweeping down behind the lower end of the same white section to the large stone at the base of Wall C.

Layers 10 and 11 are dark with moisture on the left side of the scale, and cannot be readily distinguished. There is a bedline of pebbles, however, which seems to separate the grey ashy fill into two separate layers, as was noted in the analysis of the Master Section. Layer 10 is more stony and less compact than Layer 11, as Pl. VIII.3 shows, and there is no occupation surface separating the two. The surface on top of Layer 10, where the dark red fill of Layer 9a covers it, is very level, as can be seen at the top of the large stone on the left of the meter scale in Pl. VIII.3. On the extreme left in the same photograph, part of the foundation trench, Layer 9b, has fallen out because of its crumbly and dry nature.

Small patches of the yellowish clay of Layer 12 were daubed on the face of Wall C along its base when excavated, which indicates that the stones were placed upon Layer 12 in the process of building the wall. Layer 9b, the foundation trench fill, was deposited against the base of the wall soon enough after it was built to protect the patches of clay from erosion by sun, wind, and rain. In fact, the trench must have been refilled before the first winter rains began, or else the clay would have washed off. Wall C, therefore, is set on Layer 12, and upon bedrock in places, and its foundation trench cuts through Layers 10 and 11.

The above interpretation is a revision of the view presented in a preliminary report published in 1965, immediately after the excavation of Site A. The foundation trench in Section F–F was defined at that time, but Wall C was thought to belong in a stratum preceding the first major structures (see Callaway 1965, 16) because there was no red earth of the Layer 9a fill in the trench. In sequence, the construction of Wall C preceded the depositing of Layers 9a–9, but the interval of time between the two operations must have been quite short. The original city wall enclosed an area of more than 100 dunams, so the task of building it could have required several years. After four seasons of excavations at four other sites around the city wall system, it seems certain now that the people who constructed the first city wall were those who built the first major structure at Site A, assigned to Phase III.

One further observation may be made with regard to the founding of Wall C. There was some evidence at Site C, the Lower City, that the first city wall, designated Wall C in the preliminary report (Callaway 1965, 28–31) was widened from about 5.00 meters to 5.50 meters in EB II, and that the additional width was built on the inner side of the wall. If the same widening operation occurred at Site A, and the wall was strengthened on its inner side, the evidence of the foundation trench in Section F–F would be jeopardized.

Marquet-Krause excavated Wall C at the north end of the citadel in 1934, and she noted that the wall was 6 meters wide. Excavation of the tower and wall complex in 1968, and further probing of the excavated area in 1970 indicate that Wall C was not originally six meters wide. The wall was widened in Phase IV to a width of about six meters. However, the additional width was constructed on the outside of the wall at Site A, indicating strongly that the foundation trench in Section F–F is valid evidence of the construction of the first city wall. Evidence found at the Citadel Gate, discovered in the earliest city wall about six meters north of the tower complex, reinforces this conclusion. The gate was blocked in the Phase IV widening of the wall. However, it was simply filled with stones on the inner side, with an inset blockage of the inner entrance, while the additional width of wall on the outside closed off the outer entrance. The inner face of Wall C is, therefore, undisturbed at Site A.

Phase III and Platform Z in Area II

Wall G, the semi-circular structure illustrated in Pl. VI.3, and VII.1, is a part of the foundation for Platform Z which Marquet-Krause called the Sanctuary C altar (see Marquet-Krause 1949, 30, Pl. XX:2). This was not built up to the level of the platform remnant shown in Pl. VI. 3, but it supported the fill on which the platform rests. The enclosure is open-ended toward the south, behind the platform in Pl. VI.3, and, therefore, built against the accumulated fill in the south part of Area II, against the Wall D² terrace drawn in Section H–H.

This feature of the enclosure should be noted first in order to understand its construction and apparent function. The Wall S balk upon which the platform rests, shown in Pl. VII.1, is only 50 centimeters wide, as indicated in Section A–A. The balk's south face is illustrated in Pl. VIII.2, 3, where the stones of Wall S behind the platform can be seen above the meter scale. However, there is no penetration of the balk on the south side by Wall G, the enclosure. The large stone on the left of the meter scale in Pl. VIII.3 is in Layer 10, and is not a part of Wall G. Consequently, Wall G is constructed simply in an open ended half-circle under the platform of flat stones, and it orients toward the north of Wall S. In fact Wall S is built on top of and across the open end of the half-circle.

The front, or rounded, side of Wall G is set in a trench on bedrock as Section F–F indicates. The trench is cut through Layers 10 and 11, under the meter scale in Pl. VI.2. Inside the enclosure in Pl. VI.2, the sloping surface of Layer 10 can be followed, and the cut through the layer is evident against the inside face of the stones. The base of the wall angles upward in Layer 9 from a point on the side of the half-circle toward Wall S, as indicated in Pl. II.1. The stones of Wall G are in a small trench cut into Layers 10 and 11, and the red earth of Layer 9a, is mingled with the stones.

A detailed photograph of the trench is in Pl. VIII.1. The dark-red of Layer 9a can be discerned above the grey of Layer 10 on the left side. Then the bedline of Layer 9a cuts downward toward the black section on the right end of the 25 centimeter scale to a point on bedrock in the lower right corner. The trench is located on the left side of the enclosure wall against the Wall F balk illustrated in Pl. II.1, in the left center of the photograph. On the right side of the line pointed out is the trench with red earth mixed with the stones which slope downward to bedrock. Thus Wall G seems to be a special support for the fill under the stone platform, and was, therefore, constructed when Layer 9a was placed on top of Layer 10. The wall is a Phase III structure.

Section F–F indicates a continuation of the stones of Wall G up toward the base of Wall S, and the stone platform. The continuation is suggested by some stones on the left side of Wall G found in Layer 8, above Layer 9. These can be seen in Pl. VI.3, below Wall S at the left end of the enclosure. The conjectured continuation would be along the line of the incline evident in Pl. II.1 from the base of Wall G on bedrock, to the base of Wall S above the ashy clay of Layer 8. Wall G, therefore, is an integral part of the construction of the platform, and is contemporary with Layers 9a, 9, and 8.

Layers 9a and 9 are the initial fill in Phase III, as we have seen in all sections of the site. Layer 8 is the characteristic saucer-shaped fill pointed out in Section G–G under Wall F. The platform of stones is contructed on this special fill also, along with Wall S which is bonded to Wall F on the left side of the section, as is evident in Pl. VI.3. Wall S^1, on the side of the platform next to Wall C, does not seem to be a Phase III structure, however, Its base is on a clear bedline on top of Layer 8, evident in Pl. VIII.3 above the scale on the left. There is no evident bedline under Wall S, because its foundation stones penetrate Layer 8 from a point where the platform begins just left of the top of the scale in Pl. VIII.2.

A passageway existed at Wall S in Phase III. The added Wall S^1 structure, offset to Wall S in Pl. VI.2 and Marquet-Krause Pl. XX:2, blocked the passageway in Phase IV, when Area II was extensively remodeled. The stone platform, therefore, was screened from the entrance to Area I at Wall D^1 against Wall C, by Wall S, and entrance to the platform room was gained between the west end of Wall S, located behind the altar, and Wall C.

The platform with its elaborate sub-structure was rectangular in form, and paved with '. . . deux briques et de pierres plates irrégulières, parmi lesquelles se trouvait une pierre noire d'espèce inconnue à Ay, donc importée' (Marquet-Krause 1949, 30). The surface of the platform was at floor level, and level with the surface of Layer 9 in the Master Section. There is no evidence that the flat stones were covered with a layer of *huwwar* or any kind of thin surfacing material which would conceal the stones. They must have been exposed in the Phase III floor approximately as shown in Marquet-Krause, Pl. XX:2.

Phase IV, the remodeled, or Building B, phase

A remodeling of the Phase III room in Area II resulted in the covering of Platform Z by a new Phase IV floor. The new surface is on top of Layer 8, abutting Wall S–S^1 above the platform stones. As noted in the previous discussion of Phase III, Wall S^1 apparently is a blockage of the Phase III passageway, and is therefore Phase IV. This blockage diverted traffic into the room around the east end of Wall S and over Wall F, covered by the Layer 8 fill. Thus the platform was not used in Phase IV, and the traffic pattern Area II was changed.

The Phase IV surface is Marquet-Krause's Sanctuary B floor shown in her Pl. XVIII:1, 2. In XVIII:2, a large, light-colored stone in the shape of an inverted trapezoid is located in the upper right corner, about four courses above the floor. Underneath it is a thin stone set on edge, and directly below the thin stone at the edge of the floor is a large stone with an angular corner jutting out toward the floor. The same stones are easily located in our Pl. II.1, on the left side of the Sanctuary A altar. The angular stone at the edge of the floor of her Sanctuary B is the same one above our Phase IV surface, on top of layer 8. We agree on the identification of the floor of Phase IV, and that it is above the Phase III floor and associated platform of flat stones. Our Phase III is her Sanctuary C, which rested upon 'une couche de terre rouge (*khamra*) mélangée à de toutes petites

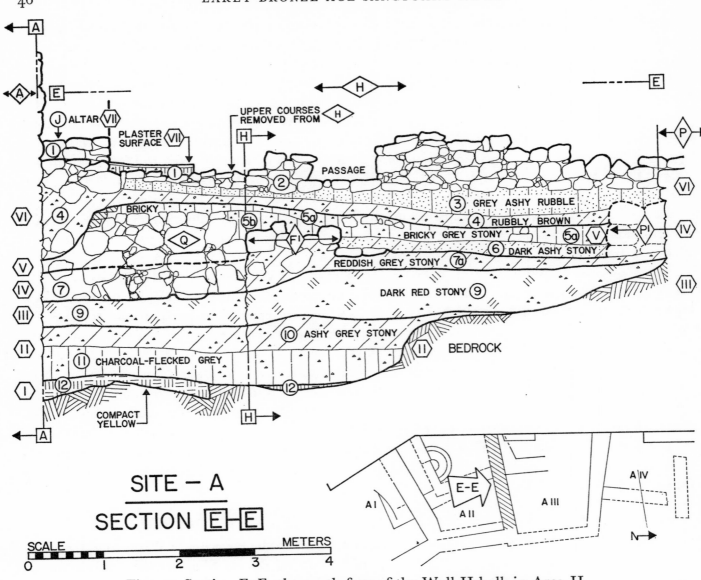

Fig. 10. Section E–E, the south face of the Wall H balk in Area II.

pierres, . . .' (Marquet-Krause 1949, 31), or Layer 9. The special saucer-shaped fill of Layer 8 is, however, immediately under the platform, set into Layer 9.

SECTION E–E AND THE STRATIGRAPHY OF AREA II

The sequence and character of layers in Area II are generally the same in Section E–E, shown in Fig. 10, as they are in the Master Section. In fact, the layers are identical from bedrock, Layer 12, up to Layer 9. There are, however, some additional features beginning with Layer 9 which are significant. An analysis of Layers 10–12, assigned to Phases I–II, is given in the discussion of the Master Section and Section F–F, because the building of Wall C is associated with a foundation trench cut through those layers in F–F. We begin here with Phase III, Layer 9.

Phase III, the split-level phase

Area II is on the slope of bedrock dropping rather sharply from Area III, requiring thicker layers of fill for the construction of Building C. Layers 10 and 11 of Phase II brought the level of Area II almost up to the surface of Layer 10 in Area III, but the thick layers of Phase III produced a two-level surface, split at Wall Q. The dark red stony fill of Layer 9 found under the Building C structure over all of the site is under the split-level surface on both sides of Wall Q.

Layer 9 covers not only the Phase II layers, but it also fills in an east-west slope in bedrock up to the top of a ledge on the extreme right of the section. A detailed view is in Pl. IV.1, where Layer 9 is visible as a wide dark band behind the top of the meter scale. This continues under Wall F¹ in the upper center of the photograph; and from Wall F¹ toward the right side, the surface is under the pebbly layer in the foreground, about midway between the pebbly surface and the white tag in the balk. The only possible remnant of Phase III Wall F, described in the analysis of Section G–G, is the tilted stone under Wall F¹, resting upon the surface of Layer 9.

The Phase III room in Area II enclosed by Wall F is therefore on a slightly lower level than the surface outside the room on the right side of the section. The room surface on the left abuts Wall Q, separating two levels of Phase III floors in Areas II–III, as noted in the analysis of the Master Section. The floor in Section E–E is 25 centimeters lower than the one across Wall Q to the north. However, the surface outside the building, on the right of Wall F¹, slopes gently from north to south without any radical step-down. For this reason, the surface of Layer 9 is higher on the right side of the section than it is on the left.

Phase IV, the remodeled, or Building B, phase

The buff clay fill of Layer 7 was placed on the surface of Layer 9 for two reasons. First, it raised the floor of the room south of Wall Q up to the same level of the Phase III floor across the wall. The surface in Area III, however, was not built higher, so it continued in use through Phase IV. Second, the fill covered the stone base of Wall F and the stone platform against Wall S and raised the entire level to a point where the building could be extended eastward, parallel with Wall E¹ to the ledge of bedrock on the right side of Section E–E.

Layer 7a on the right side of Wall F¹ is a part of the leveling operation for extension of the remodeled structure. This is a reddish-grey stony fill, pointed out above in Pl. IV.1 as the pebbly layer about 20 centimeters above the white tag. Actually, there was a packed surface on top of the pebbles, evident in Pl. IV.2 in the lower right corner of the photograph. The surface is against Wall F¹, separating the surface of Layer 7a on the right from the surface of Layer 7 under the meter scale on the left side. Wall P¹ is the wall probably enclosing the area on the right side of Section E–E. This connected with the east end of Wall E¹ in Section G–G, underneath the Phase VI extension of Wall E, and was preserved in fragments across Area II almost to the Wall H balk. Marquet-Krause shows the top of Wall P¹ as a 'banquette' in the Sanctuary A plan (Marquet-Krause 1949, Pl. C.128 our Fig. 6). This 'banquette' appears to be the top of the Phase IV wall built on Layer 7a for the remodeled room. Its location is indicated in Section E–E.

Wall F¹ in Section E–E is a later structure than Wall F² on the opposite side of the balk. Pl. II.1 shows the discontinuity between the walls. On the left side and under the meter scale, Wall F¹ is built upon pebbly Layer 7a, Phase IV, while Wall F² on the right side is constructed upon Layer 9.

A detailed view of the point of junction is in Pl. IX.1. Wall F², on the right, is set into the dark red stony Layer 9 of Phase III, and is bonded into Wall Q in the background under the left side of the altar. However, Wall F¹ is constructed upon an additional layer, No. 7a in Section E–E, and is built over the end of Wall F² and against the end of Wall Q.

Phase V, the destruction phase of Building B

Ashy destruction debris from the termination of Phase IV was pointed out on the floor of Building B in Section A–A. This extends on top of Layer 7 in Section E–E also, and ends against Wall F¹ in the center of the section. Layer 6 actually includes a 10 centimeter thickness of clay and ashes which appears in Pl. IV.2 to be two thicknesses of packed earth surface. However, in excavating the area, the apparently superimposed surfaces were not consistent, because bits of charred wood were found throughout the entire thickness of the layer. This all belongs to the terminal use of the Building B structure and probably represents a clay roof supported by wooden slats or beams.

Across Wall F¹ and on top of layer 7a, the same kind of ashy destruction debris was found which characterizes the termination of this phase. There was a considerable depth of ashy earth containing decayed and broken sun-dried mud-bricks. No complete bricks were recovered, but some were discernible on top of Wall Q as in Pl. V.2 above the 25 centimeter scale. Apparently the super-structure of Wall F¹ was of sun-dried brick tied together with evergreen oak cross-reinforcement laid among the bricks. There is evidence of wooden ties among the bricky remains on top of Wall Q in the photograph, where tubular cavities appear among the bricks and stones.

Layer 5a seems to be a part of the undisturbed destruction debris of Phase V also. The layer contains bricky debris with small stones, the kind incorporated into large sun-dried bricks and mud mortar in field-stone wall construction. Wall F¹ collapsed toward the right side of the section, covering the ruins of the roof on the floor in Layer 6. Layer 5a is a part of the wall collapse lying on top of the ruins from Wall F¹ on the left to Wall P¹ on the right side of the section.

Phase VI, and construction of Tower A and Wall H

The foundation trench for Tower A is evident at the left end of Layer 4 in Section E–E, and in Pl. IV.2. On the right of the meter scale in the photograph, the cut through Wall Q is filled with a large stone and some pebbles mixed with loose earth. A detailed view of the same is found in Pl. V.2 on the left of the 25 centimeter scale. Wall Q is cut through on the left of the large stone supporting the bricks stacked above, and the space between the undisturbed end of the wall and the tower whose stones are visible on the extreme left is filled with loose ashy earth. A few stones of the base of Wall H are visible across the top of the photograph.

Layer 4, therefore, is associated with the construction of Tower A, and also leveled the site for contruction of lateral Wall H abutting the tower. Wall H is built upon Layer 3, an ashy rubble possibly moved from the area where the tower was built above Wall C. Associated with Layer 3 is Wall P on the right end of the section. This Wall enclosed the east side of the room in Area II, and was bonded into Wall H as indicated in the section. The nature of the bonding suggests that Wall P was contructed first, then Wall H was built between Wall P and the tower. The line of Wall P¹ in the section indicates the widening of the Room in Phase VI about the same distance as in Section G–G.

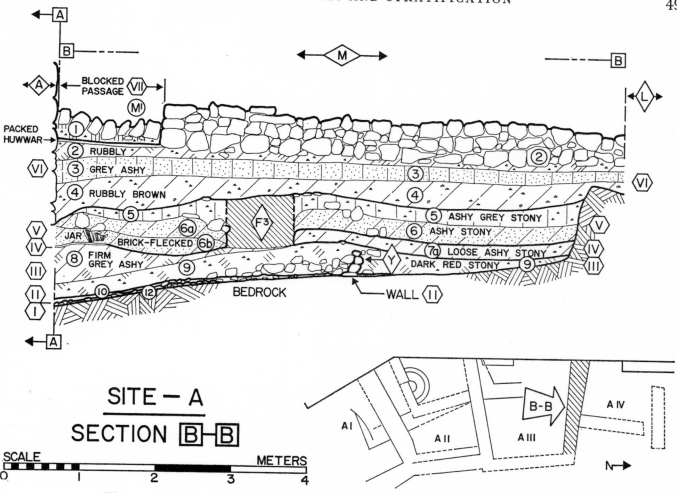

Fig. 11. Section B–B, the south face of the Wall M balk in Area III.

Wall H is our Layer 2 associated with the *huwwar* surface underneath the Phase VII floor and altar of Sanctuary A. Layer 1, the makeup and floor for the Phase VII altar, is across the balk from Section E–E, behind the partly removed Wall H in Pl. IV.2. This floor represents a second phase use of Wall H.

SECTION B–B AND THE STRATIGRAPHY OF AREA III

The most complete evidence of the four major strata of the site, from Phase II through Phase VII, is found in Area III and is represented in Section B–B, shown in Fig. 11. The section connects with the Master Section as indicated, on the left side. This is supplemented by Sections C–C and D–D on the south side of the area. They are partial, but specialized, sections detailing Phases III through VI and a Phase VII installation designated Bin N, constructed on top of a Phase VI cobblestone platform designated N[1].

Phase II and Walls R and Y

Layer 10 is a relatively thin, grey deposit on the pebbly surface of Layer 12 at the Wall M balk, as indicated in Fig. 11. Layer 12 underlies Wall Y, a lateral branch of Wall R as illustrated in Pl. II.2 and Layer 10 is against its side. Layer 12 is therefore foundational to Wall Y, as well as Wall R, pointed out in the analysis of the Master Section. The two walls are contemporary Phase II structures.

Layer 10 slopes with bedrock towards the left side of Section B–B. Wall C was not constructed at the time Walls Y and R were in use, so the building enclosed by them probably extended on to the leveled section of bedrock under the inner face of the later city wall. A deep bay in bedrock is immediately west of the Wall R house, so it is afforded some protection on that side. The Citadel Gate, located in Area A VII some 14 meters north of the Wall R building, proves that the Wall R–Y structure was a house and not part of a gate complex.

Across Tower A toward the outside of the city, a slightly curved-wall tower seems to be built against the outside of Wall C in the area of Marquet-Krause's Enclosures 123, 127 in Pl. XCIII (our Fig. 5). The tower is somewhat similar in shape to gate towers found at Tell el-Far'ah (N) dating to EB I (see de Vaux LXIX, 216, Pl. XIX). Located under Tower A, it is associated with the Phase III, or earliest, city wall. The Citadel Gate north of Tower A apparently exited with a sharp turn alongside the city wall toward Tower A, in which case the outside approach road led straight in toward the city wall with the Phase III tower on the south side, with a sharp left turn against the wall leading up toward the gate.

Like Wall R in the Master Section, Wall Y is covered completely with the dark red stony fill of Layer 9 imported to level the site for construction of Building C. There is no accumulation of ashes or occupation debris sealed on top of Layer 10, so a destruction of the Phase II structure is not indicated. The evidence of Sections A–A and B–B is that Phase II was intermediate in the development of the site, but probably represents a phase of considerable duration.

Phase III, the brick wall phase in Area III

Layers 8 and 9, identified already in the Master Section, extend across Section B–B to the ledge of bedrock on the right side in Fig. 13. The dark-red stony fill of Layer 9 covers Wall Y, as noted above, and fills in, to some extent, the space between Wall Y and the ledge of bedrock on the right, where it inclines sharply upward as indicated in Section B–B. The slope downward toward Wall C on the left, under the tower, is part of the depression left in Layer 9 for the saucer-shaped fill of Layer 8, which seems to be a special foundation for a small room enclosed by brick walls. The area was made suitable for building by the construction of Wall C which retained the fill of Layer 9.

Wall F³ in Section B–B enclosed the room on the east side, continuing Wall F² as illustrated in Pl. II.2. The stony rubble under F³ is unlike the stones of Wall F², although large stones similar to those in Wall F² can be seen in the foreground of Pl. II.2 where F³ was removed. The wall, therefore, was brick, constructed upon a stone base and possibly extended southward as Wall F in Area II to Wall D¹. Smaller lateral walls, W and X, led off from F²–F³ toward the Section A–A balk, and a third lateral wall in Area IV possibly paralleled Wall X.

The saucer-shaped fill of Layer 8 is the foundation for two rooms, therefore, enclosed by brick Walls W, X, and F³, the latter being located on the right side of the fill in Section B–B. These two rooms were constructed in Phase III, contemporary with Wall Q and the stone platform of Building C in Area II, but different in nature, and probably, function.

The surface on top of Layer 9 between Wall F³ and the ledge of bedrock on the right side of Section B–B seems to have been outside the building described above. There is a peculiar walkway-like terrace built into Layer 9 in Pl. II.1 abutting Wall F². This construction is Phase III in origin, and is a part of the landscaping outside the building. The surface on the right side of the structure in Pl. II.1 is the one appearing as Layer 9 in Section B–B.

Phase IV, the reuse of Phase III structures in Area III

It was noted earlier that Phase III in Area II was not terminated by radical destruction because there is negligible evidence of burning on the surfaces of Layers 8 and 9, where they are preserved. However, there was considerable remodeling of the Phase III building in Area II in Phase IV. The remodeling seems to have changed the orientation of the room where the stone platform was located from south to east. Wall S¹ closed the passageway into the room from the south, and a new entrance was possibly located in Wall F¹ on the east.

There is no evidence of remodeling of the Phase III structures in Area III in Phase IV. The floors of the rooms used in Phase III were level with the newly constructed Phase IV floors in Area II, and they seem to have continued in use through Phase IV. The evidence of radical destruction on the Area III floors seems to be contemporary with that on the Phase IV surfaces in Area II. Thus Phase IV in Area III is represented by continued use of the brick-wall enclosed rooms first built in Phase III.

Changes were made in the area east of Walls F²–F³ in Phase IV, however. The walkway constructed on Layer 9 in Pl. II.1 was resurfaced with a thin layer possibly indicating a change in the function of the area. If the walkway indicated an entrance into the room across Wall F², the entrance may have been discontinued, or it could have continued with no special approach marking the walkway. The evidence of resurfacing in Section B–B is in Layer 7a, against the right side of Wall F³. This appears in the balk in Pl. XVI.5 as the same kind of rubbly ashy fill as Layer 7a in Section E–E.

There seems to have been, however, a continued use of the Phase III surface on the left of Wall F³ in Section B–B, because there is no suggestion of a surface corresponding to Layer 7a. Perhaps it should be noted that Layer 7a is not really a surface foundation in the sense that Layer 7 is in Area II. This is more of a rubbly fill probably dumped from the remodeling operation in Area II and leveled outside the walls of the Phase III buildings. This additional layer of fill brought the level of the surface outside Wall F³ to a point above the level inside the building, but the uneven formation of bedrock probably contributed to this feature.

An alternative to the above interpretation is that the Phase III structure in Area III was destroyed at the end of Phase III, and not reused in Phase IV. The destruction debris of Layer 6b in Section B–B would be from the Phase III destruction instead of Phase IV. This position seems untenable, however, for the following reasons.

First, as noted earlier, the destruction evidence on the Phase III surface in Area III corresponds in depth of debris and intensity of burning to that of the Phase IV surface, on Layer 7, in Area II. There is negligible evidence in Area II to suggest that Phase III was terminated with such violence. Second, there seems to have been a conscious effort to build the level of the Phase IV structure in Area II up to the level of the Phase III floors in Area III in the remodeling of the buildings. The floors inside the rooms of the building are almost level with each other. The unevenness of surface occurs outside Walls F² –F³ in Area III, possibly a courtyard without a roof. A firepit set in Layer 7a of Section C–C suggests this. And third, the surface of bedrock rises rapidly from the north end of Area III into Area IV on the right side, encouraging the filling of Area IV outside Wall F³ to a level above that next to Wall C so that more space could be utilized. This seems to be evident in Section I–I, as we shall see.

Finally, it is evident in Pl. XVI.5, as represented in Section B–B, that severe erosion or wear of the surface on Layer 8 took place. This is also apparent in Area IV in Pl. XI.1 under the meter scale. The erosion of this surface would have occurred over a long period of use, which would include Phase IV as well as Phase III. Phase IV, therefore, is represented in Section B–B by fill layer 7a on the right side of Wall F³, indicating an accumulation outside the building, while the Phase III surface on Layer 8 continued in use through Phase IV.

Phase V, the termination of Building B

Two layers of destruction debris are identified on the surface of Layer 8 between Wall F³ and Tower A. Layer 6, covered by the collapse of Wall F³, is subdivided into 6a and 6b to distinguish between what appears to be ashes sealed by roof material immediately on the surface in 6b, and stones along with bricky debris from the destruction of walls and roof in 6a. Layer 6b near the base of Tower A is characterized by a deep layer of reddish ashy earth around the broken jar drawn in the section, and illustrated in Pl. X. 2.

Layer 6b, covering the broken jar in the photograph, extends under the base stones of the tower on the left, and under the two large stones on top of the jar. This is made up of ashy debris covering the surface shown in Pl. X.2, and is mixed with apparent roofing material in the area on the right side of the jar, extending to the left side of Wall F³. Layer 6a includes the two large stones above the jar, up to the line of the foundation trench for the tower. On the right side of the larger stone in Pl. X.2, the separation line between Layers 6a and 5 can be discerned leading under the topmost small stone on the right side of the jar. This layer line can be followed in Pl. XVI.5 to the underside of collapsed debris of Wall F³.

Layer 5 is also undisturbed destruction debris from the terminal phase of the building complex. This incorporates the decayed materials of Wall F³ covering ruins of the destroyed buildings. The settled, or semi-collapsed, appearance of the wall material in Pl. XVI.5 (Area III) and Pl. XI.1 (Area IV), suggests two things. First, a considerable period of time elapsed between the destruction of the Building B complex and the construction of Building A. This is compatible with the evidence of erosion in the passageway in Wall E¹ against Wall C, which required a period of abandonment. Second, the fairly even distribution of debris across the area suggests that water was impounded within the walls and fill of the site, creating a saturation of the area which hastened the decay and breakdown of the mud-brick walls.

Phase VI, the construction of the Building A complex

Layers 3 and 4 seem to belong with the preparation of Site A for the Phase VI buildings. Both layers lie against the east face of Tower A, and under Wall M, both Phase VI walls. Tower A was constructed first, as the foundation trench filled by Layer 4 attests. The first new structure was, therefore, the tower and associated strengthening of the city fortifications including the addition of a new wall around the entire circumference of the city. The tower covered Wall B and the Phase V destruction debris of Building B.

Layers 3 and 4 consist of materials shifted from other parts of the site, probably from the clearing for construction of the tower. This would be primarily destruction debris from Phase V, but with occasional artifacts dropped or discarded by the Phase VI builders. The purpose of the layers of fill was to build up the level of the area above the ledge of bedrock on the right side of Section B–B so the Phase VI structure could have an east wall on top of the ledge. The tower was constructed on top of the earlier citadel towers and encroached upon the limited space between the ledge and the fortification. This deepening of fill in Layers 3 and 4 enabled the extension of the building eastward on top of the ledge of bedrock, and thus reclaimed space to compensate for that lost in the encroachment by the tower.

Layer 2 is the immediate make-up of ashy rubble upon which Phase VI Wall M was constructed. The wall in this phase had a passageway against Tower A on the left, and a packed *huwwar* surface is preserved in the entrance as indicated in the section. Communication between Areas III and IV was maintained by way of this passageway in the Phase VI period. Wall M was built eastward over the ledge of bedrock on the right in Section B–B, shifting the room of Building A eastward from the location of the Building B room enclosed by Wall F³.

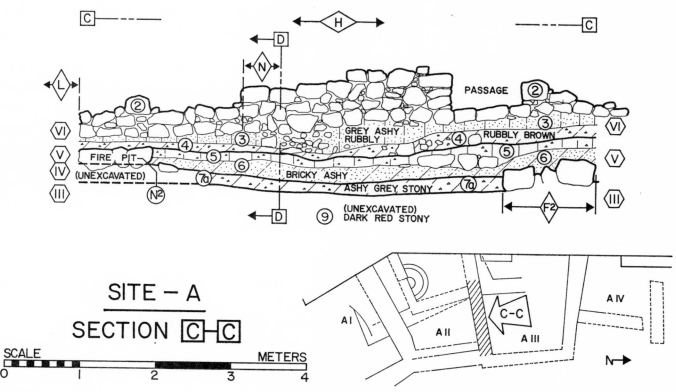

Fig. 12. Section C–C, the north face of the Wall H balk, between Walls L and F² in Area III.

Phase VII, the second, or Sanctuary A, phase

Sometime during the Building A period, a modification of the room arrangement took place. The Wall M passageway between Areas III and IV was closed by a massive blockage of stones, and Enclosure 136 was constructed in the corner where the passageway had been, from the face of Tower A in a semi-circle to Wall M. The blocked entrance is illustrated in Pl. XVIII.4, viewed from Area III and the orientation of Section B–B. The packed surface upon which the blockage was placed is evident underneath the large white stone in the center of the lowest course.

The face of Tower A, on the left of Pl. XVIII.4, is almost vertical, as the position of the meter scale indicates. However, the right side of the passageway is canted about five degrees to the right, suggesting an open passage not equipped with a door.

SECTIONS C–C AND D–D IN AREA III

Section C–C, shown in Fig. 12, is the north face of the Wall H balk in Area III. The balk is illustrated in Pl. XVII and the section is drawn along the face of the wall on the left side from the foreground to the unexcavated part of the altar against the tower in the background. The section covers the balk from Wall F^2, in front of the altar, across Bin N, where the scale lies, to the end of Wall H at the lower left of the photograph.

Phases III–V

The floor of the Building B structure is on the right side of Wall F^2, at the base of the Sanctuary A altar in Pl. II.1, 2. This is off the right side of Section C–C. However, the Phase III surface on the left side of Wall F^2, contemporary with the first use of the floor cited above, is apparently outside the building. There is a terraced construction apparently a walkway against the east side of Wall F^2. It is constructed in the Layer 9 red earth fill as illustrated in Pl. IX. 1, in the left foreground.

Phase IV is represented in Section C–C by Layer 7a, an ashy rubbly fill covering the terrace-like construction of Phase III. The Phase IV building in Area II was remodeled and widened toward the east side of the site, as noted earlier. The resurfacing in Area III was a part of the remodeling operation and a stone-lined firepit, N^2, located on the east side of Area III as indicated in the section, was constructed. The Phase IV surface is illustrated in Pl. XVII along the right side of the structures, and a few stones of the Phase III terrace which it covers are visible behind the flat stone of Bin N, in front of Wall F. The firepit is underneath Bin N in the photograph, and, consequently, not visible. One inference of the rubbly surface and crude firepit is that the area was outside the Phase IV enclosure, probably in a courtyard.

Phase V is indicated in the section by Layers 5 and 6, made up of ashy and bricky rubble covering Wall F^2 on the right side, and the firepit on the left. Deposits of charcoal and ashes are concentrated near Wall F^2, suggesting that the building enclosed by the wall burned and collapsed in that part of the area. Lighter deposits on the left side of the section around the firepit strengthen the suggestion that this was outside the main structure. Wall F^2 probably had a brick superstructure which collapsed partly in the area covered in Section C–C, and Layers 5 and 6 represent the undisturbed debris of the collapse and subsequent natural leveling of the site before the Phase VI rebuilding was begun.

Phases VI–VII

Layers 3 and 4 seem to be redistributed debris from the Phase IV buildings which was leveled for the construction of Building A. No distinction between Layers 2 and 3 was made, although Wall H itself is set in Layer 2. There is no evidence of rebuilding Wall H in an operation corresponding to the blockage of the passageway in Wall M in Phase VII. However, there is some evidence that a cobblestone platform was built against the face of Wall H in Phase VI from the point of juncture of Section D–D at Wall H to the extreme left side of Section C–C. This platform is under Bin N, and therefore is Phase VI, while Bin N is a Phase VII structure built over the platform.

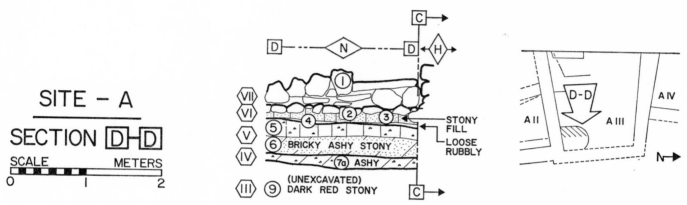

Fig. 13. Section D–D, the Bin N balk against the north face of Wall H in Area III.

SECTION D–D, THE BIN N BALK AGAINST SECTION C–C

A short balk against the west side of Bin N, drawn in Fig. 13, supports the distinction between Phases VI and VII indicated in Section B–B. The balk was drawn because Bin N was not bonded into Wall H, and, therefore, could have been either a Phase VI or Phase VII structure. The bin, illustrated in Pl. XVII, is built in a semi-circle around the half-meter scale, abutting Wall H on the left. Stones of the bin are rather carelessly laid, and the surface under the scale is of packed *huwwar*.

On the right side of the bin in Pl. XVII, and at a lower level, are the small stones of the platform-like structure upon which the bin is built. These stones join Wall H at the juncture of Sections C–C and D–D, and are upon the fill of Layer 3. The platform is therefore contemporary with Wall H, and is assigned to Phase VI. Bin N is contemporary with the blocked entrance in Wall M, Marquet-Krause's Enclosure 136, the Sanctuary A altar inside Enclosure 133, and probably Enclosure 137 and 131. The bin is therefore assigned to Phase VII. The Phase VI platform was constructed in the southeast corner of the room in Area III, therefore, and may have been a counterpart structure to the suggested platform in the southwest corner, mentioned in the discussion of Phase VI in connection with Section A–A above.

Layers 4–9 in Section D–D are extensions of the same layers identified in Section C–C and described above.

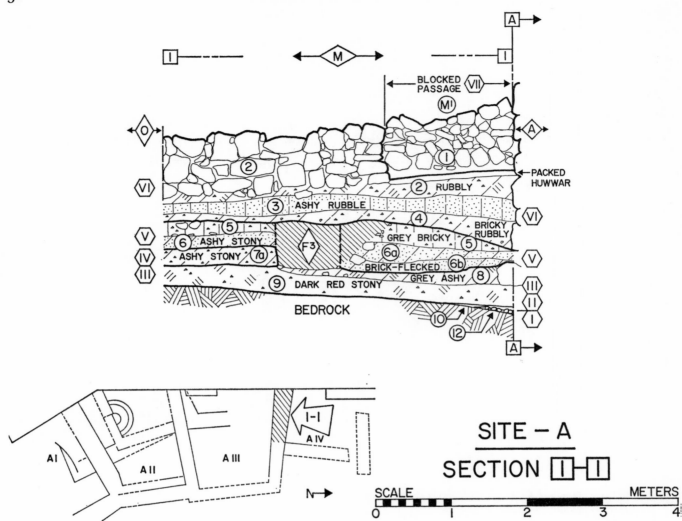

Fig. 14. Section I–I, the north face of the Wall M balk, between Wall O and Tower A in Area IV.

SECTION I–I AND THE STRATIGRAPHY OF AREA IV

Located across the Wall M balk from Section B–B and shown in Fig. 14, this section represents all that was recovered in Area IV. The area was excavated by Marquet-Krause to bedrock, and only the side of the Wall M balk and a small part of Wall O remained. Consequently Section I–I was obtained by trimming the north side of the balk which sloped at an angle from Wall M to a rise in bedrock at the end of Tower Buttress A[1] located in Fig. 81. The balk as trimmed is shown in Pl. XI.1, with a detailed photograph of brick Wall F[3] in the balk in XI.2.

Phase III

The meter scale in Pl. XI.1 lies on grey compact fill underneath the Phase III surface, a patch of which is preserved at the right end of the scale. Layer 8, under the scale, has been described in the analysis of Section B–B, but it tapers to a point under the left side of the brick wall as in B–B. Underneath Layer 8 is the red stony fill of Layer 9 extending across the area as indicated in the section. Stones of the collapse of Wall Y are among those of the fill of Layer 9, but no articulated line of the wall was picked up in Area IV. The Phase III structures are, therefore, the earliest recovered in Area IV.

Wall F³, identified already in Section B–B, is strikingly evident in Section I–I. The wall and related layers of Phases III and IV are preserved to a greater height in Area IV, possibly because of the incline in bedrock toward the north. A step upward in the level of bedrock parallels the Wall M balk about 2 meters north of the balk. The wall itself seems to have collapsed toward the right side of the section, while the left side is preserved almost vertically to Layer 5. The apparent reason for the collapse of the wall toward Tower A was reuse in Phase IV, with the surface on the left side of the section being built up, while that on the right side was not.

Phase IV

Layer 7a in Section I–I seems to be a Phase IV fill corresponding to the fill east of Wall F³ in Area III. However, this is not a rubbly ashy layer such as one would find outside a building. The layer appears in Pl. XI.1 as a very compact fill with a surface running up against Wall F³. This may be the south end of a room which extended into Area IV on the east side of Wall F³, and did not extend south into Area III. The balk in Pl. XVI.5 does not show the compact layer with its defined surface. It is impossible to know precisely whether there was indeed a room in Area IV because almost all of the area was excavated previously to bedrock. The fill in Layer 7a brought the surface of Phase IV occupation up about 25 centimeters higher than the Phase III surface on Layer 8 which was reused in Phase IV on the west side of Wall F³. This split-level Phase IV surface in Section I–I probably accounts for the collapse of Wall F³ toward the west, as noted above. Also the reuse of the Phase III surface accounts for its worn and eroded condition evident in Pl. XI.1 in Area IV and Pl. X.2 in Area III. In fact, some decay of Wall F³ may have taken place on its west side before the final destruction of the site in Phase V.

Phase V

When Building B was terminated in the holocaust assigned to Phase V, roof and wall debris fell toward Wall B on the west. Layers 6a and 6b are destruction layers containing evidence of intense burning and roof fall which have characterized Phase V elsewhere in the site. There is more debris on the right side of Wall F³ than on the left side because the wall was leaning in that direction. The wall did not fall down, however, in the initial destruction, because it seems to have remained in a decaying heap until the earth of its disintegration spread across the entire area. This suggests an elapse of time between Phase V and the rebuilding of the site in Phase VI, as has been noted elsewhere. Pl. XI.1, 2, illustrates the deposit of bricky earth in Layer 5 as drawn in Section I–I.

Phase VI

Layer 4 of Phase VI slopes toward the base of Tower A, indicating that it is contemporary with the building of the tower. Layers 4 and 3 were spread evenly across the area in the operation of leveling the site. They consist of destruction debris from the Building B ruins, along with the few artifacts dropped in the fill during the construction of Building A.

Wall M has its foundation of rubble fill as described in the analysis of Section B–B. A light line along the bedline of Layer 2 indicates *huwwar* spread over the fill of Layer 3 in preparation for construction of the wall in Phase VI. The blocked entrance of Phase VII, illustrated from the Area IV side, is evident in Pl. XI.1, with a detailed photograph in Pl. XVIII.1. The passageway is wider on the Area IV side than across the wall on the Area III side, suggesting further that no door was employed to close the opening.

Very little evidence of Wall O remained. It joined Section I–I at the left end as indicated on the location plan of the section. The few stones of the wall found were not bonded into Wall M. They abutted Wall M like the stone platform and Bin N against Wall H in Area III. A passageway through the south end of Wall O, against Wall M, is suggested by the photograph in Marquet-Krause 1949, Pl. XXI.2, although Marquet-Krause did not identify an entrance at that point. This seems a more plausible location of an entrance than the gap pictured in the north end of Wall O, against Wall q (see also Marquet-Krause 1949, Pl. XCIII), and is drawn as a possibility in Phase VI, Fig. 86.

Another possible entrance into the Area IV room is drawn in the west end of Wall q, based upon the evidence of Marquet-Krause 1949, Pl. XXI:2 and Pl. XCIII. A gap between Wall q and Tower A is left in the plan of this wall, but the opening is irregular. Pl. XXI.2 shows the juncture of the wall with Tower A before the gap was excavated, and the end of Wall q against Tower Buttress A[1] is thickened, like the west end of Wall M. Tower Buttress A[1] is a Phase VII reinforcement of Tower A, so the thickened end of Wall q against the buttress indicates that no passageway was left in Wall q in Phase VII. If an entrance was there in Phase VI, the buttress encroached upon it and caused the Phase VII builders to block the passage and strengthen Wall q on the west end as a support for the buttress.

In Phase VI, therefore, a passageway in the south end of Wall O, against Wall M, probably connected Enclosures 121/132 and 138, and a second entrance to 121/132 was located at the west end of Wall q, against Tower A. The Phase VI passageway in Wall M, against Tower A, allowed entrance into the Area III room also. However, the remodeling of Building A for Sanctuary A in Phase VII changed the character of the rooms in Area IV. Reinforcement of Tower A in Phase VII possibly had something to do with the reorientation of these rooms also.

Tower A seems to have been bulging dangerously at its north end when Phase VI was terminated, so Tower Buttress A[1] was constructed as a reinforcement around the north end. If an entrance was located in Wall q against Tower A in Phase VI, the buttress closed it and Wall q became a lateral buttress for the rebuilt tower. Also, the passageway in Wall M, against Tower A, was blocked and Wall M became another lateral buttress of the tower. Enclosure 121/132 was closed off on the north and south, and the only means of access in Phase VII was from the east, through Wall O. The room may have been abandoned in Phase VII. However, if it continued in use, the most likely place for a passageway was at the south end of Wall O, against Wall M, as indicated in Fig. 87. The rooms in Area IV, therefore, were not connected with Sanctuary A in Phase VII.

III

PHASES I–II, THE PRE-URBAN STRATUM

The earliest structure on the site is found in Phase II, preceding the building of the first city wall and Building C. The structure is founded on the original soil of the site, designated Phase I. The soil of Phase I was not sterile, yielding fifteen pieces of pottery, apparently left by the builders of the Phase II structure. Phase I, therefore, provides evidence of the beginning of the Pre-Urban occupation of the site, and Phase II is the occupation evidence itself.

PHASE I, THE BEGINNING OF THE PRE-URBAN OCCUPATION

The provenance of Phase I pottery

The yellow-to-brownish original soil of Phase I is identified in the Master Section as Layer 12, resting on bedrock. This is found in Areas II, III, and IV, although pottery was recovered only in Area II where the deposits were deepest. Two sub-areas, designated A II 102 and A II 103, yielded the pottery drawn in Fig. 15.

A II 102.11 is the provenance of the pottery found north of Wall S–S¹. The sub-area designated No. 102 was bounded by the balk of Walls H–Q on the north, the Tower A balk on the west, the Wall F¹ balk on the east, and Wall S–S¹ on the south. These are located in Fig. 82. Within Sub-area 102, the layer is No. 11, although it is No. 12 in the sequence of layers in the Master Section. Deposits were found mainly in the break in bedrock shown in Pl. IV.1, on the left side of the meter scale. As was noted in the preceding chapter, the strata of bedrock tilt upward on the west side of the site, and the decline of the *tell* toward the west is effected by a succession of breaks stepping down from the ragged end of one projecting layer to the next. The Phase I deposits were captured in the tilted pockets of these steps and resisted erosion which swept all other original soil down into the *wadi*.

Pottery labeled A II 103.6 was taken from the small sub-area No. 103, located between Wall S–S¹ and Wall E¹ in Fig. 82. The Phase I deposit was layer No. 6 in the sub-area, and a continuation of A II 102.11 as the Master Section indicates in Layer 12, Fig. 83.

The pottery forms

The fifteen pieces of pottery drawn in Fig. 15 are not enough evidence *per se* for conclusive dating of cultural associations. However, the provenance of the pottery is the lowest of a succession of layers ranging from EB I through EB III, as we shall find in the following chapters. Therefore, the stratigraphy reinforces assignment of the general horizon to EB I, indicated by type analysis, and adds weight to the limited evidence of the pottery itself.

Bowls. The more significant of the two bowls in Fig. 15 is No. 2, a large, medium-shallow, carinated platter with burnished red slip. This family of bowls begins to appear at Jericho in Phase O of Areas E III–IV, which is Kenyon's Proto-Urban B (see Hennessy 1967, 8–9, Pl. II:7, 12), and becomes common in her EB I. They appear at Arad in Stratum IV (see Amiran Early Arad, Pl. 8:4–

5), Amiran's EB I equivalent of Kenyon's Proto-Urban B at Jericho. Amiran notes that the ware, characterized by 'pinkish fat clay . . . well levigated' with 'relatively thick' walls and 'all-over red slip . . . evenly burnished' distinguishes various types of bowls, teapots, amphoriskoi juglets and jars in this period, both in the north and in the south (Amiran 1969, 42, Pl. 9:3, 6–8, 10).

The small, shallow hemispherical bowl in Fig. 15:1 is also common during EB I, and is distinguished by buff to pinkish ware with continuously-burnished red slip. This family of bowls has formal antecedents in the Chalcolithic period where crude, hand-made examples appear, for instance, in Stratum V at Arad (see Amiran Early Arad, Pl. 1:19–20), but becomes well-defined in EB I when the bowls apparently serve as oil lamps.

Jars. Medium to short-necked jars with angular to rounded flaring rims become common in EB I. The angular flaring rim of Fig. 15:3 is present in a crude form at Jericho in Proto-Urban B on the *tell* as well as in tombs (see Hennessy 1967, 8, Pl. II:16; Kenyon 1960, 38, Fig. 14:12, is similar in type) and at Arad in Stratum IV (Amiran Early Arad, Pl. 12:19, with lip of rim missing). A complete jar with the characteristics of the rim in Fig. 15:3 and the body and neck of Early Arad Pl. 12:19 is found in Megiddo Tomb 910D, dating to EB I (see Guy 1938, Pl. 4:22).

The angular form derives from a Chalcolithic motif evident in the neck and rim of churns (see Perrot 1961, 75, Fig. 39:1–8), and large store-jars, as in Arad Stratum V (Amiran Early Arad, Pl. 5:5), and at Tell Abu Matar (Perrot 1955, 81, Fig. 16:7; see also de Contenson 1956, 164, Fig. 1:5, 7). The form becomes characteristic in EB I jars as cited above, and as is evident in Meggido Tomb 903 Lower (see Guy 1938, pl. 3:37–40; also amphoriskos No. 7), and Tell el-Far'ah (N) Chalcolithique Superieur (de Vaux 1947, 409, Fig. 2:30).

The rounded, flaring rim in Fig. 15:4–6 also derives from Chalcolithic forms, evident at Abu Matar and Safadi (de Contenson 1956, 172, Fig. 5:1–12). This rim is common at Arad in Stratum IV (Amiran Early Arad, Pl. 11:1, 3; 12:3, 4, 8, 11, 12), at Jericho in Proto-Urban B (Kenyon 1960, 38, Fig. 14:10; 1965, 25, Fig. 9:2–5), and at Tell el-Far'ah (N) Tomb 2 (de Vaux 1949, 120, Fig. 6:39).

Three forms of hole-mouth jars are shown in Fig. 15:7–10. No. 10 is the oldest form, first appearing in Chalcolithic strata in numerous family variations and with burnished or painted decorations. At Arad in Stratum V, the form appears as a plain hole-mouth jar with burnishing on the outside (Amiran Early Arad, Pl. 13:8); with rope-moulding well below the rim (*ibid.*, No. 11), and with vertical loop-handles just under the rim (*ibid.*, Pl. 2:8), or high on the shoulder (*ibid.*, Pl. 6:1). This jar is less common in Stratum IV, where the form yields to types similar to those in Fig. 15:7–9. The jar is present at Ghassul in Stratum IV A with horizontal, pierced lug-handles located on the shoulder of the vessel (Mallon, 1940, Pl. 96:5).

The line-group painted design in reddish-brown over orange ware is characteristic in Proto-Urban B at Jericho, especially in Tombs A13, Levels II–I (Kenyon 1960, 51, Fig. 22:12; also No. 2 has a similar decoration on 'buff-cream-rose ware') and K2, Phase II (Kenyon 1965, 22, Fig. 7:2, 3; see also K2, Phase I, p. 16, Fig. 4:26, 27, 28, 30, which, as Kenyon notes, may belong to Phase II). Hennessy notes that the characteristic line-group and net-painted decoration of Proto-Urban B is common in Areas E III–IV at Jericho in Phase Oi (Hennessy 1967, 9, Pl. III:26), and continues in Phase L in EB I (*ibid.* p. 11, Pl. V), ending in Phase K, or EB II (*ibid.*, p. 11, Pl. VI:58b–d). The sherds found in Phase K, however, may actually derive from earlier phases.

Amiran points out that patterns of net-painting and line-group decoration are dominant in southern Palestine in EB I (Kenyon's Proto-Urban B), to the extent that she identifies a 'Southern Culture' (Amiran 1969, 49) characterized mainly by this decoration. The jar in Fig. 15:10 belongs in this culture, and in the context of the Proto-Urban B strata of Tombs A13, Levels II–I and K2, Phase II, at Jericho, and similar strata of Tombs G, C, and B at Ai.

The hole-mouth jar with squared, or flattened, rim in Fig. 15:9 belongs in a family beginning at Jericho, Areas E III–IV, in Phase Oi (Hennessy 1967, 8, Pl. III:21), or possibly Nii (*ibid.*, p. 8, Pl. III:23), in Proto-Urban B. A characteristic white slip, usually decorated with reddish-brown line painting, as in Fig. 15:15, begins in Phase Oi (*ibid.*, p. 9; Pl. III: 29) and continues in EB I and II with many variations of jar forms.

A jar with squared rim and an unusual loop-handle attached to the rim found in Beth-yerah XVI is placed in EB I with characteristic Proto-Urban B forms by Amiran (Amiran 1969, Pl. 14:10). The same jar form is common at Arad, Stratum IV (Amiran Early Arad, Pl. 8:13, 14) along with the Fig. 15:10 form (*ibid.*, 8:17), but does not appear in Stratum V. The form does continue, however, in Stratum III (*ibid.*, Pl. 18:26, 21:42), and, with variations, in Stratum II (*ibid.*, Pl. 49:15, 50:11–18).

The flattened rim, like most other forms in Phase I, appears first in Chalcolithic (Contenson 1956, 166, Fig. 2:6, with painted decoration; also de Vaux 1961, 568, Fig. 1:8, with painted red band around the exterior of the rim), and continues in Chalcolithique Superieur et Tell el-Far'ah (N) (de Vaux 1961, 572, Fig. 2:21, 37, both with red slip) in stratified deposits.

The two jar forms with thickened, rounded rims, Fig. 15:7–8, appear first in Stratum IV at Arad (cf. 15:7 with Amiran Early Arad, Pl. 8:36, and 15:8 with Pl. 8:40) and continue through Stratum II in variations. Also the flattened oval loop-handle in Fig. 15:14 is early, beginning at Arad in Stratum IV (*ibid.*, Pl. 9:10), as do the ledge-handles in Fig. 15:12–13. These forms begin in EB I, or Kenyon's Proto-Urban, and continue through EB II.

Conclusions

Phase I may be assigned to the same cultural period as Arad Stratum IV; Jericho Proto-Urban B (tombs) and Phases Oi through Nii of Areas E III–IV; Tell el-Far'ah (N) Chalcolithique Superieur; and the beginning of the use of Tombs G, C, and B at Ai.

An analysis of pottery forms from the tombs at Ai indicates that the Jericho Proto-Urban A types are not common at Ai. Only one general Type A bowl occurs in Tomb C (Marquet-Krause 1949, Pl. LXX:645), comparable to a Layer V form in Tomb A94 (Kenyon 1960, 29, Fig. 10:14), and no Type B bowls occur (Callaway 1964, 20). The Type A form is found at Tell en-Nasbeh in Tomb 66 (Wampler 1947, Pl. 51:1106) and in Tombs 2 and 5 at Tell el-Far'ah (N) (de Vaux 1949, 120, Fig. 6:7, Tomb 2; 127, Fig. 8:3, Tomb 5) indicating a spread of the form to the north and west at the same time it appears at Ai. This may be correlated with the end of the period represented in Jericho Tomb A94, Levels V, IV–III.

However, the Proto-Urban Phase II forms, represented in Tombs A94, Levels IIa, II–I, A114(A), A13, II–I, A84, A124, K1, and K2, Phase II, are common, and are represented also in the Pre-Urban, Phase II remains at Ai. Phase I, the beginning of the Pre-Urban stratum, therefore, may be more precisely located with reference to Jericho at the first appearance of the Proto-Urban B culture, possibly as a result of the influx of the same people who introduced the culture there. This conclusion, supported by an analysis of the Ai tombs' pottery, is compatible with the association of Ai, Phase I, with Phases Oi–Nii in Areas E III–IV on the *tell* at Jericho.

PHASE II, THE PRE-URBAN WALL R BUILDING

The building

As was noted in the analysis of the Master Section and Section B–B, Walls R and Y in Area III comprise the structural remains of Phase II. This is the structure noted by Marquet-Krause as '. . . les vestiges d'un muret construit a même le roc' (1949, 31) in the northern part of the site.

Wall R runs east-west, and fragments of both ends are preserved, as illustrated in Pl. II.2, on bedrock in front of the meter scale. The west extremity runs into the master balk on the right, under Tower A, and also under the Phase III fill as the Master Section in Fig. 83 shows. A detailed photograph of that part of Wall R is in Pl. III.1. The wall is built of stacked stones one-course wide, and the two stones above the 25 centimeter scale suggest that the superstructure was partly of stone. No mud-bricks were recovered, although it is possible that bricks were laid on a stone sub-structure, reaching two stones above the scale. A whitish mud-brick is evident in the balk on the right side of the top stone, although the brick seems to be a part of the saucer-shaped fill of Phase III which follows the line of rubble tilting from the upper left center of the photograph to the lower right.

In any case, a wall with a stone base up to 35 centimeters wide is certain, and the possibility that a narrower band of stones set in clay mortar enclosed the room above floor level may be allowed. The superstructure above the two-stones high band, on the other hand, may very well have been mud-bricks like the one in Pl. III.1. This is supported somewhat by the remains of Wall Y and the eastern end of Wall R, where disintegrated mud-bricks seem to cover the base stones on bedrock.

The Wall R building cannot be traced, except as shown in the plan in Fig. 25. Possibly the structure, actually little more than a hut, occupied the uneven slope of bedrock below the ledge shown on the right of Section B–B, Fig. 11, and between Wall R and Area IV as indicated in Section A–A, Fig. 83. The entrance would have been on the low side, presumably, and therefore in the west wall covered by Tower A. Since previous excavations removed all earth around the walls to bedrock, a reconstruction beyond this is unsupported by evidence.

Provenance of the pottery

Most of the pottery in Phase II is from Layers 11 and 10 in Area II, as located in the Master Section, Fig. 83. Thick deposits of ashy earth mixed with pottery and bones, presumably thrown out by the Phase II inhabitants, spread down the slope from Wall R. A few pieces of pottery were taken from scant remains of the collapse of Wall R in Area III. These are assigned to Layer 10 because they seem to be a part of the destruction debris of the structure. Layer 11, therefore, is to be associated with the occupation of the site by the Phase II inhabitants, and Layer 10 belongs with the final occupation and termination of the phase.

Layer 11. Layer 11 in Area III can be identified in Pl. VI.2, resting on bedrock and extending to the light-grey stony deposit under the scale. This layer is also behind the second white tag above bedrock on the right side of the photograph. The first tag above bedrock indicates Layer 12, below, and the meter scale is on the upper surface of Layer 10, above.

A II 102.10 is the designation of Layer 11 between Wall S–S¹ and the balk of Walls H–Q. This is a very compact ashy fill with a consistent mixture of pottery and bones throughout its depth of 25 to 35 cm. If this is indeed the midden of the Phase II inhabitants, the ash content of the earth, contributing to its compactness, would have derived from occasional cleaning of the houses at the site, and clearing of ashes from fire hearths.

A II 103.5 is a continuation of Layer 11 south of Wall S–S¹, and down to the Wall E¹ balk. This continuation is almost indistinguishable from Layer 10, above in Pl. VIII.3, behind the center section of the scale. The merging of the two layers, distinguishable in Pl. VI.2, indicates that they were shaped partly by erosion, commencing at the increased decline of the slope drawn in the Master Section, Fig. 83. Therefore, the distinction between A II 103.5 (Layer 11) and A II 103.4 (Layer 10) is not as sharply defined as that between A II 102.10 and A II 102.9 north of Wall S–S¹.

Layer 10. Layer 10 between Wall S–S¹ and the balk of Walls H–Q has been identified as the light-grey stony fill under the meter scale in Pl. VI.2. Like Layer 11, this has an ash content with a mixture of pottery and bones, but is consistently more stony in the north half of Area II. A II 102.9 is the designation of the layer from this part of the area.

A II 103.4 is a continuation of the layer between Wall S–S¹ and the Wall E¹ balk, located above A II 103.5, but with the bedline less clearly defined than was the case north of Wall S–S¹. The sub-area, No. 103, was excavated to bedrock by Marquet-Krause, so the yield of pottery was relatively small deriving principally from straightening balks and clearing corners.

A II 101.11 is from Sub-area 101 across the Wall F¹ balk east of Sub-area 102. The location may be determined by consulting the sketch plan in Fig. 82 where the balks are indicated. In Pl. IV.1, this is the grey layer on the right side of the photograph about 25 centimeters below the white tag, and a continuation of the same layer behind the upper white section of the meter scale.

A III 202.10 is reddish or bricky ashy earth among the stones of the disintegrated Walls R and Y in Area III. Very little undisturbed earth was left from the previous excavation, because Wall R was exposed almost to its eastern end. Sub-area 202 is from the Wall M balk alongside Wall Y to Wall R, and to the point toward the tower where bedrock was exposed by Marquet-Krause. The exact provenance may be seen in Pl. II.2, underneath the stones in the left foreground where Walls Y and R join.

The Phase II pottery forms

All of the pottery which could be reconstructed to any meaningful degree in drawings is found in Figs. 16–24. In general, this phase continues the forms of Phase I, and terminates by EB IC. This places Phase II in Wright's EB IB, Kenyon's Proto-Urban B at Jericho, the Chalcolithique Superieur of de Vaux at Tell el-Far'ah (N), and Amiran's Stratum IV at Arad. This is the EB Pre-Urban occupation stratum at Ai.

Small to medium bowls. The small hemispherical bowls in Fig. 16:1–4 continue the tradition of Phase I, with general deepening and rim variations common in EB IB. They are the Proto-Urban Type C bowls at Jericho, common in Tombs A114(A), A13, and A84, but scarce in Tomb A94

(Kenyon 1960, 12–13). In Tomb K2, they occur more frequently in Phase II than in Phase I, although the form may be called common in both phases (see Kenyon 1965. 4: tabulation of bowl types). Fig. 16:3 begins in stratified deposits on the *tell* in Areas E III–IV in Phase Oi (Hennessy 1967, 8, Pl. 11:2), and when the other sites on the *tell* are published, probably all forms will be represented.

The medium bowls in Fig. 16:5–15 are generally found in the context of small bowls noted above. Two of the medium bowls, Fig. 16:11 and 14, are in the family of Amiran's 'V-shaped' bowls common in Chalcolithic, and persisting in variations through EB III. The angular form, No. 11, is a variant of the V-shaped bowls found at Abu Matar and Safadi (see de Contenson 1956, 174, Fig. 6) as well as Azor (Perrot 1961, 71, Fig. 37). The form is contemporary with, and possibly a local imitation of, Wright's grey lustrous ware Type 2 (Wright 1958, 43) the nearest parallel of which is found at Tell el-Far'ah (N) in Tomb 14 (de Vaux 1951, 575, Fig. 6:2). The rim is less everted, and the thickening below the rim is not a distinct rope-molding. However, the form is strikingly similar. No. 14 is also a V-shaped form, but with the rim turns sharply upward.

Similar forms are found in Chalcolithic at Gezer, with the characteristic red band painted around the rim (see Amiran 1969, 30, Pl. 4:1), and a contemporary form occurs in Chalcolithique Superieur at Tell el Far'ah (N), also in Tomb 14 (de Vaux 1952, 581, Fig. 12:8; see also 1947, 409, Fig. 2:29, from stratified deposits). Both the Ai and Tell el-Far'ah (N) Tomb 14 bowls have lost the earlier red band characterizing the Chalcolithic form. Still later variations of the form are the Type L bowls at Jericho occurring in EB III (Kenyon 1960, 58) and in Sanctuary A at Ai (Marquet-Krause 1949, Pl. LXXV, 1383–1397, from Enclosure 122). The later forms differ from No. 14, however, in the profile of the sides, not distinctly concave, and the rims, which are not as abruptly turned upward.

Among the other medium bowls, Nos. 5, possibly 6, 7, and 8 are decorated with burnished reddish-brown slip; No. 9 has traces of a white slip; No. 12 has a burnished orangish-brown slip, and the deep bowl, No. 16, has a burnished reddish-brown slip. There is no example of pattern- or net-burnishing, a decoration beginning in EB I, and common in EB II (Amiran 1969, 55). The small bowls likewise are characterized by burnished red slip (No. 2), or reddish-brown slip (No. 5), if there is any decoration at all.

The medium bowls are found in Arad Stratum IV (Amiran Early Arad, Pl. 7:8 with Fig. 18:12; Pl. 7:5 with 18:15); and in Jericho Tombs A13, Level III (Kenyon 1960, 49, 50, Fig. 21:2 with No. 13), Level I (*ibid.*, p. 51, Fig. 22:3 with No. 11), A94, Level IIa (*ibid.*, pp. 30–31, Fig. 11:11–14, Type B.2.b, with Nos. 7–10). They are also present in Chalcolithique Superieur stratified deposits at Tell el-Far'ah (N) (de Vaux 1947, 407, Fig. 1:4, 29, and Fig. 18:7, 8, 10), and Tomb 3 (1949, 113, Fig. 1:2).

Wide medium-to-deep bowls. The forms in Fig. 16:17, 19, 25, are characterized by orange to pinkish-orange ware and white slip outside, up to the edge of the rim. Hennessy notes that a heavy white slip begins to occur in Areas E III–IV at Jericho in Phase Oi, and he cites a jar rim which has vertical stripes of reddish-brown (Hennessy 1967, 9, Pl. III:29). This type of decoration occurs at Ai on jars in Phases I and II and in the early tombs (see Marquet-Krause, 1949, Pl. LXXIII:933 Tomb G). Deeper bowls with sharply inverted flattened rims occur in EB II with characteristic white slip (Loud 1948, Pl. 4:8, Stratum XVIII), continuing the decoration with the family of forms.

Two deep bowls, Fig. 16:21, 23, continue a rim form beginning in Chalcolithic (see de Contenson 1956, 166, Fig. 2:7–9), and continuing in EB I with variations in stance and shape. This is Hennessy's 'hammer-rim' form noted first in Areas E III–IV at Jericho in Phase L, or Kenyon's EB I (Hennessy 1967, 10). This occurs first at Arad in Stratum IV, in a more upright flattened form than the two from Ai, Phase II (Amiran Early Arad, Pl. 8:1). However, the variation in stance does not seem to be chronologically significant, because variation among those cited in Chalcolithic can be noted.

Shallow platter-bowls. The large, shallow, carinated platter with burnished red slip noted in Phase I (Fig. 15:2) is also present in Phase II. Figs. 16:27–29 and 17:1–5 are variations of the same form, and all are decorated with a burnished slip in reddish-brown (16:27, 29; 17:1, 2, 4, 5), or orangish-red to brown (16:28; 17:3). Fig. 16:28 is radially-burnished inside to the carination, and is the only one with a definite pattern. Some of the rim fragments, however, are too small to indicate more than the form and rim decoration.

Fig. 16:26 seems to be a crude, carinated-platter form which, for some reason, was poorly made and not finished like those noted above. The rim is suggestive of the well-finished wheel-turned rims of the general type, but both the rim and body are thick and only roughly finished, without a decorative slip. In the context of A II 102.9, this seems to represent either an apprentice's stumbling effort or a potter's mistake, and, therefore, an aberrant of a family of distinctive forms.

Various rim forms of the large, shallow platters occur along with the distinctive carinated form. Fig. 16:18 appears in stratified deposits of Areas E III–IV at Jericho in Phase Oi, although neither this rim nor the carinated form appear in the Proto-Urban tombs. Fig. 16:20 is a slight variation of the same form, with a distinct groove marking the upward turn of the lip. Both are decorated with burnished reddish-brown slip, characteristic of the carinated forms in Phase II, as is Fig. 16:24, having a thickened flat rim with thin inverted edge.

Jars. The plain, angular, flaring rim of Phase I, Fig. 15:3, traced to antecedents in Chalcolithic, continues in a less distinctively angular form in Phase II. The angle at the base of the neck is more rounded in Fig. 17:6 and 27; and where the sharper angle is preserved in No. 28, it is combined with a more rounded, flaring rim. On the other hand, the rounded, flaring form with slight to well-rolled edge becomes more common. Also, the neckless, sharply flaring rim found on ledge-handle jars from EB I through EB III becomes common.

Fig. 17:28 is represented in the same family of forms at Arad in Stratum IV, although the Arad example has rope-molding decoration around the base of the neck (Amiran Early Arad, Pl. 12:2; see also No. 19, which has a plain neck like Fig. 17:28, but, unfortunately, has lost the rim). Fig. 17:25, and possibly 19, are variations of the same form. The rounded, flaring rim with slight to well-rolled edge is also found at Arad in Stratum IV, and continues in Stratum III. Fig. 17:14–20 are examples of the slightly rolled rim, similar to Arad forms (*ibid.*, Pl. 12:5, 3, 7, 11, and 20), while Fig. 17:22, 23, 26 and 29 are heavier rolled rims comparable to No. 4 of the Arad forms. The latter example from Arad has a more squared profile than the Ai rims; otherwise it is very similar to Fig. 17:26. No. 26 may also be compared with a complete jar from Ras el-Ain (see Amiran 1969, 57, Pl. 14:1). This jar has the same kind of flattened rolled rim, and is decorated with heavy rope-molding like that in Fig. 24:5–12.

The neckless rims becoming common on short, ledge-handled jars are shown in Fig. 17:8–10, and 13, and may be related to the same Arad Stratum IV assemblage (Amiran Early Arad, Pl. 12:12, 14, 17, and 20). They are found in the early deposits of Tomb G (Marquet-Krause 1949, Pl. LXXIII:931, 933), and at Jericho in Tombs A114(A) (Kenyon 1960, 46, Fig. 18:15, 17) and A13, IV–III (ibid., p. 50, Fig. 21:6). The heavy flaring rim in Fig. 17:27, a narrow version, and 17:30, a larger, heavier example, appears at Jericho only in stratified deposits, beginning apparently in Phase Oi (Hennessy 1967, 8, Pl. II: 16), contemporary with the neckless rims found in the tombs cited.

Almost all of the jars in Phase II are decorated with a heavy, white slip, which becomes normative for the period. Fig. 17:6–7, 9–10, 14–17, 19–20, 23, 25–26, 28–29 all have definite traces of light-to-heavy white slip. Only No. 21 has a burnished red slip, while the other examples have no definable slip of any kind. Body sherds illustrated in Fig. 24:1–12 indicate that rope-molding was a common decoration on jars, and Nos. 13–23 show that a reddish-brown vertical stripe was a popular decoration over white slip.

Hole-mouth jars. A considerable variety of both the squared, flattened and thickened, inward-rolled rim forms of hole-mouth jars found in Phase I occurs in Phase II. New forms with decorative grooves, ridges, and rope-molding outside and below the rims appear, and the rim stance varies from almost horizontal, for possible cooking-pots, to near vertical for regular store-jars.

The squared rim with flattened edge, a form continuing from Chalcolithic, is less common than the inward-rolled rim. Fig. 18:26, 28 shows two variations. No. 26, is more like the antecedent form cited in the interpretation of Phase I. The entire rim in No. 28 is bent to a horizontal stance anticipating the drooping, inturned rim form found in Kenyon's EB I at Jericho (Hennessy 1967, 11, Pl. V:48, Phase L of Areas E III–IV). Other variations occur in combination with the rolled rim, as in Fig. 18:20, 27, and 19:5, where only a part of the edge is flattened, leaving a profile more triangular than squared.

Another form, possibly a variant of the squared rim, is the bow-rim, Fig. 19:25, appearing at Jericho in Phase Oi (Hennessy, 1967, 8, Pl. II:15), and, in a slightly different form, at Arad in Stratum IV (Amiran Early Arad, Pl. 8:19, 34). A variation of this form continues in Stratum III at Arad (ibid., Pl. 18:24).

Ridges, grooves, and rope-molding are common decorations on the inward-rolled rims in Phase II. The ridge is actually a half-relief rope-molding indented diagonally in some instances, as in Fig. 24:1, or a high-relief narrow molding with indentations as in Fig. 24:2, or plain, Fig. 24:3. This type of decoration occurs in Stratum IV at Arad (cf. Fig. 21:20 with Amiran Early Arad, Pl. 8:23; Fig. 21:1 with Pl. 8:22), Phase P at Jericho, Areas E III–IV (Hennessy 1967, 8, Pl. 3:19), and Chalcolithique Superieur at Tell el-Far'ah (N) (de Vaux 1961, 572, Fig. 2:18, 19, 20). A plain groove below the rim is found on Fig. 20:4, a thickened, inward-rolled rim similar to Fig. 15:7 in Phase I.

The most common rim decoration in Phase II was apparently made by turning the completed vessel with a flat tool held against the outside of the rim. A smooth, flat surface just below the edge was fashioned, leaving a small ridge at the lower side of the turned area. The ridge was formed by the accumulation of the clay of the vessel, and is not a rope-molding or plastic decoration. This type of rim is illustrated in Figs. 19:7–24, 26, 20:1–3. This is Hennessy's 'cut-rim' beginning at Jericho in Phase Oi (Hennessy 1967, 8, Pl. III:20), and becoming more common in Phase M, or late Proto-Urban. The general type is rare in Stratum IV at Arad (see Amiran Early Arad, Pl. 8:31), and becomes slightly more numerous in Stratum III (*ibid.*, Pl. 21:4, 8, 16), though not as common as at Ai.

Upright, or wide-mouth forms are shown in Fig. 20:7, 9–20. They occur with the same rim forms and decorations as regular hole-mouth jars. These forms occurring in Phase II are of special interest because only one apparent example is reported at Arad in Stratum IV (Amiran Early Arad, Pl. 8:19) although some forms appear in Stratum V (*ibid.*, Pl. 6:4–6), and in Stratum III (*ibid.*, Pl. 13:42–43, 45). Fig. 20:16, 18, and 19 seem to belong in the same general family as the Stratum V forms in Pl. 6:4, 6. Fig. 17:32 may be included also. On the other hand, Fig. 20:9–15, 17, 20 are very similar to Stratum III forms in Pl. 13:42–43, 45. The single Stratum IV form cited is similar to the latter, though not as common. The numerous upright forms in Phase II at Ai seem to be, therefore, a regional variation.

Handles and spouts. Four pierced lug-handles of small juglets or pots are illustrated in Fig. 23:1–4. They are typical in Proto-Urban Tomb A13, II–I, at Jericho (Kenyon 1960, 51, Fig. 22:5, 11–13), and in Stratum IV at Arad (Amiran Early Arad, Pl. 10:2, 6). Ledge-handles are plain (Fig. 23:6–8, 13, 14); indented (Nos. 5, 10–12); pushed-up (No. 9); and a unique, plain serrated form (No. 15). The latter is similar in type to a handle at Tell el-Far'ah (N) with small round, not diagonally incised, indentations, found in Chalcolithique Supérieur (de Vaux 1961, 572, Fig. 2:11; cf. also 2:12, 13, and Fig. 1:30–31). Amiran notes in her review of ledge-handle forms and general typological analysis that '. . . from the very beginning, it seems to have had more than one form' (Amiran 1969, 40).

The pushed-up form in Fig. 23:9 should be later than Phase II, if a typological development is assumed. However, this form appears in Tomb A94 at Jericho (Kenyon 1960, 38, Fig. 14:10) in Phase IIA, or Proto-Urban, and a similar handle is also in Tomb A114(A) (*ibid.*, p. 46, Fig. 18:16). The twin-loop juglet handle similar to those in Fig. 23:16–17 is also found in Proto-Urban at Jericho in Tomb A94 (Kenyon 1960, 36, Fig. 13:12), but is not characteristic of later tombs. No. 18 is a unique, and probably malformed, loop-handle on a wide shallow bowl which does not appear to have parallels.

Open spouts, characteristic of cooking-pot and water-jar forms, are shown in Fig. 23:19, 21. They are found on both large and small vessels, and in a variety of forms. Nos. 19 and 21 may be cooking-pot spouts from vessels similar to a form cited by Amiran from Tell el-Far'ah (N) (1969, 57, Pl. 14:6), found also in Proto-Dynastic Egypt at Qau, as noted by Hennessy (1967), 31, Pl. XXIV:8, 9). Fig. 23:20 is a pierced spout, probably from a water jar, becoming vestigial in EB II.

Conclusions

The pottery forms of Phases I–II have been compared rather closely with similar types, or families of forms, from stratified deposits elsewhere in Palestine. Emphasis has been given to parallels at Jericho, Arad, and Tell el-Far'ah, which are post-World War II excavations. There are many other parallels than those cited which could be searched out, but the present research seems to be adequate to locate the Early Bronze pre-urban occupation at Ai both culturally and chronologically.

Cultural horizon. The material evidence of Phases I–II seems to be contemporary with the Jericho Proto-Urban B culture. The pottery assemblage is typologically related to Jericho Tombs A94, Levels IIa–I; A114(A); A13, Levels II–I; and K2, Phase II. In Areas E III–IV on the *tell*, the assemblage relates to Phases Oi–Nii, also Proto-Urban B. Elsewhere, pottery from Phases I–II is associated closely with typical forms of Arad, Stratum IV, Chalcolithique Superieur at Tell el-Far'ah (N), and less specifically with EB IA (or IB) shaft tombs at Bab edh-Dhra'.

Levels IIa–I of Jericho Tomb A94 occur in a stratigraphic sequence to Levels V–III, assigned to Proto-Urban A by Kenyon. Levels II–I of Tomb A13 are in a sequence to Levels IV–III, and Phase II succeeds Phase I in Tomb K2. Hennessy reports a similar sequence of cultures on the *tell* in Areas E III–IV, with the Proto-Urban B innovations appearing in Phase Oi. Lapp reports three instances of EB IB (Kenyon's Proto-Urban B) tombs cut into existing EB IA Proto-Urban A) tombs at Bab edh-Dhra' (1970, 107). Phases I–II at Ai, therefore, occur in the second, or EB IB, sequence of cultural development in the Early Bronze Age. In the transition from Chalcolithic, this is the second cultural sequence beyond the end of Chalcolithic, and immediately preceding the first urban phase at Ai.

Little use has been made of the significant Early Bronze Age finds at Bab edh-Dhra' because of the lack of published stratified deposits. The most extensive report with illustrations and drawings is that of Saller (1965, 137–219), based upon purchased collections of pottery and objects arranged in a sequence of four periods by Hennessy, as a result of his study of Areas E III–IV at Jericho (see Saller 1965, 148–150). Some of the forms assigned to 'the oldest stage in the history of Bab edh-Dhra' (p. 150), dated tentatively to the 34th–31st centuries B.C., are apparently contemporary with Phase II at Ai (see for instance, p. 152, Fig. 13:2, 5; p. 154, Fig. 14:11; p. 165, Fig. 18:12, 15; p. 173, Fig. 21:1, 12, 15). However, most of these forms can also be assigned to Jericho EB I, or post-Phases Q–N in Areas E III–IV, so their value as a control over the attribution of the Ai material is uncertain.

Other forms found in the shaft tombs, e.g., Tomb A76, were believed to be contemporary with the Proto-Urban A assemblage in Tomb A13, Levels IV–III, K2, Phase I, and A94, Levels V–IV at Jericho (see Lapp 1968, 26–41). Some of the Tomb A76 parallels cited in Jericho Tomb K2 (Kenyon 1965, 15–27) are indeed Proto-Urban A, e.g., Lapp, Fig. 8:2 and Kenyon, Fig. 4:8 (K2, Phase IB); Lapp, Fig. 8:5 and Kenyon, Fig. 4:19 (K2, Phase IB). Other parallels, however, are Proto-Urban B, or Phase II of Tomb K2, e.g., Lapp, Fig. 9:st 1 and Kenyon Fig. 8:12; Lapp, Fig. 9:19 and Kenyon, Fig. 8:25. All of the artifacts cited from Tomb A76 at Bab edh-Dhra' are from the undisturbed east chamber, so the implication is that the assemblage is post Proto-Urban A, although pottery with characteristic line-group painted decoration is lacking. Tomb A76, therefore, seems to be contemporary with Phase II at Ai, but the lack of clear parallels with the Phase II assemblage limits its relevance.

Tomb A43 at Bab edh-Dhra' contained pottery with line-group painted decoration (see Lapp 1966, 110) similar to that in Jericho Tomb K2, Phase II (see Kenyon 1965, 22, Fig. 7) and Tomb A13, Levels II–I (Kenyon 1960, 51, Fig. 22). These parallels from Jericho have been related to a Phase I decorated rim at Ai, shown in Fig. 15:10. Lapp suggests, however, that Tomb A43 contained forms present in the EB II charnel houses at Bab edh-Dhra', so the usefulness of Tomb A43 is also limited. The same is true of the remarkable find of line-group painted pottery at Argub el-

Dhahr (Parr 1956), where no clear distinction can be made between Proto-Urban B, or EB IB, and EB IC forms.

Chronology. No Carbon 14 dates on Phase II were obtained, so a chronology for the period has to be fixed rather loosely. Several Carbon 14 dates were obtained on the beginning of Phase III, the first great urban phase at Ai, as we shall note in the next chapter. These assays support a date of 3000–2860 B.C., for Phase III, which in turn requires a date of ca. 3100–3000 B.C. for Phases I–II.

The appearance of the pre-urban settlers would, therefore, be about 3100 B.C., with the Phase I pottery as material evidence of their beginnings. Kenyon places the beginning of the Proto-Urban A culture at Jericho ca. 3300 B.C. on the evidence of a Carbon 14 date of 3260 B.C. ± 110 from charcoal in Level IV of Tomb A94 (1960, 21). Level IV is intermediate between the earliest layer, Level V, and the appearance of the Proto-Urban B culture, contemporary with Level IIa (see Kenyon 1960, 21–25). Lapp correctly inferred that the one published Carbon 14 date of 3260 B.C. for EB IA needed additional support from other assays to be accepted with confidence (1970, 106). The assays from Phase III at Ai, interpreted in the next chapter, support a lower date, or a date on the low side of the ± range, i.e., ca. 3150 B.C., instead of 3260 B.C. for the introduction of Proto-Urban B at Jericho.

THE SETTLEMENT AND POPULATION

Phases I–II at Site A precede the building of the first walled city at Ai in Phase III, and are, therefore, pre-urban. How extensive the unfortified village was is not known. Contemporary house remains were found underneath the first city wall at Site C, Area II, so the village was at least 200 meters long. Compared with later walled cities, this indicates a fairly large settlement, although it is small in comparison with the Phase III walled city.

Amiran (1970, 84–85) surveyed the evidence of unwalled settlements in EB I and three conclusions may be drawn from her study. First, the extent of the unwalled settlements in almost every case is unknown. Thus, a village reaching a length of 200 meters at Ai is significant. Second, unwalled villages seem to have existed at some sites until EB II, or Phase IV at Ai. This places the emergence of walled cities in an irregular sequence, with some unwalled settlements never developing into walled cities. The Phase III walled city at Ai probably preceded the establishment of the Stratum II walled city at Arad, for instance. And third, Amiran's theory of a 'population explosion' early in EB I, leading to the establishment of large walled cities seems to be supported by the evidence of the unfortified village at Ai. The village was larger than the Iron Age I village at Ai in biblical times, and actually as large as many of the 'cities' of Iron Age II, a period of prosperity and extensive population which spilled over into settlements in marginal areas such as Arad.

There were no inhabitants at Ai prior to the settlement in Phases I–II, so the village seems to have been established by the overflow of population from other sites, and an increment of newcomers. Lapp proposed a population development at Bab edh-Dhra' in successive increments of new people who superimposed their culture on that of the local inhabitants (1970, 108f). The newcomers were rapidly absorbed into the local population and their culture dominated, but did not replace, that of the indigenous people. Lapp rejected the theory of overlapping but different cultures, such as Chalcolithic and Early Bronze, as well as Kenyon's theory of contemporary but culturally distinct tribal groups co-existing in settlements like Jericho (see Kenyon 1965, 5–6).

Amiran observes that '... urbanism in Canaan seems *not* to have developed out of *purely and exclusively* local conditions' (1970, 83), but that stimulation came from the Jemdet Nasr Sumerian culture. She cites the EB I spouted vessel, traced to Mesopotamian origins by Kantor, as evidence of migratory infiltrating movements from upper Mesopotamia into Canaan. An intermingling of cultural elements from Mesopotamia, and Egypt, with local traditions is evident in some objects from excavations. A locally made cylinder seal from Arad, Stratum II, is one example. The seal is crude in workmanship, but reflects the 'squat form' and 'design . . . of a general debased Jemdet Nasr flair' (1970, 88–89). Amiran's view of the influence of newcomers upon the life and culture of the in- digenous population in EB I seems to be less radical than that of Lapp.

The evidence of Phases I–II at Site A seems to support Amiran's view of population development. The artifacts reflect a mingling of cultures within the region prior to the settlement, and after the decline of Chalcolithic culture. Chalcolithic influences are evident in the angular jar neck and rim forms in Fig. 15:3 and 17:28, and the rolled, flaring rims of Figs. 15:4–6 and 17:14–20. Jars with these rim forms continue the Chalcolithic rope-molding decoration. The angular bowl in Fig. 16:14 also continues a Chalcolithic form, as does the thin, tapered jar rim in Fig. 15:10. The latter, however, is decorated with line-group painting, a new development in EB IB.

Influences attributable to newcomers in EB IB are the line-group decoration noted above and the carinate platters in Fig. 15:2, 16:26–29, and 17:1–5. These do not appear in the local Chalcolithic tradition. Also, the inward rolled rim of the hole-mouth jar is a new development, decorated various- ly with applied molding on the outside, or shaped with a cutting tool around the outside edge. Ledge handles may have originated from Chalcolithic pottery-making techniques, such as application of rope decoration or knob handles (see Amiran 1969, 36), but the true ledge handle is an EB develop- ment.

The significance of these features is two-fold. First, there seems to be a strong Chalcolithic in- fluence in the artifacts of the first settlers at Ai. This influence would be inexplicable apart from people who descended from the Chalcolithic population and retained fundamental elements of their culture. However, the submerging of these elements, or features, under the new influences attributable to newcomers in EB IB suggests that the break with Chalcolithic culture is complete, though probably not as radical as Lapp suggests (see Lapp 1970, 105).

Second, the newcomers associated with the EB IB influences eventually dominate the new settlement. Their culture persists in the succeeding phases at Ai, so they must have been fore- runners of successive migrations of people from the same general region. The immediate point of emigration for the people of Phases I–II was probably east of Ai, possibly Jericho. They were pos- sibly associated with the incursion of Proto-Urban B people to Jericho, with enough time elapsing before settlement at Ai to allow some absorption of scattered indigenous remnants into their group.

The ultimate origin of the newcomers is to be found north of Canaan. Hennessy suggests a local origin of the EB IB tradition (1967, 46), but Lapp points out a closeness to the Ciradere tradition in Anatolia, assigned by him to EB IB on the basis of stratigraphy at Alishar Hüyük (1970, 119). This Anatolian origin places the EB IB increment in the succession of an earlier EB IA migration from eastern Anatolia and Syria (Hennessy 1967, 38, 45), and as far north as southern Russia (suggested by Lapp 1970, 118). The settlers at Ai in Phases I–II, therefore, came out of diverse backgrounds, but by the time the village was built, absorption into one social unit had been accomplished.

DESCRIPTIONS OF PHASE I POTTERY, FIG. 15

Fig. 15 No.	Reg. No.	
1	4176	Rim slightly incurved to thin, rounded edge, wheel-made; buff with greyish-buff core; fine with few white and black grits; continuously-burnished, reddish-brown slip outside and inside edge of rim. A II 102.11.
2	4202	Rim carinated with wide, thinned, rounded edge, wheel-turned; red slip with thick, pinkish-brown core; medium-coarse with some medium white, and many assorted, dark-grey grits; traces of continuous wheel-burnishing over-all. A II 103.6.
3	4220	Rim inclined outward to rounded edge, wheel-made; pinkish-tan with thick, brown core; medium with many assorted grits; thin, tan slip outside; pitted and spalling inside. A II 103.6.
4	4189	Rim outcurved to flat, thin, rounded edge, wheel-made; orange with thick, dark-grey core; medium with few assorted black and fine white grits; some yellow discoloration inside, some grey incrustations over-all. A II 102.11.
5	4204	Rim sharply flared out to thinned, rounded edge, wheel-finished; buff; medium-coarse with few fine white grits; dark-grey smoke marks inside, some heavy, grey incrustations outside. A II 103.6.
6	4160	Heavy rim flared out to thickened, rounded edge, wheel-finished; buff with dark-grey core; medium-coarse with many assorted white and tan grits; traces of white slip outside and inside edge; some grey incrustations over-all. A II 102.11.
7	4190	Rim incurved to medium-wide, very thick, rounded edge; light-red with very thick, dark-grey core; coarse with many assorted white and grey grits; some brown discoloration outside, some grey incrustations. A II 102.11.
8	4191	Rim incurved to narrow, thickened, rounded edge, rim wheel-finished; tan with yellow core; coarse with many assorted white, grey, and quartz grits; thin, white slip outside; some grey incrustations over-all. A II 102.11.
9	4203	Rim incurved to thickened, squared, slightly depressed edge, rim wheel-finished; red with thick, tan core; coarse with many very large to fine, white, tan, brown, and black grits; tannish-white slip outside; very pitted inside, black smoke marks outside, dark-brown discoloration on rim. A II 103.6.
10	4158	Rim incurved to thin, tapered edge, wheel-finished; orange; medium with few large and many small and fine white grits; traces of painted, reddish-brown trellis-pattern outside; some grey incrustations over-all. A II 102.11.
11	4157	Orange with dark-grey core; coarse with some assorted grits; traces of white slip outside; very pitted on bottom. A II 102.11.
12	4177	Thumb-indented ledge-handle; buff; coarse with few fine white grits; some grey incrustations. A II 102.11.
13	4219	Small ledge-handle with thumb-indented edge; dark-orange; very coarse with many assorted white and tan grits; traces of heavy, white slip outside; some assorted pits inside, grey smoke marks outside, some grey incrustations outside. A II 103.6.
14	4221	Loop-handle fragment, flattened oval section, joined to shoulder of vessel; pinkish-buff with dark grey core; coarse with some fine white grits; very uneven surface inside from joining of handle, some grey incrustations outside. A II 103.6.

Fig. 15 No.	Reg. No.	
—	4191a	Small loop-handle fragment, oval section, flat on inside; orange with grey core; medium with some small to fine, white and tan grits; traces of burnished, reddish-brown slip over-all. A II 102.11.
15	4159	Body sherd; orange ware; medium with some assorted white grits; heavy, white slip over-all with two wide, vertical, painted reddish-orange stripes outside; some grey incrustations. A II 102.11.
—	4178	Body sherd; tan; coarse with few assorted white and brown grits; closely spaced, parallel, burnished lines outside. A II 102.11.
—	4222	Body sherd of jar with pierced spout fragment; brown; fine with many fine white grits; rough, grainy texture outside, heavy, grey incrustations over-all. A II 103.6.

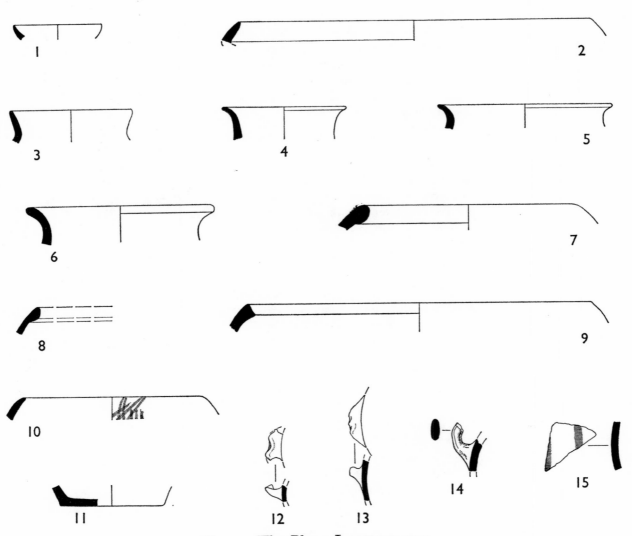

Fig. 15. The Phase I pottery. 1:4.

DESCRIPTIONS OF PHASE II POTTERY AND OBJECTS, FIGS. 16–24

Fig. 16 No.	Reg. No.	
1	4426	Rim gently upcurved to thin, rounded edge, wet-smoothed; tan with dark-grey core; coarse with some assorted white and grey grits; some assorted pits. A II 102.10.
2	4449	Rim gently upcurved to thin, rounded edge, wheel-finished; buff with tan core; medium with few fine white grits; traces of vertically-burnished, red slip outside; few assorted pits and crazing inside. A II 102.10.
3	4417	Rim upturned to straight, thin, tapered edge, very nicely wheel-finished; buff with orange-buff outside; fine ware with many fine white grits; uneven surface inside. A II 102.10.
4	4450	Rim upturned to thin, rounded edge, wheel-finished; tan with dark-grey core; medium-fine with few fine white grits; faint traces of orange slip inside; some assorted pits over-all, black smoke marks on edge indicate possible use as lamp. A II 102.10.
—	4440	Rim and body sherd of bowl, inclined out and up with thin inverted edge, wheel-finished; orange with greyish-buff core; very coarse with some assorted white quartz, grey, and tan grits; some assorted pits over-all, much flaking over-all, few dark-grey incrustations. A II 102.10.
5	4389	Rim slightly flared to thin, rounded edge, wheel-finished; orange inside with tan outside and core; medium with some assorted tan and reddish-brown grits; traces of horizontally-burnished, reddish-brown slip over-all; few small pits. A II 102.9.
6	4456	Angular side with rim slightly flared outward to rounded edge, wheel-finished; dark-grey; medium-fine with few assorted white grits; brown discoloration outside, some fine pits. A II 102.10.
7	5071n	Rim upcurved to thin, rounded edge, wheel-finished; pinkish-buff; medium with some fine white grits; traces of wheel-burnished, reddish-brown slip over-all; black smoke marks on edge indicate possible use as lamp. A II 102.9.
8	5071g	Rim upcurved to thin, rounded edge, wheel-finished; pinkish-brown, medium with many fine white grits; traces of reddish-brown slip over-all. A II 102.9.
9	5071f	Rim upcurved to blunt, rounded edge, wheel-finished; orange ware; medium-coarse with few assorted white grits; traces of white slip outside; grey incrustations over-all. A II 102.9.
10	4441	Rim upcurved to thin, rounded edge, edge wheel-finished; pinkish-tan; medium with few fine white grits. A II 102.10.
11	4421	Angular side with rim slightly flared; rounded edge with some thickening at transition, crudely wheel-finished; pinkish-orange with dark-grey core; coarse with some assorted tan and white grits; uneven surfaces over-all. A II 102.10.
12	4378	Rim slightly incurved to thin, rounded edge; orange with buff core; coarse with some assorted white and tan grits; traces of dark orangish-brown slip outside, possibly burnished; black smoke marks on rim indicate possible use as lamp. A II 102.9.
—	5071mm	Rim of bowl, incurved to thin, rounded edge, wet-smoothed; buff; medium-coarse with some assorted grey and few fine white grits; traces of wheel-burnished, reddish-brown slip outside. A II 102.9.
13	4445	Rim incurved to very thin, upturned edge, wheel-finished; buff; medium-coarse with very large to small grey grits; many assorted pits over-all, black smoke marks on edge indicate possible use as lamp. A II 102.10.
—	5071pp	Rim of bowl, slightly everted to thinned, rounded edge, wet-smoothed; orange with dark-buff core; medium with many fine, and few small, white grits; traces of wheel-burnished,

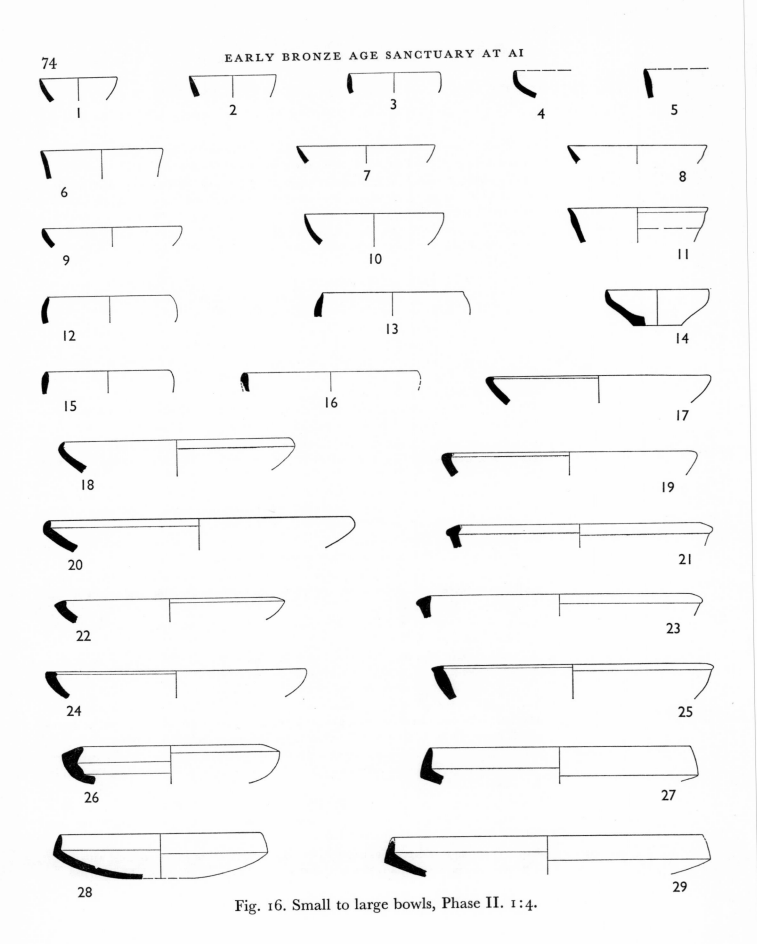

Fig. 16. Small to large bowls, Phase II. 1:4.

Fig. 16 *No.*	*Reg.* *No.*	
		reddish-brown slip outside; black smoke marks on edge indicate possible use as lamp, some grey incrustations over-all. A II 102.9.
14	4438	Angular bowl, with rim slightly upturned to thin, rounded edge, wheel-finished; buff with dark-grey core; very coarse with some assorted white quartz grits; many assorted pits over-all, black smoke marks on rim. A II 102.10.
15	4377	Rim slightly incurved to medium-wide, thickened, rounded edge, wheel-finished; orange-buff with buff core; medium-coarse with many assorted white and grey grits. A II 102.9.
16	5071v	Rim slightly incurved to thickened, rounded edge, wheel-finished; orange-buff; medium-coarse with many assorted, mostly small to fine, white grits; traces of burnished, reddish-brown slip over-all. A II 102.9.
17	4363	Upcurved, rounded, sharply inverted edge, wheel-finished; orange with thick, grey core; coarse with some assorted, mostly grey, grits; traces of white slip outside and on edge. A II 102.9.
18	4311	Upcurved to narrow, inverted, thinned edge, wheel-finished; pinkish-buff; medium-coarse with few small white grits; wheel-burnished, reddish-brown slip outside with dark red discoloration; orange discoloration inside, some grey incrustations over-all. A II 101.11.
19	4184	Incurved to rounded, flattened, inverted edge, very badly chipped; light-orange with dark-grey core; medium with many assorted white grits; traces of heavy, white slip outside and on edge; heavy, grey incrustations over-all. A II 103.4.
20	5060	Upturned to short, slightly inverted, rounded edge, rim wheel-finished; buff; medium-coarse with few assorted white and grey grits; traces of burnished, reddish-brown slip over-all; dark-grey smoke marks. A II 102.9.
21	5071z	Slightly incurved to medium-wide, triangular edge projected in, rounded ridge outside, edge wheel-finished; buff with dark-grey core penetrating to outside in places; coarse with some small to fine, white grits; some grey incrustations. A II 102.9.
22	4470	Upcurved to inverted, thickened flat edge, wheel-finished; buff; medium-coarse with few small to fine, white grits, some fine pits, light-grey smoke-mark outside. A II 102.10.
23	4490j	Slightly incurved to triangular edge projected in, rounded ridge outside, edge wheel-finished; buff with thick, dark-grey core; coarse with many assorted white and tan grits; grey incrustations over-all. A II 102.10.
24	4428	Upcurved to thickened, flat, inverted edge; inside and edge wheel-finished; brown with reddish-brown core; medium-coarse with many medium to small, white and tan grits, few large grey grits; traces of wheel-burnished, red slip outside and on edge. A II 102.10.
25	4374	Gently upturned to thickened, flat edge with slight flange outside, crudely wheel-finished; pinkish-orange; medium-coarse with few assorted white grits; traces of white slip outside; some grey incrustations. A II 102.9.
26	4392	Sharply incurved to medium-wide, thickened, angular edge inclined sharply inward; tan with pinkish-tan core; coarse with some assorted grits of mixed colors, mostly white; very rough texture, deeply pitted. A II 102.9.
27	4446	Rim thickened at angle with rounded edge, wheel-turned and finished; tan; medium with few small to fine, white and black grits; wheel-burnished, reddish-brown slip outside; many medium to small pits over-all. A II 102.10.
28	4466	Rim carinated with slight thickening at angle and thin, rounded edge, wheel-turned and finished; dark-orange with tan core; medium with many medium to small grits of mixed colors; orange-red slip, radially-burnished to carination and wheel-burnished

Fig. 16 No.	Reg. No.	
		outside and inside rim; one shallow hole drilled inside, some small pits inside and many assorted pits outside, flaking on rim. A II 102.10.
29	4488	Rim thickened at angle, chipped on edge, wheel-turned and finished; tan; medium with many small to fine, white and grey grits; wheel-burnished, reddish-brown slip outside. A II 102.10.

Fig. 17 No.	Reg. No.	
1	4459	Rim carinated with thin, rounded edge, wheel-turned and finished; medium-coarse with some small white grits; reddish-brown slip, wheel-burnished over-all; grey smoke marks along side of break in rim. A II 102.10.
2	4490k	Rim carinated with thin, rounded edge, wheel-finished; buff; medium-coarse with few assorted, and many fine, white grits; traces of burnished red slip; light, grey incrustations over-all. A II 102.10.
3	4165	Rim carinated with thin, rounded edge, wheel-turned and finished; brown with dark-grey core; coarse with some assorted white grits; wheel-burnished, orangish-brown slip over-all; many assorted pits. A II 103.4.
4	4385	Rim inverted to thin, rounded edge, wheel-finished; buff; medium with many assorted grits of mixed colors; traces of wheel-burnished, reddish-brown slip outside. A II 102.9.
5	5071t	Rim inverted to thin, rounded edge, wheel-finished; reddish-brown; medium with many assorted, mostly fine, tan grits, porous ware; faint traces of wheel-burnished, red slip outside; black smoke marks on edge. A II 102.9.
6	4691	Rim slightly outcurved to rounded edge, rim wheel-finished; buff; coarse with few assorted white grits, traces of straw temper; traces of white slip outside; few assorted pits, very uneven surface inside. A III 202.10.
7	4164	Rim of jar, outcurved to rounded edge, rim wheel-finished; pinkish-buff; medium-coarse with many small to fine, white grits; very heavy, white slip outside and inside edge. A II 103.4.
8	4692	Rim outcurved to thinned, rounded edge, wheel-finished; greyish-tan; fine with few medium to fine, white grits; few grey incrustations over-all. A III 202.10.
—	507100	Rim outcurved to rounded edge, wet-smoothed; brownish-buff; coarse with some assorted grey and tan grits. A II 102.9.
—	5071qq	Rim outcurved to rounded edge, wheel-finished; orangish-brown with buff core; coarse with some assorted white and grey quartz grits; traces of white slip outside. A II 102.9.
—	5071ii	Rim of jar, outcurved to rounded edge, hand-made; orange with greyish-buff core; medium-coarse with some medium to fine, white and grey, grits; faint traces of reddish-brown slip; grey incrustations over-all. A II 102.9.
9	4174	Rim sharply curved out to rounded edge, wheel-finished; buff; coarse with many small to fine, white grits; heavy, white slip outside with traces of white slip inside edge; grey incrustations over-all. A II 103.4.
10	5071x	Rim sharply curved out to rounded edge, wheel-finished; buff; coarse with some assorted white and tan grits; faint traces of white slip outside; grey incrustations over-all. A II 102.9.
—	5071ll	Rim, sharply curved out to rounded edge, wet-smoothed; dark-brown with dark-grey core; very coarse with some assorted white grits; grey incrustations over-all. A II 102.9.
—	5071kk	Neck fragment of jar, wet-smoothed; buff; very coarse with many assorted grey and tan grits; traces of continuously-burnished, reddish-brown slip outside; grey incrustations over-all. A II 102.9.

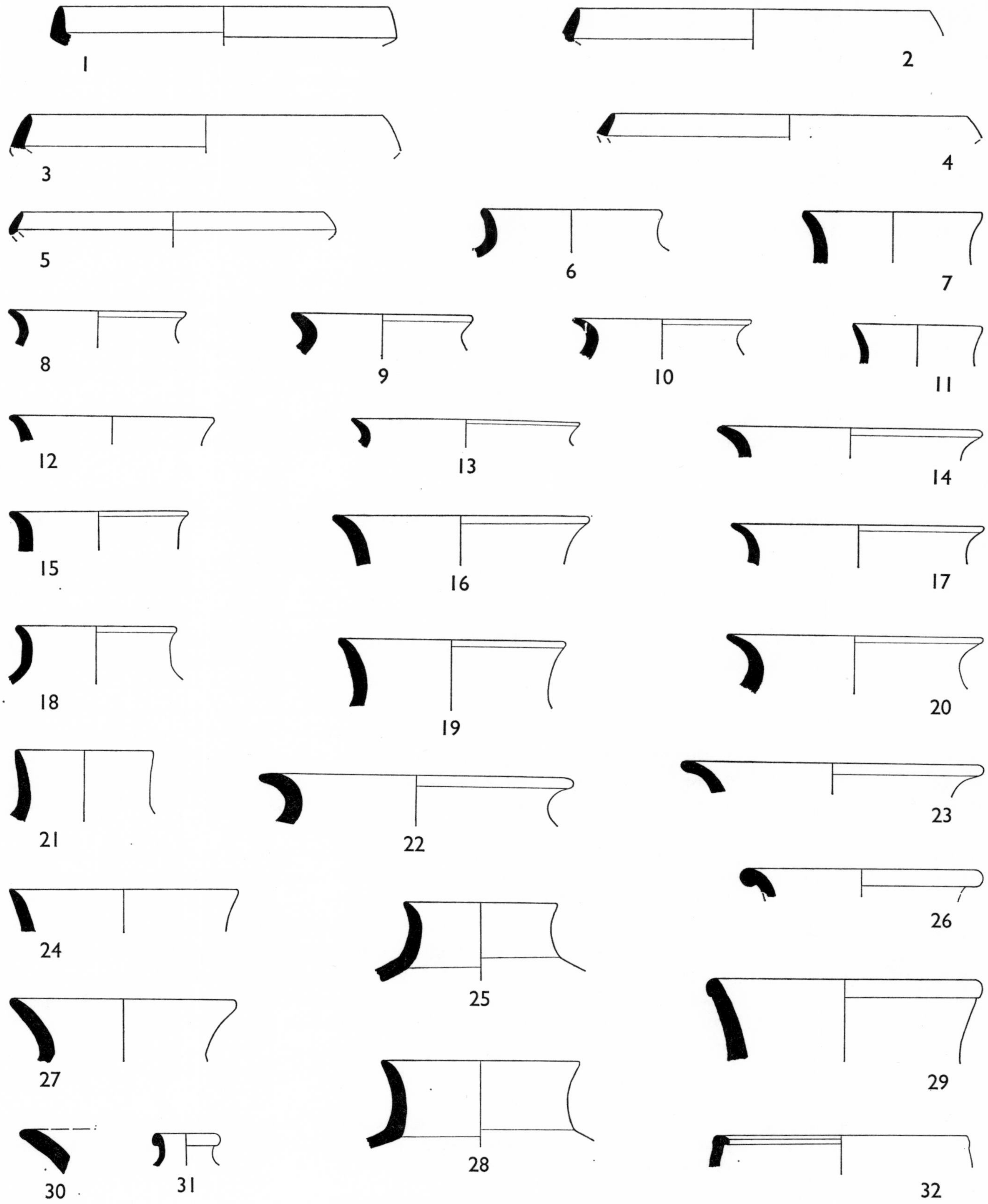

Fig. 17. Bowls and jars, Phase II. 1:4.

Fig. 17 *No.*	*Reg.* *No.*	
11	4382	Rim gently outcurved to thinned, rounded edge, wheel-finished; buff; medium-coarse with few assorted white grits; some pinkish discoloration inside; light, grey incrustations over-all. A II 102.9.
12	4187	Rim outcurved to thinned, rounded edge, wheel-finished; light-orange; many small to fine, white grits; some grey incrustations over-all. A II 103.4.
13	5071h	Rim sharply curved out to thinned, rounded edge, wheel-finished; buff; medium with some assorted white grits; dark-grey smoke marks inside. A II 102.9.
14	4183	Heavy rim, outcurved to rounded edge; buff; traces of white slip outside; very heavy, grey incrustations over-all. A II 103.4.
15	4479	Thick rim, outcurved to rounded edge, wheel-finished; greyish-tan with tan core; medium-coarse with some assorted white and grey grits; traces of white slip outside. A II 102.10.
16	4390	Heavy rim, outcurved to rounded edge, wheel-finished; tan with pinkish-tan outside; coarse with few fine white grits; traces of heavy, white slip outside; few assorted pits inside, heavy, grey incrustations over-all. A II 102.9.
17	4365	Rim sharply curved out to rounded edge, wheel-finished; pinkish-orange; coarse with many small to fine, white grits; traces of white slip outside; some grey incrustations over-all. A II 102.9.
18	4693–94 (joined)	Rim outcurved to rounded edge, wheel-finished; greyish-tan with thick, dark-grey core; very coarse with many assorted grits of mixed colors; some brown discoloration inside. A III 202.10.
19	4200	Heavy rim, gently outcurved to thinned, rounded edge, wheel-finished; pinkish-orange with tan core; very coarse with many assorted white and grey grits; traces of white slip outside; very rough texture inside, some grey incrustations inside. A II 103.4.
20	4372	Heavy rim, sharply curved out to thinned, rounded edge, wheel-finished; buff inside and pinkish-buff outside; very thick, dark-grey core; coarse with very few assorted dark-grey grits; traces of white slip outside; grey incrustations over-all. A II 102.9.
21	4437	Rim inclined out to rounded edge, wheel-finished; pinkish-tan; coarse with many large to medium, grey grits; traces of wheel-burnished, red slip outside; some light-grey incrustations. A II 102.10.
22	4373	Heavy rim, sharply curved out to thinned, rounded edge, wheel-finished; light-orange with very thick, dark-grey core; very coarse with many assorted, mostly tan, grits; roughly pitted over-all, black smoke marks inside. A II 102.9.
23	4380	Large rim, outcurved to rounded edge, wheel-finished; buff with grey core; medium-coarse with some small to fine, white grits and some large to medium, tan grits; traces of white slip over-all. A II 102.9.
24	4388	Rim inclined out to very thin, rounded edge, wheel-finished; buff; very coarse with many medium to small, white and grey grits; orange discoloration outside. A II 102.9.
25	4429	Rim outcurved to thinned, rounded edge, wheel-finished; buff with grey core; very coarse with some assorted white grits; traces of very heavy, white slip outside and inside rim; few assorted pits inside, some heavy, grey incrustations. A II 102.10.
26	5071s	Heavy rim outcurved to rolled edge, wheel-finished; buff with grey core; medium-coarse with some small to fine, white grits; traces of white slip outside and inside rim; some grey incrustations. A II 102.9.
27	4173	Heavy rim flared out to rounded edge, wheel-finished; tan with pinkish-tan outside; coarse with some assorted white grits; light-tan discoloration inside, many assorted pits. A II 103.4.

Fig. 17	*Reg.*	
No.	No.	
28	4386	Rim outcurved to thinned, rounded edge; buff inside with grey outside and core; very coarse with some assorted white and tan grits; heavy, white slip outside; many assorted pits inside, heavy, grey incrustations. A II 102.9.
29	4171	Heavy rim, inclined out to rolled edge, wheel-finished; orange with very thick, dark-grey core; very coarse with some small to fine, white grits; traces of white slip outside; grey incrustations. A II 103.4.
30	4168	Heavy rim, outcurved to rounded edge, wheel-finished; pinkish-tan; coarse with some small to fine, white grits; some assorted pits. A II 103.4.
31	4167	Straight rim with rolled edge, wheel-made; orangish-buff; fine with few small to fine, white grits; very faint traces of wheel-burnishing outside; some assorted pits. A II 103.4.
32	4695	Rim sharply inverted to drooping, flattened edge, pinkish-buff with greyish-buff core; coarse with some assorted grits of mixed colors; some assorted pits inside, grey smoke marks on rim, very uneven surfaces over-all. A III 202.10.

Fig. 18	*Reg.*	
No.	No.	
1	4490e	Rim incurved to narrow, thickened, rounded edge, wheel-finished; dark buff; very coarse with many assorted white quartz grits; some assorted pits over-all, black smoke marks outside. A II 102.10.
2	4490g	Rim incurved to medium-wide, thickened, rounded edge, wheel-finished; dark orange with greyish-brown core; coarse with very many assorted grey quartz grits; pitted and spalling outside, black smoke marks outside. A II 102.10.
3	4490d	Rim incurved to medium-wide, thickened, rounded edge; buff with grey core penetrating to outside in places; coarse with many assorted white and light grey quartz grits; very uneven surface inside. A II 102.10.
4	4468	Rim incurved to medium-wide, thickened, rounded edge with faint ridge outside, edge wheel-finished; pinkish-tan with brown outside; coarse with many assorted, mostly large, white and grey quartz grits; black smoke marks outside. A II 102.10.
5	4487	Rim incurved to wide, thickened, rounded edge, wheel-finished; brown with dark-grey core; coarse with many assorted grey quartz grits; some assorted pits, black smoke marks outside. A II 102.10.
6	4407	Rim of large jar, incurved to very wide, thickened, rounded edge; orange inside and orangish-tan outside, buff core; very coarse with many large to small, grey grits; rough and uneven surface over-all, many assorted pits. A II 102.9.
7	4465	Rim incurved to narrow, very thickened, rounded edge, wheel-finished; pinkish-orange with buff core; coarse with many small to fine, white grits; traces of white slip outside; some heavy, grey incrustations. A II 102.10.
8	4438a	Rim incurved to thickened, rounded edge, wheel-finished. A II 102.10.
9	5071i	Rim incurved to wide, thickened, rounded edge, wheel-finished; dark-orange with buff outside; coarse with many assorted dark-grey quartz grits; rough, gritty texture inside, grey incrustations over-all. A II 102.9.
10	4690	Rim incurved to wide, thickened, rounded edge, wheel-finished; buff; medium-coarse with many assorted grey and white quartz grits; orange discoloration outside. A III 202.10.
11	4490b	Rim incurved to wide, thickened, rounded edge, wheel-finished; dark-brown with dark-grey core; coarse with many assorted, mostly medium to fine, tan and grey grits; very uneven surface outside, grey incrustations over-all. A II 102.10.
12	5071r	Rim incurved to thickened, rounded edge; dark-orange inside and orangish-buff outside; coarse with very many small to fine, white grits; traces of white slip outside; many assorted pits over-all, some grey incrustations. A II 102.9.

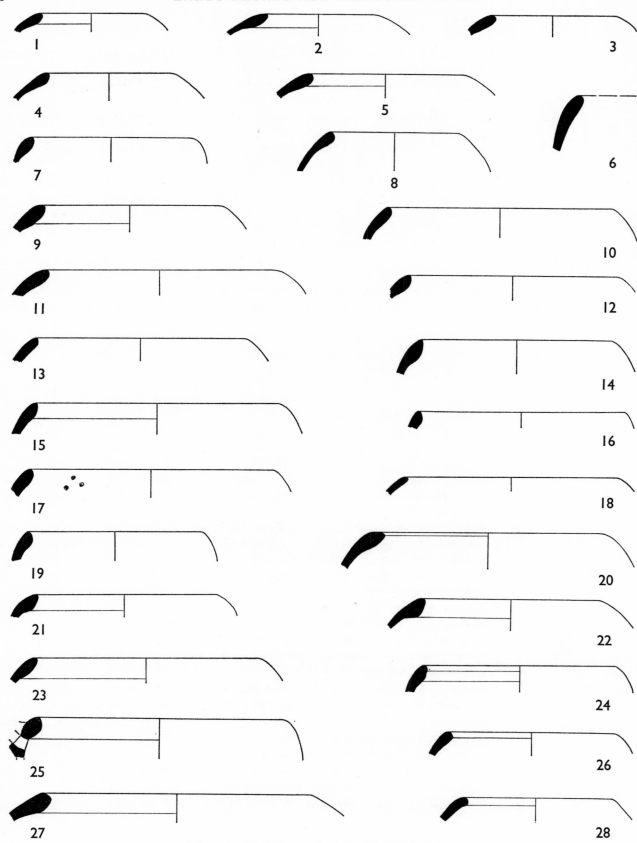

Fig. 18. Hole-mouth jars, Phase II. 1:4.

Fig. 18 No.	Reg. No.	
13	4396	Rim incurved to wide, thickened, rounded edge with faint ridge outside, wheel-finished; buff with tan core; coarse with few assorted white and grey quartz grits; some grey incrustations. A II 102.9.
14	4383	Rim incurved to medium-wide, thickened, angular edge; pinkish-buff with dark-grey core; coarse with some assorted white grits; traces of white slip outside; uneven surface over-all. A II 102.9.
15	5047	Rim incurved to wide, thickened, rounded edge with slight ridge outside, wheel-finished; greyish-tan with greyish-buff inside; coarse with some small to fine, white grits; many fine pits inside. A II 102.9.
16	5071k	Rim incurved to thickened, rounded edge, wheel-finished; buff with grey core; coarse with some assorted white grits; few assorted pits. A II 102.9.
17	5071aa	Rim incurved to thickened, rounded edge; dark orangish-buff with grey core; coarse with very many assorted white quartz grits; three holes drilled inside, two deep and one shallow; some grey incrustations outside. A II 102.9.
18	4387	Rim incurved to slightly thickened, rounded edge, wheel-finished; buff; coarse with some assorted white grits; orange discoloration outside, uneven surface over-all. A II 102.9.
19	4369	Rim incurved to narrow, very thickened, rounded edge, wheel-finished; orange with tan core; very coarse with many assorted, mostly white, grits; white slip outside; many assorted pits, some grey incrustations. A II 102.9.
20	5067	Rim incurved to wide, very thickened, rounded flat edge, wheel-finished; orange inside and tan outside, greyish-brown core; coarse with very many assorted white and grey quartz grits; pronounced crazing and spalling on edge outside. A II 102.9.
21	4469	Rim incurved to medium-wide, thickened, rounded edge, wheel-finished; orangish-brown with dark-grey core penetrating to outside in places; coarse with some assorted white grits; traces of white slip outside; many assorted pits inside and few outside. A II 102.10.
22	4391	Rim incurved to medium-wide, very thickened, rounded edge, wheel-finished; dark orangish-brown with dark-orange on edge to outside; very coarse with many assorted light- and dark-grey grits; many fine pits inside and on edge. A II 102.9.
23	50710	Rim incurved to wide, thickened, elliptical edge with faint ridge outside, wheel-finished; orangish-buff with thick, grey core; coarse with some assorted white and tan grits; some assorted pits inside, very uneven surface over-all. A II 102.9.
24	4362	Rim incurved to wide, thickened, rounded edge, wheel-finished; orange with tan outside and inside edge; very coarse with some large grits of mixed colors, mostly tan; heavy, white slip outside; some assorted pits. A II 102.9.
25	4170	Rim with spout (fragment), incurved to wide, very thickened rolled edge, wheel-finished; orangish-buff with dark-orange patches outside; coarse with many assorted white and grey grits; some assorted pits, some grey incrustations over-all. A II 103.4.
26	4453	Rim incurved to narrow, thickened, squared edge with slight groove, nicely wheel-finished; orangish-brown with buff core; coarse with many assorted grey quartz grits; many assorted pits over-all. A II 102.10.
27	4175	Rim of large jar, incurved to very wide, thickened edge, nicely wheel-finished; brown with thick, dark brownish-grey core penetrating to outside in places; coarse with many assorted grits of mixed colors; tan discoloration outside edge. A II 103.4.
28	4480	Rim incurved to drooping squared edge, wheel-finished; buff inside and orangish-brown outside; very coarse with many assorted white quartz grits concentrated inside and many dark-grey quartz grits concentrated outside; grey smoke marks outside. A II 102.10.

Fig. 18	*Reg.*	
No.	*No.*	
—	5071bb	Rim of hole-mouth jar, incurved to slightly thickened, rounded edge, wet-smoothed; pinkish-buff; medium-coarse with some assorted dark brown grits; crude, very high-relief molding outside perpendicular to rim; traces of white slip outside; pitted and flaking inside. A II 102.9.

Fig. 19	*Reg.*	
No.	*No.*	
1	4490i	Rim incurved to wide, thickened, rounded edge; dull orange; very coarse with many assorted white and tan grits; narrow, crude, high-relief molding outside. A II 102.10.
2	4489	Rim incurved to wide, greatly thickened, rounded edge, wheel-finished; orange inside and greyish-tan outside, dark-grey core; coarse with very many assorted grey quartz grits; some grey incrustations. A II 102.10.
3	4490	Rim incurved to medium-wide, greatly thickened, triangular edge; buff with dark-grey core; very coarse with many assorted white and grey grits. A II 102.10.
4	4474	Rim incurved to narrow, thickened, slightly squared edge, wheel-finished; tan with dark-grey core penetrating to outside in places; coarse with many assorted white and grey quartz grits. A II 102.10.
5	4490e	Rim incurved to slightly thickened, rounded, beveled edge, wheel-finished; dark-orange with greyish-buff core; coarse with many assorted grey quartz grits; rough, gritty texture inside. A II 102.10.
6	4482	Rim incurved to wide, greatly thickened, rounded edge with faint trace of ridge outside, wheel-finished; orangish-brown with dark-grey core; very coarse with many assorted white and grey grits; grey smoke marks over-all. A II 102.10.
7	5048	Rim incurved to wide, greatly thickened, rounded edge with slight ridge outside, wheel-finished; buff with orange inside; very coarse with many assorted white and grey grits, traces of straw temper; grey smoke marks over-all, few large pits and crazing. A II 102.9.
8	4427	Rim incurved to wide, thickened edge with pronounced ridge outside, wheel-finished; orange with dark-grey and buff core; coarse with many assorted, mostly very large to large, grey quartz grits, traces of straw temper; some assorted pits inside, some crazing outside. A II 102.10.
9	4162	Rim incurved to wide, thickened, rounded edge with pronounced ridge outside, wheel-finished; orange inside and tan outside; coarse with many assorted grey grits; smoke marks inside and on edge, some pronounced crazing on edge; some heavy, grey incrustations. A II 103.5.
10	4457	Rim incurved to medium-wide, thickened, rounded edge with low ridge outside, crudely wheel-finished; tan with dark-grey core; very coarse with many assorted white and grey grits; traces of heavy, white slip outside and over edge. A II 102.10.
11	4490c	Rim incurved to wide, greatly thickened, rounded beveled edge with faint ridge outside, wheel-finished; dark-orange with grey core; very coarse with many grey quartz grits; rough, gritty texture over-all, black smoke marks outside, some grey incrustations inside. A II 102.10.
12	4169	Rim incurved to wide, thickened, rounded edge with low ridge outside, wheel-finished; orange with buff outside; coarse with many assorted grey and dark-grey grits; many assorted pits over-all. A II 103.4.
13	4424	Rim incurved to wide, greatly thickened, rounded edge with low ridge outside, wheel-finished; orangish-buff inside and orangish-brown outside, grey core; coarse with many assorted white and grey grits concentrated inside and many assorted dark-grey quartz grits concentrated outside; many assorted pits with two large and deep pits inside. A II 102.10.

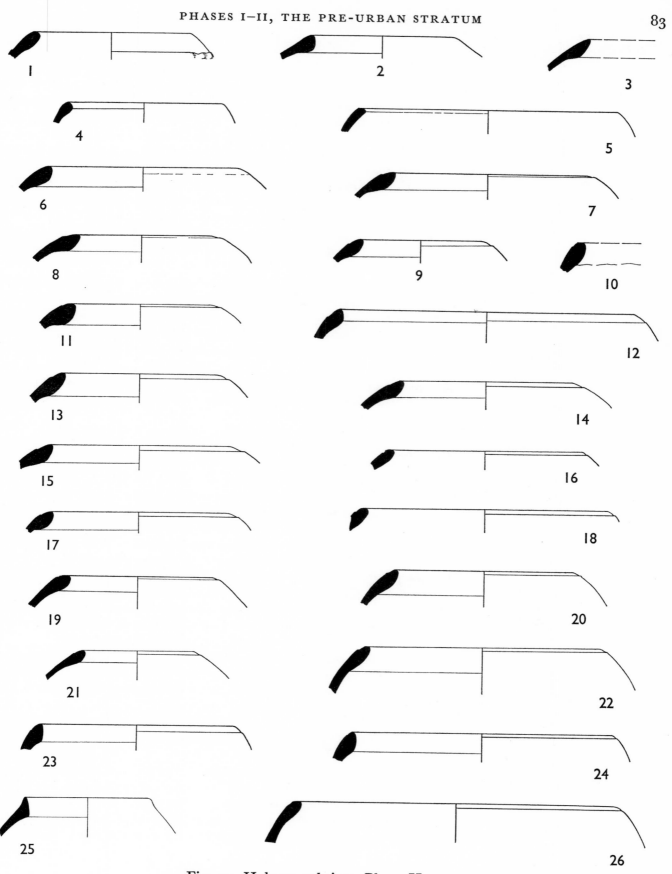

Fig. 19. Hole-mouth jars, Phase II. 1:4.

Fig. 19 *No.*	*Reg.* *No.*	
14	4410	Rim incurved to wide, thickened, rounded edge with slight ridge outside, wheel-finished; orange with dark-brown core; very coarse with many assorted, mostly very large to large, white and grey grits; dark-grey smoke marks inside, many fine pits over-all, pronounced crazing outside. A II 102.10.
15	5061	Rim of large jar, incurved to greatly thickened, rounded edge with ridge outside, wheel-finished; orangish-buff with deep-orange inside; coarse with very many assorted, mostly large, grey grits, traces of straw temper. A II 102.9.
16	4490f	Rim incurved to slightly thickened, rounded edge with ridge outside; orangish-buff with deep-buff core; medium-coarse with many assorted, mostly fine, white grits; traces of white slip outside; grey incrustations over-all. A II 102.10.
17	4490h	Rim incurved to medium-wide, thickened, rounded, beveled edge with faint ridge outside; orangish-brown with thick, grey core; very coarse with many assorted grey quartz grits; spalling outside. A II 102.10.
18	5071q	Rim incurved to thickened, rounded edge with pronounced ridge outside, wheel-finished; buff with thick, dark-grey core; very coarse with many assorted white grits; some assorted pits inside. A II 102.9.
19	4430	Rim incurved to medium-wide, thickened, rounded edge with low ridge outside, wheel-finished; brown; very coarse with many assorted grey grits; black smoke marks outside. A II 102.10.
20	4366	Rim incurved to wide, thickened, rounded edge with ridge outside, wheel-finished; brown; coarse with many assorted, mostly large, grey and white grits; some pits and dark-grey smoke marks over-all. A II 102.9.
21	4368	Rim incurved to medium-wide, thickened, rounded edge with ridge outside, wheel-finished; pinkish-buff with tan core; very coarse with many assorted white and grey grits; very large, deep, spalled spot outside associated with very large, white lime inclusion, some heavy, grey incrustations. A II 102.9.
22	4376	Rim incurved to wide, thickened, rounded edge with low, rounded ridge outside, wheel-finished; buff inside and tan outside, dark-grey core; very coarse with many assorted white and tan grits; traces of white slip outside; many assorted pits inside. A II 102.9.
23	4435	Rim incurved to wide, thickened, beveled edge with slight ridge outside, wheel-finished; brown with tan core; coarse with many assorted, mostly large, grey grits; spalling inside rim. A II 102.10.
24	5071m	Rim incurved to thickened, rounded, slightly beveled edge with ridge outside, wheel-finished; bright-orange with buff core; coarse with some assorted white grits; traces of heavy, white slip outside; black smoke marks inside edge, grey incrustations over-all. A II 102.9.
25	4201	Rim incurved to wide, greatly thickened, rounded, triangular edge, wheel-finished; buff inside and tan outside, thick, dark-grey core; medium with some assorted white and tan grits; traces of straw temper; some assorted pits over-all, spalling inside. A II 103.4.
26	6144	Rim incurved to thickened, rounded edge with slight ridge outside, wheel-finished. A II 102.9.
Fig. 20 *No.*	*Reg.* *No.*	
1	4452	Rim incurved to medium-wide, thickened, rounded edge with low ridge outside, wheel-finished; greyish-brown with dark-grey core; coarse with many assorted, mostly large, grey quartz grits; many assorted pits over-all. A II 102.10.
2	4199	Rim incurved to wide, thickened, rounded edge with low ridge outside, wheel-finished; buff inside and orange outside, thick, dark-grey core; coarse with many assorted white

Fig. 20 No.	*Reg. No.*	
		and grey grits; traces of white slip outside; many assorted pits inside with a few very large and deep, some grey incrustations outside. A II 103.4.
3	5071j	Rim of large jar, incurved to rounded, beveled edge, wheel-finished; dark-orange inside and buff outside; coarse with some assorted white and tan grits; fragment of medium-wide, ridged molding outside below rim, traces of white slip outside and inside edge; heavy, grey incrustations over-all. A II 102.9.
4	4490a	Rim of large jar, incurved to wide, greatly thickened, rounded edge with narrow, pronounced groove outside, wheel-finished; buff; coarse with many assorted white grits; traces of burnished, reddish-brown slip outside and inside edge; very heavy, grey incrustations over-all. A II 102.10.
5	4163	Rim incurved to wide, thickened, rounded edge with raised collar outside; brownish-tan; medium-coarse with many assorted grey quartz grits; grey smoke marks on edge, many assorted pits inside. A II 103.4.
6	4368a	Rim slightly incurved to wide, thickened, rounded edge, wheel-finished. A II 102.9.
7	4436	Rim incurved to elongated, thickened, rounded edge; orangish-buff with dark-grey core; very coarse with some medium to fine, white and grey grits; traces of heavy, white slip outside; many pits and flaking inside. A II 102.10.
8	4312	Rim of large jar, incurved to very wide, thickened, rounded edge with ridge outside, wheel-finished; orange with dark-grey core; medium-coarse with many large grey quartz grits; many assorted pits over-all. A II 101.11.
9	4404	Rim slightly incurved to thickened, rounded edge, wheel-finished; pinkish-tan with tan core; very coarse with few large and some fine, white grits; rough, uneven surface outside, few large and many fine pits. A II 102.9.
10	5071e	Rim incurved to rounded edge with pronounced depression and ridge outside, wheel-finished; greyish-brown; coarse with many assorted white and grey quartz grits; black smoke marks on edge. A II 102.9.
11	4197	Rim upturned to medium-wide, thickened, rolled edge, wheel-finished; dark-orange with thick, buff core; medium-coarse with some assorted white and grey grits; very rough inside at juncture of rim and body. A II 103.4.
12	4356	Rim slightly incurved to thickened, rounded edge; tan inside with dark-grey outside and core; very coarse with some assorted grey grits; traces of heavy, white slip outside; few assorted pits over-all, rough gritty texture inside. A II 102.9.
13	4384	Rim slightly incurved to wide, thickened, rounded edge with low, squared ridge outside; reddish-orange with brown core; medium-coarse with some assorted white grits; heavy, white slip outside with traces on and inside rim; some grey incrustations over-all. A II 102.9.
14	4475	Rim upturned to wide, very thickened, rounded edge; orangish-buff with very thick, greyish-brown core; very coarse with some assorted white grits; some grey incrustations over-all. A II 102.10.
15	4408	Rim slightly incurved to thickened, flattened edge inclined up and projected in, wheel-finished; pinkish-orange inside with pinkish-tan outside and core, dark-grey in parts; coarse with few small to fine, tan and white grits; very uneven surface inside, some small and fine pits. A II 102.9.
16	4432	Rim slightly incurved to greatly thickened, triangular, flat edge, very nicely wheel-finished; brown; medium-coarse with many, mostly fine, white grits; many assorted pits. A II 102.10.

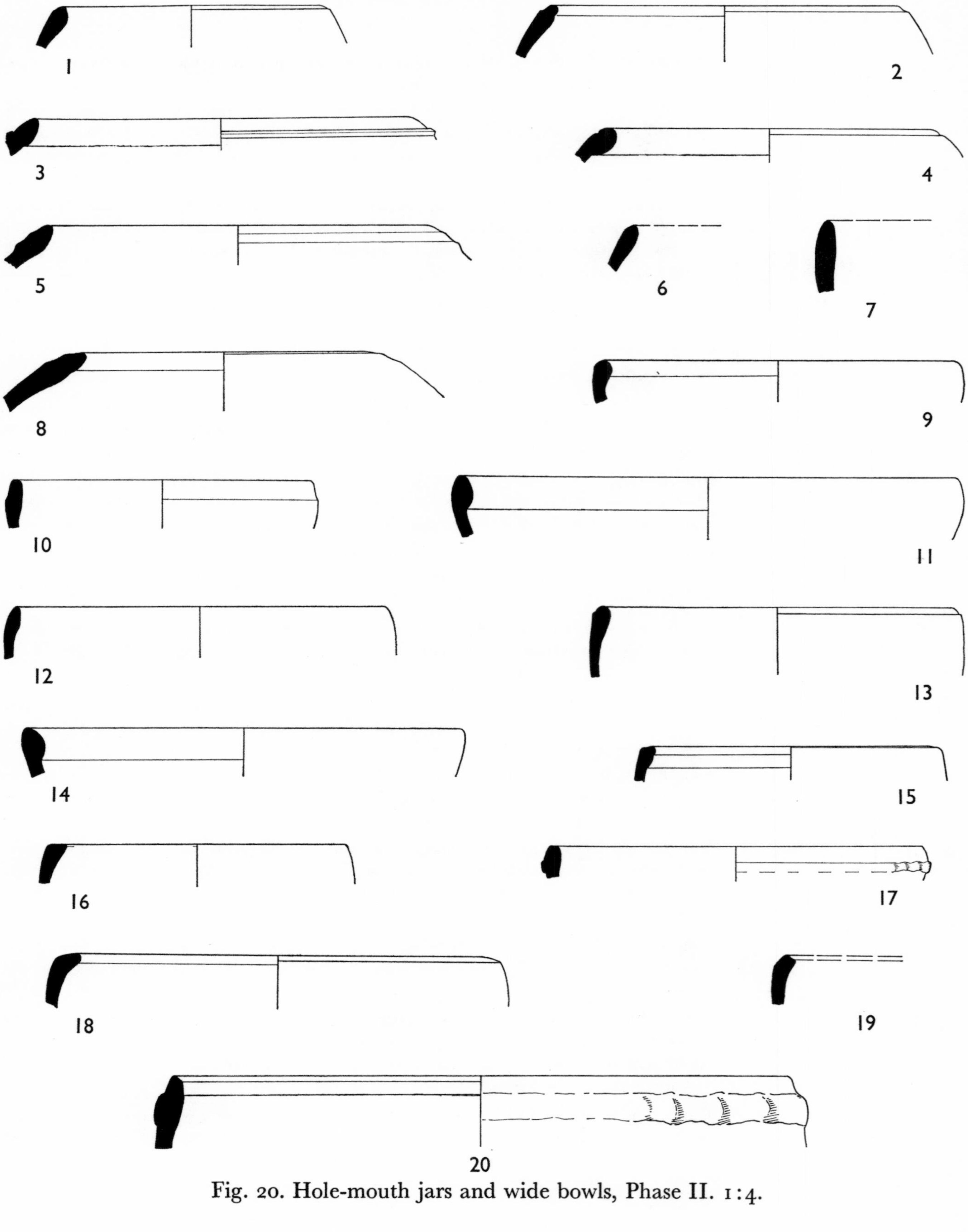

Fig. 20. Hole-mouth jars and wide bowls, Phase II. 1:4.

Fig. 20 No.	*Reg. No.*	
17	5071p	Rim slightly incurved to thick, rounded edge; brown with dark-grey core; very coarse with many assorted white grits; narrow, crude, high-relief rope-molding outside below rim. A II 102.9.
18	4375	Rim slightly incurved to thickened flat top with angular, inverted edge, very nicely wheel-finished; tan with dark-grey inside and core; coarse with some assorted grits of mixed color, traces of straw temper; some grey smoke marks outside. A II 102.9.
19	4461	Rim incurved to wide, thickened, slightly inverted, squared edge, wheel-finished; brown with greyish-brown core; medium-coarse with many assorted grey quartz grits, porous ware; some dark-grey discolorations, many fine pits. A II 102.10.
20	4444	Rim of very large, wide-mouth jar slightly incurved to thickened, rounded flat edge with low ridge inside rim, wheel-finished; buff inside and tan outside, very thick, dark-grey core; coarse with few assorted white grits, traces of straw temper; wide, crude, wavy, high-relief rope-molding outside; many assorted pits over-all with one very large and deep. A II 102.10.

Fig. 21 No.	*Reg. No.*	
1	4393	Orangish-buff with dark-grey core; coarse with many very large to medium, grey quartz grits; many assorted pits over-all, grey smoke marks on bottom. A II 102.9.
2	4472	Dark-orange inside and pinkish-buff outside, pinkish-brown core; medium-coarse with many assorted white grits; traces of straw temper; traces of white slip outside; some small and fine pits inside and a few medium pits outside, some grey incrustations over-all. A II 102.10.
3	4186	Tan with thick, grey core, penetrating to outside in places; very coarse with many assorted grits of mixed colors, mostly white and tan; traces of heavy, white slip outside. A II 103.4.
4	4401	Orange with tan inside; very coarse with some assorted white and grey grits, traces of straw temper; buff discoloration outside, some small and fine pits outside, deep pits on bottom. A II 102.9.
5	4394	Tan outside with dark-grey inside and core penetrating to outside in places; very coarse with some small white and large grey grits, traces of straw temper; rough pits on bottom, crazing outside. A II 102.9.
6	4451	Buff inside and tan outside with very thick, dark-grey core; coarse with few assorted white grits, traces of straw temper; many assorted pits over-all, very rough texture on bottom and outside near bottom, black smoke marks inside. A II 102.10.
7	4460	Buff outside with greyish-brown inside and core; very coarse with some small to fine white grits, traces of straw temper; narrow, well-defined, high-relief rope-molding outside; very uneven surfaces over-all, some large rough pits. A II 102.10.
8	4422	Dark-buff with brown core; coarse with some assorted white quartz grits, traces of straw temper; traces of white slip outside, dark-grey smoke marks inside. A II 102.10.
9	4448	Orange with buff core; coarse with some assorted white grits; very heavy, white slip outside; few assorted pits, dark-grey smoke marks inside, very rough texture outside. A II 102.10.
10	4484	Dark-grey with tan outside; coarse with few small to fine, white grits; many assorted pits inside and a few assorted pits and grey incrustations outside. A II 102.10.
11	5071u	Greyish-brown; very coarse with many assorted grey grits, traces of straw temper; rough, uneven texture over-all, black smoke marks inside. A II 102.9.
12	4442	Tan with greyish-brown inside; very coarse with many assorted grey grits; very uneven surfaces, many assorted pits and some flaking inside. A II 102.10.

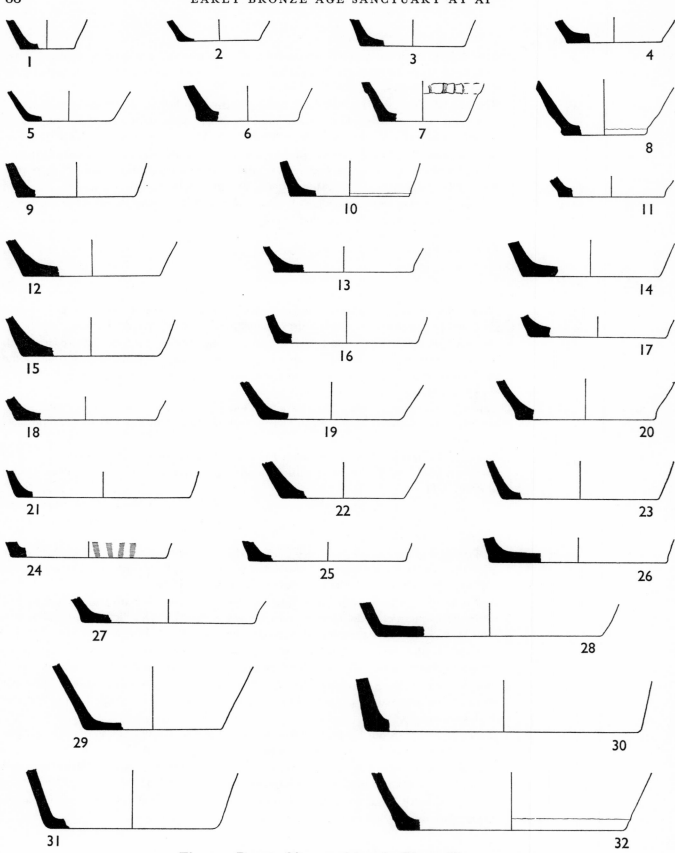

Fig. 21. Bases of jars and bowls, Phase II. 1:4.

Fig. 21 *No.*	*Reg.* *No.*	
13	4434	Buff outside and orange inside, dark-grey core penetrating to outside in places; very coarse with many assorted grey and white grits; dark-orange discoloration outside, many assorted pits inside and a few pits outside. A II 102.10.
14	4357	Tan with thick, dark-grey core; very coarse with many assorted grits of mixed colors, mostly tan, traces of straw temper; friable, very pitted with much spalling inside and on bottom. A II 102.9.
15	4310	Orange with thick, buff core penetrating to outside in places; very coarse with some assorted white and grey grits; some irregular indentations on bottom. A II 101.11.
16	44900	Orange with dark-grey core; very coarse with some assorted white grits; one very large, deep pit outside on bottom, heavy black coating over-all inside, some grey incrustations outside. A II 102.10.
17	5071b	Greyish-buff; coarse with many assorted grey grits, traces of straw temper; rough pitted texture over-all, black smoke marks on bottom and inside on broken edge. A II 102.9.
18	5071y	Brown with dark reddish-orange inside; coarse with very many assorted white and grey grits; pitted on bottom, grey incrustations over-all. A II 102.9.
19	4400	Tan inside and buff outside, dark-grey core; very coarse with some assorted white grits; dark-orange discoloration outside, some very large, and many fine, pits over-all, black smoke marks inside. A II 102.9.
20	4490n	Orange; very coarse with some assorted, mostly fine, white grits; traces of white slip outside; grey incrustations over-all. A II 102.10.
21	4402	Orangish-buff with thick, dark-grey core; coarse with some assorted white grits; some small pits over-all, uneven surface inside. A II 102.9.
22	4364	Orange with grey core; coarse with many assorted grits of mixed colors; pitted over-all with some very deep pits inside; tan and buff discolorations outside, black smoke marks inside. A II 102.9.
23	4464	Buff outside and pinkish-orange inside, grey core; coarse with few assorted white grits; some assorted pits, mostly medium to fine, over-all, bright orange discolorations outside. A II 102.10.
24	4166	Orange with grey core; very coarse with some assorted white grits; traces of white slip outside with four medium-wide, vertical, painted red stripes; black smoke marks, flaking inside, grey incrustations outside. A II 103.4.
25	4467	Orange with thick, dark-grey core; coarse with some assorted white grits; traces of white slip outside and on bottom; some grey incrustations over-all. A II 102.10.
26	4418	Buff with dark-grey core penetrating to outside in places; very coarse with many assorted white and grey grits, roughly pitted and flaking inside, uneven surface outside. A II 102.10.
27	4414	Pinkish-buff with tan core; very coarse with few small to fine, white grits; traces of white slip outside; pronounced spalling and crazing over-all, some grey incrustations. A II 102.10.
28	4486	Orange with thick, dark-grey core; medium-coarse with many small to fine, white grits; very heavy, white slip outside; many assorted pits and grey smoke marks inside, heavy, grey incrustations on bottom. A II 102.10.
29	4415	Buff with thick, dark-grey core; coarse with many assorted grey grits and some assorted white grits concentrated on outside; some small and fine pits inside, many assorted pits uniformly distributed outside, some brown and olive discolorations inside, some grey incrustations over-all. A II 102.10.

Fig. 21 No.	Reg. No.	
30	4476	Buff outside and greyish-buff inside, grey core; very coarse with some small and fine, white grits; traces of white slip outside; few grey incrustations over-all. A II 102.10.
31	4458	Buff inside and tan outside, grey core; very coarse with many small to fine, white grits, some very large white grits outside; traces of dark-grey slip outside; some dark-orange discolorations inside, many assorted pits over-all, some spalling outside. A II 102.10.
32	4490q	Light-buff with very thick, dark-grey core; very coarse with some assorted white grits; pitted and spalling on bottom, uneven surfaces and grey incrustations over-all. A II 102.10.

Fig. 22 No.	Reg. No.	
1	4172	Orangish-buff; coarse with many medium to small, white grits; white slip outside; many assorted pits inside; some grey incrustations over-all. A II 103.4.
2	4490p	Dark-grey with dark-orange inside; very coarse with many assorted grey grits; uneven surfaces, grey incrustations over-all. A II 102.10.
3	5071e	Buff inside and dark-reddish-orange outside, dark-grey core; medium-coarse with few medium to fine, white grits; rough pitted texture on bottom, heavy, grey incrustations over-all. A II 102.9.
4	4696	Buff with dark-grey core; coarse with few small to fine, white grits; traces of white slip outside; some assorted pits inside, roughly pitted on bottom. A III 202.10.
5	5071c	Orangish-buff inside and brown outside; very coarse with some assorted white grits; faint traces of white slip outside. A II 102.9.
6	4397	Buff with dark greyish-buff inside and core; coarse with very many assorted, mostly large, grey and white grits; orange discoloration inside, pitted and uneven surfaces over-all. A II 102.9.
7	4490m	Dark-grey with dark-orange outside; very coarse with some assorted white and grey grits, many fine white grits concentrated outside; traces of white slip outside; rough pitted and spalling inside, some grey incrustations outside. A II 102.10.
8	4477	Pinkish-buff outside and mauve inside, very thick, dark-grey core; medium-coarse with many assorted, mostly small to fine, white and tan grits; traces of white slip outside; some assorted pits inside, rough, deep pits on bottom. A II 102.10.
9	4425	Orangish-buff with dark-grey core; very coarse with few small to fine, white grits, traces of straw temper; traces of white slip outside; pitted and spalling over-all. A II 102.10.
10	4443	Tan outside and orange inside with greyish-brown core; very coarse with many assorted grey quartz grits; many assorted pits, uneven surfaces over-all. A II 102.10.
11	4198	Pinkish-buff with grey core, dark-grey core at bottom; very coarse with many small to fine, white grits; traces of heavy, white slip outside; some assorted pits inside and on bottom. A II 103.4.
12	4478	Pinkish-buff outside and pinkish-tan inside, very thick, dark-grey core; very coarse with few small to fine, white grits, some assorted white grits concentrated on bottom; pitted on bottom, uneven surface inside, some grey incrustations outside. A II 102.10.
13	4447	Tan outside with dark-grey inside, dark-grey core penetrating to outside in places; very coarse with many assorted, mostly large, grey quartz grits; very many assorted pits over-all, uneven surface outside. A II 102.10.
14	5071a	Buff with thick, grey core; very coarse with some assorted white and grey grits; traces of heavy, white slip outside and on bottom; uneven surfaces outside, heavy, grey incrustations over-all. A II 102.9.
15	5071d	Orangish-buff; very coarse with many assorted white and grey grits; traces of burnished reddish-brown slip outside; black smoke marks over-all. A II 102.9.

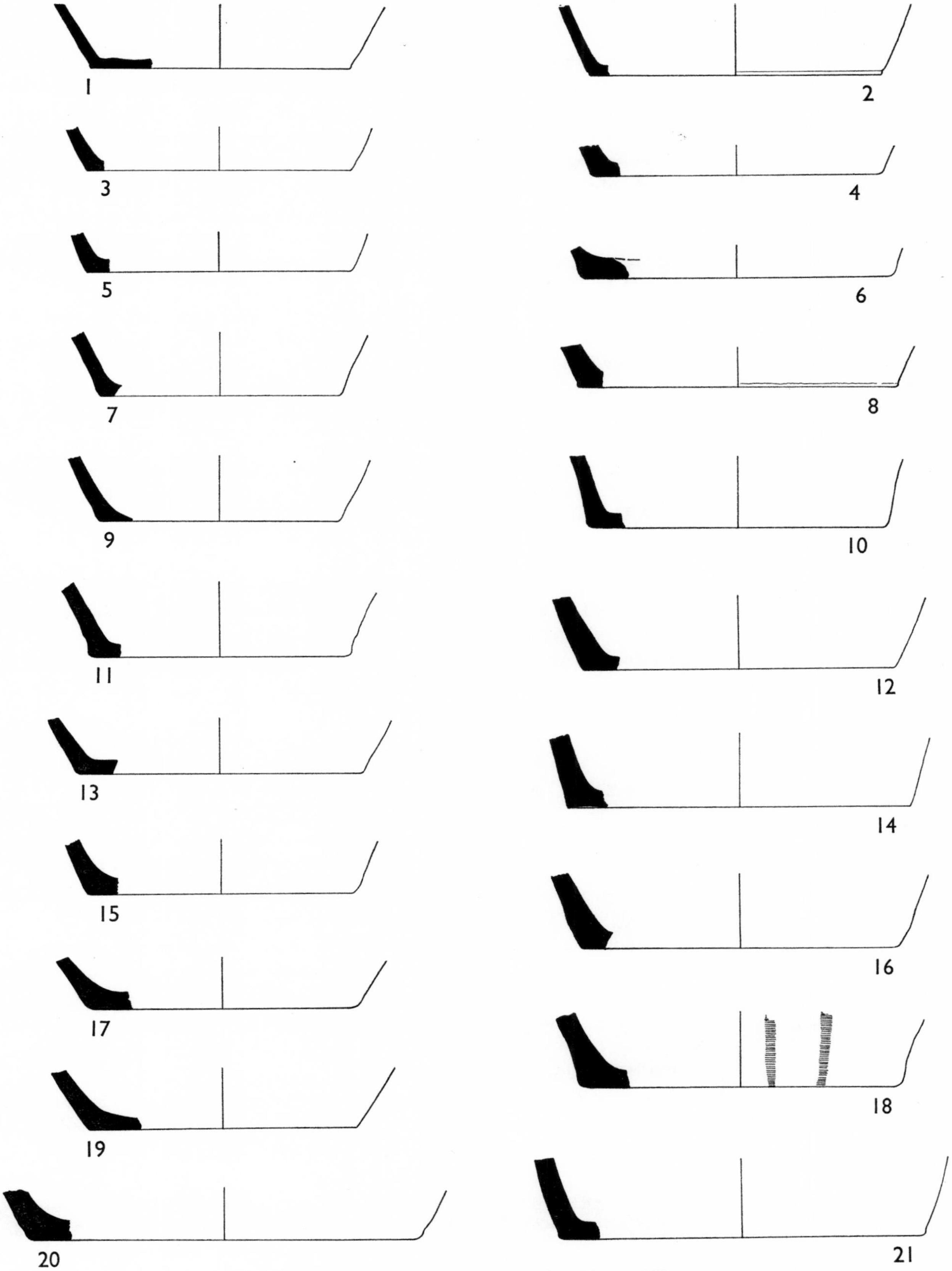

Fig. 22. Bases of jars and bowls, Phase II. 1:4.

Fig. 22 *No.*	*Reg.* *No.*	
16	4483	Pinkish-buff with tan core; very coarse with some assorted white and tan grits; traces of white slip outside; many assorted pits and flaking inside, some assorted pits outside, grey incrustations over-all, grey smoke marks inside, very uneven surfaces. A II 102.10.
17	4395	Buff with greyish-brown inside; very coarse with many assorted grits of mixed colors, mostly orange and white, traces of straw temper; traces of white slip outside; few large, deep pits outside. A II 102.9.
18	4431	Pinkish-buff with buff core; very coarse with some assorted white grits; traces of heavy, white slip outside, faint traces of two medium-wide, vertical, painted red stripes; very uneven surfaces, many assorted pits inside and on bottom, heavy, grey incrustations over-all. A II 102.10.
19	4406	Orangish-brown with brown outside; very coarse with many large to medium, grey quartz grits, traces of straw temper; many assorted pits over-all, dark grey smoke marks inside and on bottom. A II 102.9.
20	4409	Pinkish-buff with pinkish-tan inside; coarse with few very large white and dark-red grits; traces of heavy, white slip over-all with heavy, white deposit inside; deeply pitted on bottom. A II 102.9.
21	4473	Very thick; greyish-brown core with orange outside; coarse with some assorted white and grey quartz grits; traces of white slip outside; very uneven surface black smoke marks inside. A II 102.10.

Fig. 23 *No.*	*Reg.* *No.*	
1	4353	Lug-handle, rounded and pierced, horizontally located on body; tan outside with dark-grey inside and core; medium-coarse with some assorted grey and white grits; traces of dark-brown slip outside; pitted and spalling on handle. A II 102.9.
2	4370	Lug-handle, rounded and pierced, horizontally located on shoulder; buff; medium-coarse with many assorted, mostly small, grey grits; traces of burnished, dark-orange slip outside; pitted and spalling inside. A II 102.9.
3	4399	Lug-handle, rounded and pierced, horizontally located, pinkish-buff; coarse with few large grey grits; horizontally burnished, reddish-brown slip inside with faint traces of burnishing outside; many fine pits over-all. A II 102.9.
4	4352	Lug-handle, angular and pierced, horizontally located on body; tan outside with dark-grey inside and core; medium with some assorted white grits; traces of straw temper; uneven surface inside from joining of handle; some pitting over-all. A II 102.9.
5	5071dd	Ledge-handle fragment, narrow, thumb-indented edge; dark-orange; medium with few assorted white grits; very heavy, grey incrustations over-all. A II 102.9.
6	5071cc	Ledge-handle fragment, plain; dark-orange with greyish-brown core; coarse with few assorted white grits; traces of white slip outside; heavy, grey incrustations over-all. A II 102.9.
7	4423	Ledge-handle, slightly pushed up with plain edge; pinkish-tan with grey inside and core; coarse with few small to fine, white grits; traces of white slip outside; some heavy, grey incrustations outside. A II 102.10.
8	4485	Ledge-handle, plain; buff with dark-grey core in places; coarse with many assorted white and grey quartz grits; faint traces of white slip outside; many assorted pits inside; some pits outside, grey smoke marks over-all, some heavy grey incrustations outside. A II 102.10.
9	4412	Ledge-handle with pushed-up, scalloped edge; tan; medium-coarse with many assorted dark-grey grits; traces of white slip outside; grey smoke marks outside. A II 102.10.

Fig. 23 *No.*	*Reg.* *No.*	
10	5071	Ledge-handle with thumb-indented edge; buff inside and orange outside, dark-grey core; coarse with some assorted grey and white grits; many assorted pits outside with several large and deep pits. A II 102.9.
11	4161	Ledge-handle with thumb-indented edge; buff with very thick, dark-grey core at juncture with body; coarse with many assorted white grits; traces of heavy, white slip outside; pitted and flaking inside, black smoke marks on edge of handle, some grey incrustations over-all. A II 103.5.
12	4358	Ledge-handle with pushed-up, thumb-indented edge; buff outside and orange inside with brown core; very coarse with many assorted, mostly tan, grits; some assorted pits over-all, some grey incrustations outside. A II 102.9.
13	4420	Ledge-handle fragment, plain, rounded edge; dark-orange inside and pinkish-orange outside, thick, dark-grey core; coarse with some assorted grits; traces of heavy, white slip outside; some assorted pits inside. A II 102.10.
14	4180	Ledge-handle fragment, plain, pinkish-orange with very thick, greyish-brown core; coarse with some large to small, white grits; heavy, white slip outside; heavy, grey incrustations over-all. A II 103.4.
15	4411	Ledge-handle with deep diagonal pressed indentations closely and evenly spaced on edge; greenish-buff with dark-grey core; coarse with few fine white grits; traces of orangish-red slip outside; heavy, grey incrustations outside. A II 102.10.
—	5071jj	Fragment of small ledge-handle, plain; buff inside and tan outside; coarse with many small white grits; traces of white slip outside. A II 102.9.
16	5071w	Loop-handle fragment made of two coils, joined to body; dark-orange; coarse with some fine white grits; traces of white slip outside; black smoke marks over-all. A II 102.9.
17	4351	Loop-handle fragment made of two coils, joined to body; buff with dark-grey core; medium-coarse with few assorted white and grey grits; very uneven surface inside from joining of handle; grey smoke marks on handle. A II 102.9.
—	5071gg	Fragment of loop-handle, one curved, tapered coil, circular section; buff; medium with few fine white grits; very uneven surface. A II 102.9.
—	4188	Fragment of loop-handle, wide, flattened oval section; orange; medium-coarse with few small to fine, white grits; continuously-burnished outside; some grey incrustations. A II 103.4.
—	5071ee	Fragment of loop-handle, oval section; dark-orange; medium with many assorted tan grits; traces of continuously-burnished, dark-brown slip; rough gritty texture, light, grey incrustations over-all. A II 102.9.
—	5071ff	Fragment of loop-handle, rounded rectangular section; pinkish-buff; medium with few assorted reddish-brown grits; traces of white slip; some assorted pits over-all, very uneven surfaces. A II 102.9.
18	5045	Rim of bowl with wide, flattened, loop-handle, upcurved to thickened, rounded inverted edge; reddish-brown with dark-brown core; very coarse with many assorted tan grits; traces of continuously-burnished, reddish-brown slip over-all, seven holes impressed in handle at top; orangish-red discolorations inside and outside, black smoke marks outside, roughly pitted and spalling inside. A II 102.9.
19	4371	Spout fragment, flared out to thin rounded edge; tan with dark-grey core; medium-coarse with few assorted white grits; buff discoloration outside with some grey smoke marks; many assorted, mostly small to fine, pits over-all. A II 102.9.

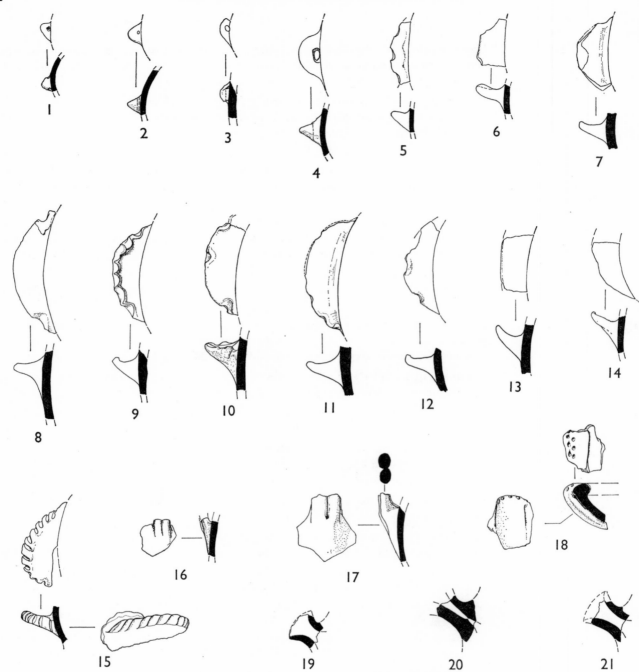

Fig. 23. Handles and spouts, Phase II. 1:4.

Fig. 23 No.	Reg. No.	
20	4419	Spout fragment with small opening; pierced from each end; orangish-buff with dark-grey core; very coarse with small to fine, white grits; some grey incrustations over-all. A II 102.10.
21	4439	Spout fragment; buff with thick, grey core; medium with some fine white and grey grits; grey discoloration outside. A II 102.10.

Fig. 24 No.	Reg. No.	
I	4405	Body sherd of jar; buff; medium with very few large to fine, dark-brown grits; medium-narrow, half-relief rope-molding outside with closely spaced diagonal indentations of various depths; one large indentation inside. A II 102.9.
2	4463	Body-sherd of jar; medium with few assorted white and grey grits; well-defined, very high-relief, ridged molding with closely spaced, diagonal indentations in crest. A II 102.10.
3	5071hh	Body-sherd; dark-orange with buff core; very coarse with few small to fine, white grits; wide, well-defined, very high-relief, rope-molding outside. A II 102.9.
4	4398	Body sherd of jar; buff with thick, dark-grey core; medium-coarse with few small to fine, white grits; medium-wide, crude rope-molding outside; some assorted pits over-all. A II 102.9.
5	4462	Body sherd of jar; buff with brown core; very coarse with few assorted grits of mixed colors; medium-wide, crude, very high-relief, rope-molding outside; some fine to medium pits inside, grey smoke marks inside. A II 102.10.
6	5071rr	Body sherd of large jar; very coarse with many assorted white, grey, and dark-brown grits; narrow, crude, half-relief rope-molding outside, traces of white slip outside; heavy, grey incrustations over-all. A II 102.9.
7	4433	Body sherd of jar; greyish-brown inside with dark-grey outside and core; coarse with many assorted grey and brown grits; medium-wide, crude, high-relief rope-molding outside; many assorted pits inside, very uneven surface inside. A II 102.10.
8	4367	Body sherd of large jar; buff with dark-grey outside; very coarse with few small grey and white grits; crude, medium-wide, slightly wavy rope-molding outside, white slip outside; some grey incrustations over-all. A II 102.9.
9	4179	Body sherd of jar; pinkish-brown with buff outside; coarse with some assorted white grits; medium-wide, very crude low-relief rope-molding outside; grey smoke marks inside, some grey incrustations outside. A II 103.4.
10	4416	Body sherd of large jar; pinkish-buff with thick, dark-grey core; coarse with few fine white grits; wide, crude, very high-relief molding outside, faint traces of white slip outside; some assorted pits over-all. A II 102.10.
11	4359	Body sherd of jar; brown outside with dark-grey inside and core; coarse with few fine white grits; well defined, medium-wide, slightly wavy, high-relief rope-molding with finger impressed-indentations, traces of heavy white slip outside. A II 102.9.
12	4413	Body sherd of large jar; greyish-brown with dark-grey core penetrating to outside in places; coarse with some assorted, mostly small to fine, white grits; very wide, well-defined, high-relief molding outside, traces of heavy, white slip outside; uneven pitted surface inside. A II 102.10.
—	5071ss	Body sherd of jar; orangish-red inside and orangish-buff outside, grey core; very coarse with some small and fine, white grits; medium wide, crude, half-relief rope-molding outside, traces of heavy, white slip outside; brown incrustations inside. A II 102.9.
—	5071uu	Body sherd of jar; buff with thick, dark-grey core; coarse with many small to fine white and tan grits; very heavy, white slip outside. A II 102.9.
—	4360	Body sherd of large jar; tan outside and brown inside, thick, dark-grey core; very coarse with many small to fine, white grits; pinkish-orange patches outside. A II 102.9.
—	4403	Body sherd of large jar; brown with dark greyish-brown inside and core; coarse with many large to fine, quartz grits; traces of brown slip outside, possibly burnished; very many small to fine pits over-all. A II 102.9.

Fig. 24 *No.*	*Reg.* *No.*	
13	4381	Body sherd of jar; reddish-brown inside with dark-grey outside and core; coarse with some small to fine, white grits; traces of white slip outside, traces of three wide, vertical, parallel painted orange stripes; few deep pits over-all. A II 102.9.
14	4481	Body sherd of jar; orangish-brown with very thick, dark-grey core; medium with some fine white grits; heavy, white slip outside, traces of four vertical, painted red stripes. A II 102.10.
15	4379	Body sherd of jar, light-orange; medium-coarse with some small to fine, white and tan grits; white slip outside, two medium-wide, vertical, parallel painted red stripes. A II 102.9.
16	4371	Body sherd of jar, light-orange; medium-coarse with some small to fine, white and tan grits; white slip outside, two medium-wide, vertical, parallel painted reddish-orange stripes. A II 102.10.
17	4354	Body sherd of jar; pinkish-tan with orange inside; medium-coarse with many assorted grey grits; faint traces of white slip outside, traces of painted brown pattern; some grey incrustations inside. A II 102.9.
18	4455	Body sherd of jar; dark-orange with buff core; coarse with many assorted white and tan grits; white slip outside, dark-orange painted stripes; uneven surface inside. A II 102.10.
19	4454	Body sherd of jar; pinkish-tan with orange inside; medium-coarse with few small and fine, white grits; heavy, white slip outside, three medium-wide, vertical, painted brown stripes; some fine pits inside. A II 102.10.
20	4355	Body sherd of jar; dark greenish-grey; coarse with many assorted white grits; medium-wide, vertical, painted brown stripe outside; some assorted pits inside. A II 102.9.
21	5071vv	Body sherd of jar; orangish-buff; medium-coarse with many assorted white and grey grits; white slip outside, traces of painted orange trellis-pattern. A II 102.9.
22	4185	Body sherd of jar; orange inside and buff outside; medium-coarse with fine quartz grits; very heavy, white slip outside, traces of two medium-wide, parallel painted red stripes; some grey incrustations over-all. A II 103.4.
23	4361	Body sherd of jar; light brown; medium with many fine white grits; heavy, white slip outside, very faint traces of four narrow, vertical, painted red stripes. A II 102.9.
—	5071tt	Body sherd; bright-orange; coarse with many assorted white grits; traces of narrow, closely spaced, parallel, burnished lines outside; some grey incrustations over-all. A II 102.9.
—	4181	Body sherd of small jug, handmade; orange with grey inside; medium with few assorted white grits; continuously-burnished, reddish-brown slip outside; some grey incrustations over-all. A II 103.4.
—	4182	Body sherd of bowl, wheel-turned; buff, medium-coarse with many small to fine, white grits; traces of wheel-burnished, reddish-brown slip outside; heavy, brown, gritty incrustations outside. A II 103.4.
—	5071ww	Body sherd, possibly from shallow bowl; dark-orange with grey core; very coarse with some small to fine, white grits; traces of burnished, reddish-brown slip outside. A II 102.9.
—	5071nn	Body sherd of small shallow bowl, wheel-turned; dark-reddish-orange; medium with few assorted white grits; wheel-burnished over-all. A II 102.9.
24	4490r	Flint blade, triangular section; golden-brown; retouched-edge on left, well-worn; grey incrustations. A II 102.10.

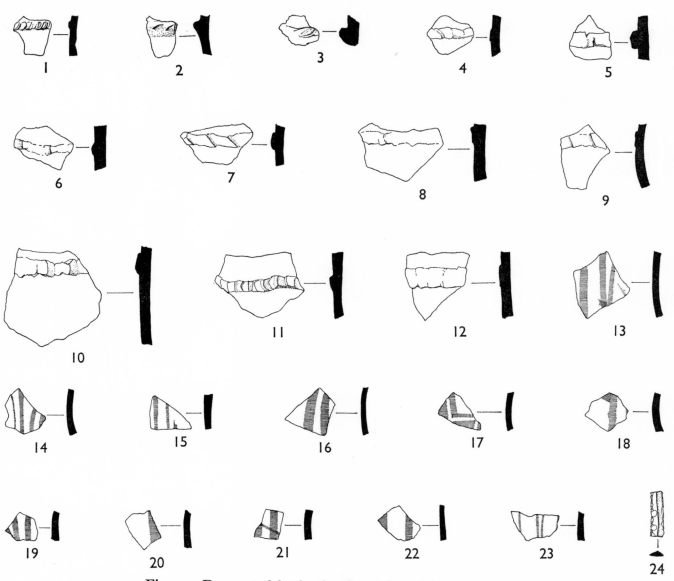

Fig. 24. Decorated body sherds; object; Phase II. 1:4.

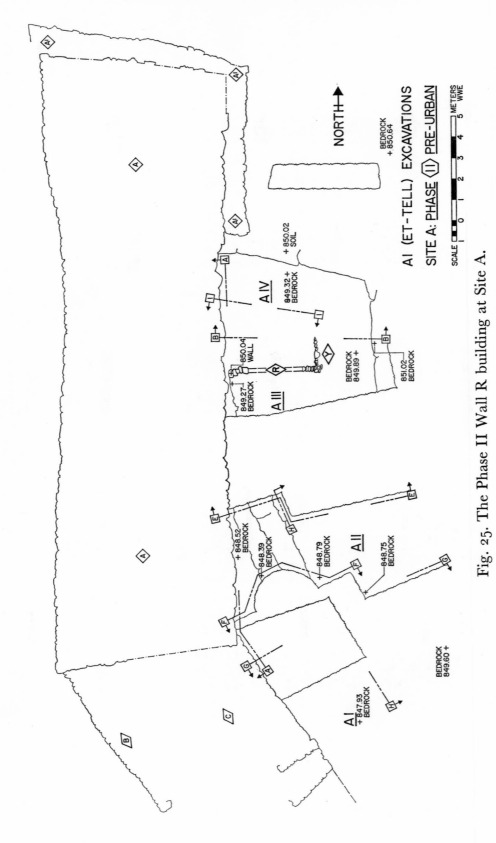

Fig. 25. The Phase II Wall R building at Site A.

IV

PHASE III, THE FIRST URBAN STRATUM

INTRODUCTION

The first city wall at Ai and the first major structure at Site A were built in Phase III. The sequence of construction, detailed in the analysis of Section F–F in Chapter II, was as follows:

First, Wall C was constructed around the original 100 dunam site, enclosing the area which was occupied by the Early Bronze Age inhabitants until the city was destroyed and abandoned in EB IIIB. The wall followed the edge of an abrupt drop in elevation around the northwest corner of the city, and the Citadel Gate was built into the original wall about 10 meters north of Tower C at Site A. Tower C guarded the approach to the gate. A foundation trench for Wall C was cut through Phase II layers 11 and 10, as shown in Section F–F, Fig. 9, and Section G–G, Fig. 7. The grey earth of Layers 11 and 10 excavated in digging the foundation trench was replaced against the inner face Wall C before Building C of Phase III was constructed.

Second, Building C was constructed on fill placed in the sequence of Layers 9b (the foundation trench fill of Wall C), 9a, 9, 8a, and 8. The Master Section shows the location of these layers which leveled the site inside Wall C for the structure. The natural slope from north to south made it expedient to construct Building C on two levels splitting at Wall Q between Areas II and III, as located in Fig. 84. The surface inside the building is about 35 centimeters lower in Area II than it is in Area III, although the same fill underlies the surface in both areas.

BUILDING C OF PHASE III

The remains of Building C were fragmentary, but enough of its walls and installations remained to allow a reconstruction, with the aid of some parts taken from the Marquet-Krause plans. Fig. 84 is the composite plan of the building. It seems to have been divided into two distinct units by Wall Q, where the split in surface levels noted above was observed. The north half, in Areas III and IV, consisted of three small rooms partitioned by narrow brick walls designated W and X, with a possible entrance by way of a ramp-like approach bordered by Walls T and U on the east side. Two larger rooms made up the unit south of Wall Q, where partition Walls S and D^1 were narrow, like Walls W and X north of Wall Q. The entrance to the south unit was apparently in Wall D^1, beside Wall C as suggested in Fig. 84. A rather wide stone-based mud-brick wall enclosed Building C on its east side, located in Fig. 84 as Walls F, F^2, and F^3 (Wall F^1 is a Phase IV rebuild of Wall F in Area II).

The north unit of Building C

Tower A and Altar J encroached upon the north unit of Building C, as Fig. 84 indicates. Wall C apparently served as the western wall of the building, and, of course, the inner face of Wall C was not uncovered in the excavation because Tower A, the later structure, was preserved and consolidated. Consequently, the extant evidence of the north unit consisted of Walls Q and F², an integral unit at the southeast corner in Area III, fragments of partition walls W and X traced into the balk under Tower A and Wall F³, a fragmentary continuation of the eastern enclosure, Wall F². Wall F³ seemed to continue northward beyond lateral Wall X, and a fragmentary floor was evident on the north side of Wall X, so a room on that side of the unit is indicated, although no evidence remained of the north enclosure wall of the building.

Rooms of the north unit. Walls Q and F² can be seen at their point of juncture in Pl. II.2. Both are made up of large field stones at the base, and Wall Q has three courses preserved. Only one course remains of Wall F². Molded mud-bricks are evident on top of the third course of Wall Q in Pl. V.1 and also in Pl. V.2, on top of the stone above the 25 centimeter scale. It is possible that Wall F² was built originally in the same manner, although the single course of large stones evident in Pl. II.2 could have supported a brick superstructure. The two walls measured from 1.10 to 1.15 meters in width, indicating that they were outer walls of the north unit. Partition walls measured regularly about 70 centimeters in width.

The evidence of Walls W and X was very fragmentary. In fact, it is possible to do little more than to confirm their existence. Pl. X.3 shows the rubbly base of Wall W associated with the same surface which continued under Altar J in Pls. X.1 and IX.1 over to the corner of Walls Q and F². The brick superstructure of Wall W was evident, as drawn in Section A–A, Fig. 83, although the weight of Tower A had pressed its flimsy remains right down on the ashy surface behind the left side of the scale in Pl. X.3. A perspective of the relationship of Wall W to the room enclosed by Walls Q and F² can be gained by consulting Pl. II.2. The large stone on which the scale rests in Pl. X.3 is visible in the right balk under Tower A in front of the one meter scale in Pl. II.2, and immediately under the surface upon which the scale rests.

Wall X was covered by the balk drawn in Section B–B, Fig. 11. It is behind the painted jar in Pl. X.2, lying upon the surface of the middle room of the north unit. The surface is traced in Section A–A, Fig. 83, but it was not preserved to a significant extent anywhere because the previous excavators removed Area III to bedrock between Altar J and Wall M. Like Wall W, partition Wall X was built of mud-bricks, crushed into the destruction debris of the building on either side as the section indicates. The surface abutting Wall X is drawn across to Wall F³ in Section B–B, although a part of it was severely eroded, as Pl. XVI.5 shows on the right side of the preserved section against Tower A. Wall F³ can be identified as the light buff bricky mass on the right front of the standing figure, and its base abuts the surface visible in the corner against Tower A.

The third, or north, room of the unit was located in Area IV, where Garstang apparently excavated to bedrock in 1928, leaving too little evidence of Building C for Marquet-Krause to reconstruct the room with any degree of certainty in 1934. The balk under Wall M, shown in Pl. XI.1, was all that remained for the present expedition. Recent findings can be seen in the photographs of Pl. XI, and Section I–I, Fig. 14.

Wall F³, in the photographs and the section, was constructed of mud-bricks upon a rubbly stone foundation. In fact, the rubble foundation seems to be a part of the destruction debris of Phase II Wall Y, shown in Pl. II.2 in the left foreground. It had a less substantial base than Wall F², enclosing the south room of the unit, possibly because the fill underneath wall F³ was already stony and not as deep as the fill under F². In any case, Wall F³ seemed to be a continuation of the eastern enclosure wall of the unit, as can be seen in Pl. XI.1. The floor of the north room, in Area IV, is visible on the right side of the one meter scale in Pl. XI.1, and the rubbly surface under the scale indicates that the surface was worn away in that area adjacent to Wall F³ by the time Wall F³ collapsed inward upon the room.

The surfaces in the north unit of Building C were reused in Building B, or Phase IV, as was pointed out in the analysis of stratification in Chapter III. The only stratified evidence of Building C in this unit was the fill underneath the floors, Layers 9 and 8, and the remnants of mud-brick walls associated with the floors. Note was taken of the unusual nature of Layer 8, the saucer-shaped fill, and further observations about its function will be made in the concluding statements about Building C which will follow the discussion of the south unit.

Entrances and passageways. One means of access to the north unit of rooms seems to have been by way of a ramp-like structure on the east side of Area III. It is actually a small terrace shaped in the Layer 9 fill by Walls U and T terminating at the base of Wall F² as indicated in Fig. 84. If the structure was indeed a ramp leading to a passageway in Wall F², the stones in Wall F² between Walls U and T served either as a threshold, or they were placed in the passageway when Building C was remodeled in Phase IV and became Building B. The stones in Wall F² at the ramp are higher than the level of Layer 9, as is evident in Pl. II.1, although there seems to be a slight rise in the level of the ramp as it approaches Wall F². The north side of the ramp, visible on the right in Pl. II.2, has been partly removed at the edge of Wall F²

No other evidence of passageways into the north unit was found. There is room for an opening in Wall Q against Wall C, where Tower A covers Wall Q. At least one meter of the wall is hidden by Tower A behind the meter scale in Pl. IV.2, so a narrow passageway could have been located there. The major problem with such an assumption is that the passageway in Wall S, discussed below, was more than one meter wide, and it is likely that an opening in Wall Q would have been wider also. Furthermore, the north unit seems to have been distinct from the south unit, with Wall Q being the separating wall between the units, so the argument for a passageway in Wall Q is not persuasive.

It is more likely that the north unit was entered from the north, near the Citadel Gate and fortification tower. All of the evidence for an entrance in Area IV, however, was removed by previous excavations, or it is covered by the northeast corner of Tower A. There is enough space in the covered parts of Walls W and X to allow openings as wide as that in Wall S in Area II, and the existence of openings at these points may be assumed on the analogy of the openings in the south unit, as well as the location of the Citadel Gate, which made the north end of Building C a focal point in the traffic pattern of the area.

The south unit of Building C

South of Wall Q, Wall F was constructed in the same manner as Wall F², except for the Phase IV rebuild, designated Wall F¹ in Fig. 85. The original Wall F continued across the east side of Area II where partition Wall S abutted it, as shown in Fig. 84, and Wall D¹ terminated the unit in Area I.

Wall S was about 70 centimeters wide, as noted above, whereas Wall F was 1.10 to 1.15 meters in width. Wall F was covered with a compact buff clay in the Phase IV rebuilding of the south unit, so the original wall was preserved to a height comparable to that of Wall F² in Area III. This was most likely the original height of the stone base of the wall, and the superstructure was probably of mud-brick. Walls S and D¹ possibly had mud-brick superstructures also, although the rebuilding of Wall S and addition of Wall S¹ in Phase IV left little evidence of the Phase III structures.

The south unit consisted of two rooms larger than the rooms in the north unit, and perhaps different in function. Two features of the unit are noteworthy. First, there seems to be definite evidence of a wide passageway leading into the unit from the south, alongside Wall C. And second, Platform Z, built into the floor of the north room over a special foundation, seems to have been a fire-hearth instead of an offering table as Marquet-Krause maintained.

Entrances and passageways. The passageway in Wall S, between its west end and Wall C as located in Fig. 84, was discussed in the analysis of Section F–F in Chapter III. Evidence of it can be seen in Pl. VIII.2, 3, where a threshold is outlined by a bedline reaching from the end of Wall S, above the meter scale on top of the balk, across the left center of the photographs to Wall C. The large stone on top of the balk above the meter scale in Pl. VIII.2 is behind a flat stone of Platform Z visible across the balk. A slight depression on the left of the large stone may mark the west end of Wall S, placing Platform Z against Wall S immediately inside the opening. The small stones above the threshold bedline are a part of the Phase IV closure of the passage. This blockage was slightly offset to the north of the orientation of Wall S, and is designated Wall S¹ in Fig. 85.

No definite evidence of an entrance in Wall D¹ was preserved. However, the extant fragments of Wall F on the east side of Building C preserved no signs of a passageway either, so its location must be conjectured on the basis of the total picture of the south unit. An opening could have been located in Wall F on the east side of the unit, because there was some evidence of an entrance to the north unit in Wall F². On the other hand, there was a wide eroded gap in Wall D¹ against Wall C, as Fig. 84 indicates, which could also mark the location of the entrance. This location against Wall C seems more plausible for three reasons.

First, the south unit maintained a slight slope toward the south even though thick layers of fill raised the area almost to the level of floors at Wall Q. Perhaps the fill settled enough to maintain the slope. In any case, the surface of Layer 9 sloped toward the south, requiring an outlet for drainage alongside Wall C. The outlet would most likely have been located in a passageway at the west end of Wall D¹. Second, the opening alongside Wall C in Wall S would be in line with a passageway in Wall D¹, and would face the built-up area of houses to the south toward which the south unit was oriented. And third, a Phase IV passageway in the end of Wall E, against Wall C, probably preserves the Phase III tradition of a south entrance to the unit. Wall E was the enclosure wall in Phase IV, so the passageway alongside Wall C may very well preserve the orientation of the unit in the previous phase.

Platform Z in the south unit. Marquet-Krause called Platform Z, located in Fig. 84, the offering table of Sanctuary C (see Marquet-Krause 1949, 30, Pl. XX:2). It is an unusual installation because of Wall G, the special foundation structure discussed in the analysis of Section F–F in Chapter II. Actually, the platform did not rest directly upon Wall G, contemporary with Layer 9 and set in a foundation trench cut through Layers 10 and 11 to bedrock. Wall G was more likely a retainer for the saucer-shaped fill, Layer 8, immediately under Platform Z. The fact that stones of Wall G penetrated Layer 8, as drawn in Section F–F, Fig. 9, indicates that Layers 8, 9, 9a, and Platform Z were all contemporary, although the sequence of construction was probably as follows:

1. Terrace Wall D² in Area I, which retained the fill imported for the foundation of Building C, was begun first.

2. Layer 9a was deposited against Wall D², and Wall G was laid in a semi-circle to retain the 9a fill on the north side. Actually, Wall D² had no finished inner side, so construction of the entire unit of Walls D², Wall G, and Layer 9a may have been carried on simultaneously to build a broad-based terrace for support of the south unit of Building C. The fact that Wall G slopes upward on Layer 9a toward Wall D², as Pl. II.1 indicates, suggests that the components of the unit were not built independently of each other.

3. Layer 9, a finer quality of fill than Layer 9a, was placed over Layer 10 in the north of Area II, and on top of Layer 9a, Wall G, and inside Wall D² in Area I.

4. The ashy clay fill of Layers 8a and 8 was laid over Layer 9 as the immediate foundation for Walls D¹, F, S, and Platform Z. This is the saucer-shaped fill found also under the floors and walls of Building C in the north unit.

5. Walls D¹, F, S, and Platform Z, the structures of the south unit associated with Wall Q in Phase IV were built in the erection of Building B.

The function of Platform Z is debatable. Marquet-Krause thought it was an offering table, or altar, because she believed that a succession of sanctuary phases was evident at Site A (see the plans of the sanctuaries in Marquet-Krause 1949. Pl. XCVIII). Identification of Building C as a sanctuary and Platform Z as an offering table, however, rests upon an assumed analogy with Sanctuary A and Installation J, its altar, more than upon demonstrable material evidence. The writer has been forced to this conclusion by a study of the evidence associated with Building C, and the view that Building C was a sanctuary, set forth in the 1964 preliminary report (see Callaway 1965, 16–21), must now be changed.

There was an altar in Sanctuary A, or Phase VII in the sequence of buildings at the site. The altar was built against the inner face of Tower A to a considerable height above floor level (see Marquet-Krause 1949, Pls. XV:1; XVI:1, 2; XVII:1), and cultic vessels, as well as remains of apparent animal offerings, were found on the altar and the floor around it. Platform Z in Building C, however, was different in form from Installation J of Sanctuary A. The platform was built in the floor of the room, and projected barely above the level of the floor.

A structure similar to Platform Z was discovered at Site G in the 1966 excavations at Ai. It is designated Pavement N in the preliminary report and is located in Area II (see Callaway 1969, 14, Fig. 10). This installation was almost rectangular in form, and was built of flat stones set into the packed earth floor of the room in which it was found. Like Platform Z, it was constructed against a wall. However, it was bordered on two sides by large stones forming low enclosure walls and setting it off from the rest of the room. The side facing the center of the room was not enclosed, and was thus open for functional use. Pavement N was found to be covered with a considerable depth of ashes apparently accumulated over a long period of use as a fire hearth. No additional discovery since 1966 has made the identification of Pavement N as a hearth untenable.

Platform Z in Building C was likely a hearth also. There is no record of what was found on the pavement at the time of excavation. Whether it was covered with a deep accumulation of ashes like Pavement N in G II is, therefore, not known. A low enclosure wall around part of Platform Z is suggested by the single large stone on the right edge of the installation shown in Marquet-Krause 1949, Pl. XX:2. The enclosure would have walled off the west side of the platform from the passage-way in Wall S, and Wall S itself enclosed the backside. Structurally, therefore, Platform Z seems to have a closer analogy in the Pavement N fire hearth of G II than it has in the Installation J altar of Sanctuary A. Chronologically, Pavement N is also closer to Platform Z, because it was a part of the earliest EB house at Site G.

Conclusions.

Two aspects of Building C are unusual enough to require further explanation and concluding statements of the writer's views. First, the saucer-shaped fill of Layers 8a and 8, a distinctive part of the foundation for Building C, apparently had a definite function which would explain its peculiar form. And, second, the designation of Building C as a sanctuary by Marquet-Krause and others must be reviewed in the light of structural features in the building and artifacts recovered from it.

The saucer-shaped fill. Layers 8a and 8, the ashy clay fill immediately underneath the floors and walls of Building C, covered almost all of the *khamra* of Layer 9. The characteristic inverted lens shape seems to have been due to a functional role served, rather than to mere accident in building.

The functional role seems to be implicit in the nature of the *khamra* fill itself. *Khamra* is very sensitive to changes in moisture content and, therefore, is not a desirable soil for exposed surfaces. When excessive moisture is taken up by the soil, either from rain or artificial sources, it becomes very sticky and slippery. On the other hand, it is soft and powdery when the moisture content is removed by evaporation or heat. Consequently, an exposed surface would always mean potential trouble. However, the soil is very stable and firm when it has the proper moisture content, and it maintains this content naturally when the surface is covered. In fact, when the soil is damp, it acquires a consistency approaching that of pottery clay, and becomes a moisture-barrier sealing out excessive wetness which might seep through from below to the surface above.

The ashy clay of Layer 8 was the kind of surfacing soil needed to provide an effective covering for the *khamra*, to preserve its moisture content, and to make a durable packed earth surface in the rooms of Building C. This surfacing material was thickened under some of the walls to give them a more stable foundation. The saucer-shaped fill, therefore, had a functional role of stabilizing the foundation of Building C for its walls and floors.

The function of Building C. There remains the question of whether Building C was a sanctuary. The writer's view that it was not a sanctuary is evident in the designation 'Building C' instead of 'Sanctuary C,' and in the interpretation that Platform Z in the south unit was a fire hearth and not an offering table or altar. This view seems to be supported by a study of the artifacts drawn in Figs. 26–33. Every object and piece of pottery recovered in the latest excavation capable of being drawn with any reasonable degree of accuracy by the artist is presented. Nothing was discarded. The same is true with regard to Fig. 34, a presentation of all the artifacts from Marquet-Krause 1949 which can be assigned to her Sanctuary C from the notes on provenance or description.

There is not one definite cult object in the lot. Actually, the pottery seems to be ordinary household ware without any distinguishing characteristics, setting it in a different category from the finds in Sanctuary A, Phase VII. Building C was most likely, therefore, an ordinary large house built against the Phase III city wall and Tower C for a function other than that of a sanctuary.

What was its function? The fact that Building C and Tower C were built almost as one unit with Wall C suggests that the two were related in function. In the Lower City, a street separated houses from the inner face of Wall C, leaving a space along the inside of the wall for communication, or defense purposes. A restudy of the buildings uncovered by Marquet-Krause has revealed a Phase III street in 'fouille V4, 1935' (see Marquet-Krause 1949, Pl. C). Room 239, adjacent to 242 on the south, is a street leading toward Site C along the inner face of Wall C. This preserves a space up to 1.75 meters wide between Wall C and the Phase III houses.

A similar style of town planning is evident at Arad also, where the housing units in the southwest quarter were separated from the city wall by a street (see Amiran 1970, 94, Pl. 10). Consequently, the location of Building C against Wall C and the tower is an exception to the rule of town planning in Phase III. Of course, the exception may be due to the unevenness of Site A, which may have made it impractical to locate a street from the Citadel Gate alongside the inner face of Wall C toward the Lower City. It seems more likely, however, that the building served some purpose in association with the tower fortifications. If this was the case, the small rooms in the north unit of Building C would most likely have been store-rooms, and the south unit would have provided living quarters for the keepers of the Citadel.

THE PHASE III POTTERY AND OBJECTS

Provenance

The presentation of pottery in Figs. 26–33 is by types assembled from Layers 9b, 9a, 9 8a, and 8. Analysis of the sections and pottery forms indicates that these layers belong in one historical stratum, although there was a sequence in the depositing of the various component layers as detailed in the preceding discussion of Building C. Pottery associated with specific layers can be isolated by consulting the descriptions accompanying the drawings, where the exact provenance of each piece is included.

A description of the layers indicated by code numbers in the pottery listings of Figs. 26–33 is given here for guidance in using the code numbers. It is also helpful in locating the exact areas and sub-areas indicated in the Sketch Plan, Fig. 82. The code numbers are in the general area locations where they belong, but the exact provenance recorded in the field record book can be determined more accurately by using the following information along with the Sketch Plan.

The north unit. A distinction between the north and south units of Building C was made in the discussion of the structure above, so the same distinction will be preserved in describing the provenance of artifacts associated with the building. The north unit was located north of Wall Q, comprising Areas III and IV as located in Fig. 84. Pottery in the north unit was taken from Layers 9 and 8, drawn in Sections A–A, Fig. 83, B–B, Fig. 11, and I–I, Fig. 14.

Layer 9. The dark red stony fill of this layer can be located under the surface on which the meter scale rests in Pl. II.2. It is the foundational fill for the floor and Wall F² in the left center. Wall R in the foreground, on bedrock, is covered, as the close-up photograph in Pl. III.1 shows in the Section A–A balk. Pl. X.3 is another detailed photograph showing Layer 9 under the fragmentary remains of Wall W, above the right end of the 25 centimeter scale. The same fill stretched into Area IV on bedrock and leveled the terrain for the north unit as indicated in Section I–I, Fig. 14, and shown in Pl. XI.1.

A III 201.13 is the designation of the entire red stony layer excavated between Wall R and the balk under the meter scale in Pl. II.2. Part of the layer was removed by Marquet-Krause at Wall R, but a substantial thickness remained in front of the balk under Wall F and the master balk under Tower A on the right of the photograph. The number was assigned to all of the preserved part of the layer from these balks to the point where it lensed out in the center of the area.

A III 201.13a is the upper part of 201.13 between Wall F, in the left center of Pl. II.2, and the left end of Wall R. A distinction was made between the stony, loose fill immediately under Wall F, extending left under the terrace, Wall T, and the more compact red layer underneath. The compact sub-layer is A III 201.13b resting upon Layer 10 of Phase II.

A III 201.14 was a fragmentary layer in the middle of Area III, east of Wall F², excavated with 201.13b and equated with it. Because of a mixture of grey stony earth with Layer 9 reddish fill, the sub-layer was given a separate designation.

A III 202.9 was the loose stony layer against the upper right side of Wall R in Pl. III.1, above the compact stony surface of Layer 10 drawn in the Master Section. The more compact reddish fill on top of 202.9 is designated A III 202.8, and comprises the upper part of Layer 9 in Section B–B between Tower A and Wall F³. Sub-layer 9 contained stones from the collapse of Walls R and Y mixed with the reddish fill which was more distinct in sub-layer 8. The two make up Layer 9 inside the corner of the Wall R building, and are under the saucer-shaped fill of Layer 8, drawn in Sections A–A, B–B and I–I.

A III 204.5 was assigned to the Layer 9 fill between Wall F² and Wall L. Sections C–C, Fig. 12, and D–D, Fig. 13, locate the layer, but the part excavated did not extend up to the balks. Pl. XVII shows the excavated area on the right, in front of the drawn balks. The 204.5 fill was a continuation of 201.13 described above, lensing out on bedrock near Wall L.

A IV 300.18 and 18a were the Area IV counterparts of A III 202.8 and 9. Sub-layer 18a was the stony debris from the collapse of Wall Y mixed with the characteristic reddish clay of Layer 9, and 300.18 was the reddish fill in the Wall M balk, drawn in Section I–I, above the Wall Y debris and underneath Layer 8.

A IV 300.14e is the Layer 9 fill on the right side of Wall Y in Section B–B, Fig. 11, visible in Pl. XVI.5 in the lower right of the photograph. The layer was reddish gray, mixed with the thin ashy deposit on bedrock ,and underlying the loose ashy deposit of Layer 7a.

Layer 8. The saucer-shaped fill of grey ashy earth described as a feature of the Phase III building in the discussion of Building C is designated Layer 8. A part of the layer drawn in the Master Section is visible in the lower right center of Pl. II.2, under Tower A on the right and over the top of Wall R in the Tower A balk. Wall W in Pl. X.3 was constructed on the lensed edge of Layer 8, and Wall X was placed over the thick center section of the layer, as drawn in the Master Section. Wall F^3 in Section B–B, Fig. 11, was on the eastern edge of the fill.

A III 202.4 was the grey ashy fill in the northwest corner of Area III, between Walls X and W in the Master Section, Fig. 83, and Wall F^3 and Tower A in Section B–B, Fig. 11. The surface under the 25 centimeter scale in Pl. X.2 is the top side of 202.4 as drawn in Section B–B and the Master Section.

A III 202.6 was assigned to the bricky remains of Wall X covered by the balk drawn in Section B–B and behind the crushed jar in Pl. X.2. The remains were meager, but definable and therefore drawn in the Master Section, Fig. 83.

A IV 300.13 was the Area IV counterpart designation of 202.6, removed in the dismantling of the Wall M balk. The sub-layer was described as compact bricky underlying A IV 300.12 and above 300.15. The latter was the equivalent of A III 202.4 described above, as was A IV 300.20, the compact grey ashy fill in the southwest corner of Area IV, pictured under the right end of the meter scale in Pl. XI.1.

The south unit. Most of the stratified remains of the unit south of Wall Q, located in Fig. 84, were projections from the master balk and undisturbed layers around and under Platform A. Comprising these remains were Layers 9b, 9a, 9, 8a, and 8, most of which bear the same general features of Layers 9 and 8 in the north unit. Layer 9b was a small foundation trench for Wall C which yielded no artifacts, and 9a was a coarse, stony sub-fill of Layer 9. The saucer-shaped fill of Layer 8 stretched across Area II under Walls S and F, and 8a was the sub-fill placed against the terrace formed by Wall D^2, drawn in Section H–H, Fig. 8.

Layer 9, including 9a. The dark red stony fill of Layer 9 was especially thick in Area II, due to the drop in the level of bedrock. Possibly to economize on labor, the builders laid a coarse fill of stones, Layer 9a, in the low places of Areas I and II, and placed the more compact fill of Layer 9 on top as preparation for construction of Building C.

The loose stony fill of Layer 9a begins in Area II as drawn in the Master Section, Fig. 83. Pl. VI.2 shows the beginning point of medium-size stones in the balk behind the left end of the meter scale. A II 103.3 is the loose stony layer between Wall $S–S^1$ and the Wall E balk, as drawn in the Master Section.

A II 102.6 is the thick, dark fill of Layer 9 in Pl. VI.2 above the meter scale, and between Wall $S–S^1$ and Wall Q at the north end of Area II. Wall Q was constructed on A II 102.6, as Pl. V.1 details. Across Wall F^1 in the northeast corner of Area II, Layer 9 continues as 101.9a, extending underneath Layer 7a as drawn in Section E–E, Fig. 10, and illustrated in Pl. III.2 above the right end of the meter scale. A II 102.5 was *huwwar* and clay surface on 102.6 belonging to Building C, and covered by grey rubbly debris designated 102.4 assigned to Phase IV. This particular deposit was the only isolated evidence of the termination of Building C.

The red fill of Layer 9 is A II 102.8 in Section F–F from the right end of semi-circular Wall G across to Wall F on the left, visible in Pl. VI.3. A II 102.8 is the same as A II 102.6 drawn in the Master section. The latter was excavated first, and the sub-area was terminated in the corner of Walls C, S^1, and G, leaving the earth inside the enclosure of Wall G to be removed later. Pl. VII.1 shows the separation of Layer 9 by the right end of Wall G, behind the lower part of the meter scale.

In Area I, Layer 9 is A I 1.7, located between the Wall E balk and Wall D². The area was excavated to bedrock by Marquet-Krause, but undisturbed parts of Layer 9 projected from the Wall E balk, and these yielded the A I 1.7 artifacts.

Layer 8, including 8a. The compact grey ashy saucer-shaped fill, designated Layer 8, covered Layer 9 in the area of Platform Z, Wall F, and the area between Walls S and D¹. In the latter area, a mixture of stones and ashy clay was found in a much thicker layer than that under Platform Z. The form of Layers 8, 8a can be seen in Section H–H, Fig. 8, giving a north-south profile, and Section G–G, Fig. 7, an east-west profile.

A II 102.7 is the grey ashy fill layer under Platform Z in Section F–F, Fig. 9, and it includes all of the layer excavated from Wall F on the left to a point where it lenses out between the right end of Wall G and Wall C. The latter point is visible in Pl. VII.1 under the stones of Wall S¹ on the upper right of the meter scale. The same layer between the balks of Wall S–S¹ and Wall E, behind Platform Z in Pl. VI.3, is designated A II 103.1. Wall F limited the sub-area on the east side.

Only fragmentary remains of Layers 8a and 8 were found in Area I, south of the Wall B balk. A I 1.6 is a continuation of 103.1 under Wall E¹ and south to Wall D¹. A thickened surface of huwwar and small stones was defined on top of A I 1.6 and it was designated A I 1.5a. The line of stones drawn in Section G–G on top of Layer 8 is visible in Pl. VI.3 under Wall E¹ in the background. A I 2.2 was a fragmentary layer at the right end of Section H–H, between Wall D² and the large undesignated stone at the end of the section. This layer and A I 2.1 were possibly associated with the south entrance to Building C. The evidence was, however, extremely meager, as the yield of pottery indicates.

The Phase III pottery forms

Drawings of all Phase III pottery are found in Figs. 26–33, with descriptions accompanying the drawings. Occasional pieces were too undistinguished to draw. They were identified and described, however, and are included in the lists with similar, drawn forms. The assemblage of Phase III pottery may be assigned to Wright's EB IC, EB I of Kenyon and de Vaux, and Amiran's Stratum III at Arad. This is equivalent to Lapp's first urban phase at Bab edh-Dhra', assigned to Wright's EB IC (Lapp 1970, 106–110).

Small to medium bowls. Small bowls, both shallow and hemispherical, continue in the traditions of Phases I and II. The shallow bowls in Fig. 26:1, 5 are similar to Fig. 15:1, traced to antecedents in the Chalcolithic period. Persistence of the form may be attributed to its function as a lamp, evident in the black smoke marks on the rim of Reg. No. 5029f, under Fig. 26:1. The same form continues at Arad in Stratum III, with a balance in proportion between the shallow and hemispherical bowls (Amiran Early Arad, Pl. 13:10, 14, 15, 16, 19, and 6, 26, 27, 30, 33). The distinctive hemispherical bowl in Phase III, Fig. 26:2, shows refinement in technique over those in earlier phases. A fine buff ware, evenly fired and tempered, and characteristic of better pottery in later EB phases, appears for the first time in this thin, delicate bowl form.

Medium bowl forms of Phase III continue the tradition of Phase II with some modifications and exceptions. The angular bowl in Fig. 16:14, Phase II, a form with Chalcolithic antecedents, does not appear in Building C, Phase III. Another form, the V-shaped bowl in Fig. 16:11, Phase II, continues in a flattened, thin-walled variation in Phase III, Fig. 26:14. Improvement in technique is evident in the finer ware and delicate form of the bowl, but a thickening of the wall just under the rim preserves a characteristic traceable to Chalcolithic antecedents. One general tendency in Phase III is toward shallower forms than those of Phase II, evident in Fig. 26:9. This tendency is markedly evident in Stratum III at Arad (Amiran Early Arad, Pl. 13:1–19), and is a hallmark of the Stratum II forms.

Noticeably absent from the Building C assemblage is the medium bowl with everted carinate rim. This is a common form in Phase IV (Fig. 35:18–23), as well as Stratum II at Arad and EB II at Jericho. However, the form first appears in Stratum III at Arad (Pl. 13:13–32) and in Phase K of Areas E III–IV and Tomb A108 at Jericho (Hennessy 1967, Pl. V:52, p. 11; Kenyon 1960, 84, Fig. 23:1–4). de Vaux cites one example of this form in Eneolithique (Chalcolithique) Superieur at Tell el-Far'ah (N) (1947, 409, Fig. 2:25), and a variety of the same forms in Ancien Bronze I (*ibid.*, 413, Fig. 4:1, 3, 4, 6, 7, 9, 10–15). Phase IV examples from Ai were taken from the reused Phase III north unit of Building C, but none was found in the construction phase of the building, i.e., Phase III.

Wide, deep bowls. Wide bowls characterized by orange to orangish-buff ware with white slip outside continue in Phase III. Variations in decoration and form do occur, however, distinguishing the Phase III assemblage. The variations in decoration are not associated with any particular new form, or variation of an old form, suggesting that the changes are not due to functional causes. Changes in forms are actually refinements, and seem to reflect a process of development rather than new functions.

One variation in form is evident in a comparison of Fig. 26:18–19 with Fig. 16:21, 23. The 'hammer-rim' is flattened on top in Phase III, and the outside ridge is more angular, while the inner lip is less pronounced. Hennessy notes that this form is common in Areas E III–IV at Jericho in Phase L (Hennessy 1967, Pl. IV:30, 32; p. 10), and observes that Pl. IV:32 has antecedents in Phase M. The ware of Fig. 16:21, 23 is buff with thick grey core. The color of the ware continues in Fig. 26:18–19, but refinements in technology seem to be evident in better firing and finer ware in Phase III. Also, Fig. 26:19 is decorated with a reddish-brown slip inside, reinforcing the evidence of better technology because a slip inside the bowl makes it less porous.

Another variation in form is seen in the transition of the rim with thinned, sharply inverted edge in Phase II, Fig. 16:17, 19, to a rolled, inward-projecting edge in Phase III, Fig. 26:21. Orangish ware characterizes the form in both phases, as does the decoration with white slip outside. This distinction is not evident in the pottery from Jericho or Arad, and, therefore, may be due to limited evidence rather than evolution in form at Ai.

The thick-walled bowl in Fig. 26:25 preserves an interesting example of Phase III decoration. Consistent with Phase III forms, e.g., Fig. 26:23, 26, this bowl is decorated with diagonal indentations in the rolled outer ridge of the rim, a motif common in Stratum V at Arad (Amiran Early Arad, Pl. 2:5–7), but found largely on the rope molding of hole-mouth jars in Strata IV–III at Arad and Phases II–III at Ai. Other decoration is confined mainly to the color and application of slip. Fig. 26:19 has traces of reddish-brown slip inside, while 26:25 has traces of brown slip outside. White slip, made from a limestone base, is found consistently on the outside of bowls in Phase III, as it is on jars.

Platter-bowls. Three observations about the Phase III platter bowls can be made. First, there is a trend toward thinner, better quality ware in Phase III than in Phase II. Descriptions of ware in Phase II indicate consistently medium to coarse ware, accounting for the heavy forms in Fig. 16:26–29 and Fig. 17:1–3. The two forms in Fig. 17:4–5 are similar to the better platters in Phase III, although the ware in these examples is medium. Only one Phase III example is described as coarse, Fig. 26:29, while the others range from medium to very fine, Figs. 26:28, 30-32; 27:1–7.

Second, pattern-burnishing becomes more common in Phase III than in Phase II at Ai. Amiran pointed out this characteristic as common in EB II, but beginning in EB I (Amiran 1969, 55), and cited an example from EB I at Tell el-Far'ah (N) (*ibid.*, p. 56:2). One platter with orange-red slip radially-burnished inside to the angle of the rim was registered in Phase II at Ai, Fig. 16:28. The same pattern occurs more frequently in Phase III. Reg. No. 4820, listed under Fig. 26:32, is typical with reddish-brown slip radially-burnished inside to the angle of the rim, then horizontally burnished inside and outside the rim. Two other examples of the same slip and pattern are in Fig. 27:4, 5. The first instance of net-pattern burnishing occurs in Phase III, Reg. No. 4309d, listed under Fig. 27:7. A reddish-brown slip is continuously burnished with parallel lines, then a burnished net pattern is superimposed both inside and outside the body of the platter.

Third, the wide, shallow platter with low, slightly inverted rim appears first in Phase III, Fig. 27:7. The Phase III platter continues a burnished reddish-brown slip decoration found on earlier forms but adds a distinct ridge on the outside of the sharply angled rim, and a slight concavity below the angle. This particular form is found also in Phase IV, Fig. 26:7, 8, and becomes common in EB III. Hennessy reported an example in Phase G of Areas E III–IV at Jericho (Hennessy 1967, Pl. VI:63), but apparently thought it belonged in Phase F, EB IIA, instead of EB II (*ibid.*, p. 12). Phase IV at Ai is EB II, and Phase III is still earlier.

Juglets and jars. The pierced lug handle juglet in Fig. 27:26 appears first at Site A in Phase III. This example is decorated with a burnished reddish brown slip. The form occurs first in Areas E III–IV at Jericho in Phase K (Hennessy 1967, Pl. V:55; p. 11) and in Tomb A108 (Kenyon 1960, 84, Fig. 23:15–18). No. 17 from Tomb A108 is decorated with a painted net pattern, as are the Phase K examples. No. 18, however, has a reddish slip with a net pattern formed by burnished lines instead of paint. Only the neck and lug handles of Fig. 27:26 are preserved, so a burnished pattern could have decorated the body of the juglet. Amiran cites a similar form with painted net pattern from Tomb G at Ai as EB I, or contemporary with Phase III (Amiran 1969, Pl. 11:13, cited from Marquet-Krause 1949, Pl. LXXII:870).

The plain rim jar form common in Phase II continues in Phase III with a trend toward fewer straight rims and more outcurving patterns. The straight rims in Fig. 27:13–14 continue the form in Fig. 17:21, but with slightly more flare in the neck and rim. Rims 15–21 of Fig. 27 continue the sharply outcurved form evident in Fig. 17:8–10, 20, 22–23, but the form becomes dominant. Two examples, Fig. 27:16–17, curve outward from neck to rim sharply enough to form a distinct angle on the inner surface. Others, in Fig. 27:15, 18–21, are bent outward almost at an angle where the rim is formed.

The heavy flared rim in Fig. 27:22 is a continuation of Fig. 17:30 in Phase II, but Fig. 27:23 seems to be a new form in Phase III. The latter is a distinctive, well-developed form, characterized by projecting, squared-edge rim and burnished reddish-brown slip outside and inside the rim. Possible antecedents in Phase II, Fig. 17:26 or 29, do not seem probable because they belong in the tradition of rolled rims illustrated in Fig. 27:24, 25, characterized by white slip decoration. The squared rim in Fig. 27:23 is a new form in Phase III at Site A, possibly comparable with Stratum III squared rim jars at Arad (Amiran Early Arad, Pl. 17:1–4), although the kind of slip on the latter is not known to the writer.

Hole-mouth jars. The bow-rim jar cited in Phase II at Site A, Fig. 19:25, disappears in Phase III, although a variation of the form is found at Arad in Stratum III (Amiran Early Arad, Pl. 18:24). The squared rim with flattened edge, Fig. 18:26, 29 in Phase II, survives in Phase III, Fig. 28:2, 5, but is not influential. Fig. 28:5 does not have a groove in the flattened surface like Fig. 18:26, and it is decorated with white slip. Fig. 28:2 actually is not a flattened rim, but it seems to continue the tradition of the drooping semi-flattened form in Fig. 18:28 with the edge more rounded. This example is similar to the 'drooping inturned rim' of Phase L in Areas E III–IV at Jericho (Hennessy 1967, Pl. V:49; p. 11). One similar form is found at Arad in Stratum III (Amiran Early Arad, Pl. 21:43).

Rims with swollen, inward rolled forms in many variations continue in Phase III, as do the ridged forms noted in Phase II. The latter are common at Arad in Stratum III. Hennessy's 'grooved and everted rim' of Phases L–J at Jericho in Areas E III–IV (1967, Pl. IV:42; p. 10) occurs in Phase III, Fig. 29:18, Fig. 30:1, but in a less pronounced form. The 'beaked rim' of Phases L, K, J (1967, Pl. V:47; p. 11) is present also in Phase III, Fig. 30:6–9. This form does not appear in Phase II, and there is no definite example of it at Arad in Strata IV or III.

Upright, or wide-mouth, jars in Phase III, Fig. 30:12–18, continue the hole-mouth jar rim form, and most of the jar characteristics found in Phase II. The rim forms generally have less variety in Phase III, evidenced by the absence of examples like Fig. 20:16, 18.

Handles and spouts. One tubular lug handle, pierced horizontally, was found at Site A in Phase III (Fig. 32:4). A similar handle on a large jar is reported by Hennessy from Area E III–IV at Jericho (1967, Pl. V:53; p. 11) in Phase K, or Kenyon's EB I. Amiran includes a small jar from Khirbet Masada with tubular lug handles pierced vertically in the 'southern culture' repertory of EB pottery (1969, 54, Photo 47). A unique globular jar with vertical, pierced tubular lugs is reported by Saller from Bab edh-Dhra' (1965, 166, Fig. 19; also 159, Fig. 16:4 and 165, Fig. 18:5). The lugs are decorated on the upper half by a bust in relief, without the head. Primitive sketches of four human figures are painted in squares on the waist of the jar between the lugs. Saller places the jar, which was obtained out of context, in Late Chalcolithic (p. 168), or EB IB of Wright, on the parallel evidence of 'somewhat similar representations' of dancing figures from Tomb 454 at Nakada. The evidence of the tubular handles from Ai and Jericho is in an EB IC stratified context, although these examples may reflect an incursion of the type from Transjordan where it could have existed in EB IB.

Loop handles are more common in Phase III than in Phase II at Site A. The twin-handle form is dominant in Phase II, Fig. 23:16–17, but does not appear in Phase III. Single loop handles with oval section (Fig. 32:16–18), or triangular oval section (No. 15) are common in the latter phase. Fig. 32:17 is a top section of a handle connected to the neck of a jug below the rim, and if the handle and body are projected to the bottom section, a connection occurs on the bulging shoulder of the vessel. This form is found in Tomb A108 at Jericho (Kenyon 1960, 84, Fig. 23:8–10), and Tomb 14 at Tell el-Far'ah (N) (de Vaux 1952, 579, Fig. 11:20). One jug in Tomb 14 has a high loop handle reaching to the rim (*ibid.*, Fig. 11:19), a form possibly similar to the incomplete handles in Fig. 32:16, 18, and parallel in type with Fig. 23:9 in Tomb A 108 at Jericho.

Open spouts of water jars and cooking pots continue in Phase III, Fig. 32:19–20, and the first instance of the vestigial spout common in EB II appears. Fig. 32:21 is actually a pierced spout like the Phase II example in Fig. 23:20, but the piercing is not complete. Both the open and pierced spouts were made separately and affixed to vessels at the leather-hard stage, and the pierced spouts were pierced from each end. The Phase III spout had apparently lost its function, because the hole was not pierced through, although the piercing was attempted.

Column handles with pierced openings appear at Jericho, Areas E III–IV, in Phase L (Hennessy 1967, Pl. V:49; p. 11), and continue into Phase J, when the piercing is discontinued (*ibid.*, Pl. VI:58a). Amiran reports unpierced column handles in Stratum III at Arad (Early Arad, Pl. 15:15–17), and one example in Stratum IV which is barely pierced (Pl. 11:6), similar to the Phase II spout at Site A, Fig. 23:20. The solid column form in Stratum III is spindly and apparently unsuitable for piercing. It is, therefore, a new form at Arad, and possibly an influence affecting the transition of the pierced spout to a column handle.

Objects

Two types of objects were recovered in the meager remains of Phase III. The first is a short, semi-flattened bone tool, in two styles, and the second is a large tusk, drawn in Fig. 33:29.

Bone tools. Object No. 87, Fig. 33:30, is apparently an awl with a finely worked point. The broad end of the awl is a semi-flattened joint of the bone with no hole for thread to be inserted. Object No. 88, Fig. 33:31 is fashioned in a similar manner, but more flattened, as the section indicates. These tools seem to have been used as thread separators in weaving, but not for sewing.

The ivory tusk. The gently curving tusk is characterized by longitudinally ribbed enamel and a flat, elongated facet on the end caused by wear. It is 18 centimeters in length, but the root is broken off so the length is only approximate. Cornwall identifies the tusk as a lower right canine of a hippopotamus, not fossilized.*

The tusk was found in Layer 9, A III 204.5, between Walls F² and L. This is outside the east wall of Building C, and in the red fill underlying Building C as well as the open area on the east. Since the red fill was brought into the city from the valley nearby, probably south of Sites A and C, it is possible that the tusk was brought in from the valley in containers of the fill. In this case, the *terminus ad quem* of the tusk would be Phase III, but its *terminus a quo* would be uncertain.

Against this view, one may argue that an 18-centimeter tusk would hardly be gathered up in earth fill in the kind of containers used in EB IC without detection, and that it probably was dropped in the open area east of Building C during Phase III. This view does not prohibit an uncertain date of origin for the tusk, because someone could have found it in the fields. However, one could posit a provenance in Phase III from a hunt in the nearby Jordan Valley, and support the view with evi-

---

* The writer is grateful to Professor Ian Cornwall of the London University Institute of Archaeology for identifying the tusk.

dence of the broken-off root, which would hardly have been broken off if the tusk had been found in a dessicated skull or if the tusk were separated from a skull by wild animals in the field.

Conclusions

In many instances, the pottery of Phase III shows improvements in technology and craftsmanship over that of Phase II, although there persists a curious inconsistency in the quality of the potter's art. This inconsistency seems to derive from the complex amalgam of traditions traceable to various cultural elements making up the Phase III city at Ai. Some pottery forms continue the indigenous traditions first identified in Chalcolithic antecedents, while others are introduced at Site A in Phase III, apparently from outside the region of Ai. Still other forms continue traditions introduced in Phases I–II, with no background in the indigenous cultures.

Identification of the distinguishing features of the Phase III pottery culture at Ai is, therefore, of primary significance. The assemblage will then be related to contemporary strata in an effort to define its cultural context, and, finally, a chronology for Phase III, the first walled city at Ai, will be proposed.

The Phase III pottery traditions. Small hemispherical and shallow bowls, used as lamps, continue the traditions of Phases I–II, and indigenous forms traceable to Chalcolithic origins. Also the V-shaped bowl in Fig. 26:14 continues an indigenous form, as does the hammer-rim deep bowl, Fig. 26:18–19. Variations in the Phase III forms are noted, but they still belong in a continuous tradition of indigenous types. Most of the jar forms seem to continue traditions traced to Chalcolithic origins in Chapter IV above. The plain, angular flaring rims in Fig. 27 belong in this group, as do the hole-mouth jar forms with squared rims. Amiran notes that the hole-mouth jar form itself begins to appear first in the Chalcolithic period (1969. 24).

Traditions of decoration found in Phase III also may be traced back to the indigenous cultures of the land. The thick-walled bowl in Fig. 26:25 is decorated with diagonal indentations in the rim, a feature found at Arad in Stratum V (Amiran Early Arad, Pl. 2:5–7), and in the Beersheba Culture (Amiran 1967, 30, Pl. 4:7). Various kinds of rope-molding on jars, Fig. 33:1–18, are found in Phase III, a feature common in Chalcolithic at Ghassul (Amiran 1969, 27, Pl. 3:4). Also, the tubular lug handle in Fig. 32:4 seems to continue a very ancient feature found in Chalcolithic at Safadi, for instance (see Amiran 1969, 31, Pl. 5:8).

These forms and decoration traditions at Ai in Phase III seem to represent a component of the first urban culture with indigenous roots. One might claim that these traditions were taken over by newcomers and do not necessarily require a continuum of the local inhabitants, but this seems highly improbable. There was an extensive population in the Chalcolithic period, although the settlements were relatively small, and elements of this population seem to have survived the events which brought new cultural elements into the land.

The pottery of Phase III is dominated by forms and decoration which appeared in the region after the Chalcolithic period, and at Site A in Phases I–II, the pre-urban settlement. Among these are the wide platters in Figs. 15:2, 16:26–29, 17:1–5, 26:28–32, 27:1–7; the wide, deep bowls decorated with white slip outside, or reddish-brown slip inside and outside, Figs. 16:17–25, 26:18–27; outcurving, flared jar rims with rolled edges, Figs. 17:22–23, 26, 29, 27:18–21, 24–25; hole-mouth jars with inward-rolled rims, cut rims, and grooved rims; and open spouts, both bell-shaped and pierced, Figs. 23:19–21, 32:19–21.

Dominant among decorative features is the burnished reddish-brown slip, noted as an EB I characteristic by Amiran (1969, 42) and others. Radial-burnishing appears in Phase II at Site A, Fig. 16:28, and net-burnishing appears in Phase III, Fig. 27:7, Reg. No. 4309d. Jugs and juglets are usually hand-burnished vertically. Another common type of decoration is the white slip found primarily on jars, with vertical painted reddish-brown stripes in various patterns and combinations, as in Figs. 21:24, 24:13–23, 33:19–27.

Some new forms appear in Phase III without antecedents in Phase II. Among these are the platter with low rim and shallow concavity under the angle of the rim, Fig. 27:7; net burnished patterns on platters, Fig. 27:7, Reg. No. 4309d; the pierced earlug amphorette, or juglet with burnished net-pattern decoration, Fig. 27:26; the sharply-finished squared jar rim in Fig. 27:23, decorated with burnished reddish-brown slip, high loop handles on jugs, attaching either at the rim, or below, Fig. 32:15–18; and the pillar handle on jars, Fig. 32:16, which may be vestigial of the pierced spout found in Phase II and continuing partial piercing in Phase III.

Notable among forms and decorations not continuing from Phases I–II to III are the twin-loop handle in Fig. 23:16–17; the angular bowl form in Fig. 16:14; and the group-line painted decoration of Fig. 15:10. These forms may appear at other sites in their equivalent of Phase III at Site A, but they do not occur in Building C.

The new pottery traditions in Phase III, evident in the low-rim platter with concavity under the angle of the rim, the pierced ear-lug juglet, the squared jar rim, and the high-loop, jug handle, probably have origins to the north of Canaan. Hennessy cites examples of the squared jar rim from Qalat er-Rouss (1967, Pl. XLIX:2H), Judeideh (*ibid.*, No. 3:J), and Tarsus (*ibid.*, No. 4:J). Painted net patterns are present at the same places, as are examples of the high-loop jug handle, found also at Byblos and Lebea (*ibid.*, Pl. XLVIII:2, 3). Pillar handle jars are found in First Dynasty Egypt, but are regarded as 'foreign ware' (*ibid.*, Pl. XLV:1–3).

Cultural context. Comparative analysis of the Phase III pottery forms and decoration places Building C in the same cultural context with Arad Stratum III, with a few forms found in Stratum II; Phases L–K in Areas E III–IV, Tomb A108, and some elements of Garstang's Level V and Tomb 24 at Jericho; Tomb 14 and Périodes I and II at Tell el-Far'ah (N); and Lapp's first urban phase at Bab edh-Dhra'. Similar cultural features are found also in Megiddo Stages V–IV and Tombs 910 and 1128, and Beth-shan Levels XV–XIV. In a wider context, the artifacts in Phase III at Site A relate to the Late Gerzean and early First Dynasty in Egypt, late Amuq F in Syria, and the Jemdet Nasr period in the upper Euphrates Valley.

Chronology. Albright places the end of EB I (Wright's EB IC) 'between the reign of Narmer, founder of the First Dynasty in Egypt, and the reign of Athothis (Djer)—that is, at some time during the twenty-ninth century B.C. . . .' (1965, 49–50). Wright is less specific in relating the termination of EB IC to Egyptian chronology, dating it simply to the end of the 'post-Ghassulian phase of Palestinian culture before the First Dynasty,' or ± 2900 B.C. (1958, 40). Lapp follows Albright's chronology, but terminates EB IC with the early First Dynasty reign of Djet, the first (or (or second) in succession to Djer (1970, 124). In this latter position, Lapp follows Hennessy (1967,

60, 89, Chart 9), but he assigns the low chronology of Albright to the period, i.e., 2950–2850 B.C. Hennessy dates EB IC to 3050–2950 B.C., or from the founding of the First Dynasty through the reign of Djet. This chronology is influenced by the Carbon 14 date of 3260 ± 110 B.C. obtained in an assay of charred wood from Tomb A94 at Jericho (Kenyon 1960, 25) and the revised *Cambridge Ancient History* date for the founding of the First Dynasty in Egypt ca. 3100 B.C. (see Hayes 1964, 4, and Hennessy 1967, 89). EB IC, in Hennessy's view, is contemporary with the reigns of Hor-aha-Djet (Uadji), down to the beginning of the reign of Den (Udimu) (1967, 85–90).

Two new considerations are introduced into the discussion of chronology of EB IC by the evidence from Ai. First, Phase III at Sites A, C, and D represents a very substantial occupation. At the beginning of this phase, an urban settlement of more than 100 dunams was enclosed by a city wall ranging from 5 to 5½ meters in width. Building C was a part of this city, built against the inner face of the wall. The observation of Hennessy, therefore, that EB I (EB IC) was 'relatively short and marks a transition . . . from the older Proto-Urban culture to the established urban civilization of Early Bronze II' (1967, 86) must be reviewed in the light of the EB IC walled city at Ai. During this period, walled and unwalled cities existed side by side, as Amiran notes (1970, 84–85), so that remains at one site may be quite less substantial than those at another location. The proximity of Ai, some 15 kilometers to the west, may have suppressed the growth of a more substantial city at Jericho in EB IC.

Second, Carbon 14 assays from Sites A, C, and D add to the cumulative evidence ultimately affecting the choice of a high or low chronology. Four assays, three of charred timbers and one of charred seeds, have a bearing upon the beginning date of Phase III, or EB IC. They are as follows:

1. *Sample No.*   *Provenance*   *Date*
    TX 1027   A IV 300.9a   4920 ± 90
                                                               2970 B.C.

Charred reinforcement timber from Wall F³ of Building C, Phase III. Wall F³ continued in use in Phase IV, and was burned in the Phase V destruction of Building B. The superstructure of mud-bricks remained standing and projected upward through the layers of debris filled in around it for the construction of Building A, and Phase VI Wall M. The fill derived from various sources, from Phase IV to Phase VI, but the timber in Wall F³ used in the assay was laid as a binder in constructing the brick wall in Phase III.

2. TX 1034   C VII 600.19   5120 ± 70
                                                               3170 B.C.

Charred seeds from the hearth area in Area C VII built against the inside of Wall C, the Phase III city wall. Building C at Site A is built against the same city wall some 200 meters north of Site C.

3. TX 1032   D IV 300.5   4940 ± 90
                                                               2990 B.C.

Charred wood from Building C, Phase III, at Site D, the acropolis. The wood was a part of the collapsed roof found on the floor of a room in Area IV. The room was abandoned at the end of Phase III and not rebuilt until the beginning of Phase VI, in EB III A.

4. GaK 2379   D IV 300.5   4980 ± 120
                                                               3030 B.C.

Charred wood from Building C, Phase III, at Site D, the acropolis, the same as TX 1032 above.

Assays TX 1027, TX 1032, and TX 1034 were done at the Balcones Research Center of the University of Texas in 1970.* GaK 2379 was done at the Science Laboratory of Gakushuin University, Tokyo, Japan, in 1969.† The calculated age of samples is based upon a half-life of 5570 years, before 1950.

The range of time covered by the assays is as follows:

1.	TX 1027	A IV 300.9a	2880–3060 B.C.
2.	TX 1034	C VII 600.19	3100–3240 B.C.
3.	TX 1032	D IV 300.5	2900–3080 B.C.
4.	GaK 2379	D IV 300.5	2910–3150 B.C.

Dr. E. Mott Davis, Director of the Balcones Research Center, pointed out in a letter to the writer 'that the stated error (±) gives the range within which there is a 2/3 chance that the true radiocarbon age falls; . . .' Furthermore, he noted that 'if the ± ranges of two dates overlap it means that statistically they are indistinguishable.' There is, therefore, considerable leeway in fixing a date for EB IC on the evidence of the Carbon 14 assays. However, the cumulative impact of four dates so close together cannot be ignored. If TX 1034 is eliminated as an aberrant assay on the high side, the remaining three are in remarkable agreement with regard to mean and ± limits. Furthermore, TX 1032 and GaK 2379 are assays of the same sample done independently of each other before the result of one assay could be known by the other laboratory. The agreement in results is impressive.

The mean dates of the three assays, excluding TX 1034 as an aberrant on the high side, average 2997 B.C. Allowing for construction of the city wall before the erection of Building C, a date of 3000 B.C. is possible. All of the three assays are of wood used in the construction of Phase III buildings, although the samples were taken from destruction debris. The deterioration of radiocarbon 14 in the wood began when the wood was cut for the buildings, not when the buildings were destroyed by fire, so the date of 3000 B.C. applies to the beginning of Phase III.

The following sample from Site C indicates a date for the termination of Phase III at ca. 2860 B.C.:

TX 1035	C I 1.31	4810 ± 90
		2860 B.C.

Charred seeds from the destruction of the EB IC building alongside Wall C in Area I of Site C. C I 1.31 is across a meter balk from C VII 600.19, and is a part of the same building.

The effect of this date of 3000–2860 B.C. for EB IC is two-fold. First, it extends the period a half-century beyond the 100 years proposed by Lapp (2950–2850 B.C.) and Hennessy (3050–2950 B.C.). Evidence of the extensive Phase III walled city supports the lengthened period required by the

* The writer is indebted to Dr. E. Mott Davis, Director, and Mr. S. Valastro, Assistant Director, for the assays, which will be published in *Radiocarbon* in 1971 or 1972. Dean Prescott Williams, Jr., of Austin Presbyterian Theological Seminary arranged the scheduling of the assays, for which the writer is grateful.

† Indebtedness to Dr. Kunihiko Kigoshi, Professor on the Science Faculty, for expediting the assay is gladly acknowledged. Another sample, GaK 2381 from C I 1.28b, gives a date of 3050 B.C. (± 120), which is aberrant because the provenance is a Phase V destruction layer. The sample assayed was charred wood, but the sample collected in C I 1.28b was charred seeds. GaK 2381 seems to be another assay of D IV 300.5 instead of C I 1.28b, and therefore supports GaK 2379 if that is the case. The assay of the C I 1.28b seeds by the Balcones Research Laboratory, TX 1030 dated to 2680 B.C. (± 70), seems to reflect the Phase V destruction.

Carbon 14 dates. Second, a mean between the high chronology of the revised *Cambridge Ancient History* and the low chronology of Albright is required, although Albright's date for the termination of the period is supported. If the half-century extension of the period is added on the high side of Albright's date, i.e., 2950 B.C. becomes 3000 B.C., the Carbon 14 dates from Ai support his chronology.

THE FIRST URBAN PHASE AND ITS POPULATION

The extent and nature of the Phase III city will be examined at length in Vol. III of the Ai reports, *The Early Bronze Age Acropolis at Ai (et-Tell)*, in connection with the report of the Phase III acropolis buildings. A completely new, and very extensive, acropolis complex with its own walled enclosure within the city was constructed in Phase III as a part of the city-building operation. Building C at Site A contributes to this first urban phase, but Site D, the acropolis, is the type-site for understanding its significance.

One point concerning the relation of Building C at Site A to the first walled city is of importance here. The process of growth from unwalled to walled settlements in Canaan is not well known, as Lapp notes in his discussion of fortified towns and settlements of EB IC–III (1970, 109–17). Kenyon states that Jericho probably had a 'fully developed occupation before the town was actually walled. . .' (1970, 107), as did Tell el-Far'ah (N) (*ibid.*, 109). Jericho and Tell el-Far'ah (N) seem to have developed flourishing EB IC towns first, which led to the construction of town walls at some point during the period. The case at Ai seems to be different.

At Site A, the town wall was constructed *before* Building C was erected alongside its inner face. This point was discussed in Chapter II in connection with Section F–F, where the sequence seems to have been (1) construction of Wall C on the fill of Phase II at Site A, (2) installation of fill over the ruins of the Phase II huts preparatory to construction of Building C, and (3) the erection of Building C alongside the completed city wall and tower protecting the Citadel Gate. The city wall and Building C seem to have been a part of the same planned city-building operation at Ai. This, of course, could be due to the auxiliary role that Building C played in relation to Tower C of the citadel and possibly is not representative of the development process, but evidence from Site C and the Lower City suggests strongly that it is representative.

Wall C at Site C is built across the ruins of the Phase II unwalled settlement, so Wall C did not develop out of that settlement. The buildings in Phase III at Site C either use Wall C as an outside wall, as in C VII, or they parallel Wall C with a road some 1.50 to 1.75 meters separating the houses from the city wall. The parallel course of building is exact, even to gentle curves, as is evident in the Marquet-Krause Lower City. Chambre 239 in Fouille V4 (Marquet-Krause 1949, Pl. C), a road alongside Wall C gently curves toward the north at the end next to Chambre 242, and the contemporary structure along its northeast side curves with the city wall, as though they were built in the same planned operation.

The evidence at Site A, therefore, indicates a planned building operation at the beginning of Phase III resulting in the establishment of a major city. At every site, the components of this city show no indebtedness to those of the previous unwalled settlement. Only the population continues to some extent, as the pottery indicates. The conclusion seems warranted that leadership for construction of the first urban phase at Ai was not indigenous, but was imposed from the outside.

The Phase III city was inhabited by a substantial element of indigenous people whose pottery culture roots back to Chalcolithic traditions. Considerable amalgamation took place by Phase III, however, in the mixture of the indigenous population elements with an increment of newcomers from North Syria and Central to Eastern Anatolia just prior to establishment of the pre-urban settlement in Phases I–II. Another increment of population at the beginning of Phase III is indicated by the new pottery forms noted earlier, most of which can be traced to Coastal and North Syria and Southern Anatolia. This group undoubtedly provided the imaginative leadership required to build the extensive Phase III walled city with its planned acropolis, gates, fortification towers, and residential area on the east terraces of the *tell*.

DESCRIPTIONS OF PHASE III POTTERY AND OBJECTS, FIGS. 26–33

Fig. 26 No.	Reg. No.	
1	5132a	Rim upcurved to thin, rounded edge, wheel-finished; orangish-buff; medium with many fine white grits; brown incrustations over-all. A IV 300.18a.
—	5029f	Rim of small bowl upcurved to thin, rounded edge; buff inside and orange outside; coarse with few assorted, and many fine, white grits; spalling over-all, black smoke marks on rim indicate possible use as lamp. A IV 300.14e.
2	4344	Rim incurved to thin, rounded, vertical edge, wheel-finished; buff; fine with many assorted white and grey grits. A II 102.8.
3	4215b	Rim slightly incurved to thin, vertical, rounded edge; orangish-buff; coarse with few fine white grits; traces of horizontal-burnishing inside and outside; black smoke marks on rim indicate possible use as lamp. A II 103.3.
4	4632	Rim incurved to thin, rounded edge; orange inside to outside edge, tan outside and core; coarse with few small white grits; some assorted pits, grey smoke mark outside. A III 202.4.
5	4823	Rim slightly upcurved to rounded edge; brownish-buff with orangish-buff core; medium-coarse with many assorted white grits; very uneven surfaces, some assorted pits, some brown incrustations outside. A III 204.5.
6	4685a	Rim upcurved to thin, rounded edge; buff; coarse with few assorted white and grey grits; rough texture inside, one very large and few assorted pits inside, pitted and spalling outside, black marks on rim indicate possible use as lamp. A III 202.8.
7	4325	Rim upcurved to slightly thickened, rounded edge; buff; coarse with some assorted white grits; very worn. A II 102.6.
8	4341	Rim upcurved to thin, rounded, vertical edge; buff with tan outside; medium with many small to fine, white grits; some grey incrustations, rough, hand-finished texture outside. A II 102.8.
9	4317	Rim upcurved to thin, rounded edge, wheel-made; reddish-orange; medium with some small to fine, white grits; radially-burnished inside and wheel-burnished outside. A II 102.6.
—	4956d	Body sherd, wheel finished; light pinkish-brown; medium-coarse with some fine light- and dark-grey grits; traces of continuously-burnished reddish-brown slip outside. A IV 300.13.
—	5029k	Body sherd of shallow bowl, wheel-turned; pinkish-buff; medium-coarse with many assorted grey and tan grits; traces of reddish-brown slip inside and outside, continuously-burnished. A IV 300.14e.

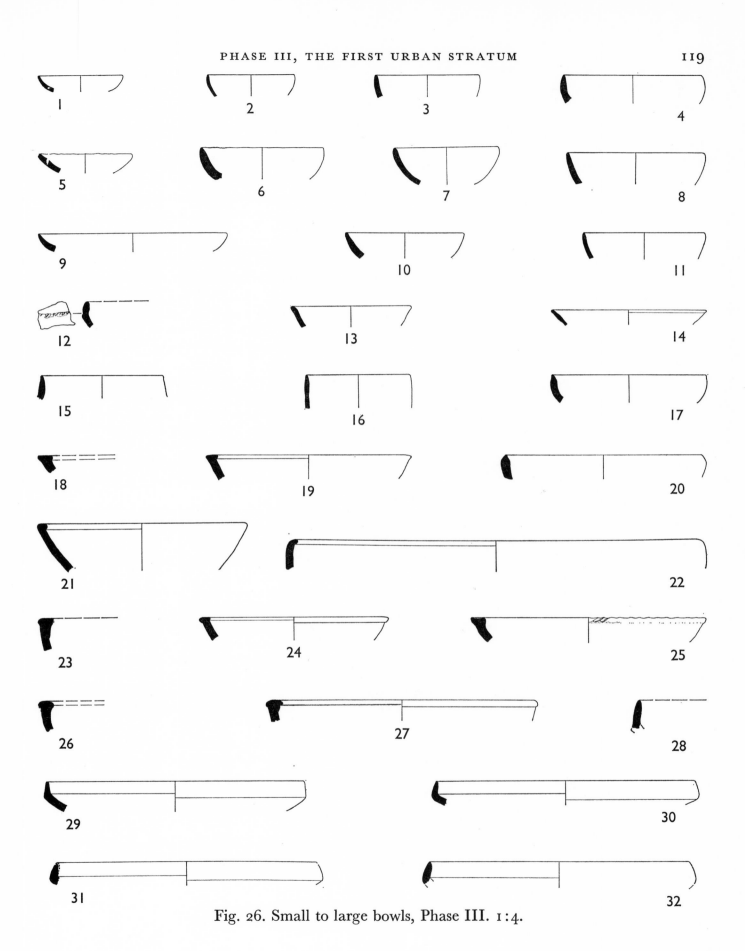

Fig. 26. Small to large bowls, Phase III. 1:4.

Fig. 26 *No.*	*Reg.* *No.*	
—	5143h	Body sherd of shallow bowl, wheel-turned; buff; medium with many small to fine, white grits; reddish-brown slip, continuously-burnished, outside, pitted and spalling inside. A IV 300.20.
10	4606	Rim upcurved to thin, rounded edge; buff; medium with some small to fine, white grits. A III 201.13a.
11	4217	Rim upcurved to thin, rounded, vertical edge, wheel-made; orangish-buff; medium-coarse with some small to fine, white grits; pronounced crazing over-all, some grey incrustations. A II 103.3.
12	5130	Rim inverted with rounded edge, some thickening at angle; buff; medium-coarse with some assorted white grits; very narrow, straight, half-relief molding at angle outside with closely spaced, diagonal indentations, faint traces of burnished, reddish-brown slip over-all. A IV 300.18a.
13	5101b	Angular wall with slightly everted rim, wheel-made; tan outside and orangish-buff inside, very thick, dark-grey core; medium with some medium to very fine, grey and white grits; traces of continuously-burnished, reddish-orange slip outside rim. A IV 300.15.
14	5125	Angular wall with slightly everted rim, slight roll outside, wheel-made; buff; medium with few assorted grits; traces of wheel-burnished, reddish-brown slip over-all. A IV 300.18a.
15	5101	Rim slightly outcurved to thinned, rounded edge, hand-made and wet-smoothed; pinkish-buff; medium with some assorted grey and white quartz grits. A IV 300.15.
16	4294	Rim upturned to straight, thin edge, wheel-made; buff with grey core; fine with many assorted white grits; traces of brown slip inside and outside, wheel-burnished rim. A II 101.10.
17	5124	Rim slightly incurved to thin, rounded edge, wheel-made; dark-grey; medium-coarse with many assorted white, grey, and tan grits; tan slip inside, traces of wheel-burnished, reddish-brown slip outside; few assorted pits. A IV 300.18a.
18	4609b	Rim upcurved to flattened edge, projected in; buff; coarse with some small to fine, white grits. A III 201.13a.
19	4343	Rim upcurved to flat edge projected in, wheel-turned inside and on edge; buff with tan outside; medium-coarse with some assorted white and tan grits, porous ware; traces of reddish-brown slip inside; pink discolorations and very rough, pitted texture outside, some grey incrustations over-all. A II 102.8.
20	4814	Rim upcurved to thickened, rounded, pointed edge, wheel-made; orange inside and buff outside; coarse with many assorted white grits and one very large, red grit. A III 204.5.
21	4215a	Rim slightly upcurved to thick, flattened edge, projected in, wheel-made; orange inside, dark-grey outside and core; traces of white slip outside, and inside edge; some assorted pits over-all, some grey incrustations. A II 103.3.
22	5029e	Rim upcurved to inverted, rounded edge projecting in, wheel-finished; buff with grey core; coarse with few assorted tan grits; traces of white slip outside; pitted inside, grey incrustations over-all. A IV 300.14e.
23	5040	Rim upright with thickened, flat edge projected in, slight rounded ridge outside; orange with very thick, dark-grey core; medium-coarse with some assorted white and tan grits, rough texture over-all. A I 1.6.
24	4342	Rim upcurved to rounded, flat edge with small inverted inner lip; rounded ridge outside; orange with thick, dark-grey core; medium-coarse with few assorted white grits. A II 102.8.

Fig. 26 *No.*	*Reg.* *No.*	
25	4609a	Rim upcurved to flat depressed edge projected slightly in, rolled ridge outside; buff; coarse with some small to fine, white grits; closely spaced, diagonal indentations in rolled ridge outside, faint traces of brown slip; uneven surfaces over-all. A III 201.13a.
26	5099	Rim slightly incurved to rounded, flattened edge, wheel-finished; buff with grey core; coarse with many small to fine, white and tan grits; rough texture outside with some grey incrustations. A IV 300.15.
27	5058d	Rim upright, slightly rounded, flat edge with inverted, drooping inner lip; orangish-buff; medium-coarse with some assorted white-grits; some grey incrustations. A I 2.2.
28	5143c	Rim slightly inverted to wide, thinned, rounded edge, wheel-turned; dark-grey; medium-coarse with some fine white grits; traces of wheel-burnished, reddish-brown slip over-all. A IV 300.20.
29	4684	Rim slightly inverted from carination, wheel-turned; buff with grey core; coarse with many assorted dark-grey, tan, white, and reddish-brown grits; traces of burnished, reddish-brown slip outside; some crazing inside. A III 202.8.
30	4612	Rim upturned to thin, rounded, inverted edge, wheel-made; buff; fine with many small to fine, white and grey grits; traces of wheel-burnished slip outside and on edge. A III 201.13b.
31	4309b	Rim inverted with medium-wide, thinned, rounded edge, wheel-turned; reddish-brown; medium-coarse with many assorted reddish-brown, dark-grey and white grits; traces of wheel-burnishing. A II 102.5.
32	4291	Rim upturned to thinned, rounded edge, wheel-made; buff with grey core; medium with few fine white grits; traces of wheel-burnished, reddish-brown slip inside and outside; some assorted pits outside. A II 101.10.
—	4820	Body sherd; buff; very fine with many fine, and few medium to small, white grits; reddish-brown slip, radially-burnished inside and horizontally-burnished outside. A III 204.5.
—	4808	Body sherd; buff with orange core; medium-coarse with many assorted dark-grey grits; traces of reddish-brown slip outside, continuously burnished. A III 204.5.

Fig. 27 *No.*	*Reg.* *No.*	
1	4822	Rim inverted to thin, rounded edge, wheel-made; buff; medium-coarse with many assorted grey grits; faint traces of wheel-burnished, reddish-brown slip outside; orange discoloration inside. A III 204.5.
2	5058e	Rim inverted with thinned, rounded edge, wheel-turned; dark-buff; medium with many small dark-grey and white grits; traces of wheel-burnished, reddish-brown slip over-all. A I 2.2.
3	4218a	Rim inverted with medium-wide, rounded edge, wheel-turned; reddish-buff; medium with some assorted dark-grey and reddish-brown grits; traces of wheel-burnished, reddish-brown slip over-all. A III 201.13.
4	4809	Rim sharply carinated with thinned, rounded edge, some thickening at angle, wheel-made; reddish-orange with thick, dark-grey core; medium with assorted, mostly fine, grey grits; reddish-brown slip continuously-burnished inside angle of carination, burnished stripe inside wall, wheel-burnished outside, continuing slightly over edge to inside; many assorted pits over-all. A III 204.5.
5	5038	Rim carinated with thinned, rounded edge, wheel-made; reddish-buff; medium-coarse with some fine white grits; reddish brown slip radially-burnished inside, wheel-burnished inside edge and outside to angle of wall; some assorted pits on unburnished portion outside, some incrustation on unburnished portion. A I 1.5a.

Fig. 27 *No.*	*Reg.* *No.*	
6	5135	Rim carinated with rounded edge, wheel-made; brown; medium with some assorted tan grits; traces of wheel-burnished, reddish-brown slip outside; pitted and flaking inside and edge, many assorted pits and some flaking outside. A IV 300.20.
7	4626	Rim slightly upcurved to inverted edge, slight thickening at angle, wheel-made; orangish-brown; fine with many assorted, mostly brown, grits; traces of wheel-burnished, reddish-brown slip inside and outside edge (4626, 4629, and 4635 joined). A III 202.4.
—	4309d	Body sherd of bowl, wheel-turned; pinkish-brown; medium with few small to fine, white and tan grits; reddish-brown slip, net-pattern of burnished lines, both sides, superimposed on pattern of parallel, burnished lines. A II 102.5.
—	4309e	Body sherd of bowl, wheel-turned; pinkish-brown; medium with few small to fine, tan grits; reddish-brown slip with random burnished lines outside. A II 102.5.
8	4350b	Rim outcurved to thinned rolled edge, wheel-finished; brownish-buff; coarse with some assorted white and grey grits. A II 102.8.
9	5058f	Rim sharply flared out to medium rolled edge, wheel-finished; tannish buff; coarse with few assorted white grits; rough gritty texture inside, grey incrustations over-all. A I 2.2.
10	4628	Rim sharply flared out to thin, rolled edge, wheel-made; buff with dark-grey core; medium-coarse with many medium grey grits; many assorted pits inside and few assorted pits outside, very rough texture inside (4628, 4633 joined). A III 202.4.
11	4610	Rim wheel-made; bright-orange inside and orangish-black outside, dark-grey core; coarse with many assorted white grits; some grey incrustations. A III 201.13b.
12	5101c	Rim outcurved to thinned, rounded edge, wheel-finished; medium-coarse with some small to fine, grey, white and tan grits; traces of white slip outside; greyish-brown incrustations over-all. A IV 300.15.
13	4500	Rim slightly flared to thinned, rounded edge, wheel-made; orange with thick, dark-grey core; medium-coarse with few assorted white grits; many pits, some grey incrustations. A I 1.7.
14	4332	Rim slightly flared to rounded edge; deep orange with grey core; coarse with some assorted white and grey grits; many small to fine pits. A II 102.7.
15	4216	Rim sharply flared out to thin, rounded edge, wheel-made; thick, dark-grey core; coarse with some assorted white grits; uneven surface inside. A II 103.3.
16	4293	Rim sharply everted with thin, rounded edge, wheel-made; dark-orange; medium with one large, some small, and many fine white grits; very rough texture inside. A II 101.10.
17	4208	Rim sharply everted with thin, rounded edge, pronounced thickening at point of bend; buff with grey core; medium-coarse with many assorted grits of various colors; many assorted pits inside and some assorted pits outside, very rough texture inside. A II 103.2.
18	4685	Rim sharply outcurved to thin, rounded edge, wheel-finished; pinkish-buff with thick, dark-grey core; very coarse with some assorted grey, white, and reddish-brown grits, porous ware; many assorted pits over-all. A III 202.8.
19	5101d	Rim sharply flared out to short, thinned, rounded edge, wheel-finished; reddish-orange with very thick, dark-grey core; medium-coarse with many fine to very fine, white and tan grits; some greyish-brown incrustations over-all. A IV 300.15.
20	4337	Rim sharply flared out to thinned, rounded edge; tan with pinkish-buff outside; medium-coarse with few assorted white grits; traces of white slip outside; few assorted pits inside and one large pit outside, some grey incrustations. A II 102.8.
—	4350c	Neck and rim fragment of jar, flared out; dark-buff with grey core; coarse with some assorted tan and white grits; some assorted pits over-all. A II 102.8.

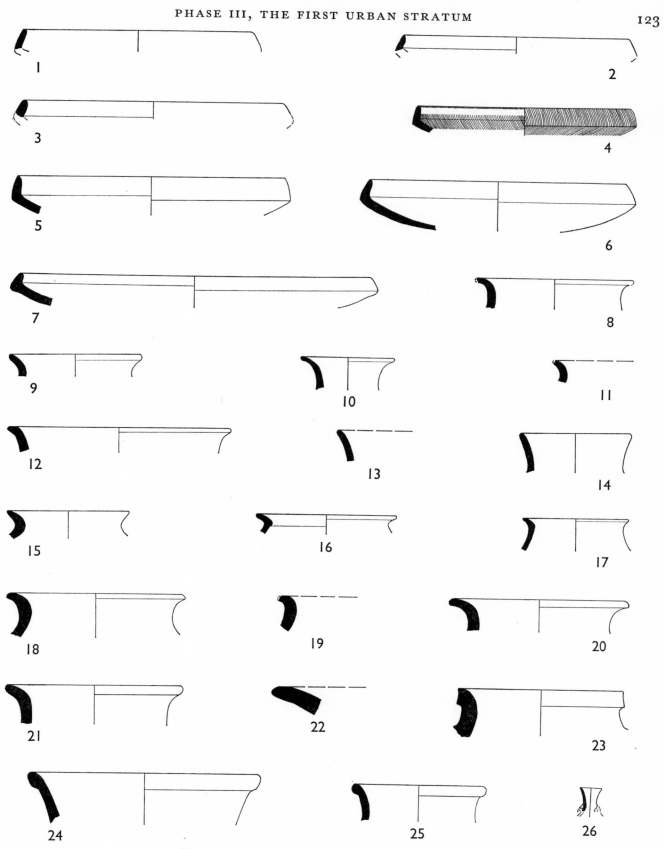

Fig. 27. Bowls and jars, Phase III. 1:4.

Fig. 27 No.	Reg. No.	
—	4824d	Neck fragment of jar, wheel-finished; buff with grey core; coarse with many fine white grits; grey and white incrustations over-all. A III 204.5.
—	4956c	Neck fragment of jar, slightly outcurved; orange with thick, dark-grey core; medium-coarse with some fine white grits; white slip, horizontal, painted red lines outside. A IV 300.13.
—	4821	Neck fragment of jar; orange outside and tan inside, grey core; medium-coarse with some medium to fine, black grits, very porous ware; traces of reddish-brown slip outside. A III 204.5.
—	4824l	Neck fragment of jar; pinkish-buff; coarse with few assorted white grits; white slip outside with traces of medium-wide, vertical, painted red stripes. A III 204.5.
21	4209	Heavy rim sharply flared to rolled edge; buff inside and reddish-orange outside, thick, dark-grey core; very coarse with many assorted grits of various colors; many assorted pits over-all, flaking outside and on edge. A II 103.2.
22	4824n	Heavy rim sharply flared out to thick, rounded edge, wet-smoothed; orange with dark-buff core; very coarse with some assorted tan and grey grits; grey incrustations over-all. A III 204.5.
23	4613	Heavy rim outcurved to well-shaped, squared edge projected out, wheel-finished; buff inside and pinkish-tan outside, greyish-tan core; coarse with many assorted dark-grey grits; traces of wheel-burnished, reddish-brown slip outside and inside rim; many assorted pits, some grey incrustations outside. A III 201.14.
24	4627	Heavy rim outcurved to rolled edge, projected out; yellowish-tan with very thick, reddish core; very coarse with many small and fine white grits; traces of heavy, white slip outside; many assorted pits inside, some grey incrustations. A III 202.4.
25	4497	Rim outcurved to rolled edge; buff; coarse with many assorted white grits; traces of heavy, white slip outside; many assorted pits inside and on edge, some grey incrustations. A I 1.7.
—	4326a	Neck fragment of jar; orangish-buff with grey core; very coarse with many fine white grits; rough, uneven surface inside. A II 102.6.
—	4824e	Neck fragment of large jar, slightly outcurved with ridged line outside of transition between shoulder and neck; pinkish-buff with grey patches inside; very coarse with some assorted white grits; white slip outside; rough spalling surface inside, brown incrustations over-all. A II 204.5.
26	4635f	Neck of juglet, slightly flared to thinned, rounded edge, remnant of two small, vertical, lug handles pierced through on either side of neck; orange; fine with some medium to fine, brown and grey grits; traces of burnished reddish-brown slip outside; some pitting over-all. A III 202.4.
—	5029j	Body sherd of juglet; tannish-buff; medium with many small to fine, dark-grey grits; continuously-burnished, reddish-brown slip outside; grey incrustations over-all. A IV 300.14e.
—	5132d	Body sherd of jug; brownish-buff; medium with some assorted dark-grey grits; continuously-burnished red slip outside; some grey incrustations over-all. A IV 300.18a.
—	5122d	Neck fragment of jug, with neck joined separately to shoulder; tan; medium with many small to very fine, black and brown grits; tool-finished outside with vertically-burnished, reddish-brown slip. A IV 300.18.
—	5143f	Neck fragment of jug; pinkish-buff; coarse with few assorted white and reddish-brown grits; traces of burnished, reddish-brown slip outside; rough, gritty texture inside; light-grey incrustations over-all. A IV 300.20.

Fig. 28 No.	Reg. No.	
1	4816	Rim incurved to wide, greatly thickened, rounded edge, wheel-finished; orangish-buff; very coarse with few medium to fine, white grits; traces of heavy, white slip outside; many assorted pits inside, very rough texture inside. A III 204.5.
2	5029d	Rim incurved to wide, very thickened, rounded, beveled edge, wheel-finished; buff inside and orangish-grey outside, grey core; medium-coarse with some assorted, mostly fine, white grits; some spalling outside edge. A IV 300.14e.
3	5129	Rim incurved to medium-wide, thickened, rounded edge; orangish-buff with dark-orangish-buff core; coarse with many assorted white and grey grits; traces of white slip outside and on edge inside. A IV 300.18a.
4	5143a	Rim incurved to medium-wide, thickened, rounded edge, folded over inside, edge wheel-finished; dark greyish-orange with dark-brown core; medium-coarse with many medium to fine, white and grey grits; rough gritty texture inside, black smoke marks on edge. A IV 300.20.
5	5029a	Rim incurved to wide, very thickened, rounded edge; dark-buff inside and reddish-brown outside; coarse with many assorted grey and tan grits; gritty texture inside, light, grey incrustations over-all. A IV 300.14e.
6	5132	Rim incurved to narrow, thickened, rounded edge; buff with dark-grey core penetrating to outside in places; medium-coarse with many assorted white and light-grey grits; very uneven surface inside. A IV 300.18a.
7	4609d	Rim incurved to wide, greatly thickened, rounded edge, outside swollen; greyish-buff with thick, dark-grey core; very coarse with many assorted white and light-grey quartz grits; rough, gritty texture over-all, very uneven surface outside. A III 201.13a.
8	4329	Rim incurved to wide, thickened, rounded edge, wheel-finished; greyish-brown with thick, dark-grey core penetrating to outside in places; very coarse with many assorted grey quartz grits; some large and assorted pits. A II 102.7.
9	4596	Rim incurved to medium-wide, thickened, rounded edge, ridge low inside edge, wheel-finished; greyish-buff with grey core; coarse with many assorted grey quartz grits. A III 201.13a.
10	4499	Rim incurved to very wide, thickened, rounded flattened edge, wheel-finished; orange with grey core; medium-coarse with many assorted white and grey grits. A I 1.7.
11	4315	Rim incurved to wide, thickened, rounded edge; buff; coarse with many assorted white and grey grits; pitted and flaking outside, some grey and white incrustations over-all. A II 102.6.
12	4608	Rim incurved to wide, thickened, rounded beveled edge; orangish-buff inside and greyish-buff outside, orange and grey core; coarse with very many assorted grey quartz grits; few large and some assorted pits, crazing on edge and outside, grey smoke marks and some flaking outside. A III 201.13a.
13	5039	Rim incurved to medium-wide, thickened, rounded edge, wheel-finished; buff with pinkish-buff core; coarse with few assorted white grits; traces of white slip outside; some orange discoloration inside, many assorted pits and very rough texture inside, some grey incrustation. A I 1.6.
14	4681	Rim incurved to narrow, rounded edge, folded in; orangish-buff inside and greyish-brown outside, dark-buff core; very coarse with many very assorted grey and white grits; many assorted pits and very uneven surfaces over-all, some crazing outside, black smoke marks inside. A III 202.8.
15	4594	Rim incurved to wide, greatly thickened, rounded, beveled edge; wheel-finished; orange with buff core; coarse with very many assorted white and grey quartz grits. A III 201.13a.

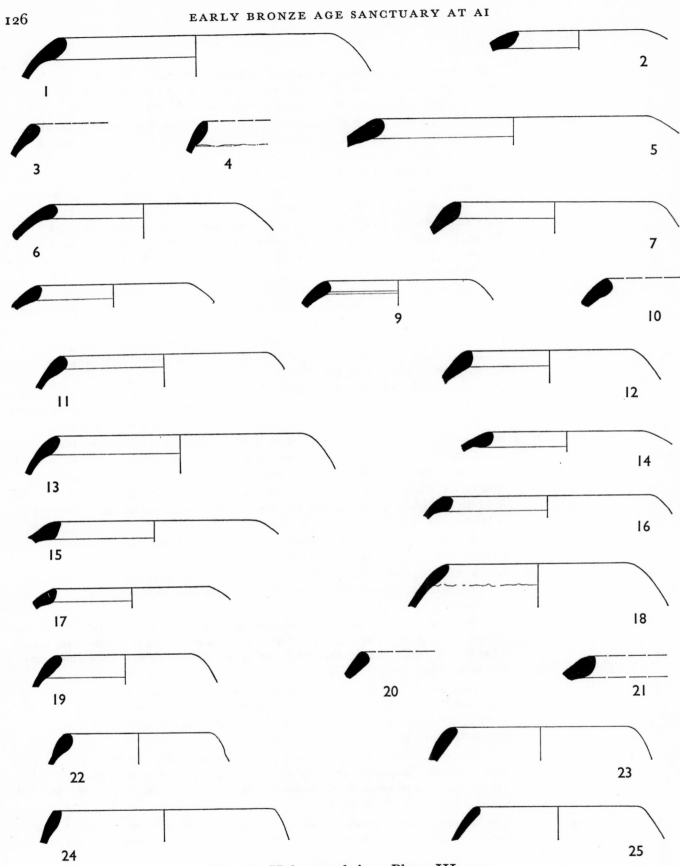

Fig. 28. Hole-mouth jars, Phase III. 1:4.

Fig. 28 *No.*	*Reg.* *No.*	
16	4630	Rim incurved to medium-wide, greatly thickened, rounded edge, wheel-finished; reddish-orange; coarse with many assorted grey and white grits, porous ware; many assorted pits over-all, grey smoke marks outside, flaking inside. A III 202.4.
17	4670	Rim incurved to narrow, thickened, rounded, beveled edge; wheel-finished; brown; coarse with many assorted grey quartz and white grits; black smoke marks on rim, spalling on rim. A III 202.6.
18	4321	Rim incurved to wide, thickened, rounded edge, wheel-finished; buff; medium-coarse with many assorted grey and white grits; orange discoloration outside, grey smoke marks inside, very rough surface inside at joint of rim fold. A II 102.6.
19	4316	Rim incurved to wide, greatly thickened, rounded edge, wheel-finished; greyish-orange; with buff inside; coarse with many grey grits; grey smoke marks. A II 102.6.
20	4609c	Rim incurved to medium-wide, thickened, rounded edge; dull orange with buff core; coarse with many assorted grey and tan grits; rough, uneven surfaces over-all. A III 201.13a.
21	4635b	Rim incurved to very wide, greatly thickened, rounded, beveled edge; dull orange; medium-coarse with many assorted dark-grey quartz grits. A III 202.4.
22	4326	Rim incurved to medium-wide, greatly thickened, rounded edge, wheel-finished; orangish-buff; coarse with many assorted white and light-grey grits; some assorted pits inside, very worn. A II 102.6.
23	4326b	Rim slightly incurved to wide, thickened, rounded edge, wheel-finished; orangish-grey with thick, dark-grey core; coarse with many assorted, mostly small, grey grits; black smoke marks outside. A II 102.6.
24	4309	Rim incurved to wide, thickened, rounded edge; tannish-buff with thick, dark-grey core, penetrating to outside in places; very coarse with some assorted white and quartz grits, very porous ware; many assorted large to fine pits. A II 102.5.
25	4346	Rim incurved to wide thickened rounded edge; buff inside and brown outside with brownish-grey core; very coarse with many assorted white and bluish-grey grits; many assorted pits, pronounced cracking and crazing, grey smoke marks over-all. A II 102.8.
Fig. 29 *No.*	*Reg.* *No.*	
1	4599	Rim incurved to medium-wide, thickened, rounded edge, wheel-finished; brown inside and tan outside, greyish-tan core; medium-coarse with many assorted grey quartz grits; very rough texture inside. A III 201.13a.
2	4211	Rim incurved to thickened, inturned, round edge; dark-orange inside and orangish-buff outside, with buff core; medium-coarse with many assorted white, grey, and tan grits; traces of white slip outside; some very large and fine pits over-all. A II 103.2.
3	4806	Rim incurved to medium-wide, thickened, tapered edge; orange with thick, dark-grey core; coarse with many assorted white grits; traces of white slip outside; one very large and few assorted pits. A III 204.5.
4	4205	Rim incurved to wide, thickened, rounded edge; buff with thick, dark-grey core; medium-coarse with many assorted grey quartz grits; some diagonal indentations inside edge, orange discoloration inside, grey smoke marks outside, many assorted, mostly fine, pits. A II 103.2.
5	4196	Rim incurved to rounded, flattened edge; orange with grey core; coarse with many small to fine, white grits; traces of white slip outside; some assorted pits over-all, some grey incrustations. A II 103.1.

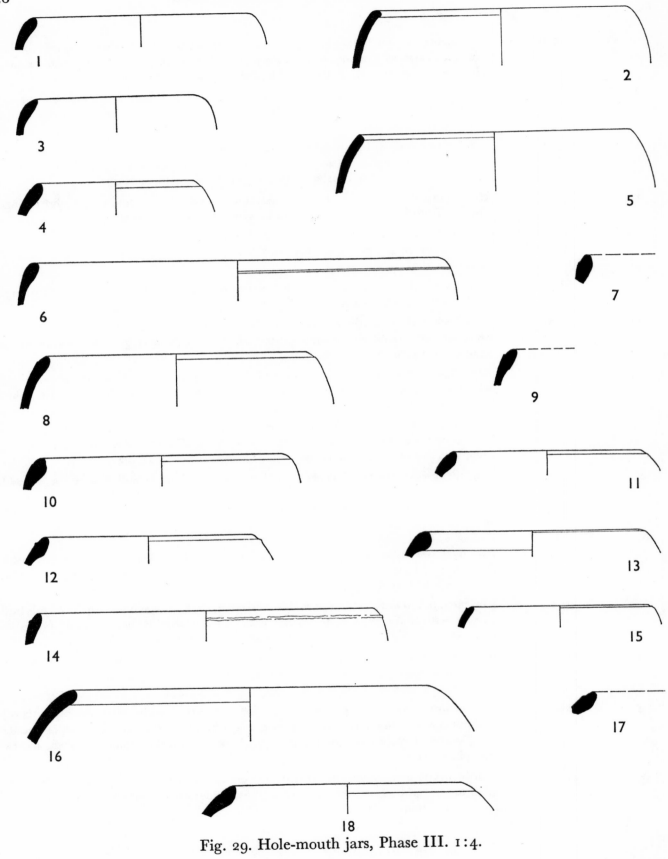

Fig. 29. Hole-mouth jars, Phase III. 1:4.

Fig. 29 *No.*	*Reg.* *No.*	
6	5139	Rim slightly incurved to wide, thickened, rounded edge with faint ridge outside; dark-grey; coarse with many assorted white grits, many assorted tan grits concentrated inside; traces of tan wash outside and on edge. A IV 300.20.
7	5101a	Rim slightly incurved to wide thickened rounded edge with low ridge outside, wheel-finished; orange outside and buff inside, grey core in thickened portion; medium-coarse with some medium to fine, white, grey quartz, and tan grits; some brownish-grey incrustations over-all. A IV 300.15.
8	5058	Rim incurved to wide, thickened, rounded edge; dark-grey; very coarse with some small to fine, white grits; traces of white slip outside; smoke marks inside, some grey incrustations. A I 1.7.
9	4600	Rim incurved to medium-wide, thickened, rounded edge with pronounced ridge outside, wheel-finished; orange with thick, dark-grey core penetrating to outside; coarse with some assorted white grits. A III 201.13a.
10	4194	Rim incurved to wide, greatly thickened, rounded edge with pronounced ridge outside; grey; very coarse with many assorted white grits; many assorted pits and rough texture over-all. A II 103.2.
11	4292	Rim incurved to wide, thickened, rounded edge with low ridge outside, wheel-finished; orange inside and dark-grey outside, thick, dark-grey core; coarse with many assorted, mostly small to fine, white grits; rough texture over-all. A II 101.10.
12	4815	Rim incurved to medium-wide, greatly thickened, rounded edge with pronounced ridge outside, wheel-finished; buff inside and orange outside, thick, grey core; coarse with many assorted white grits; one large elongated pit inside, some assorted pits on edge and outside. A III 204.5.
13	4290	Rim incurved to medium-wide, greatly thickened, rounded, beveled edge with low ridge outside, wheel-finished; orange with thick, buff core; coarse with very many assorted, mostly large, grey quartz grits; few very large pits, grey smoke marks outside and on edge. A II 101.9a.
14	4824	Rim slightly incurved to medium-wide, thickened, rounded edge with pronounced ridge outside, wheel-finished; buff with orange inside; coarse with many assorted grey grits; dark-grey smoke marks inside. A III 204.5.
15	4348	Rim incurved to slightly thickened rounded edge with pronounced ridge outside, wheel-finished; orangish-buff with dark-grey core; medium-coarse with many small to fine, white grits; black smoke marks outside. A II 102.8.
16	5096	Rim incurved to thickened, rounded edge, buff; coarse with many assorted tan and grey grits, many fine black grits; traces of burnished, reddish-brown slip outside and inside edge; grey incrustations over-all. A IV 300.15.
17	4635a	Rim incurved to wide thickened, rounded, beveled edge with pronounced ridge outside, wet-smoothed; orangish-brown with dark-grey core; very coarse with many assorted grey grits; black smoke marks outside. A III 202.4.
18	4336	Rim incurved to wide, thickened, rounded edge with shallow groove outside below edge; buff with orange inside; coarse with very many assorted grey grits; some orange discoloration outside, grey smoke marks inside. A II 102.8.
—	5143b	Rim slightly incurved to very wide, greatly thickened, rounded edge; buff with greyish-white inside core; very coarse with some assorted grey, tan, white, and reddish-brown grits; traces of heavy, white slip outside; very uneven surfaces over-all, some incrustations. A IV 300.20.

Fig. 30 No.	Reg. No.	
1	4824b	Rim incurved to medium-wide, greatly thickened, rounded edge with ridge outside; orangish-buff; coarse with many assorted grey grits; grey incrustations over-all. A III 204.5.
2	4635c	Rim incurved to wide, greatly thickened, rounded beveled edge with faint ridge outside; dull orange with greyish-buff core; very coarse with many assorted grey grits; diagonal ridges on surface outside. A III 202.4.
3	5029c	Rim incurved to wide, thickened, rounded edge with ridge outside; greyish-buff; coarse with many assorted grey grits; black smoke marks on edge, rough texture over-all. A IV 300.14e.
4	5029b	Rim incurved to medium-wide, thickened, rounded, beveled edge with low ridge outside; orangish-buff inside and grey outside; coarse with many assorted white and grey grits; spalling over-all. A IV 300.14e.
5	5126	Rim incurved to thickened rounded edge, wheel-finished; buffish-grey inside and greyish-brown outside with buff core; coarse with very many assorted white and grey quartz grits; very narrow, slightly wavy, high-relief ridged molding outside; grey smoke marks inside and black smoke marks outside. A IV 300.18a.
6	4807	Rim incurved to very wide, greatly thickened, semi-rounded, flattened edge, wheel-finished; brown inside and black outside, dark-grey core in places; coarse with very many assorted grey grits; orange discoloration outside, grey smoke marks inside and on edge. A III 204.5.
7	5119	Rim incurved to thickened, semi-rounded, edge, wheel-finished; orangish-grey inside and buff outside with thick, dark-grey core; with very many assorted grey and white quartz grits; many fine pits outside and one very large pit and flaking inside. A IV 300.18.
8	5122a	Rim incurved to very wide, greatly thickened, semi-rounded, flattened edge, wet-smoothed; brown inside and buff outside, grey core; rough, gritty texture over-all. A IV 300.18.
9	4824a	Rim of jar, incurved to thickened, flattened edge with shallow depression; dull orange; coarse with few assorted white grits; traces of white slip outside; grey incrustations over-all. A III 204.5.
10	5131	Rim incurved to wide, greatly thickened, rounded edge, wheel-finished; buff; medium-coarse with many assorted white and light-grey grits; closely spaced, large diagonal indentations outside at thickening of edge; very uneven surface inside. A IV 300.18a.
11	4824c	Rim incurved to thickened, semi-flattened edge; orangish-brown with grey core; coarse with many assorted light-grey grits; rough, uneven surfaces over-all. A III 204.5.
12	4295	Rim inclined out to wide, thickened, rounded edge; dark-grey; coarse with some assorted white grits; buff slip over-all. A II 101.10.
13	4604	Upright rim incurved to wide, very thickened, rounded edge, wheel-finished; orange inside and buff outside, grey core; medium-coarse with many assorted, mostly fine, white grits. A III 201.13a.
14	4347	Rim upcurved to very wide, thickened, rounded edge with shallow ridge outside, wheel-finished; orangish-buff with greyish-buff core; coarse with few assorted white grits; traces of white slip outside; some assorted pits. A II 102.8.
15	4319	Upright rim, slightly incurved to medium-wide thickened, rounded, edge, wheel-finished; orangish-buff with greyish-buff core; coarse with few assorted white grits; smoke marks inside. A II 102.6.
16	5100	Upright rim, crudely wheel-finished, inclined out to rounded edge; pinkish-orange with grey core; coarse with some medium to very fine, white and tan grits; very uneven surface inside below edge. A IV 300.15.

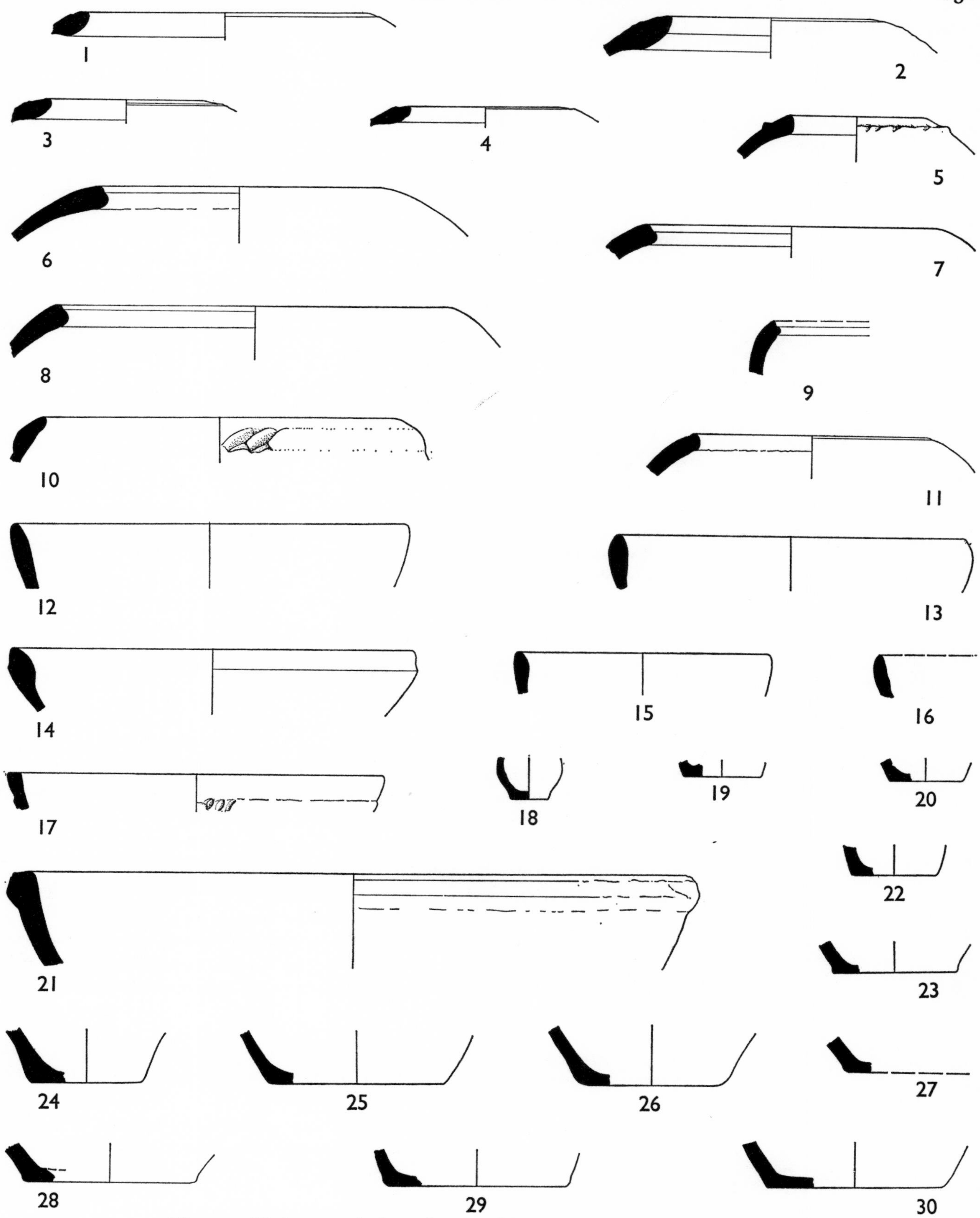

Fig. 30. Hole-mouth jars, bases of jugs and jars, Phase III. 1:4.

Fig. 30 No.	Reg. No.	
17	4328	Upright rim with rounded flat edge; reddish-brown with thick, very dark-grey core, medium-coarse with many small to fine, white grits; narrow, high-relief molding with closely spaced indentations; few assorted pits outside. A II 102.7.
18	4296	Rim upcurved to rounded, flat edge, wheel-finished; buff with very thick, dark-grey core penetrating to surfaces in places; very coarse with many assorted white grits; medium-wide, crude, high-relief rope-molding outside edge; many assorted pits. A II 101.10.
19	4819	Fragment of very small pot with flat base and crude, rough rim; brown inside and buff outside; very coarse with some assorted white grits and two very large, light-grey grits; many assorted pits and pronounced crazing over-all, very rough texture outside, black smoke marks on rim indicate possible use as lamp. A III 204.5.
20	4309a	Pinkish-brown; medium-coarse with many assorted white, tan, and reddish-brown grits; traces of continuous burnishing outside and on bottom. A II 102.5.
21	5121	Wheel-finished; buff with thick, dark-grey core; fine with assorted grey grits, very porous ware; traces of wheel-burnished, brown slip outside; many small to fine pits outside and on bottom. A IV 300.18.
22	4193	Base of jug, wheel-finished; buff with grey core; medium-coarse with few small white grits; traces of wheel-burnished, reddish-brown slip outside; pronounced crazing, many assorted pits on bottom. A II 103.2.
23	5098	Buff with thick, dark-grey core; coarse with many assorted, mostly fine, white grits; traces of white slip outside, traces of painted, reddish-brown lines outside; some assorted pits inside, black smoke marks inside. A IV 300.15.
24	4338	Dark-orange with buff core; medium-coarse with some assorted white grits; traces of white slip outside; very rough texture outside and on bottom, incrustations inside. A II 102.8.
25	4598	Buff inside and orangish-buff outside; very coarse with many assorted white grits; many assorted pits and very rough texture over-all. A III 201.13a.
26	5143d	Brownish-grey inside and brown outside, dark greyish-buff core; coarse with many assorted smokey quartz and grey grits; traces of reddish-brown slip outside; very pitted and spalling inside, rough texture outside and on bottom. A IV 300.20.
27	4956b	Buff with orange patch on bottom; coarse with some assorted grey grits; faint traces of white slip outside; pitted and spalling on bottom. A IV 300.13.
28	5029g	Grey inside and pinkish-buff outside; coarse with some assorted white grits; traces of white slip outside; brown incrustations over-all. A IV 300.14e.
29	4324	Orange with thick, dark-grey core; medium-coarse with many assorted white grits; many assorted pits, very worn inside. A II 102.6.
30	5138	Orangish-buff outside with very dark grey inside and core; coarse with many assorted, mostly small to fine, white grits; traces of white slip outside; many assorted pits outside and on bottom, pronounced crazing inside, very rough texture over-all. A IV 300.20.
Fig. 31 No.	Reg. No.	
1	4603	Wheel-finished; tan outside, grey inside and core; coarse with some assorted white grits and many assorted tan and grey grits, concentrated inside; very uneven surface inside and on bottom. A III 201.13a.
2	4607	Orangish-buff with dark-grey core in places; coarse with many assorted, mostly fine, white and grey grits; uneven surfaces over-all, very rough texture on bottom. A III 201.13a.

Fig. 31 *No.*	*Reg.* *No.*	
3	4320	Buff inside and bottom and orange outside, greyish-buff core; coarse with many assorted white and grey grits; traces of white slip outside; many assorted pits on bottom and outside. A II 102.6.
4	4214	Pinkish-tan inside and orange outside, thick, brown core; medium-coarse with many assorted white grits; traces of heavy, white slip outside; few assorted pits, some brown discoloration outside, some incrustations. A II 103.3.
5	4339	Pinkish-tan with dark-grey core; coarse with some assorted white and grey grits; white slip outside; rough texture over-all, some assorted pits inside. A II 102.8.
6	4683	Brown inside and orange outside, buff core; coarse with many small to fine, white grits; traces of white slip outside, faint traces of painted, reddish-orange net-pattern. A III 202.8.
7	4350f	Orangish-brown inside and brown outside; very coarse with many assorted grey quartz grits; very uneven surface inside, cloth impression outside, rough pitted surface on bottom. A II 102.8.
8	4689	Tan with reddish-orange outside; very coarse with some assorted white grits, porous ware; some assorted pits over-all. A III 202.9.
9	4605	Greyish-buff inside and orange outside, grey core; very coarse with some assorted white grits; traces of heavy, white slip outside; many assorted pits inside, very rough texture over-all. A III 201.13a.
10	4213	Tan with thick, dark-grey core; very coarse with many assorted white grits; flaking inside, pitted on bottom, very rough texture over-all. A II 103.3.
11	4323	Reddish-brown with dark-grey core; fine with few fine white grits, hard, well-fired ware; some black and orange discoloration outside. A II 102.6.
12	4195	Buff with pinkish-buff outside; very coarse with some assorted white and grey grits; faint traces of white slip outside; many assorted pits over-all, black smoke marks inside. A II 103.1.
13	4345	Buff inside and pinkish-brown outside, thick, dark-grey core; very coarse with many assorted white grits; traces of white slip outside; black smoke marks, some assorted pits inside, rough texture outside. A II 102.8.
14	4210	Orangish-buff with dark-grey core at angle; coarse with many assorted white and few grey grits; roughly pitted over-all. A II 103.2.
15	4810	Orange inside and buff outside; coarse with many assorted white grits; many assorted pits over-all, grey smoke marks, very rough texture outside. A III 204.5.
16	4813	Tan with dark-grey core penetrating to outside in places; coarse with very many assorted white and grey grits; few assorted pits over-all, very rough texture outside, grey smoke marks on bottom. A III 204.5.
17	4687	Orange with greyish-buff core penetrating to inside in places; medium-coarse with very many assorted white grits, porous ware; many assorted pits over-all, very rough texture outside. A III 202.9.
18	4601	Tan; coarse with few assorted white grits; traces of white slip outside; pitted and very rough texture, grey smoke marks over-all. A III 201.13a.
19	4207	Orangish-buff inside and orange outside, thick, grey core; coarse with many assorted white and few grey grits; many assorted pits over-all. A II 103.2.
20	4334	Dark-brown inside and reddish-brown outside, dark-grey core; fine with many medium to fine, white grits, porous ware; many assorted pits, tool-made facets at angle outside, very rough texture outside. A II 102.7.

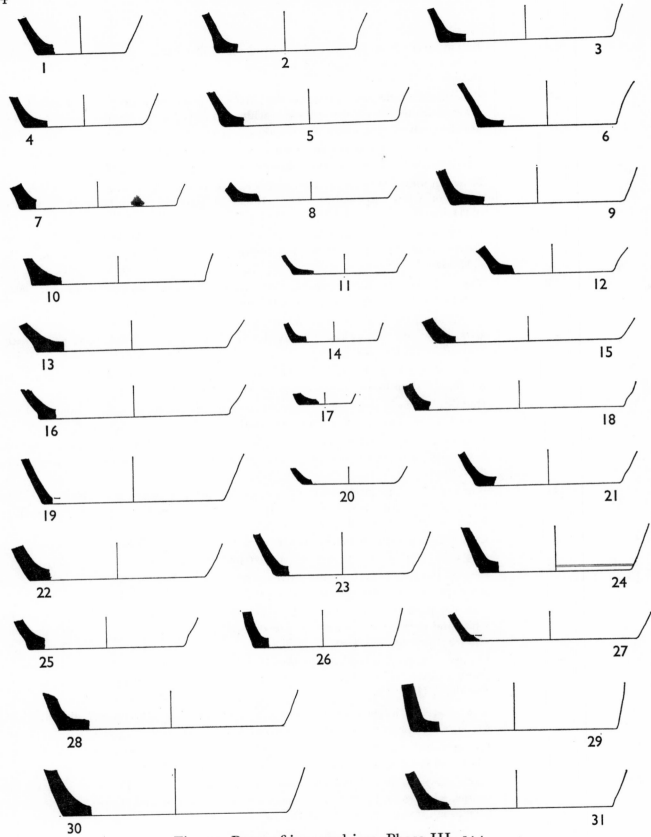

Fig. 31. Bases of jugs and jars, Phase III. 1:4.

Fig. 31 *No.*	*Reg.* *No.*	
21	5058a	Orange with thick, grey core; medium-coarse with few assorted white grits; traces of white slip outside; very uneven surface outside, heavy, grey incrustations over-all. A I 1.7.
22	4350e	Dark pinkish-tan inside and dark-orange outside; very coarse with some assorted brown grits; rough, pitted texture over-all. A II 102.8.
23	4812	Bottom appears to be made separately with wall applied; buff inside and orangish-buff outside; coarse with many assorted white and grey grits; traces of white slip outside; many assorted pits inside, dark-orange discoloration outside, very rough texture over-all. A III 204.5.
24	4322	Orangish-buff outside, dark-grey inside and core; coarse with some assorted white and tan grits; groove around base; some assorted pits. A II 102.6.
25	4350d	Brown with dark greyish-brown core; very coarse with many assorted grey quartz grits; rough, uneven surface outside and on bottom. A II 102.8.
26	4597	Brown inside and dark-grey outside; very coarse with many assorted grey quartz grits; dark-grey smoke marks, many fine pits inside, very rough texture outside. A III 201.13a.
27	5058b	Grey inside and buff outside; very coarse with some medium to fine, white and tan grits; very uneven surfaces over-all; some crazing and spalling inside, black smoke marks on bottom, light, grey incrustations outside. A I 2.1.
28	4609	Greyish-buff inside and buff outside; coarse with many assorted white and tan grits; traces of white slip outside; many assorted pits over-all, very uneven surface outside. A III 201.13a.
29	4308	Pinkish-tan with thick, dark-grey core; very coarse with many assorted white grits; very large, deep indentation outside near bottom, many assorted pits. A II 102.5.
30	4818	Greyish-brown inside and dark-orange outside, brown core; coarse with many assorted, mostly fine, white grits; traces of heavy, white slip outside; many assorted pits and very rough texture over-all. A III 204.5.
31	4330	Greyish-brown with thick, dark-grey core; very coarse with many assorted white and grey grits; orange discoloration inside, very rough texture over-all. A II 102.7.
—	4634	Flat base of jar, orange inside and dark-grey outside, tan core penetrating to outside in places; medium-coarse with very many assorted grey grits; some assorted pits outside, very rough texture over-all. A III 202.4.
—	4824m	Base fragment of shallow bowl, wheel-turned; orangish-brown; medium with some assorted reddish-brown and white grits; traces of continuous-burnishing inside and outside; rough texture on flat bottom. A III 204.5.
Fig. 32 *No.*	*Reg.* *No.*	
1	4326d	Base of large jar dark greyish-brown inside and buff outside; very coarse with many assorted white, tan, and grey grits, porous ware; traces of white slip outside and on bottom; many assorted pits and uneven surfaces over-all. A II 102.6.
2	5122	Base of large jar; greyish-buff inside and orangish-buff outside, dark-grey core in places; coarse with many assorted grey and white grits; traces of white slip outside; some very large and many fine pits inside, very rough texture over-all, some grey incrustations outside. A IV 300.18.
3	4333	Orange inside and buff outside, thick grey core; many assorted pits, rough texture inside, smoke marks over-all. A II 102.7.
4	4350	Lug-handle of small jar, elongated with two prominent knobs, located horizontally on body, pierced lengthwise; traces of burnished, reddish-brown slip outside, on handle, and on upper part of inside; few assorted pits inside, some grey incrustations. A II 102.8

Fig. 32 No.	Reg. No.	
5	5136	Rim of deep bowl, slightly incurved to rounded, flat edge; buff; coarse with many assorted white and grey grits; vestigial, vertical lug-handle outside; many assorted pits and very rough texture over-all. A IV 300.20.
6	4824i	Narrow possibly thumb-indented, edge; buff with grey core; medium-coarse with few assorted white grits; brown incrustations over-all. A III 204.5.
—	4824k	Ledge-handle fragment with thumb-indented edge; buff with grey inside; coarse with some assorted white grits; brown incrustations over-all. A III 204.5.
—	4609e	Ledge-handle fragment with slightly thumb-indented edge; brown with bright-grey core; medium-coarse with some assorted white grits; very uneven surface outside, pitted and spalling inside. A III 201.13a.
7	4218c	Traces of thumb-indentations; buff; very coarse with few fine white grits, some assorted tan grits; patches of shiny, dark-brown incrustations over-all. A III 201.13.
—	4218b	Ledge-handle fragment with three shallow finger-indentations on edge; buff with grey core; very coarse with some assorted white grits; traces of white slip outside. A III 201.13.
—	4612a	Ledge-handle fragment chipped on edge, possibly thumb-indented; pinkish-brown; very coarse with many assorted white grits, porous ware; creamy-white slip outside; very uneven surface, heavy, grey incrustations over-all. A III 201.13b
8	5029h	Narrow, slightly thumb-indented, edge; bright-orange; medium with many fine white grits; traces of greyish-brown slip outside; grey incrustations over-all. A IV 300.14e.
—	4609h	Small ledge-handle fragment, plain edge; orangish-buff; medium-coarse with many assorted, mostly small to fine, light-grey and reddish-brown grits; traces of white slip outside; rough, gritty texture inside, some grey incrustations over-all. A III 201.13a.
9	4331	Handle of large jar, slightly thumb-indented edge; orangish-buff inside with pinkish buff outside and core; very coarse with many assorted white grits; buff slip outside; dark-grey smoke marks inside, some grey incrustations. A II 102.7.
10	4612b	Thumb-indented, pushed up edge; buff, coarse with some assorted tan grits; traces of white slip outside; pitted and spalling inside, uneven surfaces over-all. A III 201.13b.
11	4609f	Deeply tool-indented edge; buff with thick, dark-grey core; very coarse with some assorted white and grey grits, rough gritty texture outside. A III 201.13a.
12	4609g	Slightly thumb-indented edge; orange inside and orangish-buff outside; coarse with some assorted white grits; faint traces of white slip outside; grey incrustations over-all. A III 201.13a.
13	5117	Slightly thumb-indented edge; greyish-brown inside with buff outside and core; coarse with many assorted white grits; grey smoke marks outside, some assorted pits over-all, very uneven surface under handle. A IV 300.18.
14	4335	Thumb-indented edge; orange inside and orangish-buff outside; coarse with some assorted white grits; grey incrustations. A II 102.7.
—	4824j	Small ledge-handle fragment with plain edge; dark-grey; medium-coarse with few assorted white grits; traces of reddish-brown slip outside. A III 204.5.
—	5132b	Ledge-handle fragment with plain edge; orangish-buff; very coarse with many small to fine, white and grey grits; rough uneven surface over-all, grey incrustations outside. A IV 300.18a.
15	4609i	Loop-handle fragment joined to body, irregular oval section; orangish-buff; medium-coarse with some small white grits; traces of reddish-orange slip outside; uneven, spalling surfaces, brown incrustations over-all. A III 201.13a.
—	4824f	Loop-handle fragment joined to body, elongated oval section; brown inside and dark-orange outside; medium-coarse with many small dark-grey and white grits; traces of

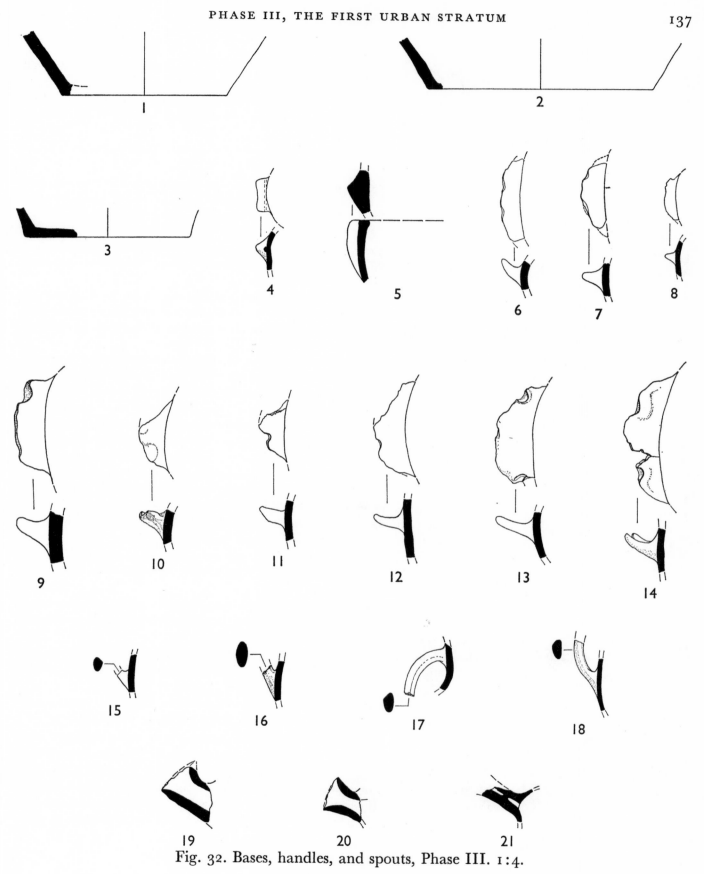

Fig. 32. Bases, handles, and spouts, Phase III. 1:4.

Fig. 32 No.	Reg. No.	
		continuously-burnished orangish-brown slip outside; brown incrustations over-all. A III 204.5.
—	5143i	Body sherd; buff with orange inside; medium-coarse with some assorted white and tan grits; continuously burnished, reddish-brown slip outside; some heavy, grey incrustations over-all. A IV 300.20.
—	4326e	Body sherd; light-orange; medium-coarse with some assorted grey and reddish-brown grits; traces of reddish-brown slip outside. A II 102.6.
—	5101f	Body sherd; burnt-orange outside and dark-brown inside, dark-grey core; medium with some assorted, mostly fine, tan and grey grits; continuously-burnished, reddish-orange slip outside; few assorted pits inside, spalling, some grey incrustations over-all. A IV 300.15.
16	4218d	Loop-handle fragment joined to body, elongated oval section; brown with thick, dark-grey core; medium-coarse with some assorted white grits; continuously-burnished, reddish-brown slip outside. A III 201.13.
17	5122b	Loop-handle fragment joined to neck of jug, oval tapering down to flattened oval section; tan; medium with many assorted, mostly small to fine, grey and few white grits; traces of continuously-burnished, orangish-brown slip outside; some grey incrustations over-all. A IV 300.18.
—	4824g	Loop-handle fragment, elongated oval section tapering to wide, flattened oval; tan; medium-coarse with very many assorted, mostly small to fine, dark-grey and white grits; traces of burnished, reddish-brown slip; some assorted mostly large pits, some grey incrustations over-all. A III 204.5.
—	4824h	Loop-handle fragment, round tapering to oval section; buff with grey core; coarse with many assorted, mostly small to fine, dark-grey grits; traces of burnished, reddish-brown slip. A III 204.5.
—	4612c	Body sherd; buff; coarse with many assorted, mostly fine, dark-grey, white, and reddish-brown grits; continuously-burnished, reddish-brown slip outside; rough, gritty texture inside, light, grey incrustations over-all. A III 201.13b.
—	4326f	Body sherd; buff with dark-buff core, medium-coarse with some assorted grey white and reddish-brown grits; reddish-brown slip outside. A II 102.6.
—	4309c	Body sherd; brownish-red with brown core; medium with some assorted tan, reddish-brown, and black grits; possibly burnished slip outside; uneven surface inside, some assorted pits outside. A II 102.5.
18	5118	Loop-handle fragment joined to body; greyish-tan; fine with many assorted, mostly small, dark-grey grits; traces of continuously-burnished, reddish-brown slip outside and on handle; many small to fine pits outside. A IV 300.18.
—	5058c	Body sherd; buff outside and greyish-yellow inside; medium-coarse with some assorted grey and white grits; traces of reddish-brown slip outside; grey incrustations over-all. A I 2.1.
—	5101e	Small, circular loop-handle fragment, oval section flattened inside; dark-orange; medium with some medium to fine, grey, white, and tan grits. A IV 300.15.
19	4817	Open, flared spout; tan inside and greyish-tan outside with thick, dark-grey core; coarse with many small to fine, white grits; very uneven surface outside, rough texture inside. A III 204.5.
20	5123	Open, flared spout; orangish-buff inside, pinkish-tan outside with orange in places; coarse with some assorted white grits; traces of white slip outside near juncture with body; pronounced crazing inside, many assorted pits and rough texture over-all. A IV 300.18a.

Fig. 32 *No.*	*Reg.* *No.*	
21	4327	Vestigial spout fragment partially pierced from each end; buff; medium-coarse with few medium white grits; traces of white slip outside and inside of vessel. A II 102.6.
—	5122c	Pierced spout fragment from small vessel; greyish-buff; very coarse with some assorted tan and grey grits; rough texture over-all. A IV 300.18.

Fig. 33 *No.*	*Reg.* *No.*	
1	4212	Reddish-orange; medium with few small to fine, white grits; narrow, straight, high-relief rope-molding outside with closely spaced, diagonal indentations. A II 103.3.
2	4669	Greyish-buff; coarse with many assorted white and tan grits; medium-wide, crude, very high-relief rope-molding with traces of white slip outside; many assorted pits inside. A III 202.6.
3	4635d	Pinkish-buff; medium-coarse with very many small to fine, white and tan grits; well defined, high-relief, ridged rope-molding, traces of white slip outside. A III 202.4.
4	4349	Brown; medium-coarse with few small to fine, white and grey grits; medium-wide, crude, high-relief rope-molding outside; dark-grey smoke marks. A II 102.8.
5	5132c	Buff; coarse with some small to fine, white grits; medium-wide, crude, high-relief, ridged molding and traces of white slip outside; some incrustations over-all. A IV 300.18a.
6	4318	Dark-grey inside and pinkish-buff outside, greyish-buff core; very coarse with many assorted white grits; narrow, straight, high-relief ridged molding outside, traces of brown wash inside; rough texture. A II 102.6.
7	4602	Orange with buff core; coarse with many assorted white grits; narrow, crude, straight, half-relief rope-molding outside; many assorted pits and very rough texture over-all. A III 201.13a.
8	4682	Buff with bluish-grey core; medium-coarse with many medium to fine, tan grits; narrow, crude, low-relief ridged molding outside. A III 202.8.
9	4206	Pinkish-buff; medium-coarse with few small to fine, white grits; narrow, crude, uneven, rope-molding applied in random vertical pattern, traces of heavy white slip outside; many assorted pits inside. A II 103.2.
10	5097	Pinkish-grey inside and buff outside with grey core; coarse with many small to fine, tan and white grits; medium-wide, crude, high-relief rope-molding, traces of very heavy, white slip outside. A IV 300.15.
11	4340	Reddish-brown with thick, dark-grey core; coarse with few fine white grits and many assorted tan and white grits concentrated inside; very wide, high-relief rope-molding, heavy, white slip outside; some assorted pits inside, some grey incrustations. A II 102.8.
12	5127	Reddish-orange with orangish-buff core; medium-coarse with many assorted, mostly small to fine, white and grey grits; medium-wide, straight, high-relief, ridged molding outside with diagonal, closely spaced, indentations in ridge; grey smoke marks outside, some assorted pits over-all. A IV 300.18a.
13	4192	Buff with grey core in places; medium-coarse with many medium to fine, white grits; medium-wide, crude, high-relief rope-molding outside; some orange discoloration outside, many assorted pits inside and few assorted pits outside, very uneven surface inside, some grey incrustation. A II 103.2.
14	4595	Buff inside with dark-grey outside and core; medium-coarse with some assorted white grits, medium-wide, crude, wavy, high-relief rope-molding, traces of pinkish-tan slip outside; few assorted pits over-all, very rough texture inside. A III 201.13a.
15	4631	Buff; coarse with many assorted white grits; wide, straight, very high-relief, rope-molding, white slip outside; some heavy, grey incrustations, many assorted pits inside. A III 202.4.

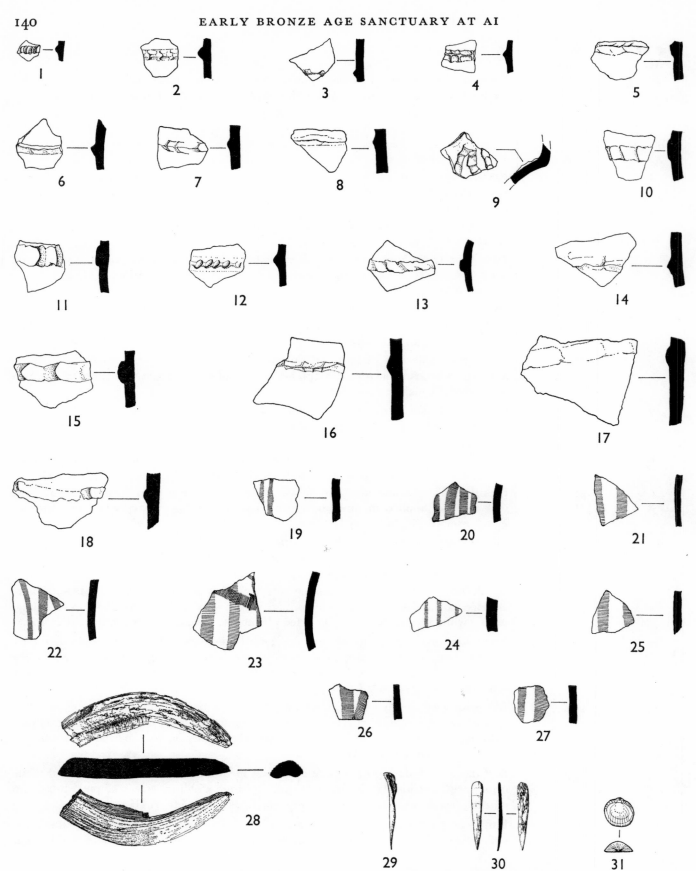

Fig. 33. Decorated body sherds and various objects, Phase III. 1:4.

Fig. 33 No.	*Reg.* No.	
16	4593	Pinkish-tan inside and pinkish-buff outside, thick, grey core; medium-wide, uneven, half-relief rope-molding, traces of heavy, white slip outside; many assorted pits inside, very rough texture over-all. A III 201.13a.
17	5128	Creamy-white with pinkish- and yellowish-white in places outside; very coarse with some assorted grits of mixed colors, porous ware; wide, crude, high-relief rope-molding, some grey and brown discolorations outside. A IV 300.18a.
18	4635e	Greyish-pink with grey core; very coarse with many medium to fine, grey grits, porous ware; medium-wide, crude, high relief rope-molding, faint traces of creamy-white slip outside; rough, gritty texture over-all. A III 202.4.
—	4350g	Body sherd; pinkish-tan; medium-coarse with few small to fine, white grits; narrow, crude, high-relief ridged molding, traces of white slip outside. A II 102.8.
—	5143e	Body sherd; red inside and reddish-grey outside; coarse with many assorted grey grits, porous ware; crude, high-relief rope-molding, creamy-white slip outside; rough, gritty texture over-all. A IV 300.20.
—	5143g	Body sherd; pinkish-orange; medium-coarse with few assorted white, tan, grey, and reddish-brown grits; white slip outside; some incrustations over-all. A IV 300.20.
—	4326c	Body sherd; brownish-buff with grey core; medium with very many fine white grits. A II 102.6.
19	5143	Tan with buff patches inside; medium with few assorted white grits; traces of white slip, two medium-wide, parallel, painted red stripes outside; flaking inside. A IV 300.20.
20	4811	Tan; coarse with some small to fine, white grits; white slip, traces of four wide, parallel, painted brown stripes outside; some grey incrustations. A III 204.5.
21	5142	Buff with dark-grey outside and core; coarse with many small to fine, white grits; white slip, wide, painted brown stripes outside; some grey incrustations inside. A IV 300.20.
22	4498	Buff with dark-grey core; medium-coarse with some assorted white and tan grits; white slip outside, with three irregular, painted, dark-orange stripes; assorted pits, dark-grey smoke marks inside, some grey incrustations. A I 1.7.
23	5137	Buff with dark grey outside and core; coarse with many small to fine, white grits; white slip and wide, painted brownish-red stripes in large net-pattern outside; some grey incrustations. (5137, 5141 joined) A IV 300.20.
24	4671	Buff; coarse with some assorted tan grits, porous ware; grey slip outside, traces of three narrow, parallel, painted red stripes, pitted and crazing inside. A III 202.6.
25	5140	Similar to Nos. 21, 23 above. A IV 300.20.
26	4688	Brown inside and orange outside; coarse with many assorted white grits; white slip, traces of two wide, converging, vertical, painted dark-orange stripes outside. A III 202.9.
27	4686	Similar to No. 26, but with vertical parallel stripes. A III 202.9.
—	4611	Body sherd of jar; orangish-buff inside and orange outside, dark-grey core; medium-coarse with many fine white grits; heavy, white slip outside with faint traces of painted red lines. A III 201.13b.
—	4218	Body sherd of jar; light-orange with dark-grey inside; medium with few large and many fine white grits; faint traces of narrow vertical painted red lines outside; some grey incrustations. A II 103.3.
—	5029i	Body sherd; orange; coarse with few assorted white grits; heavy, white slip outside with traces of medium-wide, painted red lines; white incrustations inside. A IV 300.14e.
—	4350h	Body sherd; buff; medium-coarse with some assorted grey and tan grits; traces of white slip outside with faint traces of painted, reddish-brown lines, pitted and spalling inside. A II 102.8.

Fig. 33 No.	Reg. No.	
28	4350a	White shell with drilled hole at hinge. A II 102.8.
29	0–71	Lower right canine tusk of hippopotamus, not fossilized; ivory; inside half split off; no decoration. A III 204.5.
30	0–87	Bone tool, yellowish-ivory; finely worked point. A II 103.3.
31	0–88	Bone tool, yellowish-ivory; carefully worked over-all. A II 103.3.

DESCRIPTIONS OF THE MARQUET-KRAUSE PHASE III POTTERY AND OBJECTS, FIG. 34

Fig. 34 No.	M-K Reg. No.	
1	2591	Fragment of bowl. H:116; 1.60 m.; under floor B (M-K Pl. LXXXII).
2	2592	Bowl, H:116; under floor B, under the stones of the altar (M-K Pl. LXXXII).
—	2621	Fragments of bowls: (1) wall rather inclined, slightly curved; horizontal rim, projecting short and thin over inside face; grey clay; (2) wall and rim in straight line. Fragment of bowl showing three concentric lines. Rim of hole-mouth, not thickened, edge slightly concave. H:116; 50 cm. under Altar C.
—	2589	Fragments of bowls: (1) rounded form; fine wall and rim; on rim large painted red band on outside surface, thin band on inside surface; (2) wall slightly inclined, incurved; horizontal rim in thin projection rather pronounced on the two sides. Rims of hole-mouths: (1) thin, flat edge; (2) slightly thickened over outside surface, inside surface straight; lime slip; (3) very thin, rounded edge; friable material; (4) thick, slightly thickened over sides, edge somewhat flat; (5) slightly thickened over inside surface; edge thinned. H:116; under Floor B, under C.
—	2253	Fragment of very small, very flat bowl, thin rim curved toward top; traces of wick (lamp); fragment of very fine neck; thin rim curved toward outside. Rims of hole-mouths: (1) thin, not thickened; on outside surface surrounded by a thin depression; (2) heavier, not thickened (3) very thick, very heavy, swollen over inside surface. Fragment with narrow molding in triangular projections. H:136; on the rock.
—	2254	Fragment of bowl, thin rim (wall and rim in straight line); fine and well-baked ware. Rim of hole-mouth not thickened. Fragment with brown glossy slip. Various fragments, thick and heavy ware. H:136; down to original surface just above the rock; under the first floor B.
—	2271	Fragment of bowl, . . . or round base (?). Fragment of fine neck, thin and thickened rim; well baked brown ware. Fragment: fine and well-baked red slip. Fragment: light, porous ware, mixed with gravel, white lime slip. H:116, under floor B.
—	2593	Flat loop-handle; red slip. Fragments of bowls: (1) wall very curved, thin at base, very much thickened toward top of inside surface; large horizontal rim; brown slip outside; (2) curved wall, horizontal rim, not very pronounced projection over inside surface. Rims of hole-mouths: (1) thickened over inside surface; on outside surface, near edge line in rather deep groove; (2) thickened over inside surface, rounded edge; (3) thickened over inside surface, edge thinned. Fragments with molding: (1) large; (2) projecting. H:116; under floor B.
—	2608II	Horizontal handle, type I; small half-circles pressed on edge. Circular handle. Fragment of bowl: wall very curved rather thick; flat rim nearly horizontal (slightly inclined from the base), in thin projection over inside surface, angle of rim and of wall rounded over inside surface. Neck of jug with sloping shoulder, neck very thickened, thin rim curved toward outside; line at base of neck. Rim of hole-mouth; thin, edge rather fine; thin molding set rather low on outside surface. H:116; under floor B, under Altar II.

Fig. 34 No.	M-K Reg. No.	
—	2620	Fragment of bowl: fine wall in straight line inclined at 45°; thin, long rim forming with it a slightly sharp angle. Fragment of rim of fine rounded bowl. Rims of hole-mouths: (1) heavy, not thickened, rounded edge; (2) thick, not swollen, curved, flat edge slightly projecting over inside surface; (3) very heavy; edge very much thickened and rounded over inside surface. Fragment of a type of hole-mouth; wall slightly curved toward inside, thickened toward top through the strong curvature of interior surface, flat edge rather inclined from base. Fragment of neck: fine wall and rim, very lightly curved toward outside. H:116; under floor B.
—	2663	Fragment of bowl; straight wall rather inclined, rim nearly horizontal, projecting triangularly over inside surface. Rim of hole-mouth, slightly curved, thickened edge in rounded projection over inside surface. H:116; under floor B.
3	2646	Fragment of pot with globular body carrying on shoulder a crude ear-handle, rounded shape. H:116; under floor B (M-K Pl. LXXXII).
—	2651	Fragment of neck continuing the line of the shoulder; fine rim curved toward outside; fragment of neck of jar; thin rim curved toward outside; fragment of bowl, fine wall and rim slightly incurved. H:116; under floor B.
4	2257	Slightly thickened, rounded edge. H:136; over natural soil (M-K Pl. LXXXIV).
—	2569	Horizontal handle type I, small half-circles pressed on rim. Three rims of hole-mouths: (1) thickened toward top of inside surface; edge somewhat flat; (2) thin; incised line on outside surface; (3) thin, small conical protuberance on outside surface. H:116; under the level of the altar stones.
5	2257	Slightly thickened rounded edge. H:136; over natural soil (M-K Pl. LXXXIV).
6	2606	Thin, slightly thickened toward rounded edge. H:116; under floor B; 1 m. 70 cm. (M-K Pl. LXXXIV).
7	2256	Hole-mouth type; wall thickened toward top; flat rim projecting over inside surface, outside edge has a thin, striated band over its edge. H:137; on the rock (M-K Pl. LXXXII).
8	2249	Thick and heavy, slightly swollen. H:116; 1 m. 20 cm; under floor B (M-K Pl. LXXXIV).
9	2662	Very much thickened over inside surface, rounded edge. H:116; under floor B (M-K Pl. LXXXIV).
10	2597	Rim of hole-mouth. H:116; under floor B near the new altar (M-K Pl. LXXXIV).
11	2662	Rim of hole-mouth: not thickened; on outside surface a line slightly depressed. H:116; under floor B (M-K Pl. LXXXIV).
12	2256	Rim of hole-mouths: (1) thin; (2) very thin edge, line incised on surface. H:137; on the rock (M-K Pl. LXXXIV).
13	2590	Rim of hole-mouth, flat edge. H:116; south of the wall discovered under floor B (M-K Pl. LXXXIV).
14	2591	Hole-mouth, type of large bowl; rim thickened over flattened edge; on outside surface, at edge, incised decoration. H:116; depth 1 m. 60 cm.; under floor B (M-K Pl. LXXXII).
15	2607	Rim of hole-mouth, flat edge. H:116; under Altar B (M-K Pl. LXXXIV).
16	2666	Not thickened; line projecting over outside surface. H:116; under floor B (M-K Pl. LXXXIV).
17	2256	Edge . . . rounded, slightly thickened over the two surfaces, incised line on outside surface. H:137; on the rock (M-K Pl. LXXXIV).

Fig. 34 No.	M-K Reg. No.	
—	2270	Four horizontal flat handles, some with fingerprints on interior surface; flat horizontal handle, on the rim a finger indentation; horizontal handle with raised edge; loop-handle; fragment with beginning of loop-handle; fragments with molding: (1) narrow with pronounced triangular projection; wavy; (2) barely projecting, straight; (3) projecting, straight and smooth, reddish clay; neck of small vase: narrow rim, everted; fragment of neck of jar with sloping shoulders, slightly outcurved; rim folded into pads on outside surface; fragment of neck: wall of neck perpendicular to shoulder; fragments of two small bowls: fine wall and rim incurved at the top; rims of hole-mouths: (1) thin, rounded edge slightly curved at the top, forming a slight depression on the outside surface: (2) very thin, showing a projection over the outside surface; (3) thin; rounded edge, slightly bulging over inside surface; (4) thickened toward top, flat edge curved toward the inside; (5) slightly thickened toward top, somewhat flat edge (6) edge very much rounded, thickening over the two surfaces; (7) thick, rounded edge, slightly bulging over the two surfaces. (8) very thin, fine edge; (9) thin edge slightly rounded; (10) thick elongated in form of leaf; (1) slightly bulging over inside surface, rounded edge; over the inside surface the edge of the extension is badly finished. Fragment of hole-mouth or large basin; wall very thick still more thickening toward rim over inside surface; flat, horizontal rim; coarse ware; fragments with red slip; some with design of darker lines; fragments with white slip. H:116; depth 40 cm. under floor B.
—	2225	Fragment (handle?) with a series of unequal indentations; fragments with slip, one with red slip and design of darker lines; fragment, ware speckled with white grains; 2 flints. H:136–137; under floor B.
—	2237	Two horizontal handles, type I, flat, outer edge folded over in small half-circle; flat horizontal handle, fingerprints over inside surface; fragment of circular twin-coil handle; spout, not pierced, thickened rim; neck of jar completely straight and simple, medium height; traces of red slip; fragment of bowl, wall somewhat inclined, rim nearly horizontal projecting over the two surfaces (the outside projection more pronounced than inside projection), brown clay; rims of hole-mouths: (1) thickened toward top of side of inside

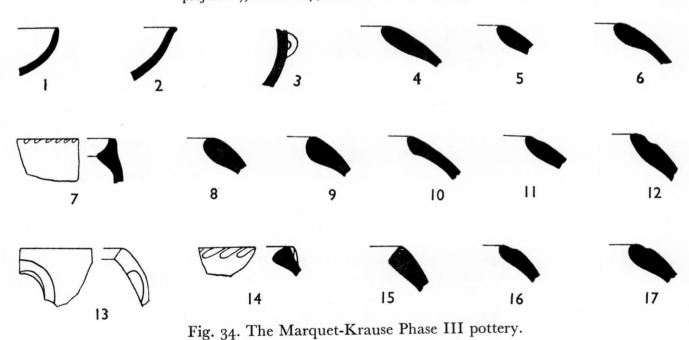

Fig. 34. The Marquet-Krause Phase III pottery.

Fig. 34 *No.*	*M-K Reg.* *No.*	
		surface, flat edge, brown clay speckled with grains of sand; (2) very thick and heavy, slightly swollen over inside surface, very rounded edge; grey ware; (3) thickened over inside surface, rounded edge. H : 136; under floor B, toward the rock.
—	2240	Horizontal handle. H : 116; under floor B near the rock, southeast corner; depth 2 m. (M-K Pl. XLVII).
—	2255	Fragment with molding. H : 116; under floor B at the south wall (M-K Pl. LI).
—	2604	Horizontal handle, type I, flat, small semi-circles on edge; thick fragment; traces of burnishing. H : 116; under floor B.
—	2619	Flat horizontal handle, type I, small half-circles on edge; circular cylindrical handle; fragment of jug with rounded shoulder, base of straight neck, brown ware, flat base; burnished fragment. H : 116; northeast corner on the rock.
—	2623	Circular cylindrical handle; fragment with molding; small flat carefully worked base; round body of small pot; rims of hole-mouths: (1) (2) slightly thickened, thin edge: (3) thin, rounded edge. H : 116; under floor B.
—	2650	Circular cylindrical handle; fragment of rather short neck, wall thick on bottom, rim sharply curved toward outside; flints. H : 116; under floor B.
—	2652	Two broken horizontal handles; fragment of small rounded bowl, very fine wall and rim; fragment of neck of jar, straight wall, rim strongly curved or rather folded toward outside, as if to form a rounded border but not adhering to wall; white slip; rims of hole-mouths: (1) (2) rounded and very thickened edges; heavy ware; (3) not thickened, curved, concave edge; heavy ware. H : 116; under floor B.
—	2654	Horizontal handle, type I, small half-circles on edge; fragment of neck, thick wall, fine rim curved toward outside; fragment with white slip. H : 116, under floor B, under Altar B.
—	2390	Pointed blade; bronze. H; Sanctuary C.
—	2586	Flint; pointed bone. H : 116; on the rock.

V

PHASE IV, THE BUILDING B STRATUM

INTRODUCTION

Adjectives such as 'creative' and 'imaginative' may be used to describe the work of the Phase III city builders at Ai. Their achievements are unprecedented in Early Bronze Age Canaan, and the EB IC city is unique. The Phase IV city, and Building B at Site A, are another story. 'Functional' more aptly describes the Phase IV modifications of the city, and 'retrenchment' seems to characterize the objectives of the new leadership.

Tower C of the Phase III citadel was stormed and burned, presumably by the people of Phase IV, and the acropolis buildings were burned to the ground. Building C, however, was not destroyed, as noted in Chapter II. The new people of Phase IV rebuilt the citadel, closing off the Citadel Gate and strengthening the fortifications at Site A. The city wall was strengthened by widening it to almost six meters, and the number of gates into the city was reduced. Gates at the citadel and Lower City used in Phase III were closed, and a single gate in the Lower City replaced them.

This kind of modification is termed 'functional' because it strengthened the weak points in the previous city fortifications. There is not a single creative innovation evident in the modification of city walls, fortification towers, or gates. What does seem to be evident is the exercise of naked power and pragmatic decisiveness in securing the city and making it operative.

A functional kind of modification is evident in Building B at Site A. Instead of constructing a new building complex with a grand new design, the people of Phase IV retained the north unit of Building C, and remodeled the south unit to serve their purposes better. The result is a curious amalgam of the old and the new, and the plan of the remodeled building has a degree of *ad hoc* character evident in the room arrangements and traffic patterns. Phase IV, therefore, reflects a period of unimaginative retrenchment in the life-style of the city.

BUILDING B OF PHASE IV

Building C was remodeled in Phase IV to enlarge the structure on the south and to build a court with outdoor firepit east of the north unit. Walls E^1, K, and P^1 enclose an additional area east of the south unit of Phase III, and Wall K apparently encloses a large room or another house unit in Area A I. The traffic pattern in Phase IV is still north-south, with a major passageway in Wall E^1 against Wall B, but there is a detour in a narrow corridor around Walls $S–S^1$, where the passageway directly in front of the one in Wall E^1 is blocked. This diversion of traffic through the corridor between Walls E^1 and $S–S^1$ apparently reorients entry into the rooms in Areas A II–III and makes them accessible from the court on the east.

The fire hearth, Platform Z in Area II, is covered by the buff fill of Layer 7 in Phase IV, and a new firepit is constructed in the court east of the north unit. This area seems to be unroofed, because the surface of the ground is loose and unfinished, as it was in Phase III. Nothing suggesting a packed floor surface was found. Building B, therefore, is remodeled in a rather awkward manner reflecting the closure of the Citadel Gate and the changed role of Site A in the life of the city. Important traffic in and out of the city no longer passed by Site A, and the rather well-planned and compact Building C of Phase III is changed into a sprawling, purely functional domestic house in the backwash of the city in Phase IV.

The Phase IV remodeling of Building C

Building C consisted of two units of two rooms each, separated by Wall Q between Areas II and III. The north unit in Areas III–IV was apparently reused in Building B with minor alterations, such as the relocation of passageways, while the south unit was extensively remodeled. An additional fill was laid in the Platform Z room of the south unit, covering the fire hearth; the passageway in Wall S was blocked by the installation of Wall S^1; and Wall E^1 was constructed across the middle of the room between Walls S–S^1 and D^1.

The reused north unit. As noted earlier, there is no evidence of additional fill placed over the Phase III surfaces of the north unit in Phase IV. Apparently the rooms north of Wall Q were not extensively damaged in the capture of the Phase III citadel, so the same walls and floors were reused in Phase IV. Evidence for this view has been presented in the analysis of Sections A–A and B–B in Chapter III. The most significant reason for holding this view is the uniform coverage of surfaces in both the north and south units by debris from the final destruction of Building B in Phase V. A considerable depth of ashes, bits of charred roof beams, clay from the roofing materials, and calcined stones is evident in Pl. IV.2, at the base of the meter scale, in the south unit, and in Pl. IX.2, against the north face of Wall Q in the north unit. Both stratigraphic and ceramic evidence support the identification of this destruction layer as Phase V, or EB II B. The surface underneath the layer in the north unit was first constructed in Phase III, so it was reused in Phase IV.

Passageways in the remodeled north unit are not identifiable because of the fragmentary nature of building remains. An entrance into the north end of the unit was proposed for Phase III because of the proximity of the Citadel Gate north of the building. With the closure of the gate in Phase IV, and the addition of a courtyard along the east side of the north unit in Building B, an entrance through Wall F^3 at some point seems required. No evidence of such a passageway was found, but adequate space for it is indicated by the dashed lines in Fig. 85, where Wall F^3 was located in the original structure. The ramp against the east face of Wall F^2 supported by Walls T–U, shown in Pl. IX.1, was covered in Phase IV, so a passageway there, if it existed in Phase III, seems to be ruled out in Phase IV.

The two, or three, rooms of the Phase III north unit, therefore, were apparently taken over with little alteration in Phase IV and reoriented toward the newly constructed courtyard on the east instead of the Phase III Citadel Gate which was blocked in Phase IV.

The remodeled south unit. A fill of compact, buff clay about 35 centimeters in thickness was placed in the Platform Z room of the south unit in Phase IV. This fill, Layer 7 in Fig. 83, is shown under the meter scale in Pl. IV.2, where the scale actually rests on the Phase IV surface. Two things were accomplished in the installation of the fill. First, the level of the south unit surfaces was brought up to that of the north unit, as the Master Section, Fig. 83, demonstrates. And secondly, the stone substructure of Wall F as well as Platform Z were covered by the fill in preparation for the remodeling of the southernmost room and construction of Wall E^1.

Platform Z is interpreted as a fire hearth in the preceding chapter, implying a purely domestic function for the room. However, the fires in the room must have created problems, even though a vent may have been built into the roof. In any case, the fireplace was moved into the courtyard in Phase IV, and the Platform Z room was used for preparation of food to be cooked outside in the courtyard. Large store-jars were found on the Phase IV floor by Marquet-Krause, as shown in Pl. XVIII:1 (Marquet-Krause 1949), and a stone mortar was set in the surface of the floor in the southwest part of the room in front of the blocked Phase III passageway. Pl. XVIII.2 shows the hole left by removal of the mortar, and its location relative to the southwest corner.

Wall F^1 was built over the base of Phase III Wall F along the east side of the room. This wall was probably constructed with a brick superstructure, and its orientation was slightly different from that of Wall F. The stones of Wall F, covered by Layer 7 fill under the meter scale in Pl. III.2, do not align exactly with the remnant of Phase IV Wall F^1 in the background, shown in a closer view in Pl. IV.1. A passageway into the room through Wall F^1 is suggested in Fig. 85, because of the proximity of the hearth in the courtyard to the adjacent room with the mortar and store-jars. Open and unrestricted access to the courtyard seems to be required.

The southernmost room of the unit was divided by the construction of Wall E^1 across its middle, as shown in Fig. 85. In Phase III, the room was enclosed by Wall D^1 on the south, Wall F on the east, and Wall S on the north. Wall E^1, a Phase IV structure, made the room into a corridor on the north side, between Walls E^1 and S–S^1, because the entrance into the Platform Z room was blocked by Wall S^1. Traffic through the open passage at the west end of Wall E^1 flowed through the corridor and into the courtyard area east of Wall F^1. The Phase IV remodeling, therefore, eliminated one of the rooms of the south unit, and moved the fireplace into a courtyard where it probably served families living on both sides of Wall Q. The family living in the south unit occupied one room, apart from the courtyard area.

Walls P^1 and K. The functions of Walls P^1 and K in the Building B complex are obscure, mainly due to an almost complete absence of related evidence. Both walls are definitely Phase IV structures, and both seem to be integral parts of Phase IV additions to the Site A complex. A projected extension of Wall P^1 is drawn in Section E–E, Fig. 10, with its base on Layer 7a, the foundation fill of the Phase IV surface between Walls P^1 and F^1. A small corner of the surface against Wall F^1 is visible in the lower right corner of Pl. IV.2.

Walls P^1 and K intersect Wall E^1 as shown in Fig. 85. The two walls are almost identical in width, and are founded upon the fill, or bedrock, allowing extension of the complex eastward from the location of Phase III Building C in the Phase IV remodeling. Wall P^1 abuts E^1 on top of Layer 7 in Section G–G, Fig. 7, and Wall K is a continuation of Wall E^1 in Area I. Apparently, Walls E^1, P^1, and K were all built at the same time.

The orientation of their extant remains supports this conclusion. Wall E^1 begins its course on the west end at almost a right angle to Wall C, apparently oriented with Wall B. However, a deflection in orientation occurs just before the intersection with Walls K and P^1. The deflection aligns Wall E^1

to bisect the angle formed by the intersection, and this suggests a concern on the part of the builders to align the internal structure of Building B with the eastern enclosure walls, as well as with the city wall on the west side.

The problem with Walls P¹ and K is the direction, and extent, of the missing ends, i.e., the north end of Wall P¹, and the south end of Wall K. No conclusive evidence of a bend toward Wall F¹ in Wall P¹ at Firepit N² remained. A bend is suggested by the bench along the base of Wall H in Marquet-Krause Pl. XIII:1, in the left center of the photograph. This bench, however, seems to be part of the base of Wall H, set in Layer 3, Phase VI, and, therefore, is not a continuation of Wall P¹.

A bend to the east around the firepit is more likely. Marquet-Krause Pl. XIII:2 indicates this course in the extension of Wall H beyond Wall P in the right center of the photograph. The extension seems to be constructed quite deep in the trench, below the level of Wall H and Wall P, so it is likely built on the north end of Wall P¹ as proposed in the reconstruction around Firepit N² in Fig. 85.

The south end of Wall K is missing, probably due to erosion on the steep slope beginning at its termination point. The wall is oriented with Wall B, but continuation toward the south alongside Wall B appears improbable because of the 2 meter drop in terrain indicated in the elevations in Fig. 85. Wall K, therefore, probably terminated in its original construction about where the last stone is drawn in Fig. 85.

A right angle bend in Wall K toward Wall B is suggested by the evidence in Section H–H, Fig. 8. The dark ashy debris of Layer 6 on the south side of Wall E¹ is Phase V destruction of Phase IV Building B. An accumulation of ashes to the depth indicated would be hardly possible unless some kind of roofed structure stood south of Wall E¹. Previous excavations and natural erosion removed all evidence south of Wall D, as shown in Fig. 8, but a continuation over the base of Wall D¹ is probable. This would leave about 2 meters of floor space for a long, narrow room alongside Wall E¹, facing south.

Wall K, therefore, is a Phase IV addition in the Building B complex enabling the construction of a possible room along the south side of Wall E¹ and west side of Wall K, and extending the built up area eastward from the Phase III building to a ledge of bedrock shown in Section G–G, Fig. 7. Wall P¹ also extended the complex eastward, and possibly enabled the construction of rooms east of the courtyard serving Building B.

Conclusions

Two conclusions with regard to the nature and role of Building B may be drawn. First, the Phase III building complex was remodeled in Phase IV to create a multiple unit domestic complex of rooms around a courtyard. Firepit N in the courtyard probably served two units of living quarters in the reused Phase III building, and one or two possible units east of Walls P¹ and K. Because Wall E¹ appears to be a major enclosure wall, the unit on its south side probably belonged to a complex down the slope from Building B. Thus Building B appears to be the dwelling place of a family, or clan, living in close proximity around a courtyard.

Second, the role of Building B in the life of the city seems to be different from that of Building C. The latter was very closely related to Tower C and the Citadel Gate fortification complex. Building B, on the other hand, was oriented about a courtyard, because the Citadel Gate was closed, and traffic in and out of the city no longer flowed by Site A. Tower B of the citadel fortifications was probably manned only in emergencies, because gate traffic was monitored elsewhere in Phase IV. Building B was, therefore, in the backwash of city life in Phase IV, whereas Building C was at the center of traffic and security of the city in Phase III.

THE PHASE IV POTTERY AND OBJECTS

Provenance

No appreciable interval seems to have occurred between the termination of Building C, Phase III, and the construction of Building B, Phase IV. The north unit actually remained usable in Phase IV, although considerable remodeling of the south unit took place. The significance of this observation is that Phase IV evidence of the construction of Building B serves two purposes. It marks the termination point of EB IC at Site A, and the beginning of EB IIA. The pottery listed in Phase IV is from the construction and remodeling of Building B.

The south room in Area I. The scant remains of the long narrow south room in Area I derive from the space between Walls D^2 and E^1 on Section H–H, Fig. 8. Actually, the fill of Layer 7 in Area II extends into Area I under Wall E^1, covering the stones of Wall F and of Wall D^1. Removal of this fill in Area I involved also the removal of stones of Wall D^1, so a possible mixture of Phase III and Phase IV pottery must be allowed. The latest pottery forms, however, may be associated with the founding of Wall E^1.

Layer 7 in Area I is the fill under the meter scale in Pl. III.2, on top of, and among, the stones of Wall F. Wall E^1 was constructed on the fill upon which the scale is resting. Another view of the same layer is in Pl. VI.1, looking west. Wall F of Building C is covered by the fill, and the foundation of Wall E^1 rested upon the smooth surface of the balk running from lower left to upper right.

Layer 1.4 is assigned to the packed surface shown in the above photographs, underlying Wall E^1. This layer includes the surface remaining in the balk under Wall E^1, as shown in Pl. VI.1, and extending to Wall D^2 in the upper left. Layer 1.5 is the same fill among the stones reaching from Walls F to D^1, underneath 1.4 which was relatively free of stones. The subdivision is made because more mixture of Phase III and Phase IV pottery may be expected in Layer 1.5. The same is true of Layer 1.5b, a sub-layer of 1.5 limited to the fill among the stones on top of Wall D^1, visible across the lower part of the photograph in Pl. III.2.

Layer 1.3 is assigned to the pottery taken from Wall E^1 itself, underneath the Phase VI rebuild, Wall E, and above Layer 7, the foundation fill. The wall is shown in Pl. VI.3, and drawn in Section G–G, Fig. 7. A heavy line across the top of Section G–G divides the Phase VI rebuild, Wall E, from the original Phase IV structure, Wall E^1, and the Phase VI blockage of the Phase IV opening against Wall C on the right is designated E^2. Layer 1.3 is from the Phase IV part of the wall only, reaching across to Wall P^1 on the left in Fig. 7.

The remodeled south unit in Area II. Layer 7, the compact buff clay fill in the Platform Z room, yielded most of the Phase IV evidence in Area II. This layer is confined to the Phase III building, reaching from Wall $F–F^1$ to Wall B, and from Wall Q to Wall E^1. Pottery from Layer 7 is, therefore, evidence of the remodeling of the Phase III rooms of the south unit, and the construction phase of Building B.

Layer 102.1 is the part of Layer 7 in the northwest corner of Area II, against Walls B and Q. Most of Layer 7 was removed in the previous excavation, but irregular projections remained against Wall Q and under Wall A. These remnants were trimmed as shown in Pl. IV.1, 2. A fairly wide section of Layer 102.1 against Wall Q is seen under the meter scale in Pl. IV.2, extending over to Wall F[1] on the right. This is drawn as Layer 7 in Section E–E, Fig. 10. The dashed line along the top of Layer 7 indicates the upper surface on which the scale rests in Pl. IV.2, before the layer was removed, exposing Wall Q behind the buff fill as seen in Pl. V.1. The fill is against the face of Wall Q on the left of the meter scale, but Wall Q is founded upon Layer 9, the *khamra* fill of Phase III.

Layer 102.3 is the continuation of Layer 7 as drawn in Section A–A, Fig. 83, in the corner formed by the intersection of Walls S[1] and B. The layer continues in Section F–F, Fig. 9, in the upper right, as part fill and part Wall S[1], the blocked Phase III entrance into the Platform Z room. This continuation is shown in Pl. VIII.3 at the upper left of the balk in the foreground, and Pl. VII.1 on the upper right of the meter scale. The part drawn in the Master Section, Fig. 83, is the light layer above the meter scale in Pl. VI.2, joining Wall S[1] on the upper left.

In the latter photograph, the light grey covering of Layer 9, the Phase III *khamra* fill, is evident above the meter scale. Layer 102.4 was assigned to this lower part of Layer 7 immediately on top of Layer 9, because its relation to Layers 9 and 7 was not clear at the time of excavation. There is undoubtedly Phase III pottery in 102.4, but no clear bedline separating it from 102.3 was distinguished so the layer is assigned to Phase IV.

The reused north unit in Area III. There was no discernible evidence of remodeling in the Phase III rooms of the north unit during Phase IV. Nothing comparable to the fill of Layer 7 was found in the unit, and the surface of Layer 9, Phase III, lay under the destruction debris assigned to Building B use. The pottery and objects from the destruction debris are assigned to Phase V, the termination of Building B, and Layer 9 is assigned to Phase III, the construction phase of Building C. No pottery was distinguished in the north unit as unquestionably Phase IV, so no evidence is presented from the north unit in the Phase IV listings.

The courtyard of the Building B complex. A distinction is made between the courtyard area, with its passageway to the south, and the remodeled Building C structure. Most of the pottery from Phase IV comes from layers foundational to the courtyard area and its new Building B walls. The courtyard probably became the focus of activity in Phase IV because the reused and remodeled rooms of Building C were oriented toward it, and possible new units east of Wall P[1] may have used it also.

In Area II, Wall P[1] is built on Layer 7a, the continuation of Layer 7 from the west side of Wall F[1], drawn in Section E–E, Fig. 10. Layer 7a was excavated as 101.9, a reddish-grey stony earth on top of the Phase III *khamra* fill, 101.10, and under the ashy destruction debris of Building B, 101.8a, b, assigned to Phase V. Layer 101.9 is shown against Wall F[1] in Pl. IV.2, in the lower right of the photograph. Across Wall F[1] in the same photograph is Layer 7, abutting Wall Q in the background.

Three parts of Area III yielded Phase IV pottery. A large section of the area was already excavated to bedrock between Firepit N[2] and the Wall M balk, so the sub-areas were excavated separately. Layers 202.5, 5a are drawn as Layer 7a in Section B–B, Fig. 11, on top of Phase III Layer 9, and against the outside of Wall F³. Layer 202.5 is the loose ashy stony fill visible in Pl. XVI.5 on top of the small balk projecting from the main balk, and running over against the lower side of the brick wall in the left center of the balk. The lower part of 202.5, on top of Phase III Layer 9 in Section B–B, is 202.5a.

The 300 sub-area is in Area IV, consisting mainly of the Wall M balk. Layers 300.14c and d comprise Layer 7a in the balk of Section B–B, Fig. 11, and are the equivalent of 202.5, 5a in Area III. The latter derive from removal of Layer 7a up to the balk. Layer 202.7 is a medium grey ashy fragment associated with Wall F³ in Area III where the wall itself was found exposed from previous excavations. This was excavated as Wall F³, but ashy earth from Layer 7a was found to be mixed, so the layer is assigned to 7a, or Phase IV.

On the south side of Area III, Layer 7a runs from Firepit N² on the east side of Section C–C, Fig. 12, to Wall F² on the west side. Pottery found in removing the stones of the firepit is designated 203.5a, and the ashy grey stony foundation of the firepit is 203.5, or the east end of Layer 7a in the section. The west end of Layer 7a, against Wall F², is 204.3, the equivalent of 203.5. A distinction was made in excavating the lower parts of both 203.5 and 204.3, where the bedline separating Layers 7a and 9 was indistinct. Pottery from this latter sub-layer was designated 203.6, under 203.5, and 204.3a, under 204.3. The sub-layer was assigned to Phase IV because of mixture at the point where the separation between 7a and 9 was not clear.

A problem was encountered in excavating the layers on top of, and around, Wall F². The remains were fragmentary, in irregular projections from the Wall H balk, so a different series of numbers was assigned to the pottery taken from Wall F² and its abutting layers. No. 204.10 was assigned to the end of Layer 7a abutting Wall F² on the east side, and is equivalent to 204.3 and 203.5. The equivalent of 203.6 and 204.3a against Wall F² is 204.11, and 204.9 is the bricky earth removed from the top of the stones of Wall F². The stones of Wall F², a Phase III structure, abut Wall F¹, a Phase IV structure at the north face of the Wall H balk, as is evident in Pl. IX.1, so the pottery taken from the top of Wall F² against the end of Phase IV Wall F¹ is assigned to Phase IV.

The Phase IV pottery forms

As noted earlier, no separation between destruction evidence of Building C and the beginning of Building B was made. The site was apparently spared total destruction evident in Tower C of Site A, or Building C at the acropolis. Tower C was subjected to intense heat, resulting in destruction of the fortification. Stones of the tower are still discolored and cracked from the extreme heat of the fire. Building C, on the east side of the tower, was apparently abandoned by the defenders of the city, and left standing when the attackers moved on to the acropolis and destroyed it. The north unit of Building C rooms was reused, and the south unit was remodeled in the Building B phase. Consequently the pottery and objects drawn in Figs. 35–43 represent the termination of Building C and the beginning of Building B, or the transition from Wright's EB IC to EB II. This is equivalent to the transition from Stratum III to Stratum II at Arad, and from EB I to EB II at Jericho and Tell el-Far'ah (N).

Small to medium bowls. Small bowls continue in Phase IV in all forms noted in Phase III, and their function as oil lamps is more evident. Black smoke marks are described on the rims of both shallow and hemispherical forms, suggesting that no particular criterion other than size determined what was used as a lamp. Examples of oil lamps are found in Fig. 35:1, 3, 4, 6, 7, 10, 16, 21, and Reg. No. 4776d under No. 21.

A new characteristic found among the small bowl forms is the semi-carinate profile in Fig. 35:6–8. No. 9 also has a slight angle in the wall below the rim, although the rim is not bent upright. This feature seems to be related to the new carinate form in Fig. 35:18–23, and not to earlier types of incurved rims. For instance, Fig. 35:8 reflects the same technique in throwing and shaping that is more sharply defined in No. 21, and is not a reappearance of the Proto-Urban incurved rim evident in Tomb A13, Levels II–I at Jericho (Kenyon 1960, 51, Fig. 22:6–9).

The carinate form in Fig. 35:18–23 is distinctively new. This is characterized by a sharp angle at the point where the rim bends upright, and a graceful outward curve from the angle to the rim. Pl. XIII.1 indicates the consistency in proportion of the bottom and wall of the bowl, and visual evidence of a sure hand in shaping it. The ware is generally grey to reddish brown, although two examples are described as buff, Fig. 35:8, 15, and two are orange, Nos. 11, 12. Rims are burnished horizontally, probably with the use of a slow wheel, down to the angle of the wall both inside and outside, and the inside bottom is hand-burnished with random, contiguous lines in somewhat crude, deep markings. The latter is illustrated in Pl. XIII.3. Generally, a slip of fine clay is applied before burnishing.

The first appearance of the above form at Jericho is in Tomb A127 (Kenyon 1960, 88, Fig. 25:3) and in Phase Kii of Areas E III–IV (Hennessy 1967, Pl. V.52, p. 11; Pl. XII.2, p. 20). A major destruction of Jericho occurred at the end of Phase K, marking the end of EB I, so the example cited from Phase Kii is in a transition context similar to Phase IV at Ai, Site A. Hennessy suggests assigning the Phase K bowl at Jericho to Phase J (*ibid.*, p. 20) and the beginning of EB II, apparently because of the difficulty in separating destruction evidence of Phase K from construction evidence of Phase J.

The carinate bowl form is more popular at sites north of Ai than at those in the south. One similar, possibly locally imitated, form is reported in Stratum III at Arad (Amiran Early Arad, Pl. 13:31), and another semi-carinate form occurs in Stratum II (*ibid.*, Pl. 22:59). The crisply-styled authentic form seems to be absent at Arad. North of Ai, however, at Tell el-Far'ah (N), numerous examples are found. A series of shallow to deep carinate forms is reported by de Vaux in Ancien Bronze I (EB IC) from the *tell* (1947, 412–413, Fig. 4, 1948, 560–561, Fig. 6:10–11). Other examples occur in Tomb 2 (1949, 120–121) Fig. 6:23, 25), and in EB Périodes 1–5, they are numerous in the first Période (1961, 580–581, Fig. 3:36–38). A pattern of movement to the south may be deduced from the occurrences of the form, because it appears at Tell el-Far'ah in EB IC (as Amiran lists it in her catalogue of forms, 1969. 56, Pl. 13:5), at Jericho in Phase Kii, a transition context from EB IC to EB II, and at Ai in Phase IV, the construction phase of EB IIA.

The two crudely made medium-wide bowls in Fig. 35:28–29 are similar to Hennessy's hammer-rim forms appearing first in Phase L at Jericho (Hennessy 1967, Pl. IV. 30; p. 10), marking the beginning of EB I (Wright's EB IC). This type also appears in Phase III at Ai (Fig. 26:26) in a deeper, straighter-walled form, but with the same coarseness of ware and thick-walled functional profile. The degenerate form and semi-handmade technique of manufacture contrasts sharply with that of the stylish carinate form appearing for the first time in Phase IV.

Wide, deep bowls. Two types of wide, deep bowls are significant in Phase IV. Both types continue forms and technology evident in Phase III, with some refinements. The first is drawn in Fig. 35:25–27, a fairly thick-walled bowl with upcurved (No. 27) to slightly incurved (No. 26) sides and a thinned everted edge. No. 25 has a burnished reddish-brown slip inside with no special decoration noted outside, while Nos. 26–27 have traces of white slip outside. These examples continue the family of forms evident in Fig. 26:15–17, 20, and a technique of slipping both the inside and outside.

The second type seems to have developed from the Phase III form in Fig. 26:18–19, 21, characterized by a flattened rim with inward projecting lip. No. 19 has traces of a reddish-brown slip inside, and No. 21 has a heavy white slip outside. The Phase IV examples in Fig. 36:3, 5 have a burnished reddish-brown slip inside and are characterized by flattened rims with inward projecting lips. The profiles of the latter are sharper and all traces of a ridge on the outside of the rim have disappeared. This refinement may be due to the influence of the platter form in its low-rim variation, examples of which are shown in Fig. 36. Fig. 36:2 seems to be a hybrid form between the latter and the former. The decoration of radially-burnished reddish-brown slip of Fig. 36:2 is found in Fig. 36:3, the deep bowl form, and in Fig. 36:14, a wide, shallow platter with low-profile rim.

Deep bowls with flattened rims and inturned edges appear at Jericho in Areas E II–IV in Phases J and H. Forms similar to Fig. 36:3 are noted in Phase J (Hennessy 1967, Pl. VI:56; p. 12), and traced to a possible origin in Phase L. Fig. 36:5 has its nearest parallel in a Phase H form (*ibid.*, Pl. VI:59), assigned to EB II. Phase L and Phase K at Jericho are assigned to EB I, but interpreted as transitional between Proto-Urban and EB II, and Phases H and J are within the EB II tradition. Fig. 36:3 is paralleled at Arad, Stratum II, in several rim styles, varying mainly in the stance of the inward-turned lip and the depth of the bowls (see Amiran Early Arad, Pl. 23:8–17). No exact parallel with Fig. 36:5 is shown in Stratum II, although No. 22 on the same plate has a horizontally flattened rim with a slight ridge on the outside opposite an inward projecting lip.

A bowl similar to Fig. 36:3 is found at Tell el-Farʿah (N) in Période 1 of Ancien Bronze (de Vaux 1961, 580–581, Fig. 3:32), and another with a sloping triangular rim similar to Fig. 36:4 is assigned to Période 3 by de Vaux (*ibid.*, 586–587, Fig. 4:15). The latter has a wide, flat base characteristic of Phase V forms at Ai, and it is possible that Fig. 36:4 does not share the base characteristic. Shipton assigns the wide, flat base form to Strata XVI–XVII at Megiddo (1939, Pl. 10:26), while the deep bowl form with flattened, inward projecting edge is assigned to Stratum XVIII (*ibid.*, No. 37). Amiran cites the latter example as a typical EB II form (1969, 60–61, Pl. 15:9).

Wide platter-bowls. The wide platter is a prominent and distinctive form in Phase IV, evidenced by the drawings in Figs. 35–36. The hallmark of platter decoration is a burnished reddish-brown slip, applied inside and outside the vessel and in various patterns. Ware is not distinctively different from that of Phase III, probably representing a leveling-off of technological improvements in pottery making. The new trend in form is toward a lower profile rim and thicker angle at the bend of the rim. A shallow concavity underneath the angle of the rim, evident in only one example in Phase III (Fig. 27:7), is recorded in two examples in Phase IV (see Fig. 36:7–8).

The wide platter with low profile rim and concavity underneath the angle of the rim reported by Hennessy in Areas E III–IV at Jericho in Phase G (Hennessy 1967, Pl. VI:63) is contemporary with the Phase IV examples cited. This form is rare at Jericho until EB IIIA, and is not reported from tombs before EB III. One example from Tomb D12 (Kenyon 1960, 119, Fig. 38:3) is of uncertain stratification, either EB II or III. This form is deeper than the Phase IV bowls in Fig. 36:7–8, and actually compares with the Phase VI form at Ai in Fig. 59:27, an EB IIIA example. Amiran reports two low profile forms from Arad in Stratum II (Amiran Early Arad, Pl. 23:1–2), the first of which is characterized by a distinct concavity in the wall underneath the angle of the rim. A slight concavity is present in No. 2, although the groove is fashioned in the thickening of the rim and not by depressing the clay of the bottom of the vessel.

One platter form with a possible concavity under the angle of the rim is reported by de Vaux from Tell el-Far'ah (N) and assigned to Période 2 of Ancien Bronze (1955, 566–567, Fig. 13:20). Another of the same type is assigned to Megiddo XIX by Shipton (1939, Stratum XIX:16, chart), although he noted that the form normally is found in Strata XVI–XVIII (see p. 37:133). Amiran places the form in EB III as typical (1969, 71, Pl. 18:1), but the occurrences noted above indicate that it was used in EB II, and the single example in Phase III at Site A indicates an introduction in EB IC, or an aberrancy caused by a mixture of artifacts while excavating. If the latter occurred, it slipped by fairly rigid controls imposed upon field excavation.

Jugs and Jars. The distinctive jug with tall cylindrical neck and high loop handle in Fig. 37:26 is a new form in Phase IV. This vessel is not as well-made as the drawing indicates, being of very coarse ware roughly finished. There is evidence of an orange-red slip vertically burnished on the neck above the high relief molding, a feature not noted in the description. The form itself is more pleasing from an aesthetic perspective than the craftsmanship evident in the jug. Other fragments of jugs are registered under Fig. 37:26, but are not drawn. All of the fragments are decorated with burnished reddish-brown slip and reflect a low level of craftsmanship, seemingly incompatible with the graceful form occurring in several variations (see Hennessy 1967, Pls. XXXIX–XLIV).

A jug similar to Fig. 37:26 is reported from Tomb G (Marquet-Krause 1949, Pl. LXXV:1451). This jug also has an applied molding around the base of the neck, at the point where the body and neck units are joined, and is decorated with a burnished red slip. The Tomb G vessel was paralleled with a counterpart form in Tomb 14 at Tell el-Far'ah (N) in an earlier study (Callaway 1964, 41) and assigned to EB I. De Vaux believed the Tomb 14 forms 'prédulent aux formes de l'Ancien Bronze' (1952, 577; see the form referred to on p. 579, Fig. 11:19) and assigned them to Chalcolithique Superieur.

The EB I (Wright's EB IC) assignment of Tomb G:1451 was made on the evidence of parallel forms in Tombs 13 and 14, classified by de Vaux as Chalcolithique Superieur, and forms in Jericho Tomb A108, Kenyon's EB I (Callaway 1964, 41). This assignment now seems valid, and possibly conservative with reference to this particular jug. Hennessy cites EB II parallels of the same family of forms from Room W, Square K6 of Garstang's excavations at Jericho (1967, 22, Pl. XII:5) and examples in First Dynasty contexts in Egypt (*ibid.*, Pls. XXXIX–XLIV). A similar form from Bab edh-Dhra' is reported by Saller (1965, 199, Fig. 31:12, p. 202) and assigned to EB II on the basis of Hennessy's type series from Area E III–IV at Jericho. The Phase IV example in Fig. 37:26 occurs in the construction phase of the EB II city at Ai, and thus is transitional from EB IC to EB IIA.

Hennessy found related forms of the high, cylindrical-necked jug with loop handle at northern sites, specifically at Qalat-er-Rouss (1967, Pl. XLIX:2M, p. 63) and Tarsus (1967, Pl. XLIX:4M, p. 63). The form appears first in EB IC, and becomes common in EB II, or Amuq G. Kantor cites examples decorated with painted geometrical designs from Abydos, Saqqara, and Abusir in Egypt dated to the First Dynasty (1965, 29, Fig. 5:A–G), or EB II. The only occurrence of the geometrical design at Site A is in Phase V, or EB IIB. No phase IV jugs or juglets were decorated with painted designs. The form seems to have appeared first in North Syria, and then moved southward to Canaan and Egypt, where it was decorated with the painted geometrical motif in EB II.

The small jar with short, everted rim in Fig. 37:27 is a new form at Site A in Phase IV. The form occurs at Arad in Stratum III (Amiran Early Arad, Pl. 14:10) and is among the forms from northern sites shown by Hennessy (1967, Pl. XLIX:2G, 3G, 4F). The jar in Fig. 37:27 has traces of a white slip, or wash, as Hennessy notes of the forms from Qalat er-Rouss (1967, 63), but the former is handmade with an uneven surface on the wall, and not burnished. The short everted rim, however, is wheel-turned. If the form derives from northern antecedents, it seems to be a poorly made local imitation.

The store-jar with squared rim drawn in Fig. 37:23, appears first at Site A in Phase III. Variations of the same form occur in Phase IV, Fig. 37:22–23, 25, 28, all of which lack the crispness of the earlier form and the excellence of its craftsmanship and finish. This poorer level of craftsmanship may be due to deterioration of the Phase III culture, or it may indicate the arrival at Ai of a new increment of people from the same general region as that of the Phase III city builders. Hennessy finds forms similar to those in Phase IV at Qalat er-Rouss (1967, Pl. LXIX:2H), Judeideh F (ibid., 3J, K), and Tarsus (ibid., 4J), suggesting a northern origin of the type in EB I.

Hole-mouth jars. There is a monotonous continuity in most hole-mouth jar forms from Phase III to Phase IV. The plain, squared rim of Fig. 29:5 is continued in Fig. 38:21, 22 with slight variation toward a flatter stance and a more pronounced point on the outer ridge of the rim. Cut rims continue, as is evident in comparing Figs. 29:8–14, 15, 17; 30:1–4 with Figs. 39:1–10, but the trend is toward a flatter stance with these also. Wide mouth jars seem to be more numerous in Phase IV than Phase III, and the Phase IV forms tend toward more incurved or inverted rims, probably reflecting the trend toward flatter stance in the jars noted above.

One Phase III form not evident at Site A in Phase IV is the beaked rim, shown in Fig. 30:6–9. This form appears at Jericho in Areas E III–IV in Phases L–K, contemporary with Phase III at Ai, and continues in Phases J–G (Hennessy 1967, 11), the equivalent of Phase IV at Ai. This form may appear at another site at Ai in Phase IV, because it recurs at Site A in Phase V.

Handles and spouts. Very few examples of loop handles occur in Building B in Phase IV. The tall, cylindrical loop form introduced in Phase IV is more rare than the rounded handle attached to the waist or shoulder of the 'metallic' ware jugs. Fig. 42:12 is a type found at Arad in Stratum III and continuing in Stratum II (Amiran Early Arad, Pl. 14:38, 27:4) associated with the elongated ovoid-shaped jar characteristic of EB II. Another form is the more rounded handle in Fig. 42:13 attached to the waist of jugs found at Arad in Stratum II (ibid., Pl. 27:1–3), and cited by Hennessy as a typical EB II form (Hennessy 1967, Pl. XII:5). This is Amiran's 'Abydos' or 'metallic' ware (1969, 59–60), found in tombs of the First Dynasty in Egypt, and recognized as foreign imports.

The column or pillar handle with no pierced aperture occurs in Phase IV, Fig. 42:26, although the form occurs at Arad in earlier strata. This form seems to continue the tradition of the pierced spout found first at Ai in Phase II, Fig. 23:20, and continuing in Phase III, Fig. 32:21. The latter is not pierced all the way through the spout, so it is vestigial in Phase III. The Phase IV example is solid, with no attempt at piercing indicated.

The Marquet-Krause Phase IV pottery

Several of the forms in Fig. 43, taken from Marquet-Krause, are assigned to Sanctuary C, or Phase III, by Hennessy (1967, Pl. XVI), so a brief apologetic for Fig. 43 seems to be required. The guidelines for the assignment in Fig. 43 are (1) that Marquet-Krause noted a provenance *under* the floor, or an installation, of her Sanctuary B, and (2) that the provenance was not specified as Sanctuary C. Phase IV is the construction phase of Building B (M–K Sanctuary B), so the provenance of pottery would agree with the stated guidelines. Phase V includes all pottery found *on* or immediately *above* the floor of Building B.

Fig. 43:11, Hennessy's Pl. XVI:33, is M-K No. 2003, listed with No. 2002 from Ch. 116 (Area II), 'sous parquet B' (Marquet-Krause 1949, 247). Since the provenance of some pottery in ch. 116 is listed as Sanctuary C, it seems prudent to assign No. 2003 to Phase IV instead of Phase III. Fig. 43:10, Hennessy's Pl. XVI:35, is M-K No. 2543, listed with several other pieces from ch. 116, 'sous parquet B' (p. 346), as is Fig. 43:6, Hennessy's Pl. XVI. 36, M-K No. 2002, cited above with No. 2003. The juglet with painted trellis design in Fig. 43:3, Hennessy's Pl. XVI:38, is M-K No. 2542, listed with No. 2543 above 'sous parquet B.' Fig. 43:7, an oval, flat-base jug, is Hennessy's Pl. XVI:37, M-K No. 2537, from ch. 116, 'sous parquet B' (p. 345). Hennessy's Pl. XVI:39, on the other hand, is not listed in Phase IV because Marquet-Krause gives its provenance as ch. 238 in Fouille V_2, in the Lower City (see No. 2536a, p. 345). Pl. XVI. 41 has been noted earlier as from Tomb G (see No. 1315, p. 159), although it is probably contemporary with Building C or Phase III.

Objects

Two objects from the courtyard in Areas II and III suggest new crafts in Phase IV. The first is a well-made basalt ring with flattened oval section, drawn in Fig. 42:39, and the second is a fired pottery palette, or brick-like object.

The basalt ring. Rings similar to this example are reported from Arad in variations of form (Amiran Early Arad, Pl. 76:1–27), where functions from beads to spindle whorls seem evident. Pierced stone disks occur in Tomb D12 at Jericho (Kenyon 1960, 124, Fig. 40:125), possibly dating to EB II. The ring in Fig. 42:39 is too large for a bead, and its rounded profile does not suggest a spindle whorl. Three larger basalt rings found in Site C (unpublished) are worn flat on one side, as though they served as tools of a craftsman. A function as a tool does not seem improbable for the ring, from Building B, because the rounded surface of the hole is worn to a polished finish.

The pottery palette. Two pieces of the thick brick-like palette in Fig. 42:40 were found in Layer 202.5, drawn as Layer 7a in Section C–C, Fig. 12. The object is made of pottery clay and fired to a medium hard consistency. Because the palette was found near Firepit N^2 in the courtyard, it may have been used in the preparation of food, or in cooking. Bread, for instance, may have been cooked on the concave surface of the palette.

Conclusions

Most of the Phase IV pottery forms continue or develop from Phase III traditions, but a few significant new types occur. The new forms belong to traditions found north of Ai, either in northern Canaan, or in Syria, and, therefore, have a bearing upon the changing locus of power in Canaan and its relation to increments of newcomers from the north.

The pottery horizon of Phase IV. The nearest stratified parallels to the Phase IV pottery are found in Phases Kii–H in Areas E III–IV at Jericho (see Hennessy 1967, 12). Some forms found in Tombs A108 and A127 also occur in Phase IV, suggesting an early EB II pottery horizon. Comparative study of the Arad pottery leaves no clear-cut equation of strata, because forms from Strata III and II occur in Building B. This supports the evidence from Jericho in placing Phase IV at the beginning of EB II, however.

Comparison with the Tell el-Far'ah (N) material results in a less precise stratigraphic parallel than with Arad. Similar forms are found on the *tell* in Périodes 1–3 of Ancien Bronze. One form, the sharply carinated medium bowl, seems to occur earlier at Tell el-Far'ah (N) than at Ai, becoming common in Période 1. The latest parallel forms seem to occur in Période 3, with considerable overlapping of Période 2. A general equation of Phase IV with Périodes 2–3 seems to be warranted, placing Phase IV at the beginning of EB II. Similar pottery forms are cited from Megiddo XVI–XVIII, although a comparison of strata is of little practical use.

In the context of the Near Eastern culture area, the beginning of Phase IV relates to the late First Dynasty in Egypt, from Djer (Albright), or Den (Hennessy and Lapp), and continues, with Phase V, into the Second Dynasty. This correlates with Amuq G in North Syria and Byblos III as Kantor arranged the sequences (1965, 27), but Kantor's high chronology is not supported by the Carbon 14 assays of materials from Ai.

A termination point for Phase IV is not indicated in the comparative study, because there is considerable overlapping with Phase V, the destruction phase of the EB II city at Ai. Phase IV does, however, mark the beginning of EB II, so it is designated EB IIA, and Phase V, the subject of the next chapter, is EB IIB.

Chronology. A date of 3000 B.C. for the beginning of Phase III is indicated by Carbon 14 assays of wood taken from buildings of the first walled city, as noted in Chapter V, and a date of 2860 B.C. is suggested for the termination of Phase III and the beginning of Phase IV. This chronology seems to be supported by the following Carbon 14 assays of wood from the roof of Building B:

Sample No.	Provenance	Date
1. TX 1028	A IV 300.16	4800 ± 90
		2850 B.C.

Charred wood from the roof of Building B, burned in the Phase V destruction of the building, but most likely constructed in the remodeling of Building C at the beginning of Phase IV. The brick walls of Building C, Area IV, were reused in Phase IV, but the roof probably did not survive the burning of adjacent Tower C, which was completely rebuilt in Phase IV. The cutting of this wood dates from the beginning of Phase IV, therefore, because its charred remains were on top of the pottery lying on the floor of Building B.

2. GaK 2382	A III 201.4a	4840 ± 130
		2890 B.C.

Charred wood from the roof of Building B, burned in the Phase V destruction of the building, but installed in the remodeling of Building C at the beginning of Phase IV. As in No. 1 above, the roof material in Area III belongs with Phase IV, although Walls Q and F² were reused Phase III structures. Tower B, which supported the west side of the roof, was built in Phase IV over the burned remains of Phase III Tower C. This sample was on top of the pottery lying on the floor of Building B, between Walls Q and W.

Two dates, therefore, may be related to the beginning of Phase IV, and one date was given for the termination of Phase III in the preceding chapter. The three dates are a cluster marking the same event, and having cumulative significance. The range of time covered in their $\pm$ margins is as follows:

1. TX 1028   A IV 300.16   2760–2940 B.C.
2. GaK 2382   A III 201.4a   2760–3020 B.C.
3. TX 1035   C I 1.31   2770–2950 B.C.

The mean dates of the three assays average 2867 B.C. TX 1028 and TX 1035 are only 10 years apart, and the low side of the $\pm$ margins is the same for TX 1028 and GaK 2382. TX 1035 maintains its 10 year plus on the low side of the margin. GaK 2382, therefore, has the effect of weighing the margin toward TX 1035, so a date for the termination of Phase III and the beginning of Phase IV of ca. 2860 B.C. is acceptable on the evidence of Carbon 14 dating.

THE TRANSITION TO THE SECOND URBAN PHASE

Two distinctive new pottery forms seem to be representative of the culture introduced at the time of transition from Phase III to Phase IV. The first is the carinate bowl with outward curving rim, drawn in Fig. 35:18–23. This bowl has a crisp, almost metallic, form in its authentic style, and does not seem to have developed from any local small or medium bowl forms. The semi-carinate bowls in Fig. 35:6–9 are probably local variations influenced by the metallic form, and not antecedent to it.

No parallels of the authentic form are reported from Arad, but numerous examples occur north of Ai, particularly at Tell el-Far'ah (N), even in EB IC. The implication is that the carinate bowl was introduced at Ai in Phase IV by people already in Canaan. The occurrence of examples in Phase Kii of the *tell* at Jericho, a destruction layer of the EB IC city, suggests that these people had something to do with the termination of the city. The appearance of the forms in construction layers of Phase IV at Ai suggests that the violent holocaust terminating the Phase III city was participated in by groups of the same people.

The second new form is the jug with a tall, cylindrical neck and high loop handle, drawn in Fig. 37:26. This vessel, along with other variations with rounded loop handles attached to the waist or shoulder, is styled with crisp lines in a hard, well-fired ware commonly described as 'metallic' (see Kantor 1965, 15). This form seems to be common at Tell el-Far'ah (N) earlier than Phase IV at Ai, but it becomes common at Arad in Stratum II, contemporary with Phases IV and V.

A movement from north to south seems to be indicated for this form, as well as the carinated bowl noted above. The examples cited from Egypt by Kantor have a painted geometric decoration similar to that found on a Phase V form at Ai, dating to the latter half of the Building B period, or EB IIB. No instances of the decoration occur in Phase IV. At Arad the geometric decoration occurs in Stratum II, but not in Stratum III, which overlaps the beginning of Phase IV. If the painted decoration originated in Egypt, it seems to have reached southern Canaan after the events bringing about the transition from EB IC to EB IIA.

The evidence seems to support a transition at Ai from Phase III to Phase IV brought about by local elements rather than an intrusion from the outside. Ultimately, outside influences can be traced to North Syria and the coastal cities, but these elements seem to have settled first in northern Canaan, perhaps during the time that the Phase III city flourished. Possibly continuing increments from the north, and increasing influence of Egypt during the reign of Den conspired together to bring about the downfall of the Phase III city and the occupation of Ai by rivals who seem to have been unworthy successors.

DESCRIPTIONS OF THE PHASE IV POTTERY AND OBJECTS, FIGS. 35–42

Fig. 35 No.	Reg. No.	
1	5038c	Rim slightly incurved to thin rounded edge; brown with grey core; traces of burnished, reddish-brown slip over-all; some assorted pits and spalling; black smoke marks on rim indicate possible use as lamp. A I 1.5b.
2	4663	Rim incurved to thickened, rounded edge; greenish-grey inside and buff outside, grey core; fine with many assorted, mostly fine, white grits; rough, uneven surfaces over-all. A III 202.5a.
3	4843	Rim slightly incurved to rounded edge, wet-smoothed; buff; medium with some small to fine, tan, reddish-brown, white, and grey grits, one very large white grit, traces of burnished, reddish-brown slip outside; black smoke marks on edge indicate possible use as lamp, many assorted pits over-all. A III 204.9.
4	4776e	Rim slightly upcurved to thinned, rounded edge; grey with orangish-buff outside; medium-coarse with some small to fine, tan and white grits, black smoke marks on edge indicate possible use as lamp. A III 203.5.
5	4747	Rim upcurved to rounded edge, wet-smoothed; orangish-buff with grey core; coarse with many medium to fine white, grey, and tan grits; very uneven surfaces over-all. A III 203.5.
6	4855	Rim slightly inverted to rounded edge, wheel-turned; medium with some assorted tan and grey grits; few assorted pits over-all, black smoke marks on edge indicate possible use as lamp. A III 204.10.
—	4662i	Rim of small bowl, slightly everted to rounded edge; tan; medium-coarse with many assorted grey grits. A III 202.5.
7	4866	Rim upcurved and slightly inverted to rounded edge, wet-smoothed; buff with grey core; coarse with many assorted tan and grey grits, few assorted reddish-brown grits; traces of orange slip over-all; many assorted pits outside, black smoke marks on edge indicate possible use as lamp. A III 204.10.
8	4871	Rim upturned and slightly everted to thinned, rounded edge, wet-smoothed; buff; medium-coarse with many assorted light-grey and tan grits, porous ware; traces of continuously-burnished, reddish-brown slip over-all; many assorted pits. A III 204.10.
9	4776	Rim upcurved and slightly everted to thin, rounded edge, wet-smoothed; buff with grey core; medium-coarse with many assorted white grits; uneven surfaces over-all, some grey incrustations. A III 203.5.
10	4854	Rim slightly upcurved to thinned, rounded edge; buff with thick, dark-grey core; coarse with many assorted tan and grey grits; faint traces of reddish-orange slip inside; black smoke marks on edge indicate possible use as lamp, many assorted pits and rough, gritty texture over-all. A III 204.10.

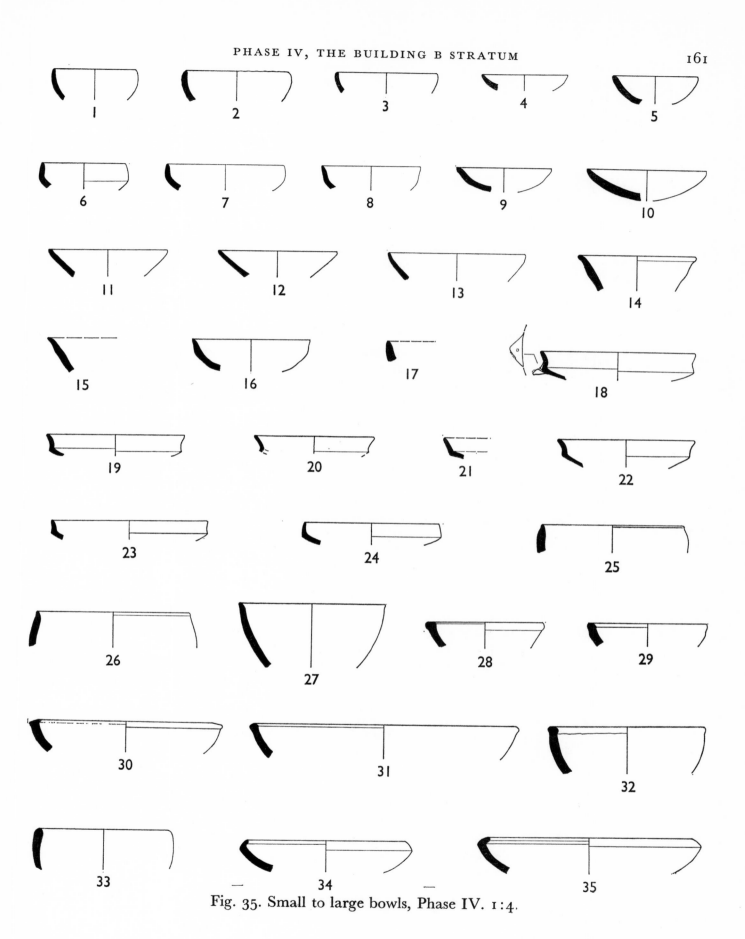

Fig. 35. Small to large bowls, Phase IV. 1:4.

Fig. 35 No.	Reg. No.	
11	4761	Rim inclined out to rounded edge, wheel-turned; orange; medium with many small to fine tan grits; traces of radially-burnished, reddish-brown slip over-all. A III 203.5.
12	4771	Rim inclined out to thinned, rounded edge, wet-smoothed; orange; medium-coarse with many assorted tan grits; traces of burnished, reddish-brown slip inside. A III 203.5.
13	4856	Angular wall with rim slightly incurved to thinned, rounded edge, wheel-turned; inside; dark-orange; medium-coarse with many small to fine tan grits; traces of burnished, reddish-brown slip inside; some assorted pits. A III 204.10.
14	4873	Angular wall with rim slightly everted to rounded edge, wet-smoothed; pronounced tool marks outside; pinkish-brown; very coarse with many assorted white and tan grits; creamy-white slip outside and on edge; very rough texture outside, grey incrustations over-all. A III 204.11.
15	4772	Angular wall with rim slightly everted to thin, rounded edge, wet-smoothed; buff; medium-coarse with many fine white, and some assorted tan, grits; traces of burnished, reddish-brown slip over-all. A III 203.5.
16	4762	Rim slightly everted with thin, rounded edge; pinkish-buff; medium-coarse with many assorted tan grits, porous ware; many assorted pits over-all, black smoke marks on edge indicate possible use as lamp. A III 203.5.
17	4637	Rim upcurved to thinned, rounded edge; buff with dark-grey core; medium with some small to fine white and grey grits; traces of reddish-brown slip over-all, traces of burnishing inside. A III 202.5.
18	4842	Carinated wall with rim everted to rounded edge, inside and edge wheel-turned; lug-handle located horizontally at angle of wall, triangular shaped and pierced; hole reduces in size from top to pinhole at bottom; brown slip; medium with many small to fine white grits; traces of crude, continuous-burnishing over-all. A III 204.9.
19	4745	Carinated wall with upper portion everted to thin, rounded rim, wheel-turned; reddish-brown; with brown slip; medium with some fine white grits; uneven wheel-burnishing on edge and crude burnishing inside and on bottom; very uneven surface on bottom. A III 203.5.
—	4870	Carinated wall with upper portion everted to thinned edge, wheel-turned; reddish-brown; medium with some assorted, mostly fine, white grits; crude, wheel-burnishing over-all. A III 204.10.
—	4872	Body sherd of bowl carinated wall, wheel-turned; reddish-brown; fine with some white grits; traces of continuous burnishing over-all. A III 204.10.
20	4857	Carinated wall with upper portion sharply everted to rounded rim, wheel-turned; grey-brown with reddish-brown slip; medium with few small white grits; traces of uneven wheel-burnishing inside rim. A III 204.10.
21	4786	Carinated wall with upper portion everted to thinned, rounded rim; buff; medium-coarse with many assorted tan and reddish-brown grits; traces of orange slip inside; rough gritty texture inside, black smoke marks on edge indicate possible use as lamp. A III 203.6.
—	4776d	Carinated wall of bowl with upper portion everted to thinned, rounded rim, wheel-turned; orange with buff core; medium-coarse with few assorted white grits; black smoke marks on edge indicate possible use as lamp. A III 203.5.
22	4852	Carinated wall with upper portion everted to thinned, rounded rim; brown with grey-brown slip; medium with many small to fine white grits; traces of crude, continuous-burnishing over-all. A III 204.10.

Fig. 35 *No.*	*Reg.* *No.*	
23	5018	Carinated wall with upper portion everted to thinned, rounded rim, inside and outside edge wheel-turned; grey with grey-brown slip; medium with many fine white grits; crude wheel-burnishing over-all. A IV 300.14c.
24	4660	Carinated wall with upright rim slightly inverted to thinned, rounded edge, wheel turned; buff; medium with many small to fine white and grey grits; traces of continuously turned; buff; medium with many small to fine white and grey grits; traces of continuously-burnished buff slip inside; rough sandy texture. A III 202.5.
25	4770	Upright rim slightly everted with thin, rounded edge, wet-smoothed; tan with grey core, medium-coarse with few small to fine white grits; traces of burnished reddish-brown slip inside. A III 203.5.
26	4847	Slightly incurved wall with thinned, upright to inverted rim, wet-smoothed; orangish-buff; medium-coarse with many small to fine tan grits; faint traces of white slip outside and inside edge; grey smoke marks inside. A III 204.10.
27	4864	Wall upcurved to thin, rounded, slightly everted rim, wet smoothed; orangish-buff with thick, dark-grey core penetrating to outside in places; medium-coarse with many assorted grey and tan grits; traces of heavy white slip outside, some grey incrustations inside. A III 204.10.
28	4785	Rim upcurved to thickened, rounded, flat edge projected out; tannish-grey with dark-grey core; coarse with few assorted grey grits; rough texture and few small to fine pits over-all. A III 203.6.
29	4769	Rim upcurved to rounded, flattened edge slightly projected in; buff with dark-orange patches, grey core in places; medium-coarse with many small to fine, white and grey grits, porous ware; very uneven surfaces over-all. A III 203.5.
30	4279	Rim upcurved to inverted edge projected out, wheel-finished; orangish-buff with buff core; very coarse with many assorted, mostly small to fine, white grits; many assorted pits, very rough texture. A II 101.9.
31	4675	Rim upcurved to flattened, inverted edge with small ridge outside; brownish-grey; medium-coarse with many assorted, mostly medium to small, dark-grey, white, and tan grits; black smoke marks inside. A III 202.7.
32	4751	Upright rim with flattened edge projected in and out, wheel-finished; buff with dark-orange patch inside; coarse with many assorted white grits; rough texture, and some assorted pits over-all. A III 203.5.
33	4739	Upright rim incurved to thickened, rounded edge, wet-smoothed; orange with patches of buff outside, thick, dark-grey core; coarse with many assorted grey quartz grits; very uneven surfaces over-all. A III 203.5.
34	4774	Rim upcurved to rounded, inverted edge; tannish-buff with thick, dark-grey core; medium with some fine white grits; traces of burnished reddish-brown slip over-all; some assorted pits and spalling outside. A III 203.5.
35	4780	Rim upcurved to rounded, inverted edge, wheel-turned; tan with grey core penetrating to outside in places; traces of burnished, reddish-brown slip inside and on edge; many small to fine pits over-all. A III 203.5a.
Fig. 36 *No.*	*Reg.* *No.*	
1	4776h	Angular wall inclined out to rounded sharply inverted rim; greyish-buff; coarse with some assorted grey, white, and orange grits; greyish-white slip outside; uneven surfaces, brown incrustations over-all. A III 203.5.
2	4867	Wall upcurved to wide, rounded, triangular inverted edge, wheel-turned; reddish-brown slip, dark-grey core; coarse with many assorted white and grey grits; radial-burnishing inside and wheel-burnishing outside and on edge. A III 204.10.

Fig. 36 No.	Reg. No.	
3	4865	Wide, slightly rounded, triangular, inverted rim, wheel-turned; reddish-brown slip, grey core; coarse with many assorted white and grey grits, traces of radial-burnishing inside and wheel-burnishing outside and on edge. A III 204.10.
4	4768	Upcurved to wide, rounded flat, triangular inverted rim, wheel-turned; buff; medium-coarse with many assorted white, tan, and dark-brown grits; traces of burnished, reddish-brown slip over-all. A III 203.5.
5	4846	Upturned to wide, slightly rounded, flat, triangular inverted rim, wheel-turned; reddish-brown slip, thick dark-grey core; coarse with very many assorted white and light- and dark-grey grits; traces of crude radial-burnishing inside and crude wheel-burnishing outside and on edge; black smoke marks inside and on edge. (4846 and 4860 joined). A III 204.10.
6	4749	Upcurved to rounded, inverted rim, wheel-turned; reddish-brown slip, dark-grey core; medium with many small to fine white, grey, and reddish-brown grits; radially-burnished inside and wheel-burnished outside and on edge; some assorted pits over-all, spalling on edge, some grey incrustations. A III 203.5.
7	4750	Upcurved to thickened, triangular, inverted rim, shallow groove underneath angle of rim, wheel-turned; orange with buff and grey core; medium-coarse with some assorted grey and tan grits; traces of wheel-burnished reddish-brown slip over-all; burned inside. A III 203.5.
8	4851	Upcurved to thickened, triangular, inverted rim, with shallow groove underneath angle of rim, wheel-turned; buff; medium with some assorted white, tan, grey, and reddish-brown grits; traces of wheel-burnished, reddish-brown slip over-all. (4851 and 4853 joined). A III 204.10.
9	4858	Slightly upcurved to thickened, slightly inverted rim, wheel-finished; buff; very coarse with many assorted tan grits; traces of burnished reddish-brown slip inside. A III 204.10.
10	4765	Upcurved to low, triangular, inverted rim, wheel-turned; orangish-buff with thick, grey core; medium with many small to fine white grits; traces of burnished reddish-orange slip over-all. A III 203.5.
—	5038d	Flattened base of wide bowl wheel-turned; tan with grey core; coarse with many assorted white grits; dark-orange slip inside and on portion of outside, continuously-burnished over-all; some grey incrustations over-all. A I 1.5b.
—	5019	Upcurved wall of wide bowl with thickened angle of low, inverted broken rim, wheel-turned; dark-orange with reddish-brown core; very coarse with many assorted light- and dark-grey, and reddish-brown grits; faint traces of wheel-burnished, reddish-brown slip inside and on edge; pitted and spalling over-all. A IV 300.14c.
—	4794	Upcurved side of platter, with rounded angle to broken inverted rim, wheel-turned; buff; coarse with many assorted grey and white grits; traces of burnished, reddish-brown slip over-all. A III 204.3a.
—	4662f	Low inverted broken rim of wide bowl, wheel-turned; buff; coarse with few assorted white grits; traces of burnished, reddish-brown slip inside; brown incrustations over-all. A III 202.5.
11	4872c	Low, inverted rim with rounded edge, wheel-turned; tan; medium-coarse with few assorted tan and reddish-brown grits; traces of wheel-burnished, reddish-brown slip over-all. A III 204.10.
12	6039	Upcurved to thickened, low inverted rim with rounded edge, wheel-turned; reddish-orange; medium with many small to fine, dark-grey, brown, and white grits; faint traces of burnished reddish-brown slip over-all. A III 203.5.

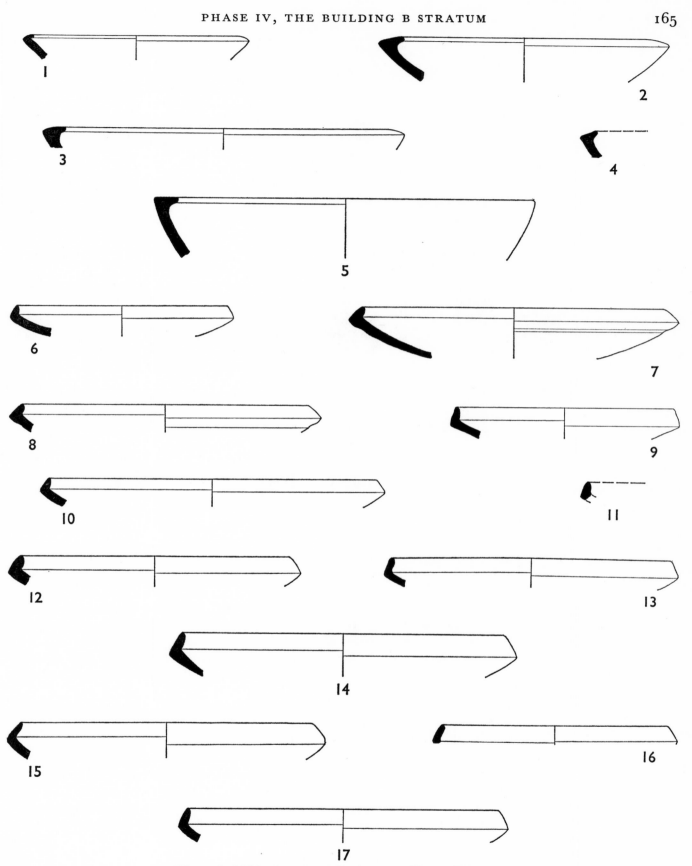

Fig. 36. Wide bowls and platters, Phase IV. 1:4.

Fig. 36 No.	Reg. No.	
13	4758	Upcurved to inverted thinned and rounded edge; tannish-buff with thick, dark-grey core; medium-coarse with some small to fine, white grits; traces of burnished, dark-brown slip over-all; some assorted pits. A III 203.5.
—	4662h	Upcurved wall of wide bowl with angle of inverted, medium-high broken rim, wheel-turned; light-brown; medium-coarse with some assorted grey and tan grits; traces of burnished, reddish-brown slip outside. A III 202.5.
—	4662k	Base of large, shallow bowl, wheel turned; light-brown; medium with many small to fine white and grey grits; continuously-burnished, reddish-brown slip outside; dark-grey smoke marks inside. A III 202.5.
14	4755	Sharply carinated wall greatly thickened at angle with high, thinned, inverted rim, wheel-turned; brick-red; medium-coarse with many assorted white and dark-brown grits, porous ware; traces of radially-burnished reddish-brown slip inside, wheel-burnished outside and on edge; black smoke marks on edge. A III 203.5.
—	4776o	Body sherd of wide bowl; buff with thick grey core; coarse with some assorted grey and reddish-brown grits; reddish-brown slip over-all, radially-burnished inside and horizontally-burnished outside. A III 203.5.
—	4872j	Body sherd of wide shallow bowl, wheel-turned; buff with grey core; coarse with many assorted light- and dark-grey grits; reddish-brown slip over-all, random radially-burnished inside and horizontally burnished outside; light, grey incrustations over-all. A III 204.10.
—	4872a	Body sherd of wide bowl, upcurved to thickened angle of inverted broken rim; light reddish-brown; medium-coarse with some assorted tan and grey grits; traces of continuously burnished, reddish-brown slip over-all; heavy, grey incrustations. A III 204.10.
15	5032	Upcurved to thin, rounded inverted edge, some thickening at angle, wheel-made; brownish-buff with thick, dark-grey core, penetrating to inside in places; medium with some small to fine, white grits; wheel-burnished brown slip inside and outside; many assorted pits. A I 1.5.
—	5024j	Body sherd of wide bowl, wheel-turned; buff with grey core; coarse with some assorted grey grits; traces of continuously-burnished, reddish-brown slip inside and outside. A IV 300.14c.
—	4680f	Body sherd of wide bowl; buff with orange inside; very coarse with some assorted grey and white grits; traces of burnished, reddish-brown slip outside; some grey incrustations over-all. A III 202.7.
—	4872k	Body sherd of wide shallow bowl, wheel-turned; buff; medium-coarse with some assorted grey and orange grits; traces of continuously burnished, reddish-brown slip over-all; light, grey incrustations. A III 204.10.
16	4307b	Upcurved to narrow, thinned, rounded, inverted rim, wheel-turned; dark brown; medium with many fine white grits; traces of wheel-burnished reddish-brown slip over-all. A II 102.3.
17	5028	Upturned to thinned, rounded, inverted rim, wheel-turned; brown, medium-coarse with many assorted tan and dark-brown grits; traces of wheel-burnished reddish-brown slip over-all; many pits and spalling. A IV 300.14d.
—	4668i	Body sherd of wide bowl; dark greyish-brown; medium with few small to fine, white and tan grits; continuously-burnished brownish slip over-all. A III 202.5a.
—	5024i	Body sherd of wide-bowl, wheel-turned; burnt-orange inside and brown outside; medium-coarse with some assorted dark reddish-brown grits; traces of burnished reddish-brown slip inside and outside; few assorted pits and brownish-grey incrustations over-all. A IV 300.14c.

Fig. 37 No.	*Reg. No.*	
I	4659	Rim outcurved to rounded edge, wet-smoothed; pinkish-tan with grey core; coarse with very many assorted tan and dark-grey grits; rough gritty texture inside. A III 202.5.
2	4313	Rim slightly outcurved to thinned, rounded edge, wheel-made; medium-coarse with many assorted grey and white grits; traces of orangish-red slip outside; one very large and few assorted pits outside. A II 102.4.
—	4776j	Neck of jar, slightly outcurved; reddish-orange; medium-coarse with some assorted white grits; vertically-burnished outside and horizontally-burnished inside neck; some spalling outside and inside neck, grey incrustations over-all. A III 203.5.
—	4792a	Neck fragment of jar; neck made separately and joined to body; dark-orange with grey core; very coarse with some assorted tan and grey grits; white slip outside; grey incrustations over-all. A III 204.3.
3	4289d	Rim outcurved to thinned, rounded edge, wet-smoothed; orange with buff core; coarse with some assorted white grits; traces of heavy, white slip outside and inside edge; some grey incrustations over-all. A II 101.9.
—	4668g	Body sherd of jar; pinkish-buff; medium-coarse with very many fine white grits; traces of white slip outside; some grey incrustations over-all. A III 202.5a.
4	4784	Rim slightly outcurved to thinned, rounded edge, wet-smoothed; orangish-buff with grey core; medium-coarse with some assorted tan and white grits; rough gritty texture and spalling inside. A III 203.6.
5	4776i	Rim sharply outcurved to rounded edge; dark-orange with buff core; medium-coarse with some assorted white and grey grits; some fine pits over-all. A III 203.5.
6	6110	Rim sharply outcurved to medium rolled edge, wet-smoothed; coarse ware. A I 1.5.
7	5022	Rim sharply outcurved to thinned, rounded edge; dark-orange; coarse with many fine white grits; traces of white slip outside and inside edge; grey incrustations over-all. A IV 300.14c.
—	5038b	Rim and neck of large jar, outcurved to thin rolled edge, wet-smoothed; orangish-buff with dark-grey core; coarse with some assorted white and tan grits; heavy, grey and yellow incrustations over-all. A I 1.5b.
8	4673	Rim sharply outcurved to thinned, rounded edge, wheel-finished; tan with thick, grey core; medium-coarse with few assorted white, grey, and tan grits; many assorted pits over-all, very rough texture inside, some dark-grey smoke marks inside. A III 202.7.
9	5037	Rim sharply flared out to thin rolled edge; pinkish-buff; medium-coarse with some assorted white grits; traces of white slip outside; few assorted pits, some grey incrustation outside. A I 1.5.
10	4307a	Rim sharply outcurved to thinned, rolled edge; pinkish-buff; very coarse with some assorted white grits; very pitted and spalling inside. A II 102.3.
11	4859	Short neck with rim outcurved to thinned rounded edge, wet-smoothed; buff with greyish-buff core; coarse with very many assorted grey quartz grits; many assorted pits over-all, black smoke marks outside. A III 204.10.
12	4289e	Rim slightly outcurved to rounded, thin rolled edge, wet-smoothed; pinkish-buff; medium with many fine white grits; few assorted reddish-brown grits. A II 101.9.
13	4863	Neck inclined in with sharply outcurved, rounded rim, wet-smoothed; buff with orangish-buff outside; medium-coarse with some assorted white and reddish-brown grits. A III 204.10.
14	5028c	Rim sharply outcurved to thinned, rounded edge, wheel-finished; orange with thick, grey core; medium-coarse with some medium to very fine white and tan grits; traces of white slip outside; some light brownish-grey incrustations over-all. A IV 300.14d.

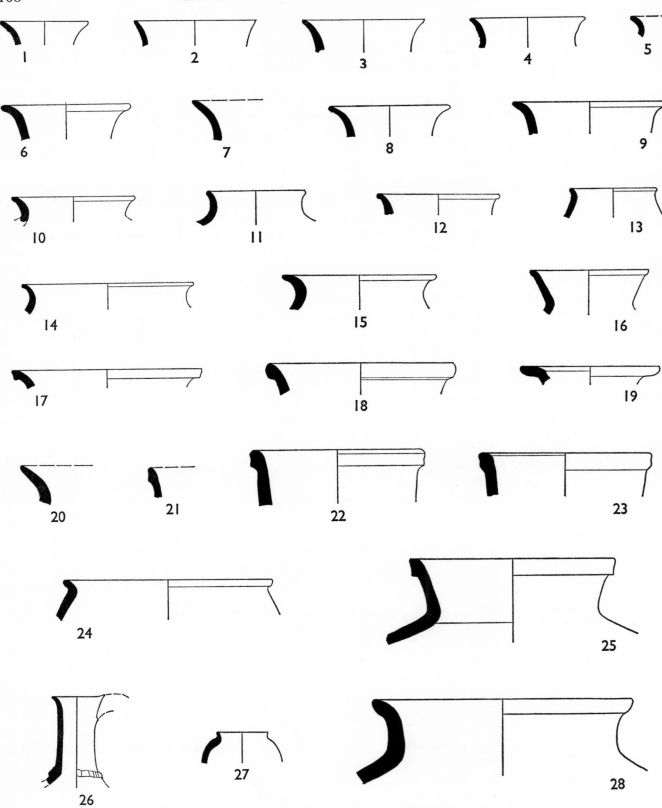

Fig. 37. Jugs and storage jars, Phase IV. 1:4.

Fig. 37 No.	Reg. No.	
15	4284	Heavy rim sharply outcurved to thinned, rolled edge; buff with grey core; coarse with some large white, grey, and many small white grits; deeply pitted inside and many assorted pits outside. A II 101.9.
16	4653	Rim flared out to thinned, rolled edge; buff with dark-grey core; coarse with very many assorted dark-grey quartz grits; pitted and flaking over-all. A III 202.5.
17	4790	Rim of jar, outcurved to flattened squared edge with narrow collar projected out, wheel-finished; buff; coarse with some assorted white and grey grits; traces of orange slip outside. A III 204.3.
18	4781	Heavy rim slightly outcurved to rolled, beaded edge; buff; coarse with many assorted white and tan grits; spalling inside and on edge. A III 203.5a.
19	4764	Rim flattened out to wide flange, beveled on inside, rounded outside; dark-orange with dark-grey core in places; medium-coarse with very many assorted, mostly fine, white and tan grits; some grey incrustations. A III 203.5.
20	4792	Heavy rim sharply outcurved to thinned, rounded edge; bright-orange with very thick, dark-grey core; coarse with some assorted grey, white, and tan grits; uneven surfaces over-all; many assorted pits and spalling inside. A III 204.3.
—	4795	Rim of large jar, outcurved to rounded edge; buff; very coarse with many assorted white and light-grey grits; some assorted pits inside, traces of orange slip over-all. A III 204.3a.
21	4776c	Rim slightly outcurved to thickened, triangular, rounded edge with collar projected out; dark-orange with buff core; medium-coarse with many assorted white, light- and dark-grey grits; uneven surfaces, some grey incrustations over-all. A III 203.5.
22	5033	Heavy rim upright with well-rounded, squared collar projected out, wheel-made; pinkish-buff with very thick, grey core; coarse with some assorted white grits; traces of wheel-burnished, brown slip outside; many assorted pits. A I 1.5.
23	6106	Heavy rim, upright with rounded squared collar projected out, wheel-made; thick grey core; coarse with assorted white grits. A I 1.5.
24	4797	Short rim sharp flared out to thinned, rounded edge, wet-smoothed; buff with brownish-buff core; coarse with many assorted white grits; many assorted pits inside, crazing over-all, some grey incrustations outside. A III 204.3a.
25	4662	Heavy rim inclined out to rounded edge with squared collar outside; pinkish-tan inside and tan outside with thick, dark-grey core; very coarse with very many, mostly fine, white grits; traces of white slip outside; pronounced crazing and spalling inside, grey incrustations over-all. A III 202.5.
—	4782	Neck fragment of very large jar; dark dull-orange with greyish-buff core; very coarse with many assorted grey, white, and tan grits, few assorted reddish-brown grits; traces of white slip outside; many assorted pits and spalling inside, grey incrustations over-all. A III 203.5a.
26	4840	High neck of large jug with thinned, outcurved rim; remnant of high loop-handle attachment at rim; greyish-tan inside and orange outside with patches of buff, thick, grey core; very coarse with many assorted white grits; narrow indented, high-relief molding around base of neck; rough texture inside with striations parallel to axis of neck, black smoke marks outside. (4840, 4841, and 4844 joined). A III 204.9.
—	4872d	Neck fragment of jug, buff; medium-coarse with few assorted white and dark-grey grits; traces of burnished, reddish-brown slip outside; grey incrustations over-all. A III 204.10.
—	4792b	Neck fragment of jug; reddish-brown; coarse with some small to fine, dark- and reddish-brown grits; traces of burnished, reddish-brown slip outside; very uneven surface inside at transition from neck to body; grey incrustations over-all. A III 204.3.

Fig. 37 No.	*Reg. No.*	
—	5024l	Body sherd of jug at transition from shoulder to neck, wheel-finished; buff with light-orange core; medium with some small to very fine white and grey grits; continuously-burnished, reddish-brown slip outside; some light-grey incrustation over-all. A IV 300.14c.
—	4662s	Body sherd of jug; grey inside and buff outside; coarse with few assorted white and dark-grey grits; continuously-burnished, reddish-brown slip outside; light, grey incrustations over-all. A III 202.5.
27	4766	Wall of small jar, incurved to thickened shoulder with short everted, thin rounded rim, wet-smoothed; buff with thick, dark-grey core; fine with few assorted grey, white, and reddish-brown grits; traces of white slip outside; very uneven surfaces, some grey incrustations over-all. A III 203.5.
28	4777	Heavy rim sharply outcurved at top to thinned, rolled collar; orange with buff patches outside, buff core; coarse with very many assorted tan and grey grits, few large reddish-brown grits; traces of white slip, some grey incrustations over-all. A III 203.5a.

Fig. 38 No.	*Reg. No.*	
I	4872b	Rim incurved to wide, thickened, rounded beveled edge, wet-smoothed; dark-orange inside and grey outside, dark-buff core; very coarse with many assorted grey quartz grits; grey incrustations over-all. A III 204.10.
—	4662e	Rim of hole-mouth jar, incurved to thickened, rounded, beveled edge; orangish-buff with grey core; very coarse with many assorted grey grits; rough texture inside, some spalling on edge. A III 202.5.
—	4668b	Rim of hole-mouth jar, incurved to very thickened, rounded, beveled edge, wet-smoothed; greyish-buff with buff core; very coarse with many assorted grey grits; grey incrustations over-all. A III 202.5a.
—	4662b	Rim of hole-mouth jar, incurved to wide, very thickened, rounded, beveled edge; dark-grey; coarse with some assorted white grits. A III 202.5.
2	4773	Rim incurved to very wide, greatly thickened, rounded edge, wet-smoothed; buff inside and orange outside, dark-grey core penetrating to surface in places; very coarse with many assorted white and dark-grey quartz grits. A III 203.5.
3	5034	Rim incurved to slightly thickened, rounded, beveled edge, wheel-finished; reddish-brown with dark-brown core; very many assorted white and grey quartz grits; brown slip inside and outside; smoke marks and crazing inside. A I 1.5.
4	4679	Rim incurved to very wide, thickened, rounded edge, wheel-finished; buff with dark-grey core penetrating to surface in places; very coarse with many small to fine, white and tan grits; wide, crude, high-relief rope-molding outside, traces of heavy white slip inside. A III 202.7.
5	4757	Rim incurved to medium-wide, thickened, rounded edge with ridge at base of inner fold; orange with black outside; coarse with very many assorted grey quartz grits; some crazing and spalling inside and on edge. A III 203.5.
6	5024b	Rim of incurved to wide, slightly thickened, rounded, beveled edge, wheel-finished; greyish-brown inside and dark-grey outside, brown core; coarse with some assorted white and grey grits; greyish-brown incrustations over-all. A IV 300.14c.
7	4845	Rim incurved to very wide, thickened, rounded edge, wet-smoothed outside and on edge; buff with orange and grey patches in places; coarse with very many assorted grey quartz and white grits; many assorted pits over-all, crazing inside. A III 204.10.
—	4668a	Rim of hole-mouth jar, incurved to thickened rounded edge; buff with grey core; coarse with some medium to fine, white grits; grey incrustations over-all. A III 202.5a.

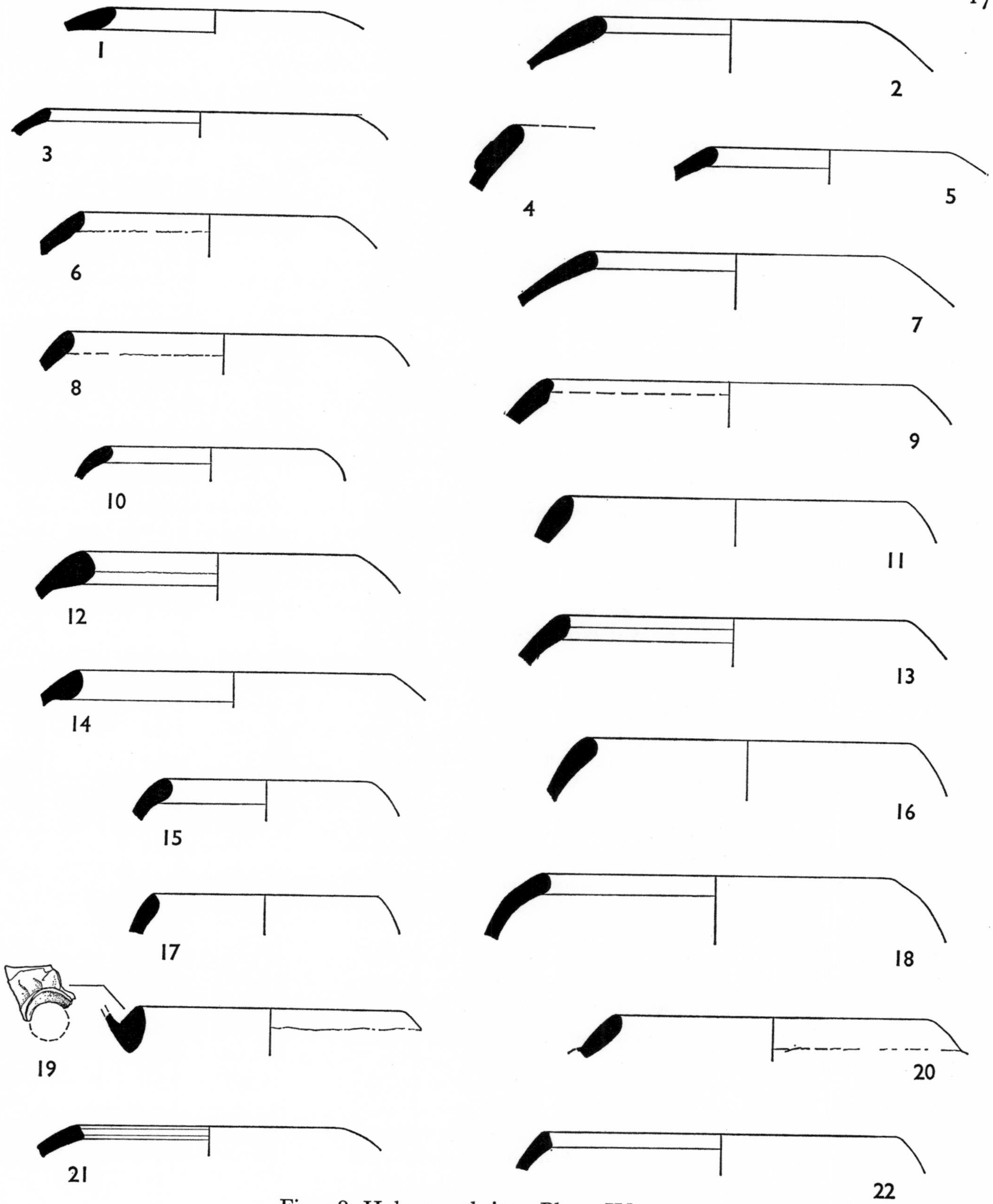

Fig. 38. Hole-mouth jars, Phase IV. 1:4.

Fig. 38 No.	Reg. No.	
8	5024a	Rim incurved to narrow, slightly thickened, rounded edge, wheel-finished; dark greyish-brown; medium-coarse with few assorted grey quartz grits; black discoloration on edge of rim, some brown incrustations inside. A IV 300.14c.
9	6103	Rim incurved to thickened, rounded edge depressed midway of inner surface, wet-smoothed; coarse ware. A I 1.4.
10	4289c	Rim sharply incurved to narrow, thickened, rounded edge, wet-smoothed; brown with dark-grey patches outside; very coarse with many assorted grey grits; some pitting and spalling outside. A II 101.9.
11	5024d	Rim incurved to very wide, thickened, rounded edge, wheel-finished; orangish-buff with buff core; medium-coarse with some small to very fine grey and tan grits, few medium grey and brown grits; traces of white slip outside and inside edge; some traces of grey incrustations. A IV 300.14c.
12	4666	Rim incurved to wide, greatly thickened, rounded edge, wet-smoothed; buff with very thick, dark-grey core; very coarse with many assorted white grits; many assorted pits over-all; rough texture inside, orange discoloration outside. A III 202.5a.
13	5031	Rim incurved to wide, thickened, rounded edge, wheel-finished; orange with greyish-brown core; coarse with many assorted white, tan and grey grits; traces of tan wash outside. A I 1.4.
14	5028a	Rim incurved to medium-wide, greatly thickened, rounded angular edge, wheel-finished; orangish-buff with grey core; medium-coarse with many assorted white and grey quartz grits; some light-grey incrustations over-all. A IV 300.14d.
—	4662a	Rim of hole-mouth jar, incurved to narrow, very thickened, rounded edge; orangish-brown with greyish-brown core; coarse with many assorted white and light-grey grits; rough, gritty texture over-all. A III 202.5.
15	4289b	Rim incurved to medium-wide, thickened, rounded edge, wet-smoothed; dark-brown with dark-grey core penetrating to surface in places; very coarse with many assorted grey quartz grits. A II 101.9.
16	4746	Rim incurved to very wide, thickened, rounded edge, wet-smoothed; yellowish-buff inside and greyish-buff outside, thick, dark-grey core; coarse with very many assorted white and grey quartz grits, porous ware. A III 203.5.
17	4307	Rim slightly incurved to medium-wide, thickened, rounded, beveled edge, wheel-finished; greyish-buff; very coarse with many assorted grey grits; black smoke marks inside. A II 102.3.
18	4753	Rim incurved to very wide, thickened, rounded edge, wet-smoothed; buff; coarse with many assorted grey quartz grits; traces of burnished reddish-brown slip outside; uneven surface inside. A III 203.5.
19	4760	Greatly thickened, incurved rim with spout fragment; orangish-buff, very coarse with some small white grits; wide, crude, high-relief rope-molding outside around spout, faint traces of white slip outside. A III 203.5.
20	5024c	Rim incurved to wide, thickened, rounded edge; brownish-buff inside and pinkish-buff outside, brown core in places; coarse with many assorted white and grey quartz grits; remnant of low-relief rope-molding outside; some heavy grey incrustations over-all. A IV 300.14c.
21	4776a	Rim sharply incurved to thickened, flattened, squared edge; brown with greyish-brown outside; coarse with many assorted tan, grey, and white grits; some small diagonal indentations outside below edge; many fine pits over-all. A III 203.5.

Fig. 38 *No.*	*Reg.* *No.*	
22	5035	Rim incurved to medium-wide, thickened, flattened, beveled edge; orange with buff core; medium-coarse with many assorted white grits; traces of white slip outside; smoke marks, very rough texture inside, some grey incrustations. A I 1.5.
—	4759	Rim of hole-mouth jar, incurved to thickened, flattened, squared edge; dark-buff with dark-orange outside; very coarse with many assorted tan, white, and grey grits; pitted, uneven surfaces over-all. A III 203.5.

Fig. 39 *No.*	*Reg.* *No.*	
1	5023	Rim incurved to very wide, thickened, rounded, beveled edge, with ridge outside, wheel-finished; buff with very thick, dark-grey core penetrating to surfaces in places; very coarse with many assorted grey quartz grits, some spalling on edge. A IV 300.14c.
—	4662d	Rim of hole-mouth jar incurved to thickened, rounded, beveled edge with ridge outside, wet-smoothed; dull orange; coarse with many assorted grey grits; some spalling and grey incrustations over-all. A III 202.5.
2	4672	Rim sharply incurved to very wide, greatly thickened, rounded edge with low ridge outside, wet-smoothed; dark-grey with buff inside; very coarse with many, assorted white and grey quartz grits. A III 202.7.
3	4301	Rim incurved to thickened, rounded edge, with pronounced ridge outside, wheel-finished; orange inside and outside edge, buff outside with buff core; medium-coarse with very many assorted white and grey grits. A II 102.3.
4	4636	Rim sharply incurved to very wide, thickened, rounded edge with two parallel ridges outside; orange with buff core; coarse with many assorted grey quartz grits; greyish-buff slip outside; some spalling on edge. A III 202.5.
5	4744	Rim incurved to wide, thickened, rounded edge, with pronounced ridge outside; orangish-brown inside and greyish-brown outside, buff and grey core; coarse with many assorted white and grey quartz grits; two large, deep pits outside, some spalling on edge. A III 203.5.
6	4649	Rim incurved to very wide, greaty thickened, rounded edge, with low ridge outside; orangish-buff with buff core; coarse with many assorted dark-grey quartz grits; some crazing and spalling on edge. A III 202.5.
7	4748	Rim incurved to wide, thickened, rounded edge, with pronounced ridge outside; dark-greyish-buff; coarse with many assorted grey quartz grits, porous ware; traces of orange slip inside and outside edge; many assorted pits outside, grey smoke marks on rim. A III 203.5.
8	4306	Rim slightly incurved to wide, thickened, rounded edge, with pronounced ridge outside, wheel-finished; buff with dark-brown outside; coarse with many assorted dark-grey grits, and some very large to medium light-grey grits; grey smoke marks inside. A II 102.3.
9	4667	Rim slightly incurved to thickened, tapered edge, wet-smoothed; buff; coarse with some small to fine white and grey grits; traces of orange slip over-all. A III 202.5a.
10	4641	Rim sharply incurved to wide, greatly thickened, rounded, beveled edge, with pronounced ridge outside; buff with dark-orange outside; very coarse with many assorted white and grey quartz grits; very rough texture, black smoke marks inside, some spalling on edge. A III 202.5.
11	4289a	Rim incurved to medium-wide, very greatly thickened, rounded edge, with very pronounced ridge outside, edge wheel-finished; dark greyish-buff; very coarse with some assorted white and grey quartz grits; rough, uneven surfaces, grey incrustations over-all. A II 101.9.

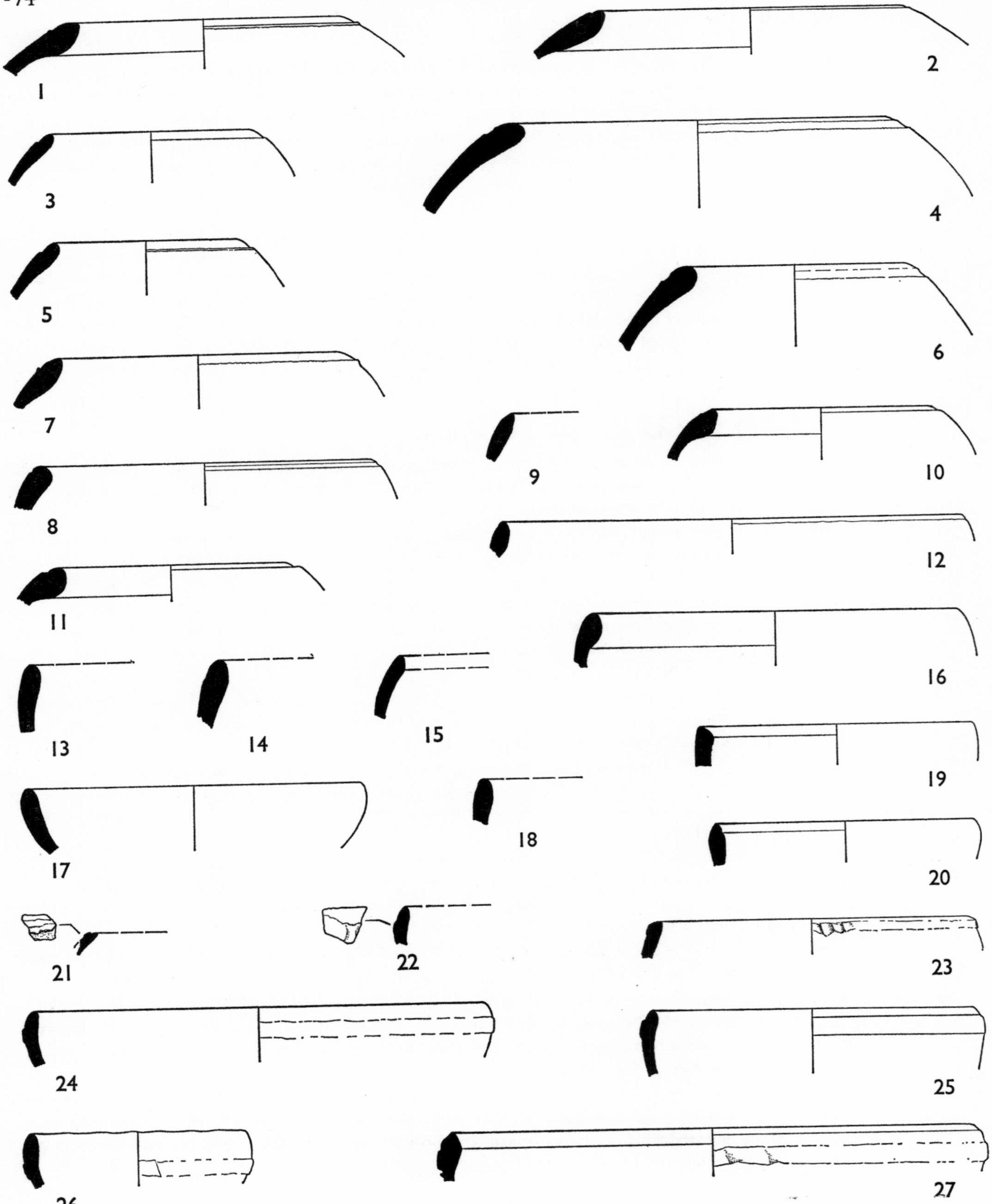

Fig. 39. Hole-mouth jars, Phase IV. 1:4.

Fig. 39 No.	Reg. No.	
12	4680a	Upright rim slightly incurved to narrow, thickened, rounded edge with shallow depression outside below edge; buff with orangish buff inside; coarse with some medium to fine white grits; few assorted pits outside, some grey incrustations. A III 202.7.
13	5027	Upright rim slightly incurved to thickened, rounded edge; greyish-buff with orange patches outside; very coarse with many assorted grey quartz grits; many assorted deep pits, grey smoke marks inside. A IV 300.14d.
14	5038a	Upright rim slightly incurved to very wide, thickened, rounded edge, with faint ridge outside, wet-smoothed; brownish-orange with grey core; very coarse with many assorted light-grey grits; some grey incrustations over-all. A I 1.5b.
15	4643	Rim slightly incurved to thickened, flattened, beveled edge; orangish-buff with greyish-buff core; medium-coarse with some assorted white grits; traces of white slip outside; grey incrustations over-all. A III 202.5.
16	4874	Upright rim slightly incurved to narrow, thickened, rounded edge, wet-smoothed; dark-orange with grey and buff core in places; medium-coarse with many light- and dark-grey quartz and white grits; rough texture inside, pronounced crazing and spalling outside. A III 204.11.
17	4664	Rim upcurved to wide, thickened, rounded edge, wet-smoothed; buff with grey core; coarse with many assorted, mostly small, white grits; traces of white slip outside; some large deep pits, rough texture inside, some grey incrustations over-all. A III 202.5a.
18	5028b	Upright rim slightly incurved to medium-wide, slightly thickened, rounded edge; orange; medium-coarse with some assorted grey, tan, and reddish-brown grits; traces of white slip outside; some brownish-grey incrustations over-all. A IV 300.14d.
19	4800	Upright rim slightly incurved to flattened, beveled edge; very dark-grey with orangish-buff on rim; coarse with some assorted white grits, porous ware. A III 204.3a.
20	4665	Upright rim with thickened, tapered edge; buff with thick, dark-grey core; coarse with many small to fine white grits; traces of reddish-brown slip outside; grey smoke marks on edge. A III 202.5a.
21	4776g	Rim of small jar, incurved to thickened, tapered edge; orange with buff core; coarse with some assorted tan, reddish-brown, and grey grits; narrow, crude, high-relief molding outside. A III 203.5.
—	4289l	Rim of hole-mouth jar, slightly incurved to triangular edge; orange outside and brownish-buff inside; coarse with many assorted white grits; narrow, well-defined, high-relief rope-molding outside along edge. A II 101.9.
22	4776f	Upright rim slightly incurved to narrow, thickened, oval edge; dark-orange; coarse with some assorted tan and white grits; medium-wide, crude, high-relief, wavy rope-molding outside, traces of white slip outside; grey incrustations over-all. A III 203.5.
23	4302	Upright rim slightly incurved to rounded, flat edge, wheel-finished; orange; coarse with many assorted white and few small grey grits; narrow, crude, low-relief rope-molding outside. A II 102.3.
24	6105	Upright rim slightly incurved to oval edge, wet-smoothed; coarse ware; crude, medium-wide, half-relief wavy rope-molding outside. A I 1.5.
25	5036	Upright rim slightly incurved to wide, thickened, oval edge; buff with grey core; coarse with some assorted white grits; crudely applied rope-molding outside; many assorted pits inside, smoke marks outside. A I 1.5.
26	4776b	Upcurved, straight rim with thickened, rounded edge; orangish-buff with grey core; coarse with some assorted white grits; medium-wide, half-relief rope-molding outside; some grey incrustations over-all. A III 203.5.

Fig. 39 *No.*	*Reg.* *No.*	
27	5016	Upright rim slightly incurved to wide, greatly thickened, flattened, beveled edge, shallow depression outside, edge wet-smoothed; buff; coarse with very many small to fine white grits and some assorted tan and grey grits; medium-wide, crude, half-relief rope-molding, traces of reddish-brown slip, dark-grey smoke marks outside. A IV 300.14c.

Fig. 40 *No.*	*Reg.* *No.*	
1	5020	Incurved rim of jar with stump of basket-handle which merges into rim; buff; medium-coarse with some assorted white, tan, and reddish-brown grits; traces of reddish-brown slip outside and on handle. A III 204.10.
2	4783	Upright rim slightly incurved to medium-side, thickened, flattened, beveled edge, wet-smoothed; tan with grey core penetrating to surface in places; very wide, crude, half-relief rope-molding outside; some assorted pits inside. A III 203.6.
3	4287	Upright rim incurved to rounded, flattened edge with raised wavy-edged bead projected up and out; orange inside and orangish-buff outside, grey core; coarse with very many assorted white grits; many small to fine pits, some grey incrustations. A II 101.9.
—	4662c	Rim of hole-mouth jar, incurved to slightly thickened, rounded, flattened edge, projected up; orange inside and grey outside; medium-coarse with many assorted white and light-grey grits; some brown incrustations over-all, uneven surface outside. A III 202.5.
—	4662g	Rim of hole-mouth jar, incurved to thickened, rounded, flattened edge, projected slightly out; dull-orange; coarse with many assorted grey grits; light-grey and brown incrustations. A III 202.5.
4	4680b	Crudely made base; grey inside and orangish-buff outside; very coarse with many assorted white and tan grits; very rough, pitted, uneven surface outside and on bottom, some grey incrustations over-all. A III 202.7.
5	5072	String-cut base; greyish-buff with grey core; medium-coarse with some assorted reddish-brown and grey grits; traces of burnished, reddish-brown slip outside; black smoke marks over-all. A IV 300.14c.
—	4289h	Body sherd; greyish-buff; medium-coarse with some assorted white grits; continuously-burnished, reddish-brown slip over-all; some assorted pits inside. A II 101.9.
—	4289g	Body sherd; greyish-buff; medium with many small dark-grey grits; continuously-burnished, reddish-brown slip outside. A II 101.9.
—	5028j	Body sherd; buff with brownish-grey inside; medium with some medium to very fine grey and white grits; traces of burnished, red slip outside. A IV 300.14d.
6	4304	Orangish-brown inside and reddish-brown slip outside, thick, dark-grey core; coarse with many assorted grey grits; very rough texture inside, many assorted mostly large, pits on bottom, black smoke mark inside. A II 102.3.
7	4848	Reddish-brown; coarse with many assorted, mostly small to fine, tan grits; traces of tan slip over-all; very pitted, spalling outside and on bottom, black smoke marks over-all. (4848 and 4849 joined) A III 204.10.
8	4654	Buff with dark-grey core; medium-coarse with many assorted white, tan, and grey grits; traces of vertically-burnished, reddish-brown slip outside; many assorted pits over-all. A III 202.5.
—	4872i	Body sherd; dark-grey with buff outside; coarse with many small to fine grey grits; traces of burnished, reddish-brown slip outside; grey incrustations over-all. A III 204.10.
—	4872m	Body sherd; tannish-buff; coarse with small to fine, tan and grey grits; traces of reddish-brown slip outside; uneven surfaces over-all. A III 204.10.

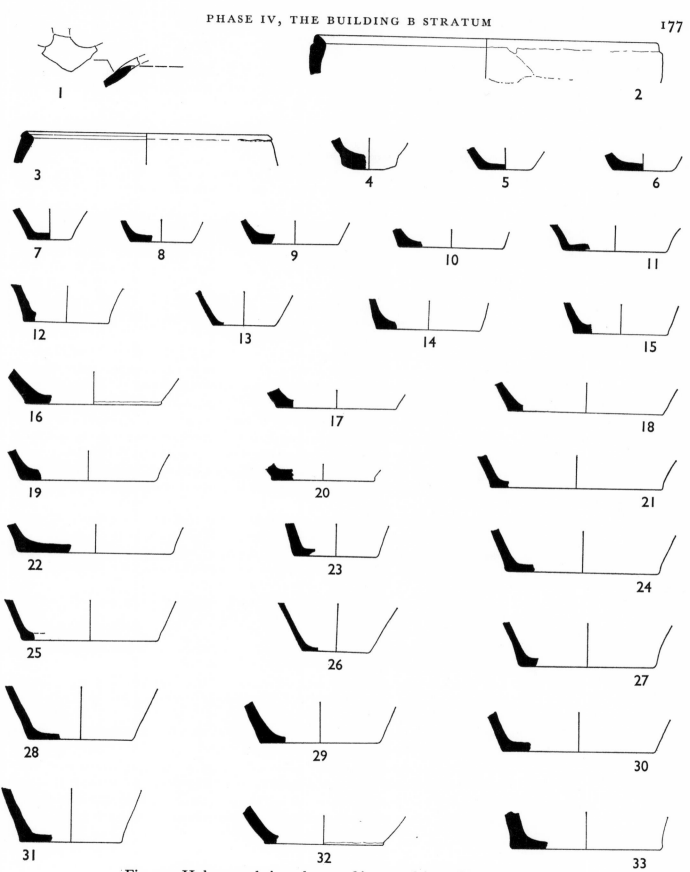

Fig. 40. Hole-mouth jars, bases of jugs and jars, Phase IV. 1:4.

Fig. 40 No.	Reg. No.	
9	4640	Buff; medium-coarse with many medium to fine, white and grey grits, porous ware; traces of burnished, reddish-brown slip outside; many assorted pits over-all, flaking inside. A III 202.5.
—	4872l	Body sherd; pinkish-buff with tannish-buff inside; coarse with many assorted white and dark-grey grits; traces of reddish-brown slip outside; rough, gritty, uneven surface inside, grey incrustations over-all. A III 204.10.
10	4756	Orangish-buff, very coarse with some assorted, and very many fine, white grits; traces of white slip outside; very rough texture over-all, dark-grey smoke marks inside, some grey incrustations. A III 203.5.
11	5013	Orangish-buff with grey patch outside; medium-coarse with some small to fine, white and tan grits. A IV 300.14c.
—	4767	Body sherd; dark orangish-buff inside and bright-orange outside, dark-grey core; medium-coarse with some assorted grey and white grits; very uneven surfaces and many fine pits over-all. A III 203.5.
12	4658	Brick-red; very coarse with many assorted tan grits; traces of vertical burnishing on inner walls and continuous burnishing on bottom inside; very pitted and spalling, some dark-grey incrustations over-all. A III 202.5.
13	4639	Reddish-orange with dark-brown core penetrating to inside in places; medium-coarse with very many assorted white grits and few assorted red grits, porous ware; traces of burnished, reddish-brown slip outside, many assorted pits over-all. A III 202.5.
—	4307d	Body sherd; orange-red; medium-coarse with some fine white grits; continuously-burnished, reddish-brown slip over-all. A II 102.3.
14	4281	Buff with dark-grey core at angle; coarse with few assorted white grits; faint trace of white slip outside; very uneven surfaces, some pitting on bottom. A II 101.9.
—	4289k	Body sherd; buff inside and pinkish-buff outside, thick grey core; coarse with some assorted white grits; rough gritty texture over-all, heavy, grey incrustations over-all. A II 101.9.
15	4286	Buff; fine with many fine white grits; many fine pits over-all with some large pits outside, near and on bottom, some striations on bottom. A II 101.9.
16	4799	Dark-orange inside and buff outside, thick, dark-grey core in places; coarse with many assorted white grits; traces of reddish-brown incrustations inside; very pitted on bottom. A III 204.3a.
17	4801	Brownish-buff; very coarse with many assorted white grits; very rough texture with pitting and spalling outside and on bottom. A III 204.3a.
18	6104	No description. A I 1.4.
19	5028e	Pinkish-orange with grey core; medium with some fine to very fine white grits; some light, brownish-grey incrustations over-all. A IV 300.14d.
—	5031a	Flat base of jar, hand made and wet-smoothed; buff with pinkish-orange outside; medium with many assorted white and grey quartz grits, some assorted black grits; some grey incrustations. A I 1.4.
20	4763	Buff with orange inside; coarse with many assorted tan and few white grits; rough texture outside, grey incrustations over-all. A III 203.5.
21	4743	Greyish-brown with black inside; coarse with many assorted grey quartz grits; many assorted pits over-all, very uneven surface and some spalling on bottom. A III 203.5.
22	4646	Greyish-buff with thick, dark-grey core on bottom; coarse with very many assorted grey quartz grits; rough texture over-all, many assorted pits on bottom. A III 202.5.

Fig. 40 No.	*Reg. No.*	
23	4869	Brown inside and dark-orange with dark-buff patches outside, thick, dark-brown core; very coarse with many assorted tan grits and a few assorted grey quartz grits; many assorted pits and some crazing over-all, very pitted and spalling on bottom. A III 204.10.
24	4661	Grey with orange surfaces; very coarse with some small to fine white grits; traces of white slip outside; very pitted and spalling inside and on bottom. A III 202.5.
—	4668c	Flat base of large jar; greyish-orange inside and greyish-buff outside; very coarse with many assorted white and tan grits; traces of white slip outside; pitted, uneven surfaces over-all. A III 202.5a.
25	4657	Brown with thick, dark-grey core, orangish-buff surface outside; very coarse with many assorted white and tan grits; very pitted on bottom. A III 202.5.
—	4662j	Flat base of jar; brownish-buff inside and dark-grey outside; very coarse with few small to fine, white grits; traces of white slip outside; rough, uneven surfaces over-all, spalling inside on bottom. A III 202.5.
26	5021	Dark reddish-orange; medium-coarse with very many medium to fine white grits; traces of vertically-burnished, dark-brown slip outside; many assorted pits over-all, spalling outside. A IV 300.14c.
27	5024e	Pinkish-buff with brownish-grey core; medium-coarse with few assorted grey and brown grits; traces of white slip outside; dark-grey smoke marks inside, some brownish-grey incrustations over-all. A IV 300.14c.
—	4796	Body sherd; buff; medium with many small to fine white grey, tan and reddish-brown grits; some grey incrustations over-all. A III 204.3a.
28	4283	Orangish-buff with grey core at angle; coarse with few assorted white and grey grits; vertically-burnished, orangish-red slip outside; heavy black smoke mark outside, flaking outside because of burning, many assorted pits inside. A II 101.9.
—	5024k	Body sherd of small jug; orange outside and greyish-buff inside, buff core; medium-coarse with some small to very fine, white and tan grits; continuously-burnished, reddish-brown slip outside; some light, grey incrustations over-all. A IV 300.14c.
—	4668h	Body sherd; orangish-buff; coarse with very many assorted white and light-grey grits; traces of burnished, reddish-brown slip outside; pitted and spalling inside, some grey incrustations over-all. A III 202.5a.
29	5024f	Brown inside and orange outside, greyish-brown core; medium with few medium to very fine white and grey grits; white slip outside; some assorted pits inside, grey incrustations over-all. A IV 300.14c.
—	4668d	Flat base of jar; dark-grey with brownish-grey inside; coarse with few assorted white grits; traces of white slip outside; pitted, uneven surface, dark-grey smoke marks inside, grey incrustations outside. A III 202.5a.
30	4650	Buff inside and orange outside; very coarse with many assorted white and grey grits; traces of white slip outside; very rough texture over-all; some grey incrustations over-all. A III 202.5.
31	4741	Pinkish-buff; very coarse with many assorted white grits; traces of white slip outside; grey incrustations over-all. A III 203.5.
32	4775	Buff; very coarse with some assorted white grits; traces of white slip outside; very rough texture over-all. A III 203.5.
33	4740	Buff with orange outside; very coarse with some assorted white grits; traces of white slip outside; very pitted on bottom, grey incrustations over-all. A III 203.5.

Fig. 41 No.	Reg. No.	
1	4644	Greyish-buff with dark-grey core penetrating to outside in places; coarse with some assorted, mostly fine, white grits; rough, gritty texture outside, some grey incrustations outside. A III 202.5.
2	4787	Orangish-buff with greyish-buff core; very coarse with few fine white and three very large, reddish-brown grits; faint traces of white slip outside; pitted and spalling outside and on bottom, some grey incrustations over-all. A III 203.6.
3	5028d	Buff; coarse with few medium to fine grey grits; heavy white slip outside; some light brownish-grey incrustations over-all. A IV 300.14d.
4	4793	Brown inside and dark-orange outside, thick, dark-grey core; coarse with many assorted white and tan grits; traces of white slip outside; some buff incrustations inside, grey incrustations outside. A III 204.3a.
5	4655	Buff inside and creamy-white outside, dark-grey core penetrating to outside in places; coarse with many assorted white grits; many assorted pits over-all, grey smoke marks inside. A III 202.5.
—	4289m	Body sherd; creamy-white outside; coarse with many assorted grey-white grits; black smoke marks inside and on one edge, flaking inside. A II 101.9.
6	4778	Reddish-brown with dark greyish-brown core; coarse with many assorted grey, white, and reddish-brown grits; many assorted pits over-all. A III 203.5a.
7	4289	Orangish-buff with dark-grey core in places; coarse with some assorted white and grey grits; deeply pitted and flaking inside. A II 101.9.
8	4754	Buff with dark-orange core; very coarse with many assorted white and grey grits; very pitted on bottom. A III 203.5.
9	4861	Dark-grey with buff outside; coarse with many assorted tan grits; rough pitted texture, dark-brown discoloration outside. A III 204.10.
10	4647	Buff with thick, dark-grey core penetrating to outside in places; very coarse with many small to fine, white grits; white slip outside. A III 202.5.
11	4868	Buff with grey patches over-all, orange core in places; coarse with many assorted white and grey quartz grits; very many small to fine pits over-all, rough texture at outside juncture of wall and bottom. A III 204.10.
12	5015	Greyish-brown; very coarse with many assorted light- and dark-grey quartz grits; many assorted pits inside and some assorted pits outside, black smoke marks inside. A IV 300.14c.
13	4850	Buff with dark-grey core in places; very coarse with some assorted white, tan, and dark-grey grits; traces of white slip outside; very pitted and spalling inside and on bottom, diagonal finger marks, pronounced crazing outside. A III 204.10.
14	4738	Orange inside and outside with pinkish tan on bottom, dark-grey core in bottom and part of side; very coarse with many fine white grits; traces of white slip outside; faint, diagonal ridges at outside juncture of wall and bottom, very pitted on bottom, grey incrustations over-all. A III 203.5.
15	4680	Orange inside and dark-grey outside; coarse with very many assorted white grits. A III 202.7.
Fig. 42 No.	Reg. No.	
1	4645	Small ledge-handle with narrow, pushed-up, thumb-indented edge; buff; medium with few assorted tan grits; traces of reddish-brown slip outside; black smoke marks over-all. A III 202.5.
2	4674	Single, deep thumb-indentation on edge; orangish buff, coarse with many assorted white grits; traces of heavy white slip outside; black smoke marks, very uneven surface inside. A III 202.7.

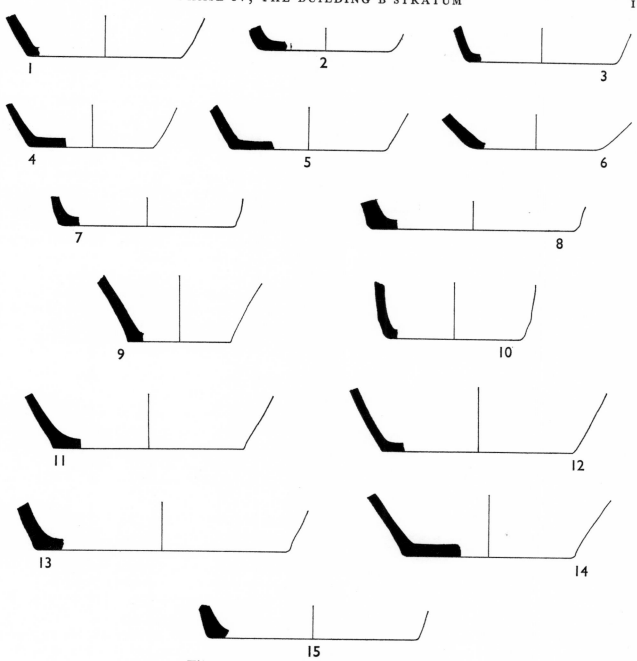

Fig. 41. Bases of jars, Phase IV. 1:4.

Fig. 42 No.	Reg. No.	
—	4289m	Ledge-handle fragment, one small indentation on edge; dark-grey, very coarse with some assorted white grits. A II 101.9.
3	4776m	Plain edge with two shallow indentations; buff; coarse with many assorted tan and reddish-brown grits; traces of white slip outside; grey incrustations over-all. A III 203.5.
—	4668e	Ledge-handle fragment, with plain edge; buff with greyish-buff core; coarse with few assorted white and reddish-brown grits; some heavy, grey and brown incrustations. A III 202.5a.

Fig. 42 *No.*	*Reg.* *No.*	
—	4662r	Ledge-handle fragment; chipped edge probably plain; dark-orange, very coarse with few assorted white grits, very rough, uneven surface over-all. A III 202.5.
4	4642	Shallow indentations on edge; orange with greyish-buff core; very coarse with few assorted white grits; traces of white slip outside; some grey incrustations. A III 202.5.
5	5030	Thin edge with shallow thumb indentations; orange with grey core; very coarse with many assorted white grits; traces of heavy, white slip outside; heavy grey incrustations over-all. A I 1.4.
6	5028h	Traces of thumb-indented edge; yellowish-buff outside and greyish-buff inside, grey core; medium with some medium to very fine grey and white grits; traces of heavy, white slip outside; surface badly spalled under handle, pronounced layer of yellowish-grey incrustation inside. (5028h and 5024h joined) A IV 300.14d.
7	5010	Rounded, thumb-indented edge; dark-orange; coarse with very many assorted, mostly small to fine, white grits, traces of heavy, white slip outside; grey incrustations over-all. A IV 300.14c.
8	4776l	Large handle with thumb-indented edge; buff outside and orangish-buff inside, thick dark-grey core; medium-coarse with many assorted white, grey, and tan grits; shallow evenly spaced depressions on bottom of handle, traces of white slip outside; many assorted pits inside and some assorted pits outside, greyish-brown incrustations over-all. A III 203.5.
9	4638	Lug-handle, horizontally pierced; grey inside and greyish-tan outside; medium-coarse with many assorted light-grey and tan grits. A III 202.5.
10	4742	Lug-handle, located vertically on shoulder, rounded and pierced; buff; medium with very many fine white grits and some assorted white, grey, and brown grits. A III 203.5.
—	5028f	Lug-handle fragment, elongated and merging into line of body, single vertically pierced hole; orangish-brown; medium-coarse with some assorted dark- and light-grey and white grits; traces of continuously burnished, reddish-brown slip outside; few assorted pits over-all. A IV 300.14d.
11	4776n	Very small lug-handle, triangular section; orangish-buff with dark-grey inside; coarse with a few assorted grey grits; uneven surfaces, some grey incrustations over-all. A III 203.5.
12	4872e	Loop handle joined to shoulder, elongated oval section; greyish-buff inside and pinkish-buff outside; medium-coarse with many assorted light- and dark-grey grits; faint traces of burnished, reddish-brown slip outside; grey incrustations. (4872e and 4872g joined) A III 204.10.
—	4681d	Loop-handle fragment, elongated oval section; dark-orange with dark greyish-brown core; medium-coarse with very many assorted white and dark-grey grits; traces of burnished, reddish-brown slip; flaking on outside surface of handle. A III 202.7.
—	5028g	Loop-handle fragment, very irregular, oval section; orangish-buff with thick, greyish-brown core; medium with many small to very fine grey and few white grits; traces of burnished reddish-brown slip outside. A IV 300.14d.
—	4662p	Loop-handle fragment, oval section flattened on one side; dark-orange with grey core; medium-coarse with few medium white grits; traces of continuously burnished; some grey incrustations over-all. A III 202.5.
—	4289i	Loop-handle fragment joined to body; dark orangish-buff with grey core; traces of burnished, reddish-brown slip outside; white incrustations inside. A II 101.9.

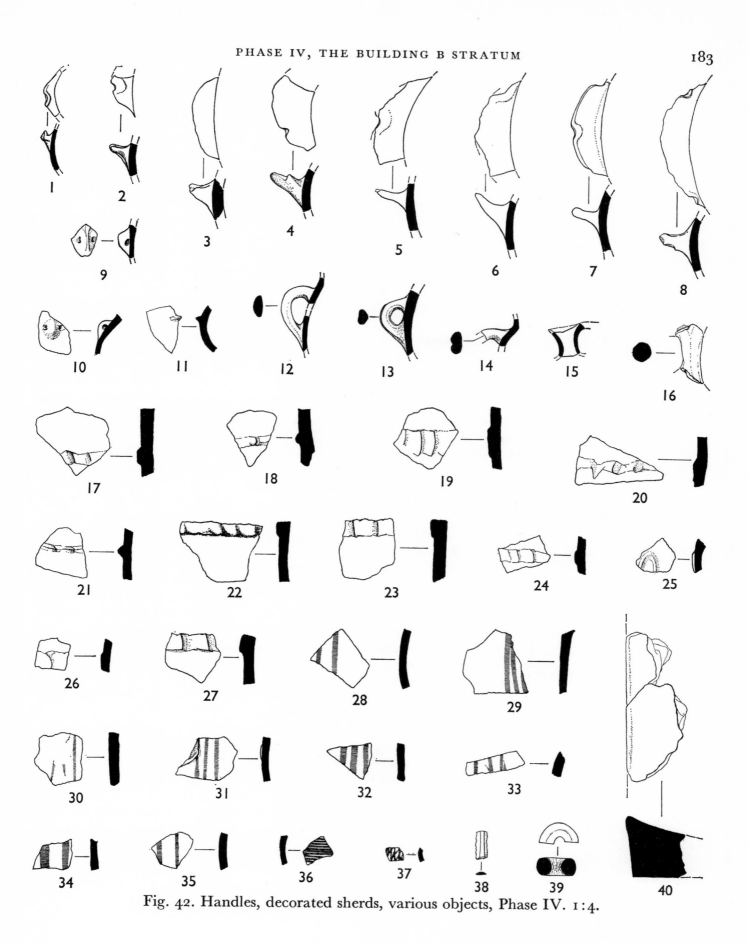

Fig. 42. Handles, decorated sherds, various objects, Phase IV. 1:4.

Fig. 42 No.	Reg. No.	
13	4280	Loop-handle joined to body at shoulder; buff; coarse with very many assorted grey grits; reddish-brown slip over-all, traces of continuous vertical burnishing outside and on handle; very rough texture, many assorted pits outside and on handle, some grey incrustations. A II 101.9.
—	4680c	Loop-handle fragment joined to shoulder, round oval section; orangish-buff with greyish-buff core; coarse with some assorted white and tan grits; rough uneven surfaces, heavy grey incrustations over-all. A III 202.7.
—	4289o	Loop-handle fragment joined to body; buff; coarse with few assorted white and grey grits; traces of burnished reddish-brown slip outside. A II 101.9.
—	4872h	Loop-handle fragment joined to body; elongated oval section; buff; medium-coarse with few assorted grey and reddish-brown grits; grey incrustations over-all. A III 204.10.
—	4662m	Loop-handle fragment joined to body, flattened, oval section; buff; coarse with few small to fine, white grits; traces of white slip outside; grey incrustations over-all. A III 202.5.
14	4872f	Loop-handle fragment joined to body at base of neck, elongated oval section with vertical groove; greyish-buff inside and pinkish buff outside; medium-coarse with many assorted light and dark-grey grits; traces of burnished, reddish-brown slip outside. A III 204.10.
—	4307c	Loop-handle fragment, single coil; round to oval section; orangish-brown; medium with some assorted, mostly fine, white grits; traces of burnished brown slip parallel to length of fragment. A II 102.3.
—	4662l	Loop-handle fragment joined to body, oval section; reddish-orange; medium-coarse with some assorted white grits; traces of continuously burnished reddish-brown slip outside; some light, grey incrustations over-all. A III 202.5.
—	4662n	Loop-handle fragment joined to body; greyish-brown; fine with some fine white and medium dark-brown grits; traces of continuously burnished reddish-brown slip outside; grey incrustations over-all. A III 202.5.
—	4776k	Loop-handle fragment joined to body, very elongated, oval section; dark reddish-orange; coarse with some assorted white grits; continuously, vertically-burnished reddish-orange slip outside; uneven surface inside, some grey incrustations over-all. A III 203.5.
—	4662o	Loop-handle fragment, elongated, oval section; dark-orange; coarse with some small to fine, white, and some assorted tan grits; traces of continuously burnished reddish-orange slip outside; spalling on handle, grey incrustations over-all. A III 202.5.
—	4662q	Loop-handle fragment, oval tapering to elongated section; tan with grey core; coarse with some assorted grey and reddish-brown grits; traces of burnished, reddish-brown slip over-all; some grey incrustations. A III 202.5.
—	4792c	Loop-handle fragment, oval section; pinkish-brown; fine with few fine black grits; burnished, reddish-brown slip over-all. A III 204.3.
—	4289j	Loop-handle fragment joined to shoulder of juglet; buff; medium-coarse with some assorted dark-grey and white grits; traces of burnished, reddish-brown slip outside; very uneven surface inside where handle joins body. A II 101.9.
15	5011	Open flared spout attached to jar rim; buff; medium with many assorted, mostly small to fine, reddish-brown grits. A III 204.10.
16	4677	Pillar-handle attached to jar rim at top; orangish-buff with very thick, dark-grey core; traces of white slip outside; very rough texture, some grey incrustations over-all. A III 202.7.

Fig. 42 No.	Reg. No.	
17	4282	Pinkish-tan inside and orangish-tan outside; coarse with many small to fine white grits; medium-wide, crude, half-relief molding outside, traces of very heavy, white slip outside, and pinkish-white slip inside; grey smoke mark inside, some grey incrustations. A II 101.9.
18	5029	Buff inside and grey outside; very coarse with many assorted white and grey grits; narrow, crude, high-relief rope-molding, faint traces of white slip outside. A IV 300.14d.
19	4496	Orange inside and dark-grey outside; coarse with many assorted, mostly small to fine, white grits; very wide, half-relief rope-molding, traces of heavy, white slip outside; some grey incrustations. A I 1.3.
—	5026	Body sherd of jar; orange with reddish-buff core, patches of grey in core; medium-coarse with many assorted grey and tan grits, few assorted reddish-brown grits; traces of white slip outside; uneven surfaces and pitting over-all. A IV 300.14d.
20	4305	Buff with thick, dark-grey core, medium-wide, irregular, high-relief rope-molding, white slip outside; grey incrustations inside. A II 102.3.
21	4285	Pinkish-red; coarse with many small to fine tan grits; narrow, high-relief ridged rope-molding, few traces of white slip outside; few assorted pits inside, some grey incrustations. A II 101.9.
22	5024	Buff; very coarse with many assorted, mostly small to fine, white and grey grits, porous ware; medium-wide, very high-relief rope-molding outside; many assorted pits, spalling outside, grey smoke marks over-all. A IV 300.14c.
—	5038e	Body sherd of large jar; reddish-brown outside and greyish-brown inside; medium-coarse with some small to fine, white and grey grits; some grey and brown incrustations over-all. A I 1.5b.
23	4303	Orange outside and dark-grey inside, thick, dark-grey core; very coarse with some assorted white grits; wide, crude, high-relief molding outside; pitted over-all. A II 102.3.
—	4307e	Body sherd of large jar; buff with orange patches outside; coarse with some assorted white and grey grits; traces of heavy white slip outside; very thick, heavy, white incrustation uniformly over-all inside. A II 102.3.
24	4678	Orange; coarse with some small white grits; medium-wide, crude, high-relief rope-molding, traces of white slip outside, faint traces of two medium-wide, intersecting, painted reddish-brown stripes over molding; some grey incrustations over-all. A III 202.7.
25	4752	Greyish-brown with brown core; coarse with many assorted tan and orange grits; narrow, high-relief, ridged molding in crescent pattern outside. A III 203.5.
26	4680e	Pinkish-buff; coarse with some assorted white and tan grits; wide, crude, half-relief rope-molding, traces of heavy white slip outside; some grey incrustations. A III 202.7.
27	5024g	Orangish-brown with brownish-buff inside; medium-coarse with some assorted grey and tan grits; wide, high-relief rope-molding, heavy, white slip outside; some greyish-brown incrustations over-all. A IV 300.14c.
28	4789	Orange inside and grey outside; medium coarse grits; white slip, two medium-wide, parallel, painted, dark-red stripes outside; grey incrustations over-all. A III 204.3.
—	5028i	Body sherd of jar; burnt-orange outside and yellowish-orange inside, greyish-brown core; medium-coarse with few small to very fine white and tan grits; white slip outside with faint traces of two medium-wide, parallel, painted red lines: grey incrustations over-all. A IV 300.14d.
29	4798	Reddish-brown; very coarse with many assorted tan grits; traces of white slip, painted red pattern outside; some assorted pits and crazing inside, grey incrustations over-all. A III 204.3a.

Fig. 42 No.	Reg. No.	
30	4791	Dark-orange with thick buff core; very coarse with many assorted white, grey, and tan grits; white slip, traces of three narrow, parallel, painted, dark-red stripes outside; some grey incrustations over-all. A III 204.3.
31	4652	Greyish-buff; very coarse with some fine white grits; traces of white slip outside, faint traces of narrow, painted red stripes; very rough texture over-all, some grey incrustations. A III 202.5.
32	4651	Buff inside and grey outside; coarse with many assorted, mostly fine, white grits; traces of heavy white slip outside, faint traces of three medium-wide painted red stripes. A III 202.5.
33	4676	Buff with dark-grey outside; very coarse with many small to fine white grits; traces of white slip outside, traces of painted, reddish-brown lines in pattern; some assorted pits inside. A III 202.7.
34	5025	Buff with thick, dark-grey core penetrating to outside; coarse with many small to fine white grits; traces of white slip outside, traces of two wide, parallel, painted, reddish-brown stripes. A IV 300.14d.
35	4668	Orangish-buff; very coarse with many assorted tan, grey, and white grits; traces of heavy white slip outside, two parallel, painted, reddish-brown stripes; rough gritty texture inside. A III 202.5a.
—	4289p	Body sherd of jar; dull-orange with grey core; coarse with few assorted tan grits; heavy, white slip outside with traces of two narrow, parallel, painted red lines; black smoke marks inside. A II 101.9.
36	4314	Body sherd of bowl; buff with dark-orange outside; fine with many assorted white and grey grits; very narrow, parallel, horizontal, painted red stripes inside; orange discoloration inside. A II 102.4.
37	4288	Body sherd of amphoriskos; greyish-brown inside and buff outside; coarse with some small to fine, white grits; traces of painted, reddish-brown trellis pattern outside. A II 101.9.
38	5038f	Flint blade; light brown; unretouched edges, some grey incrustations. A I 1.5b.
39	4289f	Fragment of stone ring with flattened oval section; black basalt; inside of hole is well polished or worn smooth. A II 101.9.
40	4648	Palette or brick-like fragment; orangish-buff with orange patches, pinkish-brown core; very coarse with many assorted white and reddish-brown grits; some grey incrustations over-all, pitted on bottom. (4648 and 5017 joined) A III 202.5.
—	4680g	Hard piece of fired clay, very irregular in shape with possible finger impression on one side, does not appear to be part of a pottery vessel; dark-reddish-brown; very coarse with some assorted white and grey grits; very rough, uneven surfaces with some deep crazing and pitting over-all. A III 202.7.
—	4668f	Shell, pinkish white; small hole in hinge. A III 202.5a.

DESCRIPTIONS OF THE MARQUET-KRAUSE PHASE IV POTTERY AND OBJECTS, FIG. 43

Fig. 43 No.	M-K Reg. No.	
I	2566	Fragment of fine small bowl (lamp), rim in the everted extension of the side; smoke traces; thick and friable ware. H : 116; under the column at side of altar stones, at their level (M-K Pl. LXXVIII).

Fig. 43 No.	*M-K Reg. No.*	
2	2190	Fragment of bowl: flat shape. H:116; under floor B (M-K Pl. LXXXII).
—	2514	Fragments of bowls: (1) inclined wall, rim projecting over surface at a slight angle with inner wall (angles slightly rounded), red slip; (2) inclined wall, rim forming an obtuse angle with inner wall; (3) very small; inclined wall slightly thickened toward top, rim slightly projecting over inside surface at right angle with wall; grey ware; rim of hole-mouth; thick, slightly rounded, thickened over inside surface; loop-handle; fragment with molding slightly projecting, with design; fragment of flat horizontal handle; edge turned up, three finger indentations. H:116; under floor B.
—	2539	Fragment of bowl; wall inclined nearly 45°; horizontal rim projecting over inside surface; rims of hole-mouths thin, not thickened, rounded at edge; spout with vertical decoration, not pierced, showing an apparent opening at top; widened rim, approaching neck of jar; fragments of necks: (1) of small, fine juglet with sloping shoulder, neck continuing line of shoulder, then curved rim toward outside; (2) larger, high, thin wall, straight, thin rim curved toward outside. H:116; under floor B.
3	2542	Fragment of amphorette; broken ear-handles; red lattice design. H:116; under floor B (M-K Pl. LXXVIII).
—	2567	Fragment of the lower part of an amphorette with lattice design; rims of hole-mouths: (1) thin, curved, rounded edge; (2) thin, rounded edge, slightly flat; (3) thick, swollen over inside surface towards edge, edge slightly flat; fragment, red slip; fragment with molding; loop-handle; flat horizontal handle; finger prints on inner surface; Type I. H:116; under floor B; 3rd sanctuary.
4	2568	Fragment of neck of jar, not very high, outcurved; wall and rim in very fine straight line. H:116; under floor B (M-K Pl. LXXXII).
—	2573	Fragment of neck: somewhat thickened, thin edge; fragment of bowl; wall inclined about 45°, thin rim forming right angle with inner wall (angle rounded), burnished; rim of thin hole-mouth: brown fragment with glossy red slip. H:116; under floor B.
5	2568	Fragment of neck of jar: fine, straight wall; extreme edge somewhat thin, curved toward outside. H:116; under floor B (M-K Pl. LXXXIV).
—	2379	Fragments of jar with neck missing, horizontal spout below rim, rounded body, flat base; molding with impressions at base of neck. H:116; interior of floor B, and below.
—	2549	Fragment of neck, somewhat raised, thick wall; thin rim, curved toward outside; fragment of bowl: wall very inclined, horizontal rim slightly projecting over the two surfaces; light brown ware. H:116; under floor B.
—	2561	Fragment of jug or jar with flat thick base, coarse pinkish-brown ware. H:116; under floor B.
—	2563	Neck of jar, somewhat raised; thin edge curved toward outside; rim of hole-mouth thick, rounded edge, on outside surface incised line, bordered below by a slight projection. H:116; under floor B.
6	2002	Flat base of small pot with pear-shaped glossy body. H:116; under floor B (M-K Pl. LXXVII).
7	2537	Upper part of a jug: high neck; rim curved toward outside; ear-handles on shoulder. H:116; under floor B (M-K Pl. LXXVIII).
—	2293	Neck of small jug: thin and extended; fragment with projecting molding, very narrow, straight; fragment of neck of jar: white slip; rim of burnt hole-mouth; bones. H:116; under floor B.
8	2568	Rim of hole-mouth: thick, swollen over inside surface, rounded edge, white slip. H:116; under floor B (M-K Pl. LXXXIV).

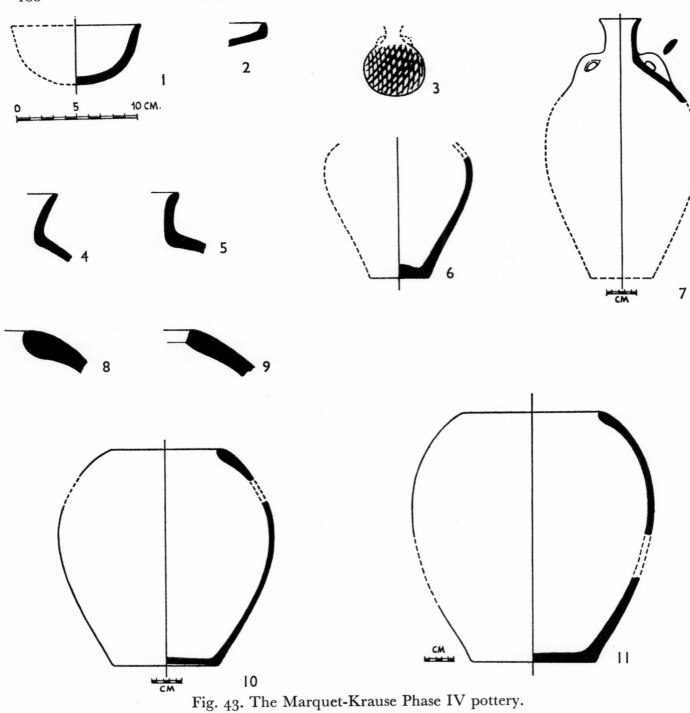

Fig. 43. The Marquet-Krause Phase IV pottery.

Fig. 43 No.	M-K Reg. No.	
—	2515	Two rims of hole-mouths; (1) thin, slightly thickened over inside surface; wavy molding (2) larger, more thickened; wavy molding; fragment with narrow molding; two loop-handles. H:116; under floor B.
—	2544	Fragment: rim of thick hole-mouth, slightly thickened over inside surface, rounded edge. H:116; under floor B.

Fig. 43 *No.*	*M-K Reg.* *No.*	
9	2568	Rim of hole-mouth: not thickened, flat edge. H : 116; under floor B (M-K Pl. LXXXIV).
—	2320	Fragment of hole-mouth or large bowl: rim inclined toward inside, rather thin, flat edge or slightly concave; on outside edge thin, striated molding, pink-brown ware; rims of hole-mouths: (1) not thickened, thin edge; wavy molding over outside surface; white slip; (2) thicker, slightly swollen over the two surfaces, thin edge, projecting molding, white slip; (3) thickened over inside surface, rounded edge; necks (of jars): thin rim, curved toward outside; fragment of bowl, curved wall, rim slightly jutting out projecting over inside surface at an angle quite sharp to the inside surface; fragment: narrow molding in triangular projections; flint knife. H : 116; under floor B, eastside.
—	2548	Rims of hole-mouths: (1) thin, curved, flat edge; (2) not thickened over inside surface; very small fragment (of small hole-mouth?) with striated rope-molding; fragment of simple neck, white slip; fragment of small flat bowl, rim incurved at top; brown ware; horizontal handles: (1) completely flat; (2) type I; flat, small half-circles on edge. H : 116; under floor B.
10	2543	Hole-mouth, globular body, rather large flat base, thickened rim. H : 116; under floor B (M-K Pl. LXXVIII).
—	2346II	Fragments of flat base, thick and coarse, doubtlessly belonging to a hole-mouth; rims of hole-mouths: (1) not thickened, flat edge; (2) slightly thickened over the two surfaces, edge slightly concave. H : 116; under floor B.
—	2466	(a) Various fragments: base of hole-mouth; fragment: red slip, glossy fragment; (b) flint. H : 116; under floor B.
11	2003	Hole-mouth. H : 116; under floor B (M-K Pl. LXXVII).
—	2378	Two flat horizontal handles, outer edge folded over itself, fold type I, on one the fold is slightly turned up; fragment of neck of simple jar, thin rim curved toward outside; fragment with a series of flutings or short incisions slightly angled. H : 116; at the interior of floor B, and below.
—	2481	Five horizontal handles, flat, broken, but still showing the edge turned upward at end of knuckle on the folded side, type I; large loop-handle, thick, red slip; fragment with projecting molding; small rounded bowls; fragment of neck: (1) thin wall and edge, rounded rim curved toward outside; (2) very fine wall and rim curved toward outside, flat edge; rims of hole-mouths: (1) thin, somewhat thickened over inside surface; (2) not thickened; on outside surface, close to edge, line in deep groove; compact and heavy ware; (3) not thickened; (4) thickened over the two surfaces toward edge, edge slightly flat. H : 116; under floor B.
—	2540	Horizontal handle; flat, on the side, outer edge folded over with finger, fingerprints on inner surface; rim, hole-mouth type thickening toward top, flat edge; curved rim of hole-mouth, rather thick, not swollen, edge somewhat thinned; fragment of neck of small juglet, thin, straight inner wall, thin rim curved toward outside. H : 116; under floor B.
—	2546	Fragment of hole-mouth; thick ware. H : 116; under floor B.
—	2547	Horizontal handles: (1) flat; (2) completely round; (3) outer edge folded over itself; fragment of bowl: wall rather inclined, thickening slightly toward top, flat rim projecting over outside surface at right angle with inside wall; projection rather thick, thinned at edge; fragment; red burnished brick. H : 116, under floor B.
—	2562	Small flat, horizontal handle; trace of fold at end of indentation on edge (fold type I); loop-handle; traces of red slip; fragment of bowl: flat form, wall very inclined, rim straightened again toward top at an angle somewhat obtuse with inner wall, rounded angle; neck of small juglet, thin rim curved toward outside rim very much thickened over inner surface and rounded at edge. H : 116, under floor B.

Fig. 43 No.	M-K Reg. No.	
—	2565	Horizontal handle with small finger indentations. H:116; 1 m. 40 cm.; under floor B.
—	2571	Broken horizontal handle; loop-handles: (1) flat; (2) cylindrical; fragment of juglet, brown slip with design of darker lines; fragment of neck; straight wall, thin rim barely curved toward outside; rims of hole-mouths: (1) rather thin, thick layer of lime; (2) very thick, rounded edge, swollen over inside surface in low and crudely formed projection; (3) very thick, rounded at edge and slightly thickened over inside surface; (4) hardly thickened over inside surface, a narrow and rather deep depression surrounding outside surface. H:116; under floor B.
—	2572	Horizontal handles: (1) on rim three impressions made by end of finger. (2) extreme rim folded over itself at end of indentation; fragment of neck, wall very thin, rim curved toward outside, flat edge; fragment: red slip; fragment: white slip with design of red lines; rims of hole-mouths: (1) (2) (3): very thin; (4) greatly thickened over inside surface, rounded edge; (5) edge very thickened and rounded on inside surface; (6) slightly thickened toward top, flat edge; curved. H:116; under floor B.
—	2545	(a) mortar; (b) donkey's jaw bone; (c) flat horizontal handle; imprint of finger tip on side; flat and large loop-handle, glossy slip; pierced spout. H:116; under floor B.
—	2424	Point or knife of bone. H:116; under floor B.

VI

PHASE V, THE TERMINATION OF BUILDING B

INTRODUCTION

A violent disaster brought the Phase IV city at Ai to an end and closed out the first great era in its history. Building B at Site A was completely destroyed and left in ruins. The destruction was radical enough to warrant the designation Phase V, because it was a watershed event in the history of the site. The characteristics of the evidence are as follows:

1. Collapsed walls of brick or stone. Bricky debris and stones from the collapse of Wall X and Tower B cover a large jar in Pl. X.2, for instance, to a depth of one-half meter. The scale in front of the jar rests upon a Building B floor, and the destruction debris covers the large stones above the jar as indicated in Section B–B, Fig. 11, Layers 5 and 6.

2. Calcined wall stones. The intense heat created by burning roof timbers partially, or completely, covered by roofing clay seems to have broken down wall stones into lime. This is particularly evident in the room between Walls Q and W, shown in Pl. IX.1 and 2. A mass of calcined stone rests against Wall Q in the left of Pl. IX.2, and small stones are broken down on the floor across the lower part of the photograph. The calcined small stones are more evident in Pl. X.1 in the lower left corner.

3. Cemented masses of pottery solidified into lumps by the calcined stone and other substances producing a molten, lava-like result. A cemented mass is shown in Pl. XV.1, where a small pot, barely discernible in the upper left center, is cemented to the outside of a large store-jar wall fragment. A close-up view of bubble holes on the outside of a store-jar neck and rim left by the molten substances is shown in Pl. X.2.

4. Baked lumps of clay with imprints of leaves, twigs, pottery, and stones pressed in the clay. The intense heat seems to have fired the clay to a consistency approaching that of pottery, leaving the imprints sharp and clear, as in Pl. XVI.1–4. These samples were on the floor shown in Pl. IX.2, in front of the balk.

5. Earthquake evidence at Site D, the acropolis. No distinctive evidence of an earthquake was observed at Site A, but the Phase IV outer wall of the acropolis building is tilted outward at a precarious angle from the curve at the northwest corner to the passageway leading into Area D II (see Callaway 1965, 32, Fig. 12, Wall B). This wall was buttressed on the outside and rebuilt in Phase VI, but the tilt was preserved in the rebuilding. The most credible reason for the tilted and partially dislodged wall is an earthquake, and the destruction layer associated with the wall is Phase V.

Phase V, therefore, is occupation evidence of Building B at the time it was terminated. In sequence to Phase IV, the construction evidence, Phase V, represents the latter part of EB II, and thus is classified EB IIB, over against EB IIA for the former. The artifacts assigned to Phase V were taken from ruins of the same Building B described in the preceding chapter, so the present chapter begins with a study of the Phase V pottery and objects.

THE PHASE V POTTERY AND OBJECTS

Provenance

The pottery and objects from Phase V are found in Figs. 44–55, and Marquet-Krause pottery assigned to Phase V appears in Figs. 56–58. Two layers are distinguished in the Master Section, Fig. 83, in the phase. Layer 6 (comprised of 6a and 6b in Section B–B, Fig. 11) includes the artifacts found on the floor of Building B, and the ashy remains of destruction debris lying on the artifacts. The bedline between layers 6 and 5 is difficult to define in places, but generally Layer 5 includes Phase V destruction debris which apparently resulted from deterioration of the ruins immediately following the initial holocaust.

For instance, in Pl. IX.1, 2, the lump of calcined stone behind the half-meter scale has a definite line of separation across its top, marked in a slight downward sweep to the right by a line of small charcoal lumps. This line is drawn in the Master Section, Fig. 83, as the upper limit of Layer 6. Layer 5, above it, reaches to the line of loose pebbles stretching from the top edge of Wall Q on the left across the entire width of the balk to the right. This layer seems to be undisturbed by builders who erected the Phase VI structures on the site, and, therefore, belongs with Layer 6 in Phase V. Layer 5, however, may have assumed its shape over an interval of time after the Phase V destruction when the site seems to have been abandoned, before the Phase VI leveling of the site took place.

The following descriptions of provenance will enable the correlation of sub-layers designated at the time of excavation with Layers 5 and 6 on the various sections. The sequence of provenance description follows that of the preceding chapter on Building B.

The south room in Area I. The only remnant of Phase V in Area I was a fragmentary layer of ashes drawn as Layer 6 between Walls E[1] and D[1] in Section H–H, Fig. 8. This Layer was largely removed in the previous excavations, and the small part remaining was exposed when the present expedition began work. The layer of ashes was removed, therefore, as a part of Wall D, and the few pieces of pottery from it are included with the Phase VI pottery. No pottery or objects with a reliable provenance in Phase V were obtained in Area I.

The remodeled south unit in Area II. Sub-layers 102.2 and 102.2a make up Layer 6 in the remodeled south room of Area II. Pottery from both sub-layers was taken from irregular projections of the Building B floor on top of Layer 7 against Wall Q and under the base of Tower A. The upper part of Layer 6 consisting of bricky and ashy earth along the base of Tower A, above the ashy surface of the Building B floor, is No. 102.2. In Pl. IV.1, 2, this is the charcoal flecked earth on the left and right of the base of the meter scale, above the black ashy floor surface. The artifacts taken from the ashy floor surface are designated No. 102.2a.

Layer 5 in the same unit is found only against the upper remains of Wall Q as drawn in Section E–E, Fig. 10, and visible also in Pl. IV. 2 on the right side of the upper quarter of the meter scale. The few pieces of pottery obtained from this provenance are designated No. 101.7a.

These three sub-layers are all that remained in the remodeled south unit assignable with any degree of reliability to Phase V. Most of the evidence from rooms of Building B was taken from the unit north of Wall Q, where undisturbed layers were preserved around the base of the Sanctuary A altar.

The reused north unit in Area III. Layer 6 in the sub-area around the base of the Sanctuary A altar is made up of several sub-layers. The thickness of the layer is evident in the Master Section, on the right side of Wall Q, and visible evidence is shown in Pl. IX.1, 2. The sub-layers make up one homogeneous unit, but the following breakdown, reading from the Building B floor up to the top of Layer 6 may be useful:

Layer 201.12–12a is the bricky ashy debris covering pottery and calcined stones lying on the Building B floor shown in Pl. IX. 1 under the end of the meter scale. No. 201.12 was assigned to the layer across the right end of the Sanctuary A altar balk, by the meter scale, and No. 201.12a designates the extension in front of the balk. This layer is about 10 centimeters thick on the right side of the balk, and increases slightly in depth where it covers the large stone in the lower right of Pl. IX.2 and sweeps upward midway of the half-meter scale to Wall Q.

Layer 201.6–6a is above No. 201.12–12a, and consists of the dark reddish layer in Pl. IX.2 above and to the left of the large stone in the lower right, and separating 201.12–12a from the less ashy sub-layer above. No. 201.11 is the same as 201.6 across the north end of the balk. The separation line seems to run through the calcined mass of stones against Wall A behind the center black section of the half-meter scale.

Layer 201.5–5a is the bricky, charcoal-flecked earth above No. 201.6–6a up to the top of Layer 6 as drawn in the Master Section, Fig. 83, and visible in Pl. IX.2 sweeping downward from the top of the large calcined mass toward the lower middle right of the photograph.

Layer 5 of the Master Section is made up of two sub-layers, reading as follows from lower to upper:

Layer 201.4–4a is above the upper bedline of Layer 6, following the charcoal-dotted line across Pl. IX.2 from the upper corner of Wall Q downward toward the right center.

Layer 201.3–3a is a truncated fragment of rubbly ashy earth on top of the right side of 201.4–4a in Pl. IX.2, and defined by loose rubbly bedlines above and below, the latter of which is evident at the extreme right center of the photograph.

These components of Layers 5 and 6 are all located in the area enclosed by Wall Q on the south, Wall F² on the east, Wall W on the north, and the Tower A balk on the west. The sub-layers of the north room of the unit have a different series of numbers, indicating a separate sub-area of Area III. The following components make up Layers 5 and 6 in the northwest corner of Area III, between Walls W and X ,and Wall F³ and the balk of Tower A:

Layer 202.3 is Layer 6 in the corner shown in Pl. X.2. This layer includes the jar behind the quarter-meter scale, and all of the bricky flecked earth up to the top of the jar, under the two large stones. The extension of this layer in Section B–B, Fig. 11, over to Wall F³, Layer 6b, is designated 300.17, because Area IV numbers are given to layers in the balk itself. Across the balk in Area IV, No. 300.19 is the counterpart of 202.3 and the same as 300.17. Layer 300.16 is No. 6a in the Master Section, between Wall F³ and the balk of Tower A.

Layer 5 of Section B–B is No. 300.12, above the two stones in Pl. X.2 and reaching from the base of Tower A across to the top of Wall F³. Layer 5 in Section I–I, Fig. 14, contains some of the decayed bricky debris of Wall F³, apparently broken down during the interval of abandonment of Site A between Phases V and VI.

The courtyard of the Building B complex. Layers 6 and 5 in Area II are found only in the northeast corner of the area between Walls F¹ and P¹. Layer 6 is the dark ashy stony debris indicated in Section E–E, Fig. 10, consisting of the residue from the destruction of Building B. The upper part of Layer 6 is designated 101.8, which was sub-divided into 101.8a, the more ashy earth adjacent to Wall F¹, and 101.8b, the more stony part of the layer near Wall P¹. The three numbers comprise one unit, however, resting on top of the Phase IV courtyard surface, Layer 7a, and covered by Layer 5a, the later component of Phase V. Layer 5a consists of Nos. 101.5, the upper part of the deposit of earth, and 101.5a, a more closely defined layer immediately above 101.8.

Layer 6 in the southeast part of Area III is drawn in Sections C–C, Fig. 12, and D–D, Fig. 13. The bricky ashy destruction debris in Section C–C, reaching from Wall F² to Firepit N² is made up of the following sub-layers:

No. 204.2–2a designates the layer between Firepit N² and the three large stones in Layer 5 above and on the left side of Wall F². The three stones were left on a small projecting balk, visible in Pl. XVII, until most of Layer 6 was excavated on each side of it. Layer 204.7 is the bricky earth on top of Wall F² on the right side of the three stones. Nos. 204.8–8a designate the extension of 204.2–2a to the side of Wall F² when the three stones were removed and all of Layer 6 was excavated down to the courtyard surface.

Layer 5 was excavated as No. 203.4a from Firepit N², in Section D–D, Fig. 13, across Section C–C, Fig. 12, to the top of Wall F². This layer was rubbly with mixed ashes and charcoal, resulting from the natural settlement of the ruins of Building B from exposure to wind, rain, and water impounded within the terraced sub-structure.

Layer 6 on the northeast quadrant of the courtyard consisted mainly of materials under Wall M. These were given Area IV numbers when the balk was removed. The ashy stony destruction layer on the courtyard surface was excavated as No. 300.14b, drawn as Layer 6 in Section B–B, Fig. 11, and Layer 5 above it is No. 300.14a.

The Phase V pottery forms

The pottery from Phase V, the Building B destruction layers, is drawn in Figs. 44–58. Physical remains of Building B are meager, being confined almost completely to Areas II–III, but the yield of pottery is relatively abundant when compared with that of other phases. The destruction of Building B apparently happened suddenly and unexpectedly, causing the inhabitants to flee and leave their belongings in the building largely as in daily use. The result is an unusually complete assemblage of pottery representing the terminal phase of EB II at Ai, designated EB IIB in the following study.

Small to medium bowls. The plain, small bowls found in hemispherical to shallow forms in Phases II–IV are less numerous in Phase V. Plain bowls tend to be medium-wide and shallow, e.g., Fig. 44:1–4, and small bowls are influenced by the carinate form appearing in Phase IV. Figs. 44:6 and 56:8 are small shallow bowls in the distinctive carinate form of those in Fig. 35:18–23, but comparable in size to those in Fig. 35:1–6. This form was anticipated in the semi-carinate forms of Fig. 35:6–9, recurring in Fig. 44:7 with the addition of a thin, rounded edge. A form comparable to 44:7 is found in Stratum I at Arad (Amiran Early Arad, Pl. 52:12). This form at Arad seems to have antecedents in Stratum II (Pl. 22:59) and Stratum III (Pl. 13:32).

Smoke marks are noted on the rims of both small and medium bowls, plain and semi-carinate forms, indicating a function as oil lamps which tended to transcend particular forms. Size, rather than form, was the criterion for selecting bowls as lamps. The form changed as new types, such as the carinate bowl, were introduced, but the range of sizes remained from small to medium, i.e., from 10 to 18 centimeters wide. Examples of lamp forms in Phase V are found in Fig. 44:1-4, 7, and Reg. No. 4258 under No. 2.

In the midst of the more sophisticated carinate and shallow bowl forms are the relatively crude and poorly fired thick-rim bowls in Fig. 44:5, 11-12. This form appeared first at Site A in Phase III (Fig. 26:26), and in Phase L at Jericho in Areas E III-IV (Hennessy 1967, Pl. IV. 30; p. 10). Phase L at Jericho lacked architectural remains, and the phase was defined from an 'enormous midden deposit' (*ibid.*) preceding the architectural evidence of Phase K. The evidence at Jericho implies an unsophisticated people associated with this form, but a people who were absorbed into the cultures of Phase K and later. If the association of pottery form and people is valid, the same cultural absorption is evident at Ai, because this crude medium bowl persists in Phase IV, Fig. 35:28-29, and Phase V, as noted above.

The bowl in Fig. 44:5 is entirely hand-made and is decorated with a white slip painted with vertical and horizontal reddish-brown stripes. The other bowls, Fig. 44:11-12, are better formed, although the technique of making these seems to have been primitive. Only the rims are wheel-finished, while the lower parts are hand-made. Two bowls found in Tomb A127 at Jericho reflect the same technique of throwing, and belong in the same family of forms (Kenyon 1960, 88, Fig. 25:5-6). The latter of these examples is described as 'lower part hand-made, rim wheel-made' (*ibid.*, p. 87). One similar form at Arad in Stratum I is drawn as though the rim is hand-made and irregular (Amiran Early Arad, Pl. 52:15), but the description is not available for more precise information.

Wide platter-bowls. The forms characteristic of EB II in Phase IV continue in Phase V with little variation. The sharply carinated form in Fig. 44:14 is similar to that in Fig. 36:14, although the stance of the rim suggests a shallower bowl, and the rim itself is lower in profile. Reddish-brown slip remains the standard decoration, burnished either in radial patterns, e.g. Fig. 44:17, 18, or in a smooth, even finish approaching a polish in appearance.

Two variations of the platter form do not seem to have antecedents in Phase IV. The flange-rim bowl in Fig. 44:13 is new, and at first sight seems to be an aberrant form, due to an error of the potter in throwing it, or of the draftsman in determining the stance. The former seems improbable in view of the unusually fine craftsmanship evident in the ware and finish of the bowl. The ware is fine and uniform, with a few white grits, and a smoothly-burnished reddish-orange slip covers both inside and outside. An error in drawing is also improbable because the stance and diameter of the sherd were double-checked by three persons. Fig. 44:13 is either a new form in Phase V, or an extreme variation of a more inverted flange-rim form found at Arad in Stratum II (Amiran Early Arad, Pl. 23:6) or a more upright flange-rim at Jericho in Tomb D12 (Kenyon 1960, 119, Fig. 38:4).

The other variation in platters is the extremely short and thick rounded, inverted rim form drawn in Fig. 44:21. This bowl has a slight concavity under the angle of the rim, a feature evident in

Phase IV, Fig. 36:7–8 ,and first found in Phase III, Fig. 27:7. The upturned rim, however, is very blunt and almost vestigial, suggesting an influence of the deeper bowl forms evident, for instance, in Phase IV, Fig. 35:32. Parallels of the blunt, inverted platter rim occur in Stratum XVII at Megiddo (Loud 1948, Pl. 5:16–17).

Wide deep bowls. The deep bowl with sloping sides in Fig. 45:1 is a common form in Phase V. This particular bowl is wheel-made and decorated with a reddish-brown slip radially burnished inside and wheel-burnished outside. Amiran cites a similar bowl from Megiddo XVIII as a typical EB II form, although the bowl cited is decorated with a white slip. White slip seems to be almost as common as reddish-brown slip, because Fig. 45:6–7 are white-slipped. The large bowl with thick, incurved wall in Fig. 45:7 is a new form in Phase V, paralleled at Arad in Stratum II (Amiran Early Arad, Pl. 23:12) and possibly at Jericho in Tomb D12. The latter in a complete bowl with wide, flat base (Kenyon 1960, 97, Fig. 33:20).

Juglets and small jars. A conspicuous new juglet form is drawn in Fig. 45:10, characterized by fine pinkish-orange ware and painted brown decoration of alternating horizontal and wavy lines from the lower waist to the base of the neck. This juglet was recovered from the floor of the room between Walls W and X in Area III, near the large jar shown in Pl. X.2.

Equally prominent is the decorated juglet, or possibly jar, drawn in Fig. 45:11, and photographed in Pl. XIV.3. Well-fired of light greenish ware, this juglet is wheel-made and decorated with a geometric and wavy line design painted in black. The provenance is the floor in front of the Sanctuary A altar balk, beside Wall Q in front of the half-meter scale in Pl. IX.2. On the same floor at the north end of the balk, in front of the meter scale in Pl. IX.1, a body sherd of a second decorated juglet was found. This piece is well-fired of dark buff ware, and has the point of a suspended triangle painted in black on the uppermost part of the sherd. The remainder of the juglet is probably on the floor covered by the altar balk. This floor of Building B is traced by way of Wall W in the Master section, Fig. 83, to the contemporary surface against Wall X on which Fig. 45:10 was found.

These decorated juglets are among Amiran's 'Abydos' ware forms (1969, 59, 62, 65, Pl. 17:6–10), now becoming increasingly known in Canaan. The type is distinguished by 'light-faced or white-slipped' ware painted in brown or red with geometric designs, and, exceptionally, a bird, in Egypt (Kantor 1965, 15). Amiran cites two Egyptian bird 'signatures,' one of which is painted on a juglet from Saqqara decorated with suspended triangles filled with dots, and a band of painted chevrons under the triangles and the bird (1968, 242, Pl. 26C–D).

The decoration is characterized by triangles, alternately plain and dotted or hatched, diamonds with similar designs, undulating horizontal lines, chevrons inside parallel horizontal lines, and alternating straight and wavy horizontal lines. Two of the three examples from Building B are decorated with black paint, which should be added to the red and brown mentioned by Kantor and Amiran.

Fig. 45:11 is decorated with a combination of the horizontal and wavy line motif found on Fig. 45:10, a band of suspended triangles filled with dots, and a fragment of chevron design around the shoulder up to the neck. The horizontal and wavy line motif is found with the triangle design at

Jericho in Tomb A127 (Kenyon 1960, 88, Fig. 88:34); in the Kinnereth tomb (Amiran 1969, 65, Pl. 17:8); at Saqqara (Kantor 1965, 29, Fig. 5A); and Abydos (Hennessy 1967, Pl. XLIV:2, 3; see also Petrie 1901, Pl. LIV for color photograph). A combination of the horizontal and wavy horizontal lines, suspended triangles, and a horizontal band of chevrons is found on the Saqqara bird vessel referred to above. More crude triangle and wavy line designs occur in Syria at Judeideh in Amuq G (and H), and at Arad on large jars in Stratum II (Amiran Early Arad, Pls. 28:2, 7, 29:4, 8, 30:4, 7, 8, and 33:1, 2). Some of the latter, e.g., Pl. 29:4, have an undulating rather than wavy line between parallel horizontal lines.

The spread of the painted forms is, therefore, from Abydos in Egypt to Judeideh in North Syria, with most examples in Egypt, an increasing number in Canaan, and a few at Judeideh. Hennessy notes that the Egyptian forms occur from the reign of Den at the beginning of EB II to the reign of Qa (1967, 51), the last king of the First Dynasty. The Tarkhan jug with the bird 'signature,' related to the painted Saqqara 'bird' juglet by Amiran (1968, 241), is from a tomb dating to the time of Uadji (Djet), the king associated with the end of EB IC by Hennessy and Lapp. Amiran points out that the Tarkhan representation of the bird is incised, not painted, and is later than the original net-burnished red-slip decoration of the jug. The implication of the provenance, however, is that it belongs at the end of EB IC, or at the beginning of EB II.

On the other hand, the stratified painted forms in Canaan seem to occur after the beginning of EB II. Phase V at Ai in Building B is the terminal phase of EB II, or EB IIB. An indefinite period of abandonment of Site A after Phase V is indicated, but Phase IV is the EB IIA, or initial, EB II period at Ai. The correlation of Building B and Arad pottery indicates that Phase IV forms overlap Strata III and II, and that Phase V correlates with Stratum II. This suggests that Stratum II, like Phase V at Ai, should be placed after the beginning of EB II.

The two occurrences of painted forms in tombs also suggest a provenance after the beginning of EB II. Tomb A127 at Jericho, dated to EB II, has Kenyon's Type E juglets, which are related to Tomb A108 but disappear in the later tombs, as well as juglets of Type F, which continue in the later tombs (Kenyon 1960, 86). The painted juglet, Fig. 25:34 (*ibid.*, p. 88), is assigned Type F.3.d, a form continuing without the painted decoration in Tombs D12, F4, F3, F2, and A114 (p. 71). Its provenance is Layer 3 of A127 (see pp. 89, 86), although Kenyon discounts the significance of layer designations in the tomb because of erosion and disturbances. Both type and layer provenance suggest, however, that the painted juglet belongs to a time after the beginning of EB II, probably contemporary with Phase V of Building B at Ai. The other examples, from the Kinnereth tomb, are dated by Amiran '. . . most probably to the very end of EB II, on the border of EB III' (1969, 66, n.2), a period contemporary with Phase V at Ai.

A problem of correlation between the painted forms in Egypt and those in Canaan emerges, because the forms seem to appear at the beginning of EB II, or EB IIA, in Egypt, while they appear in EB IIB in Canaan. This problem will be explored in the following discussion of chronology, but note should be taken here that the archaeological evidence does not seem to support the view that the style of decoration originated in Canaan. Some of the pottery forms on which the decoration is applied are known in Egypt and Canaan at the beginning of EB II, and, therefore, are probaby 'foreign ware' in Egypt. But the evidence of decorated forms is that the painted designs are known in Egypt before they appear in Canaan.

Large store-jars. Most jar forms in Phase V continue from Phase IV, with minor variations. The squared rim found first in Phase III appears in a more flaring profile than in Phase IV. Thin, folded rims are rolled at the outer edge, or pressed to a tapered edge, e.g., Fig. 45:14. In this case, two distinct ridges are molded in the long fold outside the rim. Fig. 45:15 has a flat, outward turned rim reflecting a technique of forming similar to that in Fig. 37:18, but without the inner bevel. Fig. 45:19, a thickened rim curving to an outward, overhanging point, seems to be a new form, although it may be a variation of Fig. 37:15 in Phase IV.

The complete jar drawn in Fig. 46:13 is the one shown in Pl. X.2. This jar is representative of a common form in Phase V, indicated by the numerous painted sherds in Fig. 55:7–20. A similar form is found at Arad in Stratum II (Amiran Early Arad, Pl. 33:5), decorated with vertical painted stripes. The same form is also decorated with the 'Abydos' geometric design in Fig. 33:1, 2. This correlation agrees with the Phase V evidence, because the small 'Abydos' decorated juglet in Fig. 45:10 was found on the floor of Building B beside Fig. 46:13. The complete jar in Fig. 57:6 was taken from the Phase V floor in Area II by Marquet-Krause, and, therefore, belongs in the same assemblage.

Hole-mouth jars. Applied molding decoration continues in Phase V on hole-mouths either on the top outer edge of the rim, e.g. Figs. 48:21, 49:1, or just below the rim, Fig. 48:18–20, 25. The form in Fig. 48:11 has an incurved, thickened, beveled rim ridged on top with unusual painted decoration. A creamy white slip covers the outside of the jar, and broad, reddish-brown stripes are painted horizontally around the inside beveled edge of the rim, and in a rough outline of a white triangle outside and below the rim. The triangle is similar to the 'Abydos' decoration, but the remainder of the design is broken off. Decorated forms at Arad in Stratum II are store-jars, not hole-mouths, but there is probably a relationship between the motifs on the Arad jars and the hole-mouth in Fig. 48:11.

Objects

Four objects from Phase V require special comment. These are the ceramic palette drawn in Fig. 55:21, the flint blade in Fig. 55:24, and the bronze needles in Fig. 58:29–30.

The ceramic palette. One end of a well-fired ceramic palette, shown in Pl. XIV.4 and Fig. 55:21, was recovered from the floor beside the painted juglet in Pl. XIV.3. The palette is 18.3 centimeters wide at the squared end, and 4.3 centimeters thick. No indication of its original length is apparent. Smoke marks on the edges and core suggest that the palette was already broken when the Phase V destruction of Building B occurred.

The sharply defined sides and edges of the object give it the appearance of a molded shape, but close examination proves that it is hand-made and shaped. Finger marks are evident on all surfaces, and the vertical sides are not straight. There is every indication of very careful shaping, and the ware is more free of pebbles and extraneous matter than a comparable section of a large jar would be. Also, the firing is carefully done, resulting in a hard, smoothly rubbed surface.

No ceramic palettes of this type are known to the writer. A suggestion was made in the previous chapter that a Phase IV brick-like object may have used been in cooking bread. The context of this Phase V object is a domestic house, so a similar function is possible. There is no discernible evidence that it was used in any kind of industrial operation, e.g., the casting of bronze.

The flint blade. Thin flint blades were found at Ai by Marquet-Krause (1949, Pl. XXXVII), and at Sites A, C, and K by the present expedition. Fig. 55:24 is the larger half of a broken blade, probably like the complete blade in Marquet-Krause 1949, Pl. XXXVII:290. The blade is quite thin, as the section in Fig. 55:24 indicates, and is retouched on the back side to make a sharp, beveled edge as Pl. XII.5 illustrates. This fragment measures 9.5 centimeters across the widest part, near the break, and 9 centimeters at the break. It is 8 millimeters thick in the center of the section. A blade from Arad, Stratum II is very similar in size, thickness, and form (Amiran Early Arad, Pl. 87:4).

The bronze needles. Two types of needles were found by Marquet-Krause on the floor of Building B in Area II. The first Fig. 58:29, is pointed at each end, and is about 5 centimeters long. This type is known in Egypt during the Old Kingdom from Zer to Khasekhemui (Petrie 1901, 36), and seems to be common at Ai (see Marquet-Krause 1949, Pl. XXXIX:1). The second, called a thinning needle by Marquet-Krause, is drawn in Fig. 58:30. It is widened in the middle, and has an eye formed by bending the point on one end. Variations of this form are also known in the Old Kingdom, e.g., from the tomb of Mersekha (Petrie 1901, XLIII:17), and according to Emery, are needles for leatherwork (1949, Pl. 9B).

Conclusions

Little change or development occurs in pottery forms from Phases IV to V. There seems to be a stability in traditions down to the end of Phase V. The appearance of new painted motifs in Phase V suggests widening trade patterns during the latter part of EB II reaching to Egypt. A reorientation of communications and commerce from North Syria to Egypt seems evident.

The pottery horizon of Phase V. Stratified pottery comparable to that of the terminal phase of Building B is found in Stratum II at Arad. Phase IV, as was noted earlier, overlapped forms in Strata III and II, suggesting that Phase V is contemporary with the latter part of Stratum II. At Jericho, comparable forms occur in Phases J–G of Areas E III–IV, and the painted ware in Phase V seems to be contemporary with the latter use of Tomb A127. The Building B assemblage seems to be contemporary with Périodes 3–5 at Tell el-Far'ah (N), although Phase V may terminate before the end Période 5.

The painted ware of Phase V is similar to late EB II painted forms in the Kinnereth tomb, and in the same tradition as painted forms at Judeideh, Phase G–H, also dated to late EB II, or transitional to EB III (see Kantor 1965, 17–18). These forms seem to occur earlier in Egypt than in Palestine, beginning with the reign of Den, with which the beginning of EB II in Palestine is correlated by Hennessy and Lapp, and continuing to Qa, the last king of the First Dynasty. Painted ware decoration may have been introduced into Palestine in commercial transactions with Egypt, rather than from Canaan to Egypt, as Amiran suggests.

Phase V terminates the first era of urban life at Ai, begun in Phase III, or EB IC. Also the new architectural stratum designated Building B, begun in Phase IV, terminates in Phase V. This is the equivalent of EB IIB at Ai, with EB IIA assigned to Phase IV.

Chronology. The beginning of Building B, or Phase IV, was dated to ca. 2860 B.C. in the preceding chapter on the evidence of three Carbon 14 assays, two of roof timbers used in constructing Building

B at Site A, and one of seeds burned in the destruction of Phase III buildings at Site C. Four additional samples related to the termination of Building B in Phase V, and the construction of Building A in Phase VI indicate a date of ca. 2720 B.C. for the end of Phase V at Ai. This places the beginning of EB IIA at ca. 2860 B.C., and the end of EB IIB ca. 2720 B.C. The four assays are as follows:

Sample	Provenance	Date
1. TX 1026	A III 204.6	4740 ± 90 2790 B.C.

Charred wood from the courtyard of Building B found on the surface of Layer 5 near Firepit N², drawn in Section C–C, Fig. 12, and included in the artifacts assigned to Layer 4. The Charcoal fragments are probably from Firepit N² in the courtyard, and thus date from a time near the end of Phase V. Layer 4, as well as Layer 5, derive from the ruins of Building B, but Layer 4 was disturbed in preparing the site for the Phase VI building. Sample TX 1026, therefore, belongs in Phase V, and probably should be placed near the end of the phase.

2. TX 1029	A IV 300.19	4570 ± 120 2620 B.C.

Charcoal fragments in the bricky debris between the broken pot and the base of Tower A in Pl. X.2, near the place where a white tag is pinned in the photograph. This is near the surface of the foundation trench for Tower A. The fragments do not seem to be a part of the Building B roof. They may derive from fires built on the surface of the site before, or during, the construction of Tower A in Phase VI.

3. TX 1030	C I 1.28b	4630 ± 70 2680 B.C.

Charred seeds from a store-jar in Area I of Site C, Layer 28b, the equivalent of the Phase V destruction layer at Site A. The seeds would have been grown the same year they were burned, so the date reflects the termination of Phase V at Site C. A note was made in Chapter V, p. 224, n.2, that assay GaK 2381, attributed to C I 1.28b, is of charred wood, not seeds, and therefore is probably the same as GaK 2379, an assay of charred wood from D IV 300.5. TX 1030 is an assay of the seeds.

4. TX 1031	C IX 800.10	4730 ± 90 2780 B.C.

Charred seeds from a room in Area IX of Site C, near Area I from which sample TX 1030 was taken. Layer 10 of sub-area 800 is near contemporary with C I 1.28b, and reflects the Phase V period, at or near the destruction.

This cluster of dates bears upon the end of Phase V, and the beginning of Phase VI, the subject of the next chapter. The spread of ± margins of the four assays is as follows:

1. TX 1026	A III 204.6	2700–2880
2. TX 1029	A IV 300.19	2500–2740
3. TX 1030	C I 1.28b	2610–2750
4. TX 1031	C IX 800.10	2690–2870

The mean average of the four assays is 2712 B.C. TX 1026 and TX 1031 are near the same in average and margin of error, so an aberrancy does not seem to be indicated. TX 1030 seems to be a good assay with a long count, while TX 1029 is more marginal, indicated by a shorter count and a higher margin of error. The fragments making up TX 1029 were small, and in less quantity than the others. The overall impression of the cluster is that less weight should be given to the results of TX 1029, yet TX 1030, which is lower than TX 1026 and TX 1031, is significant. A better average date may be obtained by averaging the lower margins of Nos. 1 and 4 with the higher margins of

Nos. 2 and 3, where the nearest point of coincidence among the four dates occurs. The spread of ± margins would align as follows in this arrangement:

1.	TX 1026	A III 204.6	2700–2880
2.	TX 1029	A IV 300.19	2500–2740
3.	TX 1030	C I 1.28b	2610–2750
4.	TX 1031	C IX 800.10	2690–2870

The average of the four dates in the center of the column is 2720 B.C., which appears to be a better result than the mean average of the four assays. This date for the termination of Phase V seems acceptable.

In summary, the chronology of Building B from its beginning in Phase IV to its termination in Phase V is ca. 2860–2720 B.C., the equivalent of EB IIA–B at Ai. This point of termination seems to occur before the end of the Second Dynasty, as Hennessy prefers (1967, 88), but reluctantly rejects because of the problem of 'filling in' the long span of time left for EB III. There seems to be no great problem with this correlation at Ai for two reasons. First, the termination of Phase V seems to have been caused by a natural disaster, probably an earthquake, and, therefore, does not reflect a conquest which introduces a new cultural period immediately. Evidence of abandonment of Site A for an appreciable interval indicates that the city was rebuilt over a considerable period of time.

Second, there are two city wall phases at Ai dating to EB III, probably reflecting a period as long as that of the first two city wall phases, i.e., 280–300 years. Phases III–V cover the period from 3000 B.C. to 2720 B.C., and Phases VI–VIII cover almost, if not as much as, the same total number of years.

DESCRIPTIONS OF THE PHASE V POTTERY AND OBJECTS, FIGS. 44–55

Fig. 44 No.	Reg. No.	
1	4788	Rim upcurved to rounded edge, wheel-finished; reddish-brown; medium with many small to fine white grits; black smoke marks on edge indicate possible use as lamp, spalling inside edge. A III 204.2a.
—	5166g	Body sherd of small bowl, wheel-turned; reddish-brown; medium-fine with some very fine white grits; continuously-burnished over-all; some light incrustations inside, A IV 300.17.
2	4262	Rim upcurved to thin, rounded edge, wheel-made; pinkish-tan; medium-coarse with few assorted white grits; black smoke marks on edge indicate possible use as lamp. A II 101.5a.
—	4838	Rim of small bowl, upcurved to thin, rounded edge, wet-smoothed; orangish buff with buff core; fine with many assorted, mostly small fine, grey grits. A III 204.8a.
—	4258	Rim of small bowl slightly upcurved to thin, rounded edge, wheel-made; buff; medium-coarse with some assorted white, tan, and grey grits; traces of burnished red slip inside and outside edge; black smoke marks on edge indicate possible use as lamp. A II 101.5a.
3	4529	Rim crudely made; orange with buff core; coarse with many assorted white and grey grits; rough texture outside, pronounced crazing inside, black smoke marks on rim indicate possible use as lamp. A III 201.4a.
—	4296a	Rim of small bowl, incurved to thinned, rounded edge, wet-smoothed; buff; medium with few small white grits; some grey incrustations. A II 102.2.

Fig. 44 *No.*	*Reg.* *No.*	
4	4255	Rim upcurved to thin, rounded edge, wheel-made; medium-coarse with many small to fine, white and grey grits; traces of burnished brown slip inside and outside edge; black smoke marks on edge indicate possible use as lamp. A II 101.5a.
5	4592u	Handmade; dull-orange with grey core; medium-fine with few assorted tan and grey grits; greyish-white slip outside and inside edge, several groups of three narrow, vertical, painted reddish-brown stripes, one horizontal stripe under rim. A III 201.12a.
—	4625e	Rim of bowl, slightly everted to thinned rounded edge, wet-smoothed; buff; medium-coarse with some small fine grey and white grits; traces of white slip outside and inside edge. A III 202.3.
6	4834	Carinated wall with upper portion everted to thinned, rounded edge; dark-grey; coarse with many assorted, mostly fine, white grits; traces of orangish slip over-all; very rough texture. A III 204.8a.
—	4956	Rim of bowl, carinated wall, upper portion everted to thinned, rounded edge; reddish-brown with dark, greyish-brown core; coarse with many assorted grey quartz grits porous ware; many small to fine pits over-all, edge badly chipped. A IV 300.12.
7	5002	Semi-carinated wall with upper portion everted to thinned rounded edge, inside and outside edge wheel-turned; orange with grey core; medium-coarse with many small to fine white grits; traces of burnished, reddish-brown slip over-all; black smoke marks on edge indicate possible use as lamp; heavy, grey incrustations over-all. A IV 300.14b.
—	5009z	Body sherd; greyish-orange outside and pinkish-orange inside, burnt-orange core; medium-fine with many small to very fine white and tan grits, few assorted grey grits; porous ware; continuously-burnished blackish-brown slip outside; many assorted, mostly fine to very fine, pits inside; some spalling outside. A IV 300.14b.
8	4974	Carinated wall with upper portion everted to thin, rounded edge, inside and outside edge wheel-turned, reddish-brown; medium with many assorted, mostly fine, tan grits; crude wheel-burnishing over-all; many assorted pits. A IV 300.14a.
—	5095g	Body sherd of bowl; dark reddish-brown; medium with some fine white grits; closely-spaced parallel bands of three narrow burnished lines outside, continuously-burnished inside. A IV 300.14a.
—	5095j	Body sherd of bowl, wheel-turned; brownish-red; medium-coarse with many fine to very fine white grits; continuously-burnished over-all. A IV 300.14a.
9	5080f	Rim of bowl, slightly upcurved to low, upright thinned, rounded edge; buff; medium-coarse with few small to fine white grits; traces of burnished, reddish-brown slip over-all; heavy, grey incrustations. A II 101.8b.
10	4271	Upcurved wall with medium-high, slightly inverted rim tapered to rounded edge, vertically pierced horizontal lug crudely joined to outer edge of rim; orangish-buff with buff core; medium-coarse with many assorted tan and white grits. A II 101.8a.
11	5078	Rim upcurved to rounded, flat edge projected out; orange inside and buff outside; medium-coarse with many assorted white, grey, and tan grits; some assorted pits outside, some grey incrustations. A II 101.8a.
12	5082	Rim upcurved to vertical, thickened, rounded, flat edge, projected out; buff; medium-coarse with some assorted white and grey grits; some grey incrustations over-all. A II 101.8a.
—	4261	Rim of bowl, upcurved to rounded, flat edge, wheel-made; buff with thick, dark-grey core in places; very coarse with many assorted grey grits; traces of wheel-burnished brown slip over-all; edge very chipped. A II 101.5a.

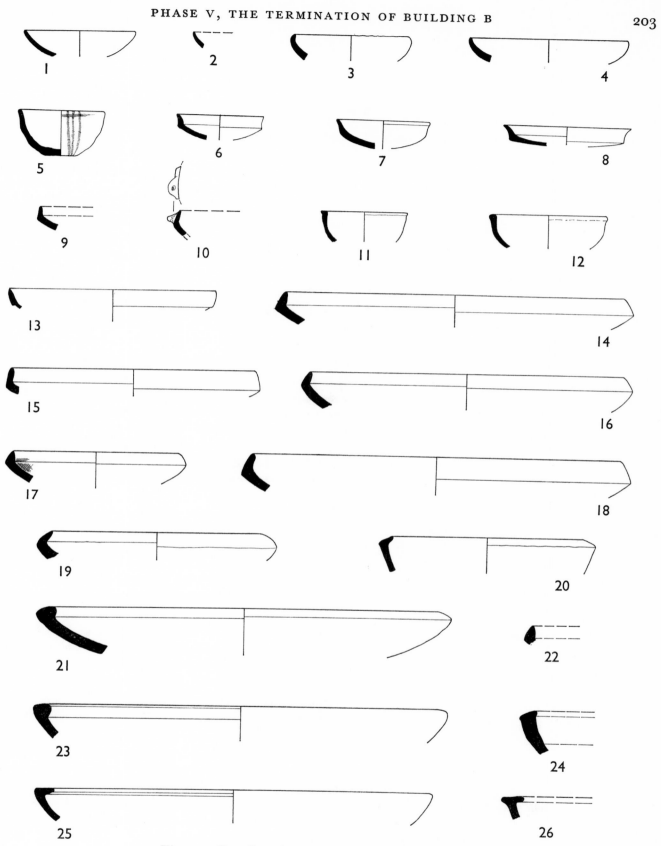

Fig. 44. Small to large bowls, Phase V. 1:4.

Fig. 44 No.	Reg. No.	
13	4300	Flange rim upcurved to pointed edge; orange; fine with few assorted white grits; traces of burnished, reddish-orange slip over-all; black smoke marks on edge. A II 102.2a.
—	4574g	Body sherd of small shallow bowl, wheel-finished inside; orangish-buff; fine with few small to fine grey and tan grits; continuously-burnished, reddish-brown slip inside and outside; some heavy, grey incrustations outside. A III 201.12.
14	5050	Rim sharply carinated with thinned, inverted edge, wheel-turned; orange; medium with very many assorted, mostly fine, white and grey grits; traces of burnished reddish-orange slip over-all; some grey incrustations. A II 101.8b.
15	4299	Upcurved to thinned, rounded slightly inverted edge, wheel-made; medium with many small to fine, white and dark-grey grits; traces of burnished, reddish-orange slip over-all. A II 102.2a.
16	5068	Upcurved to rounded, low inverted edge, wheel-made; buff with thick, dark-grey core; medium-coarse with many small to fine white and dark-brown grits; traces of burnished brown slip inside; many assorted pits over-all. A II 101.5a.
—	4831l	Body sherd of wide shallow bowl; brown with thick, dark-grey core; medium-coarse with some medium to fine, grey, tan, and orange grits; continuously-burnished, brown slip inside; greyish-brown incrustations over-all. A III 204.7.
—	4839k	Body sherd; greyish-brown; coarse with some assorted grey grits; continuously-burnished, reddish-brown slip inside. A III 204.8a.
17	4276	Upcurved to pointed, inverted edge; orange with grey core; medium-coarse with very many medium to fine, tan grits; traces of wheel-burnished, reddish-brown slip over-all, radially burnished inside; some grey incrustations. A II 101.8b.
—	4839h	Body sherd of wide shallow bowl, inside wheel-turned; orange with dark-buff core; coarse with some medium to fine white and reddish-brown grits; traces of continuously-burnished reddish-brown slip; grey incrustations over-all. A III 204.8a.
—	4831k	Body sherd of shallow bowl; dark-buff with greyish-brown core; very coarse with some medium to fine grey, tan, and reddish-brown grits; traces of continuously-burnished, reddish-brown slip over-all. A III 204.7.
18	4833	Rim carinated with thinned, rounded, inverted edge, some thickening at angle, wheel-turned; reddish-brown with dark-brown core; medium-coarse with some assorted black and reddish-brown grits; very many fine white grits; radially-burnished inside, wheel-burnished outside and on edge; black smoke marks and some grey incrustations over-all. A III 204.8a.
—	5103c	Body sherd of wide, shallow bowl, wheel-turned inside and outside; brown; medium with many medium to fine tan grits; continuously-burnished dark reddish-brown slip over-all with radial strokes inside and horizontal strokes outside. A IV 300.16.
—	5009m	Rim of small platter, inverted edge, wheel-turned; brownish-buff; medium with many fine to very fine grey, tan, and reddish-brown grits; wheel-burnished reddish-brown slip over-all; some light grey incrustations. A IV 300.14b.
—	5090	Rim of bowl, rounded carination, inverted, thinned, low edge, wheel-turned; brownish-buff; coarse with many assorted white, tan, and grey grits; traces of continuously-burnished, reddish-brown slip over-all; many assorted pits inside, very pitted and spalling outside, black smoke marks on edge. A IV 300.14a.
19	5076	Upcurved to thinned, pointed, inverted edge; buff with dark-grey core penetrating to outside in places; coarse with many assorted, mostly fine, white grits; some assorted pitting, some grey incrustations over-all. A II 101.8a.

Fig. 44 No.	Reg. No.	
—	4831i	Body sherd of bowl, wheel-turned inside, tannish-buff; coarse with some small to fine white grits; traces of burnished, reddish-brown slip over-all; very uneven surface outside, dark-grey smoke marks inside. A III 204.7.
—	4529c	Body sherd; tan; medium-coarse with some assorted tan and grey and some fine white grits; burnished reddish-brown slip inside and outside; black smoke marks inside and on broken edge. A III 201.4a.
20	4957	Wall inclined out to thinned, inverted edge, wet-smoothed; buff with grey core at thickening of edge; medium with some assorted white, and grey grits; very many fine pits over-all, some grey incrustations. A IV 300.14a.
21	5044	Rim slightly upcurved to rounded, flat, triangular, inverted edge; wide, shallow groove outside below edge, wheel-turned; greyish-buff with brownish-grey inside; very coarse with many assorted white and grey grits; faint traces of burnished brown slip inside and on edge; many assorted pits over-all, flaking inside. A II 101.5a.
22	4529a	Rim with inverted thinned, triangular, inverted edge; wheel-turned; reddish-brown; medium with many small to fine white grits; wheel-burnished brown slip over-all. A III 201.4a.
—	4831d	Rim of platter inverted to low, rounded edge with shallow depression outside, below carination, wheel-turned; pinkish-brown; fine with few small tan grits; traces of burnished, reddish-brown slip over-all. A III 204.7.
23	5053	Wall upcurved to rounded, flat, triangular, inverted greyish-buff with dark-grey core at rim; very coarse with many assorted white and tan grits; traces of burnished brown slip inside and on edge; many assorted pits and flaking over-all, some heavy, grey incrustations inside. A III 101.8a.
24	5069	Rim upcurved to thickened, flattened edge, slightly inverted; brownish-grey; very coarse with few assorted white and tan grits; traces of wheel-burnished brown slip over-all. A II 101.8a.
25	5070	Wall upcurved to wide, flat inverted rim, wheel-made; buff; coarse with many small to fine white and grey grits; traces of brown slip radially-burnished inside, wheel-burnished outside and on edge. A II 101.5a.
Fig. 45 No.	Reg. No.	
1	5056	Wall upcurved to rounded, flat inverted rim, wheel-made; orangish-brown with dark-greyish-brown core; coarse with very many assorted white, tan, and grey grits; traces of reddish-brown slip, radially-burnished inside, wheel-burnished outside and on edge. A II 101.8a.
—	5009w	Body sherd of wide shallow bowl, wheel-turned; orange with brownish-grey core; medium with many large to very fine grey and tan grits; burnished reddish-brown slip inside and outside with irregular pattern of parallel, probably radial, lines inside and possible trellis pattern outside consisting of intersecting bands of four parallel lines; traces of light grey incrustations over-all. A IV 300.14b.
—	5095i	Body sherd of bowl; orangish-buff; medium-coarse with few medium-grey grits; traces of burnished reddish-brown slip outside; some pitting and spalling. A IV 300.14a.
—	5095m	Body sherd, thin; brownish-orange outside and grey inside; fine with some assorted white grits; continuously-burnished brown slip outside; grey incrustations over-all. A IV 300.14a.
2	4543	Wall upcurved to wide, flattened, triangular inverted rim, wet-smoothed; orangish-buff; medium-coarse with many assorted white, tan, and grey grits; traces of burnished reddish-brown slip inside. A III 201.6a.

Fig. 45 No.	Reg. No.	
—	4831c	Rim of bowl, upcurved to wide, flat edge projected in; orangish-buff with dark-buff core; medium-coarse with some assorted grey and tan grits; traces of burnished, reddish-brown slip inside edge; pitted and spalling over-all. A III 204.7.
3	5042	Wall upcurved to flat, triangular, inverted rim, wheel-made; orangish-buff with very thick, dark-grey core penetrating to inside in places; coarse with many assorted white, tan, and grey grits; traces of burnished, reddish-brown slip over-all; few assorted pits, some flaking on edge, uneven surface outside. A II 101.7a.
4	5167	Wall upcurved to thickened, flat edge projected out and slightly in, wet-smoothed; dark-orange inside and brown outside, thick, dark-grey core penetrating to outside in places; very coarse with many small to fine, white grits; traces of white slip outside and on edge; grey incrustations over-all. A III 204.2.
5	5091	Wall slightly upcurved to thickened; triangular, flattened rim, projected slightly in and out; orangish-buff; coarse with many assorted grey grits; traces of white slip outside; black smoke mark outside. A IV 300.14a.
6	4250	Rim incurved to narrow, rounded, inverted edge; buff with thick, dark-grey core; medium-coarse with some assorted white grits; traces of white slip outside; very rough texture, some grey incrustations over-all. A II 101.5.
7	5043	Wall, incurved to very thickened, rounded, flat edge projected in; buff; very coarse with many assorted white and orange grits; traces of crudely burnished, reddish-orange slip over-all; very pitted and flaking, some grey incrustations over-all. A II 101.8b.
—	5085	Body sherd; greyish-brown inside and buff outside; very coarse with many assorted light- and dark-grey grits; traces of burnished reddish-orange slip outside. A IV 300.14a.
8	4541	Part of neck and loop-handle, one pierced vertical lug handle joining neck and shoulder; tan with patches of buff and orange outside; medium-coarse with very many small to fine white, tan, and reddish-brown grits; traces of white slip outside; grey smoke marks over-all, rough, gritty texture, very uneven with large lump of clay inside. A III 201.6a.
—	4592b	Body sherd; greenish-tan; medium-coarse with some assorted brown grits; white slip outside; rough, gritty texture inside, brown incrustations over-all. A III 201.12a.
9	0–81	Amphoriskos, hand-made with neck possibly wheel-made and joined to body; two pierced, vertical lug handles on either side of neck; orangish-buff; fine with many small to very fine, grey and white grits; trellis-burnished, reddish-brown slip over-all outside. A III 201.12a.
10	0–79	Fragment of juglet with stump of loop-handle; pinkish orange; fine with fine white grits; painted brown decoration of horizontal and wavy lines. A III 202.3.
—	4543b	Body sherd of juglet, very thin; dark orange inside and brown outside; fine with some small to fine white grits; continuously-burnished brown slip outside; uneven surface with few small pits, some brown incrustations inside. A III 201.6a.
—	5009t	Body sherd of juglet, including part of body and transition to neck, hand made; orange with buff patches outside, buff core; medium-coarse with many assorted dark-grey and white grits; faint traces of reddish-brown slip outside; very irregular surfaces over-all. A IV 300.14b.
—	4543a	Body sherd of juglet; buff with bright-orange patch outside; medium with some assorted grey and reddish-brown grits; continuously-burnished orange-buff slip outside; very rough, gritty, uneven surface inside, some grey incrustations outside. A III 201.6a.
—	4535	Body sherd of juglet; buff; medium with some assorted, mostly small, light- to dark-grey and reddish-brown grits; porous ware; traces of burnished, reddish-brown slip outside; many small pits over-all. A III 201.5a.
—	4526	Body sherd of juglet; buff with grey core; coarse with some assorted tan grits; traces of burnished reddish-brown slip outside. A III 201.4.

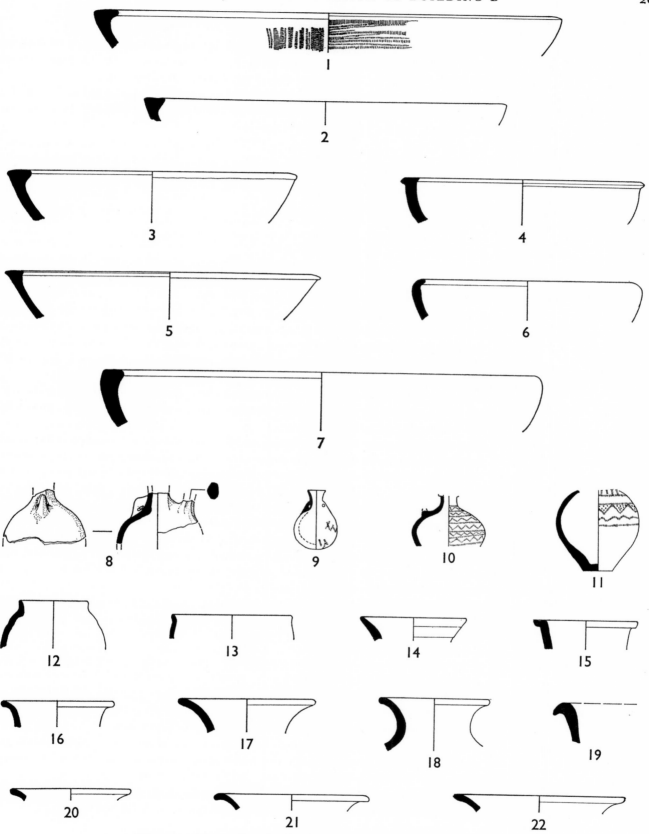

Fig. 45. Large bowls, juglets, and jars, Phase V. 1:4.

Fig. 45 No.	Reg. No.	
11	0–80	Fragment of juglet, wheel-made with pronounced ridges inside, smoothly finished outside; greenish-white; fine with some small to very fine, grey and reddish-brown grits; several horizontal bands of painted black decorations. A III 201.12a.
—	4573	Body sherd of juglet; dark-buff; medium-coarse with many assorted, mostly small to fine, dark-grey and brown grits; two very narrow intersecting, painted black lines outside; fine, gritty texture inside. A III 201.11.
12	4578	Wall incurved with short neck inclined out to thinned, rounded rim, wet-smoothed; greyish-white; medium-coarse with few small white grits; traces of creamy-white slip over-all; very uneven surface inside. A III 201.12a.
13	4737	Rim slightly everted to thinned, rounded edge, wheel-finished; brown; medium with some fine white and tan grits; faint traces of burnished reddish-brown outside; gritty texture. A III 203.4a.
—	5116i	Body sherd; light- to dark-brown; coarse with very many assorted grey and white quartz grits; traces of continuously-burnished, reddish-brown slip outside; much spalling inside. A IV 300.17.
—	4296c	Body sherd; reddish-brown; very coarse with some assorted tan and grey grits; continuously-burnished reddish-brown slip over-all; black smoke marks inside. A II 102.2.
14	4270	Rim flared out to thinned, rounded edge, wheel-made; buff with grey core penetrating to inside in places; medium-coarse with many assorted grey, white and tan grits; traces of burnished brown slip outside, some grey incrustations. (4270 and 4274 joined) A II 101.8a.
—	5009y	Body sherd; buff; medium with many medium to very fine grey and white grits; traces of continuously-burnished, reddish-brown slip outside; many small pits inside. A IV 300.14b.
15	4836	Rim slightly inclined out with flattened edge projected out in rounded collar shallow depression in top, edge and outside wheel-turned; orange; coarse with very many assorted dark-grey and some white grits; traces of wheel-burnished reddish-orange slip over-all. A III 204.8a.
16	4266	Rim sharply outcurved to rolled edge, wheel-made; pinkish-orange with reddish-grey core; coarse with very many assorted white and tan grits; few small pits outside, rough gritty texture inside. (4266 and 4273 joined) A II 101.8a.
17	4832	Rim outcurved to rounded edge, wet-smoothed; tan with grey core; coarse with many assorted tan, grey, and reddish-brown grits; rough, gritty, pitted texture inside, some grey incrustations over-all. A III 204.8.
18	5106	Neck medium-high, outcurved to rounded rim, wheel-finished, buff with patches of orangish-buff outside; coarse with very many assorted dark-grey and reddish-brown grits; many assorted pits inside. A IV 300.17.
19	5009l	Rim turned sharply out and down to thinned, pointed edge, wheel-finished; orangish-brown with bright grey core penetrating to surface in places; medium-coarse with some fine to very fine white grits; some light, grey incrustations over-all. A IV 300.14b.
20	4592d	Rim sharply outcurved to rounded edge, wheel-finished; pinkish-buff; medium with some assorted tan, grey, and reddish-brown grits. A III 201.12a.
21	4275	Rim sharply flared out to rounded downturned edge wheel-made; pinkish-buff inside and buff outside, dark-grey core; medium-coarse with many assorted white and tan grits; some assorted pits over-all, rough, gritty texture inside. A II 101.8b.
22	4542	Rim sharply outcurved to rounded edge, wheel-finished; tan with grey patch inside; coarse with many assorted grey and reddish-brown grits. A III 201.6a.

Fig. 46 No.	Reg. No.	
1	4574a	Rim slightly outcurved to rolled edge with collar projected out, wheel-finished; buff with brownish-grey core; coarse with very many assorted grey quartz and white grits; traces of reddish-brown slip over-all. A III 201.12.
2	4257	Rim outcurved to rolled edge with collar outside, wheel-made; orangish-buff; coarse with some assorted white and grey grits; some grey incrustations. A II 101.5a.
3	4581	Rim of jar, outcurved to rolled edge with wide collar outside; yellowish-tan; very coarse with many, assorted grey quartz grits; traces of reddish-brown slip over-all. (4581, 4584, and 4588 joined) A III 201.12a.
—	4538	Body sherd of jar; drab with tan outside; very coarse with many assorted smokey-quartz grits; traces of reddish-brown slip outside; very pitted and spalling inside, rough, gritty, texture over-all. A III 201.6.
4	4579	Rim outcurved to rolled, beveled edge projected out in wide collar; dark-brown with dark-grey patch inside; very coarse with many assorted grey quartz grits and some assorted tan grits; traces of reddish-brown slip over-all, traces of burnishing inside; some pitting and flaking. A III 201.12a.
5	4592e	Rim outcurved to rounded edge with heavy collar projected out, wheel-finished; dull-orange; coarse with very many assorted smokey quartz grits; traces of wheel-burnished, reddish-brown slip over-all; some dark-grey incrustations. A III 201.12a.
—	5095k	Body sherd; dull orange outside and grey inside; fine with some very fine white grits, porous ware; continulusly-burnished orange-brown slip outside. A IV 300.14a.
—	5009n	Rim of jar, sharply outcurved to slightly rounded squared wheel-finished; bright-orange; fine with some very fine and few small white, tan, and grey grits; some assorted pits and incrustations over-all. A IV 300.14b.
6	5164	Rim outcurved to rounded, beaded edge, wheel-finished; dark reddish-brown with dark-grey core; coarse with some fine white grits; black smoke marks over-all, rough, gritty texture outside. (5164 and 5165 joined) A III 204.2.
7	5116b	Rim inclined slightly and outcurved to rounded beaded edge with low ridge outside on neck, wheel-finished; brownish-buff; medium with some small to fine, tan and grey grits, porous ware; traces of white slip outside. A IV 300.17.
—	5095f	Neck fragment of very large jar; orangish-buff inside and buff outside, thick grey core; very coarse with some assorted tan and grey grits; some yellowish white incrustations inside, grey incrustations over-all. A IV 300.14a.
—	5095e	Neck fragment of large jar, outcurved; buff with grey core; coarse with some assorted tan, grey, and orange grits; rough, gritty texture outside and inside below neck, some grey incrustations over-all. A IV 300.14a.
8	5116c	Rim slightly outcurved to rounded edge; brownish-orange; medium with few medium to fine tan and grey grits. A IV 300.17.
—	4625d	Rim of jar, outcurved to thinned, rounded edge, wet-smoothed; brownish-buff; medium coarse with some assorted grey and white grits. A III 202.3.
—	4625f	Rim of jar, outcurved to rounded edge, wet-smoothed; pinkish-brown; very coarse with many medium to fine tan grits; traces of white slip outside and inside edge; pronounced spalling outside. A III 202.3.
9	5049	Rim slightly outcurved to rounded edge, wheel-made; greyish-buff with orange outside; medium-coarse with many small to fine white grits; traces of white slip outside; heavy grey incrustations over-all. A II 101.8b.
—	4586	Rim of jar slightly flared to thinned, rounded edge, wheel-finished; buff; medium-coarse with many assorted white, grey quartz, and reddish-brown grits; spalling inside, edge of rim badly chipped. A III 201.12a.

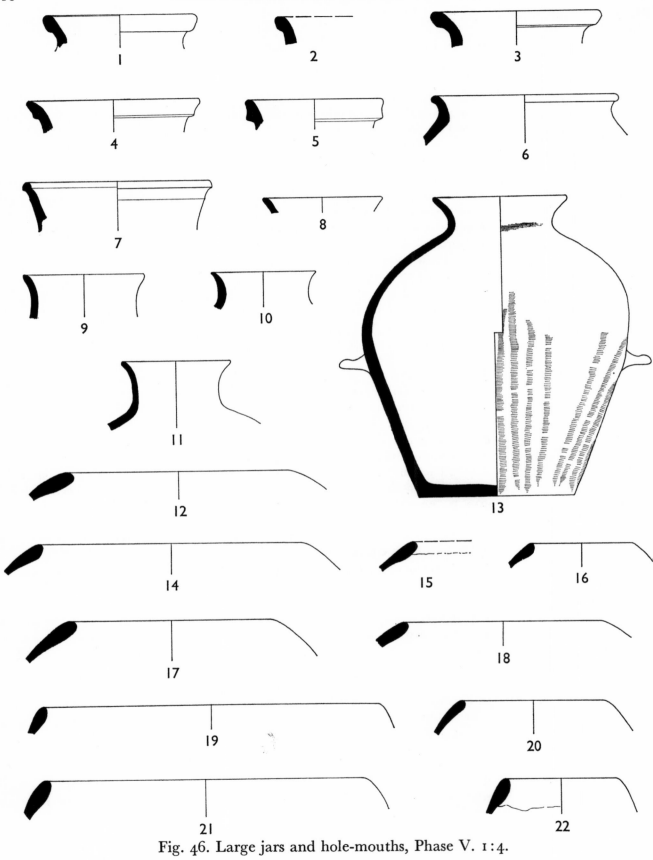

Fig. 46. Large jars and hole-mouths, Phase V. 1:4.

Fig. 46 No.	Reg. No.	
—	4537c	Rim of jar slightly outcurved to thinned, rounded edge, wet-smoothed; buff with grey core; coarse with some assorted grey grits; traces of burnished reddish-brown slip outside. A III 201.5a.
—	5009dd	Body sherd from shoulder of jar at transition to neck; orangish-buff outside and grey inside, greyish-buff core; coarse with some assorted white and grey grits; continuously-burnished, reddish-brown slip outside, some pitting and spalling outside, very uneven gritty surface inside, grey incrustations over-all. A IV 300.14b.
10	5160	Rim outcurved to thinned, rounded edge, wet-smoothed; orangish-buff with dark-grey core; coarse with some small to fine, white grits; traces of heavy, white slip outside; rough, gritty texture, grey incrustations over-all. A III 204.2.
—	4537a	Rim of jar, slightly outcurved to rounded edge, wet-smoothed; buff; coarse with some assorted white and grey grits; brown and white incrustations over-all. A III 201.5a.
—	5095d	Neck fragment of jar; pinkish-buff; coarse with some assorted tan grits; traces of white slip outside; rough, gritty texture over-all, heavy grey incrustations. A IV 300.14a.
—	4537d	Body sherd of jar; orangish-buff; very coarse with few assorted white and tan grits; traces of white slip outside; rough, gritty texture over-all, some brown incrustations. A III 201.5a.
11	4592c	High neck with rim outcurved to rounded edge, wheel-finished; buff; medium with some assorted grey and tan grits; A III 201.12a.
—	4625g	Neck fragment of jar; drab inside and orange outside, grey core; very coarse with some assorted grey and tan grits, porous ware; many assorted pits inside. A III 202.3.
12	4589	Rim incurved to wide, thickened, rounded edge, wet-smoothed outside; buff with orange patches over-all; coarse with very many assorted white and grey quartz grits; rough, gritty texture inside. A III 201.12a.
—	5009f	Rim of hole-mouth jar sharply incurved to wide, slightly thickened, oval edge, wheel-finished; greyish-buff with pinkish-orange core; medium with many assorted grey and white quartz grits. A IV 300.14b.
13	o–74	Neck outcurved to flared rim; two thumb indented ledge-handles; buff; coarse with some medium to fine white grits; white slip over-all outside; six groups of four wide, vertical, painted red stripes; one wide, painted red stripe around neck at shoulder; large black smoke mark on outside, some grey incrustations over-all. A III 202.3.
—	4575	Body sherd; orangish-buff; coarse with some assorted white and brown grits; traces of greyish-white slip outside with trace of wide painted, reddish-brown stripe. A III 201.12a.
—	5116e	Body sherd from side of jar at base; light-brown outside and dark grey inside and core; very coarse with many medium to very fine white and grey grits, porous ware; traces of heavy, white slip outside with very wide painted, dark-brown stripes; very uneven surface inside. A IV 300.17.
14	5075b	Rim incurved to wide, very thickened, rounded edge; dark-grey with patches of buff and orange; coarse with many assorted white and light-grey grits; very rough, gritty texture inside, some grey incrustations outside. A II 101.8b.
15	4298	Rim incurved to wide, thickened, rounded edge; buff with dark-orange patch outside, dark-grey core penetrating to outside in places; medium-coarse with many assorted grey quartz grits; some assorted pits over-all, black smoke marks outside. A II 102.2a.
16	4972	Rim incurved to narrow, thickened, rounded edge; dark-buff with grey patches outside, grey core; coarse with many assorted white and grey grits; some crazing and spalling outside. A IV 300.14a.

Fig. 46 No.	Reg. No.	
17	4592f	Rim incurved to wide, thickened, rounded edge, wheel-finished; orange; coarse with very many assorted, mostly medium to small, light- and dark-grey grits; traces of white slip outside. A III 201.12a.
—	4831j	Body sherd of jar; reddish-orange with brown inside; very coarse with many medium to fine white and tan grits; heavy white slip outside; white incrustations inside. A III 204.7.
—	4543e	Body sherd of large jar; orange with buff core; very coarse with many assorted smokey-quartz grits; traces of white slip outside; rough gritty texture inside. A III 201.6a.
18	5080c	Rim incurved to slightly thickened, rounded edge; dark-buff inside and dark-grey outside; very coarse with many assorted smokey quartz grits; some pitting and crazing inside and on edge. A II 101.8b.
19	5134c	Rim incurved to thickened, rounded edge, wheel-finished; dark-brown inside and core, orangish-brown outside; medium-coarse with many assorted dark- and light-grey quartz grits; gritty texture inside, spalling on edge. A IV 300.19.
20	5054	Rim incurved to medium-wide, thickened, rounded edge; dark-orange; very coarse with many assorted white and grey quartz grits; pronounced crazing outside, black smoke marks outside, flaking on edge. A II 101.5a.
21	4969	Rim slightly incurved to wide, thickened, rounded edge; dark orangish-buff with brown core; very coarse with many assorted dark- and light-grey quartz grits; many assorted pits over-all, pronounced crazing and spalling outside and on edge, black smoke marks outside. A IV 300.14a.
22	5116a	Rim incurved to wide, greatly thickened and rounded edge; burnt-orange inside and grey outside; medium-coarse with many assorted grey and white grits; some assorted pits over-all; uneven surface inside, some short parallel striations outside. A IV 300.17.
—	5009x	Body sherd of jar; burnt-orange with orangish-brown inside; medium with many fine to very fine dark-grey and tan grits, few medium to small grey and tan grits; assorted, mostly small to fine pits over-all; traces of light grey incrustations. A IV 300.14b.
—	4735	Body sherd; black with orangish-buff outside; medium-coarse with some assorted grey and white grits; two narrow parallel, inscribed lines outside intersected by a third perpendicular to them; some assorted pits over-all. A III 203.4a.
Fig. 47 No.	Reg. No.	
1	4965	Rim incurved to wide, very thickened, rounded, edge, wet-smoothed; buff inside and orange outside with very thick dark-grey core; coarse with very many assorted grey grits; many fine pits and rough texture over-all. A IV 300.14a.
2	4831a	Rim incurved to wide, very thickened, rounded edge, wet-smoothed, orange; very coarse with many assorted white and dark-grey quartz grits; very pitted and spalling outside and on edge. A III 204.7.
—	4953	Rim of hole-mouth jar, incurved to wide, greatly thickened, rounded edge; buff with orange core penetrating to surface in places; medium-coarse with many assorted white grits, some assorted dark-grey quartz grits; many assorted pits over-all, black smoke marks outside. A IV 300.12.
—	4971	Rim of hole-mouth jar, incurved to wide, thickened, rounded edge, wet-smoothed; buff with grey core; very coarse with many assorted white, light- and dark-grey quartz grits; many assorted pits over-all. A IV 300.14a.
3	4529b	Rim slightly incurved to narrow, thickened, oval edge; greyish-buff inside and greyish-brown outside, orange patch on edge and dark-brown core; coarse with many assorted

Fig. 47 No.	*Reg. No.*	
		grey quartz grits; rough gritty texture over-all, some crazing and spalling on edge. A III 201.4a.
4	4973	Rim sharply incurved to thickened, tapered edge, wet-smoothed; orangish-buff; medium-coarse with some small to fine, white grits; traces of white slip outside; some grey incrustations over-all. A IV 300.14a.
—	4839g	Body sherd of jar; buff outside and red inside, grey core; coarse with some assorted white and tan grits; heavy white slip outside; rough gritty texture inside, some grey incrustations over-all. A III 204.8a.
5	4997	Rim of hole-mouth jar, incurved to medium-wide, thickened, tapered edge, wet-smoothed; buff with thick, dark-grey core penetrating to outside in places. A IV 300.14b.
6	5005	Rim of bowl, incurved to thin, tapered edge, wheel-finished; bright-buff with dull-buff inside; medium with many medium to fine white quartz and tan grits; traces of reddish-brown slip. A IV 300.14b.
7	4576	Upright rim incurved to oval rounded edge, wet-smoothed; greyish-buff with orange inside; coarse with many assorted white and grey grits; black smoke marks on edge. A III 201.12a.
8	5009k	Angular wall incurved to thinned, slightly inverted rim, wheel-finished; orange inside and pinkish-tan outside, dark-grey core; medium with some medium to very fine white, tan, and grey grits; light, brownish-grey incrustations over-all. A IV 300.14b.
9	4619	Upright wall slightly incurved to thickened, rounded rim wet-smoothed; orange; medium-coarse with very many small to fine, white grits; rough, gritty texture over-all. A III 202.3.
10	5062	Rim sharply incurved to wide, very thickened, rounded edge; wheel-finished; dark-orange inside and buff outside, dark grey core penetrating to outside in places; coarse with very many assorted, mostly medium to fine, white grits; very rough, gritty texture, some grey incrustations inside. A II 101.8a.
11	4839a	Rim sharply incurved to rounded, beveled edge, with shallow depression outside, wheel turned; drab inside and greyish-orange outside, thick, reddish-brown core; coarse with many assorted white and dark-grey quartz grits. A III 204.8a.
12	4831b	Rim incurved to wide, very thickened, rounded edge; greyish-brown with dark-grey core; very coarse with many assorted grey grits; very pitted and spalling outside, uneven surface inside at joint of rim fold. A III 204.7.
13	4536	Rim sharply incurved to medium-wide, thickened, rounded edge, flattened on top, wet-smoothed; orange with patches of buff over-all and core; medium-coarse with many assorted light- and dark-grey quartz grits; assorted pits over-all, flaking outside. A III 201.5a.
14	4528	Rim slightly incurved to wide, greatly thickened, rounded edge; yellowish-buff inside and orange outside, grey core in places; medium-coarse with very many assorted light-grey grits; many assorted pits inside, crazing on edge. A III 201.4a.
15	4951	Rim sharply incurved to medium-wide, very thickened, rounded edge, wet-smoothed; buff with dark-grey and orange core in places, grey patches outside; coarse with many assorted, mostly small to fine, white grits. A IV 300.12.
16	4624	Rim sharply incurved to wide, very thickened, rounded edge; dark-orange; coarse with many assorted white and grey grits; very pitted and flaking inside edge, crazing and flaking, grey smoke marks outside. A III 201.5a.
17	5009d	Rim incurved to wide, greatly thickened, rounded edge, wheel-finished with pronounced wheel-marks over-all, orangish-buff with greyish-buff core; coarse with many very large to small grey quartz and some small to very fine white grits; grey smoke marks over-all. A IV 300.14b.

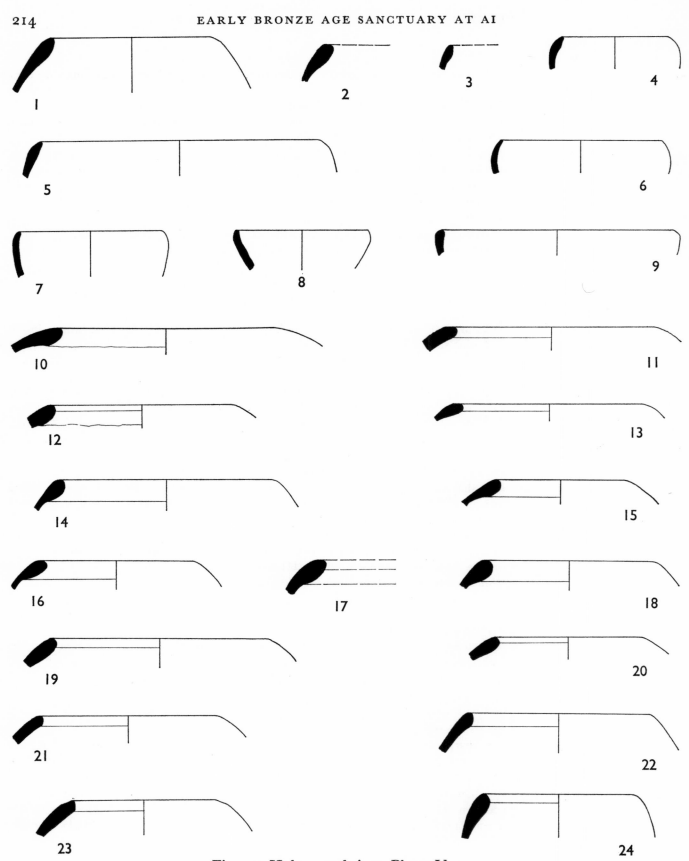

Fig. 47. Hole-mouth jars, Phase V. 1:4.

Fig. 47 No.	Reg. No.	
18	5009a	Rim incurved to wide, greatly thickened, rounded edge, very faint ridge outside; orangish-buff with very thick, dark brownish-grey core; coarse with some assorted white and light-grey grits; light, brownish-grey incrustations. A IV 300.14b.
19	5095	Rim incurved to thickened, squared edge, wheel-finished; orangish-buff; coarse with some assorted tan and grey grits; faint traces of reddish-brown slip over-all. A IV 300.14a.
20	4839b	Rim incurved to medium-wide thickened, squared edge; greyish-buff inside and greyish-orange outside; very coarse with many assorted light- and dark-grey quartz grits; few assorted tan and reddish-brown grits; rough, gritty texture inside, crazing and spalling on edge. A III 204.8a.
21	4963	Rim incurved to wide, slightly thickened, rounded, beveled edge, wet-smoothed; buff with dark-grey core; coarse with very many assorted dark- and light-grey grits. A IV 300.14a.
22	5009b	Rim incurved to slightly thickened, rounded edge; orangish-buff with greyish-buff core; medium-coarse with many medium to very fine light-grey and white grits; brownish-grey incrustations over-all. A IV 300.14b.
23	5009i	Rim incurved to very wide, slightly thickened, beveled edge, wheel-finished; orange outside and brown inside, dark brownish-grey core; medium with many medium to very fine, grey quartz grits and few large quartz and reddish-brown grits; grey smoke marks inside on edge. A IV 300.14b.
24	4837	Rim slightly incurved to wide, greatly thickened, rounded, beveled edge, wet-smoothed; orange with greyish-brown outside; coarse with very many assorted grey quartz grits; some grey incrustations inside. A III 204.8a.

Fig. 48 No.	Reg. No.	
1	4995	Rim incurved to very wide, thickened, rounded, beveled edge, wet-smoothed; buff; coarse with very many assorted white and light-grey quartz grits; dark-grey smoke marks outside, many assorted pits over-all, spalling on edge. A IV 300.14b.
2	4297	Rim incurved to narrow, very thickened, rounded, beveled edge, wet-smoothed; buff with dark-orange outside; coarse with very many assorted grey quartz grits; some assorted pits over-all, flaking outside edge, black smoke marks outside. A II 101.2a.
3	5075a	Rim slightly incurved to widened, flattened, beveled edge, wet-smoothed; buff; coarse with assorted grey quartz grits. A II 101.5a.
—	5073	Rim of hole-mouth jar, slightly incurved to rounded, beveled, flattened edge, wheel-made; buff; coarse with some assorted white grits; traces of white slip outside; heavy, grey incrustations over-all. A II 101.5a.
4	5009h	Rim incurved to slightly thickened, sharply inturned flattened edge; dark-brown with dark brownish-grey core; medium with many large to very fine white and grey grits; uneven surfaces, light, brownish-grey incrustations over-all. A IV 300.14b.
5	4985	Rim flattened incurved to very thickened edge, wet-smoothed; brownish-buff with thick, grey core; traces of burnished, reddish-brown slip outside and inside edge; grey incrustations over-all. A IV 300.14b.
6	5080b	Rim incurved to narrow, very thickened, rounded, beveled edge, wet-smoothed; greyish-buff inside and black outside; medium-coarse with few assorted black and reddish-brown grits. A II 101.8b.
7	4996	Rim incurved to wide, very thickened, rounded, squared edge, wet-smoothed; buff inside and dark-orange outside; coarse with very many assorted white and light- and dark-grey quartz grits; dark-grey smoke marks outside and on edge. A IV 300.14b.

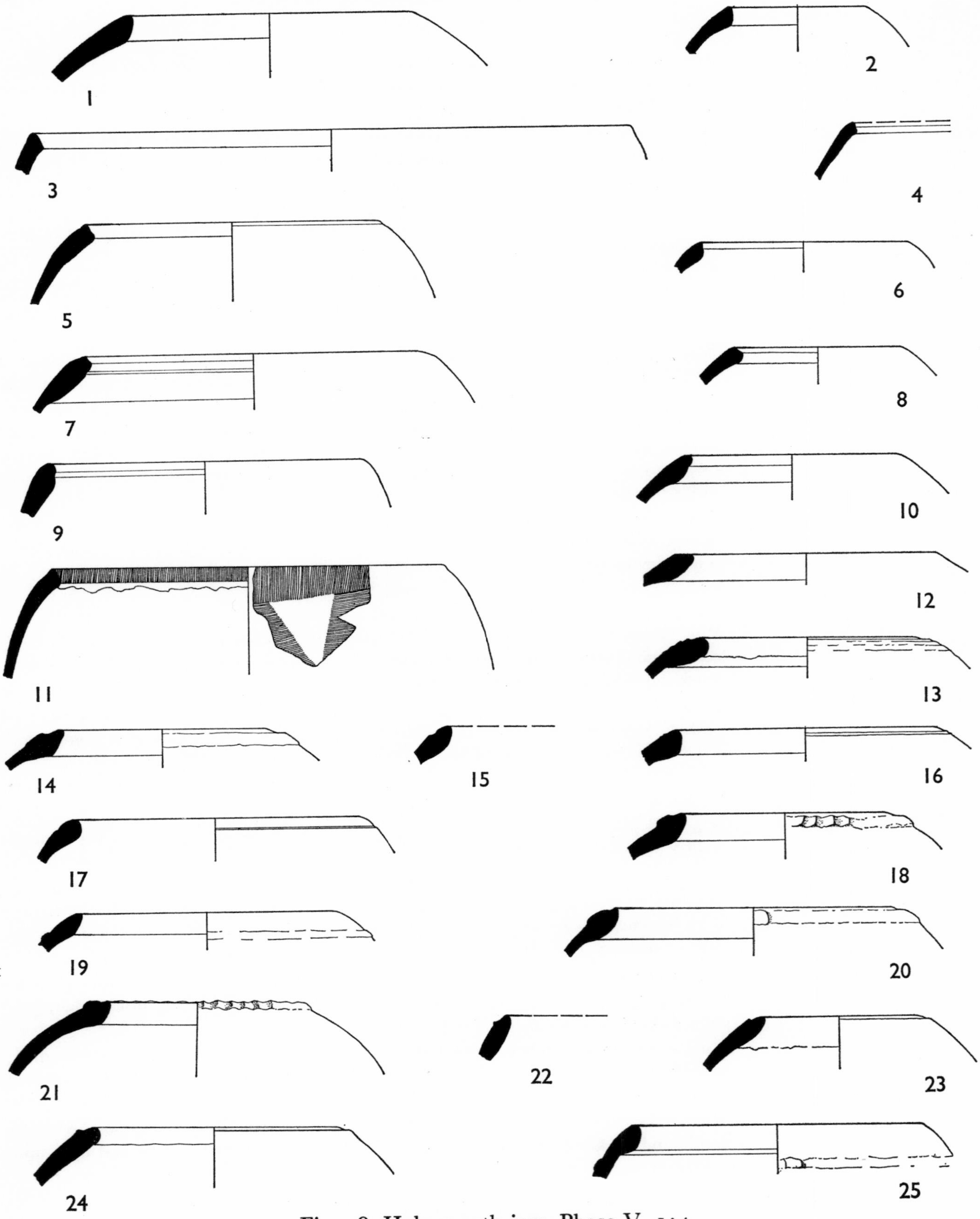

Fig. 48. Hole-mouth jars, Phase V. 1:4.

Fig. 48 *No.*	*Reg.* *No.*	
8	5080d	Rim incurved to thickened, rounded beveled edge, very faint ridge outside, wet-smoothed; dark-orange; coarse with many assorted grey quartz grits; some grey incrustations over-all. A II 101.8b.
9	5079	Rim slightly incurved to wide, very thickened, rounded depressed inner edge; buff with patches of orange inside, dark-grey outside and core; very coarse with many assorted white and grey grits; some assorted pits over-all, crazing inside, some flaking on edge, some grey incrustations inside. A II 101.8a.
10	5088	Rim incurved to medium-wide, thickened, rounded depressed inner edge, wet-smoothed; buff with dark-grey patches outside, thick, dark-grey core; very coarse with many assorted grey quartz grits; many fine pits over-all, some spalling on edge. A IV 300.14a.
11	5086	Rim slightly incurved to thickened, beveled edge, ridged on top; orangish-brown inside and buff outside; coarse with many assorted white, tan, and grey grits; creamy white slip outside, wide, painted, reddish-brown stripes outside, medium stripe inside rim. (5086 and 5087 joined) A IV 300.14a.
12	4976	Rim incurved to wide, very thickened, rounded, beveled edge, with low ridge outside; edge wet-smoothed; dark-orange with greyish-buff core; coarse with many assorted, mostly medium, dark-grey and few white quartz grits; many fine pits over-all, rough texture inside. A IV 300.14a.
13	5105	Rim sharply incurved to wide, greatly thickened, rounded edge, with three low ridges outside, edge wet-smoothed; orange inside and greyish-buff outside, buff core; coarse with very many assorted white and light-grey grits, one very large grey grit; very uneven surface inside, many fine pits with some very large pits inside, crazing over-all. A IV 300.17.
14	4955	Rim incurved to wide, greatly thickened, rounded, beveled edge, wet-smoothed; dark-orange with dark-grey core; very coarse with some assorted, mostly small, light-grey grits; wide, crude, half-relief molding outside; rough texture inside. A IV 300.12.
15	4832a	Rim upcurved to medium-wide, thickened, rounded edge, with pronounced ridge outside, wheel-finished; buff; coarse with some assorted grey and white grits; some grey incrustations over-all. A III 204.8.
16	5080a	Rim incurved to wide, very thickened, rounded, beveled edge, with ridge outside, edge wet-smoothed, brown inside and greyish-brown outside; very coarse with many assorted white and dark-grey grits; black smoke marks inside and outside edge, some grey incrustations outside. A II 101.8b.
17	4522	Rim incurved to medium-wide, greatly thickened, rounded edge, with ridge outside, wheel-finished; orange with thick, dark-grey core penetrating to outside; very coarse with many assorted white grits. A III 201.3a.
18	5134b	Rim incurved to wide, greatly thickened, rounded edge, wet-smoothed; buff with brown core in thickened portion; coarse with many assorted grey grits, few small white grits; medium-wide, high-relief rope-molding outside; very rough, gritty texture inside below edge, some assorted pits over-all, spalling on edge. A IV 300.19.
19	5003	Rim incurved to wide, thickened, rounded, beveled edge, wheel-finished; greyish-brown with thick, dark-grey core penetrating to outside in places; coarse with many assorted white and light-grey quartz grits, some very large, grey grits, very porous ware; narrow, crude, high-relief rope-molding outside; many small to fine pits inside and many assorted pits outside, spalling outside. A IV 300.14b.
20	4525	Rim incurved to wide, greatly thickened, rounded edge; orange with buff core; very coarse with many assorted tan, grey and white grits; wide, crude, half-relief rope-molding outside, traces of white slip; very pitted, flaking inside, rough, gritty texture over-all. A III 201.3a.

Fig. 48 No.	Reg. No.	
—	4543d	Body sherd of jar; drab with orange patch inside, buff outside; coarse with very many assorted grey quartz grits; traces of white slip outside; rough, gritty, uneven surface over-all. A III 201.6a.
21	5134	Rim incurved to wide, very thickened, rounded edge, wet-smoothed; orangish-buff with grey core at thickened portion; coarse with many assorted grey and tan grits; medium-wide, well-defined though crudely applied half-relief rope-molding outside, some assorted pits over-all, very rough texture inside. A IV 300.19.
22	5009j	Rim incurved to wide, slightly thickened, rounded edge, with pronounced ridge outside, wheel-finished; orange with dark-grey core penetrating to surface outside; medium-coarse with few medium to very fine, white, grey and tan grits. A IV 300.14b.
23	5041	Rim incurved to medium-wide, thickened, rounded edge, with pronounced ridge outside; buff with thick, dark-grey core penetrating to surfaces in places; medium-coarse with some assorted grey grits; some assorted pits, crazing over-all, diagonal finger marks inside and outside. A II 101.7a.
24	4981	Rim incurved to thickened, rounded edge, with high ridge outside, wheel-finished; coarse with many assorted white and grey quartz grits; many small to fine pits over-all, some crazing and spalling outside. A IV 300.14b.
25	5133	Rim incurved to medium-wide, greatly thickened, rounded edge, wheel-finished; greyish-orange with very thick dark-grey core penetrating to outside in places; coarse with many assorted white grits, two very large reddish-brown grits outside; narrow crude high-relief rope-molding outside; very many fine pits over-all with some large, elongated pits inside edge, some flaking outside, very rough texture inside edge. A IV 300.19.

Fig. 49 No.	Reg. No.	
1	5009e	Rim incurved to rounded flattened edge projecting up outside; brown; coarse with many assorted grey quartz and white grits; very uneven surface over-all. A IV 300.14b.
2	5009g	Rim incurved to wide, slightly thickened, rounded edge projecting slightly upward, shallow ridge outside, wheel-finished; greyish-brown; medium-coarse with many very large to fine, grey and white quartz grits. A IV 300.14b.
3	5095a	Rim slightly incurved to medium-wide, very thickened, rounded edge folded in; orangish-buff with thick, grey core; very coarse with many assorted dark-grey quartz and light-grey grits; rough, gritty surface inside, black smoke marks outside. A IV 300.14a.
4	4994	Rim incurved to wide, thickened, rounded, beveled edge with low ridge outside, wheel-finished; yellow with orange patch outside, greyish-brown core; coarse with very many assorted white and grey quartz grits; many assorted pits outside. A IV 300.14b.
5	4982	Rim incurved to thickened, beveled edge with depression in beveled portion, dark-orange and grey, grey core; coarse with very many assorted grey quartz grits, porous ware; many small to fine pits, black smoke marks over-all. A IV 300.14b.
6	4958	Rim incurved to narrow, very thickened, rounded, beveled edge, shallow ridge outside, wheel-finished; orange with greyish-buff core; very coarse with many assorted tan grits; some assorted pits over-all, rough texture over-all. A IV 300.14a.
7	5009c	Rim slightly incurved to wide, thickened, rounded edge, faint ridge outside; orangish-buff; medium-coarse with few assorted white and tan grits; some assorted pits inside, uneven surface over-all. A IV 300.14b.
8	5055	Rim of hole-mouth jar, incurved to wide, greatly thickened, rounded edge, wheel-finished; orangish-buff inside and pinkish-tan outside, pink core; very coarse with many

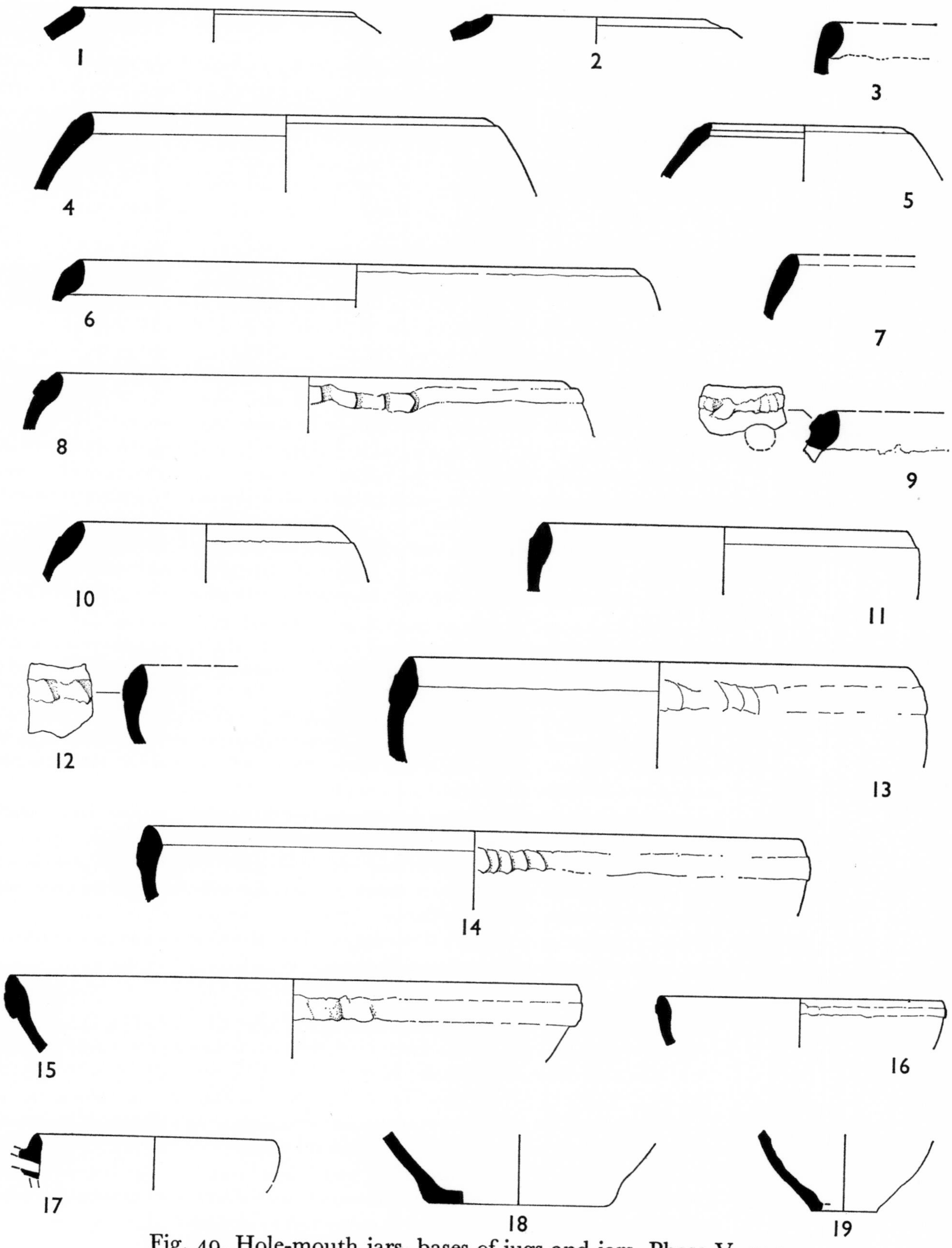

Fig. 49. Hole-mouth jars, bases of jugs and jars, Phase V. 1:4.

Fig. 49 *No.*	*Reg.* *No.*	
		assorted white and tan grits; medium-wide, crude, high-relief rope-molding outside, traces of heavy white slip outside; some assorted pits over-all, crazing outside. A II 101.5a.
9	4734	Rim incurved to wide, very thickened, rounded, beveled edge, fragment of large, pierced hole below edge; orange with buff patches; thick, dark-grey core penetrating to surface in places; coarse with some assorted white and tan grits; narrow, crude, high-relief rope-molding outside; many assorted pits over-all. A III 203.4a.
10	4964	Rim incurved to wide, greatly thickened, rounded edge with ridge outside, wheel-finished; orange inside and drab outside, buff core; coarse with very many assorted white and light-grey quartz grits. A IV 300.14a.
11	4962	Upright rim slightly incurved to medium-wide, very thickened, oval edge with ridge outside; very coarse with some assorted white, grey and tan grits; traces of heavy white slip outside and inside edge; heavy grey incrustations over-all. A IV 300.14a.
12	4620	Upright rim incurved to wide, greatly thickened, tapered edge; orange with thick grey core; coarse with many assorted tan and white grits; medium-wide, crude, half-relief rope-molding outside, traces of white slip outside with faint traces of painted orange lines; grey smoke marks over-all, some grey incrustations. A III 202.3.
13	5065	Upright rim slightly incurved to very wide, greatly thickened, tapered edge; buff with very thick, dark-grey core; very coarse with many assorted white grits; very wide, crude, high-relief rope-molding outside, traces of heavy white slip outside; some grey incrustations over-all. A II 101.8a.
14	5059	Upright rim slightly incurved to wide, very thickened, oval edge; dark-grey; very coarse with many assorted, mostly fine, white grits; wide, crude, half-relief rope-molding outside, traces of heavy white slip outside; some grey incrustations inside. A II 101.8a.
15	5083	Upright rim upcurved to wide, very thickened, rounded edge, wheel-finished; orangish-buff inside and outside edge, pinkish-tan outside and core; coarse with many assorted white and tan grits; wide, crude, high-relief rope-molding outside; many assorted pits over-all. A IV 300.14a.
16	4961	Upright rim slightly flared to thickened, rounded edge; pinkish-orange inside and mauve outside; very coarse with many assorted tan grits; narrow, crude, rope-molding outside below edge, traces of heavy white slip outside; few very assorted pits inside, spalling, some grey incrustations outside. A IV 300.14a.
17	4256	Upright rim with spout fragment slightly incurved to rounded, beveled edge; reddish-brown medium-coarse with very many assorted grey grits. A II 101.5a.
18	4999	Buff; coarse with very many assorted tan and brown grits; faint traces of possible white slip outside; orange discolorations outside, many assorted pits outside, very rough, gritty texture inside. A IV 300.14b.
19	4531	Orange with buff core; medium with many medium to fine white and grey grits; traces of continuous burnishing outside. A III 201.5.
Fig. 50 *No.*	*Reg.* *No.*	
1	4968	Base of jug, wheel-turned; pinkish-brown inside and light-brown outside; medium-coarse with some medium to fine white, tan, and reddish-brown grits; traces of continuously burnished brown slip outside and on bottom. A IV 300.14a.
—	4622	Thick flat base of jug; reddish-buff with reddish-brown outside; medium-coarse with some assorted dark-brown grits; continuously-burnished, reddish-brown slip outside; very rough texture inside, spalling outside. A III 202.3.
—	5095h	Body sherd; dark pinkish-brown inside and bright reddish-orange outside; medium with some small to fine white grits; continuously-burnished brown slip outside; uneven, gritty surface inside, grey incrustations over-all. A IV 300.14a.

Fig. 50 No.	*Reg. No.*	
—	5009aa	Body sherd; pinkish-tan; fine with some fine to very fine white grits, few medium to fine grey and reddish-brown grits; continuously burnished reddish-brown slip outside; pronounced horizontal finger marks inside. A IV 300.14b.
—	5009cc	Body sherd; tan with light-grey core; medium with some medium to fine grey and brown grits; continuously-burnished reddish-brown slip outside; spalling inside. A IV 300.14b.
—	5095l	Body sherd; brownish-red; fine with many small to very fine white grits; continuously-burnished brown slip outside; pronounced finger ridges inside, some pits outside. A IV 300.14a.
2	4831h	Buff with grey inside; medium-coarse with some fine white grits; traces of vertically-burnished reddish-brown slip outside; some black smoke marks over-all, some spalling outside. A III 204.7.
3	4533	Orange with orangish-buff patches outside and core; medium with some assorted white grits; rough texture on bottom. A III 201.5.
4	4952	Buff; very coarse with some assorted tan and reddish-brown grits; tan slip outside; many assorted pits and very rough texture over-all. A IV 300.12.
5	4265	Buff with grey core in places; medium-coarse with many assorted white and grey grits; traces of reddish-brown slip outside; very uneven surface outside, pitted on bottom, some grey incrustations. A II 101.8a.
6	4269	Dark-grey with buff outside; very coarse with many assorted grey and white grits; very chipped and flaking inside, rough texture outside, some heavy grey incrustations outside. A II 101.8a.
7	4988	Dark-grey inside and buff outside; coarse with many assorted tan, grey, and reddish-brown grits; traces of reddish-brown slip outside; many assorted pits over-all; deeply pitted on bottom, spalling outside. A IV 300.14b.
8	5008	Grey inside and greyish-buff outside; medium with very many assorted grey grits; many assorted pits over-all, very rough texture inside. A IV 300.14b.
9	4960	Wheel-finished outside; brownish-grey inside and buff outside; coarse with many assorted tan and dark-grey grits; traces of vertically-burnished reddish-brown slip outside. A IV 300.14a.
—	4537b	Body sherd of jug; reddish-brown; medium with some assorted tan and grey grits; vertically-burnished reddish slip outside; pronounced, horizontal finger marks inside, some grey incrustations outside. A III 201.5a.
10	4991	Buff; very coarse with some assorted grey grits; traces of white slip outside; rough texture outside. A IV 300.14b.
11	5163	Wet-smoothed outside; dark-orange with orangish-buff inside; coarse with some assorted white and tan grits, traces of vertically burnished orange slip outside; grey smoke marks outside, some assorted pits inside, some grey incrustations outside. A III 204.2.
12	4831g	Greyish-brown; coarse with few assorted grey and tan grits; rough texture over-all, pitted and spalling on bottom. A III 204.7.
—	4839c	Flat base of jar; greyish-tan with thick, dark-grey core; coarse with few assorted white and grey grits; uneven surface outside, many assorted pits and spalling, smoke marks on bottom. A III 204.8a.
13	4263	Buff with grey inside; very coarse with many assorted white, light- and dark-grey and tan grits; traces of vertically-burnished, reddish-brown slip outside; many assorted pits over-all, very rough texture inside, very pitted and flaking on bottom. A II 101.5a.
14	4268	Brownish-buff; very coarse with some assorted white grits; traces of heavy white slip outside; rough texture over-all, very pitted and flaking on bottom, heavy grey incrustations over-all. A II 101.8a.

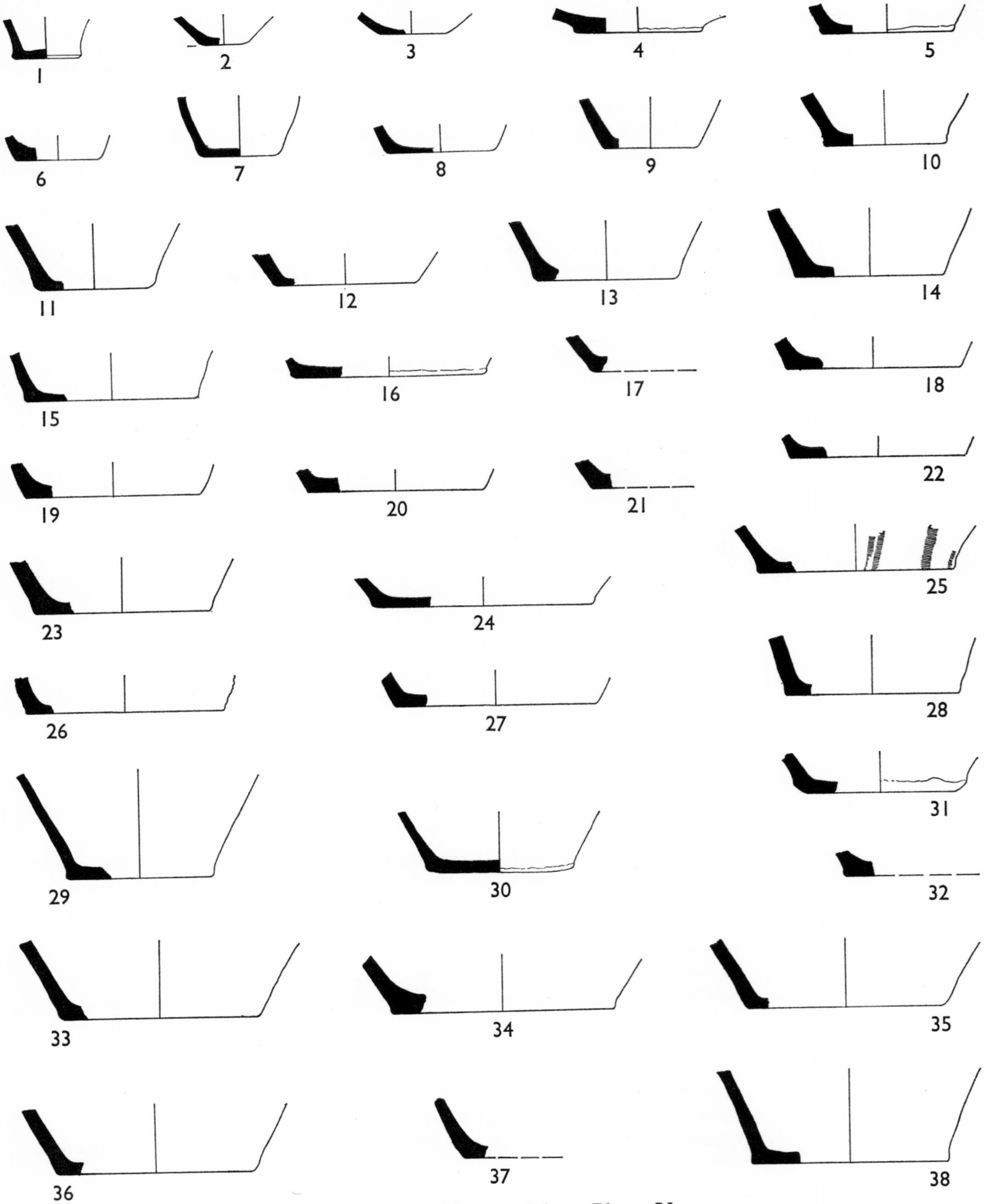

Fig. 50. Bases of jugs and jars, Phase V. 1:4.

Fig. 50 No.	Reg. No.	
15	4989	Dark-buff with dark-grey core in places; coarse with very many assorted white and grey quartz grits, porous ware; traces of reddish-brown slip outside; very many assorted pits and uneven surfaces over-all, spalling outside. A IV 300.14b.
16	5116d	Brownish-orange outside with dark grey inside and core; coarse with some assorted grey and white grits and many very fine white grits; traces of white slip outside; gritty texture inside, some pitting and spalling on bottom outside. A IV 300.17.
—	4625a	Flat base of jar; brown with orange patches outside; very coarse with many assorted grey and white grits; some crazing over-all, few assorted pits outside, some spalling inside. A III 202.3.
—	4832c	Body sherd; buff with orange patch outside, dark-orange inside; very coarse with some assorted white, grey, and tan grits; uneven surfaces over-all, very rough, gritty texture inside, some greyish-brown incrustations. A III 204.8.
17	5095b	Buff with thick dark-grey core; very coarse with some assorted white and grey grits; traces of white slip over-all; rough, gritty, uneven surface outside. A IV 300.14a.
18	4523	Orangish-buff with thick dark-grey core; coarse with some assorted white grits; rough texture outside, some assorted pits on bottom. A III 201.3a.
19	5080g	String-cut; bright-orange with light-orange core; coarse with some assorted white grits; traces of white slip outside; very uneven surface outside, heavy grey incrustations over-all. A II 101.8b.
—	4839l	Body sherd; orange inside and orangish-buff outside; coarse with some assorted white and tan grits; rough, uneven surface, grey incrustations over-all. A III 204.8a.
20	5001	String-cut; buff with orange patches inside and orangish-buff outside, orange on bottom, thick, dark-grey core; many assorted, mostly small to fine, white and grey grits; traces of white slip outside; very pitted on bottom. A IV 300.14b.
21	4998	Orangish-buff; coarse with many assorted white, tan, and brown grits; dark-grey smoke marks inside, some assorted pits over-all, one very large pit outside. A IV 300.14b.
22	4580	Tan with orange inside; very coarse with many assorted white, tan, and reddish-brown grits; traces of heavy white slip outside; rough texture over-all. A III 201.12a.
—	4839d	Flat base of jar; tan; fine with many medium to fine white grits; traces of white slip outside; uneven surface and many assorted pits inside, greyish-brown incrustations over-all. A III 204.8a.
—	4592a	Body sherd of jar; pinkish-tan; very coarse with some assorted grey and reddish-brown grits; very heavy, thick, rough, nodular incrustations over-all. A III 201.12a.
—	4839i	Body sherd of jar; tannish-buff; medium-coarse with some small to fine tan and dark-grey grits; one large red grit; traces of white slip outside. A III 204.8a.
23	4583	Dark-grey with brown bottom; very coarse with many assorted white and grey quartz grits; light-brown slip over-all; very rough texture outside. A III 201.12a.
24	5112	Bottom slightly convex; dark greyish-brown inside and buff outside; very coarse with many assorted, mostly small to fine, white, tan, and reddish-brown grits; traces of white slip outside; some assorted pits over-all, pronounced crazing inside. A IV 300.17.
25	5093	Orange; very coarse with many assorted white and grey grits; heavy white slip, traces of painted red lines outside; some assorted pits over-all. A IV 300.14a.
—	5009bb	Body sherd; burnt-orange; medium with many medium to fine grey, tan, and reddish-brown grits; faint traces of painted decoration outside; traces of light, grey incrustations over-all. A IV 300.14b.
—	4296b	Body sherd; orangish-brown inside and grey outside; very coarse with some assorted tan grits; white slip outside with traces of painted red stripe. A II 102.2.

Fig. 50 No.	Reg. No.	
—	4839f	Body sherd of jar; reddish-brown; coarse with few assorted white and tan grits; white slip outside with faint traces of medium-wide parallel, painted reddish-brown stripes. A III 204.8a.
26	5080h	Pinkish-orange with thick, grey core; very coarse with few assorted white grits; traces of white slip outside and on bottom; very uneven surface over-all, spalling outside, heavy, grey incrustations. A II 101.8b.
27	4736	String-cut; greyish-white inside and pinkish-tan outside; coarse with some assorted white grits; faint traces of white slip outside; many assorted pits over-all. A III 203.4a.
28	4970	Flat base of jar; dark-orange inside and buff outside, thick, dark-grey core; very coarse with many assorted white, and few grey and reddish-brown grits; one very large pit inside, some assorted pits over-all, pitted and spalling on bottom. A IV 300.14a.
29	5134e	Orangish-buff with grey core; medium-coarse with some assorted tan and grey grits; white slip outside. A IV 300.19.
30	5134a, d (joined)	Orangish-buff; medium-coarse with many assorted reddish-brown and tan grits; faint traces of possible white slip outside; very uneven surface inside, impressions of organic material and pitting on bottom outside, gritty texture over-all. A IV 300.19.
31	4592j, k	Tan; medium-coarse with some assorted grey, tan, and reddish-brown grits; traces of white slip outside; some grey incrustations. A III 201.12a.
32	4959	Drab with orange core in places; very coarse with many assorted light- and dark-grey quartz grits; many small to fine pits over-all, rough texture inside. A IV 300.14a.
33	4272	Orangish-buff with thick dark-grey core penetrating to bottom in places; coarse with many assorted tan and grey grits; traces of white slip outside; many assorted pits over-all; very pitted and flaking on bottom, dark-grey smoke marks inside. A II 101.8a.
34	4532	Buff; very coarse with some assorted white and grey grits; traces of heavy white slip outside; pitted inside, very uneven surface outside. A III 201.5.
35	5080i	Dark-buff with orange patches outside and in core; traces of white slip outside; uneven surfaces over-all, pitting and spalling on bottom, heavy grey incrustations. A II 101.8b.
36	4587	Flat base of jar; buff with greyish-buff inside; coarse with very many assorted grey and reddish-brown grits; very pitted and flaking inside, rough texture at outside juncture of wall and bottom. A III 201.12a.
37	4621	Brown with dark-buff core; coarse with very many assorted grey quartz grits; traces of reddish-brown slip outside; rough gritty texture over-all, pitted on bottom. A III 202.3.
38	4253	Buff; very coarse with few assorted grey grits; traces of white slip outside; potter's finger-marks over-all inside, very rough texture and few assorted pits over-all. A II 101.5.
Fig. 51 No.	Reg. No.	
1	4592l	Wet-smoothed; orangish-buff with thick, grey core; coarse with some assorted grey, tan, and reddish-brown grits; roughly pitted and spalling inside, some grey incrustations. A III 201.12a.
2	4966	Buff inside and dark-orange outside, thick, dark-grey core; traces of white slip on bottom; rough texture over-all. A IV 300.14a.
3	4839	Pinkish-buff with thick dark-grey core; coarse with many assorted tan and few grey grits; traces of white slip outside; some assorted pits over-all, spalling on bottom, some grey incrustations. A III 204.8a.
—	4625b	Flat base of jar; pinkish-buff; very coarse with some assorted grey and tan grits; traces of heavy white slip outside and on bottom; pitted and spalling inside. A III 202.3.
4	4993	Buff; coarse with many assorted white, grey, and brown grits; traces of orange slip outside. A IV 300.14b.

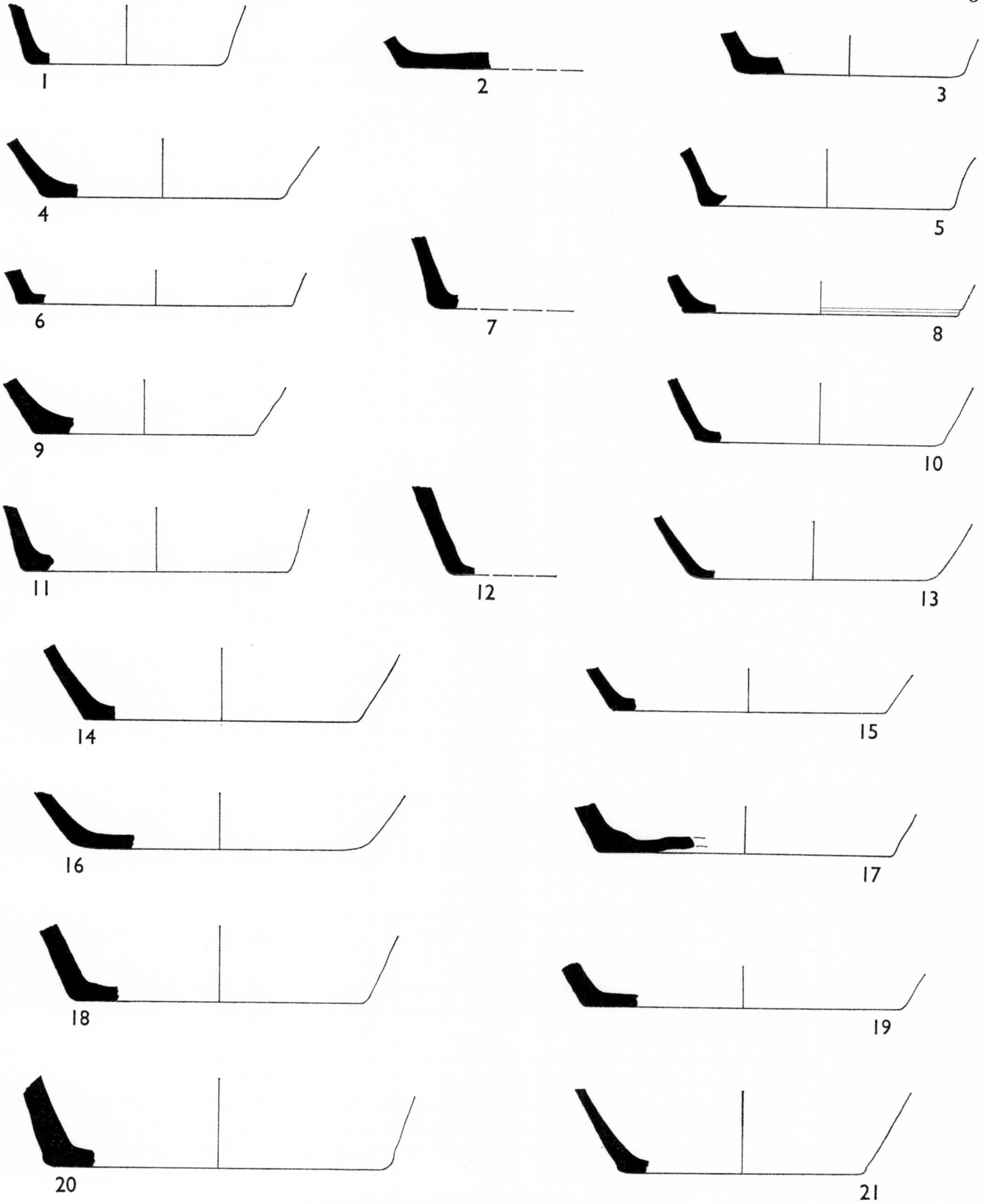

Fig. 51. Bases of jars, Phase V. 1:4.

Fig. 51 No.	Reg. No.	
5	5080e	Buff; very coarse with some assorted white and tan grits; traces of white slip outside; rough, uneven, texture, grey incrustations over-all. A II 101.8b.
6	5007	Buff with very thick dark-grey core; very coarse with many assorted, mostly small to fine grey and tan grits; traces of reddish-buff slip outside; very rough pitted texture over-all. A IV 300.14b.
7	5009p	Orangish-buff; medium-coarse with some assorted white and tan grits; some pitting outside, spalling inside. A IV 300.14b.
8	4574	Buff; coarse with many assorted white and grey grits; traces of reddish-brown slip over-all, traces of burnishing inside; some assorted pits inside, pitting and flaking on bottom, very rough texture outside. A III 201.11.
9	4592h	Wet-smoothed; orangish-brown; coarse with many assorted white and grey quartz grits; many small pits inside, uneven surface outside. A III 201.12a.
10	5108	Buff with dark-orange patches outside, pinkish-grey inside; coarse with very many assorted tan, grey, and white grits; traces of white slip outside; many assorted pits inside, some very large deep pits outside and on bottom, some grey incrustations outside. A IV 300.17.
11	5161	Orangish-buff with patches of dark-grey core penetrating to outside in places; very coarse with many assorted, mostly fine white grits; faint traces of white slip outside, traces of yellowish-tan slip inside. A III 204.2.
12	4574b	Wet-smoothed outside; dull-orange with brown core; very coarse with many assorted dark-grey quartz grits; traces of thin white slip outside; rough, gritty texture and spalling inside. A III 201.12.
13	5159	Wet-smoothed outside; dark-orange inside and on bottom, greyish-buff outside and core; very coarse with many assorted white and grey quartz grits; very pitted and spalling inside and on bottom, one large, elongated pit outside. A III 204.2.
14	4983	Buff with dark-grey core penetrating to surfaces in places; coarse with very many assorted white and grey quartz grits, very porous ware; many assorted pits over-all. A IV 300.14b.
15	5009o	Orangish-buff; medium-coarse with few assorted grey and tan grits; some assorted pits and uneven surfaces over-all, some greyish-brown incrustations. A IV 300.14b.
16	5166	Buff with thick, black core penetrating to outside in places; very coarse with many assorted grey and white grits; faint traces of white slip outside; very pitted and spalling inside and on bottom. A III 204.2.
17	4540	Buff with orangish-buff outside; very coarse with many assorted grey quartz grits, porous ware; very uneven surfaces over-all. A III 201.6.
18	4534	Buff with orangish-buff outside; very coarse with assorted grey quartz grits, porous ware; traces of grey slip on bottom; badly pitted and flaking inside, many assorted pits and uneven surface outside. A III 201.5.
19	4592g	Wet-smoothed; dark-orange with brown core; coarse with many assorted smokey quartz grits; white slip outside and on bottom; uneven surface on bottom, pitted and spalling inside. A III 201.12a.
20	5084	Dark-pink with pinkish-buff outside; very coarse with some assorted tan grits; many assorted pits over-all, pitted and spalling on bottom. A IV 300.14a.
21	4990	Buff inside and pinkish-tan outside, pinkish-brown core; very coarse with many assorted tan, reddish-brown, and few white and grey grits; many assorted pits over-all with some very large pits outside, very rough texture outside, dark-grey smoke marks inside. A IV 300.14b.

Fig. 52 No.	Reg. No.	
1	4251	Dark buff; fine with very many assorted grey grits, porous ware; traces of continuous burnishing over-all; black smoke marks inside, some assorted pits and crazing inside, many assorted pits on outside and bottom with flaking on bottom. A II 101.5.
2	4585	Dark-grey with buff outside; very coarse with many assorted grey, tan, and white grits; traces of heavy, white slip outside and on bottom; very rough, pitted and spalling over-all. A III 201.12a.
3	4733	Buff with thick dark-grey core; very coarse with many mostly fine white grits; heavy white slip outside, very rough texture inside, some grey incrustations over-all. A III 203.4a.
4	4592i	Large jar, crudely hand-made; dark-orange with thick, dark-grey core; coarse with some assorted grey and tan grits; uneven surfaces over-all. A III 201.12a.
5	4254	Buff with thick dark-grey core; very coarse with some assorted white and grey grits; some assorted pits and rough texture over-all, very pitted and flaking on bottom. A II 101.5a.
6	4527	Buff inside and reddish-orange outside, very thick, dark-grey core; very coarse with many assorted white grits; brown slip over-all, pronounced crazing, rough texture over-all. A III 201.4a.
7	4574c	Wet-smoothed outside; dark-orange; very coarse with many assorted grey quartz grits; traces of reddish-brown slip outside; rough, uneven surface inside. A III 201.12.
8	4574d	Large jar, hand-made, wet-smoothed over-all, rough jucture outside where side meets bottom; brownish-grey with dull-orange outside; very coarse with some small to fine white grits; traces of white slip outside; pronounced finger-marks and crazing inside, deeply pitted outside on bottom. A III 201.12.
—	4625l	Body sherd of large jar; greyish-white with light-orange inside; very coarse with some assorted tan and reddish-brown grits; traces of white slip outside; pronounced crazing over-all. A III 202.3.
9	4582	Brown with pinkish-brown inside; very coarse with many assorted white and tan, few assorted reddish-brown grits; traces of creamy-white slip outside; very pitted and flaking inside and on bottom, some grey incrustations over-all. A III 201.12a.
10	5116	Deep-buff with orange patches outside, pinkish-white inside, dark-grey core in places; very coarse with many assorted grey and brown grits, one very large grey grit; many assorted pits and very uneven surface over-all, pitting and spalling on bottom. A IV 300.17.
11	4984	Large jar, coil-made; pink inside and buff outside, light pinkish-brown core; very coarse with many assorted grits of mixed colors; traces of white slip outside; very rough texture and uneven surfaces over-all, very pitted and spalling on bottom. A IV 300.14b.
12	4986	Angle of wall rounded outside at juncture with bottom; orangish-buff with thick grey core in places; coarse with very many assorted white and light-grey quartz grits; many assorted pits inside, pitted and spalling on bottom. A IV 300.14b.
13	4592t	Large jar; orangish-buff with grey core; coarse with some assorted white, grey, and tan grits; wide, crude, half-relief rope-molding outside, traces of white slip outside; some grey incrustations. A III 201.12a.
14	4977	Buff; very coarse with many assorted white and light- and dark-grey grits; many assorted pits and crazing over-all, very rough, gritty texture. A IV 300.14a.
15	5006	Bright-buff; very coarse with many assorted white and light- and dark-grey grits; very rough, gritty texture and crazing over-all. A IV 300.14b.
16	5004	Greyish-brown; very coarse with many assorted dark-grey quartz and tan grits, porous ware; traces of reddish-brown slip outside; many assorted pits over-all, very pitted bottom, inside and outside. A IV 300.14b.

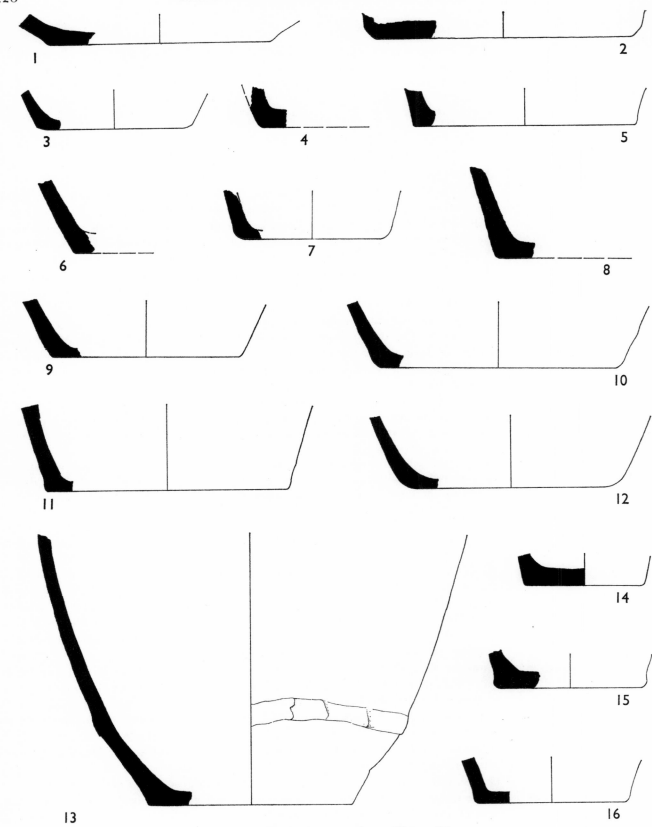

Fig. 52. Bases of heavy jars, Phase V. 1:4.

Fig. 53 No.	Reg. No.	
1	4252	Narrow, plain edge; buff, medium-coarse with few assorted red grits; traces of heavy white slip with remnants of three painted red lines outside; some grey incrustations over-all. A II 101.5.
—	4625c	Ledge-handle fragment, edge broken off; tan with grey core; coarse with few assorted white grits; traces of white slip outside. A III 202.3.
—	4956a	Ledge-handle fragment, badly chipped edge; tan; very coarse with some assorted white and tan grits; white slip outside; very rough, uneven, gritty texture over-all. A IV 300.12.
2	4987	Thumb-indented edge; dark-orange inside and buff outside; medium-coarse with some assorted grey, tan, and reddish-brown grits; traces of reddish-brown slip outside; very rough texture outside, under handle, and inside. A IV 300.14b.
—	4839j	Body sherd; orangish-buff; medium-coarse with some assorted tan and white grits; faint traces of narrow, closely-spaced, parallel burnished lines outside on background of continuously-burnished surface of orange slip. A III 204.8a.
—	5103b	Body sherd; orangish-buff; medium-coarse with some assorted light-grey and white quartz grits; continuously-burnished orange-brown slip outside; very uneven surface inside with some assorted, mostly fine, pits inside. A IV 300.16.
3	4980	Thumb-indented edge; dark-orange with thick, dark-grey core; very coarse with many assorted tan, grey, and reddish-brown grits; traces of reddish-brown slip outside. A IV 300.14b.
—	5009v	Ledge-handle fragment, deep, well-defined finger-indentation in edge; orangish-buff with orange inside, grey core; medium-coarse with some assorted grey and white quartz grits; heavy white slip outside. A IV 300.14b.
—	5009u	Ledge-handle fragment, one well-defined finger-indentation in center of edge; buff with grey core; coarse with some assorted grey, white, and reddish-brown grits; dark-grey incrustations over-all. A IV 300.14b.
4	5104 5109 (joined)	Pushed-up, thumb-indented edge; dark-grey; very coarse with many assorted grey and few white grits; traces of heavy white slip outside. A IV 300.17.
5	5115	Pushed-up, thumb-indented edge; dark greyish-brown with buff outside; coarse with very many assorted dark-grey, white, tan, and some reddish-brown grits; rough gritty texture over-all. A IV 300.17.
6	4592r	Inclined up from body, thumb-indented edge; orange with thick grey core; medium-coarse with some assorted white and grey grits; traces of white slip outside. A III 201.12a.
7	4259	Ledge-handle fragment, closely spaced, diagonal indentations along edge; reddish-orange with buff core; medium-coarse with many assorted white and grey grits. A II 101.5a.
8	4967	Lug-handle fragment of amphoriskos, vertical, merging into body, pierced; orange; medium with few small to fine, white grits; traces of painted reddish-brown trellis-pattern outside and on handle. A IV 300.14a.
9	4278	Lug-handle, located on shoulder, rounded, conical shape, pierced horizontally; pinkish-tan; medium with some small to fine white and orange grits; some assorted pits over-all, very uneven surface inside. A II 101.8b.
10	5077	Vestigial spout, flared out with opening to point of juncture with body; buff with patches of orange outside, orange inside; medium-coarse with many assorted grey and tan grits. A II 101.8a.
11	4592s	Spout fragment, wheel-made; reddish-orange; fine with some small to fine, white, dark-grey, and reddish-brown grits; continuously-burnished red slip outside. A III 201.12a.

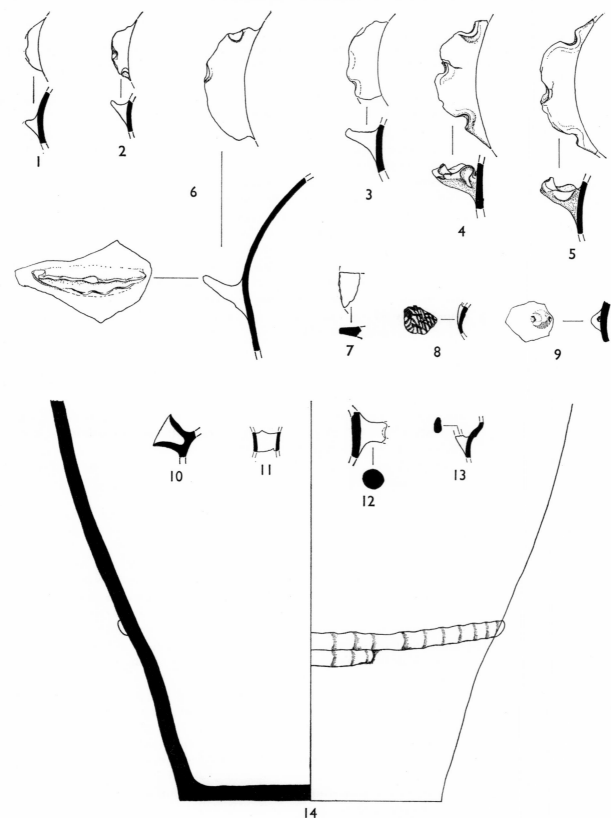

Fig. 53. Heavy jars, handles and spouts, Phase V. 1:4.

Fig. 53 No.	Reg. No.	
12	4264	Vestigial spout; buff with grey core in places; medium-coarse with many assorted, mostly small to fine, white, grey, and brown grits; traces of burnished reddish-brown slip outside. A II 101.8a.
13	5080j	Loop-handle fragment and body sherd of jug, irregular oval section; orangish-buff; medium with some assorted white and tan grits; traces of white slip outside; uneven surfaces, heavy grey incrustations over-all. A II 101.8b.
—	5009ee	Body sherd with remnant of loop-handle, wheel-made, medium-fine with many fine to very fine grey-tan, and orange grits; some small to very fine pits over-all. A IV 300.14b.
—	4832b	Loop-handle fragment joined to shoulder, large, oval section, pinkish-buff with greyish-brown inside; coarse with some assorted grey, white, and tan grits; traces of continuously-burnished, reddish-brown slip outside; some grey incrustations over-all. A III 204.8.
—	5009s	Loop-handle fragment joined to body, oval section; orange with brownish-grey core; medium-coarse with some medium to fine white, grey, and dark-red grits; traces of white slip outside; brownish-grey incrustations over-all. A IV 300.14b.
—	5009r	Loop-handle fragment joined to body elongated oval section; buff with grey inside and core; medium-coarse with many medium to very fine grey and white grits; vessel possibly burnished outside. A IV 300.14b.
—	5095c	Loop-handle fragment joined to rim of jug, elongated oval section; dull orange with grey core in places; coarse with some assorted grey, tan, and orange grits; traces of reddish-brown slip outside; light-grey incrustations over-all. A IV 300.14a.
—	4574h	Loop-handle fragment, single coil, flattened oval section; brownish-buff; fine with few small to fine, white and grey grits; burnished, reddish-brown slip over-all. A III 201.12.
—	5009q	Loop-handle fragment, irregular elongated oval section; orangish-buff with grey core; medium-coarse with few assorted grey grits; traces of burnishing over-all, some light, whitish-grey incrustations. A IV 300.14b.
14	6224	Large jar; brown inside and orangish-buff outside; grey core; medium-coarse with some assorted tan and grey grits; wide, crude, half-relief rope-molding outside; traces of white slip outside. A III 202.3.

Fig. 54 No.	Reg. No.	
1	4574f	Wet-smoothed; orange; medium with few medium to fine white and grey grits; medium-wide, crude, half-relief rope-molding outside, white slip outside. A III 201.12.
—	4625i	Body sherd of jar; drab inside and orange outside, grey core, coarse with many assorted white, grey, and tan grits; remnant of high-relief ram's horn molding and traces of heavy, white slip outside. A III 202.3.
—	5080k	Body sherd of jar; orangish-brown inside and dull-orange outside; very coarse with some assorted tan and white grits; medium-wide, low-relief rope-molding and traces of white slip outside; grey incrustations over-all. A II 101.8b.
2	4592m	Hand-made wall; brownish-orange with thick, grey core; medium with some medium to fine tan and grey grits; wide, crude, half-relief rope-molding outside, traces of greyish-white slip outside. A III 201.12a.
3	4592n	Hand-made wall; brownish-orange with thick, dark-grey core; medium-coarse with many medium to fine tan and grey grits; wide, crude, high-relief rope-molding outside, traces of heavy, creamy-white slip outside. A III 201.12a.
4	5094	Pinkish-tan with pinkish-orange outside; coarse with very many tan and pinkish-brown grits; medium-wide, crude, high-relief, wavy, rope-molding outside, traces of white slip outside; many assorted pits over-all, rough, gritty texture inside. A IV 300.14a.

Fig. 54 No.	Reg. No.	
5	4530	Hand-made wall, wet-smoothed outside, very rough inside at overlapped juncture of bands; brownish-buff inside and buff outside, dark-grey core; very coarse with many assorted white and grey grits; medium-wide, crude, half-relief, rope-molding outside, traces of white slip outside, rough, gritty texture over-all. A III 201.5.
6	4831e	Bright-orange with dark-grey outside; very coarse with some assorted white grits; very wide, crude, high-relief rope-molding, traces of heavy, white slip outside; heavy, greyish-brown incrustations over-all. A III 204.7.
7	4590	Hand-made and wet-smoothed outside; very rough texture inside where bands overlap; dark-grey; very coarse with many assorted grey and tan grits, porous ware; narrow crude, high-relief rope-molding outside, slip over-all with traces of white slip outside. A III 201.12a.
8	4574e	Hand-made wall with bands roughly overlapped inside, wet-smoothed outside; greyish-orange; coarse with some medium to fine grey and tan grits; wide, crude, high-relief molding outside, traces of greyish-white slip outside; rough, gritty texture inside. A III 201.12.
9	4277	Pinkish-orange with thick grey core, very coarse with many assorted white and tan grits, porous ware; narrow, crude, high-relief rope-molding outside, traces of heavy white slip outside; very many assorted pits inside and on molding; some grey incrustations over-all. A II 101.8b.
—	5103	Body sherd of jar; pinkish-brown with reddish-brown patches outside; very coarse with many assorted, mostly small to fine, grey grits; narrow, crude, high-relief rope-molding and creamy-white slip outside; spalling outside, rough, gritty texture over-all. A IV 300.16.
10	5080	Buff, dark-orange outside; coarse with many assorted white and tan grits; very wide, crude, high-relief rope-molding outside; pitted and flaking inside, some grey incrustations outside. A II 101.8b.
11	4539	Dark-grey, brown outside; coarse with many assorted light-tan and grey grits; medium-wide, crude, high-relief rope-molding outside, two bands of body joined at location of rope molding, traces of heavy white slip outside; very rough texture inside and on molding. A III 201.6.
—	4839e	Body sherd of jar; brown with thick dark-grey core; very coarse with few assorted white and grey grits; medium-wide, high-relief rope-molding outside. A III 204.8a.
12	5113	Deep-pink inside and buff outside, reddish-orange core; very coarse with many assorted, mostly small, tan grits; wide, crude, high-relief rope-molding outside, traces of white slip outside; rough gritty texture over-all. A IV 300.17.
—	4625k	Body sherd of large jar; greyish-pink inside and buff outside, thick dark-grey core; very coarse with some assorted reddish-brown and grey grits; wide, crude, low-relief molding outside; rough gritty texture on molding. A III 202.3.
13	4572	Dark-grey with buff outside; very coarse with many assorted white and grey grits; wide, crude, high-relief rope-molding outside, traces of very heavy, white slip outside; crazing and fine pits inside. A III 201.11.
14	4979	Light pinkish-brown; very coarse with some assorted white grits; wide, crude, half-relief rope-molding, traces of white slip outside; some assorted pits over-all, uneven surfaces inside. A IV 300.14b.
15	4591	Hand-made wall, wet-smoothed outside, very rough inside at overlap of bands; dark-grey with brown outside; coarse with very many assorted white and tan grits, porous ware; wide, crude, high-relief rope-molding, traces of heavy white slip outside; some crazing and pitting. A III 201.12a.

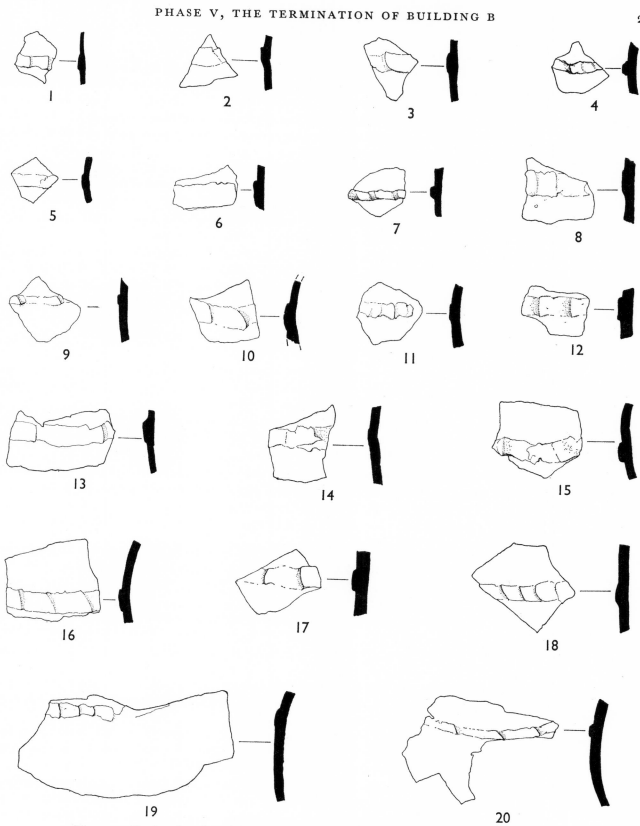

Fig. 54. Body sherds with applied, molded decorations, Phase V. 1:4.

Fig. 54 No.	Reg. No.	
16	4625	Grey inside and buff outside; very coarse with many assorted tan and white grits; wide, crude, high-relief rope-molding, traces of orange slip outside; many assorted pits inside. A III 202.3.
17	4992	Orangish-buff with dark-orange outside; coarse with many assorted, mostly small to fine, white grits; wide, crude, very high-relief wavy, rope-molding and faint traces of white slip outside. A IV 300.14b.
—	4831f	Body sherd of jar; buff; coarse with some assorted white and tan grits; very wide, crude, high-relief rope molding and traces of white slip outside; some brown incrustations over-all. A III 204.7.
18	4267	Orange with greyish-buff core; wide, crude, low-relief rope-molding outside; many assorted pits, some grey incrustations over-all. A II 101.8a.
—	4625j	Body sherd of large jar; brown inside and orangish-buff outside; very coarse with some assorted tan and white grits; very wide, crude, low-relief molding outside at joint of two parts of body; rough gritty texture on molding. A III 202.3.
19	4592p	Large jar, hand-made; brownish-orange with thick, grey core; medium-coarse with some assorted white and grey grits; medium-wide, uneven, half-relief rope-molding outside, traces of white slip outside; pronounced diagonal finger-marks inside, dark-grey incrustations over-all. A III 201.12a.
—	5116f	Body sherd of jar, brownish-orange outside and purple inside, pinkish-red core; coarse with many medium to very fine tan and few white grits; remnant of medium-wide, crude, half-relief molding outside; gritty texture inside. A IV 300.17.
—	4625h	Body sherd of large jar; grey inside, orange and drab outside; coarse with many assorted white, grey, and tan grits; medium-wide half-relief molding and traces of heavy white slip outside. A III 202.3.
20	5103a	Rosy-brown with patches of pink and tan outside; coarse with many assorted tan and grey grits; medium-wide, crude, high-relief rope-molding, traces of white slip outside; rough, gritty texture over-all. A IV 300.16.

Fig. 55 No.	Reg. No.	
1	5114	Deep pinkish-grey inside and buff outside, very thick, dark-grey core in places; very coarse with many assorted, mostly fine, grey and tan grits; medium-wide, crude, half-relief rope-molding outside, traces of white slip outside; rough, gritty texture inside. A IV 300.17.
2	5009	Pinkish-brown with pinkish-grey core in places; very coarse with some assorted grey and tan grits; very porous ware; medium-wide, very crude, low-relief rope-molding outside, creamy white slip outside; very rough texture over-all, many assorted, mostly large, pits. A IV 300.14b.
3	4592	Dark-grey with brown outside; with many assorted, mostly fine, white and tan grits, porous ware; very wide, crude, high-relief rope-molding, traces of heavy white slip outside. A III 201.12a.
4	4592o	Large jar, roughly wet-smoothed, dark-grey with brownish-orange outside; medium-coarse with some small to fine tan and grey grits; wide, crude, uneven, high-relief rope-molding, white slip outside; grey incrustations over-all. A III 201.12a.
5	4592q	Large jar, hand-made with band-construction of wall, bands roughly overlapped inside and wet-smoothed outside; greyish-brown with dark-grey patches inside; medium-coarse with some medium to fine, white and tan grits; traces of greyish-white slip outside. A III 201.12a.

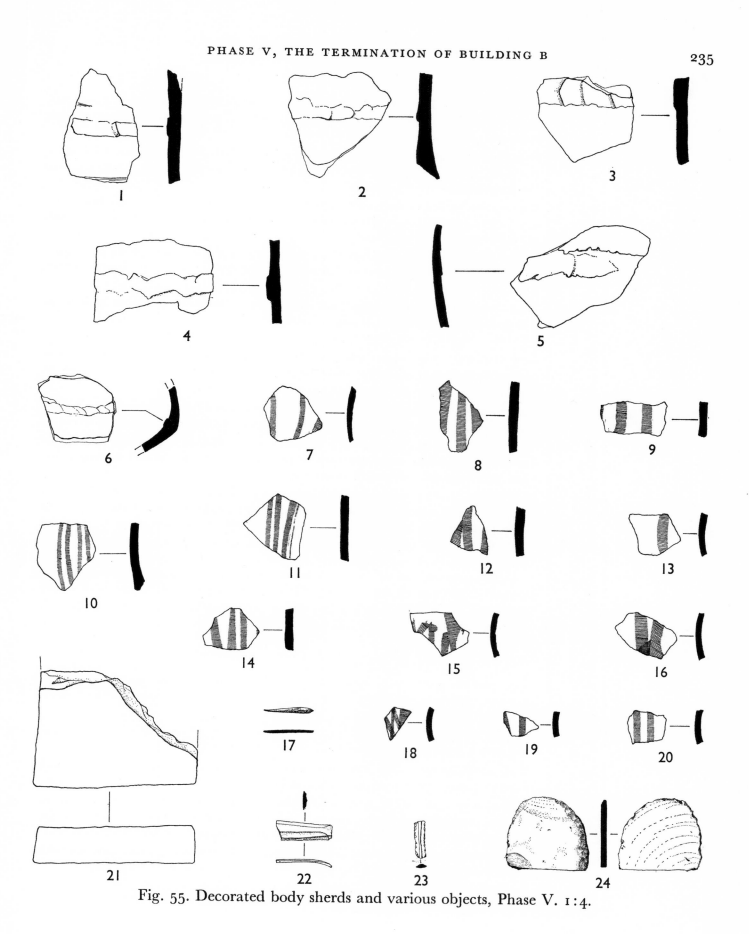

Fig. 55. Decorated body sherds and various objects, Phase V. 1:4.

Fig. 55 No.	Reg. No.	
6	4537	Neck fragment of jar; dark-orange with patches of tan outside, buff core; coarse with many assorted white, grey, and brown grits; narrow, crude, high-relief rope-molding and traces of white slip outside. A III 201.5a.
7	4975	Orange with grey core; medium-coarse with some assorted grey, tan, and white grits; white slip outside, traces of three wide, painted, red stripes outside; some grey and black incrustations. A IV 300.14a.
8	5110	Brown with thick dark-grey core; very coarse with many assorted, mostly fine, white grits; white slip with traces of three parallel, painted, dark-brown stripes outside; rough, gritty texture over-all. A IV 300.17.
9	5107	Brown with thick, dark-grey core; very coarse with many assorted, mostly fine, white grits; white slip with traces of three parallel, painted, dark-brown stripes outside; rough, gritty texture over-all. A IV 300.17.
10	4978	Whitish-brown inside and orange outside, buff core; very coarse with some assorted tan and reddish-brown grits; white slip with traces of four medium wide, roughly parallel, painted, dark-red stripes outside; very uneven surfaces over-all. A IV 300.14a.
11	4954	Buff with grey core; very coarse with some assorted white, grey, and reddish-brown grits; heavy white slip and traces of four parallel, painted red stripes outside. A IV 300.12.
12	5111	Similar to 56:8, reg. no. 5110. A IV 300.17.
13	4260	Buff; coarse with many assorted tan grits; white slip and faint traces of wide, painted orange stripes outside; some assorted pits inside, some grey incrustations. A II 101.5a.
14	4835	Pinkish-buff; very coarse with some assorted tan and dark-brown grits; white slip and traces of four painted, reddish-brown stripes outside; very pitted and spalling inside, some grey incrustations over-all. A III 204.8a.
15	5092	Row of diagonal impressions inside indicate two parts of vessel joined together; reddish-brown; medium with many small to fine white grits; crudely painted, dark-brown net pattern outside, continuous burnishing over-all outside. A IV 300.14a.
—	5116h	Body sherd; orange inside and brownish-grey outside, very thick grey core penetrating to outside; medium-coarse with some assorted grey and tan grits; traces of white slip outside; somewhat uneven surfaces over-all with bands of parallel striations outside (perhaps from finishing with a clump of grass); some assorted pits inside. A IV 300.17.
16	5102	Dark-orange inside and grey outside; coarse with many medium to fine white grits; traces of white slip with very wide, painted orange stripes outside, grey incrustations over-all. A IV 300.16.
17	0–50	Bone awl, worn smooth around point. A IV 300.14b.
18	5000	Tan; medium-coarse with many assorted brown and reddish-brown grits; traces of painted reddish-brown trellis pattern outside; very rough, gritty texture inside. A IV 300.14b.
19	4524	Buff inside and orange outside; medium-coarse with some assorted white grits; white slip outside with two well-defined painted red stripes. A III 201.3a.
20	4623	Buff; medium-coarse with some fine white grits; white slip and traces of two wide, parallel, painted orange stripes outside. A III 202.3.
21	0–67	Fragment of brick palette, well-fired, pinkish-tan and orange with greyish-tan patches outside, thick, dark-grey core; coarse with some assorted grey, tan, and reddish-brown grits, grey incrustations over-all; black smoke marks on one side. A III 201.12a.
—	4543c	Kiln-fired brick fragment, very thick; orangish-buff; very coarse with many fine white grits, some assorted grey and tan grits; some grey incrustations. A III 201.6a.

Fig. 55 No.	Reg. No.	
22	5354	Flint blade, four facets on back, curved at end, finely and evenly pointed, unretouched; dark-brown. A IV 300.19.
23	4831m	Flint blade with trapezoidal section; greyish-brown; retouched edges well worn. A III 204.7.
24	0–17	Flat flint scraper; dark-brown, thin yellowish-white limestone layer on one side; blade is relatively flat on one side, retouched edges on other side. A II 101.8a.

DESCRIPTIONS OF THE MARQUET-KRAUSE PHASE V POTTERY AND OBJECTS, FIGS. 56–58

Fig. 56 No.	M-K Reg. No.	
1	1428	Fragment of very small bowl very low projection of rim forming a sharp angle with wall; wall very inclined. H : 120, down to the rock (M-K Pl. LXXXV).
2	1428	Fragment of small, very fine bowl, flat bottom lightly curved, without base, sharp rim forming first a right angle with the bottom, then curved toward outside (cf. 742 and 1529), red burnished. H : 120; down to the rock (M-K Pl. LXXXV).
3	2197	Fragment of small fine bowl. H : 116; on floor B, east side (M-K Pl. LXXXII).
4	1556	Fragment of bowl; wall inclined at 45°, vertical rim. H : 129; above the rock (which is almost level) (M-K Pl. LXXXI).
5	2127	Fragment of bowl, fine vertical rim; red slip on both sides. H : 136; down to floor B (M-K Pl. LXXXII).
6	2127	Fragment of large bowl. H : 136; above floor B (M-K Pl. LXXXII).
7	2321	Fragment of flat bowl. H : 116; on floor B (M-K Pl. LXXXII).
8	1556	Fine bowl, rim curved toward outside. H : 129; above the rock (which is almost level) outside. H : 129; (M-K Pl. LXXXV).
—	1464	Rim of bowl (bowl form), thin rim, a little below rim horizontal ear-handle, trace of wick of lamp; long and thin neck of medium jug, burnished, fragment of bowl, flat form, thin rim folded toward inside at a sharp angle; rims of bowls projecting over inside surface, burnished, large wavy molding on body of bowl; fragment of very fine neck, rim curved toward outside; white slip; horizontal handles: (1) completely flat; (2) flat: on 3 points of rim, impression accompanied by a slight projection toward top; circular cylindrical handle, long and thin, bent on top. H : 128; locus 7 west wall.
9	2197	Fragment of bowl with thick flat bottom, thin rim curved upward; non-glossy red slip. H : 116; on floor B, east side (M-K Pl. LXXXII).
10	1428	Fragment of bowl . . . rim projecting very low forming a sharp angle with the inner wall, wall very inclined. H : 120; above the rock (M-K Pl. LXXXV).
11	2193	Fragment of bowl; wall somewhat at right angle with inner wall. H : 136; floor B (M-K Pl. LXXXII).
12	2193	Fragment of bowl: (1) very fine; very inclined wall; thin nearly vertical rim, design of brown lines on one side concentric, on the other running from rim to the base. H : 136; floor B (M-K Pl. LXXXII).
—	1442	Fragments of bowls: (1) brown slip, burnished; inside design of black concentric bands; (2) type of flat base, wall somewhat inclined, horizontal rim projecting over inside surface. H : 128; locus 6 of west wall.
13	2236	Fragment of bowl, wall very much inclined; thin and long rim forming a right angle with inner wall; angle rounded. H : 136–137; floor B, lower (M-K Pl. LXXXIV).

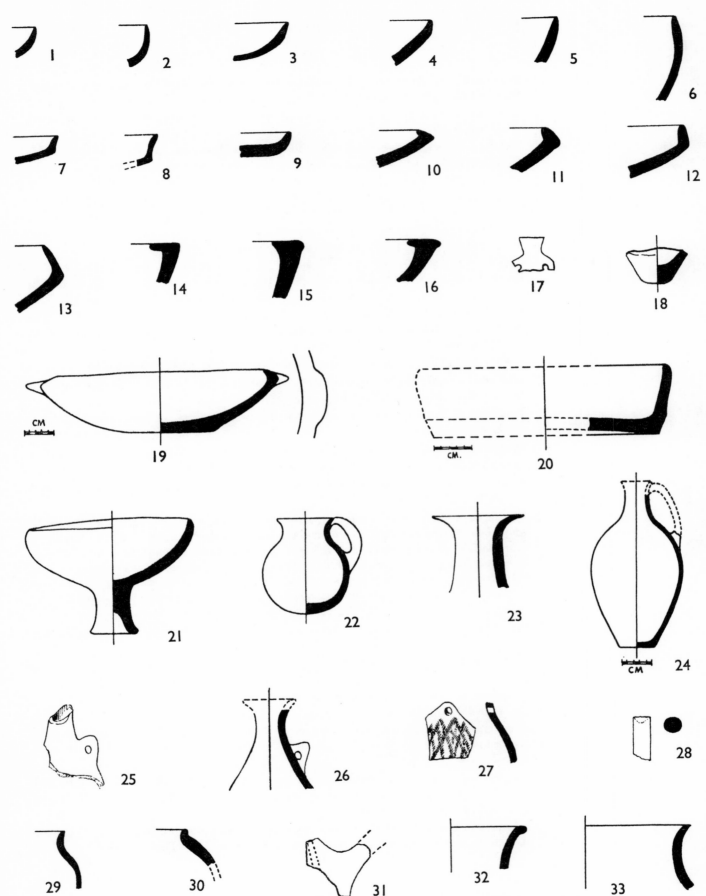

Fig. 56. Bowls, juglets, jugs, and jars, Phase V, from Marquet-Krause.

Fig. 56 *No.*	*M-K Reg.* *No.*	
14	1426	Fragment of bowl: wall slightly inclined, horizontal rim projecting long and thin over inside surface. H:120; 30 cm. under stone table. (M-K Pl. LXXXV).
—	1553	Various fragments; rims of bowls projecting over inside surface; fragments of small deep bowl; flat base, sharp rim; wall nearly vertical, slightly curved; loop-handle. H:129; above the rock (which is level).
15	2354	Fragment of bowl; inner wall quite inclined; horizontal rim projecting over the two surfaces, slightly over the outside surface. H:116, floor B (M-K Pl. LXXXII).
—	1567	Wavy handle; two folded handles; rim bowl projecting horizontally slightly over the two surfaces, wall somewhat inclined, curved. Fragment of simple neck, thin rim curved toward outside; flat thick base of large jar, cf. 216; fragment with corded molding; brick (cf. bricks of palace). H:129; above the rock.
16	1428	Fragment of bowl: horizontal rim of bowl projecting over the two surfaces. H:120; above the rock (M-K Pl. LXXXV).
—	1578II	Fragment of bowl, rim an extension of the wall, rounded edge; rim projecting over the two surfaces; wavy molding. H:128; locus 6, west wall.
17	2165	Neck of amphorette: high, flared, with two ear-handles. H:136–137; floor B (M-K Pl. LXXXI).
—	1493	Amphorette light-brown ware; two ear-handles (neck missing) globular body, flat base, dark brown lattice design. H:132; under wall constructed over charred stratum.
18	2193	Round base, narrow; red slip. H:136; floor B (M-K Pl. LXXXII).
19	2013II	Bowl: flat base, rim projecting over inside surface, flat horizontal handle; diam. 45 cm. H:116; 80 cm. under floor A (M-K Pl. LXXVII).
20	1444	Fragment of bowl; flat base, wall somewhat inclined, rim nearly sharp; thick material, grey with white grains. H:128; locus 6 of west wall (M-K Pl. LXXV).
21	2014	Bowl on foot, hemispherical body; glossy paint. H:116; 80 cm. under floor A (M-K Pl. LXXVII).
22	2016	Juglet; spherical body, one handle. H:116; in the burned layer in the corner, 80 cm. under floor A (M-K Pl. LXXVII).
23	2149a	Neck of jug, long and thin, flared rim. H:136–137; almost on floor B (M-K Pl. LXXXI).
24	2538	Jug with flat base, high neck, one handle. H:116; floor B, at the foot of the north wall, in charcoal (M-K Pl. LXXVIII).
—	1574	Long and narrow neck of small jug; loop-handle starting from rim; rim of bowl curved toward inside, striated, corded molding. H:132; loci 10–11, west wall.
—	1544II	Fragment of jug: loop-handle, corded on top, then long and straight; flat base; red slip; two horizontal handles, completely flat; on each side of edge impression made by end of finger; fragments of hole-mouths, type: cf. 1283 and 1310; rim of bowl projecting over inside surface, traces of red slip, concentric lines on rim; type: cf. 259; loop-handle; fragments, white slip. H:128; trench, above the rock.
25	2197	Fragment of amphorette. H:116; on floor B, east side (M-K Pl. LXXXI).
26	2197	Fragment of amphorette; high and thin neck, flared rim; triangular ear-handles mounted vertically on shoulder. H:116; on floor B, east side (M-K Pl. LXXXIV).
—	1587	Two horizontal handles: wavy edge; digital impressions; fragment of ear-handle in triangular form, burnished; fine and burnished fragments; fragment of bowl, rim forming an obtuse angle with inner wall; traces of burnishing, cf. 868; fragments of rims of hole-mouths: (1) simple, band thickened; (2) flat edge, projecting over outside surface; fragment of very short neck, rim curved toward outside; fragment of higher neck, rim curved toward outside. H:132; loci 9–10, above the rock.

Fig. 56 No.	M-K Reg. No.	
27	2354	Fragment of amphorette, lattice design in heavy lines over body. H:116; floor B (M-K Pl. LXXXVII).
—	2017	Neck of small jar with one handle; paint. H:116; in the burned stratum in the corner, 80 cm. under floor A.
28	2626	Loop-handle, nearly cylindrical. H:116; under the niche; floor B (M-K Pl. LXXXI).
—	1552	Two fragments of horizontal handles with raised edge; loop-handle on body of jug, or bowl; wide neck, sharp rim; rim of hole-mouth, not thickened; rim flattened to form a sharp angle with inside surface, an obtuse angle with outside surface. H:129; above the rock (which is level).
29	2193	Fragment of small jar with narrow neck, rounded shoulder, red slip. H:136; floor B (M-K Pl. LXXXII).
—	2161	Fragments of jar with flat base; well-baked (clay) material with red, glossy slip. H:137; floor B.
30	1448	Rim: (3) barely thickened, rim turned up toward top. H:128; locus 6 of north wall (M-K Pl. LXXXIV).
—	2638	Rim of small jar with molding; greenish ware. H:116; sanctuary B (M-K Pl. LI).
31	2197	Fragment of handle (?) H:116; on floor B, east side (M-K Pl. LXXXI).
32	1428	Neck of jar with wide rim: fine, rounded rim on edge. H:120; above the rock (M-K Pl. LXXXIII).
33	1428	Neck of jar with wide rim: (2) fine, rounded rim on edge. H:120; above the rock (M-K Pl. LXXXIII).
—	1549	Neck of jar, short, sharp rim, curved toward outside; fragment of very narrow neck; fragment of not very deep bowl, rim slightly curved toward top, fragment of circular cylindrical and bent handle, very small. H:132; loci 8–9.
—	2373	Fragment of neck of jar, straight: flat base, with projection; rims of hole-mouths: (1) not thickened, rounded edge; (2) somewhat thickened. H:116; on floor B.
—	2376	Neck of jar: medium height, simple and straight wall and rim, nearly at right angle with shoulder; fragments of hole-mouth; rim of thick hole-mouth. H:116; floor B.
—	1584	Flat horizontal handles: at three points, edge folded over itself in little semi-circles, forming a slight impression; flat, loop-handle; fragments of necks of jars: (1) very thin rim curved toward the outside; (2) rim sharply curved toward outside; then very low, edge thinned; fragment of bowl, flat form, curved base, rim forming an angle with the base toward the inside, then curved toward outside; very fine material. H:120; under base of the stone table, 50 cm.

Fig. 57 No.	M-K Reg. No.	
1	1428	Neck of jar with wide rim: (3) thicker, simple. H:120; above the rock (M-K Pl. LXXXIII).
—	1590	Necks of jars: (1) wall perpendicular at shoulder, rim folded toward outside in rounded pads; (2) rim curved toward outside, projecting concave edge; fragment of neck, wall perpendicular to shoulder; rim of thin hole-mouth, line incised over outside surface. H:132, west; at 50 cm. under the buttress wall which consolidates the citadel.
—	2464	Fragment of neck, straight wall, rim folded over outside surface with rounded border but the lower edge not adhering tightly to wall; fragment of bowl, straight wall; flat edge at right angle with inner wall, slightly projecting over inside surface (which curves slightly); rather thin rim of hole-mouth; fragment with projecting molding; lime slip. H:116; under floor B, intermediate.

Fig. 57 No.	M-K Reg. No.	
2	2125	Fragments of jar, flat base, neck outcurved, rim projecting in flat edge; grey ware with white grits, red slip not burnished. H : 136; above rock, floor B (M-K Pl. LXXXI).
3	2125	Fragment of neck (similar to 58 : 2). H : 136; above the rock, floor B (M-K Pl. LXXXIV).
4	1428	Neck of jar with wide rim: (6) concave edge. H : 120; above the rock (M-K Pl. LXXXIII).
5	1428	Neck of jar with wide rim: (4) coming from a large jar, rim forming a flat edge over outside surface. H : 120; above the rock (M-K Pl. LXXXIII).
6	2022	Jar, medium neck, rim curved toward outside, flattened at edge; on body two loop-handles, vertical painted lines. H : 116; under floor A (M-K Pl. LXXVII).
—	2360	Horizontal handle; loop-handle; fragment: white lime slip with design of red lines; fragment: red slip: fragment of bowl; thin wall, inclined, straight; long and thin rim forming right angle with inner wall; red slip; rims of hole-mouths: (1) slightly thickened over inside surface, rounded edge; (2) thick not bulging; (3) thin, not thickened, rounded edge, projection around outside surface; (4) thick, not swollen, slight impression on outside surface; (5) thickened over inside surface, incised or impressed line on outside surface; (6) thin, barely thickened over inside surface, rounded edge, slight impression on outside surface; (7) thickened over outside surface; thinned edge; sharply curved toward inside, on the thickening of the outside surface wavy, rather wide, molding; lime slip; fragment of neck of jar, rim a little curved toward outside, rounded at edge, projecting in slightly thick edge over outside surface. H : 116; east side, on the rock.
7	2021	Jar; pear-shaped body, flat base. H : 116; 80 cm. under floor A (M-K Pl. LXXVII).
—	2217	Fragments of flat bases; fragments of widened necks. H : 116; on floor B.
8	2051	Jar: grey ware; three bands on body; neck broken. H : 116; on floor B (M-K Pl. LXXVII).
—	1579	Three horizontal handles with raised edge, thick, fragment of neck of jar with corded band; three rims of hole-mouths: (1) rounded; (2) (3) corded band. H : 129, above the rock.
—	2192	Fragment with decorative molding barely projecting resembling that of the jar found on floor B of room 116, but larger; rim of hole-mouth very greatly thickened over inside surface toward edge; fragment of thick base, grey ware speckled with grains of sand, friable material; fragment of grey ware with white slip. H : 136; above floor B.
—	2126	Fragments of jar; white lime slip; thick neck, white lime slip; various fragments with moldings some narrow and projecting, some larger and less projecting; well-formed brick; red stone (colored?). H : 136; above floor B.
9	1428a	Rim of hole-mouth: (1) even, not thickened. H : 120; above the rock (M-K Pl. LXXXIV).
10	1428g	Rims of hole-mouths: (6) thicker, without decoration, very inclined. H : 120; above the rock (M-K Pl. LXXXIV).
11	2149f	Rims of hole-mouths: (4) flat edge. H : 136–137; almost on floor B (M-K Pl. LXXXVII).
12	2321	Rim of hole-mouth, thick and bulging edge. H : 116; on floor B (M-K Pl. LXXXVII).
—	1462	Various fragments: rims of rounded hole-mouths; rounded base of small pot; fragment of horizontal handle, edged with folds. H : 120; under locus 7, south wall.
13	2193	Rim of hole-mouth very greatly thickened over inside surface toward edge. H : 136; floor B (M-K Pl. LXXXVII).
—	2463	Rim of hole-mouth, thick and heavy, somewhat swollen; rim of fine small bowl, rounded; glossy slip. H : 116; under floor B, intermediate.

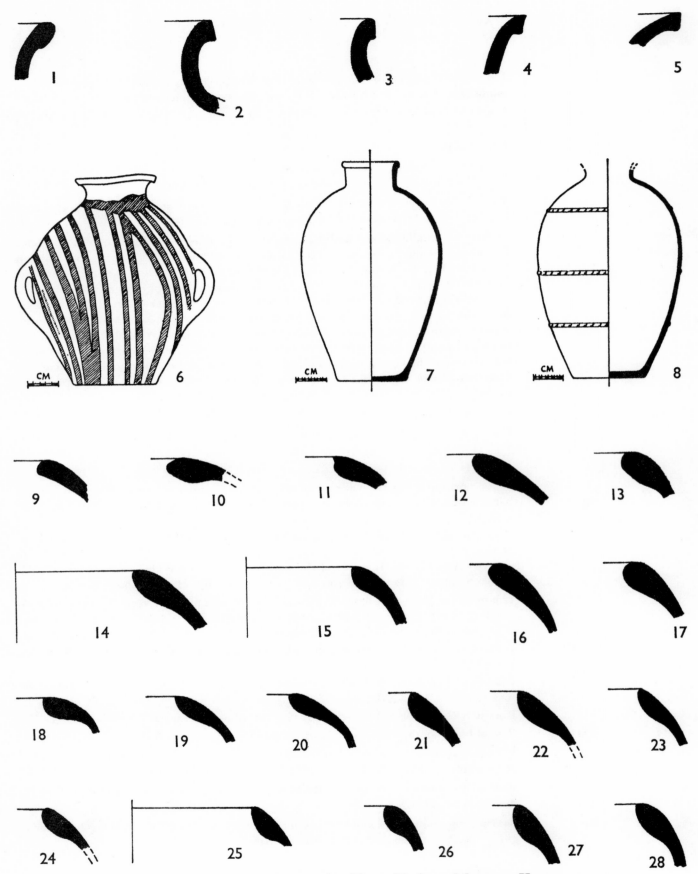

Fig. 57. Jars and hole-mouths, Phase V, from Marquet-Krause.

Fig. 57 No.	M-K Reg. No.	
14	2196a	Rims of hole-mouth: (1) thickened over inside surface. H : 136; floor B, lower (under the middle one) (M-K Pl. LXXXVII).
15	2164a	Rim of hole-mouth: somewhat thickened over the inside surface, rounded edge. H : 136; above floor B, after intermediate floor (M-K Pl. LXXXVII).
16	2512	Rim of hole-mouth, thick. H : 116; on floor II, under the niche of the south wall (M-K Pl. LXXXIV).
17	2196	Rim of hole-mouth: (4) thick, edge very rounded. H : 136; floor B, lower (under the middle one) (M-K Pl. LXXXIV).
18	2149e	Rim of hole-mouth: (5) edge with groove. H : 136–137; above floor B (M-K Pl. LXXXVII).
19	2196d	Rim of hole-mouth: grey ware with white grits; (3) very thin. H : 136; floor B, lower (under the middle one) (M-K Pl. LXXXVII).
20	2196c	Rim of hole-mouth: grey ware with white grits; (3) very thin. H : 136; floor B, lower (under the middle one) (M-K Pl. LXXXVII).
21	2164	Eight rims of hole-mouths; thin, or more often thickened over inside surface, rounded edge or slightly pointed; one has an incised line over outside surface; another, not thickened; another has on the outside surface near the edge an impression at right angle (thereby thinning the edge). H : 136; somewhat below floor B, after intermediate floor (M-K Pl. LXXXIV).
22	2164	See No. 21 above.
23	2626	Rim of hole-mouth. H : 116; under the niche, floor B (M-K Pl. LXXXIV).
24	2149	Rim of hole-mouth: (2) thin, in the form of a leaf. H : 136–137; above floor B (M-K Pl. LXXXIV).
25	2162	Rim of hole-mouth: (2) thickened over inside face; grey, white grits. H : 136; above floor B (M-K Pl. LXXXVII).
26	2232	Rim of hole-mouth: thickened and rounded edge. H : 116; on floor B (M-K Pl. LXXXIV).
27	2196	Rim of hole-mouth: (5) rounded edge and greatly thickened over inside surface. H : 136; floor B, lower (under the middle one) (M-K Pl. LXXXIV).
28	2164	See No. 21 above.

Fig. 58 No.	M-K Reg. No.	
1	2164b	Rim of hole-mouth: somewhat thickened over the inside surface, edge rounded, slightly pointed. H : 136; above floor B, after intermediate floor (M-K Pl. LXXXIV).
—	1446	Horizontal handle, edge raised in three points; rim of hole-mouth thickened over inside surface, sharp edge; fragments of bowls, type of flat base, wall slightly inclined, rim projecting over inside surface; (1) very large, (2) rim at right angle with inner wall. H : 128; locus 6 of west wall.
2	2196b	Rim of hole-mouth: (2) thickened over inside surface. H : 136; floor B, lower (under the middle one) (M-K Pl. LXXXVII).
3	2624	Rim of hole-mouth: (1) thin edge very much thickened over inside surface. H : 116; under the niche, on floor II (M-K Pl. LXXXVII).
4	2149d	Rim of hole-mouth: (3) very thickened. H : 136–137; above floor B (M-K Pl. LXXXIV).
5	1428	Rim of hole-mouth: (2) thin, edge thickened, decorated with incised line. H : 120; above the rock (M-K Pl. LXXXIV).
—	1468	Rims of hole-mouths with rounded edge; idem, on outside surface incised line bordered below by slight projection; idem, corded molding; fragments of neck: (1) simple, wide;

Fig. 58 No.	M-K Reg. No.	
		(2) wide, rim folded in pads over outside surface; fragment: white slip, bands of grey paint; fragment with decorative molding: (1) wavy; (2) corded or in semi-circular projections. H : 128; locus 7, west wall.
6	2024	Hole-mouth: flat base. H : 116; floor B (M-K Pl. LXXVII).
7	2009	Fragment of hole-mouth. H : 116; on floor B (M-K Pl. LXXXIV).
8	2164c	See 59 : 1 above. H : 136; above floor B, after intermediate floor (M-K Pl. LXXXVII).
—	1946	Fragments of two hole-mouths; grey ware. H : 116; sanctuary B I.
—	1947	Fragments of two hole mouths; grey ware. H : 116; sanctuary B I.
—	1965	Rim of hole-mouth; grey ware. H : 116; sanctuary B.
9	2203	Rim of hole-mouth: thickened over inside surface, thin edge; over outside surface incised line bordered below by a slight projection. H : 116; floor B (M-K Pl. LXXXIV).
10	2140	Fragment of hole-mouth; rim thickened over inside surface; sharp edge, light relief over outside surface. H : 116; floor B (M-K Pl. LXXXIV).
11	2197	Thin edge, very sharply flattened on outside surface, bounded by a projecting line. H : 116; on floor B, east side (M-K Pl. LXXXIV).
12	1428	Rim of hole-mouth: (7) very fine, edge somewhat flattened, belonging to a quite small hole-mouth.
—	2377	Fragments of hole-mouth, fine ware; fragment with molding. H : 116; floor B.
13	2009	Fragment of hole-mouth, thin wall, flat on inside surface, incised lines on outside surface; very fine grey material. H : 116; on floor B (M-K Pl. LXXVII).
14	2009	Fragment of hole-mouth. H : 116; on floor B (M-K Pl. LXXXVII).
15	1426	Rim of hole-mouth thickened over inside surface, wavy decorative molding with a projecting ridge above. H : 120; 30 cm. under stone table (M-K Pl. LXXXIV).
—	2119	Fragment with narrow and even molding; fragment of pot, material speckled with white grits. H : 116; floor B.
16	1428	Rim of hole-mouth: (4) rather thin slightly thickened over inside surface, decorated around rim with an incised line and with a button projecting in the form of a lozenge, placed lengthwise. H : 120; above the rock (M-K Pl. LXXXIV).
—	1577	Handle with raised edge; fragment of flat loop-handle; moldings: (1) with digital impressions; (2) even and projecting; fragment decorated with small horns in relief. H : 129; above the rock.
17	2197	Rim of hole-mouth: thin edge molding close to edge. H : 116; on floor B, east side (M-K Pl. LXXXII).
18	2197	Rim of hole-mouth: (1) decorative molding. H : 116; on floor B, east side (M-K Pl. LXXXII).
19	2140	Fragment of hole-mouth with projecting molding. H : 116; floor B (M-K Pl. LXXXII).
20	2263	Rim of hole-mouth: thin, thickened over inside surface, decorative molding. H : 116; on floor B, east side (M-K Pl. LXXXVII).
—	1472	Various fragments: rims of hole-mouths; one surrounded by decorative corded molding. H : 120; last stratum.
—	1544	Various fragments: horizontal handles; rims of hole-mouths, one with decorative corded molding; loop-handle, burnished. H : 120; last stratum.
21	2263a	Rim of hole-mouth: thin, thickened over inside surface, decorative molding. H : 116; on floor B, east side (M-K Pl. LXXXVII).
22	2385	Rim of hole-mouth: thick, long enlargement over inside surface, edge of rim thinned; wide wavy molding over outside surface. H : 116; floor B (M-K Pl. LXXXII).

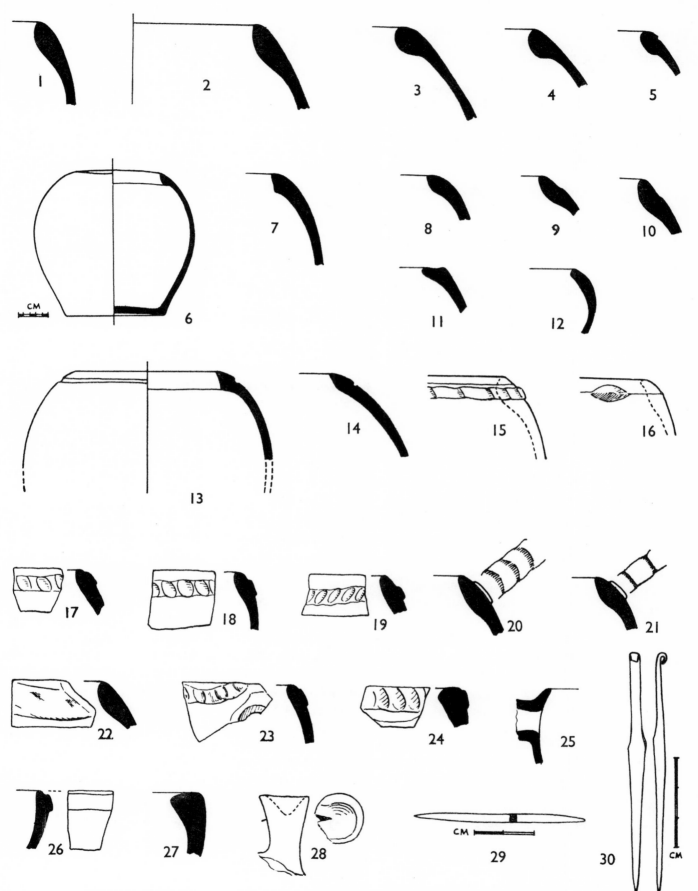

Fig. 58. Hole-mouth jars, spouts, objects, Phase V, from Marquet-Krause.

Fig. 58 No.	M-K Reg. No.	
23	2203	Rim of hole-mouth: thick edge with molding (and spout below rim). H:116; floor B (M-K Pl. LXXXII).
—	2218	Rims of hole-mouths: (1) thick and heavy, not swollen, molding close to edge; (2) heavy, not thickened; (3) thickened over inside surface. Fragment with very projecting molding. H:116; on floor B.
24	2203	Rim of hole-mouth: thick edge with molding. H:116; floor B (M-K Pl. LXXXII).
25	2149b	Thin rim of hole-mouth with spout. H:136–137; above floor B (M-K Pl. LXXXI).
—	1575	Fragment of bowl with spout, design on spout; fragment of bowl, horizontal rim: over outside edge thin striated cord; rims of hole-mouths more or less thickened: one very thickened over inside surface; incised line on outside surface; fragment: burnished with darker lines; folded horizontal handle; fragment of small juglet, burnished, with handle. H:132; locus 9, west wall.
26	2124II	Fragment of hole-mouth, very thin, narrow wavy molding. H:136; on floor II (M-K Pl. LXXXII).
27	2624	Thick rim of large bowl, grey ware, badly finished work. H:116; under the niche, on floor II (M-K Pl. LXXXII).
28	2193	Decorative spout not pierced, very high, rim slightly flared. H:136; floor B (M-K Pl. LXXXI).
—	2015	Flat horizontal handle; in three places: small depression, rim folded over at end of finger indentation. H:116; in the burned stratum, in the corner, 80 cm. under floor A (M-K Pl. XX).
—	2462	Horizontal handle, flat, edge turned up at end of indentations at three points (fold type I); fingerprints on interior surface; two broken horizontal handles, one very long still carries fingerprints on inside surface. H:116; under the niche of the south wall, floor B (under the intermediary).
—	2194	Flat horizontal handle. H:137; floor B.
—	1594	Various fragments, flat horizontal handle. H:128; above the rock (M-K Pl. XX).
—	1944	Two horizontal handles nearly triangular, outer edge turned up in three points. H:120; sanctuary B¹.
—	2323	Various fragments with white slip, rim of fine hole-mouth. H:116; under intermediate floor, on floor B.
29	2026	Needle, bronze. H:116; floor B (M-K Pl. XXXIX).
—	1949	Small needle, bronze. H:116; sanctuary B.
30	2291	Thinning needle, bronze. H:116, floor B (M-K Pl. LXXVII).
—	2018	Stone granite, cut in form of ring. H:116; 80 cm. under floor A.
—	2019	(a) Stone, basalt, cut in form of ring; (b) rim of bowl. H:116; 80 cm. under floor A.
—	2020	Stone, white, cut in form of ring. H:116; 80 cm. under floor A.
—	2050	Stone, basalt, fashioned and hollowed (mortar?); height, 16 cm.; diameter, 27 cm. H:116; on floor B.
—	2369	(a) Point of bone, flat, large and fine; (b) two flint blades.
—	2367	Five different flint blades. H:116; sanctuary B.
—	1950	Various fragments of flint knives. H:116; sanctuary B.
—	2025	Tools, flint. H:116; floor B.
—	2204	Various bones. H:116; floor B.

VII

PHASE VI, THE BUILDING A STRATUM

INTRODUCTION

As noted in the analysis of Section G–G, Fig. 7, the threshold of the passageway in Wall E[1] against Wall C eroded badly between the Phase V destruction and reconstruction of the site in Phase VI. Also Wall F[3] in Section I–I, Fig. 14, shows evidence of decay from exposure to rain and sun, with decayed mud-bricks spread over the debris in rooms adjacent to the wall. Considerable time elapsed, therefore, at Site A between the destruction of Building B in Phase V and the construction of Building A in Phase VI. How much time passed in the interval is difficult to ascertain, but a period of twenty to forty years seems reasonable in view of the present-day rate of deterioration of excavated sites.

Reconstruction of the city at Ai in Phase VI proceeded slowly for two apparent reasons. First, the Phase V city seems to have been totally destroyed. Building B at Site A was a complete ruin, with stubs of walls protruding through the debris of collapsed roofs and overturned brick walls. The acropolis also was an uninhabitable ruin. Wall B, the curved outer enclosure of the building complex, tilted outward and the upper half collapsed, leaving 1 meter of wall and roof materials on the floor inside (see Callaway 1965, 33. Fig. 13 is a photograph of the fallen debris inside Wall B, the curved outer wall drawn in Fig. 12, p. 32). Houses excavated at Site C in the lower city were apparently shaken down in the same destruction, because brick walls in Area I were either tilted at a precarious angle, or overturned and lying in semi-articulated masses over and among the fallen roof materials (*ibid.*, p. 28). The destruction was thorough enough to prevent the reuse of any building discovered by the present expedition, so the Phase VI inhabitants at Ai were faced with the mammoth task of completely rebuilding the city. The order of priorities in the reconstruction apparently left Building A at Site A near the end of the process, accounting for the evidence of abandonment and erosion.

Second, there is evidence of Egyptian involvement in rebuilding the city in Phase VI. The evidence is two-fold, related to the acropolis and sanctuary site. First, there are construction features in Temple A at the acropolis which are understood best if attributed to Egyptian craftsmen. Foremost among these features are the raised-top column bases of Temple A, which superseded the flat-top bases of Buildings C and B. The sharply defined rectangular top of the Phase VI bases was shaped by sawing four thin grooves 3 centimeters deep in the top of large, flat stones to form a rectangle. After the sawing was completed, all stone outside the grooves was chipped away to the bottom of the cut, leaving the center rectangle 3 centimeters above the base (see *ibid.*, p. 36, Fig. 15). Copper saws capable of shaping the raised-top bases are known in Egypt from the reign of Zer in the First Dynasty. A cache of six saws was found in Tomb 3471 at Saqqara, in Box 2, Room 5, by Emery (1949, 19, Pl. 5B).

Another feature is the manner of construction of the 2-meter wide wall of hammer-dressed stones, laid in mud mortar like bricks. This unique way of building a wall of stones without a rubble core is

Egyptian, dating to the beginning of the Third Dynasty. The technique is evident in the Tomb of Hesy, built of mud bricks faced with plaster (Quibell 1913, Pl. IV:1, 2) and the pyramid complex of Zoser (Firth and Quibell 1935, Pl. 73). Quibell notes that the core of the temenos wall enclosing the pyramid is made of 'coursed rubble masonry of local limestone set in clay' and that the facing is 'fine paneled masonry of white silicious limestone from the quarries at Tura' (1935, 1).

The Tomb of Hesy has brick walls faced with plaster, like the stone walls of the Phase VI temple on the acropolis. Mud mortar like that between the bricks of the core is spread over the face of the wall, and plaster covers the mortar, leaving a fine white finish which is decorated with painted designs (Quibell 1913, Pl. IV: 2).The plaster covering the Phase VI temple walls at Ai is in three layers, consisting of a base of the same grey mud used between the stones, an intermediate layer of red clay, or *khamra*, mixed with straw, and a final layer of thin, white *huwwar* (Callaway 1965, 38, Fig. 16). Black patches of plaster photographed by Marquet-Krause (1949, Pl. VI:2) suggest that the Phase VI temple walls were decorated with a painted design.

The Phase VI temple walls are, therefore, typically Egyptian core structures dating to the beginning of the Third Dynasty, and the plastered finish covering the walls is Egyptian-influenced also. The same plaster is applied in a thicker layer from the walls to the column, or pilaster, bases, making a floor of exceptional quality.

The second evidence of Egyptian involvement consists of the imported alabaster and stone vessels found in the ruins of Sanctuary A, or Phase VIII of the present report. Phase VIII is the terminal phase of Sanctuary A, which was built in Phase VII. The Egyptian vessels were installed, therefore, in the Phase VII remodeling of Building A, when the building was made into a sanctuary. The vessels themselves have been associated with First and Second Dynasty parallels in Egypt, so they must have been brought to Ai in Phase VI, not Phase VII, and were transferred to Sanctuary A in Phase VII (see Amiran 1970, 177).

No remains of broken alabaster or stone vessels were found in the construction layers of Building A, Phase VI, or the remodeled walls and floors which changed Building A into Sanctuary A in Phase VII. Building A preserves no evidence of being the repository of the cultic vessels in Phase VI. However, two large alabaster bowls like those from Sanctuary A were found in Temple A of the acropolis, the Phase VI structure with the raised-top column bases and elaborately finished plastered walls and floors. Amiran examined the bowl fragments and original field records (in Hebrew) and confirmed that Bowl No. 514+692 is from ch. 42 and Bowl No. 344+399 is from ch. 22 of Fouille G, the acropolis (1970, 177). The provenance of No. 344 is given in the French publication (Marquet-Krause 1949, 53) as Fouille D, but the original records in Hebrew indicate that the provenance is Fouille G, where matching piece No. 399 was found (see Amiran 1970, 177 n. 25).

Temple A at the acropolis, constructed in Phase VI, seems, therefore, to be a sanctuary dating to the beginning of EB IIIA. This view is supported by Amiran (1970, 179). Wright advocates the view that the acropolis buildings constitute a temple complex in all periods, and that Sanctuary A was a storage house for the temple vessels in Phase VII, and not a sanctuary (Wright 1970, 306). His proposals are based upon a comparative study of the acropolis building plans, arrived at before the stratigraphy of Sites A and D was completely worked out for final reports. Wright's view is, therefore, compatible with the present conclusions, with minor modifications.

In any case, the association of the Egyptian vessels with the Phase VI acropolis building reinforces the interpretation of Egyptian involvement in rebuilding the city at Ai in Phase VI, and accounts for the lack of interest in rebuilding Site A until fairly late in the reconstruction program. Arranged in an order of strategic priorities, the construction of Building A may be placed in the following sequence of Phase VI components of the city:

1. Construction of City Wall A, a 4-meter wide fortification of stone built against the outside of Wall B around the entire city. Concurrent with this, Tower A was built at Site A before Building A was constructed; the Corner Gate at Site K was blocked and a square (or rectangular) tower seems to have been built over the round tower of Phase IV; the Wadi Gate at Site J was rebuilt as a minor entrance and fortified with a long oval tower on top of the wall (see Callaway 1970, 20, Fig. 8) as well as a projecting square tower on the north side of the gate. A major Phase VI gate was constructed in Wall A at Site C, the lower city, located in Area V (see Callaway 1969, 11, Fig. 7; the wall designated B is now Wall A, because Wall B of Phase IV was found to be the 5.50-meter wide structure designated C in Fig. 6, p. 10, Wall C of Phase III is a 5-meter wide fortification underneath Wall B, first detected but inaccurately reported in Callaway 1965, 28).

2. The acropolis was completely rebuilt, and the inner rectangular Temple A was constructed with unique architectural features unmatched in previous phases. This building seems to have been the Phase VI sanctuary, furnished with a lavish collection of imported Egyptian alabaster and stone cult vessels which were moved to Sanctuary A in Phase VII.

3. A large paved reservoir capable of storing 1815 cubic meters of rainwater was constructed inside the blocked Corner Gate at Site K, providing an emergency water supply inside the walls of the Phase VI city (see Callaway 1970, 29, Fig. 16).*

4. Building A of Site A was constructed against the inner face of Tower A after completion of the city wall and fortification tower, possibly several years afterward.

The entire rebuilding of the city took considerable time, therefore, because of the magnitude of the task, and because continuing interaction with Egypt throughout the project seems to be required. Alongside the important components of the city at other sites, Building A at Site A appears relatively unimportant in Phase VI. The house in Areas II–III, however, is larger than a normal residence, suggesting that a prominent citizen lived there.

BUILDING A OF PHASE VI

Until 1964, there was no distinction between Sanctuary A of Phase VII and Building A of Phase VI, both of which are EB III buildings. The first evidence of Building A was the blocked passageway in Wall M, against Tower A, reported in 1965 (Callaway 1965, 23, Fig. 5), and shown in Pl. XVIII.1, 4. Analysis of the Master Section, Fig. 83, indicated two phases also, the first of which preceded installation of Altar J, a Phase VII structure. Correlation of the Master Section, Fig. 83, and Section B–B, Fig. 11, supported this distinction between Phases VI and VII because Enclosure 136, drawn in Fig. 5, was built against the Phase VII blockage of the passageway in Wall M. Enclosures 131 and

* **Dr. George R. Glenn**, School of Engineering, Rutgers University, studied the reservoir and calculated its capacity in an unpublished report to the National Geographic Society, Washington, D.C., in 1970.

137, Fig. 5, were assigned to Phase VII because they seemed to be contemporary structures with Altar J and its Enclosure 133, and Enclosure 136 against the blocked passageway in Wall M.

Further support for the identification of two EB III phases was found in renewed exploration of the citadel complex in 1968 and 1970. Tower A was found to be associated with Wall A, a new fortification erected in Phase VI around the entire city. In Phase VII, Tower A was reinforced at the north end by construction of Buttress A[1], drawn in Fig. 87, and an additional 4-meter wide city fortification, Wall A[1], was built against the outside of Wall A, beginning in Area VII of Site A and continuing across the south side of the city to Site K. The Phase VII addition was traced also in Site H on the east side (see Callaway 1970, 25, Fig. 13, and p. 26), and to the Wadi Gate at Site J (*ibid.*, p. 21, Fig. 9).

Building A, therefore, is a part of the significant EB IIIA Phase VI city at Ai, preceding the re-modeling in Phase VII, or EB IIIB, which converted the building into Sanctuary A.

The courtyard in Area III

The irregular shape and size of Area III, and its special installations, suggest that it is the court-yard of a house with an associated room in Area II. The rooms in Area IV are oriented toward a passageway alongside Tower A, or an open area east of Wall O.

Both the shape and size of Area III seem to make it unsuitable for a roof structure. Walls H and M are not parallel, and the distance between them at Tower A is 7.5 meters. Also Wall L and Tower A are not parallel, and the distance alongside Wall H is 8.5 meters. A span of about 3 meters is the maximum feasible space between roof-support pillars, so Area III would require at least two rows of pillars if the entire area were covered by a roof. No evidence of either pillars or bases is re-ported from the Marquet-Krause excavations. The absence of positive evidence of a roof, and the unusual shape and size of the area, seem to warrant the conclusion that it was not covered by a roof.

One special installation, Platform N[1], seems to be a fireplace, supporting the conclusion that Area III is a courtyard. A few stones of the platform are visible underneath Bin N in the lower right center of Pl. XVII, and in Pl. XIV of Marquet-Krause 1949. Bin N is a Phase VII structure, and Platform N[1] is Phase VI, constructed over Firepit N[2] of Phase IV as drawn in Sections C–C and D–D, Figs. 12 and 13. The Phase IV tradition of a fireplace seems to continue in Phase VI, and the courtyard tradition also continues, but the enclosure is in a different form.

There are possibly two other special installations in the courtyard. The stone base of Wall H at the entrance, shown in Pl. XX.2, seems to be integral with a row of stones leading north of Wall H at a right angle, under the Phase VII wall of Enclosure 133. This row of stones possibly borders a low, earth-filled platform in the southwest corner of the area, as drawn in Fig. 86. The function of the platform is not clear, because the row of stones bordering it was removed in 1934, and the Phase VII altar outlined in Fig. 86 was left intact in 1964. Objects from the area of the platform include scattered pieces of the platter in Fig. 59:27 and several of the small bowls in Fig. 59.

Apparently associated with the stone border of the platform is the other installation, a horseshoe-shaped enclosure of stones shown in Pl. XX.2. There is a gap between the end of the enclosure and the row of stones leading to Wall H where stones connecting the enclosure with the platform apparently were removed. Nothing of the enclosure remained from the 1934 excavation, and no artifacts can be associated with it. The enclosure appears to be a silo for storage of food, a common courtyard installation.

Two definite passageways lead from Area III to more confined and regular-shaped areas on the north and south. The entrance in Wall H, shown in Pl. XIV of Marquet-Krause 1949 and drawn in Fig. 86, seems to be suitable for a door. This suggests that Area II was a living area for a family, and that Area III was their courtyard. The north passage in Wall M, however, is 1.5 meters wide, which is too wide for a door. This passage may be a major exit for Building A, leading alongside Tower A to another possible Phase VI passage in the undesignated wall in Fig. 86 (Wall q in Pl. XCIII of Marquet-Krause 1949). The location and nature of the passageways on either side of Area III seem to support the conclusion that it was a common area serving as a courtyard for the occupants of the large room in Area II and possibly those in Area IV.

The room in Area II

Wall E on the south side of Area II is reconstructed on the evidence of fragments preserved on top of Wall E^1, drawn in Section H–H, Fig. 8, and the plans and photographs in Marquet-Krause 1949. Wall E^1, a Phase IV structure, remained standing after the Phase V destruction of Building B, and water eroded a deep gulley in the E^1 passageway between the time of the Phase V destruction and the erection of Building A in Phase VI.

The first operation in construction of the room in Area II was to fill the gulley in the Phase IV passage in Wall E^1 as indicated in Section G–G, Fig. 7, after which the blockage of stones designated E^2 was installed in the passage. Blockage E^2 is shown in Pl. VI.3, in the upper right of the photograph. Comparison of Section G–G with Pl. VI.3 enables the reader to follow the outline of Blockage E^2 as interpreted in the section. Facing stones in the original passage are laid horizontally with the outer edge perpendicular, while the stones of Blockage E^2 are angled in the first courses. Apparently, the passageway was blocked and fill was deposited in the eroded corner of the area before Wall E was constructed on the upper remains of Wall E^1 and the fill inside the Phase IV wall.

Wall E is oriented parallel with Wall H, as drawn in Fig. 86, and therefore diverges from the course of Wall E^1. The orientation with Wall H seems to have designed the room for a roof requiring one row of support pillars from east to west, between Wall P and Tower A. No evidence of partitions subdividing the room appears in the photographs, but the charred remains of one pillar were found in the center of the Phase VII room, in front of the Wall H door, as shown in Pl. XIV of Marquet-Krause 1949. This pillar was evocative of an *asherah* to Père Vincent in view of the sanctuary furnishings (Vincent 1937, 249), but Marquet-Krause seems to have accepted his interpretation reluctantly (1949, 18). Since the pillar was burned to charcoal, the 1.25 meter length of surviving fragments does not necessarily represent its original dimensions. It could, therefore, have been a roof-support pillar with an original length of 1.60 to 1.80 meters.

The original Wall E of Phase VI seems to be the southernmost of the two small walls between Rooms 116 and 140 drawn in Marquet-Krause 1949, Pl. XCIII. The same wall is visible in the extreme left side of Pl. XIII:2 of Marquet-Krause 1949, and is outlined in Pl. C. In Pl. XIII:2, Wall E continues under the undesignated Phase VII enclosure of the 'stairs,' and is likely what is designated as the stairs. The two courses of stones in the lower left of the photograph seem to be a continuation of the wall, and the third course, running underneath the Phase VII addition to Wall E inside Area II, as drawn in Fig. 87, is the surviving top of Wall E[1]. Wall E, therefore, is located as drawn in Fig. 86, and is comparable in width to Walls P and H.

A feature of the room in Area II common to EB houses is the 'banquette,' or bench constructed against Walls P and H. Wall P is constructed over the outer edge of Phase IV Wall P[1], leaving the inner side of Wall P[1] projecting above floor level to the height of a bench. A similar bench is evident alongside Wall H in Pl. XIII: 1, 2 (Marquet-Krause 1949), and possibly the north side of Wall E[1], exposed on the inside of Wall E as noted above, served as a bench also in the southeast corner of the area. The 'stairs' of Marquet-Krause 1949, Pl. XCIII belong in Phase VII. Photographs indicate that the identification as stairs is questionable, and an alternate reconstruction of the south entrance to Sanctuary A will be presented in the next chapter.

One further observation about the room in Area II concerns the entrance to the room. The door in Wall H is definite, leading to the courtyard in Area III. No positive evidence of another door survived the 1934 excavations, but two possibilities seem evident from the photographs and plans. The first is, of course, the 'stairs' mentioned above. Since the stairs seem to be the top inner and outer courses of Wall E, enclosed by a Phase VII wall built over Phase VI Wall E, an entrance at this point is untenable in Phase VI however.

The second possibility is the narrow opening between Wall E and Wall C designated Locus 135 by Marquet-Krause in Pls. XCIII and C. Entrances were located at this place in Buildings C and B, and it is possible that a small 'back door' to the Room in Area II continued the tradition. The Phase VII bin of Sanctuary A in Room 116 would have been formed by blocking this small door to the Phase VI room.

The room in Area II seems to be therefore, a private residence oriented toward the courtyard in Area III. It is rather large, requiring at least one roof-support pillar, and apparently a single room without permanent partitions. In a room the size of Area II, however, temporary partitions of cloth or skins could have been used without leaving any trace.

The north rooms in Area IV

Possibly two rooms in Area IV were a part of Building A in Phase VI. The passage in Wall M against Tower A was open, connecting the south unit in Areas II–III with Area IV as drawn in Fig. 86. Reconstruction of the north unit of rooms and their function is largely conjectured because only traces of the south end of Wall O remained in Area IV. Marquet-Krause Wall q, drawn in Fig. 5, had been removed. The following observations, however, seem to be supported by available evidence in photographs and the reconstruction of the south unit presented above.

First, the two rooms separated by Wall O in Area IV seem to be a distinct unit, separate from the rooms of the south unit. Two possible passages in Area IV favor this interpretation. The first passage seems to be a door in Wall O against Wall M, as drawn in Fig. 86, leading into the east room of the area. A straight vertical facing in Wall O at the conjectured location appears to be the side of a door in Pls. XIII: 2 and XXI: 2 of Marquet-Krause 1949. The gap in the north end of Wall O, drawn in Pls. XCIII and C of Marquet-Krause 1949 is irregular in shape, and appears to be the result of digging through the wall by either Garstang or Marquet-Krause.

The second passage is purely conjectural, but seems to be required in the west end of Wall q of Marquet-Krause 1949 against Tower A. The photograph in Pl. XXI: 2 of Marquet-Krause

1949 shows Wall q widened against Buttress A¹ very much like the widened end of Wall M against Tower A. The latter is the result of blocking the Wall M passage and buttressing Tower A with Wall M in Phase VII. Buttress A¹ of Phase III probably was constructed in an open passage at the west end of Wall q, and the remaining part of the opening was blocked, forming a buttress against the weakened tower with Wall q, on the analogy of Wall M. In Phase VI, however, an open passage in Wall q against Tower A probably existed. This would have been the major exit from Building A to the city in Phase VI. The two rooms in Area IV seem to be oriented toward this exit, and not toward the courtyard in Area III.

The second observation concerns the relationship and functions of the Area IV rooms. If a passageway to Area III from Wall q existed alongside Tower A, the west room in Area IV probably is a small courtyard. The area is much smaller than the courtyard in Area III, but it is large enough for a small family. The room east of Wall q seems to be small also, although the east wall of the room could have been located beyond the line of Wall L in Fig. 86. A small offset eastward from the corner of Walls L and M would provide space for a covered room without roof-support pillars. The niche in the east side of Wall O, located in Fig. 86, is probably a place for a lamp inside the room, analogous to the niche in the west wall of the Phase VI acropolis building. This contained a small bowl which must have served as a lamp (see Marquet-Krause 1949, Pl. VIII:3).

The north unit of two rooms in Area IV, therefore, seems to consist of Wall q, a small living room on the east side of Wall q, and a small courtyard facing the passageway alongside Tower A west of Wall q. The unit is a smaller version of the large living room-courtyard south unit in Areas II–III.

Conclusions

Two significant conclusions regarding the nature and purpose of Building A emerge in the preceding study, and both contribute to understanding of the political and religious situation at Ai in Phase VI.

First, there is the new evidence of an EB IIIA phase preceding Sanctuary A. This evidence of Building A was found in the analysis of sections at Site A, and is supported by the identification of two EB III city wall phases at the citadel and at Site C. Four major building phases are identified at Site A, the third of which is Building A of Phase VI, and four EB city wall phases at the citadel relate to the building phases.

Second, Building A has the characteristics of a domestic complex of two living units, and no evidence that it was a sanctuary preceding Sanctuary A in Phase VII can be identified. The first living unit consists of a large single room in Area II, requiring at least one roof-support pillar and an associated open courtyard in Area III where a fire-place and storage silo are located. A second unit is in Area IV, where there is a smaller room and possibly a small courtyard on the west side of Wall O facing Tower A. The major entrance to the Building A complex is alongside Tower A in Area IV, through the passageway in Wall M and probably a second passage in Wall q of Marquet-Krause 1949, located against Tower A before Buttress A¹ of Phase VII was constructed.

The implications of these conclusions bear upon an understanding of the political situation at Ai in Phase VI. First, the presence of two Egyptian alabaster bowls in what seems to be a Phase VI context at the acropolis implies that a temple was built there in Phase VI, which explains the absence of any cultic evidence at Site A during the same phase. Second, the extensive evidence of Egyptian involvement in constructing and furnishing the temple implies a relationship which is more intimate than one would expect in purely commercial agreements. This evidence is found at the seat of power in the rebuilt city, and it follows an unprecedented disaster which left the city in ruins, and presumably bankrupt. Egyptian involvement in rebuilding the acropolis and temple, and re-establishing the city in Phase VI, implies political as well as commercial relationships, and the presence of an Egyptianized temple at the acropolis instead of Site A reinforces this conclusion.

THE PHASE VI POTTERY AND OBJECTS

Provenance

The pottery and objects drawn in Figs. 59–66 were excavated in Layers 2–4 of the sections discussed in Chapter II. Layer 4 consists of the earth and decayed building materials from the Phase V destruction; but it also contains the earliest Phase VI artifacts. Natural forces redistributed the Phase V debris during the period of abandonment noted earlier. Rebuilding of the city walls and acropolis began prior to reconstruction of Site A, and Tower A in particular appears to have been built when Layer 4 was being shaped. In Sections B–B and E–E, Figs. 11 and 10, Layer 4 is against the base of Tower A, indicating that the layer fills the Tower A foundation trench, and, therefore, dates its construction.

Layer 3 seems to be Phase V and later accumulated materials redistributed artificially to level the site for construction of Building A. Artifacts in this layer would include more items belonging specifically to Phase VI. Layer 2 is the immediate Building A structure itself, including some earlier remains gathered up in making the floors and walls.

The Phase VI assemblage is arranged by forms, without distinctions among Layers 2–4. Layer distinctions can be obtained, however, by consulting the following discussion of provenance and referring to the provenance code listed with the descriptions. The discussion of provenance is organized by units of the Building A complex noted in the interpretation of the building.

The south wall of the room in Area II. Pottery was obtained from the following three components of the south wall of Building A:

1. Wall E. Layer 1.2 in the pottery listings is the fragmentary remnant of Wall E, drawn in Section H–H, Fig. 8, and located in the sketch plan in Fig. 82. This corresponds to Layer 2 in the Master Section, because it consists of the construction materials of the wall itself, i.e., earthen base and mortar of the field stones.

2. Blockage E². Layer 1.2c is the silty deposit in the Wall E¹ passage underneath the Phase VI blockage, E², drawn in Section G–G, Fig. 7. Silt accumulated during the period between the Phase V destruction and Phase VI blockage of the passage. The layer is assigned to Phase VI because it belongs in Layer 4 of the section sequences. Phase VI activity in building Wall A and Tower A was carried on prior to installation of Blockage E² in the open passage. Artifacts from the E² blockage itself are designated 1.2b, and, therefore, immediately precede 1.2, the Wall E structure erected on top of Wall E¹ and Blockage E².

3. Terrace Wall D. Layer 1.2 is from the fragmentary Wall D in Area I, apparently a small terrace wall constructed against the outer face of Wall E on the south side, and on top of ashy

earth from the Phase V destruction. Pottery in this layer is a mixture from Phase V and Phase VI, because the ashy base of Wall D was excavated with the wall. It belongs in Layer 2 of the section designations because Wall D itself was removed along with its foundation layer.

The room in Area II. Fragmentary remains of the room in Area II were preserved on the north and east sides only, along Walls H and P, and may be located in Section E–E, Fig. 10, and the sketch plan in Fig. 82.

Layer 4 is rubbly brown ashy earth covering the remains of Wall Q in Section E–E, and resting against the inside of Wall P[1] on the east side of Area II. The layer consists of two designations from the field book. No. 101.6 is the rubbly brown earth reaching from the top of Wall Q eastward to Wall P[1]. This layer seems to have covered the Phase V ruins uniformly across the area. No. 101.7 is taken from the foundation trench of Tower A, visible in Pl. IV.2 on the right side of the meter scale, and in Pl. V.2, there is a closer view on the left of the 25 centimeter scale. The construction of Tower A preceded Building A by a considerable period, as noted earlier, but occurred in Phase VI, after the Phase V destruction.

Layer 3 is the make-up under Walls H and P in Area II. Following the construction of Tower A and Wall A, the site was prepared for the floors and walls of Building A. This layer is found under Walls H and P as ashy earth mixed with pebbles and larger stones. No. 101.4 is the designation of Layer 3 from the base of the entrance in Wall H westward to Tower A, and No. 101.3 is the same layer eastward from the entrance to Wall P. No. 101.2a is the fill underneath Wall P along the east side of Area II, continuing Layer 3 toward the south from Wall H toward Wall E.

Layer 2 is the construction materials of Walls H and P in Area II. No. 101.2 designates artifacts taken from Wall H, and 101.2a is from Wall P on the east side of the area.

The courtyard in Area III. Most of the Phase VI remains of Building A are found in Area III, located in four sub-areas. No. 201 is the southwest corner of the courtyard, including the fill and stone-lined platform under Altar J of Phase VII. The sub-area along the Wall M balk, across the north side of the courtyard, is designated 202, but all of the 202 layers excavated south of the balk belong in Phase V or earlier. The balk itself is assigned to Area IV and therefore carries numbers in the 300 series. These are a part of the courtyard because they designate artifacts from Wall M and its fill underneath. No. 203 is the southeast corner of the area, around Fireplace N[1], and 204 is along the Wall H balk between Fireplace N[1] and Altar J. These locations with field designations of layers are found in Fig. 82.

Layer 4 in sub-area 201 is rubbly brown to grey-brown fill with field designations 201.2, 2a, 9, 9a, and 16. The numbers are not in sequence because the lowest numbers, 2 and 2a, represent the layers identified in shaping the north side of the Altar J balk, shown in Pl. IX.1 beside the meter scale. An irregular balk supported the large stones at the top of the altar, and angled outward, to the right of the meter scale, toward bedrock in the lower right side of the photograph. Layer 4 is the grey rubbly fill above the calcined stones beside Wall Q, as drawn in Fig. 83, and to the top of the ruins of Wall Q.

201.9 and 9a designate the same layer in the new sequence of layers from top to bottom on the front side of the altar balk. The series ran from 201.1 at the top to 201.6 on the bottom of the north side of the altar balk, and from 201.7 to 201.12a on the east, or front, side of the same balk.

No. 201.16 is part of a third series of layer numbers on the front side, assigned when the projecting balk in front of the altar shown in Pl. XVII was removed, leaving the front as shown in Pl. IX.1.

Layer 4 in Sections C–C and D–D covers the ruins of Wall F and Firepit N^2 of Phase V, as drawn in Figs. 12 and 13. The layer here consists of brownish to grey ashy earth mixed with stony rubble. No. 204.6 is the field designation of Layer 4 under the door in Wall H, and westward to the Altar J balk. The same layer between the door and Fireplace N^1 is designated 204.1, because it was the first part of the sub-area excavated. In the Fireplace N^1 balk drawn in Section D–D, this layer is No. 203.4, a continuation over the Phase V firepit, but much thinner than that on the west side of the courtyard.

In Section B–B, Fig. 11, the 300 series of field numbers is assigned to the Wall M balk as noted above. Layer 4 is against the base of Tower A, as in Section E–E, Fig. 10, indicating that it is contemporary with the founding of the tower. The earth is bricky to grey ashy in color, and consists of much decayed material from the stump of Wall F^3, a brick structure originally built in Phase III, and destroyed in Phase V. Between the base of Tower A and Wall F^3, as drawn in Sections B–B, Fig. 11, and I–I, Fig. 14, Layer 4 has the field designation 300.11 for the lower part, on the bedline separating it from Layer 5, and 300.9b for the upper part, below the Layer 3 bedline. On the east side of the area, the same layer is designated 300.10a for the lower part, and 300.10 for the upper part.

Layer 3, the immediate make-up for constructing Building A is also bricky to grey ashy in Section B–B, Fig. 11. This layer is against Tower A, indicating that the tower was already constructed and Layer 4 had accumulated, or was placed, against its base as shown in Sections B–B and E–E. The field number assigned to Layer 3 in the Wall M balk is 300.9a. A part of Layer 3 was excavated as 300.9 east of Wall F^3, but the lower part of Layer 2 was also given this number, so all of the 300.9 artifacts are assigned to Layer 2.

Layer 3 in the Altar J balk, drawn in Fig. 83, is also a grey ashy fill redistributed to level the southwest corner of the area against Tower A for construction of Wall H. Field numbers assigned to the layer are 201.1b, 201.8, 8a, and 201.15. The same layer in the Wall H balk, Section C–C, Fig. 12, is designated No. 200.1a between the door in Wall H and Altar J, and 200.1b east of the door, to Fireplace N^1. In Section D–D, Fig. 13, Layer 3 is No. 203.3 under Fireplace N^1.

Layer 2 is the designation of the Building A structures and foundation materials, as noted above. Fireplace N^1 is No. 203.2, and the stone-bordered platform under Altar J opposite Fireplace N^1 in the courtyard is Nos. 201.1, 201.7a, and 201.10. This includes the *huwwar* surface on top of Layer 2, and under Layer 1 of Phase VII, drawn in Fig. 83, and evident on top of the projecting balk in Pl. XVII. Wall H between Tower A and Fireplace N^1 is designated No. 204.4. Layer 2 in the Wall M balk, on the north side of the courtyard is a part of the north unit of rooms in Area IV, and is described below.

The north unit in Area IV. Layers 4 and 3 carry the same numbers noted in connection with the courtyard, with the addition of the first 300 series numbers assigned in the initial straightening of the balk drawn in Section I–I, Fig. 14. No. 300.3 is assigned to Layer 4 between Wall F^3 and Tower A, the equivalent of 300.9b; and No. 300.4 is the east half of the layer, equivalent to 300.10a. Layer 3 is No. 300.2, equivalent to 300.9a against Tower A, and 300.5, equivalent to the same on the east side of Wall F^3.

Layer 2 in the Wall M balk in Area IV is No. 300.1a, the foundation of Wall M, and Wall M itself is 3001.b. No. 300.1a is the equivalent of 300.9. The layers were given a new series of designations when the balk was removed, beginning with 300.7, 7a, and 8 for the Phase VII blockage of Wall M, drawn in Fig. 14.

Layers 3 and 2 are found in the Wall O balk, dividing the two rooms of the north unit. The former is designated 301.3, continuing 300.9a under the fragmentary remains of Wall O, and the latter, Wall O itself, is designated 301.2.

The Phase VI pottery forms

The meager yield of Phase VI pottery is drawn in Figs. 59–66, and the few pieces from Marquet-Krause 1949 attributable to Phase VI are in Fig. 67. The latter pieces are assigned to Phase VI because the provenance is given as 'under floor A,' 'between floors A and B,' or other indication that it is not on top of the Sanctuary A floor. Descriptions of pieces not drawn, but attributable to Phase VI for the same reasons as the drawn pieces, are included in the listing under apparently similar drawn pieces.

Small to medium bowls. The shallow medium bowl forms characteristic of Phase V continue in Phase VI with little variation, but small hemispherical bowls are scarce. In fact, the latter, represented in Fig. 59:11, may be a Phase V form appearing in Phase VI because of the redistribution of fill materials in preparation for constructing Building A. One significant new medium bowl form appears, and is drawn in Fig. 59:9. This is a shallow bowl similar to Phase V forms except that it has a distinct base, often string-cut.

The same bowl form appears in the acropolis building as a possible lamp in a niche of the inner wall (see photograph in Marquet-Krause 1949, Pl. VIII:3, and drawing, Pl. LXV:893). The form becomes very common in Sanctuary A, Phase VIII, evident in the eleven bowls recovered in Area III, and drawn in Fig. 79:2–12. The string-cut base form does not appear at Arad, and Hennessy does not report instances from Areas E III–IV at Jericho. However, it is a common form at Jericho in Tombs D12 (Kenyon 1960, 97, Fig. 33:17–18; 110, Fig. 36:8), F3 (*ibid.*, 149, Fig. 51:14), F2 (*ibid.*, 158, Fig. 67:27), F5 (*ibid.*, 172, Fig. 64:1–2), A114(B) (*ibid.*, 175, Fig. 67:7–9), and Garstang's Tomb A (1932, Pl. IV:4). North of Ai, the form is found at Megiddo on the *tell* (Shipton 1939, Chart, Strata XVI–XVII:17; XVIII:14), and in Tomb 1101–2 Lower (Guy 1938, Pl. VI:21, No. P4126 drawn, P4134 not drawn).

This form seems to have developed in Egypt during the first two dynasties as a pottery copy of stone and alabaster dishes. It is Emery's Class 32 of pottery vessels from the Archaic Period (1961, 209, Fig. 122:32), possibly developed in the Saqqara area. Similar forms with more upright angular walls are found in Tomb 3477 of the Second Dynasty, excavated by Emery (1962, 11, Fig. II:6, 10), and almost identical forms in alabaster and slate are found in First and Second Dynasty tombs at Saqqara excavated by Quibell (1923, Pl. XIV:5, 7, 9, 10, 14).

A second new bowl form is drawn in Fig. 60:11. This is imitation Khirbet Kerak ware, the first to appear at Site A. The example cited is from Layer 2 of the Wall M balk, Field No. 300.9, the make-up under Wall M, and, therefore, the construction phase of Building A. Exemplar forms are found at Jericho in Tomb D12 (Kenyon 1960, 119, Fig. 38:29–30) and in Beth-shan XII (Fitzgerald 1935, Pl. VIII:4). One local imitation occurs at Jericho in Tomb F4 (Kenyon 1960, 130, Fig. 43:21), suggesting the popularity of the new pottery forms with local potters.

The deep bowl, or krater, drawn in Fig. 60:8 also seems to be imitation Khirbet Kerak ware, almost identical with a bowl rim reported by Marquet-Krause from ch. 93 of Fouille V (1949, 144, No. 1261), and identified as a Khirbet Kerak ware form by Amiran (1967, 186). Ch. 93 is adjacent to Site C, where one authentic Khirbet Kerak ware sherd was found in the final EB III remains in 1964 (Callaway 1965, 40, n. 29). Exemplar forms similar to the deep bowl are found at Jericho in Tomb D12 (Kenyon 1960, 119, Fig. 38:35) and in Beth-shan XII (Fitzgerald 1935, Pl. VII:4).

The presence of Khirbet Kerak ware forms in the Phase VI construction layers is significant, because it indicates a peaceful introduction of the Khirbet Kerak culture in the interval between the Phase V destruction of the city and the reorganization and rebuilding which began in Phase VI. Hennessy identifies two large settlements of the newcomers from North Syria and Anatolia at Khirbet el-Kerak (the type-site) and Beth-shan (1967, 75), and evidence of trade or cultural interchange with numerous other places north of Ai and Jericho. There is no evidence that the people from the north introduced their culture by force at Jericho or Ai, so they cannot be associated with the Phase V destruction at Ai.

The two Khirbet Kerak bowl forms in Phase VI have further significance. They are similar to forms in Beth-shan XII, which is the initial settlement stratum of the newcomers. Therefore the spread of the new culture as far south as Ai occurred in the initial period of settlement in Canaan, and acceptance seems to have increased with the passing of time, because a Khirbet Kerak ware horseshoe-shaped stand is found in Sanctuary A of Phase VIII at Ai (see Fig. 73:8).

Wide platters. The large platter drawn in Fig. 59:27 is characteristic of Phase VI, and is distinguished by three features. First, the concavity under the rim noted in examples from earlier phases has become a recurved profile supporting a low, almost vertical, rim. Fig. 60:3 has a sharply grooved concavity, but the tendency in Phase VI seems to be toward making the concavity a gentle outward curve instead of a groove cut by a tool. Second, the rim is low in profile and more blunt on the edge than the earlier, higher profile rims. In fact, the rim tends toward a flange form, evident in Fig. 60:1, a form known at Site A in Phase V, Fig. 44:13, in an unusual, shallow outcurved rim. Third, the inside of the platter is decorated with a rich reddish-brown slip, burnished in concentric circles in the center and radial lines from the inner circles out to the upward bend of the rim.

This form becomes common at Jericho in Areas E III–IV in Phase F, EB IIIA (Hennessy 1967, 13, Pl. VII:68), and continues through EB IIIB. It occurs also in Tomb D12 (Kenyon 1960, 119, Fig. 38:3). Similar platters are found in Beth-shan XII (Fitzgerald 1935, Pl. VIII:25) and Megiddo XVIII (Shipton 1939, Chart, Stratum XVIII:19), and apparently continue through EB III. At Ai, the same form is found in Sanctuary A of Phase VIII, drawn in Fig. 74:8.

Unlike the string-cut base bowl, which seems to be a copy of Egyptian alabaster and stone forms, and the Khirbet Kerak ware bowls, whose origins can be traced to North Syria and Anatolia, the wide platter is a locally developed form in Phase VI. This platter, along with the bowl forms other than the two noted above, suggests a substantial continuation of the indigenous population at Ai in Phase VI.

Jars and juglets. The storejars continue earlier forms with variations in Phase VI. Fig. 61:6, 7, 9, 10, 12 are variations of ledge handle jar rims common at Site A throughout EB. Rims of large jars, drawn in Fig. 61:21–25 are derived from the rolled-rim form common throughout EB. Fig.61:28 seems to be developed from the earlier triangular rim of Phase V, drawn in Fig. 45:14.

A new jar form is drawn in Fig. 61:30. This unusual recurved rim appears at first to be an Iron I cooking pot among EB forms, but close examination indicates that it is an EB form also. The ware is yellowish-orange like much of the other EB ware at Site A, and is tempered with white grits of assorted sizes. The rim is folded over and flattened on top, then recurved to flare out as indicated in the drawing. Since the rim was found in Firepit N[1], it probably is part of a cooking pot.

One complete jar of this type is registered from Tomb C. This form has vertical loop handles at the waist of the vessel, and two lug handles under the rim (see Callaway 1964, Pl. XVII:145[II]). Marquet-Krause notes that the complete jar is '. . . un très beau vase à parois extrêmêment fines', decorated with a brown slip 'lustré avec dessin de lignes plus foncées' (1949, 44). Similar jar forms, but with a different rim, occur in Tombs F4 and F2 at Jericho (Kenyon 1960, 144, Fig. 47:4; 170, Fig. 62:3). Amiran assigns the form to EB II, apparently on the analogy of a jar from Beth-yerah XIIIB (1969, 63, Pl. 16:2, 3), but it seems to belong to EB IIIA on the evidence of the form in Fig. 61:30.

The spouted jar drawn in Fig. 64:3 is a common EB III type, although this example seems to be formed with better proportions than most. Kenyon's Type E spouted jars at Jericho are similar in type, but more crudely styled (1960, 122, Fig. 39:13, 14, Tomb D12; 144, Fig. 47:7, Tomb F4; 170, Fig. 62:6, 7, Tomb F2).

The tall stump base of a juglet, drawn in Fig. 64:5 is a new form in Phase VI. This example was found in Layer 4, in the foundation of Fireplace N[1]. Comparable forms appear at Jericho in Areas E III–IV in Phase F (Hennessy 1967, Pl. VII:73; p. 13), assigned to EB IIIA, and continue in EB IIIB in a more pointed base form (see *ibid.*, Pl. IX:92; p. 15), from Phase C. The semi-pointed stump base seems to be a local development, possibly influenced by EB II stump base jugs found in First Dynasty contexts in Egypt, which becomes almost a hallmark of EB III in Canaan. Numerous examples in many variations are found at Jericho in Tombs D12, F4, F3, F2, and A114(B) (see Kenyon 1960, 100–177).

Conclusions

Variations of Phase V forms continue in Phase VI, suggesting a continuity in the local population even though the Phase V destruction of the city apparently was total in dimension. Significant new forms appear, however, indicating at least commercial contacts with the people associated with Khirbet Kerak ware, and some degree of involvement with Egypt at the beginning of the Third Dynasty. Evidence of Egyptian influence in pottery at Site A, and in the temple on the acropolis, suggests that the dominant influence in Phase VI is Egyptian, and that the newcomers associated with Khirbet Kerak ware were possibly arrested in their infiltration of the central hill country by Egyptian power localized in the rebuilt and refortified city at Ai.

The pottery horizon of Phase VI. Phases F–D in Areas E III–IV at Jericho seem to be the nearest local stratified parallels to Phase VI at Ai. Those phases are designated EB IIIA by Hennessy (1967, 22–23), a designation suitable for the Ai materials also. Phase VI pottery forms are found in Tombs

D12, F4, F3, F2, A114(B), and Garstang's Tomb A at Jericho, but no distinction can be made between EB IIIA and EB IIIB in the evidence from the tombs.

Imitation Khirbet Kerak ware in Phase VI indicates the arrival of newcomers in the north of Canaan who settled at Beth-yerah and Beth-shan. The few parallels traceable to Khirbet Kerak ware forms associate Phase VI with Beth-shan XII, or the first phase of the new settlement at Beth-shan in EB III. This seems to be contemporary with Phase H at Judeideh in North Syria, where Khirbet Kerak ware makes up a large proportion of the total pottery.

Egyptian parallels in pottery and stone can be placed in the Second Dynasty, and architectural parallels of Temple A on the acropolis, contemporary with Building A at Site A, are found in the Tomb of Hesy and the pyramid complex of Zoser, both of the early Third Dynasty. Phase VI rebuilding of the city, therefore, seems to have been completed in the early Third Dynasty, at least by the reign of Zoser.

Chronology. The Carbon 14 dates for the termination of Phase V ca. 2720 B.C. give a beginning point for the chronology of Phase VI. Evidence of abandonment of Site A, possibly during the time that the new city wall system and acropolis complex were being constructed, suggests a period of up to forty years for the rebuilding of the city. This would place the beginning of Phase VI about 2720–2680 B.C., and would span the transition from the Second to Third Dynasties in Egypt. Completion of the construction phase of the EB IIIA city, therefore, is possible by the time of Zoser's reign early in the Third Dynasty.

Hennessy dates the introduction of Khirbet Kerak ware in Canaan ca. 2700 B.C., or at the end of the Second Dynasty, on two lines of evidence (1967, 88). First, inscribed materials in Byblos VI, dated to the reign of Khasekhemui, seem to be in an EB IIIA context, suggesting a beginning for the period in North Syria at the end of the Second Dynasty. And second, a Carbon 14 date for local Khirbet Kerak ware in south Russia of 2800 B.C. ± 90 gives a beginning point for the migration of newcomers who settled Beth-yerah and Beth-shan XII. He allows 100 years for the migration, which seems to be generous for the establishment of settlements in North Canaan, but more realistic for the penetration southward to Jericho and Ai. The date of 2700 B.C. falls within the 2720–2680 B.C. period suggested for Phase VI, and in the absence of Carbon 14 dates from Phase VI materials, may be used as a mean date for the beginning of EB IIIA at Ai.

A new era in the history of the city at Ai begins, therefore, ca. 2700 B.C., under the influence of Egypt. The Egyptian presence seems to have grown out of increasing trade relations with the region in Phase V, or EB II, and the emergence of rulers in the late Second Dynasty with imperialistic ambitions. By the beginning of the Third Dynasty, a threat to Egyptian interests was apparently posed by migrations of newcomers from the north who settled at Beth-yerah and Beth-shan, and the threat was met by Egyptian involvement in rebuilding the city at Ai and making it an outpost guarding against further encroachment from the north. This involvement was more intimate than mere trade relations would suggest, because the seat of political and religious leadership of the city on the acropolis was Egyptian-planned and built. A vassal-relationship seems to be required, because the city at Ai had nothing to offer Egypt at the beginning of Phase VI other than its strategic location and history of dominance in the immediate region.

DESCRIPTIONS OF THE PHASE VI POTTERY AND OBJECTS, FIGS. 59–66

Fig. 59 No.	Reg. No.	
1	4571	Rim gently upcurved to rounded edge, wheel-made; buff inside and orange outside; fine with many assorted white and grey grits; traces of wheel-burnished brown slip over-all, with evenly spaced, diagonally-burnished lines inside; black smoke marks on edge indicate possible use as lamp. A III 201.10.
—	4571f	Body sherd of bowl; burnt-orange; medium-coarse with few assorted tan grits; burnished greyish-brown slip inside and outside. A III 201.10.
—	4805h, i (joined)	Rim of small bowl; dark-orange; medium with some small to fine tan and grey grits; continuously-burnished, reddish-brown slip inside. A III 204.4.
—	4885d	Body sherd of small bowl, thin; dark reddish-brown; fine with few very fine tan grits; continuously-burnished reddish-brown slip over-all. A IV 300.4.
2	4510	Rim upcurved to thinned, rounded edge, wheel-made, greyish-brown; medium-coarse with some assorted grey grits; traces of burnished reddish-orange slip over-all; many assorted pits. A III 201.1.
3	5158b	Rim slightly incurved to rounded edge; orangish-buff with thick, light-grey core; fine with few fine to very fine white and tan grits; some light tan incrustations over-all. A IV 301.3.
—	4616g	Body sherd, thick, wheel-finished on one side; orangish-buff on one side and grey on the other; coarse with some assorted grey and tan grits. A III 201.15.
—	4732k	Body sherd; wheel-finished; brownish-buff with grey core; medium with some small to very fine white grits; black smoke-mark on edge. A III 203.4.
4	4616	Rim upcurved to thinned, rounded edge, wheel-finished; orangish-buff; medium with very many assorted white grits; continuously-burnished reddish-brown slip inside with evenly spaced, narrow, diagonally-burnished lines. A III 201.15.
5	4567	Rim slightly incurved to thinned, rounded edge; dark-orange; medium-coarse with very many small to fine tan and grey grits. A III 201.9a.
—	4229	Rim of medium bowl, vertical with rounded edge; tan; medium-coarse with many small to fine white grits; some assorted pits inside, rough texture over-all. A II 101.3.
—	4571a	Rim of small bowl; upcurved to pointed edge; burnt-orange with grey core; medium-coarse with some assorted grey and tan grits; traces of reddish-brown slip over-all; black smoke mark on rim indicates possible use as lamp. A III 201.10.
6	4564	Rim upcurved to thinned rounded edge, wet-smoothed; orange with very thick, dark-grey core; medium-coarse with many assorted white, tan, and dark-brown grits; some assorted pits over-all. A III 201.9a.
—	5158c	Rim of medium bowl, hand-made; wet smoothed; bright-orange; medium with some assorted tan and grey grits; gritty texture over-all. A IV 301.3.
7	5051	Rim upcurved and slightly everted to rounded edge; buff; medium-coarse with few assorted white and grey grits; rough texture inside, uneven surface outside. A II 101.2a.
8	4883	Rim slightly upcurved to thin, rounded edge, wheel-made; orange with buff outside and core; medium with many small to fine white and grey grits; traces of wheel-burnished reddish-brown slip over-all. A IV 300.4.
9	0–5	Small bowl, flat base, sides upcurved to thin, rounded edge, hand-made with rim wheel-finished (base string-cut); pinkish-orange; medium with some assorted tan and grey grits, few medium to fine, white quartz grits; reddish-brown slip over-all, continuously burnished inside and wheel-burnished outside, no slip on bottom. A III 204.4.

Fig. 59 No.	Reg. No.	
10	4242	Rim upcurved to uneven, rounded edge; orangish-tan; coarse with some assorted tan and brown grits; some assorted pits over-all, black smoke marks. A II 101.2a.
11	4571b	Base of small bowl; buff with dark-orange patches in places, brownish-buff core; coarse with many assorted dark-grey grits, few assorted white grits; traces of burnished reddish-brown slip outside; spalling over-all, pitted outside. A III 201.10.
—	4562e	Flattened base of small bowl, very thin, possibly wheel-turned; burnt-orange; medium with few assorted, and many very fine, white, grey, and reddish-brown grits; random radial burnishing over-all inside; many assorted pits over-all. A III 201.9.
12	4513	Rim upcurved to thinned, rounded edge, wheel-finished; orange inside and tan outside; medium with some assorted white grits; traces of reddish-brown slip inside and outside edge. A III 201.1.
13	4550	Rim upcurved and slightly everted to thinned rounded edge; brownish-buff; medium with many assorted light- and dark-grey grits; traces of burnished reddish-brown slip inside and outside edge. A III 201.7a.
14	6117	Rim upcurved to slightly everted rounded edge; buff; medium with light- to dark-grey grits. A II 101.2a.
15	4877, 4879, 4880 (joined)	Carinated wall with upper portion everted to thin, rounded edge, wheel-turned; reddish-brown with thick black core in places; medium with many fine and some small white grits; burnished over-all, wheel-burnished on upper wall, burnished with long, parallel strokes inside and on bottom with curved strokes on portion of bottom, several sets of parallel incisions on bottom. A IV 300.3.
—	4885c	Fragment of carinated wall with everted rim of medium bowl, wheel-turned; dark-brown; fine with few very fine tan grits; continuously-burnished brown slip over-all. A IV 300.4.
—	4732f	Rim of small bowl, carinated wall with upper portion slightly outcurved to thin, rounded edge, wheel-turned; reddish-brown; fine with some fine white grits; wheel-burnished reddish-brown slip over-all. A III 203.4.
16	4803	Carinated wall with upper portion everted to thinned rounded edge, wheel-made; inside wheel-turned; brown; fine with very many fine white grits; burnished trellis-pattern inside body, very narrow wheel-burnished bands inside and outside edge, rough texture outside below rim. A III 204.4.
17	5081a	Rim slightly incurved to thinned, rounded edge; wheel-finished; reddish-brown with greyish-buff core; medium with few small to fine, grey and tan grits; wheel-burnished, reddish-brown slip over-all. A II 101.2a.
—	4884	Rim of bowl, slightly incurved to thin, rounded edge; buff; medium-coarse with many assorted tan grits. A IV 300.4.
18	4559	Rim gently incurved to thinned, rounded edge; dark grey with buff inside; medium-coarse with some medium to small tan and grey grits; traces of continuously-burnished reddish-brown slip inside and outside edge, un-slipped portion of outside surface also burnished. A III 201.9.
19	4560	Rim incurved to slightly thickened, rounded edge, wet-smoothed; orange with buff core; coarse with many assorted white and tan grits; rough texture inside. A III 201.9.
20	4917a	Rim of platter, wheel-turned; tan; medium-fine with few medium to fine reddish-brown grits; horizontally-burnished, reddish-brown slip over-all. A IV 300.9.
21	4932	Rim upcurved to rounded edge, wheel-made; orangish-buff with greyish-pink core; very coarse with many assorted tan grits; traces of continuously-burnished reddish-brown slip inside and outside edge; many assorted pits over-all, rough texture outside. A IV 300.10.

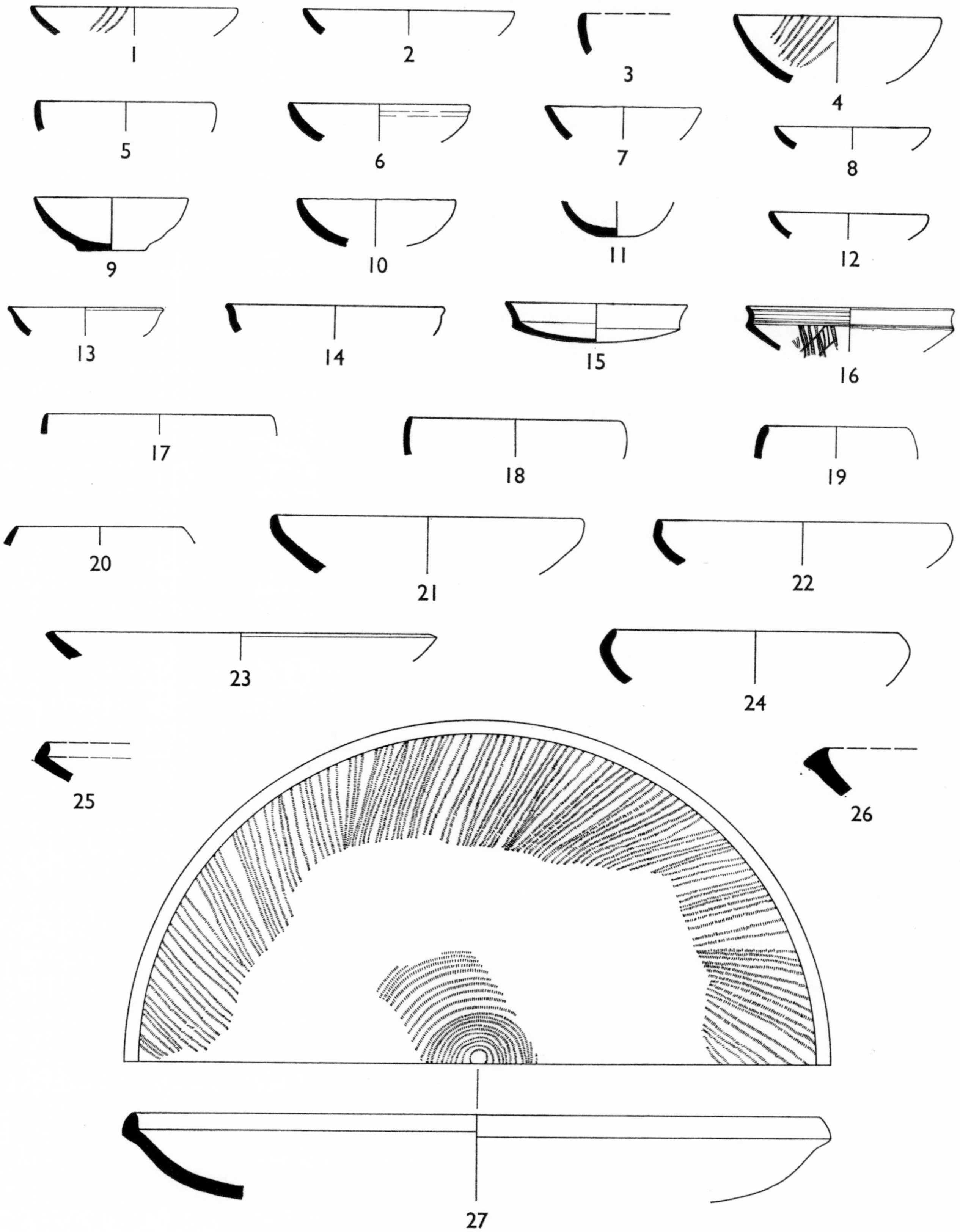

Fig. 59. Small to large bowls, Phase VI. 1:4.

Fig. 59 No.	Reg. No.	
22	4241	Rim upcurved to thinned, rounded, slightly inverted edge; buff with grey core; medium-coarse with some assorted tan, grey, and white grits; traces of white slip inside; some assorted pits outside, grey incrustations inside. A II 101.1a.
23	4494	Rim slightly upcurved to thinned, rounded, flattened edge, wheel-finished; tan inside and buff outside, dark-grey core; medium with many small to fine white and grey grits; traces of burnished brown slip outside; many assorted pits, very rough texture inside, some crazing outside. A I 1.2c.
24	4917	Rim upcurved to thinned, rounded, inverted edge; orangish-buff with thick dark-grey core; medium-coarse with many assorted white and grey grits. A IV 300.9.
25	4940	Carinated wall inclined out to low inverted edge, wheel-turned; buff with reddish-orange inside; medium-coarse with many assorted reddish-brown grits; wheel-burnished reddish-orange slip over-all. A IV 300.10.
26	4237	Rim slightly upcurved to rounded, flattened edge projected in and out; yellowish-buff inside and orangish-buff outside, reddish-pink and grey core; coarse with many assorted white and tan grits; faint traces of continuously burnished orange slip over-all; some assorted pits. A II 101.4.
27	5778–80 4551d 4552f 4553 4804 4805f, g	Wall upcurved to rounded, low, inverted rim, shallow groove outside below rim, wheel-turned body and wheel-finished rim; orange with buff core; medium with some assorted grey, tan, white, and reddish-brown grits; reddish-brown slip with burnished, concentric circles in center and burnished lines radiating out to rim from inner circles. A III 200.1a; 201.7a; 201.8a; 201.10; 204.4.
—	4569a	Body sherd of large shallow bowl, carinated with shallow depression outside below angle; brown with grey core; medium-coarse with some small to very fine white and tan grits; continuously wheel-burnished reddish-brown slip inside with traces outside and on edge. A III 201.9a.
—	4732e	Rim of wide shallow bowl, inverted to low rounded edge, wheel-turned; buff; fine with few assorted tan grits; traces of wheel-burnished, reddish-brown slip over-all. A III 203.4.
—	5158g	Body sherd of wide shallow bowl, wheel-turned; bright reddish-brown with thin yellowish-grey core; fine with few fine to very fine white grits; radially-burnished reddish-brown slip inside with random strokes of burnishing outside. A IV 301.3.
—	4552e	Body sherd of large, shallow bowl; brown with dark-grey core; medium with many fine to very fine white and grey grits; continuously-burnished brown slip over-all. A III 201.8a.
—	4917b	Body sherd of shallow bowl, very thick, wheel-turned; dark-brown; medium-coarse with some assorted white grits, few medium grey and reddish-brown grits; continuously-burnished brown slip inside. A IV 300.9.
Fig. 60 No.	Reg. No.	
1	4920	Rim inclined out to thinned, rounded low, straight edge, some thickening at angle with rounded protuberance outside; dark-orange with buff and dark-grey core; fine with many medium to fine, white and grey grits; traces of wheel-burnished reddish-brown slip inside and outside edge. A IV 300.9a.
—	4569b	Body sherd of wide shallow bowl, very thick; orange with buff and grey core; medium-coarse with some assorted grey and tan grits; traces of burnished reddish-brown slip over-all. A III 201.9a.
2	4248	Flattened, inverted rim; orangish-buff with dark-grey core in places; very coarse with many assorted white grits; rough texture over-all, some black smoke marks, some grey incrustations outside. A II 101.2a.

Fig. 60 No.	*Reg. No.*	
3	4230	Wall gently inclined out to low, inverted rim, wide groove outside below edge, wheel-turned; reddish-orange with brown core; medium with many assorted dark-brown grits, many small to fine tan grits; traces of wheel-burnished red slip over-all; many assorted pits. A III 101.3.
—	4950f	Body sherd of wide shallow bowl, wheel-turned; bright reddish-brown; medium-fine with many small to very fine white and tan grits; burnished reddish slip over-all; much spalling. A IV 300.10a.
4	4515	Rim slightly everted to medium-wide, thickened, beveled edge; buff with grey core; coarse with some assorted white grits; traces of white slip outside and inside edge; rough texture over-all. A III 201.2.
5	4878	Inclined out to thinned, rounded, low, inverted rim, some thickening at angle; reddish-orange with grey core; radially-burnished inside body, wheel-burnished inside edge and outside; some assorted pits over-all, dark-grey smoke marks on edge. A IV 300.3.
6	4723	Upcurved to thickened, rounded, inverted rim projected slightly out, wet-smoothed; pinkish-buff; coarse with many assorted tan grits. A III 203.4.
—	5155	Rim of small bowl, slightly everted with low ridge outside, rounded edge, wheel-made; bright-orange; fine with some small to fine white grits. A IV 301.3.
7	4787b	Carinated with thinned, rounded edge, wheel-turned; brownish-red; medium-coarse with many small to very fine white grits and few assorted tan and reddish-brown grits; continuously-burnished brown slip over-all; many assorted pits and some spalling, light grey incrustations. A III 204.1.
—	4950h	Body sherd, wheel-turned; greyish-brown; fine with some fine to very fine grey and dark-brown grits; burnished brown slip inside; some light brown incrustations. A IV 300.11.
8	4571g	Curved wall with upright rim slightly everted to thinned, rounded edge; buff; coarse with many assorted tan grits; continuously horizontally-burnished reddish-brown slip over-all. A III 201.10.
9	4944	Slightly upcurved to rounded, inverted rim; orange inside and reddish-orange outside; fine with many assorted brown grits; radially-burnished reddish-orange slip inside, wheel-burnished outside and on edge. A IV 300.10.
10	4562	Upcurved to narrow, rounded, flat edge, projected in; orange inside and buff outside with thick grey core; coarse with many assorted tan and grey grits; traces of burnished reddish-brown slip over-all, pitted and flaking. A III 201.9.
11	4908	Curved upright wall everted to thinned rounded rim wheel-made; fine with many assorted white grits; continuously-burnished reddish-brown slip outside and inside edge; some grey incrustations. A IV 300.9.
12	4521	Carinated with thinned, rounded low, inverted rim, some thickening at angle; brown with thick dark-grey core; medium-coarse with many assorted white grits; traces of brown slip radially-burnished inside body, wheel-burnished on both sides of edge; some grey incrustations. A III 201.2a.
13	4708	Slightly upcurved to wide inverted edge; buff with thick dark-grey core; coarse with few assorted white grits; many assorted pits over-all, very worn. A III 203.2.
14	5150	Upcurved to flat edge projected in and out, wheel-finished; orangish-buff with buff core; medium-coarse with some assorted light- and dark-grey grits; traces of wheel-burnished, reddish-brown slip inside, on top of, and just outside edge; assorted pits over-all, flaking inside. A IV 301.2.
15	5066	Slightly upcurved with rounded, triangular inverted edge, wheel-turned; orangish-buff with dark-grey core; very coarse with many assorted white, tan, and grey grits; faint traces of burnished reddish-brown slip over-all; many assorted pits. A II 101.2a.

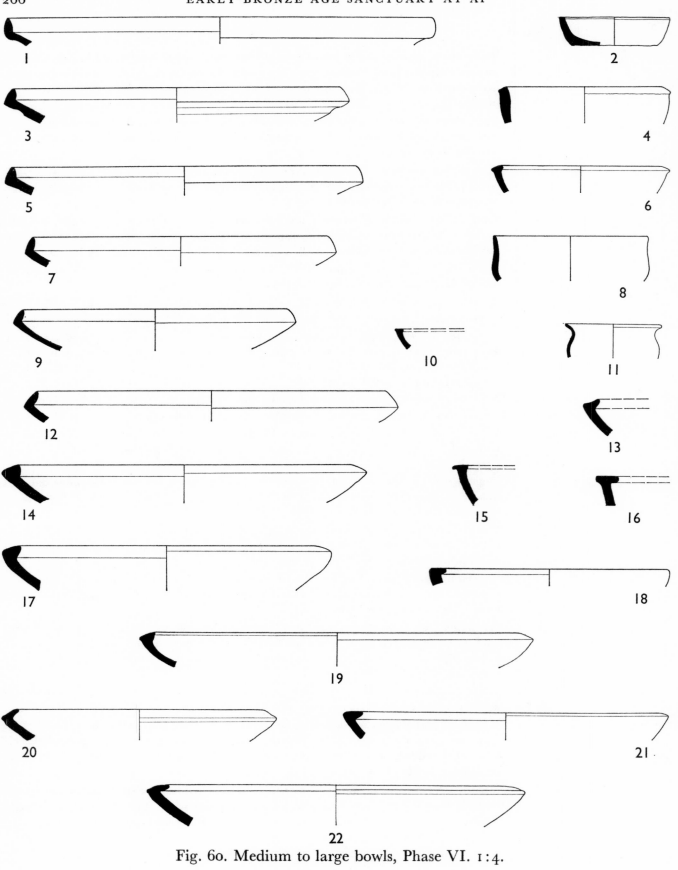

Fig. 60. Medium to large bowls, Phase VI. 1:4.

Fig. 60 *No.*	*Reg.* *No.*	
—	4917c	Body sherd of wide shallow bowl, wheel-turned, orangish-tan; medium-fine with few medium to small dark-brown, grey, and white grits; continuously-burnished reddish-brown slip outside. A IV 300.9.
—	4551c	Body sherd of wide shallow bowl, wheel-turned; orangish-brown outside with dark-grey inside and core; medium-fine with very many small to very fine white grits; continuously-burnished reddish-brown slip outside; rough, uneven, gritty texture inside. A III 201.7a.
16	4931	Sharply upcurved to thickened, rounded, flat edge projected out; buff with thick, dark-grey core; very coarse with some assorted white and tan grits; traces of burnished dark-orange slip inside and on edge; rough texture over-all. A IV 300.10.
17	4508	Slightly inclined out to wide, flat, inverted edge projected out; wheel-made; buff with orange inside; medium-coarse with many assorted white, greyish-tan, and brown grits; traces of burnished reddish-orange slip on edge, many assorted pits over-all, rough, gritty texture inside. A III 201.1.
18	4718	Upcurved to rounded, triangular inverted edge, wheel-turned; buff; coarse with many assorted grey, tan, and reddish-brown grits; faint traces of burnished reddish-brown slip over-all. A III 203.4.
—	4569c	Body sherd of wide shallow bowl, wheel-turned; greyish-buff; medium-coarse with some assorted tan and grey grits; wheel-burnished reddish-brown slip over-all. A III 201.9a.
19	4913	Sharply upcurved to thickened, flat inverted edge; reddish-brown; medium-coarse with some assorted reddish-brown and grey grits; porous ware; traces of wheel-burnished reddish-brown slip inside and on edge; many assorted pits over-all, flaking outside, black smoke marks on edge. A IV 300.9.
20	4240	Upcurved to triangular, inverted edge, wheel-turned; buff; coarse with some assorted white and tan grits; traces of burnished dark-purple slip over-all; black smoke marks on edge and outside. A II 101.1a.
21	5149	Upcurved to wide, thinned, inverted edge; wheel-finished; pinkish-orange; coarse with some assorted black and tan grits; traces of creamy-white slip outside and on edge; some assorted pits and rough texture over-all, some grey incrustations. A IV 301.2.
22	4730	Upcurved to wide, triangular, sharply inverted edge; buff with thick dark-grey core; medium coarse with some assorted tan and grey grits; traces of wheel burnished reddish-brown slip inside and on edge. A III 203.4.
23	4714	Slightly upcurved to rounded, thinned, inverted edge, wheel-turned; orange with thick grey core; coarse with many assorted grey and white grits; traces of wheel-burnished reddish-brown slip over-all; many small to fine pits. A III 203.3.
—	5158f	Body sherd of wide, shallow bowl, wheel-turned; burnt-orange; medium with some small to very fine grey and white quartz grits; burnished reddish-brown slip inside; spalling outside. A IV 301.3.
—	4551e	Body sherd of wide shallow bowl; wheel-turned; light-orange; medium-coarse with many assorted tan and grey grits; continuously-burnished reddish-brown slip over-all, horizontal strokes inside rim. A III 201.7a.
—	4946j	Body sherd; buff inside and orange outside, grey core; medium with many small to fine dark- and light-grey grits; outside smoothly burnished. A IV 300.10.

Fig. 61 *No.*	*Reg.* *No.*	
1	4233	Upcurved to thickened, flattened rim; orangish-buff with thick, dark-grey core; very coarse with many assorted grey grits; faint traces of continuously burnished orange slip on edge and inside; many assorted pits and flaking inside, some assorted pits outside. A II 101.4.

Fig. 61 No.	Reg. No.	
2	4939	Upright wall slightly everted with rounded, wide, inverted rim, wheel-made; reddish-orange; medium-coarse with some assorted white and many small reddish-brown grits; wheel-burnished reddish slip inside and on edge, small hole drilled inside; very rough texture outside. A IV 300.10.
3	4712	Slightly upcurved to flat inverted edge, wheel-made; orange; very coarse with many assorted tan grits; traces of continuously burnished orange slip outside; many assorted pits over-all. A III 203.2.
4	4493	Upcurved to vertical, flat edge projecting in and out; buff with orangish-buff places in core; coarse with many assorted grits of mixed colors; very rough texture over-all, dark-brown discoloration inside. A I 1.2c.
5	4228	Slightly incurved to flattened edge, slightly projected in and out; buff; coarse with many assorted tan grits; traces of burnished orange slip over-all; very pitted and flaking; grey smoke marks inside. A II 101.3.
—	4915	Rim of bowl, upcurved to rounded, flat edge projecting in and ridged outside, brownish-grey with thick, dark-grey core; coarse with many assorted white grits; traces of wheel-burnished orangish-buff slip inside and on edge; some assorted pits over-all. A IV 300.9.
—	4787c	Rim of wide bowl inclined out to wide, flat edge projecting in, rim crudely wheel-finished; light brownish-orange with grey core; coarse with few small reddish-brown and tan grits; some grey smoke marks on edge. A III 204.1.
6	5152	Rim outcurved to thinned, rounded edge, wheel-made; dark-orange with buff core; coarse with many assorted white grits; very pitted inside. A IV 301.3.
7	4556	Rim outcurved to rounded edge, wheel-made; buff; medium with some assorted grey and tan grits, porous ware; some assorted pits over-all. A III 201.9.
8	4552	Rim upcurved to rounded inverted edge; dark-grey with orangish-brown inside and orange on edge; medium-coarse with many small to fine white grits; traces of white slip outside; rough, gritty texture over-all. A III 201.8a.
—	4618	Body sherd, thin; orange with grey core; medium with some medium to very fine white grits; traces of white slip outside. A III 201.16.
—	4516	Body sherd of jar; dark-orange with buff surfaces; medium with some small to fine white, grey, and tan grits; white slip outside; some assorted pits and spalling inside. A III 201.2.
9	4614	Rim flared out to thinned, rounded edge, wet-smoothed; buff with orange patch outside; medium-coarse with many medium to small grey grits. A III 201.15.
10	4925	Rim flared out to thinned, rounded edge, wheel-made; buff; medium-coarse with very many assorted dark-grey and reddish-brown grits; creamy white slip; grey smoke marks, some assorted pits over-all. A IV 300.9b.
11	4562b	Rim slightly upcurved to triangular, slightly inverted edge, wheel-made; tan with grey core; medium with some assorted, and many fine to very fine, grey and tan grits; faint traces of burnished reddish-brown slip inside and on top of edge. A III 201.9.
12	4916	Rim flared out to thinned rounded edge, wheel-made; light buff; medium-coarse with some assorted white grits; creamy white slip; one very large pit, and rough texture inside. A IV 300.9.
13	4551	Rim outcurved to thinned, rounded edge, wet-smoothed; buff with grey core; medium-coarse with many small to fine white grits, many assorted buff grits. A III 201.7a.
—	4930c	Neck and shoulder fragment of jar; greyish-tan with brown core; medium-coarse with some assorted grey and brown grits, few medium reddish-brown grits; dark-grey smoke marks over-all. A IV 300.9b.

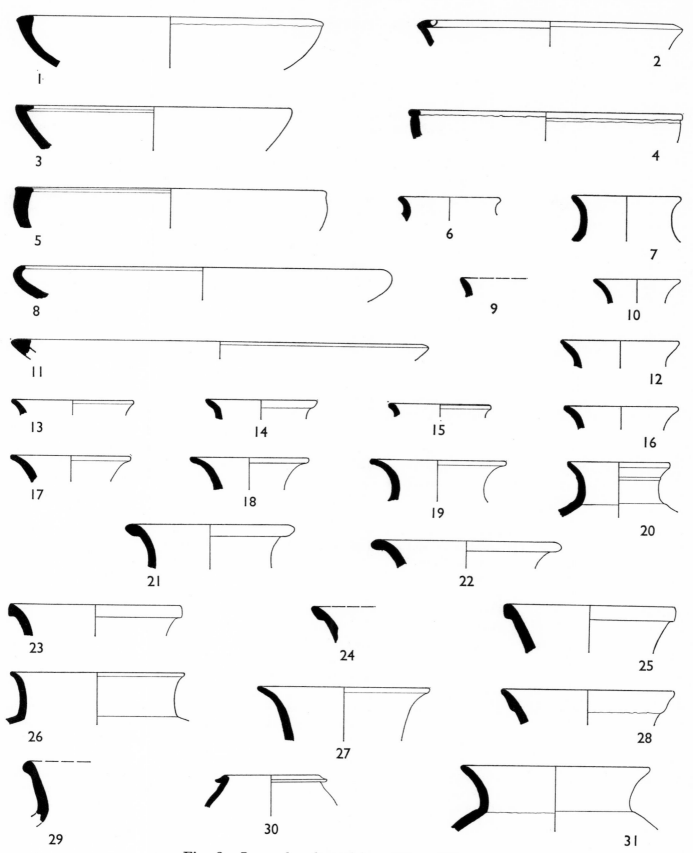

Fig. 61. Large bowls and jars, Phase VI. 1:4.

Fig. 61 *No.*	*Reg.* *No.*	
14	4223	Rim flared out to thin, folded edge, wheel-made; buff; medium-coarse with some assorted grey grits; traces of white slip outside. A II 101.2.
—	4571d	Body sherd, thin; brownish-buff with grey core; coarse with some assorted tan and grey grits; traces of white slip outside; very uneven surface with some assorted pits inside. A III 201.10.
15	4507	Rim outcurved to rounded edge; dark-orange; medium-coarse with very many assorted white grits; traces of burnished reddish-brown slip inside edge and outside. A III 200.1.
—	4551b	Rim of jar, slightly outcurved to thinned, rounded edge; wheel-finished; orange with orangish-buff core; medium with many fine to very fine, and few small, white grits; traces of continuously-burnished reddish-brown slip outside. A III 201.7a.
16	4519	Rim outcurved to rounded edge, wheel-made; buff; medium with many assorted grey and white grits; some assorted pits inside. A III 201.2a.
17	4946c	Rim flared out to thinned rounded edge, wheel-finished; pinkish-buff; medium with some medium to fine white and grey grits; some light grey and white incrustations over-all. A IV 300.10.
18	4732d	Rim sharply outcurved to rounded edge, wet-smoothed; dark-orange with reddish-orange core; coarse with very many assorted tan grits; rough gritty uneven surface inside, grey incrustations over-all. A III 203.4.
—	4732h	Rim of large jar, outcurved to thinned, rounded edge with raised band outside, below edge; dark-orange with buff core; coarse with some assorted grey grits, traces of white slip outside and inside edge, grey incrustations over-all. A III 203.4.
19	4909	Rim sharply outcurved to thinned, rounded edge, wheel-made; buff with greyish-buff inside; coarse with very many assorted white, dark-grey, and reddish-brown grits; many assorted pits inside, some pits outside. A IV 300.9.
—	4930b	Neck fragment of jar, outcurved to thinned edge, edge badly chipped, crudely wheel-finished; orangish-buff with brownish-grey core; medium-coarse with few assorted grey and tan grits; white slip outside. A IV 300.9b.
20	4563	Rim outcurved to rounded pointed edge, very narrow raised band around neck, neck wheel-made and joined to body; buff; medium with many assorted white, grey, and brown grits, porous ware; traces of white slip inside rim; few assorted pits. A III 201.9a.
—	4949	Body sherd of jar, hand-made; burnt-orange inside, light- and dark-grey outside, tan core; medium-coarse with many assorted white and grey, few medium to small reddish-brown grits; traces of heavy white slip outside; fine pitting and crazing over-all. A IV 300.10a.
21	4707, 10 (joined)	Rim outcurved to rolled oval edge, projected out; brown inside and reddish-brown outside, thick, dark-grey core penetrating to inside in places; very coarse with many assorted white and tan grits; traces of dark-orange slip outside; many assorted pits over-all. A III 203.2.
22	4907	Rim sharply outcurved to rolled edge, wheel-made; pinkish-tan; coarse with many assorted white and reddish-brown grits; traces of heavy, white slip outside; many assorted pits over-all, crazing inside, rough gritty texture, some grey incrustations. A IV 300.9.
23	4729	Rim outcurved to squared edge projected out, wheel-finished; dark-grey inside and buff outside; medium-coarse with many assorted tan, brown, and grey grits; traces of orange slip outside. A III 203.4.
—	4728	Rim and neck of jar, outcurved to rounded, slightly squared collar projected out, shallow depression inside of rim collar, wet-smoothed; greyish-buff; coarse with very

Fig. 61 *No.*	*Reg.* *No.*	
		many assorted grey and tan grits; tan slip outside; many small to fine pits over-all, some spalling inside, grey incrustations. A III 203.4.
—	4950g	Neck fragment of jar, neck slightly outcurved, hand-made; dark-grey with greyish-buff patches; medium-coarse with some assorted grey, tan, and reddish-brown grits; white slip outside; black discoloration outside. A IV 300.11.
—	4930e	Body sherd of jar; fine with many assorted white and black grits; very uneven surface outside, gritty texture with some assorted pits over-all. A IV 300.9b.
24	4828	Rim slightly outcurved to rolled, beveled edge projected out; yellowish-tan inside and orange outside; very coarse with many assorted white grits; very heavy white slip outside. A III 204.6.
—	4616b	Body sherd of large jar, thick; burnt-orange; coarse with very many assorted white and light-grey quartz grits; white slip outside; gritty texture with some spalling inside. A III 201.15.
—	4571c	Body sherd of large jar, thick; burnt-orange with thick dark-grey core penetrating to outside surface in places; coarse with some assorted tan and grey grits; white slip outside; some assorted pits inside, grey smoke marks inside. A III 201.10.
25	5156	Rim slightly flared to rolled, squared edge; buff; very coarse with many assorted white and grey grits; traces of white slip outside; many assorted pits and crazing over-all. A IV 301.3.
26	4943	Rim slightly outcurved to thinned, rounded edge, wheel-made; buff with grey core; coarse with some assorted grey and reddish-brown grits; few assorted pits over-all. A IV 300.10.
—	4924	Body sherd of jar; orangish-buff with grey inside; medium-coarse with some medium to fine white and grey grits; very uneven pitted surface inside. A IV 300.9b.
27	5064	Rim sharply flared out to thinned, rounded edge, wheel-made; pinkish-tan with grey core; coarse with some assorted tan grits; many assorted pits over-all, crazing inside. A II 101.2a.
28	4875	Rim flared out to medium wide, folded collar, wheel-made; orange with thick dark-grey core; medium-coarse with some assorted white grits; traces of white slip over-all; rough texture outside at bottom of collar, some grey incrustations. A IV 300.3.
—	4930d	Neck and shoulder fragment of jar; orange with thick grey core; medium with some medium to small tan and brown grits; white slip outside; very uneven surface inside. A IV 300.9b.
—	4950b	Rim of large jar, slightly outcurved, edge badly chipped, rim wheel-finished; pinkish-orange with pinkish-tan core; medium-coarse with some assorted white and tan, and few reddish-brown, grits; traces of heavy white slip outside; brown incrustations over-all. A IV 300.10a.
29	4491	Rim of jar, inclined out to rounded, thickened, edge; orange inside and buff outside; very coarse with many assorted white grits; many assorted pits inside, heavy, grey incrustations over-all. A I 1.2.
30	4709	Rim slightly incurved to rounded, recurved edge, wheel-made; yellowish-orange; medium-coarse with many assorted, mostly small to fine, white grits; many assorted pits over-all. A III 203.2.
31	4938	Rim sharply flared out to thinned, rounded edge, wheel-made; orangish-buff; coarse with many assorted white grits; some assorted pits inside with two very large deep pits, very rough texture inside. A IV 300.10.
—	4933	Neck fragment of jar, wheel-finished; orangish-buff; medium-coarse with some assorted tan grits. A IV 300.10.

Fig. 61 *No.*	*Reg.* *No.*	
—	4513a	Neck and shoulder fragment of large jar, neck and body made separately and then joined; brownish-buff with dark-grey core; coarse with some assorted grey and tan grits; uneven, gritty texture over-all, some grey incrustations over-all. A III 201.1b.
—	4562f	Neck and shoulder of large jar, neck slightly outcurved, wheel-finished; orange outside and brown inside, very thick dark-grey core, medium-coarse with some assorted tan and reddish-brown grits; light grey incrustation over-all, black smoke-marks inside neck. A III 201.9.

Fig. 62 *No.*	*Reg.* *No.*	
1	6115	Rim incurved to inward rolled, greatly thickened rounded edge, wet-smoothed; buff with dark grey core; coarse with many large to small grey and white grits. A II 101.2a.
—	5074	Rim of hole-mouth jar, incurved to wide, greatly thickened, rounded edge; orange inside and buff outside, thick, dark-grey core; very coarse with some small to fine white grits; medium-wide, crude, half-relief rope-molding outside edge, traces of very heavy white slip outside; rough texture with some assorted pits over-all, some grey incrustations. A II 101.2a.
—	4805b	Rim of hole-mouth jar, incurved to medium wide, greatly thickened, rounded edge, rim wheel-finished; burnt-orange with brown core; coarse with very many assorted grey quartz grits; gritty texture over-all, outside edge badly spalled, grey smoke marks on edge. A III 204.4.
2	4551a	Rim incurved to narrow slightly thickened rounded edge, wheel-finished; dark-grey; medium-coarse with few small to very fine white grits. A III 201.7a.
3	4509	Rim incurved to thickened, rounded edge; dark-grey with patches of brown inside; very coarse with some small to fine white grits; traces of heavy white slip outside and inside edge; rough texture inside. A III 201.1.
4	5052	Rim incurved to wide, thickened, rounded edge, wheel-finished; buff with orange core penetrating to surface at edge; medium-coarse with very many assorted white and grey quartz grits; many small to fine pits over-all, flaking on edge, black smoke marks outside. A II 101.2a.
—	4805a	Rim of hole-mouth jar, incurved to wide, greatly thickened, rounded edge; orangish-buff outside and orange inside, orangish-grey core; medium-coarse with some assorted white and grey quartz grits; some dark-grey quartz grits concentrated outside; badly spalled over-all. A III 204.4.
5	4950a	Rim slightly incurved to wide, thickened, rounded edge, wheel-finished; dull orange with buff core; coarse with many assorted grey quartz, tan and few reddish-brown grits; traces of burnished reddish-brown slip outside; light grey and brown incrustations over-all. A IV 300.10a.
6	5046	Rim incurved to medium-wide, thickened, rounded edge, wheel-finished; brown inside with patches of orange and dark-orange outside; very coarse with many assorted white and grey quartz grits; many small to fine pits over-all, crazing inside edge, rough, gritty texture inside. A II 101.2a.
7	4937	Rim incurved to medium-wide, thickened, rounded edge, wheel-finished; buff with very thick, dark-grey core penetrating to outside; coarse with many assorted grey quartz grits; many assorted pits over-all. A IV 300.10.
8	4249	Rim incurved to very wide, thickened, tapered edge; dark-brown inside and orange outside with patches of buff; coarse with many assorted white and grey quartz grits; rough, gritty texture over-all. A II 101.2a.

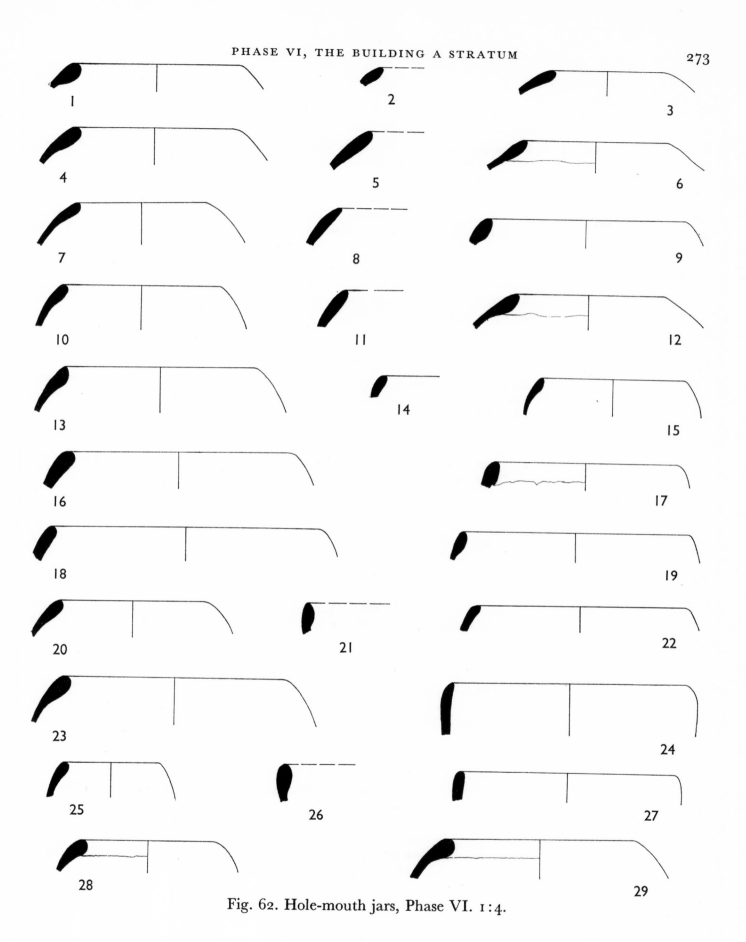

Fig. 62. Hole-mouth jars, Phase VI. 1:4.

Fig. 62 No.	Reg. No.	
9	6114	Rim slightly incurved to inward rolled, rounded edge, wet-smoothed; coarse with medium to small grey and white grits. A II 101.2a.
10	6120	Rim slightly incurved to wide, thickened, slightly flattened edge, wet-smoothed; light-grey with dark-grey core; coarse ware. A II 101.6.
11	6112	Rim slightly incurved to wide, thickened, oval edge, wheel-turned; dark-grey with buff-grey core; coarse to medium-fine grey grits. A II 101.1a.
12	4945	Rim incurved to wide, very thickened, rounded edge, wheel-finished; dark-grey with patches of yellowish-buff inside and core; coarse with very many assorted grey quartz grits; many assorted pits over-all. A IV 300.10.
13	5057	Rim incurved to wide, very thickened, rounded edge, wheel-finished; orange with patches of buff, thick, dark-grey core penetrating to outside in places; coarse with many assorted dark and light-grey grits; many assorted pits over-all with one very large and deep pit on edge, some grey incrustations inside. A II 101.2a.
14	6150	Rim slightly incurved to thickened, rounded edge, wheel-finished; buff-grey with dark grey core; coarse with assorted grey to white grits. A IV 300.9.
15	5157	Rim slightly incurved to narrow, thickened, oval edge, wheel-finished; dark-orange with thick, dark-grey core penetrating to outside in places; very coarse with many assorted white and tan grits; traces of thin, creamy white slip outside; rough, gritty texture over-all. A IV 301.3.
16	4566	Rim slightly incurved to wide, greatly thickened, rounded edge; buff with patches of orange outside and on edge, dark-grey core in places; very coarse with many assorted white and grey quartz grits; flaking outside on edge, rough, gritty texture inside. A III 201.9a.
17	4552b	Rim slightly incurved to medium-wide, greatly thickened, rounded edge folded over inside, wheel-finished with ragged edge inside; light-orange with greyish-buff core; coarse with many assorted white and grey quartz grits; dark-grey smoke marks outside. A III 201.8a.
—	4495	Rim of hole-mouth jar, slightly incurved to rounded edge, wheel-finished; orange with thick, tan core; medium-coarse with some assorted white and tan grits; very large pit on edge, some assorted pits inside, very rough texture over-all. A I 1.2c.
18	4226	Rim slightly incurved to wide, thickened, rounded edge, wheel-finished; orange inside and buff outside, greyish-buff core; coarse with many assorted grey grits; black smoke marks outside. A II 101.3.
19	4504	Rim slightly incurved to medium-wide, thickened, rounded edge, wheel-finished; buff with grey core; coarse with some assorted white and grey grits; few assorted pits over-all, grey smoke marks inside. A III 200.1b.
20	4720	Rim incurved to medium-wide, thickened, rounded edge; dark-buff inside and black outside, thick, dark-grey core; coarse with many assorted white and grey quartz grits; very porous ware; many assorted pits over-all. A III 203.4.
21	4552c	Upright rim slightly incurved to narrow, thickened rounded edge; orange with brown core; medium with some small to very fine white grits. A III 201.8a.
22	4910	Rim incurved to thickened, beveled edge, wheel-finished; orangish-buff with thick dark-grey core; medium-coarse with many assorted white grits and one very large grey grit. A IV 300.9.
23	4243	Rim slightly incurved to wide, greatly thickened, rounded edge; buff with orange on edge; medium-coarse with many assorted white and light-grey quartz grits, porous ware; many small to fine pits over-all; some flaking on edge. A II 101.2a.

Fig. 62 No.	Reg. No.	
24	4713	Upright rim slightly incurved to thinned, tapered edge, wheel-made; buff with thick dark-grey core; coarse with many assorted white and grey grits; traces of burnished orange slip over-all; some assorted pits. A III 203.2.
—	4732l	Body sherd, hand-made; with very uneven surface inside; pinkish-buff; medium-coarse with few assorted tan and reddish-brown grits; continuously-burnished orange-buff slip outside. A III 203.4.
25	4923a	Rim slightly incurved to medium-wide, thickened, rounded edge; wheel-finished; dark orangish-brown with grey core penetrating to surface in places; very coarse with many assorted grey grits. A IV 300.9a.
26	4562a	Upright rim slightly incurved to medium-wide, greatly thickened, rounded edge; wheel-finished; dark-orange and buff inside and orange and brown outside, dark-grey core; coarse with many assorted grey quartz grits. A III 201.9.
27	4552a	Upright rim gently incurved to slightly thickened rounded edge, wheel-finished; pinkish-tan with grey core; medium-coarse with many small to very fine white and grey grits; white slip outside. A III 201.8a.
—	4520	Body sherd of jar; pinkish-brown; medium-coarse with some assorted tan grits; white slip outside; gritty texture. A III 201.2a.
28	4787a	Rim incurved to wide, greatly thickened, rounded edge, wheel-finished; brown with dark-grey core penetrating to outside in places; coarse with some assorted tan and grey grits; some spalling outside. A III 204.1.
29	4236	Rim incurved to wide, greatly thickened, rounded edge, wheel-finished; dark-orange with greyish-buff core penetrating to outside in places; medium-coarse with many assorted white and grey grits. A II 101.4.

Fig. 63 No.	Reg. No.	
1	4501	Rim incurved to thickened, rounded edge, wheel-finished; orangish-buff inside and greyish-buff outside; coarse with many assorted grey and white grits, one very large brown grit, very porous ware; many assorted pits over-all, pronounced crazing inside, flaking on edge, black smoke marks outside. A III 200.1b.
2	5158a	Rim slightly incurved with thickened, rounded edge, hand-made; orangish-buff with grey core; medium-coarse with many assorted smokey quartz and white grits; light tan incrustations over-all. A IV 301.3.
3	4826	Rim incurved to wide, greatly thickened, rounded edge, wheel-finished; orange inside and outside with buff in places outside, very thick dark-grey core penetrating to outside in places; coarse with many assorted white and grey grits; some assorted pits over-all, very uneven surface outside, rough, gritty texture inside. A III 204.6.
4	4722	Rim incurved to narrow, thickened, rounded edge; dark-orange with buff core; coarse with many assorted white and grey quartz grits; very many assorted pits over-all, some spalling outside and on edge, grey smoke marks outside. A III 203.4.
5	4503	Rim incurved to very wide, greatly thickened, rounded edge, wheel-finished; buff inside and orange outside, dark-grey core in places penetrating to outside and edge; coarse with very many assorted grey and white grits; many assorted pits over-all, some flaking on edge. A III 200.1b.
6	4724	Rim incurved to narrow, thickened, rounded edge; buff with patches of orange on edge, grey core penetrating to outside in places; coarse with many assorted white and grey quartz grits, very porous ware. A III 203.4.

Fig. 63 No.	Reg. No.	
7	4919	Rim incurved to medium-wide, greatly thickened, rounded edge, wheel-finished; orangish-buff with greyish-buff core; medium-coarse with many assorted, mostly medium to small, white quartz grits. A IV 300.9a.
8	4946a	Rim incurved to wide, thickened, rounded edge, wheel-finished; burnt-orange with grey core; coarse with many assorted smokey quartz grits. A IV 300.10.
9	4732b	Rim incurved to wide, greatly thickened, rounded, beveled edge; orange; very coarse with many assorted light- and dark-grey grits; rough gritty texture over-all, some spalling outside, some grey incrustations. A III 203.4.
10	4239	Rim incurved to wide, thickened, rounded edge, wheel-finished; orange with patches of buff and buff core; coarse with very many assorted white and grey grits; many assorted pits over-all, some crazing outside, rough, gritty texture inside, some grey incrustations. A II 101.7.
11	4517	Rim incurved to medium-wide, very thickened, rounded, squared edge; orange with buff inside; coarse with very many assorted grey grits; black smoke marks outside, crazing and flaking inside and on edge. A III 200.2a.
12	4946b	Rim incurved to narrow, slightly thickened, squared edge; orange with orangish-buff core; coarse with many assorted white and tan grits. A IV 300.10.
13	4882	Rim severely incurved to thickened, slightly rounded, beveled edge, wheel-finished; greyish-orange inside and dark-grey outside; coarse with very many assorted grey and white quartz grits. A IV 300.4.
14	4238	Rim incurved to wide, greatly thickened, rounded, beveled edge, wheel-finished; yellowish-grey inside and pinkish-buff outside with orange and tan in places, dark-grey core; very coarse with many assorted, mostly very large, white and light-grey grits; very rough texture over-all, flaking outside. A II 101.4.
15	4802	Rim incurved to wide, greatly thickened, rounded, beveled edge with faint trace of ridge outside, wheel-finished; greyish-orange with grey core; very coarse with many assorted light- and dark-grey grits; some assorted pits over-all, crazing inside and on edge, grey smoke marks inside. A III 204.4.
16	4886	Rim incurved to thinned, slightly rounded, beveled edge, wheel-finished; greyish-tan with thick, dark-grey core penetrating to outside in places; medium-coarse with very many assorted white and tan grits; some assorted pits over-all, rough, gritty texture over-all. A IV 300.5.
—	4732a	Rim of hole-mouth jar, incurved to thickened, rounded, beveled edge; dark-orange with grey patches outside; very coarse with many medium to fine white grits; medium-wide, crude, half-relief rope-molding outside below edge; some grey incrustations over-all. A III 203.4.
17	4232	Upright rim slightly incurved to rounded, beveled edge, wheel-made; buff with orange patch inside edge; coarse with some assorted white grits; some grey incrustations. A II 101.3.
—	4726	Rim incurved to wide, thickened, squared edge, wet-smoothed; buff inside and grey outside, dark-orange core penetrating to surface in places; very coarse with many assorted dark-grey quartz grits; many assorted pits over-all, some spalling outside. A III 203.4.
18	4885	Rim incurved to medium-wide, thickened, rounded, beveled edge; dark-grey; coarse with very many assorted grey quartz grits; traces of orange slip over-all. A IV 300.4.
19	4950	Rim incurved to narrow, thickened, rounded edge; buff with very thick, grey core, very coarse with some assorted white and tan grits; narrow, crude, high-relief molding outside, rough texture inside. A IV 300.10a.

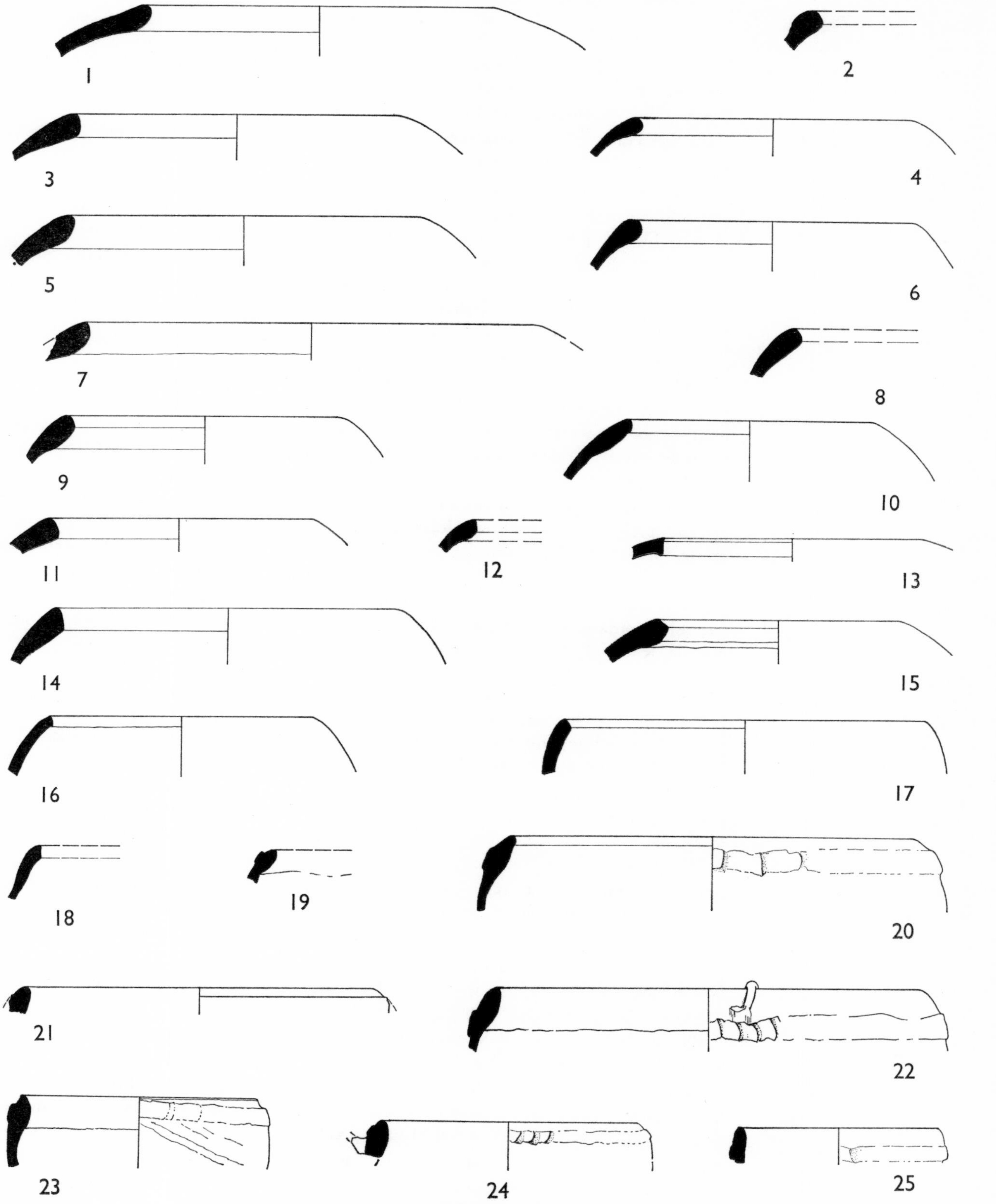

Fig. 63. Hole-mouth jars, Phase VI. 1:4.

Fig. 63 No.	Reg. No.	
20	4732c	Upright rim slightly incurved to wide, thickened, oval edge; buff; coarse with some assorted white and tan grits; medium-wide, uneven, half-relief rope-molding outside, traces of heavy, white slip outside; grey incursions over-all. A III 203.4.
—	4950d	Body sherd of jar; thick; buff; coarse with many assorted tan and grey grits; very porous ware; heavy white slip outside. A IV 300.10a.
21	4885a	Rim with rounded edge pronounced ridge outside, wheel-finished; dull orange with greyish-brown core; medium-coarse with very many assorted white and grey quartz grits. A IV 300.4.
22	4947	Upright rim slightly incurved to wide, thickened, rounded edge; orangish-buff inside and tan outside, thick dark-grey core penetrating to outside in places; coarse with some assorted white grits; wide, high-relief rope-molding outside, one of two original coils wrapped over edge from rope-molding to inside, faint traces of white slip outside; rough texture inside. A IV 300.10a.
23	4829	Upright rim slightly incurved to very wide, greatly thickened rounded, beveled edge, wheel-finished, buff with thick, dark-grey core penetrating to inside; very coarse with many assorted white and tan grits; medium-wide, straight, crude, half-relief rope-molding outside, traces of heavy white slip outside; very rough, gritty texture over-all. A III 204.6.
24	4934	Upright rim with pierced spout fragment, slightly incurved to wide, thick, rounded edge; creamy tan inside and buff outside, coarse with some assorted white grits; medium-wide, crude, high-relief rope-molding outside; some assorted pits over-all, grey smoke marks on edge. A IV 300.10.
25	4731	Upright rim very slightly incurved to rounded edge; buff with thick dark-grey core; coarse with many assorted grey, tan, and white grits; narrow, high-relief rope-molding outside, traces of reddish-orange slip over-all. A III 203.4.

Fig. 64 No.	Reg. No.	
1	4719	Rim inclined out to rounded edge; orangish-buff with pinkish-tan core; coarse with many assorted tan, white, and reddish-brown grits; wide, crude, high-relief rope-molding outside edge, faint traces of reddish-brown slip outside and inside edge; some assorted pits and rough texture over-all. A III 203.4.
—	4930g	Body sherd; orange inside and grey outside, greyish-brown core; medium with some small to fine tan and black grits; continuously-burnished orange slip outside. A IV 300.9b.
2	5081	Rim slightly incurved to narrow, thickened, rounded edge; pinkish-buff with buff core; medium-coarse with some assorted tan grits; medium-wide, straight, high-relief rope-molding outside, traces of white slip outside; some assorted pits over-all, rough texture inside, some grey incrustations. A II 101.2a.
3	5063	Rim of jar with spout, slightly everted to thinned, rounded edge; buff; medium-coarse with few small to fine white grits. A II 101.2a.
—	4569d	Body sherd of jar; tan; medium-coarse with few assorted tan and pink grits; rough, grainy texture inside. A III 200.9a.
4	4565	Upright rim upcurved to wide, greatly thickened, rounded edge, wheel-finished; pinkish-buff with grey core; very coarse with some assorted white and tan grits; traces of white slip outside; some spalling over-all, rough texture inside. A III 200.9a.
5	4721	Base of juglet; dark-grey inside and buff outside; medium-coarse with many assorted white, dark-grey, tan, and reddish-brown grits, porous ware; traces of burnished reddish-brown slip outside; many small to fine pits over-all. A III 203.4.

Fig. 64 No.	Reg. No.	
6	4922	Yellowish-tan inside and orange outside, buff core; medium with very many medium to fine white, brown, and reddish-brown grits; rough texture outside. A IV 300.9a.
—	4569e	Body sherd of jar; orangish-buff outside and grey inside; medium with some medium to very fine grey, tan, and reddish-brown grits; few assorted pits. A III 201.9a.
7	4555	Dark-orange with grey core penetrating to outside in places; coarse with many assorted grey and tan grits; many assorted pits and uneven surfaces over-all. A III 201.9.
8	4554	Pinkish-brown inside and tan outside, reddish-brown core; medium with very many fine, and few assorted, white grits; very pitted and flaking over-all. A III 201.9.
9	4511	Wheel-turned; greyish-buff; medium-coarse with some assorted white, grey, and red grits; traces of orange slip over-all; many assorted pits, very rough texture on bottom. A III 201.1.
10	4561	Orange with buff core; coarse with many assorted tan and grey grits; rough texture over-all, very uneven surfaces on bottom, some grey incrustations outside. A III 201.9.
11	4557	Pinkish-buff with grey core penetrating to bottom in places; medium-coarse with many small to fine white grits; rough texture over-all. A III 201.9.
12	4732	Orange with dark-grey core; medium-coarse with very many assorted tan and reddish-brown grits; some assorted pits outside and on bottom. A III 203.4.
13	4570	Buff inside and orange outside; very coarse with many assorted white, grey, and tan grits; traces of burnished, reddish-brown slip inside; very rough texture outside, many assorted pits, some very large and deep, over-all. A III 201.10.
—	4616e	Body sherd; pinkish-buff with orange inside; medium-coarse with few small to fine tan and grey grits; possible reddish-brown slip inside. A III 201.15.
14	4247	Grey inside and tan outside; coarse with very many assorted white, dark-grey, and brown grits; many assorted pits on bottom and outside, rough texture over-all, black smoke marks inside. A II 101.2a.
15	4946f	Hand-made; black with brownish-buff inside; medium with some medium to very fine tan and grey grits; traces of white slip outside on bottom. A IV 300.10.
16	4936	Greyish-tan inside and buff outside; very thick, dark-grey core; coarse with many assorted light-grey grits; many assorted pits over-all, very rough texture outside. A IV 300.10.
17	4942	Greyish-buff outside with dark-grey inside and core; very coarse with many assorted white grits; many assorted pits over-all, flaking on bottom. A IV 300.10.
18	4245	Orangish-buff with thick grey core; very coarse with many assorted white and tan grits; traces of white slip outside; pitting and flaking on bottom, very rough texture over-all, some grey incrustations. A II 101.2a.
19	4930a	Greyish-brown with grey inside; coarse with very many assorted smokey quartz grits; traces of reddish-brown slip outside; very gritty texture inside. A IV 300.9b.
—	4705	Body sherd of jar; thick; dark buff with thick dark grey core; coarse with some assorted tan and grey grits, few assorted white grits concentrated at surface outside; traces of reddish-brown slip outside, few assorted pits inside. A III 203.2.
20	4923d	Orangish-buff with grey outside; medium-coarse with some small to fine dark-grey and tan grits; white slip outside and on bottom; grey incrustations over-all. A IV 300.9a.
—	4616f	Body sherd of jar; burnt-orange inside and dark-grey outside, greyish-brown core; medium-coarse with very many assorted white and grey quartz grits; light, brown incrustations over-all. A III 201.15.

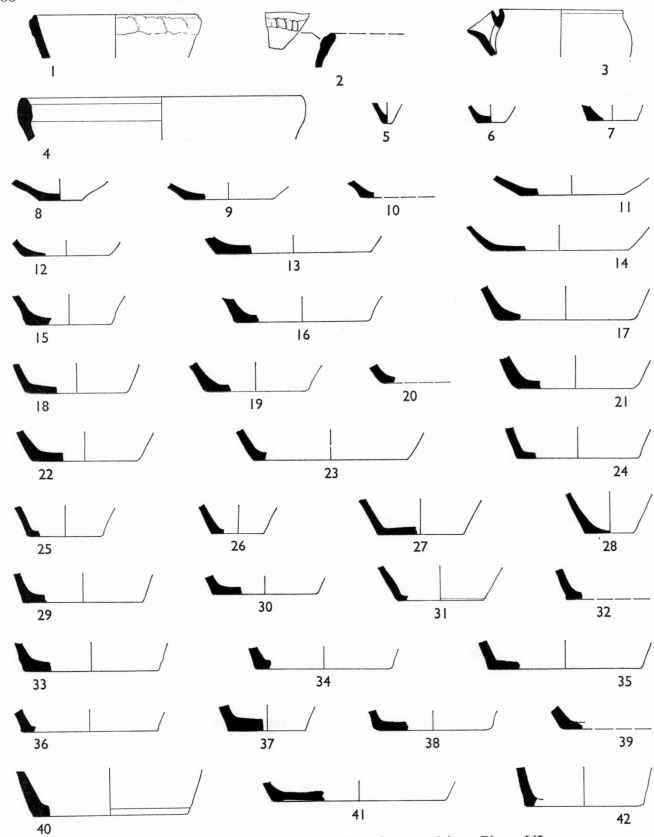

Fig. 64. Hole-mouth jars, bases of juglets, jugs, and jars, Phase VI. 1:4.

Fig. 64 No.	Reg. No.	
21	4827	Buff with grey patches inside; very coarse with some assorted white and red grits; faint traces of white slip outside; very rough texture and some assorted pits over-all. A III 204.6.
22	4926	Grey inside and greyish-tan outside, very thick, dark-grey core; very coarse with many assorted grey and tan grits; faint traces of burnishing outside; some very large pits inside and on bottom, rought texture over-all. A IV 300.9b.
23	4948	Buff; coarse with many assorted tan and grey grits, one very large reddish-brown grit; many assorted pits outside and on bottom, rough texture outside, black smoke marks inside. A IV 300.10a.
24	4706	Buff with thick grey core; coarse with some assorted white grits; many assorted pits over-all, very worn. A III 203.2.
25	4502	Greyish-orange inside and dark-orange outside; medium-coarse with some assorted white grits; faint traces of white slip outside; some assorted pits outside, very rough texture over-all. A III 200.1b.
—	4616d	Body sherd; brownish-orange; medium-coarse with many small to very fine white and reddish-brown grits; white slip outside. A III 201.15.
—	4552d	Body sherd of jar, brownish-orange with buff core in places; medium-coarse with many large to fine grey and white grits; some assorted pits outside, some spalling inside. A III 201.8a.
26	4512	String-cut; orange inside and greyish-brown outside; coarse with many assorted white and tan grits; rough texture inside, dark grey smoke marks outside. A III 201.1.
27	4617	Buff with grey core in places; very coarse with many, mostly fine, white grits and some assorted reddish-brown grits; traces of reddish-brown slip inside; very uneven surface inside, some assorted pits over-all. A III 201.16.
28	4927, 29 (joined)	Yellowish-buff outside with dark-grey inside and core; very coarse with many assorted grey and tan grits; faint traces of burnished reddish-brown slip outside; some very large pits inside and on bottom, rough texture over-all. A IV 300.9b.
—	4941	Body sherd; tan outside and bright-grey inside; medium-fine with many medium to fine black and grey grits, very porous ware; traces of burnished reddish-brown slip outside; many medium to small pits over-all. A IV 300.10.
—	5158d	Body sherd; tan with light-grey inside; medium-coarse with many medium to fine grey and black sandy grits; traces of burnished reddish-brown slip outside; spalling over-all inside. A IV 301.3.
—	4950i	Body sherd; orange-buff; fine with few assorted tan and reddish-brown grits; traces of burnished reddish-brown slip outside; spalling inside leaving a rough gritty surface. A IV 300.11.
29	4881	Buff; coarse with some assorted white grits; faint traces of white slip outside; some pitting on bottom, rough texture over-all, some grey incrustations. A IV 300.4.
30	4911	Brown inside and orange outside, very thick, dark-grey core; coarse with many assorted white grits; bottom pitted and flaking, rough texture over-all. A IV 300.9.
31	5081b	Possibly coil-made; pinkish-tan; medium with few small to fine reddish-brown, tan, and grey grits; burnished reddish-brown slip outside; uneven and irregular surface inside; black smoke mark on broken edge. A II 101.2a.
—	5158h	Body sherd of jar, hand-made; tan; coarse with some medium to fine white, tan, and reddish-brown grits; continuously-burnished reddish-brown slip outside; rough and uneven surface inside. A IV 301.3.

Fig. 64 No.	Reg. No.	
—	4923i	Body sherd; tannish-buff; fine with few small to very fine reddish-brown and grey grits; traces of burnished reddish-brown slip outside; very uneven surfaces inside. A IV 300.9a.
32	4923b	Burnt-orange with dark-grey inside; coarse with many assorted grey quartz grits; very uneven surfaces over-all; gritty texture inside. A IV 300.9a.
33	5158	Brown with thick, dark-grey core; very coarse with many assorted white and grey grits; traces of reddish-orange slip outside; rough gritty texture over-all. A IV 301.3.
34	4562c	Orangish-brown with dark-grey core; coarse with few small to very fine white grits. A III 201.9.
35	4558	Wet-smoothed outside; dark-grey with dark brownish-grey inside; very coarse with many assorted grey quartz grits; many assorted pits over-all, flaking inside. A III 201.9.
36	4562d	Wheel-finished outside; bright-orange inside and tan outside; medium-coarse with some small to fine, and two very large, white and grey grits; some assorted, mostly fine, pits over-all, with some very large inside, dark-grey smoke marks inside. A III 201.9.
37	4928	Greyish-buff inside and orange outside; coarse with very many assorted white and tan grits; traces of vertically-burnished dark red slip outside; many assorted pits over-all, very rough, gritty texture inside. A IV 300.9b.
—	5158e	Body sherd; thick, hand-made; orangish-tan with grey core; medium-coarse with some assorted dark-grey grits; reddish-brown slip over-all outside; some spalling and fine pitting inside. A IV 301.3.
—	4930f	Body sherd; orange; medium with some assorted grey grits; continuously-burnished reddish-brown slip outside. A IV 300.9b.
—	4923h	Body sherd, thick; brown; coarse with many assorted grey quartz grits; burnished, reddish-brown slip outside. A IV 300.9a.
38	4569	Dark-grey with greyish-orange outside; very coarse with many small to fine grey grits; rough, gritty texture over-all. A III 201.9a.
39	4950c, e (joined)	Pinkish-orange with greyish-buff core; coarse with some assorted tan and grey grits, very porous ware; traces of heavy white slip outside and on bottom; brown incrustations over-all. A IV 300.10a.
40	6119	Orangish buff; coarse with assorted white and grey quartz grits. A II 101.6.
41	4716	Orangish-buff inside and greyish-brown outside; very coarse with many assorted white and grey grits; many small to fine pits over-all, very uneven surfaces, some crazing inside. A III 203.3.
42	4923c	Orangish-buff; coarse with some small to fine tan grits; white slip outside; very uneven surface on bottom, greyish-brown incrustations over-all. A IV 300.9a.

Fig. 65 No.	Reg. No.	
1	6113	No description. A II 101.1a.
2	4946e	Hand-made; bright orangish-brown; medium-coarse with many small to very fine white and tan grits; traces of white slip outside on bottom; light brown incrustations over-all. A IV 300.10.
3	4732g	Buff; medium-coarse with some fine white grits; traces of heavy white slip outside and on bottom; uneven surfaces outside, some grey incrustations over-all. A III 203.4.
4	4830	Buff inside with dark-grey outside and core penetrating to inside in places; very coarse with many small to fine white grits; many assorted pits over-all. A III 204.6.
5	4549	Buff; medium-coarse with many assorted tan grits, traces of white slip over-all. A III 201.7a.

Fig. 65 No.	Reg. No.	
6	4946	Greyish-tan with thick, dark-grey core penetrating to surface in places; very coarse with many assorted grey grits; many assorted pits over-all, rough texture inside. A IV 300.10.
7	4235	Buff inside and greyish-buff outside, dark-grey core in places penetrating to inside; very coarse with many assorted white and light-grey grits; some assorted pits inside, very rough texture over-all. A II 101.4.
8	4946d	Very thin bottom, juncture of wall and bottom well-rounded, hand-made; pinkish-brown inside and dark-grey outside; medium-coarse with some assorted grey and tan grits; traces of burnished, reddish-brown slip over-all; black smoke marks on bottom. A IV 300.10.
—	4562i	Body sherd; buff-brown; fine with some very fine tan and dark-brown grits; continuously-burnished reddish-brown slip outside. A III 201.9.
—	4787f	Body sherd, varying thickness; brown with dark-grey inside and core; medium-coarse with some medium to fine white grits; continuously-burnished reddish-brown slip outside; very uneven surface inside. A III 204.1.
—	4571e	Body sherd of large jar, thick; brownish-buff with thin grey layer inside; medium-coarse with some assorted reddish-brown and grey grits; faint traces of burnished greyish-brown slip outside; some assorted pits over-all inside. A III 201.10.
9	4715	Buff with dark-grey core at angle; coarse with some assorted tan and reddish-brown grits; traces of heavy, white slip outside; some grey incrustations over-all. A III 203.3.
10	4930	Reddish-orange outside with thick dark-grey core, pinkish-grey inside; coarse with very many assorted white and tan grits; traces of vertically burnished red slip outside; very rough texture inside, flaking on bottom. A IV 300.9b.
—	4930h	Body sherd; reddish-brown; medium with some medium to fine white and tan grits; continuously-burnished reddish-brown slip outside. A IV 300.9b.
11	4727	Buff; coarse with many assorted white and grey grits. A III 203.4.
12	4918	Orange inside and dark-grey outside, grey core; coarse with very many assorted white quartz grits, porous ware; many assorted pits inside, some pits and flaking on bottom, rough texture over-all. A IV 300.9a.
13	4914	Buff with dark-orange inside; very coarse with many assorted white, grey and tan grits; many fine pits over-all, some pits and flaking on bottom, rough texture, some grey incrustations. A IV 300.9.
14	4244	Buff inside and tan outside; coarse with very many assorted white, grey and tan grits; many assorted pits inside, rough texture on bottom, grey smoke marks inside. A II 101.2a.
15	4615	Buff with grey core at angle; very coarse with many assorted white and tan grits; traces of heavy white slip outside; rough texture inside, grey smoke marks inside. A III 201.15.
16	4831	Orange inside and buff outside, grey core in places penetrating to surfaces; coarse with very many assorted white and light-grey grits; some assorted pits outside. A III 204.6.
17	4732i	Very small lug-handle fragment, pierced; buff; coarse with few assorted grey and reddish-brown grits; traces of heavy white slip outside; some grey incrustations over-all. A III 203.4.
18	4725	Lug-handle, rounded and pierced, poorly jointed to body; buff with dark-orange outside; coarse with many assorted tan grits; many assorted pits over-all. A III 203.4.
19	4946i	Thumb-indented edge; bright orangish-buff with grey core; medium with many small to fine grey and tan grits; traces of heavy white slip outside; light grey incrustations. A IV 300.10.

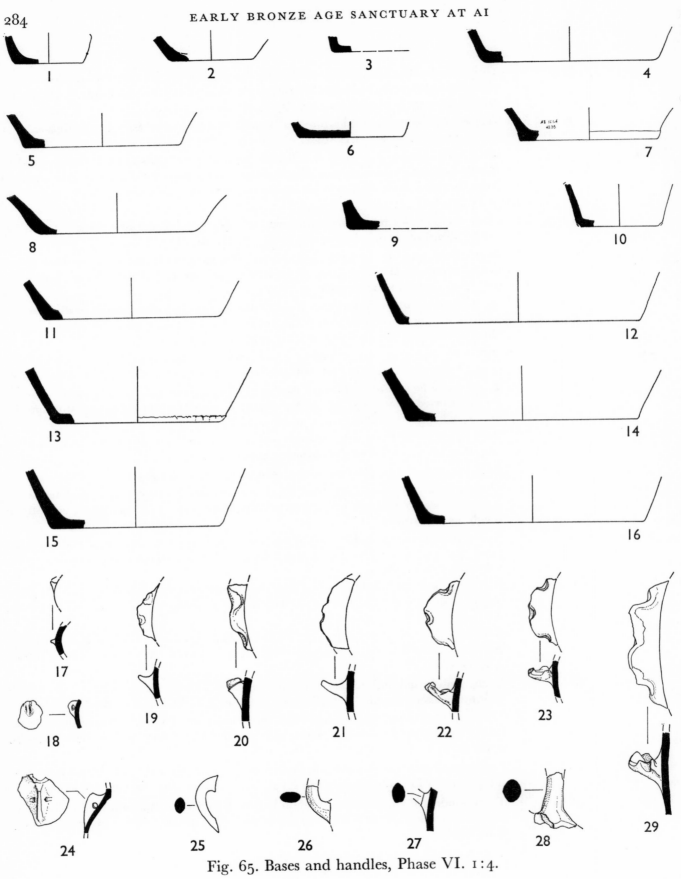

Fig. 65. Bases and handles, Phase VI. 1:4.

Fig. 65 No.	Reg. No.	
—	4923e	Ledge-handle fragment, thumb-indented edge; orange with grey outside, greyish-brown core; medium-coarse with some medium to very fine white and grey grits; white slip outside; greyish-brown incrustations. A IV 300.9a.
—	4805c	Ledge-handle fragment, edge badly chipped; orange with grey core; medium-coarse with many mostly very fine grey grits; uneven, grainy texture. A III 204.4.
—	4562h	Small ledge-handle fragment, thumb-indented edge; orangish-brown with brownish-buff inside and core; medium-coarse with some assorted white and grey grits; possible reddish-brown slip outside; few assorted pits. A III 201.9.
—	4569f	Body sherd; bright-grey with brown core; medium-fine with some small to very fine white and reddish-brown grits. A III 201.9a.
20	4912	Narrow, pushed-up, thumb-indented edge; dark greyish-brown with thick, dark-grey core; very coarse with many assorted white and reddish-brown grits, porous ware; some assorted pits inside. A IV 300.9.
21	4946g	Thumb-indented edge; vessel hand-made; light-brown with grey patches; medium with many fine to very fine tan and grey grits; traces of white slip outside; brown incrustations. A IV 300.10.
22	4946h	Slightly pushed-up, thumb-indented edge; hand-made; dark-grey; medium-coarse with many medium to fine grey, tan, and reddish-brown grits; white slip outside; brown incrustations. A IV 300.10.
23	4921	Thumb-indented edge; grey with thick, dark-grey core penetrating to surface in places; coarse with very many assorted light- and dark-grey grits; many assorted pits, very rough texture with flaking inside. A IV 300.9a.
24	5148	Located vertically on shoulder of amphoriskos, pierced; orangish-buff outside and tan inside; medium-fine with some medium to fine white and tan grits; traces of burnished-reddish-brown slip outside; assorted pits over-all, some flaking outside. A IV 301.2.
25	4923f	Small loop-handle, flattened oval section; dark-brown; medium-coarse with some assorted grey, white, and tan grits; continuously-burnished reddish-brown slip. A IV 300. 9a.
—	4805e	Body sherd; bright-grey with brown core; medium-fine with many small to very fine white and tan grits; continuously-burnished brownish-grey slip outside. A III 204.4.
26	4234	Loop-handle fragment joined to body oval section; buff with greyish-brown core; medium-coarse with very many assorted grey grits; traces of white slip and painted red stripes outside. A II 101.4.
27	4732j	Stump of loop-handle attached to body, irregular oval section; buff with grey core; medium with some small to very fine grey and white quartz and tan grits; vertically-burnished reddish-brown slip outside. A III 203.4.
—	4562g	Small loop-handle fragment joined to body, flattened-oval section; orange with brownish-buff core; medium with some medium to very fine tan grits; some light grey incrustations. A III 201.9.
28	4568	Pillar-handle fragment; pinkish-buff; coarse with some assorted white grits; traces of white incrustations, some assorted pits. A III 201.9a.
29	4717	Pushed-up edge; dark-orange with thick, dark-grey core in places; traces of white slip outside; grey incrustations. A III 203.3.
—	4805d	Ledge-handle fragment, pushed up thumb-indented edge; orangish-buff; medium with some small to fine white and tan grits; heavy white slip outside; grey incrustations. A III 204.4.

Fig. 65 No.	Reg. No.	
—	4787d	Ledge handle fragment, pushed up thumb-indented edge; burnt-orange outside with dark-grey inside and core; medium-coarse with many medium to very fine white grits, one large, dark-brown grit; reddish-brown slip outside; many assorted pits inside. A III 204.1.

Fig. 66 No.	Reg. No.	
1	4923	Orangish-buff inside and brown outside, thick, dark-grey core penetrating to outside; coarse with very many assorted white and grey grits; medium wide, crude, half-relief rope-molding outside; very uneven surface inside. A IV 300.9a.
2	4935	Orange inside and creamy-white outside; very coarse with many assorted tan grits, porous ware; wide, high-relief rope-molding outside; many assorted pits over-all, very rough texture inside. A IV 300.10.
3	4787e	Large jar; yellowish-tan; coarse with some assorted brown and reddish-brown grits; medium-wide; crude, half-relief rope-molding and heavy white slip outside; many assorted pits inside; brown incrustations. A III 204.1.
—	4616a	Body sherd of large jar; buff with greyish-brown inside; medium-coarse with some assorted tan grits; medium-wide band of very high-relief crude rope-molding and traces of white slip outside. A III 201.15.
4	4704	Neck fragment of large jar; dark brownish-grey inside and dark-brown outside, dark-grey core; coarse with very many assorted white and tan grits, porous ware; wide band of high-relief decorative crescents closely spaced outside at joint of neck and body, traces of orange slip outside; rough texture inside, many assorted pits. A III 203.2.
5	4876	Orangish-buff; medium-coarse with many medium to small white, grey, and pink grits; wide, straight, crude, half-relief rope-molding outside, traces of heavy white slip outside; many assorted pits and flaking inside. A IV 300.3.
—	4616c	Body sherd of large jar; very thick; pink outside and greyish-buff inside; grey core; medium-coarse with many fine to very fine white grits, few assorted grey and tan grits; wide very low relief molding outside at joint of two sections of wall of vessel. A III 201.15.
6	5153	Orange; medium with some assorted, mostly small to fine, white grits; creamy-white slip and painted red trellis pattern outside; some grey incrustation. A IV 301.3.
—	5154	Body sherd of jar; orange, medium-coarse with some assorted white grits; white slip outside with traces of painted reddish-brown vertical lines in possible net-pattern; grey incrustations over-all. A IV 301.3.
7	5151	Creamy-white with grey core; medium-coarse with many medium to fine orange and grey grits; traces of painted reddish-orange trellis pattern outside; some grey incrustations. A IV 301.3
8	4825	Buff with orange inside; medium-coarse with some small to fine white and grey geometric grits; traces of narrow painted brown stripes in geometric pattern and one dot outside, traces of continuous-burnishing on lower part; some grey incrustations. A III 204.6.
9	4885b	Orangish-brown with greyish-brown core; coarse with some medium to fine white and tan grits; white slip and one wide painted red stripe outside; grey incrustations. A IV 300.4.
10	4246	Orangish-buff; medium-coarse with some assorted white grits; white slip outside, one wide, painted orange stripe outside; some grey incrustations. A II 101.2a.
11	5081c	Pinkish-tan; medium with some small to fine grey quartz, tan, and white grits; white slip outside, one wide painted, reddish-brown stripe outside. A II 101.2a.
—	4923g	Body sherd of jar; buff-brown outside and grey inside; medium-coarse with some medium to very fine grey and tan grits; heavy white slip outside with traces of two painted vertical reddish-brown stripes. A IV 300.9a.

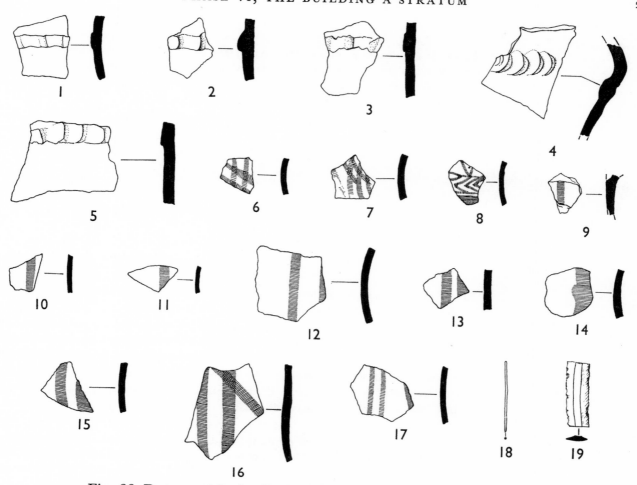

Fig. 66. Decorated body sherds and various objects, Phase VI. 1:4.

Fig. 66 No.	Reg. No.	
12	4227	Tan inside and orange outside, thick, dark-grey core; coarse with some assorted white grits; white slip outside, faint traces of two painted orange stripes, very rough texture inside, some grey incrustations outside. A II 101.3.
13	4492	Orange inside and buff outside; coarse with some assorted grey grits; white slip outside, two wide, parallel, painted, reddish orange stripes outside; grey incrustations. A 1.2a.
14	4506	Buff; medium-coarse with some assorted white grits; trace of one wide painted reddish-orange stripe outside; many assorted pits, grey incrustations outside, rough gritty texture over-all. A III 201.1.
15	4225	Buff; medium-coarse with some assorted grey grits; traces of white slip outside, two wide painted reddish-orange stripes outside. A II 101.2.
16	4805	Tannish-buff; coarse with very many assorted tan grits; traces of white slip and trellis pattern with wide painted dark brown stripes outside; very rough, gritty texture, few very large pits inside. A III 204.4.
—	4224	Body sherd of jar; buff, medium-coarse with few assorted white grits; white slip outside with traces of painted, reddish-brown net pattern; rough texture inside, some grey incrustations over-all. A II 101.2.

Fig. 66 No.	Reg. No.	
17	4231	Buff with grey core; medium-coarse with some assorted white grits; white slip outside, faint traces of three medium-wide painted orange lines outside, rough, gritty texture inside, grey incrustations. A II 101.3.
18	0–1	Bronze pin, pointed on one end, broken in middle. A II 101.1a.
19	0–3	Retouched blade, trapezoidal section; greyish-tan with whitish-marbling; light tan incrustations. A III 203.2.
—	4562j	Shell, white with hole in hinge; light grey incrustations. A III 201.9.

DESCRIPTIONS OF THE MARQUET-KRAUSE PHASE VI POTTERY AND OBJECTS, FIG. 67

Fig. 67 No.	M-K Reg. No.	
1	2085	Rounded bowl: pink burnished, design of lines inside. H:116; under floor A (M-K Pl. LXXVII).
2	2004	Two large bowls, shallow; flat base, wall very inclined, first slightly curved toward top, then somewhat bent; rim forming obtuse angle with inside wall and nearly vertical, red burnished with design of darker red lines. H:116; just under floor A (M-K Pl. LXXVII).
3	1941	Fragment of small bowl (resembling the stone bowl found in sanctuary A in the same room); wall straight, slightly inclined, horizontal rim projecting over inside surface; base slightly concave, concavity accentuated by a ring. H:116; under floor A (M-K Pl. LXXXIV).
—	2495	Fragment of bowl, straight wall rather inclined, flat rim with triangular projection (with rounded angle) over inside surface, making a very slight angle with inner wall; rim of thin hole-mouth, barely projecting over inside surface; pointed edge; decorative molding; fragment: grey burnishing. H:116; under floor II (under outside wall N.–S.).
—	2265	Fragments of bowls: (1) wall very inclined; rim forming a right angle with inner wall; fine ware; trace of wick; (2) wall less inclined, rim more elongated forming also a right angle with inner wall; rim of thick hole-mouth, thickened, very round; neck of jar; various burnished fragments; red, brown, grey. H:120; between floors A and B.
4	1980	Fragment of body of jar with primitive ear-handle; fragment of bowl: fine inside wall very inclined; curved, horizontal rim projecting very thin and very short over the inside surface. H:116; 20 cm. under floor A (M-K Pl. LXXXII).
—	2292	Rim of bowl projecting over inside surface; outcurved neck (of jar); flint fragment. H:116; under floor A.
5	2296	Rim of bowl; white ware, burnished. H:116; under floor A, column of the south wall (M-K Pl. LXXXII).
—	2380	Fragment of bowl; wall straight, somewhat inclined, horizontal rim slightly projecting over two surfaces; on body circular ring; neck of small juglet, high and thin, rim flared, loop-handle. H:116; under floor A.
6	2357	Fragment of bowl; wall rather inclined, horizontal rim slightly arched in projection over the two surfaces, less pronounced over inside surface. H:133; 1 m. 30 cm. depth; under floor A (at the foot of the altar of sanctuary A). (M-K Pl. LXXXII).
—	2092	Fragments of bowls: (1) straight wall, rather inclined, horizontal rim projecting over the two surfaces; (2) wall inclined 45°, horizontal rim projecting triangularly over inside surface; (3), (4) same type, rim projecting elongated over inside surface; (5) fine, flat,

Fig. 67 No.	*M-K Reg. No.*	
		thin rim slightly curved toward top; fragments of two small hole-mouths, fine, covered with brown slip; rim of hole-mouth, very thin, barely thickened over inside surface; fragment of neck, inside wall and rim thin, curved toward outside; fragment of neck of jar, fine ware, rim slightly outcurved, folded over itself in rather thin pads; fragment of neck of jar, rim thickened into pads; burnished white slip; fragments with irregular moldings; fragment with brown slip, design of darker lines; broken horizontal handle. H:116; under floor A.
7	2459	Fragment of bowl; wall inclined, horizontal rim in thick projection over two surfaces. H:116; under the wall at the niche (south) between floors A and B intermediate (M-K Pl. LXXXII).
8	2459	Fragment of neck of jar; simple rim, thickened over the outside surface, sharply curved toward outside. H:116, under the wall at niche (south) between floors A and B intermediate (M-K Pl. LXXXII).
—	1932	Fragments of jar, pink ware, well-baked, traces of red lines. H:116; directly under floor I.
—	2460	Fragments: white slip; fragments: brown slip. H:116; under the wall at the niche (south) between floors A and B intermediate.
—	2461	Various fragments of a jar; fragment of shoulder and of base of neck (short neck nearly perpendicular at shoulder, rounded angle); flat base; fragments of bodies with molding barely projecting; white slip. H:116; under the wall at niche (south) between floors A and B intermediate.
—	2359	Spout, not pierced; fragment of neck of jar, outcurved, very thin wall and rim, barely curved; base of small jug with red slip; fragment with decorative molding; fragments, white slip; brick fragment. H:120; under the bench which borders the wall of room 133, under floor A.

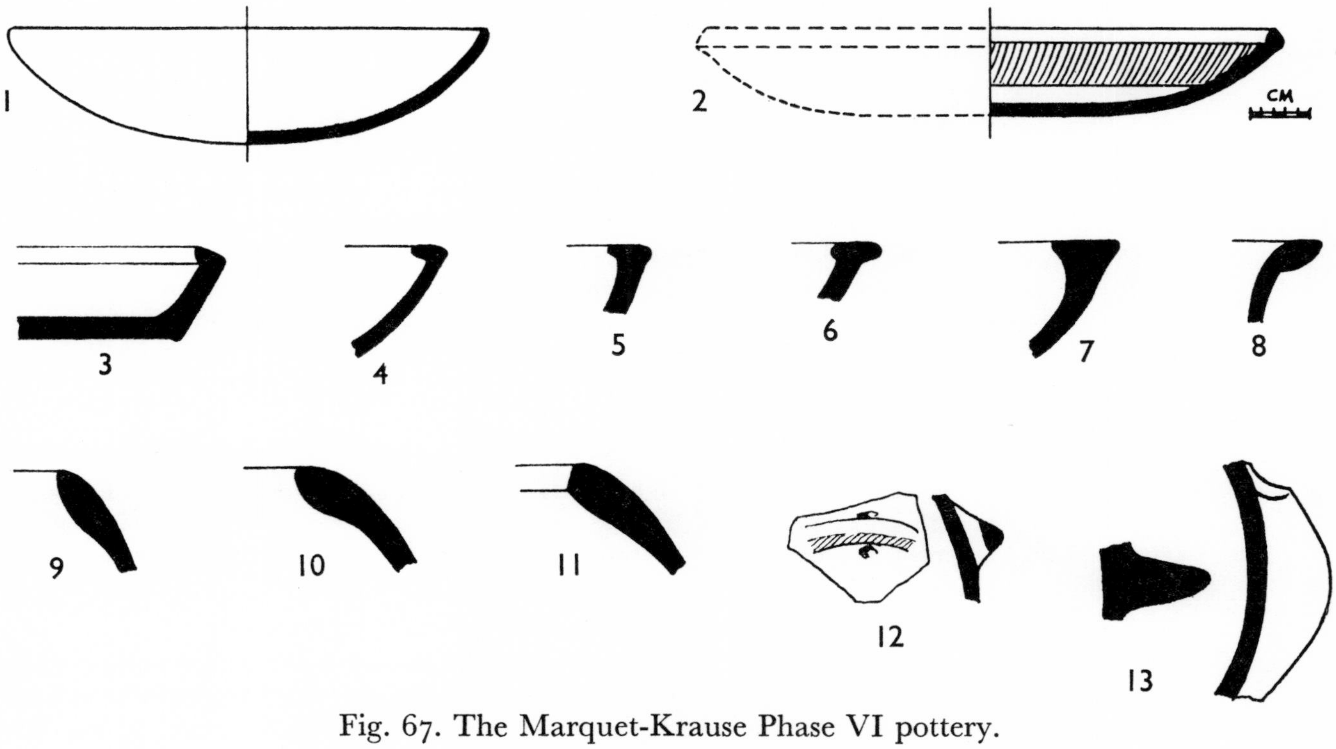

Fig. 67. The Marquet-Krause Phase VI pottery.

Fig. 67 No.	M-K Reg. No.	
9	2296	Rim of hole-mouth. H:116; under floor A, column of the south wall (M-K Pl. LXXXVII).
—	2465	Rim of hole-mouth; thin, with molding; H:116; between floors A and B intermediate (M-K Pl. LI).
10	1997	Three horizontal flat handles; one very long, another with finger impressions on side at joint. H:116; under floor A (M-K Pl. LXXXVII).
—	2353	Two rims of hole-mouths: (1) thickened over inside surface. (2) not thickened, rounded edge, flat bases. H:116; under the large stone of floor A.
—	2493	Rim of hole-mouth; thick and heavy, greatly thickened over inside surface toward edge; fragment of neck, simple, rim curved toward outside, rounded edge; fragment of rim of jug, red slip; fragment with narrow and projecting molding. H:116; under floor II.
—	1931	Fragment with decorative molding, type I. H:116; directly under floor I.
11	2322	Rim of hole-mouth; rim slightly inclined, thickened toward top of inside surface, flat edge. H:116, between floors A and B, south wall (M-K Pl. LXXXVII).
—	2354 II	Rim of bowl or hole-mouth, curved, slightly thickened toward top, edge flat; fragment of neck of jar; thin inside wall and rim, edge curved toward outside; fragment of neck, red slip; broken horizontal handle. H:116; 15–20 cm. under floor A.
12	2357	Triangular ear-handle. H:133; 1 m. 30 cm. depth; under floor A (at the foot of the altar of sanctuary A) (M-K Pl. LXXXVII).
13	1997	Three flat horizontal handles; one very long; another with finger indentations on the sides; rims of hole-mouths: (1) thin: brown, (2), (3) thin, barely thickened; brown; (4) thin, very much thickened on inside surface, brown with white grits; (5) thick and swollen. H:116; under floor A (M-K Pl. LXXXVII).
—	2088	Broken horizontal handle; flat loop-handle; fragment of jug, carefully worked and fine base, blackened by fire; fragment of neck of jar somewhat thickened rim curved toward outside and rounded in pads. H:116; under floor A.
—	2093	Completely flat horizontal handle; bowl, rounded form; fragment with triangular, rectangular projection striated at top. H:136; under floor A.
—	2094	Broken horizontal handles; fragment of small juglet, round base, globular body, dumpy form; fragment of bowl, very fine wall and rim, red slip; two rims of hole-mouths: (1) with molding; (2) very thin; fragment of slightly flared neck, rim forming a somewhat thick padding over outside surface. H:136–137, under floor I.
—	2198	Two flat horizontal handles; fragment with projecting molding; fragment with narrow molding in triangular projection; neck of small jug, very fine wall and rim curved toward outside; neck of jug, loop-handle; rims of heavy hole-mouths: (1) slightly thickened over inside face; (2) edge forming a very rounded and thick extension over inside surface. H:136–137; under floor A.
—	2397	Flat horizontal handle; base of small juglet. H:116; under the south wall of Sanctuary A.
—	2252	Horizontal handle, type I, white slip; two rims of thin hole-mouths; very small loop-handle, pink ware; small flat base, very narrow (d., 2 cm.), concave inside; various fragments of a base. H:116; between floors A and B, under the large stone, east side.
—	2494	Flat horizontal handle, elongated, red slip; fragment; brown slip, fragments of flint. H:116; under floor II (under outside wall N.–S.).
—	2582	Flat, broken, horizontal handle; two rims of hole-mouths, thickened over inside surface; one has rounded edge, the other barely thinned; flint. H:116; under the niche between intermediate floor and floor B.

Fig. 67 No.	M-K Reg. No.	
—	2625	Flat horizontal handle; imprint of end of finger on rim; rim of bowl projecting over inside surface. H:116; under the niche, under floor A.
—	2427	Fragment; white slip with bands of white paint; fragment of hole-mouth; fragment; brownish-red slip. H:116; under floor A.
—	2258	Various fragments. H:116; between floors A and B, under the east stone of floor A.
—	2324	(a) Various fragments; fragment: red slip, large brown concentric bands; brick; (b) bones; snail shell. H:116; between floor A and B, column of the south wall.
—	1933	Various fragments. H:116, directly under floor I.
—	2295	Brick; rim of hole-mouth. H:116; under floor A, east side.
—	2612	Carbonized olive seeds. H:116; under floor A, under the niche.
—	2614	Various flints. H:116; under floor A, under the niche.

VIII

PHASES VII AND VIII, SANCTUARY A STRATUM

INTRODUCTION

There is no evidence that Building A was destroyed at the end of Phase VI. No ashes indicating a general destruction are found on top of Layer 2 under the Phase VII altar in Pl. XVII, drawn in Fig. 83, or in the passage under Blockage M¹ in Wall M, drawn in Section B–B, Fig. 11. Walls H and M show no evidence of destruction and rebuilding between the original construction in Phase VI and final destruction in Phase VIII. The transition from Phase VI to Phase VII of Building A seems to have been non-violent.

However, the reflection of events in the evidence of Building A must be deceptive, because revolutionary changes occurred in the city at Ai in the transition from Phase VI to Phase VII. The changes can be attributed in part to external influences, because the Phase VI city wall at the citadel is black with smoke marks in front of Tower A. An assault on the city seems to have taken place, but the absence of general destruction evidence inside the walls suggests that changes were effected by introducing new leadership, probably dictated by the aggressors, and the general population continued under a new political orientation.

Evidence of significant changes at the acropolis and Site A seems to presume a new political orientation in local government, and strengthening of city fortifications suggests that the changes were effected at the risk of retaliation from external forces. In summary, the evidence is as follows:

1. A fourth EB city wall, A¹, was constructed against the outside of Wall A from Area VII at Site A (see Fig. 81) along the entire south side to Site K at the southeast corner, and from Site K to Site J, the Wadi Gate site. No excavation northwest of Site J has been done, but the contour of the *tell* suggests that Wall A¹ continues to the northwest bend in the city wall, near contour 815 in Fig. 2. The fourth wall, built in Phase VII, encompasses about 80% of the city. Wall A is reused in the remaining 20% along the deep Wadi el-Jaya. The objective of strengthening the fortifications is evident at Site H, where the combined width of Wall A–A¹ is about 8 meters, and the height is 7 meters (see Callaway 1970, 25–26, Fig. 13).

2. The house and courtyard of Building A in Areas II–III at Site A were remodeled and converted into a sanctuary. The courtyard remained uncovered, and an altar was constructed against the inside of Tower A. The north unit of Building A in Area IV was excluded from the sanctuary by Blockage M¹ in the Wall M passage. In Area II, a partial wall was built inside Wall E, and the entire room, covered by a roof supported by wooden pillars, was converted into a holy place, furnished with incense burners, various plates and bowls, and the Egyptian alabasters presumably used in the Phase VI temple at Site D.

3. The Phase VI temple complex at Site D was constricted in Phase VII to the central rectangular temple building surrounded by strengthened fortifications. The open rooms around the rectangular building seem to have been filled with earth and stones in Phase VII, leaving only the

rectangular building open. Living quarters around the temple were, therefore, converted into fortifications, and a decision was apparently made to move the sanctuary to Site A. The temple building, now heavily fortified, probably became the seat of government and residence of the ruler at Ai.

If the Phase VI temple at Ai reflects Egyptian political involvement, which seems to have been the case, the changes effected in Phase VII indicate a downgrading of Egyptian influence, and possibly a political reorientation recognizing the increasing influence of newcomers who introduced the culture characterized by Khirbet Kerak ware. Sanctuary A of Phase VII, therefore, came into existence in the backwash of political and military events which must be inferred, but which probably occurred in some fashion approaching the above reconstruction. The sanctuary, as a result, would have minimal value as an architectural type, and because of the political implications associated with the imported Egyptian cultic vessels, the cult would not necessarily reflect local indigenous religion at Ai.

SANCTUARY A OF PHASE VII

There is no evidence indicating the status of the north unit of Building A in Area IV in Phase VII, except that it was excluded from Sanctuary A by Blockage M¹ in Wall M. The south unit consisting of the room in Area II and the courtyard in Area III was extensively remodeled within the Building A structural framework, and converted into Sanctuary A. The latter, therefore, is of primary interest in this chapter.

The open court in Area III.

The Phase VI courtyard in Area III seems to have been adapted to an altar area because it was not roofed. No evidence of a roof over the area in Phase VII remained; indeed the same arguments against a roof in Phase VI are valid also in Phase VII, with additional reinforcement from the presence of Altar J. Altars that are known in later times are usually in open courts. One entrance to the court was through the door in Wall H. No evidence of an outside entrance through Wall L is preserved, although the logical place for a passageway would be in Wall L instead of the ramp entrance to Area II reconstructed by Marquet-Krause.

Altar J. Three stones of the enclosure wall of Altar J are preserved in Pl. IX.1, on the balk at the top of the meter scale. The stones are resting on the surface of Layer 2, as drawn in Fig. 83, and the *huwwar* surface on top of Layer 1, the floor of Sanctuary A, abuts the inside of the base stones. The wall, J¹, is a Phase VII structure, because the Phase VI surface on Layer 2, underneath Wall J¹, is smoothly finished underneath the stones. Wall J¹ is reconstructed in Fig. 87 from the plans of Marquet-Krause 1949.

Altar J rests on top of the smooth surface of Layer 2 of Phase VI also, and the *huwwar* surface of Sanctuary A abuts the base of the altar as shown in Pl. IX.1. The front of the altar is 1.75 meters wide, and each side is oriented parallel with related walls, i.e., the north side is parallel with Wall J¹ and at a 90° angle to Tower A, while the south side is parallel with Wall H, and not at a 90° angle with Tower A.

The photograph in Pl. XVI:2 of Marquet-Krause 1949 shows *huwwar* plaster on the front of the altar, reaching from the floor to the top edge, 72 centimeters above the floor (cf. elevations No. 42, 851.61, the floor, and No. 43, 852.33, the altar, in Pl. XCIX of Marquet-Krause 1949). A small cup is shown in the photograph on top of the altar with a crude enclosure of stones around it, as though they sheltered a flame burning in the cup from gusts of wind whipping against Tower A. The stones around the cup are not a permanent part of the altar. In the same photograph, the small bin at the north end of the altar, against Wall J¹, seems to be a temporary structure also, because the plaster facing on the altar does not extend to the stones forming the bin. Apparently, the original altar had an open recess on each side reaching back to the face of Tower A.

All of the plaster facing and most of the upper structure of Altar J were eroded away when excavation of the site was resumed in 1964, because the structure had been left uncovered for 30 years. Because of the erosion, it was possible to observe the inner materials of the altar and the manner of construction. Pl. IX.1 shows the facing stones, covered by plaster in the Marquet-Krause photographs, but now obviously the same kind of hammer-dressed stones found in the walls of the acropolis building. The stones are set in mud mortar like those of the acropolis structure built in Phase VI. One large mud brick, drawn in Fig. 83 and visible in Pl. IX.1, is built into the base course of the altar. The brick is about the same size as the stones, and seems to be interchangeable with them.

The technique of building Altar J is significant, because it is the bricklayer's technique used in constructing the Phase VI temple on the acropolis. Stones hammer-dressed to approximately the size and shape of bricks are laid in mud mortar like bricks, without any rubble core or fill. This manner of construction was first pointed out by Yeivin when the Phase VI temple was excavated by Marquet-Krause (Yeivin 1934, 189ff.).

The bricklayer's technique of construction is not used in Building A of Phase VI at the sanctuary site, and it is evident only in Altar J of Sanctuary A. Possibly the small altar, or projection inside the widened Wall E of Area II, was constructed in the same manner. Altar J actually has one mud brick in the base course, drawn in Fig. 83, and visible in Pl. IX.1 midway of the altar structure. It seems, therefore, that special care was given to construction of Altar J to insure that this altar was built in the same manner as the Phase VI temple on the acropolis.

Structural continuity would thus be maintained in a symbolic way when the cult was moved from the acropolis to Site A in Phase VII. The poorer quality of workmanship evident in the altar structure suggests that local craftsmen imitated the work of the Phase VI temple builders. This observation is supported by the quality of plaster covering the altar, shown in Pl. XVI.2 of Marquet-Krause 1949. A rough layer of plaster is applied over the stones and mud mortar of Altar J, contrasting markedly with the plaster in the Phase VI temple which was applied smoothly over a base layer of red clay tempered with straw (see Callaway 1965, 38, Fig. 16).

The enclosures and Bin N. The horseshoe-shaped enclosure in the upper center of Area III is assigned to Phase VI, as noted in the preceding chapter. An elevation from Pl. C of Marquet-Krause 1949 places the top of the enclosure wall at 851.39, as noted in Fig. 87, which is the same as the threshold of the door in Wall H, and lower than the floor of the enclosures along Tower A. The Sanctuary A floor probably covered the Phase VI enclosure, leaving only the Altar J enclosure wall, and the three irregular enclosures along Tower A between the altar and Wall M.

Wall J¹ enclosed the altar, as photographed in Pl. XX.2. The wall was faced on each side with field stones, and rubble of earth and pebbles, like that in Walls H and M, formed the core. Built to a width of about 75 centimeters, Wall J¹ could have supported a roof over Enclosure 133. The entrance was about 75 centimeters wide, and probably closed off the room with a door, or curtain. It is possible that the door and wall simply screened the altar from public view, however, and that the altar was not covered by a roof.

Enclosures 137, 131, and 136 against Tower A seem to be less permanent structures than Wall J¹, and probably were not much higher originally than pictured in Pl. XX.2. They have the improvised appearance of the small bin wall on the right side of Altar J, and the stones around the cup on Altar J shown in Pl. XVI:2 of Marquet-Krause 1949. If the litter of bones and pottery on the floor of the Altar J enclosure is any indication of the quality of housekeeping in Sanctuary A, the three enclosures may very well have been 'favissae' for the deposit of garbage from operation of the cult. On the other hand, Enclosure 137, 131, and 136 actually yielded almost no pottery or objects (see Fig. 80), and no record of unusual deposits of bones or other materials is preserved.

Bin N, drawn in Fig. 87, is also a loosely constructed enclosure built on top of Fireplace N¹ of Phase VI. The bin wall apparently was very low, like that of Enclosure 136, because the remains cleared in 1964, shown in Pl. XVII, are substantially the same as found in 1934, evident in Pl. XIV of Marquet-Krause 1949. The photographs in both instances show Bin N built against, but not bonded into, the side of Wall H. Bin N seems to have been a storage place for the bowls used possibly in cultic meals at Sanctuary A. Eleven bowls and a small cup with perforated bottom were recovered from the installation in 1934. They are assembled together in Pl. 79, from ch. 122 of Marquet-Krause 1949.

The remodeled room in Area II

Most of the rich yield of objects from Sanctuary A are from the room in Area II, ch. 116 of Marquet-Krause 1949, indicating that it was the most important part of the sanctuary. The burned timber found on the floor by Marquet-Krause probably was a roof-support pillar that rested on the base drawn in ch. 116 in Pl. XCIII, so the room probably was covered by a roof as it had been in Phase VI. The changes in Phase VII were the result of remodeling the back, or south, part of the room, opposite the entrance in Wall H, and the addition of a wall at the southeast corner to enclose what Marquet-Krause thought was a stepped entrance into the sanctuary (1949, Pl. XCIII:143).

The additions to Wall E. The rear of ch. 116 is difficult to reconstruct from the Marquet-Krause plans and photographs because remains of Phases VI and VII are presented as one phase in the 1949 report. Wall E is reconstructed in Phase VI, Fig. 86, as a simple, straight wall from Tower A to Wall P enclosing the south side of the room. A possible 'back door' is located at the west end of the wall, against Tower A, because Marquet-Krause leaves a narrow space about 60 centimeters wide in Pl. C at Locus 135. If this door is not a rear entrance to the Phase VI room, the triangular space drawn in Pl. C seems to be meaningless, because a storage area would hardly take this form. Furthermore, the E² blockage in Wall E¹ preserves no trace of the sharply angled space drawn in Locus 135.

An addition to the inside of Wall E was apparently constructed in Phase VII, either widening

Wall E as drawn in Pl. C, or adding a second wall with some space between it and the original Wall E, as drawn in Pl. XCIII. The former is probably more accurate, because the photographs in Pls. XII–XIII do not show a clearly defined facing of stones on the back side of the additional wall, and this is reflected in the wavy line marking the edge of the addition in Pl. C. The technique of wall construction seems to be the same as that used in building the Wall A¹ addition to the city defenses, i.e., an outer face is constructed of well-placed field stones, and the space between the newly constructed face and the Phase VI wall is filled with rubble. This view is reflected in the reconstructed plan drawn in Fig. 87.

The addition to Wall E seems to have had a two-fold purpose. First, the comparatively narrow south wall was strengthened by the buttress-like projection of the inner wall. Wall E was originally constructed on a considerable depth of fill, and its course did not coincide with that of the earlier Wall E¹, so its foundations in Phase VII may have been weakened from uneven settling. The addition in Phase VII buttressed the section of Wall E constructed on the north side of Wall E¹, and, therefore, prevented a collapse inward, into ch. 116.

Second, the addition served as a backdrop for whatever rituals were carried out in ch. 116. A small projection from the strengthened wall into ch. 116, about the same height above the floor as the altar in Enclosure 133, i.e., 71 centimeters, seems to have been a small altar. In view of the discovery of such objects as the ivory and bone knife handles (Fig. 72:1–3, 5), this may have been a more important altar than Altar J. The niche, or bin, at the west end of the addition seems to have been a storage place, much like the niche on the right side of Altar J. Consequently, the cult objects found in the niche in ch. 115 probably were used in the same room, in some ritual associated with the small altar-like projection built against the addition to Wall E.

The entrance to ch. 116 in Area II. Marquet-Krause planned a major entrance to Sanctuary A at the southeast corner of Area II, where the 'stairs' are located in Pl. XCIII. The enclosure for the entrance is an undesignated terrace wall reaching from the east end of the Phase VII addition to Wall E southward across Wall D, and then eastward to the line of Wall K. Photographs of the terrace wall are found in Pl. XII: 1, 2 of Marquet-Krause 1949, but no remnants of it survived for study in the 1964 excavations. The terrace wall may have enclosed a ramp, or stairway, leading into Area II in the manner reconstructed in Fig. 87. An approach to it would be from the east, leading down from the acropolis buildings.

There are problems, however, with this reconstruction. The first, and most obvious, one is the absence of clearly defined steps across the top of Walls E and E¹ in Pl. XII.2. With other passages in the sanctuary so clearly defined, the absence of definite stairs or steps in the terraced enclosure makes a major entrance there questionable. Second, the entrance at the top of the ramp is 2.75 meters wide, which seems to be unusually wide for an entrance to a roofed structure. One-fourth of the room enclosed by the south wall would be open, because the width of the passage at the top of the 'stairs' would be too much to close off with doors. And third, a major entrance to the sanctuary in ch. 116 would seem inappropriate in view of the reconstructions proposed for Areas II and III. Area III was probably an open court with Altar J screened off, or even roofed, in the southwest corner, while Area II seems to have been completely roofed. Entrance to the sanctuary should be in the open court in Area III, and access to the covered room in Area II should be more controlled and exclusive. If there is the equivalent of a 'holy of holies' in Sanctuary A, it is the room in Area II, not the court in Area III. A major entrance to the sanctuary through the 'holy of holies' would be inappropriate and unlikely.

The passage reconstructed at the southeast corner of Area II is, therefore, questionable. Any other reconstruction of the corner is also conjectural, because the only evidence is the photograph in Pl. XII:2 of Marquet-Krause 1949. No pottery or objects which would throw light on the problem are registered from Locus 143 of Pl. XCIII, the area of the ramp and stairs. Possibly the southeast corner was closed by an extension of Wall E, and the small walls on the ramp below Wall E supported terrace walls. This leaves the location of an entrance to Sanctuary A indefinite.

An appropriate place would be in Wall L between Bin N and the corner of Wall M, but there is no positive evidence in either plans or photographs. The sketch plan in Pl. XCVIII of Marquet-Krause 1949 has Wall L dotted in, as though no Phase VII wall was found there in 1934. although the stones outlined by dots in Pl. XCIII are not differentiated from Wall r, which is clearly a wall in Pl. XIII.1. Wall H seems to extend toward the east in Pl. XIII.1 even more than the plans indicate, so there may not have been a wall along the line of the reconstructed Wall L in Fig. 87. In this case, the court possibly extended farther to the east in Phases VI and VII than indicated on the plans, and a major entrance to Sanctuary A could have been located in the east side of the court in Phase VII, as indicated in Fig. 87.

Conclusions

Four conclusions emerge from the study of Sanctuary A and its special installations. First, the building was a remodeled residence originally constructed in Phase VI. The larger Building A unit discussed in the preceding chapter was closed off from a north unit of rooms in Area IV by Blockage M¹ in Wall M, and the orientation of the larger unit was changed. There is, therefore, an *ad hoc* character to the building plan of Sanctuary A which limits its relevance as a sanctuary type.

Second, Area III seems to have continued from Phase VI to Phase VII as an open courtyard. Altar J was screened by Wall J¹, and possibly roofed, but the larger area enclosed by Walls H, L, and M was not roofed. This conclusion weakens the interpretation of Marquet-Krause that Area III was a 'holy of holies,' because an open court in later sanctuaries, where the altar was usually located, was preliminary to the holy of holies.

Third, the covered room in Area II (ch. 116 of Marquet-Krause) seems to have been the equivalent of a 'holy of holies', because the major yield of cult objects came from this room, and against the addition to the structure of Wall E was built a small altar-like projection on the south side of the room. This conclusion, along with the lack of positive archaeological evidence of the 'stairs' in the entrance to Sanctuary A proposed by Marquet-Krause, brings into question the southeast entrance to the sanctuary. A more appropriate place would be in the east side of the court in Area II, between Bin N and Wall M.

Fourth, Altar J in Area III seems to have been constructed in a special manner, employing the bricklayer's technique used in constructing the Phase VI temple on the acropolis. This technique is intrusive in the building style at Site A, and probably represents an effort to maintain continuity with the temple when the sanctuary was moved to Site A in Phase VII.

THE PHASE VII POTTERY AND OBJECTS

Provenance

Only three distinctively Phase VII installations remained at Site A in 1964, so the small assemblage of pottery in Fig 68 is from these places. They are Altar J, Blockage M¹ in Wall M, and Bin N, all in Area III. In the sequence of layers in the Master Section, the Phase VII pottery and objects are in Layer 1.

Altar J. Layer 1 in Altar J is Field No. 201.7, excavated in the space between the Phase VI surface shown on the projecting balk in Pl. XVII and the *huwwar* surface at the base of Altar J. Only the projecting balk was removed, because a possibility existed that the remnant of Altar J against Tower A might be permanently preserved, or moved to a museum. Neither possibility has been realized, so the altar is covered by a protective mound of earth and stones at the present writing.

Bin N. Field No. 203.1 designates the pottery found in the stones and ashy earth of Bin N, shown in the left foreground of Pl. XVII and drawn as Layer 1 in Section D D, Fig. 10. The bin was removed down to the cobblestones of Fireplace N¹ of Phase VI, visible on the right side of the bin enclosure in the same photograph.

Blockage M¹ in Wall M. Blockage M¹ is shown in Pl. XVIII.1, 4, and drawn in Sections B–B and I–I, Figs. 11 and 14. Grey earth under the blockage, and on top of the compact pinkish grey surface of the Phase VI passage exposed in Pl. XVI.5, is designated by Nos. 300.7a and 8. The blockage itself is No. 300.7.

The Phase VII pottery forms

Stratigraphically, the pottery of Phase VII belongs at the end of EB IIIA and the beginning of EB IIIB at Ai. The forms recovered and drawn in Fig. 68 are too limited, however, to build a representative assemblage. They do correlate with EB III forms having a provenance after the beginning of the period, but late EB IIIB forms are absent, either because of the limited selection, or because the last EB phase at Ai begins well before the end of EB III in Canaan. The latter seems preferable.

Bowls. Body sherds of hand-made small bowls were found in the make-up of Altar J, but they are not drawn because neither rims nor bases could be reconstructed. One platter, Fig. 68:1, decorated with reddish-brown slip but otherwise undistinguished, is registered from the fill under Blockage M¹, above the threshold of the passage. Similar forms with more sharply inturned rims occur at Jericho in Areas E III–IV in Phase C (Hennessy 1967, 15, Pl. IX:87) and in Beth-shan XI (Fitzgerald 1935, Pl. VIII:2).

The deep bowl drawn in Fig. 68:2 continues a Phase VI form in Fig. 60:23 with slight variation in stance. A new form at Site A is the flat-base platter in Fig. 68:5, found in Blockage M¹ of Wall M. The rim profile is similar to a Phase F form in Areas E III–IV at Jericho (Hennessy 1967, Pl. VII: 66), but the shallow wall and wide, flat base seem to be characteristic of EB IIIB. Another bowl with similar base and wall profile, but different rim, is found in ch. 116 of Sanctuary A, and drawn in Fig. 74:9.

Juglets and hole-mouth jars. The stump-base juglet drawn in Fig. 68:15 is similar to the Phase VI form in Fig. 64:5, but there is less swelling of the walls above the base. The varieties of this base form, from stump to spike profile, are cited in the discussion of the Phase VI example, and seem to occur throughout EB III, although the spike base becomes common in EB IIIB.

Hennessy notes the trend toward upright hole-mouth forms with pointed or beveled rims in EB IIIA at Jericho (1967, 14, Pl. VIII:83). The example drawn in Fig. 68:13 indicates a similar trend at Ai in Phase VII. Earlier forms with flatter stance occur in Phase V (Fig. 48:18, 20–21). The Phase VII hole-mouth is decorated with an irregular, indented molding around the outer edge of the rim. Ledge handles on this type of jar in Phase VII are predominantly the pushed-up form drawn in Fig. 68:24–26.

Conclusions

The Phase VII pottery forms are too meager at Site A to be significant in assigning a pottery horizon to the construction phase of Sanctuary A. A distinct stratigraphic break does occur in the history of the city between the end of Phase VI and beginning of Phase VII, because the Phase VI citadel walls at Site A are smoke-marked from the fire that occurred at the termination of Phase VI, and a new city wall is added outside the Phase VI wall around most of the city in Phase VII. However, there is no destruction evidence in the remains of Site A at the end of Phase VI, and the transition to Phase VII seems to be immediate. The few pottery forms which can be related to those from contemporary sites indicate a horizon well into EB III, possibly near the transition from Phases D to C at Jericho in Areas E III–IV, and from Stratum XII to Stratum XI at Beth-shan.

No Carbon 14 assays of Phase VII remains were possible, so other lines of evidence will be followed in suggesting a chronology for the end of Phase VI and the beginning of Sanctuary A in Phase VII in the concluding section of this chapter.

THE PHASE VIII POTTERY AND OBJECTS

All of the Phase VIII pottery and objects were found by Marquet-Krause in the ruins of Sanctuary A, built in Phase VII. Pl. XIV of Marquet-Krause 1949 shows the Sanctuary A installations intact, so the provenance given seems to be reliable. One check on the reliability of provenance is the total absence of any alabaster or pottery cult vessels in levels earlier than Phase VIII.

The only mixture of pottery evident would be that from Phases VI or VII in the center of Area III where no distinction was made between the two EB III building phases, but this would not involve sanctuary artifacts. The Sanctuary A floor was removed around the Phase VI horseshoe-shaped enclosure and over to the base of the entrance in Wall H. Apparently the yield of whole pieces of pottery from Sanctuary A in Area II was of such quantity that sherds from the mixed layers in Area III were not registered, because very few pieces are attributed to ch. 120. The mixture, therefore, is insignificant, and the Phase VIII materials retain their integrity as an assemblage.

Comparative studies of Sanctuary A artifacts have been made by Marquet-Krause (1949, 16–21, 29–31) Albright (1935, 209–212), Hennessy (1967, 24–25, 69–71), and Amiran (1970, 170–179). Marquet-Krause and Albright selected objects comparable to Egyptian artifacts with the objective of locating Sanctuary A chronologically and culturally in the historical milieu of the third millennium

B.C. They discovered the wide historical spread of the objects, suggesting reuse of some from earlier phases, but Marquet-Krause's failure to define the two EB III building phases at Site A made reconstruction of the history difficult.

Hennessy studied the sanctuary artifacts from the point of view of foreign imports and chronology. He, too, confirmed the extensive chronological range of the objects, from Dynasties II to V, and the wide geographical spread of comparative pieces, reaching from Egypt to Anatolia and North Mesopotamia. The objects are listed by types, but a complete catalogue of Sanctuary A artifacts is not given in his study.

Amiran's study of the Egyptian alabasters found in Sanctuary A is thorough and very important, because she identifies for the first time the segmented jar, two sections of which are joined in Fig. 70:1, and the alabaster model of a waterskin, reconstructed in Fig. 69 (see Amiran 1970, 170–179). Also, two alabaster vessels from the acropolis are associated with Temple A of Phase VI, before the sanctuary was moved to Site A in Phase VII. However, Amiran dates the introduction of the alabasters at Ai to EB II, which would be Phase IV of the present study, contemporary with the latter part of the First Dynasty in Egypt. The overall evidence of Sites A and D seems to support an introduction of the vessels in Phase VI at Temple A, or at the beginning of the Third Dynasty. This is EB IIIA at Ai. The transfer of the vessels to Sanctuary A occurred in Phase VII, or EB IIIB. Amiran's study, therefore, lacks the dimension of final phasing at Site A.

The present study of the Sanctuary A artifacts adds little to the preceding contributions in new information about the objects. However, it is an exhaustive catalogue of the materials assembled according to place of provenance in the sanctuary, and the assemblage is placed in a carefully constructed stratigraphy. The presentation of the objects in Figs. 69–80 by groups according to provenance and general type seems to be the best way of reporting the results of the present study.

Most of the artifacts from Sanctuary A are from Room 116, interpreted as the equivalent of a 'holy of holies' in this report. The artifacts from Room 116 cannot be grouped according to provenance from specific areas of the room, so they are presented here in collections determined mainly by general types of objects for convenience in study.

The alabaster zoomorphic vessel. The enigmatic animal figure from Room 120 reconstructed by Marquet-Krause as drawn in Fig. 78:1 and photographed in Pl. XXIII:1, 2 resisted interpretation for a generation because the head was missing. Marquet-Krause associated this with a hippopotamus (1949, 186:1459), identified by Hennessy as a representation of Ta-weret, the Egyptian hippopotamus deity of fertility and childbirth (1967, 70). De Vaux suggested that this represented a pig, with its feet tied and ready for sacrifice (1957, 567).

Amiran eventually found the key to the enigma by associating the carved thongs with which the feet of the animal were tied with the bands tied around the neck of a large alabaster jar fragment from Room 116, drawn in Fig. 71:2 (1970, 185). Placing the jar rim and neck in juxtaposition to the body of the figure as drawn in Fig. 69b, she found that the neck was carved in correct proportion to the body of the figure, and that the ties around the feet and neck of the vessel were similar in form and workmanship. The animal figure found in Room 120, therefore, belonged with the jar rim and neck from Room 116.

The unusual vessel reconstructed from the two parts was found to be similar in general form to a 'model waterskin' reported by Petrie at Abydos and dating to the late First Dynasty (Amiran 1970, 174, 176–177, Fig. 5, Pl. 42). The model was carved in marble, with a jar-type neck and rim instead of an animal head, as shown in Amiran's Pl. 42. Petrie's vessel differs from the zoomorphic vessel in Sanctuary A in size, because the former is 'very small . . . a sort of miniature in the model vessel category' (*ibid.*, p. 174), while the latter is life size, in the 'size and shape of an actual waterskin' (p. 175). Also the neck and rim of the Sanctuary A vessel are different, having a rolled rim similar in form to that of the alabaster jar drawn in Fig. 71:1, and redrawn by Amiran (*ibid.*, p. 174, Fig. 4).

The marble vessel from Abydos, with its hole-mouth type rim, is, therefore, of limited value in dating the Sanctuary A vessel, and Amiran observes that the jar in Fig. 71:1, found with the rim of the zoomorphic vessel, 'is a common type of such long duration that it is of limited chronological value' (*ibid.*, p. 175). However, Hennessy notes that the splaying base of the cylinder jar marks it as comparatively late, i.e., dating to the Third and Fourth Dynasties (1967, 70), and parallels from Qau and Gizeh are cited (*ibid.*, Pl. LVI: 9, 11). In Petrie's chart of cylinder jar forms, the slightly obtuse angle of the rims of Figs. 71:1 and 69b places them late in the Second Dynasty, to the reign of Khasekhemui (1937, 3, Pl. XIIId, Rims), and the slightly concave sides become common in S. D. 81 and continue to the Third Dynasty (1937, 3, Pl. XIIIE, Sides). A date in the late Second or early Third Dynasty for the zoomorphic vessel in Fig. 69, and the alabaster cylinder jar in Fig. 71:1 is, therefore, probable. This agrees with the chronology of Phase VI at Site A developed in the previous chapter.

The segmented alabaster jar. Amiran discovered that the two bowls without bottoms, drawn in Fig. 71:3, 4 actually are two segments of one jar, joined as drawn in Fig. 70:1 (1970, 170–171). Segmented jars of stone and alabaster are known in Egypt from the beginning of the Dynastic period, and Amiran cites several examples dating to the First Dynasty, or EB II in Canaan. The form of the segmented jar is associated with that of a two-segment stone jar from Tomb 3503 at Saqqara, dating to the reign of Djer (1970, 171, 173, Fig. 2:2, Pl. 40A). This association is possible if the missing base of the Ai vessel is formed like the base segment in Fig. 2:5 (*ibid.*). However, if the base is like that of the two-segment jar cited from Naga ed-Der, from Group 3150, type S IV, dated to the Second Dynasty (*ibid.*, p. 173, Fig. 2:4), the jar from Sanctuary A belongs in EB IIIA, or Phase VI at Site A, instead of EB II as Amiran prefers.

The degenerate handle identified on the side of the upper segment of the Ai vessel by Amiran (*ibid.*, 172, Pl. 39b) is also cited as evidence of an EB II form. The handle seems to be comparable to a vestigial loop, like that on the jar shown in Pl. 403 (*ibid.*), instead of a degenerate vertical lug, as shown on jars in Pl. 40 C–D. Loop handles are degenerate on EB II jars, as Hennessy shows in Pl. XII:5 (1967) from Tell el-Far'ah (N); in Pl. XLII:6 from Jericho; and Pl. XLVII:1–3 from Saqqara and Abydos. The loops, however, are not as vestigial in appearance in these EB II examples and the example from Arad cited by Amiran as that on the segmented jar from Ai. The latter can, therefore, date to EB IIIA and belong in the Phase VI assemblage at Ai.

The alabaster bowls. Two wide, medium shallow alabaster bowls are reported from Sanctuary A and drawn in Fig. 70:2–3. Bowl No. 3 is drawn by Marquet-Krause (1949, Pl. LXVI:1489) but No. 2 is described only (1949, 194–195:1520). A photograph of the No. 2 fragments, however, is given in Pl. XXIII of Marquet-Krause 1949. Amiran recovered the fragments of Bowl No. 2 and reconstructed its profile in a new drawing (1970, 178, Fig. 6:1; photograph in Pl. 43B). The new drawing is reproduced in Fig. 70:2, along with a redrawing of Marquet-Krause No. 1489 in Fig. 70:3. The original drawing of the latter is in Fig. 71:5.

The two bowls are characterized by flat bases, convex walls, inverted rims with the edge at an obtuse angle, and incised circles or grooves in the bottom. The circles are projected out of perspective in the Amiran drawings to indicate the type (for the true perspective, see photograph of No. 1520 in Pl. 43B of Amiran 1970). This type of bowl begins in the First Dynasty, as cited by Amiran (1970, 175), but continues in the Second and Third Dynasties as Marquet-Krause noted (1949, 19). In fact, Marquet-Krause cited direct parallels at Saqqara from the reign of Neteren of the Second Dynasty. Albright noted that similar forms are found at Mycerinus, which takes them into the Fourth Dynasty (1935, 209–210), while Reisner observes that the Third Dynasty bowls of this type are characterized by more convex than straight angular sides (1931, 170).

Hennessy had difficulty with the form of Bowl No. 5 in Fig. 71, because the sides are drawn almost straight (1967, 69), and straight sides characterize the early forms. However, Amiran's redrawing of the same bowl in Fig. 70:3 indicates a more convex form of the sides above the base section, which allows it to be typed as late as the Third Dynasty, or Phase VI at Ai. The two alabaster bowls from Sanctuary A can, therefore, be later than the First Dynasty, and probably date to the beginning of the Third Dynasty, when Phase VI begins at Ai in EB IIIA. The bowls belong with the two deep bowls reported by Amiran from Temple A of the acropolis in Phase VI, and were probably moved to Sanctuary A in Phase VII.

The shallow stone platter. The pink stone disk drawn originally as shown in Fig. 71:6 is redrawn by Amiran as in Fig. 70:4. Conspicuous in the new drawing is the absence of a circular groove drawn in the original. This platter belongs in the same context as the alabaster bowls discussed above, and is possibly a top for a table stand, as Hennessy suggests, but the stand is not the alabaster segmented jar which he proposes (1967, 69). One of the incense stands found in the same room (Figs. 73:3; 74:1) could have served as a support for the platter. The stands seem to be designed for a bowl-top of some kind.

The ivory knife handle. Hennessy cites a late Pre-Dynastic curved pommel of an undecorated ivory handle as a comparable form to the handle from Sanctuary A, drawn in Fig. 72:1, but the decoration of the latter indicates a later date (1967, 71). Carved triangular patterns on wood occur in the First Dynasty, but continue into the Third Dynasty. Kantor identifies the decoration of 'excised whirligigs' as an Egyptian motif, and associates this with a painted decoration in the Tomb of Hesy, a Third Dynasty tomb contemporary with Zoser (1956, 157). She points out that the pattern ceases to be used after the Third Dynasty. This association of the decorated handle with the reign of Zoser is in accord with the dating of Temple A on the acropolis in EB IIIA, and indicates that the handle and sheath belong with the assemblage of alabaster vessels moved from Temple A on the acropolis to Sanctuary A in Phase VII.

Decorated bone tubes and cups. The bone tubes drawn in Fig. 72:2–3, 5 are similar to a carved tube found at Jericho in Tomb F4 (Kenyon 1960, 146, Fig. 48:2), dating to EB III. Hennessy cites parallel motifs from Egypt, Syria and Anatolia (1967, 82–83) ranging in date from EB I to EB III. The patterns on the tubes from Sanctuary A are nearer to examples reported from North Syria (see Prausnitz 1955, 21, Fig. 2), dating to EB III. In fact, the tubes from Sanctuary A seem to belong with the Khirbet Kerak ware culture. Tomb F4 at Jericho has both authentic and imitation Khirbet Kerak ware with the decorated tube cited, and Sanctuary A has a Khirbet Kerak plaque or stand (Fig. 73:8) in the same room with the three tubes drawn in Fig. 72.

The tubes have been called handles for knives by Hennessy and Prausnitz. It is probable, however, that they were paint containers, like Petrie's *kohl* tubes from Egypt (1927, Pl. XXII:25–38). Hennessy acknowledges moreover, the similarity of the Ai tubes with paint containers at Syros (1967, 82, Pl. LXXVII:15), which date to the end of EB III. Chronologically, the tubes seem to belong to EB IIIB, and, therefore, are later than the alabasters transferred from the Phase VI temple on the acropolis. They probably are a Phase VII addition to the assemblage of sanctuary artifacts.

Hennessy identifies the decorated cups drawn in Fig. 72:6–7 as breast coverings for a female dancer. The statue of the wife of Sapunikau, from Saqqara in the Fifth Dynasty, 'shows the lady wearing beadwork with breast cups of light blue and dark blue concentric rings' is cited as evidence that the cups are breast coverings, and a pierced shell found with the cups at Ai suggest that a bead or net garment was worn (1967, 71). The shells and beads would rattle when the lady danced, according to Hennessy. This may, indeed, be a plausible identification and reconstruction, but the evidence is not convincing. The cups are about 5 centimeters in diameter, a size too small for a breast covering, and the presence of one pierced shell of a type found commonly at every site excavated on the *tell* is not enough to support a theory of a dancing lady in the sanctuary. The cups may have had a function related to that of the bone tubes, either as paint containers, or as vessels for mixing the paint placed in the tubes.

Plaque or pot stand. The small stand drawn in Fig. 73:8 is a part of the Khirbet Kerak ware assemblage of Sanctuary A, identified by Amiran (1967, 186, Fig. 1:9) and Hennessy (1967, 78). Hennessy cites parallels from Beth-shan and Kirbet Kerak in Canaan, Judeideh and Ta'yinat in Syria, and several sites in Anatolia (1967, Pl. LXXI:1–9). The function of the stand is not clear, but it appears in the context of the decorated bone tubes possibly used as paint containers, and the decorated bone cups. Perhaps the stand was used in a ritual involving the use of paint also. Marquet-Krause notes that 'cinq pierres plates, peintes en rouge, forment sur l'autel une petite niche découverte' (1949, 19; however the field report to the Department of Antiquities dated November 10, 1934, notes 'une niche faite de trois pierres curieusement disposèes, dont l'une garde des traces de couleur rouge'). The stones are laid around a pottery votive cup on top of Altar J in Marquet-Krause 1949, Pl. XV:2. If the bone tubes, which seem to belong in the Khirbet Kerak, or northern-oriented assemblage, are in fact paint containers, the Khirbet Kerak components of the sanctuary artifacts may be associated with the painted stones on Altar J.

Votive cups. Numerous votive cups like that found on Altar J are reported from Room 116 (Fig. 73:1–2, 4–7), Room 133, the altar enclosure (Figs. 76:1–16, 77–4), Room 120 (Fig. 78:2), and Room 122 (Fig. 79:1). Two examples are pierced in the bottom, apparently to serve as funnels (Figs. 77:4, 79:1). One possible prototype made of alabaster is reported from Room 116 (Fig. 71:1).

The cup found *in situ* on Altar J, surrounded by the five flat stones decorated with red paint, indicates that at least some of the vessels were votive cups.

The alabaster cup in Fig. 71:1 is an Egyptian import, a type common in Egypt from the First through the Sixth Dynasties. Pottery copies of the alabaster and stone prototypes occur during the same period, and the examples from Sanctuary A are generally considered to be Egyptianized vessels. The alabaster cup from Room 116 may be a prototype of the pottery vessels, as evidenced by numerous Egyptian parallels cited by Hennessy (1967, Pl. LVIII: 10-11, 13, 16-17).

Similar pottery cups are reported from Beth-shan XII–XI, however, in the context of dominant Khirbet Kerak ware (Fitzgerald 1935, Pl. IX:24–25). One vessel, No. 25, is very similar to those in Fig. 73, especially in the characteristics of flaring base and markedly concave body. Hennessy cites one example from Ur with the same characteristics (1967, Pl. LVIII:9), a vessel certainly outside Egyptianizing influences. The votive cups of Sanctuary A, therefore, may reflect a significant non-Egyptian influence and actually may belong with the Khirbet Kerak assemblage in the sanctuary. The cult at Ai in Sanctuary A may, in this case, be much more Khirbet Kerak oriented than has been thought.

The incense stands. Two incense stands, drawn in Figs. 73:3 and 74:1, are reported from Room 116. Both stands are handmade of pottery clay, roughly squared with fenestrations in each side, and without bottoms. Jar-type necks and rims are shaped above the squared bodies of the stands, and angled incised markings decorate the neck.

The rims and necks of the stands are similar to jar rims and necks of local origin at Ai. One example is reported from Room 116 (Fig. 74:2), and another is from destruction debris in the acropolis area (Marquet-Krause 1949, Pl. LXVIII:115a). Many rims of this type have been found by the present expedition in EB sites, indicating that the form is a common one. The incense stands probably are locally made, therefore, and not copies of either Egyptian or Khirbet Kerak stands. Typical Khirbet Kerak stands are waisted, as evidenced by the examples cited by Hennessy (1967, Pl. LXX:1–6), and Egyptian stands are usually made of stone. As suggested earlier, the Sanctuary A stands probably supported the wide, flat stone or pottery platters like the one drawn in Fig. 70:4, and incense would have been burned in the platters.

Votive bed. The pottery votive bed drawn in Fig. 77:2 was found in the altar enclosure of Sanctuary A. A similar object is reported also from ch. 235 in the lower city (Marquet-Krause 1949, Pl. LXXVII. 1961). Hennessy finds parallels to the votive beds to the north of Canaan, in Mesopotamia (1967, Pl. LXXVII:1, Tepe Gawra: 3, Telloh), dating to the end of the Early Dynastic period, and later. The beds apparently have symbolic significance, since some examples from Mesopotamia support nude female figures.

Ivory combs. Two fragments of ivory combs drawn in Fig. 77:3 were recovered from the altar enclosure. The fragments belong to two separate combs, because the width from decoration to end of teeth differs 1 centimeter, a variation too great to allow the pieces to be joined as suggested in Fig. 77. Ivory combs are known in Egypt from the First Dynasty, and continue through the Old Kingdom. The ivory combs in Sanctuary A seem to be Egyptian imports, like the decorated knife handle in Fig. 72:1, and may have been a part of the assemblage of Egyptian imports in Temple A, Phase VI, on the acropolis before the transfer to Sanctuary A in Phase VII.

Conclusions

The pottery and objects from Sanctuary A make up a unique assemblage of artifacts from three phases in EB III. Egyptian alabaster and stone vessels used in the Phase VI temple on the acropolis from the beginning of EB IIIA were apparently transferred to the sanctuary at the beginning of Phase VII, or EB IIIB. New additions to the assemblage in Phase VII would be the Khirbet Kerak ware and objects of northern origin, along with local pottery not identifiable. The entire accumulation through Phases VI and VII remaining at the time of destruction in EB IIIB makes up the assemblage of Phase VIII. The final collection, therefore, is heterogeneous, shaped by the political vicissitudes of the city at Ai through three significant phases of its history in EB III.

The cultural horizon of Phases VII–VIII. A downgrading of Egyptian influence seems to have occurred in Phase VII, when the Egyptianized temple on the acropolis was probably taken over as a residence by the new ruler at Ai, and the cult was installed in a remodeled residence at Site A. In view of this sequence of events, it is unlikely that new Egyptian artifacts were introduced in Sanctuary A in Phase VII. The significant new element in Sanctuary A is Khirbet Kerak ware and other objects of northern origin. This new element was recognized by Amiran and Hennessy, but its implications as well as penetration of the Phase VII cult were not evaluated.

The present study indicates that northern-oriented artifacts in Sanctuary A include the decorated bone tubes and cups which were probably paint containers, the votive bed found near Altar J, and possibly the pottery votive cups, one of which was found on Altar J. Paint from the bone containers probably decorated the five flat stones forming a niche around one votive cup on Altar J. This indicates, if the reconstruction is allowed, a northern orientation of cult in Phase VII which effectively supplanted the Egyptian-oriented cult of Temple A in Phase VI.

The cultural horizon of Phases VII–VIII, therefore, includes Beth-yerah IV and Beth-shan XII–XI in north Canaan, and related strata at other sites. At Jericho, Phases C–A of Areas E III–IV seem to be contemporary, although Phase VIII may be earlier than the terminal phase of EB III at Jericho. Tombs F3 and F2 at Jericho contain close parallels, but there too the point of termination cannot be correlated with that of Sanctuary A.

Chronology. A date of ca. 2700 B.C. is assigned to the beginning of Phase VI, or EB IIIA, on the basis of Carbon 14 assays of Phase V destruction evidence. This date seems relatively secure because it is supported by four different assays. There is, however, only one additional Carbon 14 date which bears upon the succeeding phases, and it reflects the termination of the city in Phase VIII, or EB IIIB.

A sample of charred wood from Area VI of Site G yielded the Phase VIII date. Site G is located on contour line 835, north of Site C in Fig. 3. Area VI is rather barren, containing only one small EB wall on bedrock (see Callaway 1969, 14, Fig. 10), but it is adjacent to a house with rounded corners which suggests a residential area. The small wall in Area VI may be part of a court of another house, or part of a terrace on the steep slope of the site. Technical information on the sample taken from the area is as follows:

TX 1033	G VI 500.6	4400 ± 80
		2450 B.C.

Layer 500.6 is the sixth layer down from the surface, at the top of Wall H. Iron Age I pottery is found through

500.4, because the site was terraced and cultivated in the Iron Age. Unmixed EB pottery is found from 500.5 to bedrock. Layer 500.6 seems to be destruction debris from the termination of the EB city, while 500.5 is an accumulation of earth eroded from the slope above Site G during the period of abandonment before the Iron Age village was founded. Wall H seems to be part of the courtyard of a house west of G VI.

The date of Phase VIII may be placed as late as 2370 B.C. on the evidence of this sample, or ca. 2450 B.C. if the mean date is accepted. The latter allows about 250 years for the two major building phases of EB III at Ai, over against 280 years for the first two major city wall phases two hundred and fifty years may be inadequate, because Phase VII seems to be of longer duration than Phase VI. The period could easily have lasted until ca. 2400 B.C.

Assignment of dates within EB III is more difficult, because the termination of Phase VI seems to have been brought about by local revolution, or at least internal struggle in the land of Canaan, and not by foreign invasion. Phase VI began in the transition from Second to Third Dynasties in Egypt, and the EB IIIA city was profoundly influenced in the reign of Zoser. Hayes assigns a total of 74 years to the duration of the Third Dynasty, and about 120 years to the Fourth Dynasty (1964, 6–8), or a total of nearly 200 years to the two dynasties.

Egyptian interests in the Fourth Dynasty turned to pyramid building, and resentment against excessive demands for labor and resources became widespread in Egypt. Internal conditions in Egypt probably caused a relaxation in whatever controls or ties there were with Canaan in general and Ai in particular. Influence from northern-oriented peoples at Beth-yerah and Beth-shan penetrated southward and contributed to local unrest and the creation of dissident groups. The time for change probably came during the Fourth Dynasty, well before the beginning of the Fifth Dynasty. A date of ca. 2550 B.C. seems suitable in this context, allowing 150 years for Phase VI. The termination of Phase VI would occur about a half-century before the end of the Fourth Dynasty.

Phase VII, with its destruction layer, Phase VIII, seems as long, or longer, in duration than Phase VI. Material evidence of city-building is less impressive, with about 80% of the Phase VI city wall widened and strengthened. The acropolis building complex was made into a fortress-palace by filling the rooms around the inner rectangular temple structure and buttressing exterior walls. However, the citadel at Site A has two sub-phases of Buttress A^1, constructed to strengthen the Phase VI Tower A during Phase VII. This suggests a considerable length of time for the duration of Sanctuary A, requiring as much as 150 years for Phases VII–VIII, and allowing the city to terminate by ca. 2400 B.C. The period may have been even longer, and further study of other sites may require an adjustment toward 2370 B.C. for the end of EB IIIB at Ai.

In this reconstruction, Phase VIII, or the destruction of the city at Ai, falls within the Fifth Dynasty of Egypt, against the view of de Vaux who places it in the Sixth Dynasty (1966, 23). There are explicit records of military campaigns against the Asiatic 'dwellers of the sands' during the Sixth Dynasty which can account for the final subjugation of rebel cities in Canaan at the end of EB IIIB. However, de Vaux himself notes that possible Fifth Dynasty expeditions to Canaan also occurred (1966, 29). A scene in the tomb at Inti at Dishashi depicts the capture of a Canaanite city, and a mutilated inscription names two of the cities, neither of which can be identified. The inscription indicates that the expedition was extensive enough to be significant. If the city at Ai did carry out a revolt against Egypt during the Fourth Dynasty, it would be among the first places targeted for capture in any Egyptian plans to regain control of Canaan. A date ca. 2400 would be suitable for the fall of Ai during the Fifth Dynasty, and would usher in the 'dark age' which Wright calls EB IV (1971, 285).

DESCRIPTIONS OF THE PHASE VII POTTERY, FIG. 68

Fig. 68 No.	Reg. No.	
—	4548d	Body sherd of small bowl, very crudely made; orange with grey core; medium-coarse with some assorted grey and white grits. A III 201.7.
—	4548h	Body sherd of small bowl, hand-made, varying thickness; orange inside and brown outside with patches of orange, thick, grey core; coarse with many assorted white and grey quartz grits concentrated at surface outside; much spalling outside associated with white grits, very uneven surface over-all. A III 201.7.
1	4894	Upcurved to thinned, inverted edge, orangish-buff with buff core; medium-coarse with some assorted white grits; traces of burnished, reddish-brown slip over-all. A IV 300.7.
—	4548b	Rim of wide, shallow bowl, inverted, rounded edge, wheel-turned; light-orange; medium with few assorted reddish- and dark-brown grits; horizontally-burnished reddish-orange slip over-all. A III 201.7.
—	4548e	Flattened base of large, shallow bowl, wheel-turned; dark-orange with thick, grey core; medium-coarse with some assorted reddish-brown and grey grits; wheel-burnished orange slip inside; some assorted pits in bottom outside. A III 201.7.
—	4905	Rim of wide, shallow bowl, inverted with shallow depression outside below angle of wall, badly chipped, wheel-finished; brown with dark-grey core; traces of wheel-burnished brown slip inside. A IV 300.8.
2	4888	Rim upcurved to wide, inverted, flattened edge, projected in and out, wheel-made; buff with thick, dark-grey core; very coarse with some assorted grey grits; rough texture over-all. A IV 300.7.
3	4546	Rim upcurved to triangular, inverted edge, wheel-made; pinkish-tan with thick, dark pinkish-grey core; very coarse with many assorted grey and white grits; many assorted pits and rough texture over-all. A III 201.7.
4	4897	Rim upcurved to indented, inverted edge projected slightly out, wheel-made; greyish-buff with dark-grey core in places; coarse with some assorted grey grits; some white incrustations outside and on edge, flaking outside. A IV 300.7.
5	4902	Rim, wall and flat base of platter, rim indented and projected in and out, wheel-finished; orangish-buff with thick dark-grey core penetrating to outside in places; coarse with many assorted white, grey, and tan grits; rough texture and crazing over-all. A IV 300.8.
6	4901	Rim upcurved to low, inverted edge wheel-made; light-brown inside, light-grey outside and edge, thick, dark-grey core; coarse with very many assorted white and tan grits; rough texture over-all. A IV 300.7a.
7	4903	Angular wall with rim everted to thinned, rounded edge, wheel-made; dark-orange with dark-grey core; medium-coarse with many assorted white, grey, and tan grits; faint traces of burnished, reddish-brown slip outside and inside edge; many assorted pits over-all, crazing outside. A IV 300.8.
8	4544	Rim sharply incurved to wide, greatly thickened, rounded edge, wheel-finished; orangish-buff inside with buff outside and core; medium-coarse with very many assorted grey and white grits; grey smoke marks outside, rough texture inside below fold of rim. A III 201.7.

Fig. 68 *No.*	*Reg.* *No.*	
9	4900	Rim incurved to medium-wide, thickened, tapered edge; orange with patches of buff outside, buff inside with thick, grey core; medium-coarse with very many assorted grey quartz grits; two small and deep diagonal indentations outside edge, many small to fine pits. A IV 300.7a.
—	4548c	Rim of hole-mouth jar with slightly incurved, rounded edge; light-orange with grey core; medium with some assorted grey and tan grits. A III 201.7.
10	4895	Rim outcurved to rounded edge, wheel-made; buff with grey core; coarse with many assorted white and grey grits; traces of white slip over-all; rough, gritty texture outside. A IV 300.7.
—	4548f	Body sherd of jar; dark pinkish-orange; coarse with some assorted white, tan, and reddish-brown grits; traces of heavy, white slip outside. A III 201.7.
—	4548g	Body sherd of jar, thick; orange with brown core; medium-coarse with many small to very fine white and few assorted grey and reddish-brown grits; traces of white slip outside; few assorted pits. A III 201.7.
11	4898	Rim outcurved to rounded edge, wheel-made; buff with very thick, dark-grey core penetrating to inside in places; medium-coarse with many assorted grey grits; some white incrustations. A IV 300.7.
12	4700	Rim incurved to thickened, rounded, beveled edge, wheel-finished: dark-orange inside with buff outside and core; coarse with very many assorted grey and white grits; grey smoke marks outside, many assorted pits inside. A III 203.1.
13	4702	Upright rim slightly incurved to wide, greatly thickened, rounded edge, wheel-finished; orange inside with orangish-tan outside and core; very coarse with many assorted tan grits; medium-wide, crude, wavy, half-relief rope-molding outside, traces of white slip outside; many assorted pits inside, rough texture over-all. A III 203.1.
14	4548a	Rim incurved to narrow, slightly thickened, rounded edge; orange; medium-coarse with many medium to fine, grey quartz grits; outside of edge very badly chipped or spalled, few medium to small pits inside, black smoke marks outside. A III 201.7.
15	4701	Base of juglet; orange; very fine with some assorted white and grey grits, porous ware; traces of continuously-burnished, orange slip outside; many small to fine pits outside, very rough texture inside. A III 203.1.
16	4547	Coarse with few assorted white grits; bottom very pitted. A III 201.7.
17	4899	Orangish-buff; coarse with very many assorted white and reddish-brown grits; very pitted and flaking inside, pitted outside and on bottom, very worn. A IV 300.7.
—	4906	Flat base of jar; orange inside and brownish-grey outside, buff core; coarse with very many assorted grey quartz grits, few assorted reddish-brown grits. A IV 300.8.
18	4890	Dark-grey with buff outside; medium-coarse with some assorted grey and tan grits; some assorted pits inside, rough, gritty texture over-all. A IV 300.7.
19	4887	Buff with thick, dark-grey core; coarse with many assorted grey grits; some assorted pits over-all A IV 300.7.
20	4896	Buff with dark-grey core; very coarse with some assorted grey grits. A IV 300.7.
21	4548	Orangish-buff inside and dark greyish-buff outside and core; medium-coarse with very many assorted white quartz grits; one very large and some assorted pits outside and on bottom, rough texture outside, grey smoke marks outside and on bottom. A III 201.7.
22	4904	Brownish-buff with very thick, dark-grey core penetrating to inside; very coarse with many assorted white and grey grits; rough gritty texture over-all. A IV 300.8.
23	4698	Buff; very coarse with some assorted white grits; white slip outside; inside very pitted and flaking, some pitting on bottom, rough texture outside. A III 203.1.

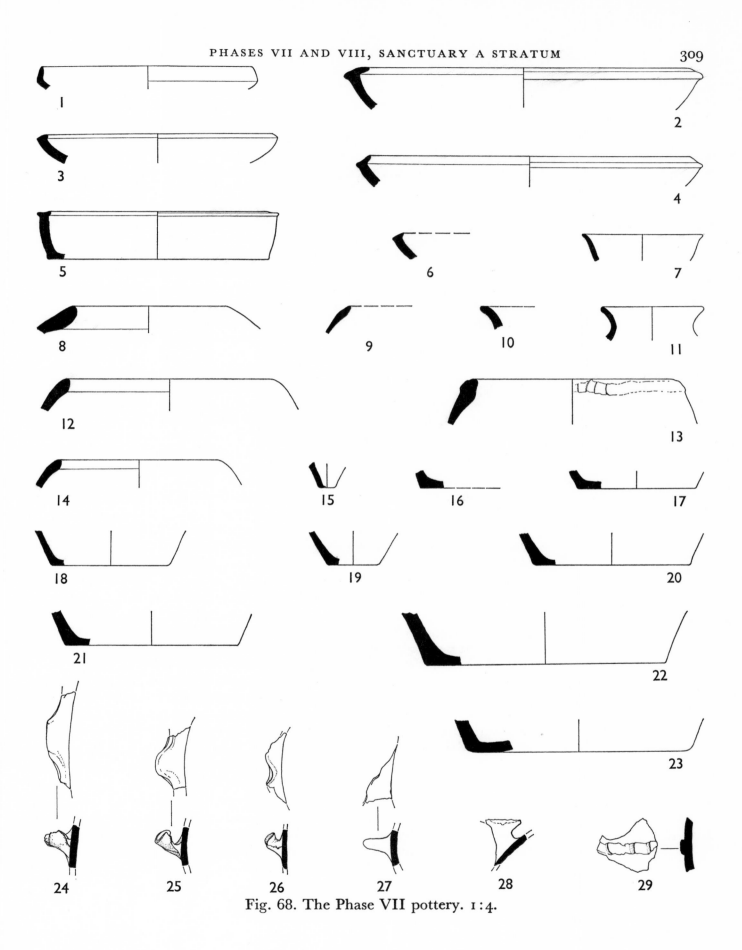

Fig. 68. The Phase VII pottery. 1:4.

Fig. 68 No.	Reg. No.	
24	4891, 92 (joined)	Pushed-up, indented edge; dark-grey with buff outside; coarse with many assorted white grits; rough texture over-all. A IV 300.7.
25	4893	Pushed-up indented edge; dark-grey inside and pinkish-buff outside; coarse with many assorted white grits; many small to fine pits. A IV 300.7.
26	4697	Pushed-up indented edge; greyish-tan inside and orange outside, thick, dark-grey core; medium-coarse with some assorted, mostly fine, white grits; many assorted pits. A III 203.1.
27	4703	Slightly thumb-indented edge; buff with grey core; some assorted grey grits; traces of continuously-burnished, reddish-brown slip outside; very rough texture inside. A III 203.1.
28	4699	Vestigial spout fragment, shallow depression in the bowl of spout; orange inside and buff outside, thick dark-grey core; fine with many small to fine, white grits; traces of white slip outside; rough texture, some grey incrustations. A III 203.1.
29	4545	Buff inside and pinkish-tan outside, dark-grey core; medium-wide, crude, straight, high-relief rope-molding outside, traces of white slip outside; many assorted pits over-all. A III 201.7.

DESCRIPTIONS OF THE MARQUET-KRAUSE PHASE VIII POTTERY AND OBJECTS, FIGS. 69–80

Fig. 69 No.	M-K Reg. No.	
1	1459	Egyptian alabaster; zoomorphic vessel in the shape and size of a water-skin; rear view. H:120; after Amiran 1971 (see original in Fig. 78:1).
2	1498, 59	Same, bottom view (reconstructed); leather thongs around jar neck (M-K Reg. 1498; Fig. 71:2; H:116) match those around skin of rear legs (M-K Reg. 1459; Fig. 78:1; H:120). After Amiran 1971.
3	1498, 59	Same, side view (reconstructed). After Amiran 1971.

Fig. 70 No.	M-K Reg. No.	
1	1485, 84 (fitted)	Egyptian alabaster jar, in two sections consisting of M-K Reg. 1485, upper, and 1484, lower, fitted together; vertical depression on either side of No. 1485; H:116; after Amiran 1971 (see originals in Fig. 71:3, No. 1485; 71:4, No. 1484).
2	1520	Egyptian alabaster bowl, reconstructed from fragments of M-K Reg. 1520. H:116; after Amiran 1971; original listed in Fig. 71 after No. 6, photograph of base fragment in M-K Pl. XXIII.
3	1489	Egyptian alabaster bowl, redrawn from original, shown in Fig. 71:5, photograph in M-K Pl. XXIII, H:116; after Amiran 1971.
4	1491	Very shallow bowl of pink stone, redrawn from original, shown in Fig. 71:6, photograph in M-K Pl. LIII (numbered 1419 in error). H:116; after Amiran 1971.

Fig. 71 No.	M-K Reg. No.	
1	2366	Egyptian alabaster libation cup; thin waist, enlarged toward flat base and toward top, horizontal rim projecting over outside surface. H:116; in the niche of the south wall; sanctuary A (M-K Pl. LXVI).

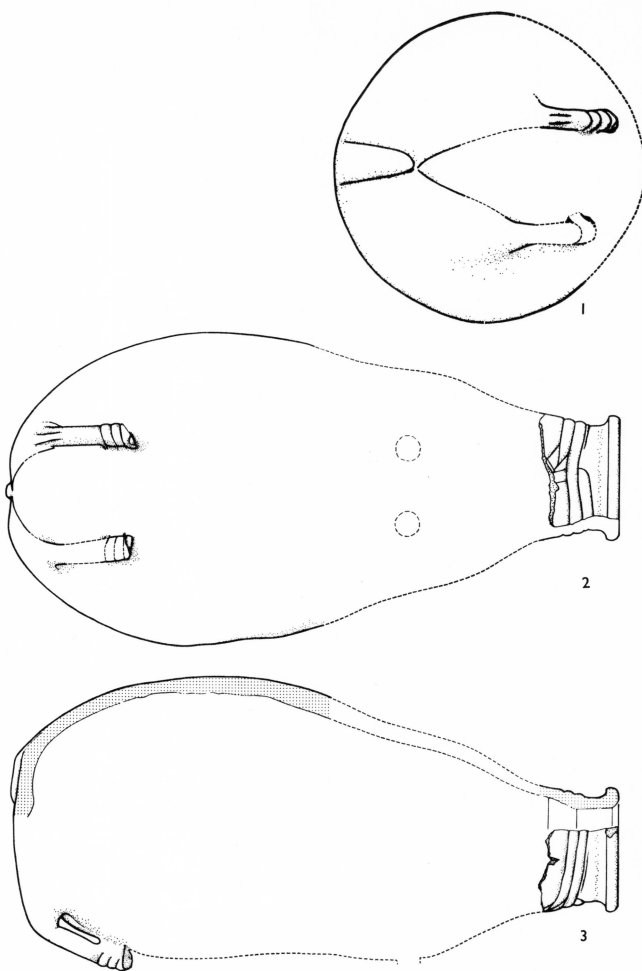

Fig. 69. Zoomorphic vessel in the shape and size of a water-skin. Phase VIII, Room 116, 120 (Area II–III), after Amiran 1971. 1:4.

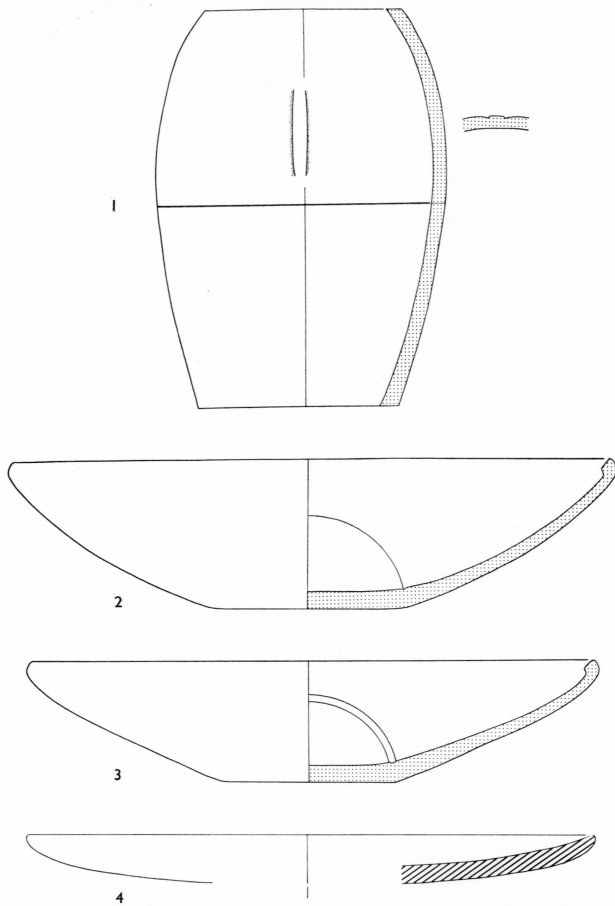

Fig. 70. Egyptian alabaster jars and bowls, Phase VIII, Room 116 (Area II), after Amiran 1971.

Fig. 71 No.	Reg. No.	
2	1498	Upper part of alabaster jar: wall slightly inclined toward inside, rounded rim curved towards the outside; below, small band in relief winding twice around neck; the end of the upper band passes underneath the second turn of the band and reappears descending to the end of the lower band, which descends also before beginning a third turn. H:116; (sanctuary A). (M-K Pl. LXVI).
3	1485	Jar without bottom resembling No. 1484, but globular; white alabaster with grey marbling; on the upper half of the jar, a small relief stretching to the top and ending in a point. H:116 (M-K Pl. LXVI).
4	1484	Jar without bottom shaped like a truncated cone; white alabaster with grey marbling; wall slightly inclined, imperceptibly curved, horizontal rim on two sides. H:116 (M-K Pl. LXVI).
5	1489	Bowl: diameter, 31 cm.; alabaster; flattened form, flat base, wall very inclined, very lightly curved; rim very slightly thickened over the inside surface at the edge; on the inside, the base of the bowl is bordered by an incised circle (very incomplete). H:116 (M-K Pl. LXVI).
6	1491	Bowl: diameter, 30 cm.; pink stone; very flat form, barely curved; rather sharp rim (very incomplete). H:116 (M-K Pl. LXVI).
—	1520	Bowl: diameter, 30 cm.; alabaster; flat base; wall very inclined, slightly curved, rim very lightly projecting triangularly over inside surface; on the inside a small incised circle bordering the base. H:116; behind the south-west door.
—	1893	Small fragment of bowl: alabaster, horizontal rim projecting over inside surface. H:116; sanctuary A floor.

Fig. 72 No.	M-K Reg. No.	
1	1533	Handle of knife: ivory; decorated by a juxtaposition of small triangles, rectangles, and rhomboids incised in relief; edge decorated with hatchings forming a network of angles, or superposed chevrons. H:116; at the side of the niche of the south angle (of wall). (M-K Pl. LXVI).
2	2251	Handle of worked bone; design of squares and incised lines. H:116; sanctuary A, in the niche of room 116 (M-K Pl. LXXVIII).
3	2349	Fashioned handle (of bone). H:116; sanctuary A in the south wall A (M-K Pl. LXXVIII).
4	1497 II	Vase without bottom, bone. H:116 (M-K Pl. LXVI).
5	2350	Fashioned handle (of bone). H:116; sanctuary A, in the south (part). (M-K Pl. LXXVIII).
6	1497a	Fragment of very small bowl; bone; round rim, two horizontal lines, forming two bands divided by a series of small diagonal lines; at the level of the second band, little circles hollowed out at equal distances. H:116 (M-K Pl. LXVI).
7	1497b	Fragment of very small bowl; bone; hemispherical body, projecting flat base; incised decoration around base, stippling forming a series of little isosceles triangles. H:116 (M-K Pl. LXVI).
—	1895	Remains of fashioned bone and alabaster. H:116; sanctuary A.

Fig. 73 No.	M-K Reg. No.	
1	1524	Cup: height, 6.5 cm., brown ware; flat base, wall widening more and more toward the rim, sharp rim. H:116; (sanctuary A). (M-K Pl. LXV).

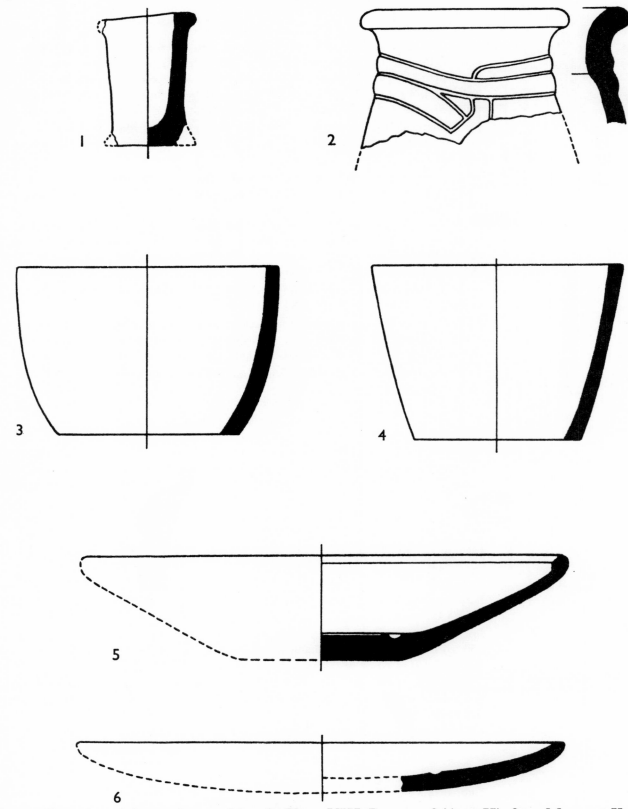

Fig. 71. Egyptian alabaster jars and bowls, Phase VIII, Room 116 (Area II), from Marquet-Krause 1949. 1:4.

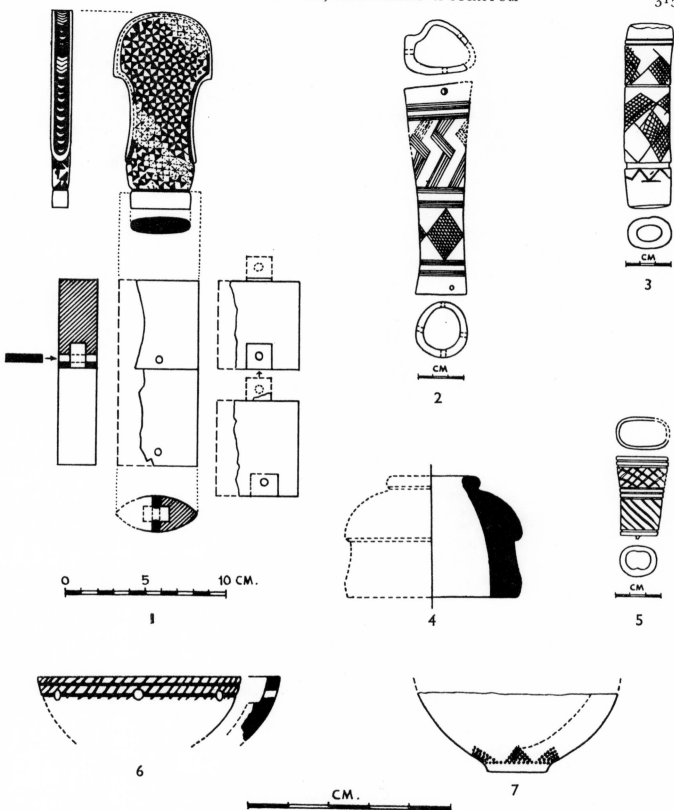

Fig. 72. Ivory knife handle and sheath, decorated bone objects, Phase VIII, Room 116 (Area II), from Marquet-Krause 1949. 1:4.

Fig. 73 No.	M-K Reg. No.	
2	1496	Fragments of cup: light brown ware; thin waist, widening toward base and toward top; sharp, very flared rim. No burnishing. H:116; at the side of the burned beam (M-K Pl. LXXV).
3	1506	Incense stand: height, 37.5 cm., light brown ware; without bottom; four sides nearly rectangular (imperceptibly inclined towards inside), each pierced by a rectangular opening in the upper part; round neck, outcurved, lower part surrounded by a series of small incisions. H:116; southeast of the burned beam (*asherah*). (M-K Pl. LXV).
4	2297	Cup: diameter aperture, 9 cm.; thin waist becoming larger toward flat base; flared rim. H:116; floor A (column of the south wall). (M-K Pl. LXXVIII).
5	1526 II	Fragments of cup: height, 8 cm.; flat base, wall nearly vertical, base projecting over side (forming almost a kind of collar), rim slightly curved toward outside, but barely extended (nearly the same diameter as base). H:116; (sanctuary A). (M-K Pl. LXV).
6	1526	Fragments of cup: flat base, wall inclined toward inside; rim curved toward outside; brown slip, burnished. H:116; (sanctuary A). (M-K Pl. LXXV).
7	1509	Cup: height, 8.2 cm.; light brown ware; vertical wall, flat base, rim curved toward outside. H:116; (sanctuary A). (M-K Pl. LXV).
8	1521	Fragment of plaque, decorated with small reliefs; (M-K describes the object as 'base of a bowl', but it seems to be a brick-like plaque or palette). H:116 (M-K Pl. LXXV).

Fig. 74 No.	M-K Reg. No.	
1	1507	Incense stand: height, 34 cm.; light-brown ware; same type as 71:2, sides narrower toward the bottom (rim and upper part of neck missing). H:116: on the northwest of the burned beam (M-K Pl. LXVI).
2	1476	Fragments of (two) large jars. H:116; in the fallen stones. (M-K Pl. LXV).
3	1525	Fragments of bowl: flat base, slightly projecting; angled wall slightly upcurved, sharp rim. H:116 (M-K Pl. LXV).
—	2403	(a) Fragment of small bowl, flat projecting base; *idem*, fine wall and rim, straight, fragment of large bowl; (b) pestle (?) of stone. H:116; in the niche of the south wall, sanctuary A.
4	2358	Fragment of bowl: small; wall and thinned rim curved toward top. H:116; sanctuary A, in the niche of the south wall (M-K Pl. LXXVIII).
5	2396	Bowl: oval, one side forming spout, flat base (lamp). H:116; in the niche of the south wall; sanctuary A (M-K Pl. LXXVIII).
6	2395	Bowl: flat, flat base; rim projecting over inside surface; beginning of a handle on outside edge. H:116; in the niche of the south wall; sanctuary A (M-K Pl. LXXVIII).
7	1475	Bowl: white stone; large base, flat and fine; horizontal rim projecting over inside surface. H:116 (M-K Pl. LXVI).
8	2023	Bowl: raised rim, forming an angle with inside wall; pink slip, burnished with design of darker lines. H:116; floor A (M-K Pl. LXXVII).
9	1529	Bowl: diameter, 31 cm.; light brown ware; flat base, wall nearly vertical; rim lightly curved toward inside (cf. 1508). H:116 (M-K Pl. LXV).

Fig. 75 No.	M-K Reg. No.	
1	2394	Bowl: diameter of opening, 27 cm.; deep; flat base, rim projecting over inside surface. H:116; in the niche of the south wall, sanctuary A (M-K Pl. LXXVIII).

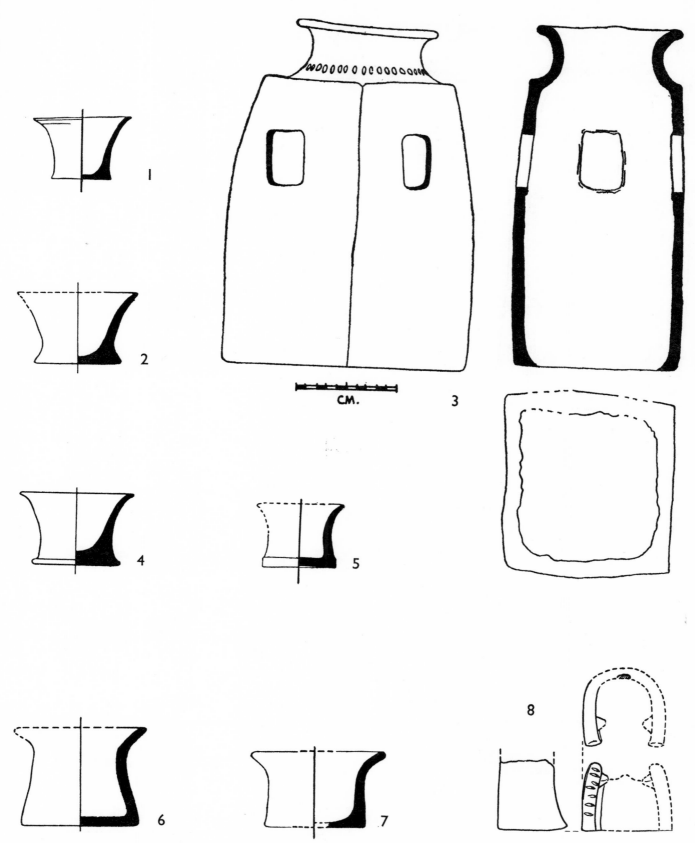

Fig. 73. Incense stand and pottery vessels, Phase VIII, Room 116 (Area II), from Marquet-Krause 1949. 1:4.

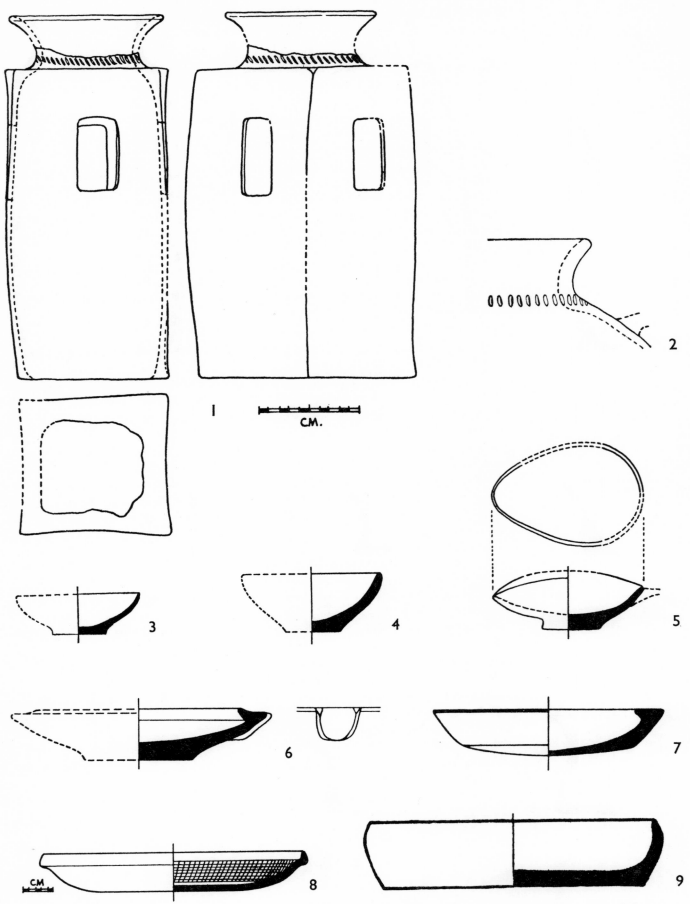

Fig. 74. Incense stand, pottery and stone vessels, Phase VIII, Room 116 (Area II), from Marquet-Krause 1949. 1:4.

Fig. 75 No.	M-K Reg. No.	
2	1531	Bowl: diameter 24 cm., brown ware; flat base, wall not very inclined; rim projecting over inside surface at a nearly straight angle with inner wall, surface slightly concave. H:116 (M-K Pl. LXV).
3	1530	Bowl: diameter, 26.5 cm.; pinkish-brown ware; flat base, wall inclined 45°; rim projecting long and sharply over surface at a less pointed angle with the inner wall, surface somewhat convex; smoke marks. H:116 (M-K Pl. LXXVI).
—	2384	Fragment of bowl: wall inclined, thin rim forming an obtuse and rounded angle with inside wall; rims of hole-mouths: (1) thick and heavy, slightly thickened over outside surface; (2) thin, folded over on inside surface (thus forming an enlargement); (3) slightly thickened over two surfaces, extremely flat. H:116 on inside of floor A, and above.
4	2005	Neck and half of body of a small jar with horizontal handles. H:116; floor A (M-K Pl. LXXVII).
—	2404	Fragment of jar; globular body, very short and wide neck; fragment (of bowl, without doubt), rim pierced by a hole, red slip; very flat loop-handle; fragment of flat and smooth stone (having perhaps served as a plate). H:116; in the niche of the south wall, sanctuary A.
—	2650 II	Neck of small jar. H:116; in floor A.
5	1512	Bowl: same type (as Nos. 2, 3 above); rim at right angle to inner wall (angle somewhat rounded). H:116 (M-K Pl. LXXV).
6	1532	Bowl: diameter 27 cm.; same type (as Nos. 2, 3, 5 above); rim projecting over inside surface, but curving slightly upward. H:116 (M-K Pl. LXXVI).
7	1479	Fragments of hole-mouth: rounded rim, somewhat thickened; the jar seems to have been of elongated form. H:116 (M-K Pl. LXV).
—	2458	Broken horizontal handle; rim of thin hole-mouth; fragment of neck, thin rim curved toward outside; flat base of small jar with rounded body; fragment with finger-indented molding; 3 pierced shells. H:116; in the niche of the south wall, floor A.
8	1478	Large bowl: flat base, wall slightly inclined, toward outside; rim projecting sharply over inside surface nearly at right angle with inside wall; loop-handle on body. H:116 (M-K Pl. LXV).
—	2374	Three fragments of deep bowl, wall somewhat inclined; horizontal rim projecting over the two surfaces, more pronounced over inside surface; fragment of neck, red burnished. H:116; on floor A.
9	2447 II	Thickened neck of jar, outcurved to rounded rim. H:116; in the niche of the south wall; sanctuary A (M-K Pl. LXXXII).
—	1415	Necks of jars with thickened rims; neck of small jar; wavy horizontal handle; fragments of hole-mouths; discoidal base. H:116; on the floor (of sanctuary A).
—	2307	Jar: flat base, diameter 22 cm.; two horizontal handles, loop-handle reaching to edge of shoulder. H:116; just above floor A, south wall at side of column.
10	2202	Rim of hole-mouth: clear brown ware; thickened toward top, flat edge. H:116; floor A (M-K Pl. LXXXVII).
—	2206	Various fragments: rim of hole-mouth, rather thin, barely thickened, incised line on outside surface bordered below by slight projection. H:116, floor A.
—	2201	Various fragments; rim of hole-mouth, heavy, thick, rounded edge; fragment with molding. H:116; floor A.
—	2090	Fragment of hole-mouth. H:116; in floor A.
—	2266	Rim of hole-mouth, thickened over inside surface; flint blade; bone. H:116; floor A, stone bench.

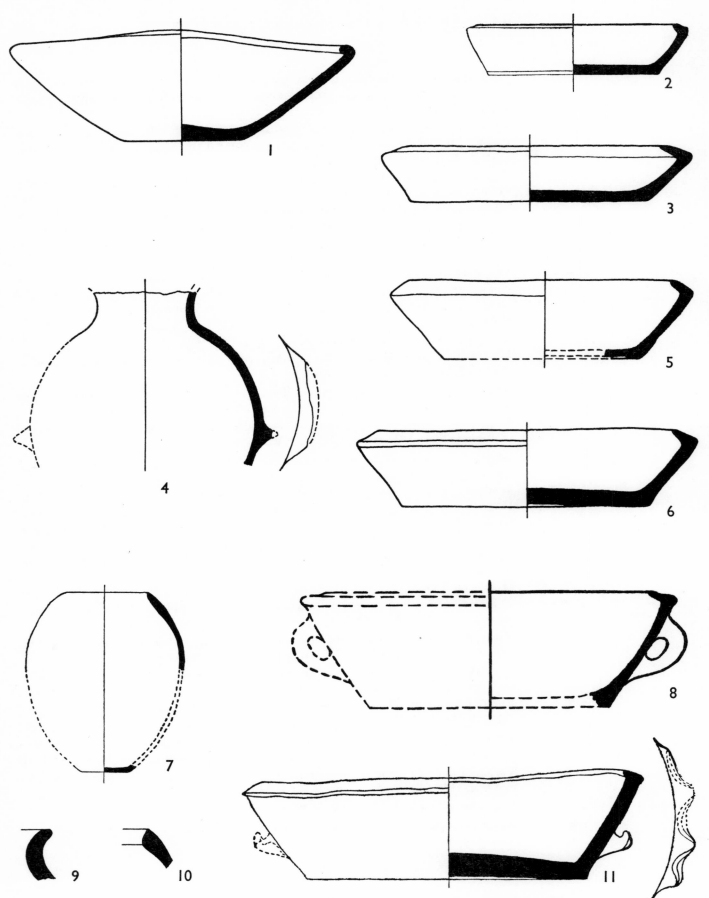

Fig. 75. Bowls and jars, Phase VIII, Room 116 (Area II), from Marquet-Krause 1949. 1:4.

Fig. 75 No.	*M-K Reg. No.*	
—	2375	Fragments of hole-mouths. H:116; floor A.
—	2383	Rim of hole-mouth, very rounded edge projecting slightly over inside surface; flat bases. H:116, floor A.
11	1562	Fragments of large bowl: flat base, thickened on inside; wall straight, rather inclined; rim slightly projecting, two sides at obtuse angle (and rounded) with inside wall; handles with raised edges. H:116 (M-K Pl. LXV).
—	1558 II	Two horizontal handles with raised edges; horizontal folded handle, somewhat projecting; fragments with decorative molding consisting of projecting undulations; small relief; (rough handle?); fragment of bowl: thick wall slightly inclined, horizontal rim projecting thin and short over the two surfaces; over inside face, below rim, horizontally projecting line; fragments of deep bowl, wavy molding, large, somewhat projecting over outside face, trace of loop-handle, light brown. H:116; sanctuary A.
—	1935	Horizontal handles with raised edges; flattened loop-handle; fragment of bowl; wall and rim thin, lightly curved; fragment of bowl rim perpendicular to inner wall, red slip burnished. H:116; sanctuary A.
—	1939	Horizontal handles with raised edge. H:116, sanctuary A (M-K Pl. XX).
—	2294	Horizontal handle with raised edge; edge folded over, horizontal handle, rim of hole-mouth thickened over inside surface toward edge; decorative molding. H:116; floor A; column of the south wall.
—	1953	Various fragments of pottery. H:116; on floor A.
—	2438	Various fragments of pottery. H:116; in the niche of the south wall, sanctuary A.
—	2441	Fragment, red burnished; pierced shell; three flints. H:116; in the niche of the south wall, sanctuary A.
—	2513	Various fragments of pottery. H:116; south corner of east wall, floor A.
—	2239	Small horizontal handle with raised edge; fragment decorated with heads and horns of stylized animals in relief; fragments of bowls: (1) flat base, wall slightly inclined, horizontal rim projecting rather long over inside surface, slightly over the other surface; grey ware; (2) very sharply inclined wall, slightly curved, horizontal rim slightly projecting over inside surface; fragment of bowl, rounded, not very deep, fine rim curved upward, pinkish-brown ware; rim of thin hole-mouth; fragment with white slip. H:116; on the bench of stone, floor A.
—	1514	Two bronze points, four-cornered (quadrangled), rounded at the end. H:116; loci 7–8, among the fallen stones (M-K Pl. XXXIX).
—	2371	Bronze point. H:116; in the niche of the south wall, sanctuary A.
—	2368	Three flint blades. H:116; in the niche of the south wall, sanctuary A.

Fig. 76 No.	*M-K Reg. No.*	
1	1499	Cup: flat base, wall slightly thickened toward base, rim curved toward outside; black smoke traces. H:133; at the foot of the altar (M-K Pl. LXXV).
2	1519	Cup: flat base, wall straight slightly inclined toward inside; rim curved toward outside; red slip, burnished. H:133 (M-K Pl. LXV).
3	1541	Bowl: light brown ware; cup form; narrow base, wall flared, sharp rim. H:133 (M-K Pl. LXXVI).
4	1536	Bowl: pinkish-brown ware; near cup form, cf. 1534; flat base, narrow wall much flared, curved toward outside; sharp edge. H:133 (M-K Pl. LXV).
5	1534	Cup: fine brown ware; narrow wall thickening toward base; wall sharply flaring toward top, sharp rim. H:133 (M-K Pl. LXV).

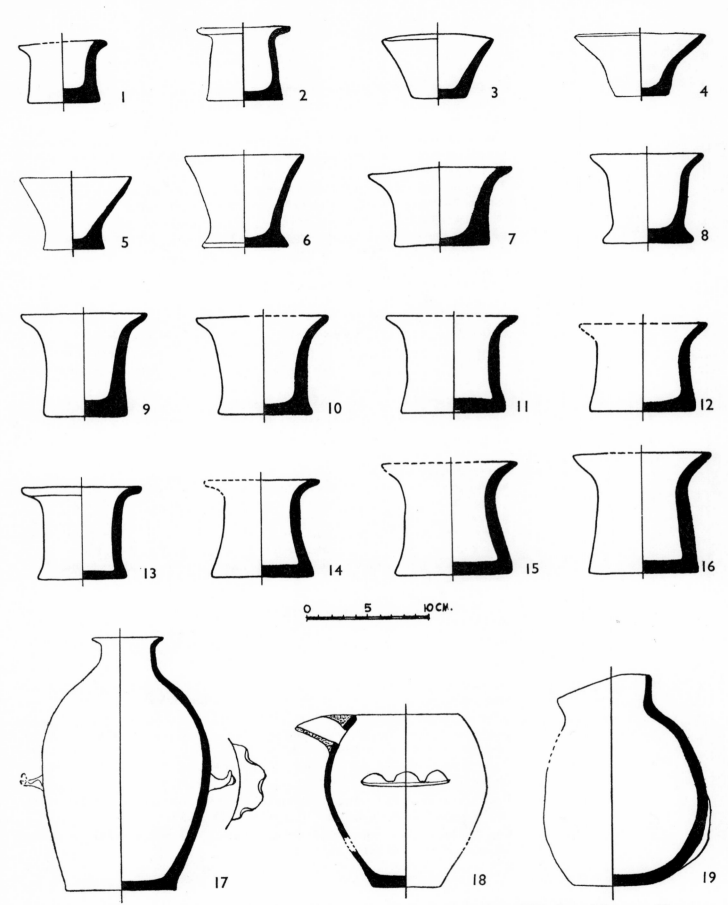

Fig. 76. Cups and jars, Phase VIII, Room 133 (the altar enclosure, Area III), from Marquet-Krause 1949. 1:4.

Fig. 76 No.	M-K Reg. No.	
6	1486	Cup: thin waist, enlarging toward base and toward top; sharp rim, dark-red slip, burnished. H:133; near the horn No. 482 (M-K Pl. LXV).
7	1537	Cup: cylindrical lower part; rim flared. H:133 (M-K Pl. LXXV).
8	1488	Cup: same type; body nearly cylindrical, base sharply projecting outside; rim abruptly curved toward outside; red slip, burnished. H:133; at the foot of the altar (M-K Pl. LXXVI).
9	1487	Cup: same type, but more cylindrical, sharp rim abruptly curved toward outside, red slip, burnished, inside and outside. H:133; in the niche of the altar. (M-K Pl. LXXV).
10	1513	Cup: flat base, wall nearly straight, widened at base; upper part and rim curved toward outside; brown slip, burnished; traces of white lime. H:133 (M-K Pl. LXXV).
11	1538	Cup: brown ware; straight body widening slightly toward flat base; rim flared; traces of brown slip, burnished; traces of smoke and lime incrustations (incomplete). H:133 (M-K Pl. LXXV).
12	1540	Cup: body widened slightly toward base; rim flared; brown slip, burnished (incomplete). H:133 (M-K Pl. LXXV).
13	1501	Cup same type, body more cylindrical, base less widened; thick dark red slip. H:133; at the foot of the altar (M-K Pl. LXXV).
14	1500	Cup: light brown ware; very large base, traces of light brown slip, without burnishing. H:133; at the foot of the altar (M-K Pl. LXXV).
15	1502	Cup: brown ware; same type, very widened toward base, without slip. H:133; at the foot of the altar (M-K Pl. LXXV).
16	1504	Fragment of cup: light brown ware; wall widened toward flat base and toward rim. H:133 (M-K Pl. LXXV).
—	1523	Cup: grey ware; flat base, rim very flared; brown slip, burnished (very much broken). H:133.
17	1503	Fragments of jar: light brown ware; flat base, sloping shoulder; neck continuous with line of shoulder, flared rim; wavy edge horizontal handle, raised edge, projecting; traces of white lime slip. H:133 (M-K Pl. LXV).
18	1510	Upper part of jar without neck: pink ware; ovoid body, flat base; spout just below rim, extending in shape of beak; at middle of body, two horizontal, folded handles, barely projecting. H:133; on the altar (M-K Pl. LXV).
19	1518	Fragments of jar: pink ware; very asymmetrical; round base slightly flattened; pear-shaped body; short neck, wide, nearly straight; thick lime layer. H:133 (M-K Pl. LXV).
—	1482	Horn of large bovine, 24 cm. long. H:133; at the foot of the altar, under a large stone.

Fig. 77 No.	M-K Reg. No.	
1	1499	Bowl: oval, one side forming spout; flat base; traces of handle. H:133; at the foot of the altar (M-K Pl. LXV).
2	1494	Small votive bed, fashioned in thick (2 cm.) clay; rectangular frame with the sides projected; remains of legs; on inside of frame, diagonal incised lines forming a lattice; probable indications of straps or bands (one half missing); red slip, burnished. H:133; near the altar (M-K Pl. LXV).
3	1505a, b	Two fragments of combs: left, 6 cm. wide, yellow ivory; right 7 cm. wide, ivory; very high, the teeth occupy only one-third of comb; pierced hole in upper part. H:133; (sanctuary A). (M-K Pl. LXVI).
4	1399	Cup: height, 3.5 cm.; straight rim; flat base slightly projecting, pierced hole in center (of base) H:133; (sanctuary A). (M-K Pl. LXV).

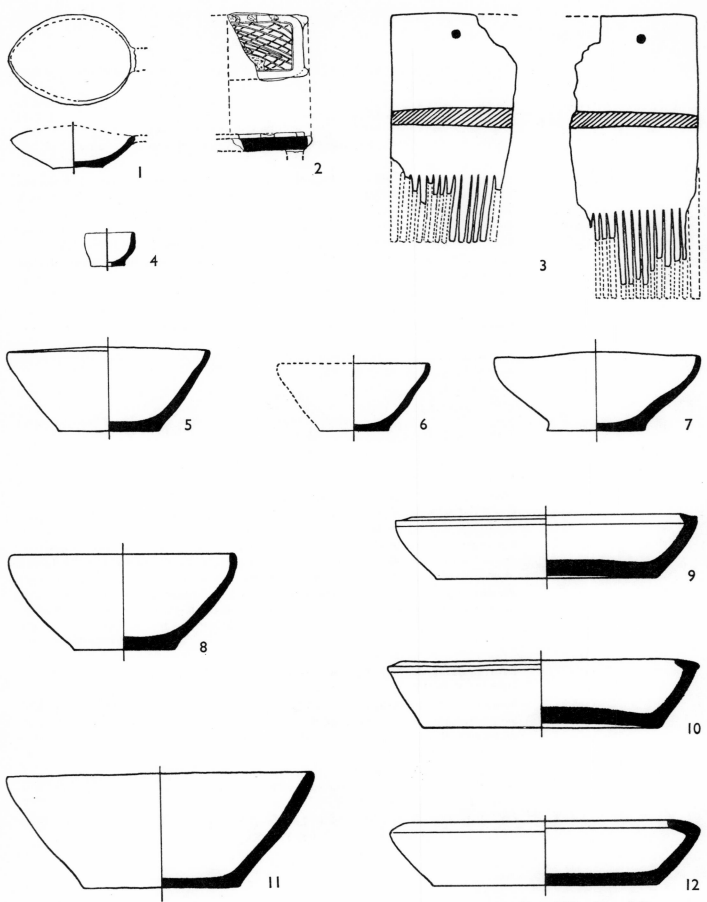

Fig. 77. Bowls and objects, Phase VIII, Room 133 (the altar enclosure, Area III), from Marquet-Krause 1949. 1:4.

Fig. 77 No.	M-K Reg. No.	
5	1517	Bowl: width of opening, 16 cm.; flat base, rim (slightly) projecting over inside surface; red slip, burnished; H:133; (sanctuary A). (M-K Pl. LXXV).
6	1528	Bowl: flat base, sharp rim, slightly curved toward inside; brown slip, burnished on inside; pink-brown band around rim, not burnished. H:133; near the altar. (M-K Pl. LXV).
7	1481	Bowl: light brown ware; flat base slightly projecting; thickened wall, thin rim. H:133; on the altar, in front of the niche (M-K Pl. LXXV).
8	1492	Bowl: width, 19 cm.; flat base barely projecting; wall inclined at about 45°, thin rim slightly curved toward inside; red slip, burnished. H:133; at the side of the altar (M-K Pl. LXXV).
9	1508	Bowl: width, 25 cm.; light pink ware; large flat base; rim projecting over inside; slightly concave inner surface. H:133; at the foot of the altar (M-K Pl. LXXV).
10	1522	Bowl: width, 26 cm.; bright pink ware; flat base, convex (arched) on the inside, straight wall slightly inclined; rim projecting over inside surface almost at right angle with inner wall, projecting barely over inside surface. H:133; (sanctuary A). (M-K Pl. LXXV).
11	1495	Bowl: width, 29 cm.; flat base, wall inclined almost 45°, straight; thin rim; brown (slip), burnished on outside. H:133; (sanctuary A). (M-K Pl. LXXV).
12	1511	Bowl: width, 25 cm.; light brown ware; flat base, wall inclined at 45°, rim projecting long and thin over inside surface at angle not very sharp with inner wall. H:133; at the foot of the altar (M-K Pl. LXXV).
—	2430	Fragment of bowl: thick wall sharply upcurved, vertical on top; horizontal rim in slight projection over inside surface, projection barely visible over other surface; rim of heavy hole-mouth, rounded edge; not thickened; fragment with narrow molding; fragment with red slip. H:133, north wall, on floor A.

Fig. 78 No.	M-K Reg. No.	
1	1459	Numerous thick fragments of zoomorphic object (see Fig. 69:1): white alabaster; traces of tail and feet. H:120; near the stone table (M-K Pl. LXVI).
2	1490	Cup: thin waist, widened toward base and toward top; sharp rim; flat base; red slip on the outside. H:120; in the middle of the room, on the stone bench south-north (M-K Pl. LXXV).
—	1421	Upper part of cup: thin at waist, very much widened toward flat base (the missing rim would have to curve sharply toward the outside); grey ware with grits; traces of red slip; pointed base ending in long and thin foot, nearly cylindrical (type Jericho); two horizontal, folded handles; rims of hole-mouth, (1) barely thickened; sharp edge; decorative molding; (2) not thickened, flat edge; decorative molding; (3) barely thickened, sharp edge; incised line on outside surface; fragments of bodies of jars with wide corded decorative molding; white slip; three fragments of small, not very deep, bowls, 'lamp' form; shoulder and neck of jar surrounded by projecting line. H:120; locus of the north wall.
3	1527	Fragment of small bowl, round form, thick-rim projecting over the inside surface; light brown slip, burnished on the outside. H:120 (M-K Pl. LXV).
—	1408	Fragments of hemispherical bowl, rim slightly curved toward inside: brown (slip) burnished; fragment of cup, flat base, body narrowed at waist, waist narrower than base, rim curved toward outside; red (slip), burnished. H:120; locus 4.
—	1424 II	Fragment of hemispherical bowl, small; rounded rim; fragment of bowl with sharp rim; fragment of bowl: wall inclined about 45°, sharp rim forming a right or barely sharp angle with inner wall; fragment of cup, with large base; fragment of horizontal handle (type 1). H:120; north part; locus 3 of the north wall.

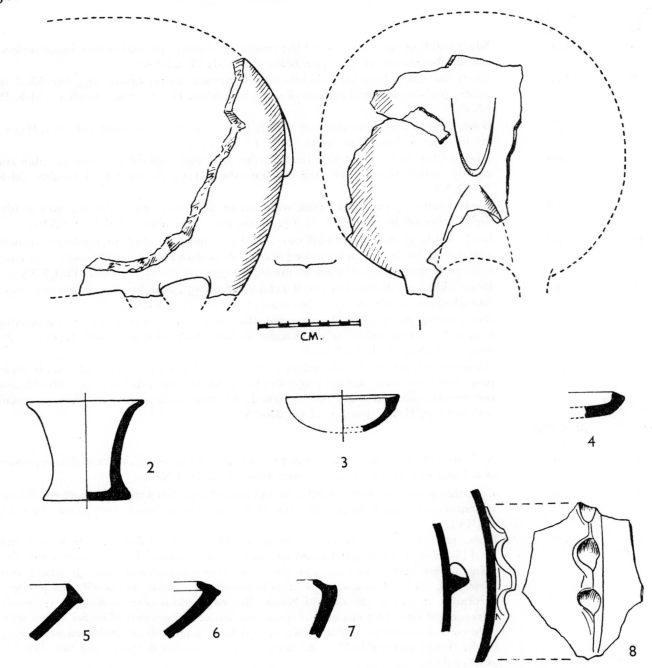

Fig. 78. Objects and pottery, Phase VIII, Room 120 (Area III), from Marquet-Krause 1949.
1:4.

Fig. 78 No.	M-K Reg. No.	
4	1433	Rim of bowl, very flat; projecting over inside surface. H:120; south wall; locus 6 (M-K Pl. LXXXI).
5	1443	Rim of bowl: (2) rim projecting over the two surfaces, at right angle with the inner wall, wall inclined at 45°. H:120; south wall; locus 6 (M-K Pl. LXXXV).

Fig. 78 No.	*M-K Reg.* No.	
—	1427	Fragment of bowl, horizontal rim projecting over the two surfaces; fragments of bowls, rim projecting over inside surface; fragment of small bowl; fragment of lamp, doubtlessly flat; fragment with rather coarse relief; fragment of neck with decorative corded molding; rim of hole-mouth, slightly thickened. H:120; locus 3 of the east wall.
—	1463	Fragment of deep round bowl, vertical inner wall and rim, rim rounded at edge; rims of bowls projecting over inside surface, red slip; very long and narrow neck of small jug; fragments of wide necks: (1) simple thin rim; (2) rim forming thick pads over outside face; (3) curved rim over outside surface, edge vertically flattened, small horizontal, flat handle; horizontal handle (broken), folded; wavy molding. H:120; northwest corner; locus 3; north wall.
6	1453	Fragment of bowl: wall rather inclined, rim projecting over inside surface at almost a right angle with inner wall. H:120; north wall; locus 6 (M-K Pl. LXXXV).
7	1443	Rim of bowl: (1) with flat base, wall somewhat inclined; rim projecting over inside surface, surface lightly concave; red slip on inside and over rim. H:120, south wall; locus 6 (M-K Pl. LXXXI).
—	1424	Fragment of bowl, flat; bottom slightly curved, without base, rim forming a right angle with inner wall, then curving toward outside; sharp edge; very fine ware, well fired; dark red, without burnish; fragment of large bowl, thick straight wall, very inclined; horizontal rim projecting barely over the two surfaces forming a sharp angle with inner wall; dark red; fragment of bowl, same type but less inclined and less straight; brown; rim of hole-mouth slightly thickened over inside surface, rounded edge; horizontal handle with raised edge; fragment of shoulder with round ear-handle, red slip. H:120; north part; locus 3 of the north wall.
8	1433	Horizontal handle: (1) very folded. H:120; south wall; locus 6 (M-K Pl. LXXXVII).
—	1466	Horizontal handles: (1) folded: (2) flat; base of small jar, button projecting but not detached from body; fragment of neck of jar, wide, rim folded toward outside in rounded patches. H:120; floor (A).
—	1461	Horizontal handle; (1) flat. H:120; out from the base of the table of stone (M-K Pl. XLVIII).
—	1413	Various fragments of pottery. H:120; floor (sanctuary A).
—	1425	Various fragments of pottery. H:120; floor (A).

Fig. 79 No.	*M-K Reg.* No.	
1	1402	Cup: globular body, thin, very slightly curved toward inside; flat base projecting, pierced by a hole in the centre; thick ware. H:122; east (M-K Pl. LXXV).
—	1400	Fragment of small cup: alabaster; rim very sharp. H:122; upper layer above the stone table.
2	1383	Wide bowl: diameter 11 cm.; flat projecting base. H:122 (M-K Pl. LXXV).
3	1390	Wide bowl: diameter, 11.4 cm.; brown ware; flat base projecting and badly formed. H:122 (M-K Pl. LXXV).
4	1391	Wide bowl: diameter, 11 cm.; brown ware; flat base projecting and badly formed. H:122 (M-K Pl. LXXV).
5	1397	Wide bowl: diameter, 12.7 cm.; bright pink ware; curved wall, flat base projecting. H:122 (M-K Pl. LXXV).
6	1387	Wide bowl: diameter, 11.5 cm.; bright pink ware; flat projecting base. H:122 (M-K Pl. LXXV).
7	1384	Wide bowl: diameter, 11 cm.; light ware; flat base projecting. H:122 (M-K Pl. LXXV).

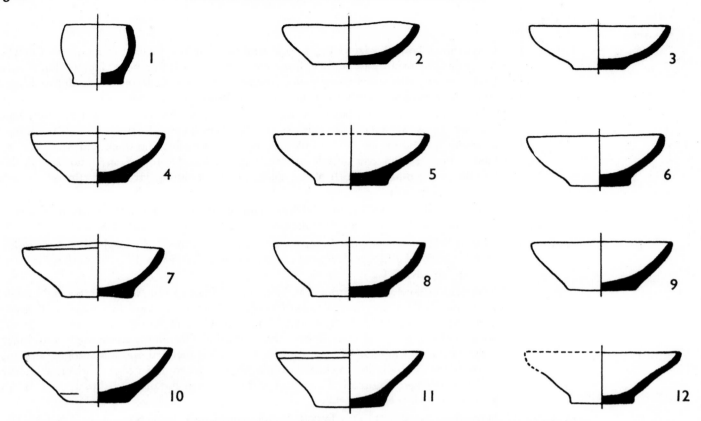

Fig. 79. Cups and bowls, Phase VIII, Enclosure 122 (Area III), from Marquet-Krause 1949.
1:4.

Fig. 79 No.	M-K Reg. No.	
8	1393	Wide bowl: diameter, 12.5 cm.; brown ware; flat base projecting. H:122 (M-K Pl. LXXV).
9	1386	Wide bowl: diameter, 11.5 cm.; bright pink ware; flat base barely projecting. H:122 (M-K Pl. LXXV).
10	1388	Wide bowl: diameter, 11.8 cm.; brown ware: flat base not projecting. H:122 (M-K Pl. LXXV).
11	1385	Wide bowl: diameter, 11.5 cm.; light brown ware; flat base projecting. H:122 (M-K Pl. LXXV).
12	1394	Wide bowl: brown ware; flat base projecting; broken. H:122 (M-K Pl. LXXV).
—	1382	Wide bowl: diameter, 14 cm.; light brown ware; wall slightly curved, sharp rim, flat base hardly projecting. H:122.
—	1389	Wide bowl: diameter, 14 cm.; brownish-pink ware; flat base, little projection and badly formed. H:122.
—	1398	Wide bowl: light brown, very fine ware; curved wall, flat base projecting; (incomplete). H:122.
—	1392	Wide bowl: brown, fine ware; flat base projecting; broken. H:122.
—	1395	Wide bowl: light grey ware; (upper part missing). H:122.
—	1401	Numerous fragments of bowls (type 1385). H:122.

Fig. 79 No.	*M-K Reg.* No.	
—	1410	Fragment of neck of jar, rim curved toward outside, rounded at edge; fragment of bowl with flat base, wall curved, rim projecting over inside surface. H:122, on the rock.
—	1412	Fragment of neck with decorative molding (half-circular); wide decorative molding, somewhat projecting, even. H:122; east, on the rock.
—	1381	Five flint blades, sharp on two sides: 4, clear brown; 1 dark grey; white hemispherical stone, pierced by a hole in the centre; curved surface, decorated by lines. H:122.

Fig. 80 No.	*M-K Reg.* No.	
1	1457	Fragment of bowl, wall inclined; (1) flat form, rim forming a right angle with inner wall. H:132; south wall, locus 6 (M-K Pl. LXXXV).
2	1452	Fragment of bowl: (2) light brown, burnished; rim thin, forming a right angle with inner wall. H:132; in the extension of the east wall (M-K Pl. LXXXV).
3	1452	Fragment of bowl: rim slightly projecting over the two surfaces. H:132; in the extension of the east wall (M-K Reg. LXXXI).
—	1441	Fragments of bowls: (1) wall slightly inclined, flat rim projecting over the two surfaces, at right angle with inner wall; (2) painting on inside; burnished lines, fragment of elongated neck; rims of hole-mouths, thin, and thickened slightly; rounded or sharp edges; flared necks; flat base, slightly projecting; half-folded, horizontal handle. H:132; locus 6 of south wall.
4	1452	Fragments of bowl: rim slightly projecting over the two surfaces. H:132; in the extension of the east wall (M-K Pl. LXXXI).
5	1457	Fragment of bowl: (2) rim slightly projecting over the two surfaces. H:132; south wall, locus 6 (M-K Pl. LXXXV).
—	1454	Neck of large jar: wide; decorative corded molding, made of half-circles; two horizontal rims of bowls projecting over inside surface, one projecting long and thin. H:131; locus 4.
—	1474	Folded, horizontal handles; fragments of necks of small jars, flared rims; pieces of clay painted with brown bands. H:132; loci 7–8.
—	1456	Rim of hole-mouth: rounded edge, slight projection over outside surface; flat base, white slip. H:136; locus 4.

Fig. 80. Pottery and objects, Phase VIII, Enclosures 131 and 136 (Area III) and 132 (Area IV), from Marquet-Krause 1949. 1:4.

IX

SUMMARY TABLES OF STRATA AND LAYERS

TABLE OF STRATA AND CHRONOLOGY

Stratum	Phase	Chronology	Period	Description
Pre-Urban	I–II	3100–3000 B.C.	EB IB	Domestic house
Building C	III	3000–2860 B.C.	EB IC	Domestic house
Building B	IV–V	2860–2720 B.C.*	EB IIA–B	Domestic house
Building A	VI	2700–2550 B.C.	EB IIIA	Domestic house
Sanctuary A	VII–VIII	2550–2400 B.C.	EB IIIB	Sanctuary

* Site abandoned briefly between Phases V and VI.

TABLE OF LAYERS AND POTTERY INFORMATION

Field No.	Layer No.	Phase	Description	Registration Nos.	Period	Section
(Area I)					—	—
1.1	—	—	Surface, unstratified	Cancelled		
1.2	—	VI	Wall E	4491	EB IIIA	H–H
1.2a	—	VI	Wall D	4492	EB IIIA	H–H
1.2b	—	VI	E² Blockage	None registered	EB IIIA	H–H
1.2c	6	V	Silty grey earth	4493–5	EB IIB	H–H
1.3	—	IV	Wall E¹	4496	EB IIA	H–H
1.4	7	IV	Compact buff clay	5030, 31, 31a	EB IIA	H–H
1.5	7	IV	Compact buff clay	5032–37	EB IIA	H–H
1.5a	8	III	Compact ashy grey	5038	EB IC	H–H
1.5b	8	IV	Wall D¹	5038a–f	EB IIA	H–H
1.6	8a	III	Ashy compact	5939–40	EB IC	H–H
1.7	9	III	Dark red stony	4497–4500, 5058–8a	EB IC	H–H
2.1	—	III	Grey earth against Wall D²	5058b–c	EB IC	H–H
2.2	—	III	Ashy grey earth	5058d–f	EB IC	H–H
(Area II)					—	—
100.1	—	—	Surface, unstratified	None registered	—	—
101.1	—	—	Surface, unstratified	None registered	—	E–E
101.1a	—	VI	Wall P, above Wall P¹	4240–1	EB IIIA	E–E
101.2	3	VI	Grey ashy fill under Wall H	4223–5	EB IIIA	E–E
101.2a	3	VI	Grey ashy fill under Wall P	4242–9, 5046, 51–2, 7, 63–4, 6, 74, 81, 1a–c	EB IIIA	E–E

Field No.	Layer No.	Phase	Description	Registration Nos.	Period	Section
101.3	3	VI	Grey ashy rubble under 101.2	4226–32	EB IIIA	E–E
101.4	3	VI	Grey ashy rubble under 101.2a	4233–8	EB IIIA	E–E
101.5	5a	V	Bricky grey stony, Wall F¹	4250–3	EB IIB	E–E
101.5a	5a	V	Same as 101.5, east to Wall P¹	4254–63, 5044, 54–5, 68, 70, 72, 75a	EB IIB	E–E
101.6	4	VI	Top of Wall Q, under Wall H	None registered	EB IIIA	E–E
101.7	4	VI	Foundation trench, Tower A	4239	EB IIIA	E–E
101.7a	5a	V	Bricky top of Wall Q	5041, 1a, 2	EB IIB	E–E
101.8	6	V	Dark ashy stony, east of Wall F¹	Assigned to 101.8a	EB IIB	E–E
101.8a	6	V	Same as 101.8, upper part	4264–74; 5053, 6, 9, 62, 5, 9, 76–9, 82	EB IIB	E–E
101.8b	6	V	Same as 101.8, lower part	4275–8, 5043, 9, 50, 75, 80, 80a–k	EB IIB	E–E
101.9	7a	IV	Reddish-grey stony, under 101.8	4279–89, 9a–p	EB IIA	E–E
101.9a	9	III	Dark red stony, under 101.9	4290	EB IC	E–E
101.10	9	III	Dark red stony, under 101.9a	4291–6	EB IC	E–E
101.11	10	II	Ashy grey stony	4310–12	EB IB	E–E
102.1	—	—	Surface, unstratified	None registered	—	A–A
102.2	6	V	Bricky ashy debris	4296a–c	EB IIB	A–A
102.2a	6	V	Bricky ashy debris	4297–300	EB IIB	A–A
102.3	7	IV	Compact buff clay	4301–7, 7a–e	EB IIA	A–A
102.4	7	IV	Grey rubbly earth above 102.5	4313–14	EB IIA	A–A
102.5	9	III	Ashy surface of 102.6	4308, 9, 9a–f	EB IC	A–A
102.6	9	III	Dark red stony clay	4315–26, 26a–f, 27	EB IC	A–A
102.7	8	III	Grey ashy fill under Platform Z	4328–35	EB IC	F–F
102.8	9	III	Dark red stony under 102.7	4336–50, 50a–h	EB IC	F–F
102.9	10	II	Ashy grey stony earth	4351–9, 61–402, 4–9, 5043, 7–8, 60–1, 7, 71, 1a–aa, cc–dd, hh, rr, vv	EB IB	A–A
102.10	11	II	Charcoal-flecked grey earth	4410–39, 41–90, 90b–o, q, s, u	EB IB	A–A
102.11	12	I	Compact yellow clay	4157–60, 76–8, 89–96	EB IB	A–A
102.11a	11	II	Bedline of 102.10	None registered	EB IB	A–A
103.1	8	III	Ashy grey under Wall S, same as 102.7	4195–6	EB IC	G–G
103.2	9	III	Dark red stony clay, same as 102.8	4192–4, 4205–11	EB IC	G–G

Field No.	Layer No.	Phase	Description	Registration Nos.	Period	Section
103.3	9a	III	Loose stony red clay, under 103.2, same as 102.6	4212–18 (15a–b)	EB IC	F–F
103.4	10	II	Grey flecked stony, under 103.3	4163–75, 79–80, 83–7, 97–201	EB IB	F–F
103.5	11	II	Bedline of 103.4, above 103.6	4161–2	EB IB	F–F
103.6	12	I	Brownish stony on bed-rock	4202–4, 19–22	EB IB	F–F
(Area III)						
200.1	—	—	Surface, unstratified	None registered	—	C–C
200.1a	3	VI	Assigned to 200.1b.	None registered	EB IIIA	C–C
200.1b	3	VI	Grey stony fill, under Wall H entrance, same as 200.1a	4501–4	EB IIIA	C–C
200.1c	—	—	M-K dump, unstratified	None registered	—	—
201.1	2	VI	Ashy rubble fill	4506–13	EB IIIA	A–A
201.1b	3	VI	Grey ashy fill, same as 201.8	4513a	EB IIIA	A–A
201.2	4	VI	Grey-brown rubbly fill, same as 201.9	4515–6	EB IIIA	A–A
201.2a	4	VI	Same as 201.2	4517–21	EB IIIA	A–A
201.3	5	V	Reddish ashy, balk trimming	None registered	EB IIB	A–A
201.3a	5	V	Reddish ashy, under 201.2	4522–5	EB IIB	A–A
201.4	5	V	Reddish ashy, under 201.3a	4526	EB IIB	A–A
201.4a	5	V	Reddish ashy, north of altar balk	4527–9, 9a–c	EB IIB	A–A
201.5	6	V	Loose ashy brown, under 201.4	4530–4	EB IIB	A–A
201.5a	6	V	Loose ashy brown, north of altar balk	4535–7, 7a–d, 4624	EB IIB	A–A
201.6	6	V	Yellowish bricky ashy, same as 201.12a	4538–40	EB IIB	A–A
201.6a	6	V	Yellowish bricky ashy, north of altar balk	4541–3, 3a–e	EB IIB	A–A
201.7	1	VII	Ashy rubble under Altar J	4544–8, 8a–h	EB IIIB	A–A
201.7a	2	VI	Ashy rubble fill under 201.7	4549–51, 1a–e	EB IIIA	A–A
201.8	3	VI	Grey ashy fill, same as 201.1b	4552, 2a–f	EB IIIA	A–A
201.8a	3	VI	Grey ashy fill, balk trimming	None registered	EB IIIA	A–A
201.9	4	VI	Rubbly brown fill, under 201.8a	4554–62, 2a–j	EB IIIA	A–A
201.9a	4	VI	Rubbly brown fill, same as 201.9	4563–9, 9a–f	EB IIIA	A–A

Field No.	Layer No.	Phase	Description	Registration Nos.	Period	Section
201.10	2	VI	Same as 201.7	4570–1, 1a–f	EB IIIA	A–A
201.11	6	V	Bricky ashy, balk trimming	None registered	EB IIB	A–A
201.12	6	V	Bricky ashy, balk trimming	None registered	EB IIB	A–A
201.12a	6	V	Bricky ashy destruction debris	4375–92, 2a–u	EB IIB	A–A
201.13	9	III	Dark red stony, under 201.12a	4218a–d	EB IC	A–A
201.13a	9	III	Dark red stony, under 201.13	4593–609, 9a–j	EB IC	A–A
201.13b	9	III	Dark red stony, under 201.12a	4610–12, 12a–c	EB IC	—
201.14	9	III	Grey stony mixed with red clay	4613	EB IC	—
201.15	3	VI	Grey ashy fill, same as 201.8	4614–16, 16a–g	EB IIIA	A–A
201.16	4	VI	Rubbly brown fill under 201.15	4617–8	EB IIIA	A–A
202.1	—	—	Surface, unstratified	None registered	—	—
202.2	—	—	M-K dump, unstratified	None registered	—	—
202.3	6b	V	Bricky ashy destruction debris	74, 4619–25, 5a–l	EB IIB	B–B
202.4	8	III	Compact grey ashy, under 202.3	4626–35, 35a–f	EB IC	B–B
202.5	7a	IV	Loose ashy stony, east of Wall F³	4636–62, 62a–s	EB IIA	B–B
202.5a	7a	IV	Same as 202.5	4663–8, 8a–j	EB IIA	B–B
202.6	8	III	Wall F³ bricks	4669–71	EB IC	B–B
202.7	7a	IV	Grey-ashy against Wall F³	4672–80, 80a–g	EB IIA	B–B
202.8	8	III	Compact grey ashy, same as 202. 4	4681–5, 5a	EB IC	B–B
202.9	9	III	Compact ashy stony, above Wall Y, under 202.5a	4686–9	EB IC	B–B
202.10	10	II	Red clay against Wall R	4690–6	EB IB	B–B
203.1	1	VII	Inside surface, Bin N	4697–703	EB IIIB	D–D
203.2	3	VI	Foundation earth under Bin N	4704–10, 12–3	EB IIIA	D–D
203.3	4	VI	Among stones of Platform N¹	4714–7	EB IIIA	D–D
203.4	4	VI	Firm reddish earth under N¹	4718–32, 2a–l	EB IIIA	D–D
203.4a	5	V	Fill over Firepit N²	4733–7	EB IIB	C–C
203.5	7a	IV	Dark ashy earth against N²	4738–76, 6a–o, 6039	EB IIA	C–C
203.5a	7a	IV	Firepit N²	4777–8, 80–2	EB IIA	C–C
203.6	7a	IV	Ashy brown under 203.5	4783–7	EB IIA	C–C

Field No.	Layer No.	Phase	Description	Registration Nos.	Period	Section
204.1	4	VI	Loose rubbly under Wall H	4787a–f	EB IIIA	C–C
204.2	6	V	Bricky ashy stony	5159–61, 63–7	EB IIB	C–C
204.2a	6	V	Same as 204.2	4788	EB IIB	C–C
204.3	7a	IV	Ashy grey stony, under 204.2	4789–92, 92a–c	EB IIA	C–C
204.3a	7a	IV	Ashy grey under 204.2	4793–801	EB IIA	C–C
204.4	2	VI	Wall H and rubble core	4802–5, 5a–i	EB IIIA	C–C
204.5	9	III	Dark red stony under 204.3a	4806–24, 24a–n	EB IC	C–C
204.6	4	VI	Loose rubble under Wall H	4825–31	EB IIIA	C–C
204.7	6	V	Bricky reddish, above Wall F^2	4831a–l	EB IIB	C–C
204.8	6	V	Bricky ashy against Wall F^2	4832, 2a–c	EB IIB	C–C
204.8a	6	V	Same as 204.8	4833–9, 9a–l	EB IIB	C–C
204.9	7a	IV	Among stones of Wall F^1 in Wall H balk	4840–4	EB IIA	C–C
204.10	7a	IV	Ashy grey in Wall H balk, same as 204.3	4845–72, 2a–m, 5011, 5020	EB IIA	C–C
204.11	7a	IV	Same as 204.3a	4873–4	EB IIA	C–C
300.1	—	—	Surface, unstratified	None registered	—	I–I
300.1a	2	VI	Balk trimming under Wall M	None registered	EB IIIA	I–I
300.1b	—	—	Top of Wall M, unstratified	None registered	—	I–I
300.2	—	VI	Balk trimming, under Wall M	None registered	EB IIIA	I–I
300.3	4	VI	Bricky rubbly above Wall F^3	4875–80	EB IIIA	I–I
300.4	4	VI	Same as 300.3, east of Wall F^3	4881–5, 5a–d	EB IIIA	I–I
300.5	3	VI	Ashy rubbly, under Wall M	4886	EB IIIA	I–I
300.6	—	—	Balk trimming, unstratified	None registered	—	I–I
300.7	1	VII	Blockage in Wall M passage	4887–99	EB IIIB	I–I
300.7a	1	VII	Makeup under stones of Blockage M^1	4900–1	EB IIIB	I–I
300.8	1	VII	Ashy earth on threshold under Blockage M^1	4902–6	EB IIIB	I–I
300.9	2	VI	Ashy rubbly fill under Wall M	4907–17, 17a–c	EB IIIA	I–I
300.9a	3	VI	Ashy bricky under 300.9	4918–23, 23a–i	EB IIIA	I–I
300.9b	4	VI	Foundation trench for Tower A	4924–30, 30a–h	EB IIIA	I–I

Field No.	Layer No.	Phase	Description	Registration Nos.	Period	Section
300.10	4	VI	Bricky rubbly, under 300.9a	4931–46, 46a–j	EB IIIA	I–I
300.10a	4	VI	Same as 300.10	4947–50, 50a–f	EB IIIA	I–I
309.11	4	VI	Same as 300.9b	4950g–i	EB IIIA	I–I
300.12	5	V	Bricky grey, under 300.9b	4951–6, 6a	EB IIB	I–I
300.13	8	III	Compact bricky, Wall X	4956b–d	EB IC	A–A
300.14a	5	V	Grey bricky stony, under 300.10a	4957–78, 5083–95, 5a–m	EB IIB	I–I
300.14b	6	V	Ashy stony, under 300.14a	4979–5009, 9a–ee	EB IIB	I–I
300.14c	7a	IV	Loose ashy stony, under 300.14b	5010–3, 15–24, 4a–g, 4i–l	EB IIA	I–I
300.14d	7a	IV	Same as 300.14c	5024h, 25–8, 8a–j, 9	EB IIA	I–I
300.14e	9	III	Compact reddish grey under 300.14d	5029a–k	EB IC	I–I
300.15	8	III	Compact grey, same as 300.14e	5096–101, 1a–f	EB IC	I–I
300.16	6a	V	Ashy flecked debris, under 300.12	5102–3, 3a–c	EB IIB	I–I
300.17	6b	V	Bricky debris, same as 202.3	5104–16, 16a–i	EB IIB	I–I
300.18	9	III	Compact grey, under 300.14e	5117–9, 21–2, 2a–d	EB IC	B–B
300.18a	9	III	Ashy stony over Wall Y, same as 202.9	5123–32, 32a–d	EB IC	B–B
300.19	6	V	Bricky red, against Wall X	5133–4, 4a–e	EB IIB	A–A
300.20	8	III	Compact dark grey, same as 202.4	5135–43, 43a–i	EB IC	B–B
301.1	—	—	M-K dump, unstratified	None registered	—	—
301.2	2	VI	Wall O remnant, and fill under base	5148–50	EB IIIA	I–I
301.3	3	VI	Grey rubbly makeup under Wall O	5151–8, 8a–h	EB IIIA	I–I

PLATE I

A general view of Ai (et-Tell), looking northeast. Rammun (Rimmon) is across the valley on the upper left.

PLATE II

1 The Early Bronze Age structures at Site A, with Sanctuary A altar against Tower A in the background.

2 Phase II Wall R on bedrock in the foreground, covered by the massive Tower A on right. Wall R is under the Phase III surface on which the meter scale rests, which is also under Tower A.

PLATE III

1   Detail of Wall R, under the scale, underneath Tower A in the upper
    background.

2   A general view of Buildings B and C stratification in Area II. The meter scale rests on Wall F,
    which continues in the right background over the dark red stony earth fill, but under Phase
    IV Wall F¹. The Building B floor is seen as a dark ashy line on top of a compact buff layer of
    fill over the reddish layer.

PLATE IV

1 Detail of fill layers in Area II underneath the Building B floor at ashy line. See Master Section A–A for layer designations.

2 The Building B surface in Area II, supporting the meter scale. Wall Q, on the right of the scale, is founded on the dark reddish layer underneath the buff fill of the floor, and decayed bricks of its superstructure are underneath the EB III Wall H, at the upper right of the scale.

PLATE V

1   The Buildings C and B Wall Q, with the buff fill layer removed, exposing the wall foundations on the dark reddish fill shown in Plate IV.2 above.

2   Detail of Building B mud-brick superstructure remains on top of Wall Q in Area II. Analysis of charred wood found between the bricks indicates that evergreen oak cross-reinforcement was used to strengthen the brick walls.

PLATE VI

1 Packed *huwwar* surface of Building B in Area II, against Wall F on the right, drawn in Section G–G. The surface is underneath Wall E¹, which has been removed.

2 Fill layers in southwest side of Area II, from bedrock to the Building B surface indicated by ashy line above buff fill. Layer designations may be found in Master Section A–A.

3 The Building C platform of flat stones, associated with semi-circular Wall G which is set on bedrock.

PLATE VII

1 The Building C platform in Area II, with flat stone surface resting on saucer-shaped fill. The stones of Wall G in the left foreground are set in a trench cut to bedrock. (See Marquet-Krause 1949. Pl. XX:2.)

2 Detail of grey stony earth fill between Wall G on the left and Wall C on the right, in Area II. The dark red stony layer, seen in Pl. VII.1 is above the meter scale.

PLATE VIII

1 Detail of trench cut in grey fill layer for construction of Wall G support for flatstone surface of Building C platform. The trench is on the left side of Wall G, shown in Pl. VI.3.

3 Detail of fill layers underneath the Building C platform surface in Area II, south of Wall S–S¹. The layers of fill are against Wall C on the left.

2 Fill layers in Area II, with Wall S–S¹ balk behind meter scale, and Wall Q balk behind workman in the background. The Building B floor is against Wall Q at the right of the workman's head.

PLATE IX

1   The Building B surface in Area III. The meter scale rests on the surface which is covered by Phase V destruction debris. Wall F² is in the foreground.

2   Detail of Phase V destruction layer, behind half-meter scale, on the Building B floor and against the north face of Wall Q in Area III.

PLATE X

1 Detail of the Building B floor at the north end of the Sanctuary A altar balk with Phase V layer at the left of the half-meter scale.

2 Crushed ledge-handle jar on Building B floor in Area III, against Wall M balk (See Fig. 46:13).

3 Detail of Phase III Wall W, above fill covering Phase II Wall R, and underneath Tower A. See Master Section A–A for relationship to the surface shown in No. 1 above.

PLATE XI

1   The north face of Wall M balk in Area IV, with Wall M and Phase VII blocked entrance on the right against Tower A. A brick wall and plaster surface of Phases III–IV are at the left of the meter scale.

2   Detail of Wall M balk showing section of the Buildings C and B brick wall underneath Building A Wall M at the top. At the upper right is a corner of the blocked passageway in Wall M.

PLATE XII

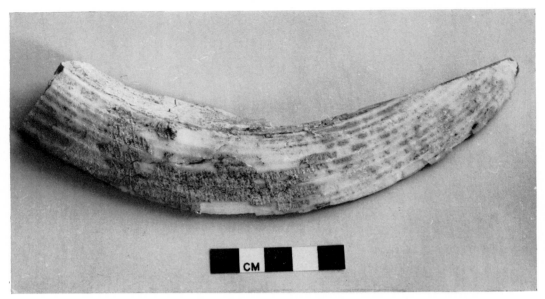

1 Lower right tusk of hippopotamus, found in dark reddish fill layer of Phase III, Building C, Area III.

3 Unretouched flint blade. From Phase V, Area III.

2 Half of basalt stone ring, with inside polished from use, Phase IV, Area II.

5 Detail of prefabricated, open spout attached to storage jar, Phase III.

4 Flint scraper from Phase V, Area II.

PLATE XIII

I

2 Detail of a small globular juglet recovered from the Building B floor, between Wall F² and Tower A.

1, 3 Shallow carinated bowl showing hand burnishing, Phase IV, Area IV.

3

4 Imprint of woven cloth on base of jar, Phase III, Area II.

PLATE XIV

1 Restored pottery found on Building B floor in Area III, Phase V. The large jars were found in the northwest corner, against the Wall M balk; the small vessels were among the destruction debris in the south-west corner between Wall F² and the Sanctuary A altar balk.

2 Juglet with vertical pierced lug handles and painted trellis decoration from Building B floor, Phase V, Area III, against Wall Q.

3 Small jar with painted geo-metric decoration from Build-ing B floor, Phase V, Area III, against Wall Q.

4 Baked brick-like object, recovered from the floor of Building B, and the ashes of Phase V in Area III.

PLATE XV

1 Small flat-base jar in calcined mass cemented to outside of large store-jar sherd, from the ashes of Phase V in Area III.

3 Fragment of baked pottery object, from Phase V, Area III, against the west face of Wall F².

2 Calcined deposits on rim and neck of store-jar, Phase V, Area III.

PLATE XVI

1

2

3

4

5

1 Impressions of leaves in Phase V destruction debris on Building B floor, Area III. The coin is Jordanian fifty fils.

2 Leaf imprints in baked clay, Phase V, Area III.

3 Impressions of leaves in baked clay, Phase V, Area III. The coin is Jordanian fifty fils.

4 Leaf imprints in baked clay, Phase V, Area III.

5 The south face of the Wall M balk in Area III, drawn in Section B–B, Fig. 11.

PLATE XVII

Bin N, around the half-meter scale in the foreground, associated with Building A, Wall H on the left, and the Sanctuary A altar in the background. The altar is constructed against Tower A.

PLATE XVIII

1 Detail of Phase VI passageway in Area IV blocked in Phase VII use of Wall M.

2 Typical sea shell found at Site A, in all major building periods.

3 Bronze pin from Phase VI, Area II.

4 Detail of Phase VI passageway in Wall M blocked for Phase VII use, seen in northwest corner of Area III.

PLATE XIX

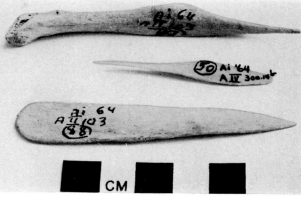

2 Bone awls from Buildings C and B, Areas II and IV.

1 Detail of hand-burnishing on shallow bowl fragment, Phase VI, Area III.

3 EB III pottery from Building A, Phase VI, Area III.

4 Retouched flint from Building A, Phase VI, Area III.

5 Inside of store-jar sherd coated with heavy layer of limestone plaster, Phase IV, Area II.

PLATE XX

1   Sanctuary A, Phase VII (after Marquet-Krause 1949. Pl. XIII:1).

2   The altar room of Sanctuary A, Phase VII (after Marquet-Krause 1949. Pl. XV:1).

PLATE XXI

1 Niche and top of Sanctuary A altar, Phase VII
(after Marquet-Krause 1949. Pl. XV:2).

2 Altar and sacrificial remains of Sanctuary A, Phase VII (after Marquet-Krause 1949. Pl. XVII:1).

PLATE XXII

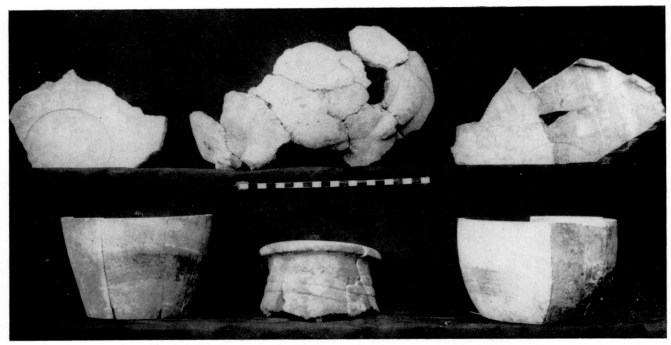

1 Alabaster fragments of zoomorphic and other vessels from Sanctuary A, Phase VIII (after Marquet-Krause 1949. Pl. XXIII:1).

2 Alabaster fragments of zoomorphic vessel in the shape of a water-skin from Sanctuary A, Phase VIII (after Marquet-Krause 1949. Pl. XXIII:2).

PLATE XXIII

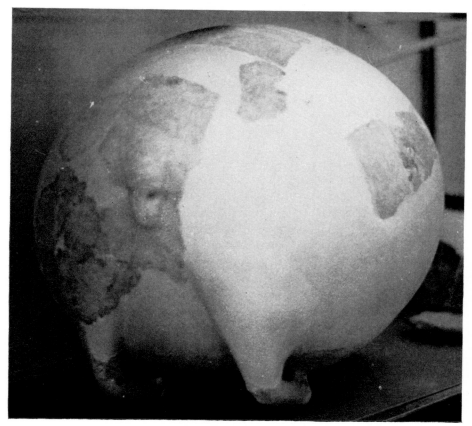

1   Restored alabaster vessel in the shape of a water-skin, rear view, found in Room 120 (Area III) by Marquet-Krause (See Fig. 69). At the Rockefeller Museum, Jerusalem.

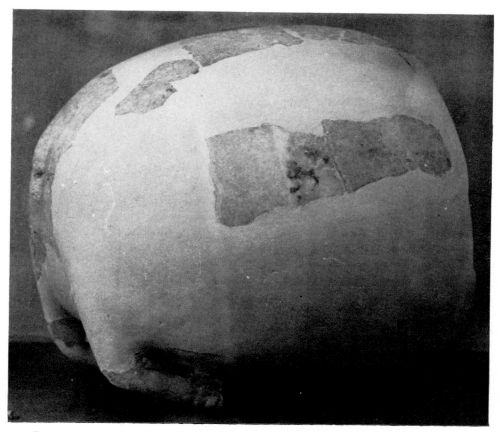

2   Restored alabaster vessel, side view. At the Rockefeller Museum, Jerusalem.

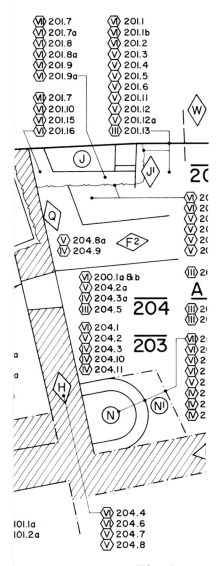

Fig. 82

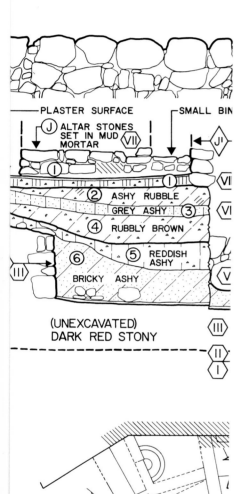

Fig. 83

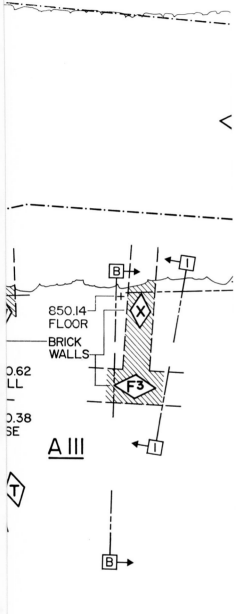

850.14
FLOOR

BRICK
WALLS

0.62
LL

0.38
SE

A III

Fig.

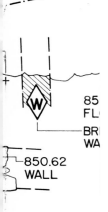

85
FL

BR
WA

850.62
WALL

A III
POSSIBLE
COURTYARD

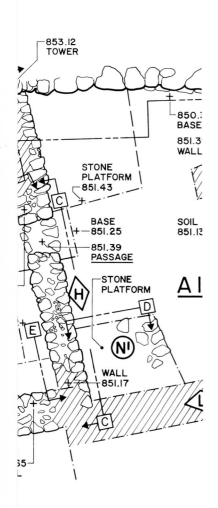

853.12
TOWER

850.3
BASE

851.3
WALL

STONE
PLATFORM
851.43

BASE
851.25

SOIL
851.13

851.39
PASSAGE

STONE
PLATFORM

A l

WALL
851.17

Fig. 86

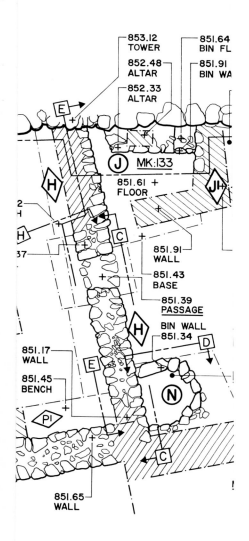

Fig. 87

AUTHOR INDEX

GENERAL INDEX